EFFECTIVE MANAGEMENT INFORMATION SYSTEMS

EFFECTIVE MANAGEMENT INFORMATION SYSTEMS

Accent on Current Practices

Second Edition

Robert J. Thierauf

MERRILL PUBLISHING COMPANY
A Bell & Howell Information Company
Columbus Toronto London Melbourne

Published by Merrill Publishing Company
A Bell & Howell Information Company
Columbus, Ohio 43216

This book was set in Frutiger.

Administrative Editor: Vernon R. Anthony
Production Coordinator: JoEllen Gohr
Cover Designer: Cathy Watterson

Library of Congress Catalog Card Number: 86-62993
International Standard Book Number: 0–675–20745–2
Printed in the United States of America
1 2 3 4 5 6 7 8 9—91 90 89 88 87

PREFACE

Since their inception over two decades ago, management information systems (MIS) have reached maturity. Now their output is treated as a sixth corporate resource needing careful direction, just as money, materials, machines, men (i.e., people), and management do. Seen from this broad perspective, management information systems can provide vital new types of information. They enable organizational personnel at all levels not only to perform the *control* function, but also to carry out the *planning* function that is so crucial today. This new task involves going beyond just *problem solving* by focusing on *problem finding.* Overall, management information systems place "first things first"—that is, they relate all the relevant external environmental factors to the internal ones to provide a sound starting point in the planning process. This processed information provides a trustworthy basis for short-, medium-, and long-range plans. Short-run planning, in turn, becomes the basis for controlling organizational activities through the coming year. Such an orderly approach to MIS activities provides all organizational personnel (management and non-management) with the information they must have to manage the company's resources.

These premises about effective management information systems underlie the purpose of this book; namely, to broaden one's total knowledge of effective MIS. Going beyond a thorough coverage of the essentials of analysis and design of management information systems, the text comprehensively documents the application of MIS for a progressive manufacturing company—the XYZ Corporation—in a six-chapter case study. In this case, systems are developed and implemented for all major corporate areas: corporate planning, marketing, manufacturing, accounting and finance, and personnel. The result of this approach to the study of MIS is a combined theoretical and practical look at what really constitutes effective management information systems. Additionally, our approach integrates the newer directions in MIS—distributed data processing (DDP) systems and decision support systems (DSS)—into current practices using Lotus 1-2-3® (a spreadsheet) and IFPS (a fourth-generation language).

This book can be used at the undergraduate or the graduate level to fulfill the requirement for a management information systems course within an information system or a computer science curriculum. The text is useful for several audiences: future systems analysts, programmers, or computer operations managers. For this audience, every effort has been made to observe the curricula suggestions of the Association for Computing Machinery (ACM) in their course ISA3, and of the Date Processing Management Association (DPMA) in their course CIS-10.

In addition, the book is designed for all business students—potential managers who will someday utilize the output from MIS. Similarly, managers and information systems professionals currently practicing in the field can benefit from this text. Managers must know how to use management information systems; information systems personnel must understand the needs of management. From this perspective, the book helps all parts of an organization ensure that "the right hand knows what the left hand is doing" in order to bridge the communications gap.

Because the book can be used both as a teaching tool and a manager's guide, it contains features to assist all students of effective management information systems:

□ *Issues* to be raised and explored, set forth at the start of each chapter to stimulate the reader's interest.
□ *Outlines* presenting the major topics and subtopics in each chapter.
□ *Current practices* of effective MIS—actual practices by large companies and current thinking by respected writers on MIS.
□ *Summaries* highlighting important points covered in each chapter.
□ *Questions* and *problems* at the end of each chapter, exploring various aspects of management information systems.
□ *MIS projects* that give the student an opportunity to analyze or design some part of an effective management information system.
□ *Lotus 1-2-3 exercises* that provide a means for the student to solve typical real-world problems. A diskette of the Lotus 1-2-3 programs in the text is available from the publisher.

The structure of the text follows an orderly flow for a comprehensive treatment of current effective management information systems based largely on microcomputers (personal computers). *Part One* is an introduction to management information systems emphasizing information needs at various management levels, including problem finding as well as problem solving. It highlights past and current management information systems and introduces real-time, distributed data processing, and decision support systems along with expert systems for business. Also, information centers are stressed. *Part Two* discusses different ways of viewing decision making. It also covers mathematical and statistical models used in the decision-making process, both on microcomputers and computer mainframes. In addition, the real essence of problem-finding and problem-solving approaches is presented.

Part Three illustrates and evaluates the computer hardware in typical management information systems, and emphasizes distributed data bases and data communication networks. This part also covers the software used by organization personnel in obtaining essential information from the management information system. Accent is placed on available preprogrammed packages such as Lotus 1-2-3 and IFPS, which can answer a wide range of "What If?" questions. The first chapter of *Part Four,* then, stresses the systems approach to management information systems, focusing on system flowcharts and structured design methodologies. The next chapter enumerates the important steps in analyzing and designing effective management information systems. A subsequent chapter covers selecting equipment and implementing MIS. Finally, the vital and timely subject of control over the MIS is thoroughly covered in a separate chapter.

Part Five unifies the preceding topics and expands on them in concrete detail in a comprehensive application of MIS. An overview of a typical management information system for the XYZ Corporation is first given. In succeeding chapters, the major subsystems included in this master case study are illustrated. Corporate planning—from long-range planning to the short run—is shown to benefit greatly through MIS. MIS benefits for the major parts of the marketing subsystem are examined; the same is accomplished for manufacturing and accounting and finance in subsequent chapters. A discussion of the inner workings of the personnel subsystem concludes the text. In each chapter of this part, the use of Lotus 1-2-3 is illustrated through a variety of examples.

In this revision, the author is indebted to many people; first, to Joseph Whitacre of Xavier University for developing the Lotus 1-2-3 programs. Second, I wish to thank the following individuals for their helpful suggestions: Professor Richard Bialac, Xavier University; Professor John B. Griffiths, University of Pittsburgh; and Dr. Karen A. Forcht, James Madison University. I would also like to thank Dr. Richard Abel for his insights and constructive suggestions throughout the entire revision process.

Robert J. Thierauf

CONTENTS

PART FOUR
DEVELOPMENT, IMPLEMENTATION, AND CONTROL OF EFFECTIVE MANAGEMENT INFORMATION SYSTEMS 215

PART ONE

Overview of Effective Management Information Systems

Chapter 1 relates managers at the various levels to information and stresses the need for management information systems. Past and current directions in management information systems are discussed in chapter 2.

CHAPTER 1

An Introduction to Effective Management Information Systems

ISSUES

What is the important relationship between information and any type of system?

Why should information be treated as a sixth major resource of a typical business organization?

What is the relationship between management levels and operational, tactical, and strategic information?

What are the characteristics of effective management information systems that are found in business organizations today?

How should effective management information systems be defined?

What is the relationship of MIS analysts to users in the development of effective management information systems?

INTRODUCTION TO EFFECTIVE MANAGEMENT INFORMATION SYSTEMS

In a fast-changing world, there is a great need for timely and accurate business information. Generally in the past, it has been undervalued, underestimated, and underused. After the human element, it is a manager's most important resource. A major problem facing today's managers is the volume of information crossing their desks. It is so voluminous as to be almost unmanageable; yet, good planning and control over operations via effective decisions must be based on a steady flow of quality, up-to-date information. As John Naisbitt points out on the first page of his best seller, *Megatrends,* "Although we continue to think we live in an industrial society, we have in fact changed to an economy based on the creation and distribution of information." He calls this a *megashift,* an explosive transformation from an industrial to an information society. This change has profound impact on all of us, particularly on the manner in which daily business is conducted.

Given these conditions and the accelerating pace of business, there arises a definite need for the manager to change his or her working habits to accommodate a new member of the information management team, the computer. A dialogue between the manager and the computer is essential if he or she is to be productive and effective. The computer should not interfere with a manager's thought processes; instead, it should augment the individual's capabilities and become an extension of his or her mind. It is from this perspective that the need for an effective management information system (MIS) arises. Fundamentally, this book focuses on what constitutes effective MIS that is capable of assisting not only the manager, but also operating personnel who have need for such a system.

This chapter first discusses information as a sixth resource of a company and its relationship to problem finding and problem solving. After the basic functions of a manager are listed, the importance of microcomputers and computer mainframes to assist in these basic functions are explored from a managerial viewpoint. The types of information needed by top, middle, and lower management for effective decision making are discussed. Next, the characteristics of management information are enumerated, followed by an exposition of information resource management and its tie-in with effective MIS. The second half of this chapter explains the need for effective manage-

3

ment information systems. Both the characteristics of management information systems and effective MIS are defined. For an MIS project to be successful, it must be backed by top management. Similarly, the user must be involved in the project from the onset. Thus, effective MIS does not just happen; it requires complete managerial involvement with MIS analysts.

THE IMPORTANCE OF INFORMATION

Information—the logical output of a system—is of vital importance to the managers of an organization to achieve short-, intermediate-, and long-range goals. Management needs a fairly accurate measurement of its sales and costs factors for various time periods. It must maximize its income through optimum selling prices and inventory turnover while it minimizes the costs of products and services. In short, management wants a combination of selling prices, turnover, costs, and profit per unit that will provide the highest return on invested capital. Given adequate information on these essential facts, management can rely more on deductive and analytical methods than on guesses and intuitive judgment, which it is forced to employ when many of the relevant facts are missing. Many wrong decisions have been the result of insufficient or inadequately processed information.

There is and continues to be an awareness in society that accurate and timely information is a vital resource of any organization, and that an effective management information system is a means of providing the needed information. Many in top management are finding that information is a source of competitive power. It gives them the ability to out-maneuver their rivals at critical times, especially when introducing new products. If the management information system does not produce the information necessary for management to handle its operations effectively, an "out-of-control" condition may result from which the organization may never recover. An examination of business organizations that have experienced difficult times over the years will verify this fact.

Information as a Sixth Major Corporate Resource

In past and current computer conferences that are held around the world today, two major points are typically emphasized about management information systems. The first is the need for management in the late 80s and beyond to treat information as a sixth major corporate resource, recognizing that corporate strategic plans cannot be accomplished without information systems support. The second point is the need for MIS management to recognize that developing an effective management information system requires a thorough knowledge of the enterprise and its functions as well as technical expertise. The speakers at these conferences address reality, not just theory. Their experience and reputations are based on "doing," not "prescribing."

If information is recognized as a sixth major corporate resource, it assumes a value just as any of the 5 M's—money, materials, machines and facilities, men (i.e., people), and management. Seen from this perspective, information provided by the management information system can assist managers at all levels in performing their managerial functions of planning, organizing, directing, and controlling available corporate resources. This relationship is exemplified in figure 1.1 and is demonstrated throughout the text.

In terms of an economic perspective that recognizes information as a valuable resource, the processing of data into information costs money. As such, information may be judged with the "value added" concept. Value is added to a product as it moves from the raw material state up to the point of consumption by the consumer; the same can be said for the conversion of data to information as a resource. Information has a specific dollar cost associated with it just as if it were purchased from an outside vendor. The loss of a company's competitive edge occurs when critical information is not produced or is lost (i.e., an opportunity loss). Information can thus be looked upon as a value-added good that is useful to managerial and operating personnel in a typical company for planning, organizing, directing, and controlling organizational activities.

Information as Related to Problem Finding and Problem Solving

Information is essential to managers and operating personnel in resolving planning, organizing, directing, and controlling problems whether in a problem-finding or a problem-solving mode. As will be seen in the text, information that is retrieved from an effective MIS is helpful in *problem finding*—identifying future problems that need to be brought back to the present time and solved. In addition, information usage centers on *problem solving*—pinpointing current problems that need to be solved now. Thus, information from management information systems is essential to solving the entire range of present and future problems that confront company managers and operating personnel.

A most distinguishing characteristic of management information systems is that they are forward-looking. Fundamentally, a *forward-looking system* emphasizes integrating future and current operations so that the company obtains information for making effective decisions that affect its future well-being. In addition to receiving information from the system in time to satisfy current decision-making requirements, users can, for example, project the life cycles of products in developing strategic plans. This approach is extremely desirable in the increasingly complex business world. The environmental factors that affect success and failure are so dynamic that users must be able to understand and react to them quickly and decisively. Hence, within an MIS environment, a new management principle—*management by perception*—is required for problem finding. This principle refers to the ability of management to perceive future external and internal trends before they occur and to determine their impact on new products so as to improve overall organizational performance. This principle is forward-looking as opposed to the

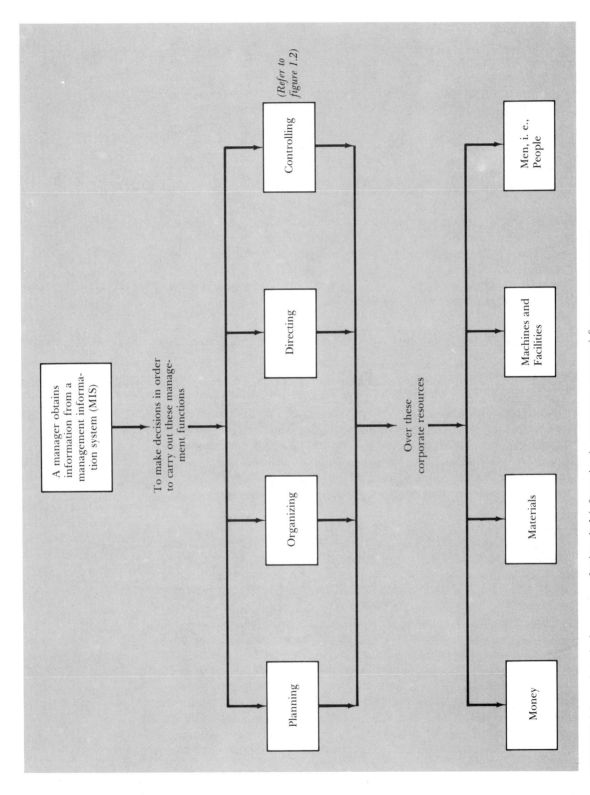

FIGURE 1.1 A typical manager obtains vital *information* (a corporate resource) from a management information system (MIS) to make *decisions* in order to carry out the managerial *functions* over corporate resources.

backward-looking *management by exception* for problem solving, which focuses on comparison after the fact. However, both have their place in an MIS.

To elaborate further on management by perception, management must be able to perceive developing political and social trends relevant to the organization. By perceiving these trends before they occur, management can adjust its strategic plans for new products and, in turn, optimize its tactical and operational plans for these products. Top management can thus improve overall performance for the organization. In effect, they need to stand back and look at the total context in which the organization operates. A forward-looking approach is illustrated by: setting long-range plans and objectives for an entire organization that are fully integrated into the MIS's major subsystems and their related parts; planning and evaluating new products over their life cycles; acquiring short-, intermediate-, and long-term capital funds as needed for the entire organization; and determining profit profiles on large alternative plans. These examples encompass a broad planning view, generally making it easier for top management to accomplish desired company goals and objectives.

THE MANAGER AND INFORMATION

The importance of information to the manager for problem finding and problem solving is paramount: it *is* a sixth major corporate resource. From this perspective, information—strategic, tactical, and operational—needed by the various levels of management is discussed below. However, before exploring these important areas, the basic functions of a manager and his or her relationship to information are defined.

Basic Functions of a Manager

Over the years, management has been defined in many ways. Early definitions consisted primarily of planning, organizing, directing, and controlling. It would seem that this generalized definition, which probably evolved from the work of Henri Fayol at the turn of the century, is the accepted and traditional description of management found in a number of textbooks. But this definition is inadequate. Its major problem probably lies in the *inherent trait* approach—its attempt to describe management in terms of what a manager does. For our purposes, it is more appropriate to define the essence of what management *is* rather than what a manager *does*.

A comprehensive definition of management incorporates the process of achieving organizational objectives:[1]

> ... the process of allocating an organization's inputs (human and economic resources) by planning, organizing, directing, and controlling for the purpose of

[1]Robert J. Thierauf, Robert C. Klekamp, and Daniel W. Geeding, *Management Principles and Practices, A Contingency and Questionnaire Approach*, Santa Barbara, Calif: Wiley/Hamilton, 1977, pp. 10–11.

producing outputs (goods and services) desired by its customers so that organization objectives are accomplished. In the process, work is performed with and through organization personnel in an ever-changing business environment.

These management functions can be related to information, as depicted in figure 1.2. In the material that follows, an overview of each managerial function is given.

PLANNING. The act of planning is the determination of short- to long-range plans—specific strategies, programs, and policies to meet organization objectives. Planning activities for a typical organization include decisions concerning product lines, marketing activities, inventories, purchasing, research, production, workforce, financial resources, exports, and similar items.

For a complete business plan, the physical levels (quantities to be manufactured) as well as the corresponding dollar amounts must be determined. This information is captured quantitatively in the budget—a type of formalized short-range plan. While budgets for the coming year will be extremely detailed, the ones for the next several years—medium- to long-range—will be more general. Nevertheless, the starting point for budgets is reliable financial information. Before the plans can be finalized, they must be coordinated with the overall goals and objectives to insure compatibility.

ORGANIZING. Once the plans are placed into effect, some mechanism or organizational structure must facilitate their successful achievement. The *structure* must relate *people, tasks,* and *technology* to the objectives. Duties and responsibilities must be clearly set forth within this framework.

MANAGEMENT FUNCTIONS

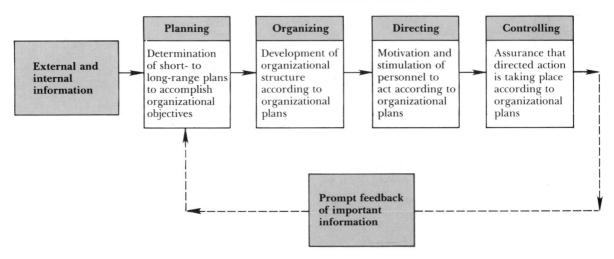

FIGURE 1.2   Information is a vital resource for performing management functions effectively.

Organizing means developing a logical structure to effect change. Information systems managers are unusual in the amount of change they experience. Theirs is a highly volatile field to begin with; in addition, they must cope with changes in other parts of the organization. They frequently find themselves pushing the limits of their department's abilities to adapt, yet they may have no idea what those limits are.

DIRECTING. Directing or activating the organization is equal in importance to other managerial functions. This function is concerned with motivating and stimulating personnel to achieve organizational plans. As such, it includes the dissemination of information in the form of orders and the acceptance and execution of those orders. Whatever action results from the directing function forms the basis of information for the control function.

Because directing requires motivating people to meet the goals of the organization, the way it is carried out by managers can make or break any MIS organization. Frequent personnel changes have a very strong impact. Fundamentally, an MIS department can tolerate a certain amount of change without serious disruption of its performance. The manner in which change is directed determines the quality of the services delivered.

CONTROLLING. Without the information necessary for proper coordination of the organization's activities, management will find it difficult to control according to plan. Control consists mainly of overseeing and comparing actual results with those originally forecasted; it assures that directed action is taking place according to organization plans and within the confines of the organization structure. Control devices can include the following: use of standards; monitoring variances from the budgeted amounts; return on investment analysis; breakeven, cost, volume, and contribution analyses; and ratio analyses. These typical management control devices permit the comparison of actual data with planned data, indicating favorable or unfavorable results. Management is concerned with any variances greater than acceptable limits. This timely information provides input to the appropriate levels of management for review and action.

The last managing function, control, closes the system loop by providing *feedback* about significant deviations from planned performance. As indicated in figure 1.2, the feedback of pertinent information from the controlling function can affect the planning process.

INTEGRATION OF MANAGEMENT FUNCTIONS. Within a typical business organization, the time spent on planning, organizing, directing, and controlling is proportional to the organization level, as illustrated in figure 1.3. At higher management levels, planning is the major task, organizing is next, and directing and controlling are least important. At the lower levels, the major management emphasis is upon directing and controlling; planning is of a short-term nature, and organizing is somewhat limited. At the middle levels of management, there is a mixture of all the basic managerial functions.

9

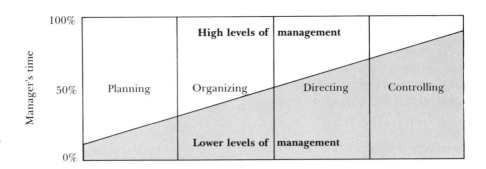

FIGURE 1.3
How management time
is spent.

How Microcomputers Assist in Basic Functions

Computers have helped managers carry out their basic functions for years. However, the type of computers in use is changing. In the 1960s and early 1970s, two economic laws reigned supreme in the world of computers. The *first*—based on economies of scale—stated that the larger the computer, the better its price and performance. The *second* applied to large systems shared by many users, the norm at that time, and stated that economies of scale were to be gained from sharing software and support resources among similar applications. These economic laws no longer apply to many recently introduced computers and business applications. Economies of scale may still apply, but only within narrow categories of equipment. With the economies derived from large-volume production of integrated circuit chips, microcomputers and superminicomputers often show better price and performance than the large machines.

The earlier benefits of spreading the costs of software and support among many users via timesharing are being challenged. Inexpensive microcomputers and relatively cheap, easy-to-use software packages can be operated by novice managers and their staff. At the same time, applications most suited to large computers, such as high-volume transaction systems and interactive data base applications serving many users, are becoming increasingly complex. The result is that the computer resources required to run such a system are increasing.

Although it is difficult to extrapolate economic rules of the past to plan computer systems of the future, the trend today is toward the use of microcomputers or personal computers (PCs) throughout a company. Now, as in the mid-1980s, we continue to witness explosive growth in microcomputer-based workstations and microcomputers, including home use. Due to a competitive market, microcomputers' prices are falling precipitously. Such a volatile marketplace continues to erode the more established minicomputer and computer mainframe markets.

Perhaps the strongest impetus to the rise of microcomputers (as well as minicomputers before them) is that lower hardware costs have been accompanied by proportionately lower software, operational, and support personnel costs. Microcomputers would have remained a curiosity if their software and support were priced at the same level as for computer mainframes. Perhaps the main reason futurists and planners did not anticipate the rapid rise in PC sales was the unexpected availability of low-cost software packages and equipment that could be easily operated by novices. The drop in hardware and software costs for microcomputers resulted from the large number of units produced. The production cost for additional copies of software is negligible compared to the cost of developing the initial product.

In light of the economics of scale gained with microcomputers, they will continue to provide managers with new ways for carrying out the managerial functions of planning, organizing, directing, and controlling. Microcomputers tend to be more user friendly than computer mainframes for managers and their staff. As noted below, the emphasis is on a manager–machine interface to assist in the problem-finding and problem-solving processes whether it be a micro or mainframe approach.

The Manager–Machine Interface

Whether the manager or assistant is using a microcomputer or a CRT terminal attached to a computer mainframe is not important. What is important is an interactive manager–machine interface that answers recurring problems as well as ad hoc "What If?" questions. As shown in figure 1.4, the human–machine interface provides comprehensible answers to managers and their assistants as well as operating personnel, when the information is needed and under their control. Hence, effective management information systems are intended to help managers throughout the company in solving their myriad problems. The merging of computer outputs with the subjective feelings of the manager provides a better basis for decision making.

Due to rapidly decreasing costs of computer storage and improvements in data entry and data base management systems, it is increasingly likely that much or all of the information a manager needs can be stored on-line in the data base (refer to figure 1.4), making MIS the logical tool for analysis and solution to user problems. In addition, since personnel costs already exceed 50 percent of most data processing budgets, the cost of providing information for managers can be reduced. This reduction alone should justify newer management information systems, together with the improved management productivity and improved decisions that result from increased use of management science (i.e., quantitative) models.

THE MANAGER AND TYPES OF INFORMATION

Because the output of MIS is directed toward management, we need to identify the type of information needed by different levels of management. They are:

- strategic information for top management
- tactical information for middle management
- operational information for lower management

11

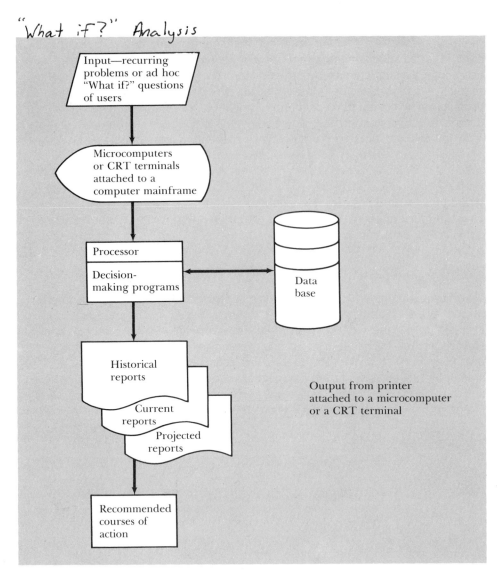

FIGURE 1.4
Emphasis on a human–
computer interface
within an effective MIS
operating mode for
interactive decision
making.

The type of information supplied is based on the relative position of the manager in the organization's hierarchy and the activities which the information describes—the internal environment of the organization or the external environment in which it operates. Internal information should be increasingly summarized as the level of management for which it is prepared rises in the hierarchical structure, with top management receiving summary reports. The rationale is that internal data are control-oriented, and the lower and middle echelons of management are the most *control-oriented;* top management, on the other hand, is more *planning-oriented.*

Information concerning the external environment of the organization should be summarized exactly opposite to that describing the internal environment. Because the upper levels of management are more planning-oriented, and because planning requires more information about the organization's external environment, information concerning the external environment should be increasingly summarized and selective as the position of the receiver decreases in the managerial hierarchy. Thus, time spent on planning and controlling for lower, middle, and top management complement one another in a management information system, as illustrated in figure 1.5.

Strategic Information for Top Management

Strategic information is used primarily by top management and their staff for long-term planning—generally 1 to 5 years. This type of information is used for planning and to discover the underlying reasons for specific problems or situations. In many cases, the objective of using strategic information is to answer *why* rather than *what* or *where*. Examples are found in table 1.1. Emphasis is on problem finding versus just problem solving.

Strategic planning concerns itself with the establishment of organization objectives and policies that will govern the acquisition of resources needed to achieve those objectives. It is normally conducted at the highest level of management. Primarily, it requires large amounts of information derived from or relating to areas of knowledge outside the organization. Finally, strategic planning is original and covers the entire spectrum of the organization's activities.

To translate this task into the information systems area, top management must be directly involved in

- □ setting directions for computer use to accomplish organization objectives
- □ setting priorities so that the limited computer resource can serve the whole organization
- □ setting criteria for selecting MIS alternatives
- □ insisting that computer-use planning be as thorough as other tactical and operational planning

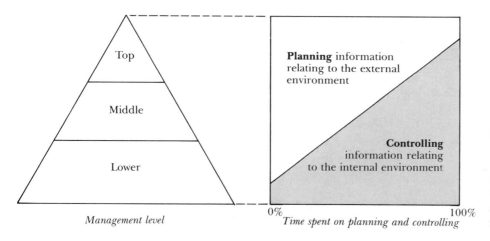

FIGURE 1.5 The relationship of the managerial levels to time spent planning and controlling, and to the summarization of information.

TABLE 1.1 Typical operational, tactical, and strategic information needed to achieve organizational objectives for the functional areas of a manufacturing company.

Functional Area	Examples of Operational Information	Examples of Tactical Information	Examples of Strategic Information
Corporate planning	Weekly and monthly sales and cost factors	Forecast of yearly sales and cost factors	Forecast of five-year sales and costs
Marketing	Open sales orders	Accurate market forecasts	Projected forecasts of product lines and new markets
Research and development	Uncompleted research and development orders	On-going research and development progress reports	Long-range evaluation of pure and applied research
Engineering	Engineering specifications	Engineering progress reports	Product design of new products
Manufacturing	Uncompleted manufacturing orders	Proper loading of machinery and equipment for current orders	Optimum allocation of present manufacturing facilities as well as projecting future plant needs
Inventory	Inventory on hand—raw materials, work in process, and finished goods	Periodic inventory summaries	New methods and models to minimize inventory
Purchasing	Open purchase orders	Vendor performance evaluation	New sources for buying at lower prices
Physical distribution	Outgoing freight routes and rates	Shipping schedules between company plants and warehouses	More efficient transportation methods from company to customers
Accounting	Payroll and cost records	Periodic department (actual vs. budget) reports	Projected financial statements for five years
Finance	Cash on hand and in short-term securites	Alternative investment opportunities for return on short-term assets	Future long-term capital needs from outside sources
Personnel	Personnel history and information needs	Negotiations with labor unions	Present and projected personnel requirements

□ following through to ensure that broad plans are being achieved and objectives realized

Tactical Information for Middle Management

Tactical information covers relatively short time periods (not greater than twelve months); it is used by middle management to implement strategic plans at functional levels. It centers around the delineation of subordinate plans necessary for implementing a particular strategy, and then maintaining and controlling the actual performance against the defined plans. For middle management, the concerns and the decisions revolve mostly around specific funding, responsibility delegation, and follow-through. As with operational information, tactical operational data are used by a large number of people. Examples are a functional budget report comparing actual to estimated amounts, a production report evaluating assembly operations, and a vendor performance evaluation report that rates overall vendor performance. Examples of tactical information are shown in table 1.1.

At the middle management level, inspiring management commitment in support of system development is important. A well thought-out application can significantly affect the company's profits. Hence, management must participate in the project prioritization process, select the best alternatives based upon cost-benefit tradeoff relationships, and approve the relevant expenditure of the resources required to make things happen. They must also participate in the coordination between various organizational entities to resolve conflicts that may arise between the different user groups contending for limited information systems resources.

Operational Information for Lower Management

Operational information, being at the lowest level, is concerned with structured and repetitive activities that are measurable in achieving specific results. It allows line managers, such as plant foremen and department heads, to measure performance against predetermined goals, including standards and budgeted figures. Similarly, operational information allows lower management to evaluate operating standards and policies and how they can be improved to assist day-by-day operations. The feedback of essential information from this low level keeps higher levels of management aware of any significant changes or results. Illustrated in table 1.1 is typical operational information for the major systems of a manufacturing company.

To the information systems department, the information user is most important, because the user triggers the development of systems and ultimately determines the success or failure of the system. But for systems to be successful, managers at the operational level who are system users must discharge certain responsibilities. They must re-examine the patterns of the past and creatively conceive new systems to increase corporate profitability, better control and manage the function, and improve efficiency of the operation. Before going forward with new systems, they should ensure that the development project is sound—that it is both economically justified and operationally feasible. Also, they should be creative, and yet not automate for the sake of automation.

Summary: The Manager and the Types of Information

Strategic information normally helps *top management* set priorities, develop strategies, initiate programs, and establish policies to govern the acquisition, use, and disposition of the organization's resources to achieve organizational objectives.

Tactical information is employed by *middle management* to implement overall strategic planning and specific plans for the organization's functional areas.

Operational information is used by *lower management* for controlling structured and repetitive activities that are measurable by specific results.

Characteristics of Management Information

As noted previously, different levels of management require different information. The higher the level of the decision maker, the more data the individual needs about external conditions. The lines in figure 1.5 cannot be delineated precisely. In a real situation, the lines between categories of decision making are blurred and tend to overlap. MIS analysts must, however, be aware of these types of decision making and how the management information system can be designed to meet differing information requirements.

In figure 1.6, the characteristics of management information as related to the three categories of decision making (strategic, tactical, and operational) are set forth. For each decision-making activity, information needed for planning and control of organization activities must be determined.

Both the systems analyst and the user must consider the scope of coverage, degree of detail, and the contents of reports, as well as the frequency of reporting, period of time to be covered, and distribution and communication methods. The principal user of the information should be given considerable leeway in determining the information requirements and the conditions of processing and communication for effective decision making.

For example—as shown in figure 1.6—the amount of "What if?" information (i.e., "If I modified a certain factor in the problem, what impact would it have on the problem's solution?") for strategic decision making is normally very high for the manager in an effective management information system. Similarly, needs for predictive information on long-term trends and dependence on external information are very high for strategic decision making. As noted in the previous section, the focus of strategic information for top management is on a long time span and not on what will happen in the next day, week, or month. Management information at this level sets the direction for the entire organization by employing problem finding. It anticipates future organizational activities and, thus, often includes external information merged with internal information to result in predictive information centering on trends.

Characteristics of Essential Management Information	CATEGORIES OF DECISION MAKING		
	Strategic	Tactical	Operational
Information that is "What if?" in nature	Very High	High	Low
Predictive information centering on long-term trends	Very High	High	Low
Predictive information centering on short-term trends	High	Very High	Moderate
Dependence on external information	Very High	Moderate	Very Low
Dependence on internal information	Moderate	High	Very High
Information capability of on-line availability	Moderate	High	Very High
Information capability of being reported periodically	Moderate	High	Very High
Current performance information	Moderate	High	Very High
Historical information	Low	High	Very High

FIGURE 1.6
Characteristics of management information as related to the three categories of decision making. Note: *very high, high, moderate,* and *low* refer to the manager's needs.

RELATIONSHIP OF INFORMATION TO INFORMATION RESOURCE MANAGEMENT (IRM)

Now that the essentials of information have been discussed, we explore the relationship of information to a concept known as Information Resource Management (IRM). IRM is the effective management of the organization's information resources. It centers on gathering, storing, and processing data so that the organization can produce the best information with which to make decisions and take appropriate actions. One might ask, "Isn't IRM just an updated form of management information systems developed many years ago?" The answer is "not really." IRM takes into account certain important factors that were not in the realm of MIS at the time. These factors focus on all levels of management making a commitment to IRM and a planning approach that determines how to accomplish the implementation of IRM.

Two Important Factors Governing IRM

The first factor is the commitment of management to information as a major resource (the sixth, as mentioned previously). Finances, people, raw materials, and capital equipment are the most common resources with which management commonly deals. The information resource is often overlooked in preparing for success and working to achieve it. Information is a resource and the business itself is the process that converts this resource into assets. Management is responsible for that conversion, and each manager must know the information requirements of his or her position. Each manager should be asked what information is needed to get the job done. This is essential in converting to the idea of information as a resource.

In addition to knowing what information is needed, each manager must recognize the nature of information required, be it facts and evidence, an estimate based on facts, or a judgment based on experience. Is the requirement for details or a summary? For a summary or an estimate, what range of facts is needed? These considerations help clarify which resources to tap to meet the information requirements. "Data litter" may result from an ill-advised application that uses too few facts to produce summaries or estimates, when a judgment based on experience is required.

The second factor of IRM is planning. Management's commitment to information-as-resource must be expressed in terms of specific events and processes needed to satisfy requirements for information formation and use. This requires an integrating approach throughout the organization and applications of electronic media—uses of mainframes and microcomputers—whenever deemed appropriate. The charter of the planning function must support the goal of providing high-quality information; that is, data provided in a meaningful form and context, when and where they are needed, using means that are practical and cost effective. The planning function's scope encompasses the art and science of organizational management and a blend of overlapping technologies related to data, image, voice, and text processing. The primary means used to span this scope and to achieve the goal is easy-to-use software that provides information for nontechnical end users. A secondary means is to use specialized hardware devices that plug into the processing facility.

Wide Usage of Software Packages for IRM

Within the goal, scope, and methods provided, planning resolves the central issue of IRM: what data to put into a computer data base and how extensively to relate the data deposited there. This involves a number of software packages. The *first* one is a data base management system (DBMS). A DBMS provides many of the necessities for managing information resources: a language for data definition, facilities for acquiring and storing data, a data model for integrating applications, and facilities for "ad hoc" browsing in the data base. A *second* important software package is a data dictionary and directory. Closely integrated with the DBMS, this package is used to document and control the information resource, to monitor data uses, and to analyze the impact of change.

Going beyond DBMS for IRM implementation, application software is a *third* important type. These packages are ready for end (i.e., nontechnical) users, interface directly with the data base, and provide processes and processing options for such varied tasks as order entry and production line balancing. A *fourth* type of software provides aids for developing information systems. Tools for systems analysts, programmers, and administrators help to define the role the computer will play in information formation and communications processes. Beyond the initial development effort, these tools are used to revise and extend the system; to audit system operations, monitor performance, and balance the use of resources; and to troubleshoot and correct problems. *Last* but not least, other pertinent software includes interfaces between the data base/DBMS and the data communications facilities, existing applications software, software utilities, and user interface software and hardware devices such as plotters, graphic terminals, and text, voice, or image processors. Although the above software packages are not mentioned per se in the next section on the essential characteristics of MIS, the framework they provide will be evident in chapter 4 (Computer Hardware) and chapter 5 (Computer Software).

In summary, information resource management recognizes the value of information as a resource and the need to control that resource. It promotes the direct, active management of corporate data and proposes to make information work for the organization in a rational, organized, and well-coordinated manner. The IRM approach challenges the attitude that technology is desirable for its own sake without regard for its larger role in an organization's business. It puts organization goals first, focusing on how to achieve them through applied and integrated technologies. Likewise, IRM focuses on organizational *productivity*. With IRM in place, organizations can capitalize on computer technology to make better decisions and increase productivity at all organizational levels. Essentially, then, the IRM concept provides an underlying framework for effective MIS to assist management in reaching stated goals and objectives.

THE MANAGER AND EFFECTIVE MANAGEMENT INFORMATION SYSTEMS

As indicated previously, the output of a management information system is directed toward assisting management and operating personnel, especially in planning and controlling organization activities. To produce this desired output, the management information system must contain certain characteristics that make this capability feasible. Hence, the characteristics of effective MIS are set forth before we define it. Initially, however, let us discuss the need for such systems.

The Need for Effective MIS

The need for an effective management information system is paramount to the organization now and in the future. The organization does not operate in a vacuum; it must coordinate its operations with the business universe. Of prime importance is information about its markets, current knowledge of its customers and competitors, availability of capital, capabilities of available personnel, and sources of supply. Increasing prices of purchased materials, rising labor costs, and foreign competition signal the need for an information system that describes the organization's economic environment and coordinates the external environment with the internal factors to provide management information.

The management information system, in addition to recognizing environmental trends external to the organization through problem finding, must treat changes that have occurred and will occur in the internal business environment. Advancements in the behavioral sciences and management science and increasing utilization of paperless computer output terminals must be reflected in the design of the management information system. Interdepartmental approaches have transcended the traditional, functional lines of business in complex systems. Still other advances in development have been made regarding methods, procedures, computer equipment, and data communications equipment. By no means is this listing of internal factors complete, but it does serve to exemplify what is causing the organization's MIS to change.

The changes taking place inside and outside the organization generally do not stand alone; each advancement tends to affect and overlap another. As a result, an effective management information system capable of integrating these advances with the needs and capabilities of the organization is needed. More frequent and more accurate information leads to better decisions, thereby enhancing managerial and operational efficiency.

Characteristics of Effective MIS

Over the years, various types of systems have been developed for satisfying the needs of managerial and operational decision making. As will be seen in the next chapter, they have varied from a narrow perspective of accounting to a much broader one that has included the entire organization. Where the accent has been on providing managers with information for the decision-making process, these types of systems have been called *management information systems.*

Figure 1.7 sets forth desirable characteristics of effective management information systems. *First,* effective MIS is a forward- and backward-looking system with integrated subsystems, which can plan and control business activities that are clearly definable within a problem-finding or problem-solving mode. The accent is as much on the planning aspects of an organization as it is on controlling what is happening now in terms of the physical flow and corresponding information flow. The time frame the system comprehends can be relatively short range, today and up to several months, or long range, such as up to five or more years in the future.

Second, reports are prepared to assist management in planning and controlling both current and expected business activities. In addition, periodic reports are prepared for management to show the results of past operations. *Third,* the "management by perception" and the "management by exception" principles are employed to highlight future and current deviations from objectives and financial plans via company-wide long-range plans, including medium- and short-range plans.

Final

1. Type of System

Forward- and backward-looking system with integrated subsystems where the accent is on planning and controlling business activities using problem-finding and problem-solving approaches.

2. Reports Prepared

Assist in planning and controlling current and future business activities. Additionally, control reports are distributed to management that show the results of past operations.

3. Exception Reporting

The "management by perception" and "management by exception" principles are employed to highlight future and current deviations from long- to short-range plans.

4. Great Use of Microcomputers and CRT Terminals of Computer Mainframes

Microcomputers and CRT terminals are used to allow users to retrieve timely information about planning and controlling operations as well as to permit transactional processing of data.

5. Processing Mode

Interactive processing is emphasized for producing desired information quickly. In addition, batch processing is used where necessary.

6. Data Elements

A data base is employed to store the data elements needed by authorized users.

7. Type of Files

Random or direct-access storage files allow the manager to obtain information on line.

8. Mathematical Models

Standard and custom-made mathematical models of management science are employed to plan and control operations.

discuss the eight items dealing w/ effective mgt. system

FIGURE 1.7
Characteristics of effective management information systems.

Fourth, to retrieve timely information about controlling operations as well as to permit transactional processing of data, microcomputers and CRT terminals are utilized. *Fifth,* the accent is on interactive processing for a timely response. Batch processing can be employed for applications that lend themselves to this treatment. Both the interactive- and batch-processing modes are found in effective management information systems; circumstances dictate which mode is best for a specific application.

Sixth, an essential part of effective MIS is the use of data elements to store frequently accessed data. The data elements are accessible only to authorized users. *Seventh,* for many systems, random or direct-access storage is the medium of storing data so that information can be extracted by the manager relatively quickly. *Eighth,* with the storage of on-line data, standard and custom-made mathematical models (taken from the discipline of management science) can be brought into play with these data to produce meaningful output for planning and controlling operations.

Overall, the foregoing characteristics of an effective MIS focus on producing timely information not only to plan and control present and future operations (through problem solving), with an accent on exception items, but also to pinpoint potential problems that need to be rectified by management (through problem finding). From this enlarged perspective, effective management information systems have important capabilities. This will be evident in the next chapter when one of the latest thrusts in MIS—decision support systems—is discussed.

Effective Management Information Systems Defined

Using the capabilities of computers to their fullest, an effective management information system goes beyond problem solving by employing problem finding. It also relies on the decision maker's insights and judgment at all stages of the problem—from problem definition, to choosing the relevant data for analysis, to selecting the approach to be used in generating solutions, and on to evaluating the solutions presented to the decision maker. In essence, effective MIS is comprehensive. By integrating the talents of the decision maker with computing capabilities, it adds a new dimension to the decision-making process for planning and controlling organizational activities.

Integrating the foregoing comments with the essential characteristics of MIS previously enumerated produces a definition of effective management information systems:

✳ Effective management information systems allow the decision maker (i.e., the manager) to combine his or her subjective experience with computerized objective output to produce meaningful information for decision making. They make use of interactive processing whereby query capabilities can be used to obtain desired information for decision making. When appropriate, they utilize mathematical models for problem finding or problem solving. From an overall standpoint, effective management information systems stress a broad perspective by allowing a conversational mode between the decision maker and the computer throughout the entire problem-finding and problem-solving processes.

EFFECTIVE MIS PRACTICE—MANAGERIAL AND USER INVOLVEMENT WITH MIS ANALYSTS

The effective practice of management information systems includes managerial involvement. Management participation in MIS starts at the highest level in an organization. The installation of MIS requires the backing of top management as well as managers below that level that have impact on the system. Lack of their support normally results in less than optimum results for MIS expenditures. Similarly, managerial involvement must be extended to the entire systems development process, thereby greatly reducing the chances of failure in implementing an effective management information system.

Before exploring managerial involvement in effective management information systems, it is wise to take a look at how information systems technology is implemented, whether it be a microcomputer or a computer mainframe. It occurs in four stages. In the *first* stage, potential users begin to see information opportunities for cost reduction or increased productivity in a new technology and they try the technology. The *second* stage becomes a little more serious as new users begin to understand the value of the new information technology and begin to master it. However, the users have not yet started to consider the implications of their tools. In the *third* stage, users are getting sophisticated, shifting from mechanizing procedures to automating functions; they begin to explore the processes—what people actually do instead of how they do it. At the *fourth* and final stage, the functional integration that began earlier with an exploration of processes continues, interweaving automated equipment and activity into the management process.

As the organization progresses through these phases, top management support for the new technology often shifts from disinterest to incipient support to full sponsorship. Indeed, their support and direction is critical for successful survival of the inevitable transitions from the present system to newer forms of management information systems. It is clear that the technology and related services are available today—most of them in an economical form—to allow the involvement of management. It is imperative that managers be at the center of this changing process so that the organization can reap the full benefits of effective management information systems.

For the most part, only managers and their support personnel can define the organization's information needs; the MIS analysts cannot. The managers know what it takes to manage their functions effectively. Managers, therefore, must be directly involved in planning and controlling this changing way of processing information through personal involvement. When a new management information system is designed, what is really being done is changing the ''how'' of an existing system, that is, changing an existing process, be it manual or already computer-based. What happens is that user management gets a totally new way of doing things. But it is impossible to bring about this change effectively if management sits on the sidelines. Through involvement, resistance to change is reduced; the system development process is less difficult.

The most effective management information system is designed when the user conceives the solution because, in the end, it is his or her system. And to make this happen requires meaningful involvement through active user participation. Only when the ultimate user of the system makes the relevant decisions will it be her or his system. Involvement provides one with an opportunity ''to be in on things'' that affect one's own function, an opportunity to contribute ideas, a feeling of satisfaction with the courses of action agreed upon, an understanding of the problems of change, and a sense of responsibility for the success of change. By working together, the expected results are not forever in some grey area. There are no surprises for managers or MIS

23

analysts. There are no misunderstood objectives or fuzzy specifications. There are no unexpected commitments. There are no gaps between promises and results. The need for interaction of users with analysts is paramount in any type of new MIS. This is particularly true for the newer management information systems, since they are designed to support managers in improved decision making, thereby enhancing managerial and operational effectiveness in organizations.

Overall, a close relationship is needed between MIS analysts and managers. Analysts must extend themselves into the manager's world, not the other way around. It is the responsibility of analysts to understand managerial and operational needs and see that resources are put in place to serve those needs. In other words, the MIS analysts need to be able to ''talk'' the language of management for effective MIS.

CHAPTER SUMMARY

This introductory chapter focused on the management of information. Not only was the importance of information stressed, but also its impact on the organization as a sixth major corporate resource, right alongside the traditional 5 M's. Information needed by the various levels of management—lower, middle, and top—was discussed, and the characteristics of information needed at these levels detailed.

From the relationship of the manager to information, our coverage was extended to include the manager's place in effective management information systems and IRM. We stressed the obvious need for effective MIS; we set forth the characteristics of such systems (which will serve as a basis for comparison in the next chapter to other types of information systems). These characteristics formed the underlying framework for defining effective management information systems. Lastly, the effective practice of MIS stresses the need for gaining the backing of management, especially at the top, and for bringing about managerial involvement throughout the system development process. This type of interface of the MIS analysts with the ultimate users in an organization is a must for a successful MIS project.

QUESTIONS

1. **a.** Of what value is information to management? To operating personnel?
   b. Is there such a thing as ''too much'' or ''too little'' information?
2. **a.** Distinguish between problem finding and problem solving.
   b. Distinguish between ''management by perception'' and ''management by exception.''
3. What is the relationship of information and MIS to the management functions and corporate resources?
4. Why should information be considered a sixth major corporate resource just as money, materials, machines, men (i.e., people), and management—(the 5 M's)—are?

5. What is the relationship of the management functions to an MIS?

6. How do information needs of top management differ from those of lower and middle management?

7. What is the relationship of the classification of information to the three categories of decision making?

8. **a.** Define information resource management (IRM).
   b. What is the relationship of information to IRM? Explain thoroughly.

9. What characteristics found in management information systems have proven to be effective for meeting an organization's needs?

10. Distinguish between a forward-looking control system and a backward-looking control system.

11. Why is it necessary to have the backing of top management before undertaking an MIS project?

12. How important is managerial and user involvement in the development of effective management information systems?

13. How can computers, i.e., micros and mainframes, assist managers and their staff in fulfilling their basic functions of planning, organizing, directing, and controlling?

PROBLEMS

14. Information is a vital resource for performing the management functions of planning, organizing, directing, and controlling. Hence, management information systems have been developed to help managers perform their essential functions. On the other hand, what type of information systems have been developed for operating personnel under managers? Are they termed "operational information systems?" If not, what type of information systems are useful to assist these operational people in terms of planning and controlling day-by-day operations? Explore thoroughly.

15. Inasmuch as every system is a part of a larger system, which, in turn, is a part of a much larger system, discuss the relationship of information as developed and produced by each of the various-sized systems. In your discussion, relate the information needs of top, middle, and lower management to one another. Also, consider the relationship of the varied-sized systems to the management functions of planning, organizing, directing, and controlling.

16. Typical types of operational, tactical, and strategic information were given in table 1.1. Using the functional areas of marketing, develop a list of at least six examples of tactical information that is useful to middle-level managers in marketing. Also, develop a list of six examples of strategic information that is helpful for a top-level finance vice-president.

ch. 12 marketing
ch. 14 finance

PROJECTS

17. In figure 1.1, it was shown that a typical business manager obtains information from a management information system to make decisions over his or her functional area. Based upon this information flow, draw a block diagram that depicts

25

the flow of all sources of information that are available to a marketing manager or a manufacturing manager in a typical business organization. Consideration should be given to information received daily, weekly, monthly, or over some other period, in terms of output (such as weekly orders processed) or reports (such as monthly departmental budget versus actual report).

18. The marketing department of the Kenmore Corporation has under consideration ten new products. It must evaluate and select what products best serve the corporation's needs currently. Because this new-product planning cuts across many functions of the organization, state what these functional areas might be. Also, state what important information is needed from the management information system to support managerial decision making in the evaluation and selection of the proposed new products. Write a memorandum to the marketing manager summarizing all of this.

19. Mr. Robert Johnson is the MIS manager of the Lipson Company, a small but decentralized organization with a diversified product line. Recently, the executive vice-president of the company said to him: "Bob, I would like to find out if our management information system for the whole company is really helping management improve their decisions. I am not interested in the efficiency of computer operations per se in this connection, but rather in managerial decision making at all levels of the company."

In the role of Mr. Johnson, write a memorandum to reassure the executive vice-president that the MIS organization is assisting in managerial decision making. Include in your memo a list of areas that you have investigated to ensure improved managerial decision making within the present MIS environment.

BIBLIOGRAPHY

Ackley, D., and Ackley, P. "Can MIS Lead the Push for Productivity?" *Computerworld,* March 11, 1985.

Allen, B. "An Unmanaged Computer System Can Stop You Dead." *Harvard Business Review,* November-December 1982.

Appleton, D. S. "Information Asset Management." *Datamation,* February 1, 1986.

Argyris, C. "Organizational Learning and Management Information Systems." *Data Base,* Winter-Spring 1982.

Ashkenas, R. N., and Schaffer, R. H. "Managers Can Avoid Wasting Time." *Harvard Business Review,* May-June, 1982.

Axelrod, C. W. "The New Economics of Computers." *Infosystems,* June 1985.

Bitran, G. R. "Productivity Measurement at the Firm Level." *Interfaces,* May-June 1984.

Bryce, M. "Information Resources Mismanagement." *Infosystems,* February 1983.

Buss, M. D. J. "Penny-Wise Approach to Data Processing." *Harvard Business Review,* July-August 1981.

Buzacott, J. A. "Productivity and Technological Change." *Interfaces,* May-June, 1985.

Carter, J. C. "Establishing a MIS." *Journal of Systems Management,* January 1980.

Cerveny, R. P., and Clark, T. D., Jr. "Conversations on Why Information Systems Fail—And What Can Be Done About It." *Systems, Objectives, Solutions, 1,* 1981.

Chandler, J. S., Trone, T., and Weiland, M. "Decision Support Systems Are for Small Businesses." *Management Accounting,* April 1983.

Connell, J. J. "The Fallacy of Information Resource Management." *Infosystems,* May 1981.

Diebold, J. "Computers Are Changing the Way Your Company Competes." *Infosystems,* March 1985.

Durell, W. "The Politics of Data." *Computerworld,* September 9, 1985.

Edelman, F. "The Management of Information Resources—A Challenge for American Business." *MIS Quarterly,* March 1981.

Franz, C. R., and Robey, D. "Organizational Context, User Involvement, and the Usefulness of Information Systems." *Decision Sciences,* Vol. 17, 1986.

Freedman, D. H. "The CEO & MIS: A Promising Partnership." *Infosystems,* February 1986.

Friendly, D. "Helping Corporate Executives Wade through Data to Find Information." *Data Communication,* September 1986.

Gallant, J. "Third Era of Info Systems—DSS—Examined." *Computerworld,* March 15, 1984.

Gluck, F. W., Kaufman, S. P., and Walleck, A. S. "Strategic Management for Competitive Advantage." *Harvard Business Review,* July-August 1980.

Gordon, R. M. "Information as a Corporate Asset." *Management Technology,* June 1983.

Hallam, T. A. "Control of MIS: A Comprehensive Model." *Journal of Systems Management,* January 1983.

Harris, C. L. "Information Power." *Business Week,* October 14, 1985.

Highsmith, J. "Synchronizing Data with Reality." *Datamation,* November 1981.

Hoover, T. B. "Decision Support at Conrail." *Datamation,* June 1983.

Horton, F. W., Jr. "The Knowledge Gateway System to Information Access." *Computerworld,* December 5, 1983.

Judson, A. S. "Productivity Strategy and Business Strategy: Two Sides of the Same Coin." *Interfaces,* January-February 1984.

Katzan, H. Jr. *Management Support Systems.* New York: Van Nostrand Reinhold, 1983.

Kellerher, J. "Tackling Information Management." *Business Computer Systems,* October 1985.

Koprowski, E. "Exploring the Meaning of 'Good' Management." *Academy of Management Review,* July 1981.

Lance, P. H., and Barbaro, R. D. "MIS Executives Face Changing Times." *Financial Executive,* August 1981.

Lecht, C. P. "Users Trail Galloping Progress of Technology." *Computerworld,* April 15, 1985.

Levine, A. "Manage Information Systems: 'The New MIS'." *Infosystems,* September 1981.

Lipner, L. D. "Tomorrow's Information Demands Could Bowl You Over." *Business Software Review,* May 1986.

Mandell, M. "MIS/DP: Apocalypse Now." *Computer Decisions,* November 5, 1985.

Markel, E. N. "Will We Manage Technology or Will Technology Manage Us?" *Information Management,* July 1984.

Matlin, G. L. "IRM: How Will Top Management React?" *Infosystems,* October 1980.

McEnaney, M. "DSS Playing Larger Part in End-User Productivity." *Computerworld,* June 3, 1985.

McFarlan, F. W.; McKenney, J. L.; and Pyburn, P. "The Information Archipelago—Plotting a Course." *Harvard Business Review,* January-February, 1983.

————. "The Information Archipelago—Governing the New World." *Harvard Business Review,* July-August 1983.

————. "The Information Archipelago—Maps and Bridges." *Harvard Business Review,* September-October 1982.

McKibbin, W. L. "Awaiting the Intelligent Computer." *Infosystems,* August 1983.

Mehra, B. K. "Putting Management Back Into MIS." *Computerworld,* August 10, 1981.

Miles, M. "Information Management: Becoming a Specialist's Game?" *Computer Decisions,* November, 1984.

Miller, F. W. "Will Top Management's Attitude Sink the MIS Ship?" *Infosystems,* February 1981.

Minicucci, R. "DSS: Computer Wizardy for the Executive." *Today's Office,* June 1983.

Morey, R. C. "Estimating and Improving the Quality of Information in a MIS." *Communications of the ACM,* May 1982.

Morgan, H. "The Microcomputer and Decision Support." *Computerworld,* August 19, 1985.

Murray, J. P. "MIS and a State-of-the-Art Environment." *Computerworld,* April 9, 1984.

————. "MIS Decisions Can Make or Break a Firm." *Computerworld,* March 12, 1984.

Nolan, R. L. "Managing the Crises in Data Processing." *Harvard Business Review,* March-April 1979.

————. "Managing Information Systems by Committee." *Harvard Business Review,* July-August 1982. ✻

O'Riordon, P. D. "Trends in Information Technology." *Information Management,* January 1985.

Papageorgiou, J. C. "Decision Making in the Year 2000." *Interfaces,* April 1983.

Pearson, W. H. "Information: Using It As a Profitable, Strategic Asset." *Management Information Systems Week,* April 28, 1982.

Pezar, P. P. "Planning in the 80s." *Managerial Planning,* March/April 1981.

Pomerantz, D. "Managing Information in the Eighties." *Today's Office,* February 1983.

Poppel, H. "New Partners in Information." *Computerworld,* May 6, 1985.

Powell, D. B. "Future Smart." *Computerworld,* September 12, 1983.

Rhodes, W. L., Jr. "Information Systems Management, A Hybrid Blossoms." *Infosystems,* January 1981.

Rittersbach, G. H. "The 'Computer-Illiterate' Executive." *Financial Executive,* January 1982.

Roach, J. M. "Simon Says . . . Decision Making Is a "Satisficing' Experience." *Management Review,* January 1979.

Rochart, J. F. and Treacy, M. E. "The CEO Goes on-Line." *Harvard Business Review.* January–February, 1985. ✻

Roman, D. "MIS on the Attack." *Computer Decisions,* February 26, 1985.

Salerno, L. M. "What Happened to the Computer Revolution?" *Harvard Business Review,* November-December, 1985. ✻

Saunders, C. S. "Management Information Systems, Communications, and Departmental Power: An Integrative Model." *The Academy of Management Review,* July 1981.

Sayles, L. R. "Managerial Productivity: Who Is Fat and What is Lean?" *Interfaces,* May-June 1985.

Schultz, B. "Business Prepares to Embrace MIS." *Computerworld,* December 28, 1981, and January 4, 1982.

————. "Data as a Corporate Resource." *Computerworld,* December 28, 1981, and January 4, 1982.

Settanni, J. A. "Information Systems Management Values." *Administrative Management,* April 1986.

Shoor, R. "Micro Managers: New Skills & Problems." *Infosystems,* January 1986.

Solomon, S. H. "The Politics of Systems." *Datamation,* December 1983. ✻

Stonecash, J. C. "The IRM Showdown." *Infosystems,* October 1981.

Strassman, P. "Information Payoff." *Computerworld,* February 11, 1985.

Synnott, W. R. "Changing Roles for Information Managers." *Computerworld,* September 21, 1981.

Synnott, W. R., and Gruber, W. H. *Information Resource Management.* New York: John Wiley & Sons, 1981.

Thierauf, R. J. *Decision Support Systems for Effective Planning and Control—A Case Study Approach,* Englewood Cliffs, NJ: Prentice-Hall, 1982.

Thierauf, R. J., and Reynolds, G. W. *Effective Information Systems Management.* Columbus, OH: Charles E. Merrill Publishing Company, 1982.

Venkatakrishnan, V. "The Information Cycle." *Datamation,* September 1983. ✻

Vincent, D. R. "Information as a Corporate Asset." *Computerworld,* September 26, 1983.

Zannetos, Z. "Strategies for Productivity." *Interfaces,* January-February 1984.

Ziehe, T. W. "What Management Should Know About IRM." *Computerworld,* October 13, 1980.

CHAPTER 2

Development of Effective Management Information Systems

ISSUES

What significant information systems have been developed over the years in response to new computer developments?

What is the important distinction between backward-looking and forward-looking information systems?

What types of management information systems are in use today?

What is the relationship of information centers to MIS?

What impact are expert systems making on business currently?

How can a typical business organization reap the benefits of important developments in management information systems?

EFFECTIVE MIS PRACTICE—DISTRIBUTED
DECISION SUPPORT SYSTEMS
   Improved Approach to Problem Finding and
     Problem Solving

CHAPTER SUMMARY
QUESTIONS, PROBLEMS, AND PROJECTS
BIBLIOGRAPHY

INTRODUCTION TO EFFECTIVE MANAGEMENT
INFORMATION SYSTEMS

Today, the computer has moved out of the data processing center into the manager's office. Whether it takes the form of a microcomputer or a multi-function management work station is unimportant. What is important is that the computer is the manager's "partner" for supporting more effective decision making. One of the major factors responsible for bringing the computer into the manager's office has been the growth of distributed data processing (DDP) systems. Basically, these types of systems allow computers to be dispersed throughout the organization, giving managers immediate access to decision-making information. As a result, computer power can be made available for applications—and at locations—that were previously considered uneconomical.

To put present management information systems in proper perspective, systems predating MIS developments are noted initially in the chapter. They include custodial accounting systems, responsibility reporting systems, and integrated data processing systems. This is followed by a discussion of the essentials of integrated MIS, real-time MIS, distributed DP, and decision support systems. Next, a tie-in of information centers to these management information systems is given. Finally, expert systems for business, the latest development in MIS, are explored. As well as being an overview, this background material sets the stage for the entire book, in particular for the master case study. This example depicts the implementation of an MIS at a typical company, the XYZ Corporation; it is presented later in the text.

SYSTEMS PRIOR TO MANAGEMENT INFORMATION
SYSTEMS

Systems prior to management information systems have been *backward looking;* that is, they have concentrated on producing various types of historical reports, particularly accounting reports. For the most part, they were not designed to produce relevant information for controlling current operations or planning future operating conditions. These backward-looking systems centered around the following:

□ custodial accounting systems
□ responsibility reporting systems
□ integrated data processing systems

30   Each of these systems is explored in the following pages.

CUSTODIAL ACCOUNTING SYSTEMS. Because information systems prior to the introduction of computers were concerned generally with historical facts (in particular, the company's balance sheet and income statement), there was little concern for control of operations day by day or hour by hour. Emphasis was on what had *occurred,* not on what *might be done* to plan and control current operations. This orientation led to what is now termed *custodial accounting systems.*

In custodial accounting systems, manual methods, bookkeeping equipment, and punched card equipment were used to process batched data. The company's major functional areas were treated as separate entities in record keeping. No attempt was made to integrate records that might serve several functions at the same time. Not only was there a proliferation of excess records in the company, but it also generally took a long time to produce historical reports. By the time data were assimilated, it was much too late for meaningful analysis. Currently, the custodial accounting system approach is used by very small businesses.

RESPONSIBILITY REPORTING SYSTEMS. An outgrowth of custodial accounting systems was the preparation of reports on the basis of responsibility assignments. *Responsibility reporting systems* accumulate historical data for specific time intervals according to the company's various activities and levels of responsibility. The basis for determining responsibility is the company's organization structure. Responsibility reporting is concerned with activities that are directly controllable and accountable by the individual.

Under responsibility reporting, each manager, regardless of level, has the right to participate in the preparation of the budget by which the individual is evaluated monthly. Although *noncontrollable* costs are included in the reports distributed, the manager is held accountable only for unfavorable deviations of *controllable* costs from the predetermined plans or the budget. The budget is constructed from the top level of management to the lowest level, that of a foreman, department head, or supervisor. Only in this manner is the individual held accountable for costs that he or she controls directly.

An examination of the responsibility reporting approach indicates that its initial accounting applications were discrete and were processed individually. There were several reasons for this approach. First, computers were regarded as large accounting machines that represented only a further mechanization of the accounting section. For example, first payroll was designed and programmed, followed by accounts receivable, then inventory, and so forth. Second, this piecemeal approach was the result of following traditional organizational boundaries. Third, these installations were justified not on the basis of giving management more information and control over their entire operations, but on the basis of the computer's ability to perform accounting jobs faster and more economically. Because of the stress on accounting applications, the computer system generally became a part of the accounting department within its existing framework.

Overall, responsibility reporting systems are an improvement over custodial accounting systems. Although output is oriented toward historical reporting of accounting activities, such systems fail to take into account the integration of a company's systems (i.e., marketing, manufacturing, etc.) with accounting. Responsibility reporting systems, then, are extremely narrow in perspective, although they are still in use by small businesses.

INTEGRATED DATA PROCESSING SYSTEMS. As time passed, systems designers saw that operations go considerably beyond the accounting aspects. They recognized the great need for a system that integrated all systems and related subsystems that can be logically interrelated. The system must integrate people, machines, money, materials, and management in conformity with the company's objectives, policies, methods, and procedures. The net result is a unified system, commonly known as an *integrated data processing system.*

In addition to embracing a network of related systems and subsystems for carrying out an organization's major functions, integrated data processing systems have other distinguishing characteristics. An example is single data entry for multiple uses. Data entered into the system are based on the *single record concept.* In essence, single data entry for multiple uses transcends organizational boundaries. Data are stored in a machine-processible form that can be used by many functional areas. Records that are kept for one purpose may actually have several other uses. Related elements in different processing activities are combined into common, coordinated procedures and work flows.

The integration of many data processing activities not only reduced the duplication of data, but also improved the coordination of the company's major functions with one another. However, the integration of major functional activities does not in itself guarantee optimum results. In addition to historical output reports prepared for various operating levels, output for planning and controlling current operations is needed. Thus, reports that could better facilitate management functions were lacking in integrated data processing systems. Despite this major deficiency, this type of system is still in use where the main accent is on batch processing.

PAST AND CURRENT MANAGEMENT INFORMATION SYSTEMS

The previously discussed systems focused on historical reporting, particularly in the form of financial reports. Because of this narrow perspective, the real needs of management were not being met; that is, the manager's ability to plan and control current as well as future organization activities was not being enhanced. A broader perspective was needed to satisfy management needs. Through continued improvements over time, various types of management information systems were developed, among them:

- integrated management information systems
- real-time management information systems
- distributed data processing systems
- decision support systems

Each type is important and is discussed here in detail. In addition, expert systems in business environments are explored.

Integrated Management Information Systems

Several of the shortcomings of the integrated data processing system were remedied by improving upon its basic concepts. Among the improvements were the preparation of output reports for all management levels and the programming of routine decision making, where feasible. An integrated management information system involves more than a mechanical linking together of various organizational functions. It also aids management by taking over routine decision making. If a manager can completely define the decision process, the decision can be computerized. Thus, management can concentrate its efforts on those areas that are not routine.

The net result of this system upgrading was an integrated management information system—a system designed to provide selected decision-oriented information needed by management to plan and control the activities of the organization. It emphasizes profit planning, performance planning, and control at all levels. It contemplates the integration of all required business information subsystems, both financial and nonfinancial, within the organization.

REPORTS TO ASSIST MANAGEMENT. Formerly, the primary interest of business information systems lay in developing financial statements. When an integrated MIS is installed, its major purpose is the production of reports that will assist management. The periodic financial reports are secondary, a by-product of the information processed that assists in controlling current operations. Thus, integration of data processing records serves several uses, thereby reducing the costs of obtaining essential managerial reports.

INTEGRATED MIS FOR A TYPICAL ORGANIZATION. The introduction of a customer order creates an open order file that forms the basis for preparing invoices and for later updating the accounts receivable file. The customer order also affects the raw material orders, manpower scheduling, production scheduling, finished goods inventory, shipping orders, sales commissions, and marketing forecasts. Incoming orders, through their effect on inventory levels, may trigger an automatic computer reordering subroutine through the issuance of a purchase order. (The reorder quantity is based on reorder levels and quantities determined by mathematical formulas designed as part of the system.) The purchase orders, in turn, create a liability, requiring payment to vendors. In such a system, the operations aspects of order entry, billing, accounts receivable, inventory control, purchasing, and accounts payable are interwoven. This approach is shown in figure 2.1.

Data input from the major business functions (such as that which illustrated the parts of the foregoing integrated MIS) is sent to a computer system on some predetermined periodic basis. There it joins inputs from previous periods on master files of data on customers, employees, inventories, and all other business phases accumulated from previous processing cycles. As current data

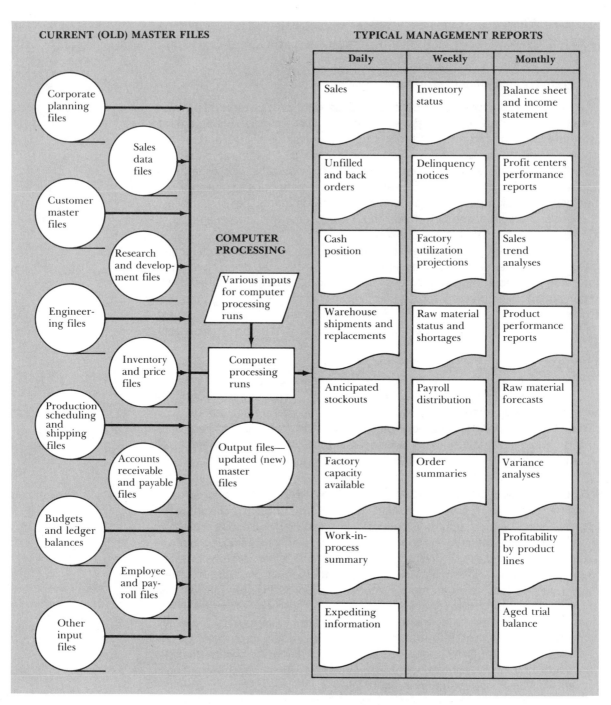

FIGURE 2.1   Integrated management information system for a typical manufacturing company where data are stored on magnetic tape files. Data files can be used to produce a wide range of management reports.

are processed by the computer system, the appropriate master files are updated. From these files, documents, forms, and reports are prepared automatically. The kinds and number of control and information reports generated from the basic data are dictated by the needs of management and the capabilities of the equipment.

Although the preceding discussion emphasized sequential access files, integrated MIS can also employ random access files. Random access files are not illustrated in figure 2.1.

ESSENTIAL CHARACTERISTICS OF INTEGRATED MIS.   An integrated management information system, then, is a network of related subsystems, integrated to perform the functional activities of an organization. Its essentials include producing meaningful output for management and taking over routine decision making. Transactions that are common to all departments are stored in a data file or data bank. Those that affect more than one functional area are captured only once and then processed in a manner appropriate for all users of the information. It is, therefore, a considerable improvement over prior systems.

SHORTCOMINGS OF INTEGRATED MIS.   Even though the integrated management information system went beyond an accounting orientation and is clearly a business information system that provides feedback in the form of management reports throughout its various subsystems, it still remains deficient in one important respect. Data must be batched, that is, accumulated for a period of time, before processing becomes feasible. Whether sequential (i.e., magnetic tape) or random access (i.e., magnetic disk) files are used, there is still the problem of time lag. For this reason all prior systems, whether they are custodial accounting, responsibility, integrated data processing, or integrated management information systems, are called *backward-looking control systems*. The methods, procedures, and equipment look to past history before reports are produced for feedback. What is needed is a *forward-looking control system*—one that looks to the present and future. Such an approach is found in a real-time management information system.

Real-Time Management Information Systems

Although integrated management information systems are in fact operating in organizations of various sizes, one newer trend in management information systems is the implementation of real-time management information systems, sometimes referred to as on-line real-time systems. Typical applications for such a system include accounts receivable, airline reservation systems, bank deposit and withdrawal accounting, hotel accounting and reservations systems, law enforcement intelligence systems, patient hospital records, savings and loan deposit accounting, and stock market information.

An essential characteristic of this type of system is the on-line real-time concept. All information is *on line,* that is, all data are sent directly into a computer as soon as they come into being. The whole operation is in *real*

35

time, which means data are processed and fed back to the appropriate source in sufficient time to change or control the operating environment. Basically, then, any system that processes and stores data or reports them as they are happening is considered to be an on-line real-time system. Company personnel receive a response from the system in time to satisfy their own real-time environmental requirements. The response time may range from a fraction of a second to minutes, hours, and even days, depending on the attendant circumstances.

To illustrate the concept of on-line real-time systems, we use the example of a production planning department that has developed a computerized on-line daily scheduler. Since all variable manufacturing data are entered as they occur in the local on-site computer system, the on-line data base for this function as well as others is always up to date. At the start of each day, the computerized scheduler simulates the activities of the factory for that day. Knowing what has occurred during the previous day, where jobs are backed up or behind schedule and where production bottlenecks are currently occurring, this manufacturing simulation model can determine what will happen as the day begins and alert the foremen and plant supervisor to critical areas that need immediate attention. A response, then, has been fed back in sufficient time to control the upcoming manufacturing activities.

INTEGRATION OF SUBSYSTEMS. A real-time system must be integrated in order to be effective. Data acquired from one source are often present in many subsystems. If an integrated approach is not used, there is much wasted effort and extra cost, since each subsystem must treat the same data without taking advantage of processing accomplished by other subsystems.

COMMON DATA ELEMENTS. The integrated data accumulated from the many detailed on-line transactions are commonly referred to as the data base elements or the organization's data base. In addition to having all data collected in one place (basically secondary on-line storage), the same data are useful for many departments. The same inventory data base may be used by a number of departments, such as sales, manufacturing, production control, inventory control, purchasing, and finance. In another example, a data base element might be an employee number that is used in preparing weekly payroll, referencing personnel records, filling new job openings, preparing contract negotiations, and the like. Thus, a data base refers to elements or data bits in a common storage medium that form the foundation for operational information.

REPORTS TO LOWER AND MIDDLE MANAGEMENT. Designing a data base structured to accommodate the various levels of management (lower, middle, and top) is a formidable task. Currently, systems satisfy the needs of lower and middle management for organizing, directing, and controlling activities around the established plans, being in conformity with the organization's objectives. Hence, real-time management information systems are focused on such areas as improved forecasting for all phases of the organization, optimum marketing budget, improved shipping schedules and service to customers, better utilization of production facilities, improved vendor performance, higher return on short-term assets, and improved negotiations with labor.

ON-LINE INPUT/OUTPUT DEVICES.   Within the MIS environment, a number of on-line input/output (I/O) devices are located throughout the organization's operations. CRTs and printers can both send and receive information. They may be miles away from one another, but are linked through a data communication network extending from the local computer and/or regional computer to the central computing facility.

REAL-TIME MIS FOR A TYPICAL ORGANIZATION.   A real-time system at the home office, for example, may be so designed that input data from an I/O device will trigger a production order when inventory reaches a predetermined level. The number of units to be produced will be based on an economic order quantity conforming to a mathematical model. The computer program will scan the present production schedules of plants throughout the country and determine which plant will produce the order, based on its capabilities and previous production commitments. Likewise, the computer program will indicate to which warehouse the products will be shipped, based on proximity to the factory and the level of present inventory. During this on-line processing, the computer files are updated simultaneously to reflect these changing conditions. Such an approach is shown in figure 2.2.

Input data (from the major business functions) for the real-time management information system is sent to the computer system as it is entered (as shown in figure 2.2). In some cases, it may be necessary to process the input data against the on-line data base to produce desired output. This may take the form of the output illustrated in figure 2.3. The types of outputs generated from real-time processing are a function of the needs of management and operating personnel to control present and future operations.

ESSENTIAL CHARACTERISTICS OF REAL-TIME MIS.   There are many essential characteristics of a real-time management information system. A real-time MIS, being a forward-looking control system, maintains data base elements on line so that they are available to the computer system when needed. The organization's data base (locally, regionally, or centrally located) is always updated as events occur and can be interrogated from many I/O terminals. With source data being entered as they happen, the real-time approach reduces repetitious recording, makes data available to all subsystems needing them, and reduces the errors in conflicting reports that arise from varying coding methods or interpretations and unsynchronized timing. As a result, all departments work with the same information, thereby making it possible to tie in their decisions with those of other functions. Also, information stored on line can be obtained upon request from a number of locations at a distance from the main computer system. It is possible to process data in real time so that output may be fed back almost instantaneously to control current operations. The on-line computer's ability to provide timely, important information

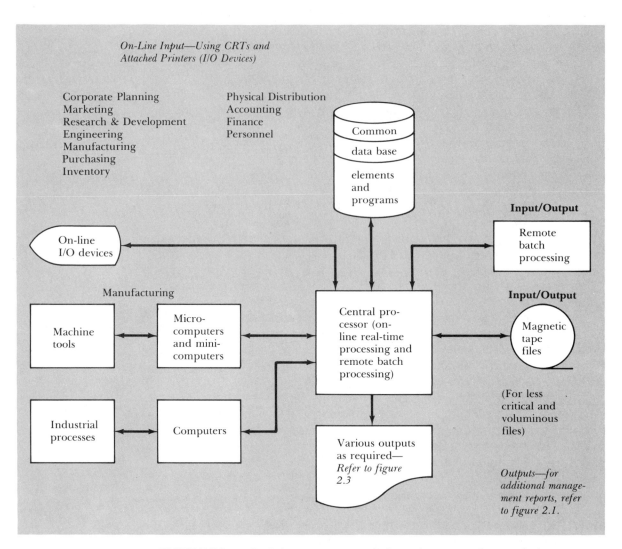

On-Line Input—Using CRTs and
Attached Printers (I/O Devices)

Corporate Planning   Physical Distribution
Marketing   Accounting
Research & Development   Finance
Engineering   Personnel
Manufacturing
Purchasing
Inventory

Common
data base
elements
and
programs

On-line
I/O devices

Input/Output
Remote
batch
processing

Input/Output

Manufacturing

| Machine tools | Micro-computers and mini-computers |

Central pro-
cessor (on-
line real-time
processing and
remote batch
processing)

Magnetic
tape
files

(For less
critical and
voluminous
files)

Industrial
processes

Computers

Various outputs
as required—
*Refer to figure
2.3*

*Outputs—for
additional manage-
ment reports, refer
to figure 2.1.*

FIGURE 2.2   Real-time management information system for a typical
manufacturing company where data are stored on magnetic disk files. The common
data base can be used to produce a wide range of management reports.

is its greatest asset. Management can learn of trends, exceptions, and results
of recent decisions in order to initiate corrective action that meets predetermined business plans. Environmental feedback alerts the manager as to how
the total business is operating, whether favorably or unfavorably, in relation
to internal and external conditions.

SHORTCOMINGS OF REAL-TIME MIS.   Even though a real-time MIS gives
lower and middle managers updated information about the organization's
basic business operations through input/output devices, the same cannot be

TYPICAL ON-LINE OUTPUT (TYPED OR VISUAL)

Corporate Planning
Budget information
Short-range planning
information
Medium-range planning
information
Long-range planning
information

Marketing
Customer order status
Back order status
Finished products
for sale

Research & Development
Research references for
review
Graphic displays
Pure and applied
research results

Engineering
Plotted engineering
data
Results of mathematical
calculations
New engineering designs

Manufacturing
Production order status
Inventory levels on
specific items
Production control
information

Purchasing
Purchase order status
Results of vendor
comparison

Inventory
Shipments received
Location of stock items
Items available in stock

Physical Distribution
Routing information
Shipping schedule data

Accounting
Net profit to date
Accounts exceeding
budget
Accounts receivable
status on accounts
Credit check
Accounts payable by
vendors
Overdue invoices

Finance
Cash flow status
Capital projects
information
Cost of capital
information

Personnel
New personnel needs
Payroll forecasts
Available in-house
personnel to fill new
job openings

FIGURE 2.3
Typical on-line output
(printed or displayed)
of a real-time
management
information system for
a typical manufacturing
company.

said for top management. Although the system does respond to the managerial needs of the first two levels, it falls short of the information relevant to top-level executives. Those in top management are responsible and accountable for the full range of business activities. Their principal task is formulating long-range, strategic plans. No matter what name is used for future planning, a real-time system does not provide long-range information per se. However, it does respond with immediate feedback on present operations, which is essential data for modifying future plans. For further information on these management information systems, consult the author's book on real-time MIS[1] and references at the end of the chapter.

Distributed Data Processing Systems

Distributed data processing, one of the major thrusts in systems today, is widely used by all sizes of organizations to oversee their widely dispersed operations. Because distributed data processing systems adhere to the characteristics of MIS set forth earlier (chapter 1), they can be referred to as distributed management information systems. However, they are designated in the literature as distributed data processing (DDP) systems or simply as distributed systems.

Distributed data processing can be defined as an approach that places low-cost computing power at the various points of data entry and links these points where necessary with a centralized computer via a distributed communications network. In effect, it places computing power where it is needed for efficient and economical DP operations. It is a viable alternative to centralized data processing due to the declining costs of programmable terminals, microprocessors, microcomputers, minicomputers, personal computers, and small business computers. Because the focus of current distributed data processing systems is on placing computer power at the lower levels in an organization, generally their output serves to assist operational (lower) and functional (middle) management.

80–20 RULE OF DATA PROCESSING..   Historically, most computing capabilities depended on one or more large central processing units that were programmed to perform various DP functions. The use of centralized systems created input bottlenecks. Likewise, they created situations where the feedback of business data necessary to run an organization occurred after substantial delays. Distributed data processing thus arose out of the need to get computing power where it is needed—at the lower levels in an organization. Another way of viewing the need for distributed processing is applying the 80–20 rule, which puts computer processing power where 80 percent of the work is done or where results are needed. In general, distributed data processing makes economic sense if 80 percent of the data generated at a downline site is used primarily for that site. Otherwise, other DP approaches, such as those enumerated previoulsy, may be more suitable for meeting an organization's data processing needs.

DISTRIBUTED PROCESSING NETWORK—AN OVERVIEW AND TYPES.   An essential part of a distributed processing system network is the use of data transmission equipment from remote processors to the central computer facil-

---

[1]Robert J. Thierauf, *Systems Analysis and Design of Real-Time Management Information Systems,* Englewood Cliffs, NJ: Prentice-Hall, 1975.

ity. Such an environment has certain operational characteristics. The system should:

□ allow a number of small computers (i.e., microcomputers, personal computers, minicomputers, and small business computers) to be combined to form an operational DP center at more than one location. A network of these centers sharing computerized files provides a powerful data processing capability at local and regional levels.
□ provide on-line data entry to the local and regional data bases for concurrent processing of multiple independent jobs. An operational DP center performs the required DP needs of the remote site while it maintains concurrent high-speed communication with the central computer and other DP centers in the network.
□ permit the development of distributed applications that can be created by the existing DP staff where simplicity of operations is required.
□ provide for generating reports within the network that give operational management control over their operations, as well as summary information for higher levels of management.

Based upon these characteristics, different network configurations can be developed by connecting network elements through communications lines. The more popular types of distributed processing networks are: (1) point-to-point, (2) hierarchical or tree, (3) star, (4) fully connected ring, and (5) hybrid type.

1. POINT-TO-POINT NETWORK

In this simplest type of distributed network, a communications line links two computers together. For this configuration, one machine can be used primarily to process data and the other to perform communications control, message switching, and the like. Each computer performs a complementary function, as illustrated in figure 2.4.

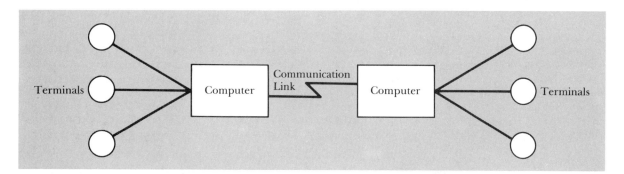

FIGURE 2.4   Point-to-point network of a distributed data processing system (first type).

2. HIERARCHICAL OR TREE NETWORK

In a hierarchical (i.e., tree) network approach, processors, microcomputers, minicomputers, or computers at the local sites perform a determined task and are linked to another, usually larger, computer at the regional sites that monitors their activities and serves as backup should one fail or encounter a problem it cannot handle. In turn, the larger computer is also monitored and controlled by yet another larger computer that may also carry out higher-order processing at the central site. Thus, there is a hierarchy of communications among the machines at the local, regional, and central sites (i.e., at different levels) but and not among the machines at the same level. Many manufacturing-oriented and service-oriented organizations of all sizes make great use of this approach. Because most current distributed data processing networks are of this type, the master case study in chapters 10 through 15 describes such a configuration. A typical example of this network is found in figure 2.5. Local sites feed summary information to the regional sites, which in turn forward summary information to the central site.

3. STAR NETWORK

In this type of configuration, all processors, microcomputers, minicomputers, or computers at the remote sites report to the central site. Although the star is similar organizationally to a two-level hierarchy, it differs in supporting a heavy flow of communications back and forth between the remote machines and the central unit (as found in an airline reservation and ticketing system). In such a network application, a small processor maintains a local file, formats the tickets, and causes them to be issued. In turn, a large computer connected to the smaller ones draws on a master file to determine seat availability on any one of numerous flights. Also, it updates the master file to reflect new reservations or current cancellations. A typical example of the star network configuration is set forth in figure 2.6.

4. FULLY CONNECTED RING NETWORK

For this network configuration, processors, microcomputers, minicomputers, or computers that have powerful local or regional processing capabilities communicate directly with the others. Many times, interactive processing is employed, wherein distributed data communication lines connect each machine with the other machines. A common example of the fully connected ring network is found in banking. If one machine goes down, any of the other machines from another site can be used for processing customer accounts until the disabled computer is up again. An example of a fully connected ring network is illustrated in figure 2.7.

5. HYBRID-TYPE NETWORK

Using the preceding network types as a basis, a hybrid-type network can be configured to meet the user's needs. For example, several central computers can each be surrounded by a separate star network of remote processors. They also can be connected together by a star network of their own. This multi-star network configuration is an alternative to a high-cost ring network when the main computers are remote from one another. To illustrate the fore-

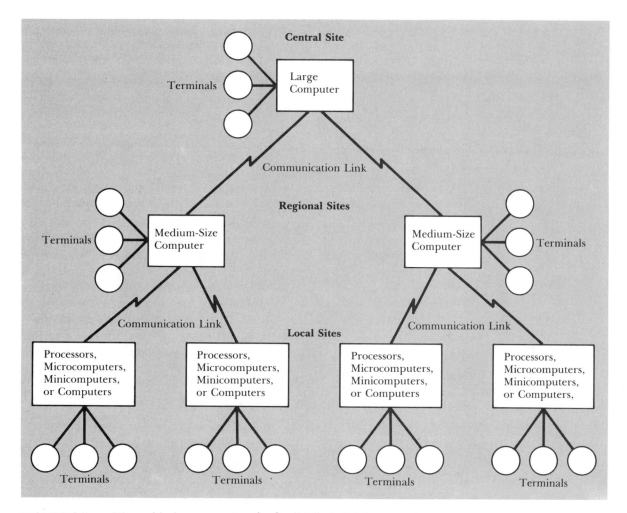

FIGURE 2.5 Hierarchical or tree network of a distributed data processing system (second type).

going DDP network, say a hybrid-type network is used by a large department store chain. To serve the chain in one city, each store has a computer that is linked to point-of-sale cash registers in a star configuration. The computers of all stores are tied together in a star via direct communication lines. Also, one of these is the host to the other computers as well as its own satellite computers. In such an arrangement, department 'store management at the home office can obtain current inventory information, sales data, and other desired information deemed important by management quickly, broken down by individual store performances or applied to the chain collectively.

DISTRIBUTED DATA BASES. To overcome objections to a large, centralized common data base, DP strategists came up with the idea of distributed data

43

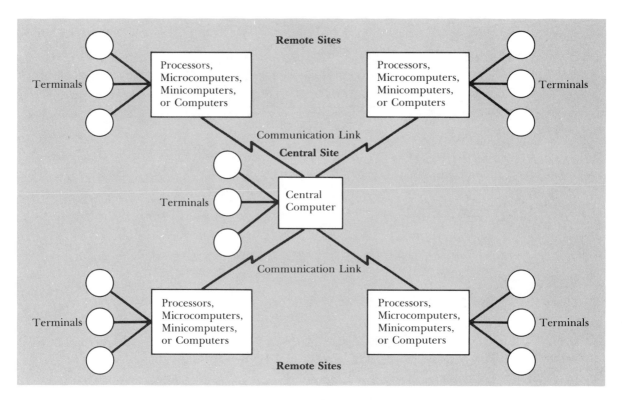

FIGURE 2.6   Star network of a distributed data processing system (third type).

bases where the user's files are placed at or near the point where transactions occur. This way, the user's data are always available; concern about data communications failures is no longer necessary. In addition, distributed data bases caught on for other reasons. Low-cost minicomputers have peripherals and processing power equal to general-purpose computers of yesterday. If the local processing load is taken off the main computer, large-scale systems at the central headquarters level become more manageable since the data base becomes smaller, as does the size of the application programs. Distributed data processing systems can then operate more autonomously at the local and regional levels and, at the same time, become an important part of a processing cooperative. The distribution of data bases at the local, regional, and home-office levels not only makes for more manageable data files, but also allows the data to be located where they are needed most in an organization.

A distributed data base may consist of a single copy of a set of information divided into subsets that are stored at the various locations. This approach is called a *partitioned data base.* Likewise, a distributed data base may consist of a set of information all or selected parts of which exist at two or more locations. This storage scheme is called a *replicated data base.* A distributed system, then, may store data in either of these arrangements, and

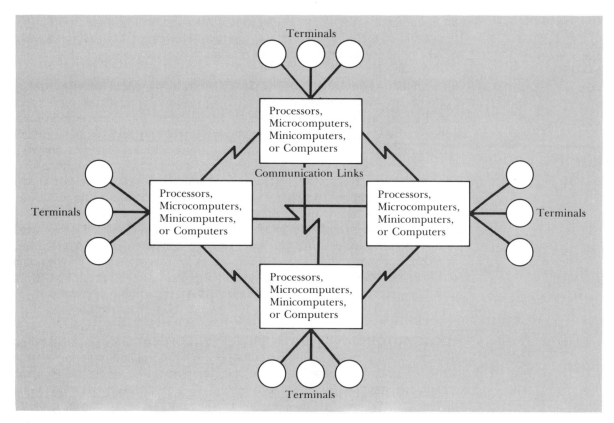

FIGURE 2.7 Fully connected ring network of a distributed data processing system (fourth type).

some systems may include data sets of both types. This gives an organization several ways to distribute processing power and data. For example, a network configured along hierarchical lines may support a replicated data base. Often this is desirable when the master data base is used for summary analysis and periodic, scheduled reporting, while the local and regional data bases are used daily and are frequently updated. Also, the hierarchical distribution of power may support a partitioned data base. This approach is often useful for subdividing along corporate lines—headquarters versus geographically dispersed divisions.

There are still other possible versions. For example, a company with offices on both coasts may partition the master data base among horizontally configured processors. Within each of these horizontal processing configurations, the company can establish hierarchical structures with replicated data bases. The result is a *hybrid system.* When determining whether multiple copies of the data will exist, whether the data base will be partitioned, or whether a hybrid will be implemented, the nature of the applications and the corporate

45

organization are the key considerations. An additional consideration is the time value of the information, that is, where information has to be and when it must be there in order to achieve maximum operational effectiveness.

SIMPLIFIED APPROACH TO PROGRAMMING AND IMPLEMENTATION. Currently, many distributed data processing systems being installed are capable of being programmed and used by operating personnel. Operating managers at the local level, as an example, are employing easy-to-operate data-entry equipment that existing personnel can use without extensive training. Such a source data input system provides computer power during processing of input data. Likewise, operating managers employ easy-to-use distributed processing equipment to sort data into meaningful operating categories and produce timely management information for themselves before the data are transmitted to the DP center. In effect, management information is produced as a normal by-product of a distributed data processing system, operated by non-computer personnel. Such an approach minimizes the impact on the home office data processing staff, preventing it from being spread too thin. Distributed computer capabilities are available to the user without the necessity of distributing computer experts among the lower levels for long periods.

LOCAL AUTONOMY OF DATA PROCESSING OPERATIONS. A distributed data processing system provides autonomy at the local and regional levels in terms of both hardware operation and processing requirements. From an equipment standpoint, the remote system keeps working, performing complete transaction processing even during temporary lapses or unavailability of the centralized computer system. In addition, unique or critical processing requirements can be handled at the operating level because of the ease of program development on a small independent system. Overall, control over local and regional data processing operations is assured.

Not only is there better control over hardware and processing requirements at the operating levels, but also more autonomy results in terms of DP applications. Operational activities and extraordinary items, peculiar to one particular operational system, can be accommodated more easily in a distributed processing environment, resulting in more flexibility. This added dimension of flexibility makes the system more accommodating to the user. Overall, development of distributed data processing applications for unique, operating-level requirements ensures responsive service to management and their staff.

DISTRIBUTED MIS FOR A TYPICAL ORGANIZATION. A manufacturing company operates four plants located throughout the country. In these facilities the company manufactures its finished products. All of these products must be accounted for, both for billing and to ensure that goods are received when the customers order them. As illustrated in figure 2.8, distributed processing is currently in operation at the four plants, from which important information is sent to the central office.

Using CRT units, operators enter information from source documents

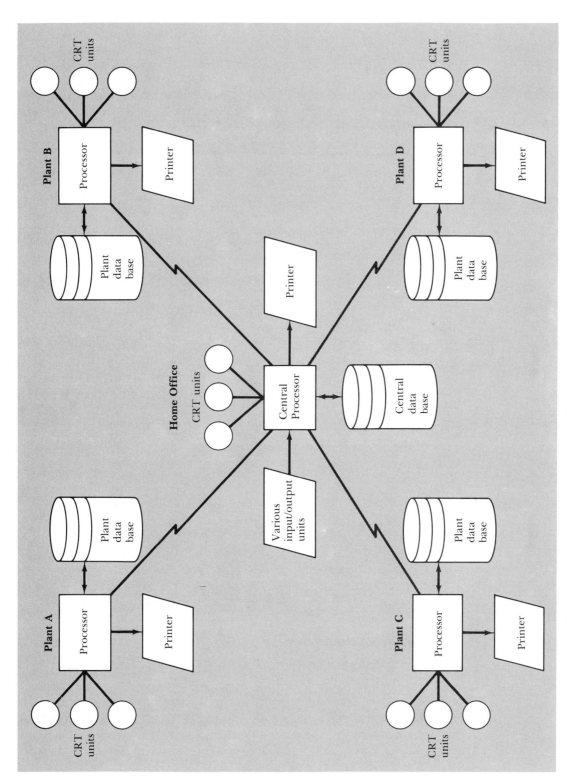

FIGURE 2.8 Distributed data processing system (i.e., distributed management information system) for a typical manufacturing company where there are distributed data bases. The central data base and the plant data bases can be used to produce a wide range of management reports.

about movements of inventory within and out of the plants to customers and for associated billing purposes. The operators can use the screens to display a sequence of preprogrammed formats corresponding to the source documents being processed. The terminals are programmed to reject certain types of entries if they fail to conform to preset range guidelines or symbol conventions. These equipment features help to reduce input errors from source documents, which caused confusion and unnecessary cost in the past.

Terminal units are used to generate many critical documents and lower-level management reports, such as production of finished products and delivery of products to customers. Special instructions for stored goods handling can be introduced into the account file. Duplicate copies of delivery orders can be used as the basis for "picking" instructions for warehouse employees. In addition, the random access memory units allow each operator access to information on the location of every product stored in the plant, facilitating more efficient utilization of time and equipment.

ESSENTIAL CHARACTERISTICS OF DISTRIBUTED DATA PROCESSING SYSTEMS. Fundamentally, distributed data processing can be characterized as an approach aimed at making computer systems more amenable and responsive for use by humans. Instead of having one or two large central processing units perform most of the data processing work, often inefficiently, distributed processing means adding to the system a series of linked minicomputers, personal computers, or microcomputers where terminals can be programmed to react more quickly to the user's needs. With smaller "building blocks" or "modules," users can assemble systems to meet highly specific needs. For example, point-of-sale terminals and bank cash machines can be configured to make operating decisions for personnel at the local level for source data entry. In a similar manner, various types of "intelligent" terminals can be programmed to do much of the processing of data before they communicate and interact with divisional or central computers. Thus, DP needs in an organization can not only be met at the local and regional levels, but also can be integrated with DP operations at central headquarters. In addition, DP operations can be undertaken at less cost in the field (local and regional levels) than at the central office level for making short-range to long-range decisions.

For further information on distributed processing systems, refer to the author's book[2] or others on the subject. In addition, selected references on current DDP articles are given at the end of this chapter.

Decision Support Systems

To satisfy the information needs of management in a "future" environment, the need arose for a new direction in management information systems, frequently referred to as decision support systems. Fundamentally, decision support systems (DSS) are *systems* designed to *support* the *decision-making pro-*

[2]Robert J. Thierauf, *Distributed Processing Systems,* Englewood Cliffs, NJ: Prentice-Hall, 1978.

cess of managers (and of some operating personnel in certain situations, i.e., redesigned work structures). They incorporate features found in prior management information systems and employ mathematical models from the discipline of operations research (management science). They emphasize direct support for managers in order to enhance the professional judgments required in making decisions, especially when the problem structures tend to be semistructured or unstructured. Emphasis is on helping the manager make decisions rather than on actually making decisions for the manager. This interplay results in a total effort that is greater than the manager or the computer operating independently, thereby providing synergistic decision making. Also, only selected information is presented, as opposed to presenting all information that might be useful. Decision support systems thus build upon present management information systems as well as complement them. This relationship is illustrated in figure 2.9 and will be obvious when the functional areas of the XYZ Corporation are designated (refer to chapters 10 through 15).

UTILIZES "MANAGEMENT BY PERCEPTION." Within a DSS environment, *management by perception* is required. As noted in a previous chapter, this principle refers to the ability of management to perceive future external and internal trends before they occur and to determine their impact on new products so as to improve overall organizational performance. It represents a forward-looking as opposed to the backward-looking approach of *management by exception,* which focuses on comparison after the fact. However, it should be pointed out that both have their place in a decision support system.

Representative examples of a forward-looking approach that utilizes the "management by perception" principle include:

- setting long-range plans and objectives for an entire organization that are fully integrated into the major subsystems and their related parts
- planning and evaluating new products over their life cycles
- determining manpower requirements and allocating organization personnel so that the best personnel are placed in the appropriate jobs
- allocating factory capacity most effectively for the entire organization

	Decision Support System	**Prior Management Information Systems**
Problem Structure	Semi-structured and unstructured along with well-structured.	Well-structured.
Decision-Making Capability	Manager–machine interface where the manager retains control over the decision-making process.	New information produced using analytical techniques for specific decision-making situations.
	Synergistic decision making.	Summarization of information in the form of control reports.

FIGURE 2.9
Comparison of decision support systems to prior management information systems in terms of problem structure and decision-making capability.

□ determining material requirements that reduce overall costs for the entire organization

□ acquiring short-, intermediate-, and long-term capital funds as needed for the entire organization

□ determining profit profiles on large alternative investment plans

□ indicating improvements in operating revenues and costs

These representative examples of a broad-based view generally make it easier for top management to accomplish desired organization goals and objectives.

HUMAN–MACHINE INTERFACE.   A fundamental characteristic of decision support systems is the human–machine interface, whereby the decision maker retains control throughout the problem-finding and problem-solving processes. This approach not only results in bringing decision-making information directly to the decision maker, but also goes a step further than typical management information systems by allowing the individual to react to the output. Hence, with the computer, the decision maker can react by getting answers to a series of "What if?" questions rather than just one answer. In this manner, the computer does not have the final say in the problem-solving process, but is simply a tool of the decision maker for evaluating alternatives so that the best decision can be made.

The focus of the human–machine interface is on learning, creativity, and evaluation rather than on replacement, automation, and routine procedures. A DSS approach allows the decision maker to look inside a problem to see what makes it "tick." When doing so, the decision maker will discover new aspects of the problem that were not obvious before. The individual will want to isolate certain parameters and ask a series of "What if?" questions about these selected parameters; that is, "*What* happens to the final results *if* we change this aspect of the problem?" This interplay between the decision maker and the computer provides a new way of arriving at answers to problems.

FACILITATES THE DECISION MAKER'S REASONING PROCESS.   To utilize the capabilities of DSS to their fullest, decision makers use query capabilities to make the system an extension of their reasoning processes. Models of the business environment allow one to envision possibilities for the future, foresee consequences, and evaluate alternative solutions. Based on this view, DSS provides the ability to retrieve information in such a way that meaningful patterns and correlations can be discerned. Hence, the user's reasoning process is augmented. With the use of modeling languages, managers can become competent in constructing and solving models in an interactive, exploratory manner that corresponds loosely to the facilities of memory and reasoning.

Going one step further, query capabilities of decision support systems should be capable of supporting various approaches to decision making. A model of the decision-making process has been developed by Herbert Simon (explored in some depth in the next chapter). He characterized three main steps in the process: (1) intelligence (searching the environment for conditions calling for decision), (2) design (inventing, developing, and analyzing possible courses of action), and (3) choice (selecting a course of action from those available). Overall, an interactive processing mode should provide the decision maker with the capability of facilitating his or her own decision-making process.

EASY-TO-USE APPROACH. The hallmark of an effective decision support system is its ease of use. A DSS should not only support the user in decision making via a human–machine interface, but should also be a natural extension of the user in problem solving. The importance of this characteristic is underscored by the discretionary latitude the user has to develop newer approaches to solving problems that is not normally supported within an MIS framework. It may well be that the user decides to try new ways of combining external information with internal information for solving the problem under study.

By not being constrained by rigid requirements, such as those found in traditional MIS, the DSS user finds the system valuable and convenient to use for solving a difficult problem. Successful DSS should be compatible with the user's modus operandi. The individual should feel that the system really assists rather than threatens or intimidates. The system should allow the user to pursue her or his own natural tendencies toward problem solving. Thus, a decision support system should earn the user's allegiance by being not only valuable and supportive, but also convenient and easy to use.

USE OF MICROCOMPUTERS OR CRT TERMINALS LINKED TO COMPUTER MAINFRAMES. For a human–machine interface, microcomputers or CRT terminals are linked to computer mainframes. In many cases, there is need for graphic capabilities to provide immediate feedback that answers "What if?" questions posed by the decision maker. When a microcomputer or a CRT terminal linked to a computer mainframe with graphic capabilities is on practically every desk, and the power to use this technology is in the employee's hands—and that includes all levels of management—there will be unprecedented acceptance and use of computer technology.

By having appropriate computer power distributed throughout an organization, the human–machine interface will be taken for granted just as the telephone is today. The end result is that the "love-hate" relationship with the computer will mature into a friendship similar to that enjoyed by people and automobiles in the past. Until now, managers have used the computer to analyze past performance; they have shied away from predicting the future with the help of mathematical and statistical models. In the future, there is expected to be a quantum leap in human–machine interaction. The "friendly computer" will be an increasingly powerful analytic tool. It will be relatively easy to use and will provide a convenient extension to the essentially human management process within a DSS environment.

SUPPORT DECISION MAKING FOR SOLVING ALL TYPES OF PROBLEM STRUCTURES. Typically, a decision support system provides assistance in decision making regardless of the type of problem encountered. Because past

MIS provides decision support for many well-structured problems, there is a tendency for DSS to place emphasis on semistructured and unstructured decisions. However, it should be emphasized that structured decisions are provided for managers and their personnel in a DSS environment. A decision is said to be *well structured* if the decision maker can identify all elements of the decision process and quantify them for determining an answer. The approach may range from a simple, straightforward role or procedure all the way to a very complex, computerized mathematical model. The approach is not as important as the capability of apprehending all of the important parameters surrounding the decision. On the other hand, if the decision maker cannot precisely identify the significant parameters within the decision process, the decision is said to be *unstructured,* since human intuition and judgment are generally needed to reach a decision. Between these two extremes is the *semistructured* decision, which contains both well-structured and unstructured elements.

Within a DSS environment where a decision process is fully structured, computer automation is generally desirable since an appropriate mathematical/statistical model can be employed to reach a good decision. Where it is unstructured from the perspective of the decision maker, computerized mathematical/statistical models are generally inappropriate. For the most part, making a decision requires managerial experience, know-how, intuition, and judgment. In the middle, the semistructured decision makes use of both computerized decision making and human judgment, balancing the two. For example, the investment decision process is considered to be semistructured. From one viewpoint, a systematic search through data on portfolios and securities is required, which can be effected through retrieval, reports, and display via a CRT terminal using mathematical and statistical models. At the same time, the criteria for making investments for a specific portfolio need to be left to the manager's judgment. Thus, output from the computer is combined with the portfolio manager's judgment to select appropriate securities.

USE OF MATHEMATICAL/STATISTICAL MODELS AND MODELING LANGUAGES. An effective decision support system should utilize an appropriate mathematical or statistical model whether standard or custom made, simple or complex. Using the on-line, interactive capabilities of computer terminals, managers and their support staff are able to participate in structuring some of the characteristics of the very models they will use. As part of this flexible modeling structure, managers are able to insert their own assumptions about key problem characteristics. Multiple runs are made to determine results under a variety of conditions. Thus, instead of a single optimum result from the model, several outputs are obtained to answer "What if?" questions. This enables solutions to be judged by managers on a variety of criteria, including risk, robustness, and performance.

For many problems confronting the manager in a DSS environment, the real world is far too complex to be completely described by a series of equations; objectives are too poorly defined and diffused to be captured precisely, and many similar complicating factors exist. It is therefore necessary either to use standard or develop appropriate custom-made mathematical/statistical models that approximate the real world in order to make problems computationally feasible. Linear relationships, for example, may have to be employed in place of more complex nonlinear relationships, which in fact more closely reflect reality. Or a single fixed value may be used in place of several estimated values. In reality, some accuracy may have to be sacrificed to gain computational efficiency.

In addition to the foregoing mathematical and statistical models, DSS makes great use of modeling languages. More recently, modeling languages have been developed that provide a way of formulating interrelationships among variables which, in turn, permit a way of answering a number of "What if?" questions. For example, the Interactive Financial Planning System (IFPS) of EXECUCOM is a computerized simulation system designed for use by non-DP–managerial personnel in the planning process. It is terminal oriented and uses an English-like modeling language for problem solving by means of "building a model." The model is developed in the form of a matrix, consisting of rows and columns. The rows (or lines), represent variables, and the columns represent time periods. The IFPS model allows the user to describe how each of the variables is expected to change over time. The fundamentals of this language and others are described in chapter 5.

ADAPTIVE SYSTEM OVER TIME. Throughout the design phase of DSS, there is a substantial amount of interaction between the managers and support personnel (i.e., the users) and the systems analysts. However, the final design should allow for changing the system over time. In effect, the changeability factor is an integral part of the DSS design. This contrasts with the traditional MIS approach, where the final design is set in place for a period of time and reviewed periodically, perhaps every three to five years, for necessary changes. Hence, a DSS design approach can be thought of as an adaptive system in which the user is able to confront new problems caused by changes from a variety of sources and, at the same time, solve these problems by adapting the system to changing conditions. The time horizon has shortened from three to five years with traditional MIS to a few weeks or possibly several months for DSS. This capability to effect system changes relatively quickly is an important advantage of decision support systems.

DECISION SUPPORT SYSTEM FOR A TYPICAL ORGANIZATION. To highlight the difference between an MIS approach and a DSS approach, consider a plant manager who relies on a mathematical scheduling model to plan manufacturing operations. In turn, the output from this model is also used to control day-to-day operations. Although this approach has worked well for planning/controlling purposes, there is always the problem of frequently received marginal orders. (Marginal orders are defined as those received at less than full sales price.) In the past, they have been declined for the most part, especially if the factory is busy. However, in a DSS environment, the plant manager's assistant can use a mathematical scheduling model via a CRT terminal to determine the effect of making changes to the present schedule on end completion dates. Using a human–machine interface, if changes can be made to the production schedule such that present shipping dates can be met and there is a contribution toward fixed costs from the marginal order(s), the acceptability or nonacceptability of such an order(s) can be established. Likewise, counterproposals can be made to customers if the sales price is too low or there is need to accept a later shipping date. In this example (figure 2.10), the decision maker—i.e., the plant manager—has complete control over marginal orders.

ESSENTIAL CHARACTERISTICS OF DECISION SUPPORT SYSTEMS. The most important characteristic of decision support systems is the human–machine interface, with the decision maker retaining control over the decision-making process. This approach not only results in bringing decision-making information directly to the manager, but also goes a step further than typical management information systems by allowing the decision maker to react to the output. Hence, the decision maker can interact with the computer by getting answers to a series of "What if?" questions, rather than just one answer. In this manner, the computer does not have the final say in the decision-making process, but is simply a tool of the manager for evaluating alternatives so that an effective decision can be made. The capability of the individual to retain control over the decision-making process is not only useful for solving well-structured problems, but also helpful in solving semistructured and unstructured problems. Thus, decision support systems give the decision maker the ability to engage in problem finding as well as solve a wide range of problems that must be confronted and resolved in an effective, economical manner. Also, DSS come closest to meeting the characteristics of management information systems as set forth in the prior chapter (figure 1.7). For further information on decision support systems, see the references at the end of this chapter, in addition to the author's own work on the subject.[3]

Summary—Past and Current Management Information Systems

Integrated management information systems—these systems stress the integration of related subsystems. Essentials include producing historical managerial reports as well as taking over routine decision making. Transactions that affect more than one functional area are captured once only and processed in a manner appropriate for all users of the information.

Real-time management information systems—these systems provide the capability to send data into a computer system as soon as they come into being and are able to feed back information to the appropriate source in sufficient time to change or control the operating environment.

Distributed data processing systems—these systems take advantage of the latest advances in computer technology by placing low-cost computing power starting at the points of data entry and linking these points—where deemed necessary—with a centralized computer via a distributed data communication network.

---

[3]Robert J. Thierauf, *Decision Support Systems for Effective Planning and Control: A Case Study Approach,* Englewood Cliffs, NJ: Prentice-Hall, 1982.

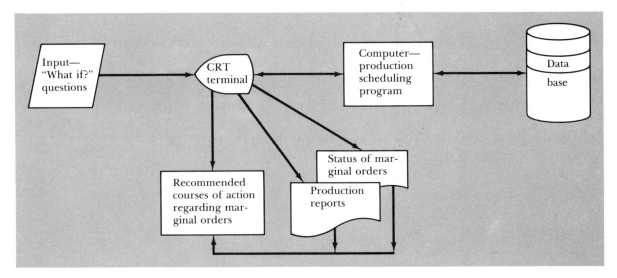

FIGURE 2.10 A decision support system utilizing interactive decision making to answer "what if" questions for a typical manufacturing company.

Decision support systems—these systems incorporate the features of prior management information systems and a mathematical modeling approach to problem solving. They are designed to support the decisions of managers (and some operating personnel). The manager–machine interface provides answers to "What if?" questions that arise in the course of everyday business.

A recap of the important characteristics of past and current management information systems is set forth in table 2.1. A comparison of these characteristics with systems prior to management information systems indicates significant improvements in systems development over time.

RELATIONSHIP OF INFORMATION CENTERS TO MANAGEMENT INFORMATION SYSTEMS

Going beyond past and current trends in management information systems to assist end users, there is an important new resource to help them accomplish their tasks: *information centers* at the home office and remote locations. Initially, an information center was defined as walk-in offices that offer advice on which microcomputers or personal computers to buy. Currently, it is defined by IBM as a new function that can exist within or alongside traditional MIS departments. It interfaces with end users, guiding them in applying easy-to-use interactive tools, program packages, and techniques to solving their problems. It should provide the following benefits:

□ greater responsiveness to end-user requests
□ improved assistance to end users and to upper management

Final Exam ✳

TABLE 2.1   Essential characteristics of management information systems.

Essential Characteristics of Management Information Systems	Integrated Management Information System	Real-Time Management Information System	Distributed Data Processing System	Decision Support System
1. Type of system	Backward-looking control system	Forward- and backward-looking control system and integrated subsystems	Forward- and backward-looking control system and integrated subsystems	Forward- and backward-looking planning and control system along with integrated subsystems
2. Reports prepared	Output reports directed to all levels of management for past operations	Output reports directed mainly to lower and middle management for past, current, and future operations	Output reports directed mainly to lower and middle management for past, current, and future operations	Output reports directed to all levels of management and some operating personnel for past, current, and future operations
3. Exception reporting	Management exception reports	Current plans and budgets used for management exception reports	Current plans and budgets used for management exception reports (distributed)	Future plans are tied in with "management by perception," while current plans and budgets are related to management exception reports
4. Information orientation	Output oriented	Input/output oriented with I/O terminals	Input/output oriented with I/O terminals	Input/output oriented with CRT and graphic terminals
5. Processing mode	Batch processing mode	On-line real-time processing	Interactive processing and remote batch processing	Interactive processing where the user retains control over the decision-making process
6. Data elements	Common data bank	Common data base	Distributed data bases	Enlarged data bases
7. Types of files	Sequential and random access file storage	Accent on random access on-line file storage	Accent on random access on-line file storage (distributed)	Great accent on random access on-line file storage
8. Mathematical models	Limited use of standard operations research models	Use of standard and some complex operations research models	Use of standard and complex operations research models	Great use of standard and complex operations research models

- potential reduction in maintenance
- improved productivity
- faster application development
- greater awareness of the potential uses of data processing

To provide you with a better understanding of information centers, their essentials are set forth below with examples.

The Nature and Direction of Current Information Centers

Several underlying factors affect information centers in any size corporation today. *First,* the information center concept is gaining and is expected to continue in popularity. Information centers are growing about as fast as anything that brings about a change in human behavior can grow. A recent survey has shown that most medium-size and larger firms have two or more information centers. *Second,* the computer industry is going to have to live with them. Information centers are a reality; they are not going to go away. *Third,* the information center concept could have a significant impact on one's career as a manager. How the individual deals with this issue may determine whether or not one emerges as a hero. *Fourth,* with the advent of microcomputers, end-user oriented software packages, and fourth-generation computer languages, the demand for access to computing resources has taken a quantum leap. The pressure from end users has grown enormously as these user-friendly products come out and the knowledge level of the user increases.

Fifth, the impetus for many centers comes from the users themselves, particularly in instances where users think the MIS department is not giving them the service they feel they deserve or need. An information center at one Wall Street brokerage firm, for example, was organized after end users formed a kind of de facto vigilante committee and threatened to go outside and buy a number of micros if their internal MIS department did not meet their demands. In another situation, corporate management and end users at a large corporation completely circumvented data processing and unilaterally set up an information center. Today, that center is run as a separate entity, totally outside the MIS department. *Sixth,* and last, the fundamental difference between the information center approaches is determined by the need to access the corporate data base. Basically, there are two classes of information centers: those where accessing the corporate data base on line is required and those where it is not. In the latter case, micros are included as part of the center, but otherwise micros are not feasible on other than a stand-alone basis because the tools are simply not there to connect them effectively to the mainframe.

Examples of Current Information Centers

At a major New York–based stock brokerage firm, different users need different tools; the information center is a central location for the end users to come and get the tools they need. It is a computerized version of a library. The user comes not knowing how to get what he or she wants. The user asks the information center to solve an information problem, and the center dispenses the tools for microcomputers, intelligent or smart terminals, and external and internal data base access codes. This is the information center's solution to the hodgepodge of hardware and software that has grown up in many companies. From this viewpoint, the center differs from distributed data processing in that it is usually built around a special walk-in facility where the end users come for data and word processing help from the technical staff that is there to support them.

As another example, Merrill Lynch offers debugging assistance to non-DP employees who have written software for their microcomputers. Drexel Burnham Lambert has developed standardized software packages for its information center clients. E.F. Hutton has an internal newsletter with advice for microcomputer or terminal users, including critiques of new software and data base services, and columns by other users on their latest projects.

Information centers can differ significantly in the way they are structured. The one developed by the Essex Group, a major wire and cable manufacturer, couples personal computers and IBM 3279 color display terminals with its mainframe, relying on a micro-mainframe mix. Others, such as Northrop's center, rely on the mainframe exclusively such that the IBM mainframe functions effectively as an internal time-sharing center. Notably, Northrop, which had received significant flack from end users who claimed its MIS department was unresponsive to their needs, initially set up a center to bring these users back into the MIS fold. Northrop now plans to set up additional information centers throughout the company, linking them together via satellite. At this point, IBM PCs or other microcomputers do not figure at all in this multicenter network.

In other cases, organizations have based their information centers on outside time-sharing center services. This was the case with Bechtel Power, which decided to tie into the IBM Information Network rather than put the information center on its own IBM mainframe. The rationale was that its own mainframe did not have the immediate capacity needed by the information center.

CURRENT AND FUTURE ARTIFICIAL INTELLIGENCE DEVELOPMENT

The foregoing developments in management information systems and information centers do not represent the end point in new systems, but represent continuing ones. The latest trend in continuing system developments focuses on artificial intelligence (AI). AI is on the threshold of becoming a mainstay technology in both the business and personal lives of people. Many computer systems that use AI technology already are in place in many corporations across the United States and abroad. During the years to come, AI technologies will become integrated into the workplace, driven by the same economic forces that are automating the office and the factory. Some observers predict that artificial intelligence will set off an explosion in information services greater than the microcomputer. Others more phlegmatically predict that AI will be the driving force for business and industry in the next century.

As AI leaves university and corporate laboratories, MIS will find itself responsible for implementing and managing these new technologies as part of its information environments. In fact, MIS and AI will become working partners. MIS managers may find their lives a little more complicated when they are faced with arbitrating conversations between humans and machines. The rationale is that artificial intelligence machines, also known as "fifth-generation" computers, differ from today's information processing machines. Computers in the typical MIS environment perform huge computational tasks based on programmed mathematical formulas. AI computing, on the other hand, involves machines that communicate in simple English, reason solutions to problems, and explain how they arrive at conclusions. AI computers also can expand their *knowledge base* from the user environment. (The term *knowledge base* will be explained in the next section.)

Today, the science of AI includes expert systems, natural languages, and robotics. The latter includes both speech recognition and vision systems. For the most part, MIS personnel will be dealing primarily with expert systems and natural language programming as these techniques lend themselves most readily to commercial applications.

Overall, management is attracted to AI because it assists them in coping with a changing environment. Additionally, AI can reduce costs and maintain reliability while improving productivity. Since expert systems are somewhat developed at this time, they are explored in the next part of the chapter. Typical reasons given by management for developing and implementing expert systems for business are set forth in figure 2.11. A similar set of reasons can be developed for other AI areas mentioned above.

□ To effect corporate change and implement goals and plans.

□ To have greater amounts of relevant expert knowledge available to managers at all levels.

□ To manage better the complexity of operations throughout the company.

□ To improve customer service through a better understanding of customer needs.

□ To improve production flow through more effective manufacturing planning and scheduling.

□ To increase the quality of products.

□ To reduce costs of personnel, rework, and similar items.

□ To provide less trained people with a higher level of knowledge.

□ To preserve and accumulate knowledge from departing company personnel.

□ To foster internal cooperation among technical and functional groups.

FIGURE 2.11
Typical reasons for undertaking the design and implementation of expert systems for business.

Expert Systems for Business

In addition to addressing the same areas as AI, expert systems for business are a solution to a critical problem handicapping the manager today—the inability to consume and utilize quantitative information and knowledge effectively. The stock market provides an excellent model for illustrating what happens when financial managers make decisions without evaluating relevant information. When they want to invest excess funds of the company in the stock market, they typically evaluate the Dow Jones average. When it starts to inch upward, the financial managers take notice, but do not make a decision. As the Dow continues to go up, they feel a certain amount of anxiety and fear until, finally, the lure of fast money spurs them to invest, usually after the market has peaked. Later, the Dow starts to decline, again causing fear and anxiety, but not enough to precipitate a decision. When the Dow continues to decline, the financial managers face a decision that they are not informed to make, and this is when they tend to sell. The net result is that the financial managers buy at the wrong time and sell at the wrong time. Hence, there is need for an expert system to assist the manager in buying and selling at the proper time.

WHERE EXPERT SYSTEMS ARE APPLIED. The question can be asked: "Under what conditions do company personnel really need expert systems?" In other words, what criteria can be applied that are useful to determine the feasibility of using an expert system in a selected functional area of a company? Fundamentally, expert systems are generally limited to solve problems that take human experts anywhere from a few minutes to a few hours. If the decision takes less than a few minutes, the operation cannot be too critical or the expert would spend more time on it. Chances are that automating that function would be waste of time and money. In contrast, if more than a couple of hours are involved, years could be spent watching the experts, waiting for that infrequent situation when a special rule applies. Problems requiring extensive analysis are also not good candidates, since knowledge is difficult to develop, not to mention changing rules or environment changes. On the other hand, critical situations that require the services of a highly skilled expert are likely candidates for expert system applications. In manufacturing, systems that respond to change and reschedule operations based on that change are other likely candidates. Within service organizations, expert system applications usually deal with standardization of the delivery of a service. In summary, the attendant circumstances regarding the problem to be solved by human experts determine the feasibility or infeasibility of expert systems.

HOW EXPERT SYSTEMS FUNCTION. Expert systems arrive at intelligent solutions to queries by developing the answers using the rules within the system's *knowledge base*. A knowledge base consists of *IF-THEN* rules, mathematical formulas, and the like to represent the knowledge of experts in a certain domain. The expert system scans through its knowledge base to find the appropriate rules, formulas, and so on that apply to the problem at hand.

60

Knowledge for such a system is extracted from human experts, called domain experts, on the subject in which the expert system is expected to specialize. The knowledge in the form of rules is then stored in the expert's knowledge base for use when needed.

As illustrated in figure 2.12, a *knowledge engineer*—one who has been trained in the techniques of obtaining knowledge from *domain experts*—procures the knowledge necessary to develop rules that apply to the problem under study. In effect, one or more knowledge engineers develop the expert system that is designed to parallel decisions made by recognized experts in a field by acquiring knowledge about the particular problem and applying appropriate rules. Once the rules are captured and programmed, a panel of domain

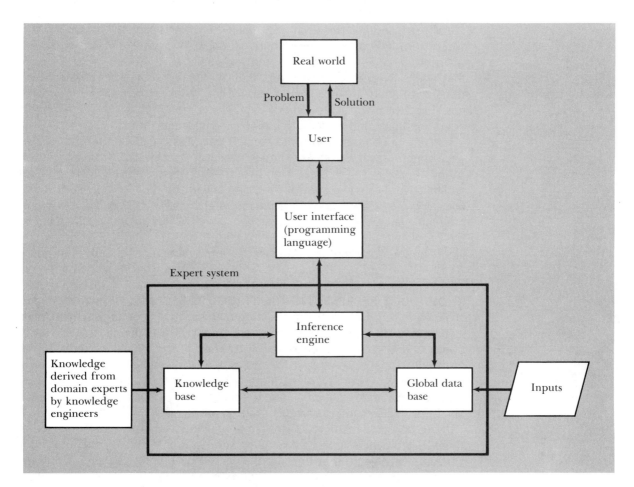

FIGURE 2.12   The relationship of domain experts, one or more knowledge engineers, and user within a typical expert system environment. The user employs a programming language to interface with the inference engine that is linked to the knowledge base and, in turn, to the global data base for obtaining solutions to the problem under study.

experts reviews the program's recommendations in a series of test cases to verify the newly designed expert system.

Most often, knowledge is stored in the form of "If . . . , Then . . . " statements known as rules. One example is: "*If* the car won't start, *then* it may be out of gas." On the other hand, additional information about the car's inability to start can cause the system to reason: "*If* the car's lights do not operate, *then* there may be a dead battery." This collection of rules is interpreted by an *inference engine* as shown in figure 2.12. Fundamentally, the inference engine navigates through the knowledge base much like a human would reason through a problem. Each rule can have one or more statements in its *If* and *Then* parts. If all the premises of the *If* part hold *true,* the conclusions reached by the expert system in the *Then* parts are also *true* and the rule is said to "fire." Furthermore, the conclusion of a certain rule may exist as a premise of another rule that may itself "fire" and "ignite" other rules in succession, until a final conclusion is reached. This process is known as *forward chaining.* Essentially, then, the expert system program looks for rules that apply. By executing each rule that applies, the computer creates additional data about the problem at hand. Then, it begins to search for another rule that applies to the new set of data. The computer then goes through this operation again and again until it reaches a final conclusion.

A more complex control strategy is *backward chaining.* Here, the inference engine traverses the knowledge base rules backwards, from conclusion to initial premises. There are even hybrid expert systems with both forward- and backward-chaining control. To utilize any of the chaining approaches, the user employs a *programming language interface,* like LISP or PROLOG (programming languages for expert systems), which allows the individual to define the problem under study. The relationship of the user and the programming language interface within an expert system environment is shown in figure 2.12.

KNOWLEDGE REPRESENTATION STRUCTURES. Forward- and backward-chaining expert systems require a large memory to accommodate many rules in the knowledge base. The more rules a system accommodates, the more powerful and accurate it becomes. In addition to the basic knowledge representation structure; that is, *If-Then* rules and mathematical formulas that are widely used in expert systems, there are several other approaches to representing knowledge for both forward- and backward-chaining expert systems. These include semantic networks, frames, and scripts.

To conserve memory space, *semantic knowledge representation,* sometimes called *semantic networks,* is sometimes used. Here, nodes represent concepts or objects that are interconnected by pointers to ease inference engine reasoning. The pointers symbolize the relationship between the nodes, a relationship that is expressed in the form of "is-a," "has-a," "lives-in," "is-made-of," statements. For example, a node can represent the word "Lincoln." This node can also be connected by an "is-a" pointer to another node representing the word "car." The latter node may be further connected by an "is-made-of" pointer to a node representing the word "metal." Thus, the expert system's inference engine can reason that a Lincoln is a car made of metal. Additional pointers can also be attached to and from the Lincoln node, providing other information such as the model year, to create a useful knowledge base. Besides conserving memory space, the network facilitates deductive reasoning.

A more recent innovation is the utilization of *frames* for knowledge representation. Nodes are made up of two-part frames. One part is fixed and specifies the permanent features of an object (e.g., the color and make of a typewriter). The other part is a changing one that identifies the object's variables status (e.g., the typewriter's age, when and in what office is it used). Framing greatly increases deductive reasoning power. It allows expert systems to expand their knowledge by fitting random information into a pre-existing conceptual framework.

Another knowledge representation structure is *scripts.* Essentially, they are frame-like structures for representing stereotypical sequences of events. For example, a restaurant script outlines the events that take place from the time a person enters to the time the individual pays and leaves. The scripts provide the computer program with stereotyped concepts that enable the program to fill in the missing context of events it is told about. As such, scripts specify a sequence of events as well as exceptions and possible error situations.

In addition to the methods of knowledge representation in the knowledge base, there is need for a *global data base,* as shown in figure 2.12, for an expert system. The global data base is the information that is built up by the system. It represents the system's data structure, which is modified as deemed necessary.

OVERVIEW OF EXPERT SYSTEMS.   As shown in figure 2.12, an expert system consists of three parts: (1) the knowledge base, (2) the global data base, and (3) the inference engine. The inference engine manipulates the knowledge and explains decisions. The knowledge base contains the knowledge about the system needed to make decisions. The global data base contains the data the system makes decisions about. The knowledge base is organized in modular fashion, so "chunks" of knowledge can be changed or added easily without affecting other parts of the program. The knowledge is accessible to furnish an explanation of why the computer makes the decisions it does, thereby making users more willing to accept computer solutions.

Expert systems differ from prior management information systems in a number of ways—in particular, in how they are programmed. For most expert systems in business, knowledge is contained in a series of *If-Then* rules. These rules are processed in a strict order of deductive or inductive inference. Expert systems allow conclusions to be reached with less than complete certainty. They can be programmed to explain the line of reasoning for the conclusions it draws. In addition, expert systems try to capture the manager's judgment in the program.

Overall, expert systems are sophisticated problem-solving techniques that utilize inference engines along with knowledge bases and global data

63

bases to solve problems beyond the reach of conventionally programmed computers. Because decision-making procedures included in expert systems are often modeled after the cognitive processes by which human experts make decisions, an important component of expert systems is a natural, user-friendly interface allowing company personnel without extensive computer skills to use the systems. In addition, the expert system must be able to explain its reasoning and justify its conclusions, so that users can evaluate the validity of results. As such, expert system technology can be applied to many domains in which expertise can be formalized. Expert systems, for example, are now in use or being developed in such fields as computer-aided design and engineering, intelligent diagnostic and test systems, financial analysis, bioengineering, and manufacturing.

Japanese Artificial Intelligence and the American Response

Going beyond expert systems, it is helpful to look at those developmental efforts that are going on where expert systems end. Notably, this trend takes the form of AI research efforts and their consequential developments. In April, 1982, the Japanese Ministry of International Trade and Industry launched a 10-year crash program called "Fifth-Generation Computer Systems." Implementation of the plan began with the establishment of the Institute for New Computer Generation Technology (ICOT). ICOT is a collaboration involving eight of Japan's major electronics manufacturers and encompasses some 24 individual projects. Collectively known as the Fifth Generation Computing Project, these individual programs have the common goal of developing an intelligent Fifth Generation knowledge information processor with a natural language interface. This KIP (knowledge information processor) will be a knowledge-based computer with 10 to 100 gigabytes of physical memory that will process information at incredibly high speed.

Japan has projected that the Fifth Generation project will achieve its intended goals by 1990, and its government has committed a half-billion dollars to the effort. ICOT is a separate, independent, neutral organization that is to be sustained for about three years by government funding. Thereafter, the eight cooperating companies will take financial control of the project and will share costs and profits equally. Essentially, Japan is taking a two-pronged approach to the Fifth Generation. In addition to ICOT, the country has instituted a massive research and development program to enhance "traditional" computing. This effort, the National Superspeed Computer Project (NSCP), is aimed at producing an ultra-fast processor—a computer 1000 times faster than a CRAY 1. Like ICOT, the NSCP involves multiple vendors and government seed money. Japan's six largest computer manufacturers are participating in the project, and their initial efforts have been subsidized with 100 million dollars in startup money.

Japan's geography and economy have a great deal to do with the country's bold Fifth Generation game plan. Faced with a dense population, lack of resources, and an economy consequently based more on services than on goods, Japanese leaders had the foresight to realize that knowledge will be power in the coming post-industrial society. Thus, their plan involves attaining the leading edge in the knowledge processing business. In the service-based post-industrial world, the country occupying this position will likely be the dominant economic power. Japan's avowed goal is to become this power, but the country faces some stiff competition.

The United States, needless to say, has not been oblivious to Japan's attempts to build Fifth Generation knowledge information processors. The Japanese challenge is being met with intensive Fifth Generation research and development projects of our own. Many of these projects are under the aegis of the federal government, but significant private sector efforts are also under way. One element of our response is the Microelectronics and Computer Technology Corporation (MCC). Based in Austin, Texas, MCC is a nonprofit cooperative joint venture forged among a dozen major U.S. computer and electronics firms. The cooperative was initially headed by retired Admiral Bobby Inman (former director of the supercomputer-intensive National Security Agency) and staffed by computer scientists, engineers, and researchers "loaned" to the corporation by their parent firms. The list of MCC participants reads like a "Who's Who" of American computer and electronics manufacturers. CDC, NCR, Motorola, RCA, and Sperry are involved, as is Digital Equipment Corporation. These highly competitive manufacturers are united by the common goal of producing a state-of-the-art Fifth Generation knowledge information processor. To achieve this objective, the MCC is concentrating on research in four general areas: microelectronics packaging, advanced software technology, CAD/CAM, and computer architecture. Overall, the American response to the Japanese challenge has been a very positive one to remain on the leading edge of new computer technology.

EFFECTIVE MIS PRACTICE—DISTRIBUTED DECISION SUPPORT SYSTEMS

As noted in the chapter, the initial developments of integrated management information systems, further refined as real-time management information systems, represent significant improvements over prior information systems. As indicated above, however, the systems which can be called "classical" MIS are not the end state of MIS development. In fact, many organizations have spent considerable sums of money to reach one of these MIS models, only to find that they were unable to realize the benefits of such systems. For this there were several reasons. First, personnel turnover was an ever-present problem. The systems analysts designing the system often left midway through a sophisticated and costly project. Second, some organizations had to cut back on ambitious projects due to enormous capital requirements. This was particularly true of the costly large mainframes, random access storage devices, and remote I/O terminals required. Third, years were required to develop such systems, from the feasibility study to final implementation. Fourth, these large systems created processing bottlenecks that resulted in undue delays for users. In view of these realities and others, many organizations have moved or are moving in the direction of simpler and easier to use management information systems—particularly, decision support systems that operate in DDP environment. Not only may the costs be lower, but also the time to implement such systems may be substantially less.

Improved Approach to Problem Finding and Problem Solving

Because professional judgment and insight are critical in effective decision making, distributed DSS is designed to support a manager's skills at all stages of decision making—from problem identification to choosing the relevant data with which to work, picking the approach to be used in making the decision, and evaluating the alternative courses of action. Distributed decision support systems are intended to help managers dispersed throughout the organization at all levels in problem finding and problem solving. The merging of computer output, that is, objective findings, with the subjective feelings of the decision maker provides a better basis for managerial decision making.

The rapidly decreasing costs of computers, improvements in data entry, and data base management systems operating in a DDP environment currently make it increasingly likely that most of the information a manager needs to reach a decision can be stored on line, thereby making DSS a logical tool for analysis and solution to managers' problems. In addition, since personnel costs already exceed 50 percent of most data processing budgets, costs of providing information for the manager can be reduced. This reduction alone should be enough to justify *distributed decision support systems* along with improved management productivity and improved decisions that result from increased use of mathematical models.

Fundamentally, distributed DSS goes beyond a two-dimensional perspective of prior MIS where the computer gives a periodic answer indicative of what should have been done or what should be done to control operations. In contrast, this newer system approach centers on the third dimension, that of the decision maker retaining control over the computerized decision-making process while bringing personal judgment, skill, and experience to bear on the whole process of problem finding and problem solving. From this broadened perspective, the manager is able to take a wider view of problems.

CHAPTER SUMMARY

Prior to management information systems, different approaches to business information systems were designed by systems analysts for managerial use. The initial system approaches (i.e., custodial accounting, responsibility reporting, and integrated data processing) satisfied management during the early generation of computers. The dynamics of an ever-changing world, however, plus the volume and complexity of needed managerial information and the recognition of the computer's potential by personnel in the data processing field, provided the initial thrust for better systems. Simultaneously, management began to realize that the information potential of the computer had not been fully exploited. Based on these initial developments, integrated data processing systems were developed, which were further refined into integrated management information systems. These systems and prior ones were backward-looking and generally batch-processing oriented.

The state of the art in both computer hardware and software progressed toward the development of real-time MIS. A real-time MIS has been shown to be a forward-looking control system maintaining data base elements on line which can be made available to the computer when needed. The computer's ability to interact on line with people from many locations remote from the main computer on a timely basis is its greatest asset. Management can be made aware of trends, exceptions, and results of recent decisions in order to initiate corrective action that meets predetermined business plans. However, a more practical, easy-to-use, and less costly approach for many business applications was found in distributed data processing, an approach to reducing the bottlenecks experienced with centralized systems. Low-cost computer capabilities are placed at the lower (local and regional) levels in an organization.

In contrast, an important current state-of-the-art development in terms of MIS is the decision support system. As will be shown throughout the text, especially in the master case study on the XYZ Corporation, DSS can complement the present management information systems operating in a distributed data processing environment. Because DSS allows for a manager (or assistant)–machine interface, the individual retains control over the decision-making process. For the most part, problems tend to be of the semistructured and unstructured types versus the well-structured types found in previous MIS. Decision support systems take a very broad perspective of the organization by merging both external and internal information. Although they represent enhancements to past information systems, it should be recognized that DSS is simply another stage in the ever-evolving state of the MIS art. Today, emphasis is on expert systems; tomorrow the direction will be toward Fifth Generation AI systems.

QUESTIONS

1. Distinguish between a responsibility reporting system and an integrated data processing system.
2. In what ways is an integrated management information system better than an integrated data processing system from:
   a. a management point of view?
   b. an operating point of view?
3. What caused the development of management information systems? Explain fully.
4. Distinguish between integrated management information systems and real-time management information systems.
5. Why is output from a real-time MIS directed basically toward lower and middle management?
6. What is the relationship of distributed data processing to real-time management information systems and decision support systems?

7. What is meant by synergistic decision making within a DSS environment?

8. How are distributed decision support systems better than previous management information systems? Explain thoroughly.

9. Which types of information systems described in the chapter come closest to meeting the characteristics of effective MIS set forth in figure 1.7 of the prior chapter?

10. **a.** What are the essential functions of an information center?
    b. How are information centers tied to the MIS department?

11. **a.** What are the essential characteristics of expert systems for business?
    b. How do they differ from prior management information systems?

12. What might be the direction of future computing activities beyond expert systems as found in a typical business organization?

PROBLEMS

13. Systems predating management information systems, namely, custodial accounting systems, responsibility reporting systems, and integrated data processing systems, were noted in the chapter. Currently, these systems are being utilized by various types of organizations. Give at least two examples of each type of system and the reason why organizations are still using them.

14. In the prior chapter, the important characteristics of effective management information systems were given (refer to figure 1.7). Compare the essential characteristics of integrated management information systems to effective MIS. Compare in terms of how they are alike and how they differ. Which of the two systems best meets management needs at the higher level? Perform the same analysis for real-time management information systems and effective MIS.

15. The fundamental characteristics of effective management information systems were given in the preceding chapter (refer to figure 1.7). Compare the essential characteristics of distributed data processing systems to effective MIS; that is, how they are alike and how they are different. Which of the two systems would be preferred by lower, middle, and top management? Perform a comparable analysis for decision support systems and effective MIS.

PROJECTS

16. The Tipton Company, a small organization engaged in the service of industrial products, has all of its sales and service operations in one large city, Chicago. It has a computerized information system that utilizes magnetic tape as the basic means of storing data electronically. The present system is a batch-oriented system that is used for service order processing, receivables, payables, payroll, and like areas. Inasmuch as customer service is not what it should be—reports are produced too late for managerial action, among other shortcomings—the manager of information systems has asked you to prepare a list of the important advantages and disadvantages of current information systems that could be used by the company to improve its computer operations. Based upon this listing, which one (or ones) of the current management information systems appears to be a feasible alternative for the company?

17. The manager of information systems for the Pleva Corporation recognizes that the present system is completely out of date, since it is too heavily dependent on punched card input and magnetic tape processing for producing desired output. The corporation has its central headquarters in a large midwestern city and has six manufacturing plants scattered around the country. In addition, there is a network of twenty sales offices in the large cities of the United States and Canada. In order processing, the placement of an order by a customer leads to a whole series of interdependent business activities with other functional areas. Orders can be placed, for example, by customers throughout a twenty-four hour day. In the past, there has been a problem of taking orders since sales people sometimes place a followup order, thereby causing a duplication of orders.

In view of these facts, what types of management information systems should the manager of information systems consider in the feasibility study of a newer order processing system? Using these MIS types, list the advantages and disadvantages of each. Additionally, draft a memorandum to the IS manager that determines which MIS seems best suited for the corporation.

18. The Janson Corporation operates three factories, turning out a wide assortment of finished products for the home market. These products are sold through ten regional sales offices (scattered around the United States) to department stores. Presently, computerized inventory reports (to take a single example of IS weaknesses) are two weeks late, but executives would like to know on Monday the inventory position of the previous Friday. One of the reasons for the late report is the lack of coordination among the plants. The vice president of manufacturing is wondering whether the manufacturing plants and regional sales offices should be tied together or connected to a central information center. He would also like to see improved sales forecasting and financial planning.

In view of the foregoing difficulty of untimely inventory reports plus many other delayed reports, the information systems manager has asked you to prepare a report outlining the newest thrusts in management information systems and how they can be applied to the Janson Corporation. Particular emphasis is to be placed on improving the inventory reporting situation.

BIBLIOGRAPHY

Abbott, L. "Information Center Staffing: A Distraught Manager's Guide." *Infosystems,* January 1986.

Ackley, D., and Ackley, P. "Can MIS Lead the Push for Productivity?" *Computerworld,* March 11, 1985.

Ahituv, N., and Sodon, B. "Learning to Live in a Distributed World." *Datamation,* September 15, 1985. ✳

Alesandrini, K. "Graphics: A Two-Edged Sword." *PC Magazine,* June 11, 1985.

Allen, L. "Who Are End Users?" *Computerworld,* November 19, 1984.

Beach, S. "Distributed Data Processing." *Information Management,* November 1984.

Belardo, S., and Pazer, H. L. "Scope/Complexity: A Framework for the Classification and Analysis of Information-Decision Systems." *Journal of Management Information Systems,* Spring 1986.

Bernstein, A. "Decision Support Graphics Draw a Better Bottom Line." *Business Computer Systems,* August 1985.

Blakeney, S. "DSS Seen Moving Ahead in Information Area." *Computerworld,* May 10, 1982.

Bobrow, D. S.; Mittal, S.; and Stefik, M. J. "Expert Systems: Perils and Promise." *Communications of the ACM,* September 1986.

Booker, M. "Computers Help You Win the Game." *Computer Decisions,* December 15, 1984.

Borgmann, M. "Visual Information Systems: New

Hope for Decision Makers." *Computerworld Focus,* April 17, 1985.

Buday, R. "MIS Works to Bridge the Gap with Corporate Management." *Information Week,* January 6, 1986.

Burch, J. G. "Will This Finally Be the Age of Systems Integration?" *Infosystems,* May 1986.

Burch, J. S., and Grudnitski, G. *Information Systems Theory and Practice,* fourth ed. New York: John Wiley & Sons, 1986.

Carter, N. "We Must Plan to Include the Users." *Software News,* March 1983.

Cerveny, R. P., and Clark, T. D., Jr. "Conversations on Why Information Systems Fail And What Can Be Done About It." *Systems, Objectives, Solutions,* Vol. 1, No. 3, 1981.

Chen, M. C., and Henschen, L. J. "On the Use and Internal Structure of Logic-Based Decision Support Systems." *Decision Support Systems,* Vol. 1, No. 3, 1985.

Colby, W. "The Graphics Triangle." *Infosystems,* August 1985.

Davis, M. W. "Anatomy of Decision Support." *Datamation,* June 15, 1984. ✳

Dery, D., and Mock, T. J. "Information Support Systems for Problem Solving." *Decision Support Systems,* Vol. 1, No. 2, 1985.

DeSanctis, G., and Gallupe, B. "Group Decision Support Systems: A New Frontier." *Data Base,* Winter 1985.

Desmond, J. "Window to MIS: Graphics Focuses Business Picture." *Software News,* April 1986.

———. "Repositioning of DSS Leaders Seen by 1990." *Software News,* September 1986.

Dickson, G. W.; De Sanctis, G.; and McBride, D. J. "Understanding the Effectiveness of Computer Graphics for Decision Support: A Cumulative Experimental Approach." *Communications of the ACM,* January 1986.

Donnelly, R. M. "Keep Up with Decision Support Systems." *Financial Executive,* August 1983.

Dooley, B. "A Micro for Every Top Manager? Not Yet." *Micro Manager,* September 1984.

Dunn, K. L., and Schuster, D. R. "Running the Information Systems Organization Like a Business," *Journal of Information Systems Management,* Spring 1986.

Ely, E. S. "Don't Be Afraid of Computer Phobia." *Computer Decisions,* December 10, 1985.

Freedman, D. "The CEO & MIS: A Promising Partnership." *Infosystems,* February 1986.

Garnto, C., and Watson, H. J. "An Investigation of Database Requirements for Institutional and Ad Hoc DSS." *Data Base,* Summer 1985.

Gillin, P. "DSS-DP Conflict Worrying Users." *Computerworld,* July 4, 1983.

Gold, J. "The Art of Low-Cost Graphics." *Computer Decisions,* July 30, 1985.

Gordon, R. M. "Information as a Corporate Asset." *Management Technology,* June 1983.

Gremillion, L. L., and Pyburn, P. "Breaking the System Development Bottleneck." *Harvard Business Review,* March-April 1983. ✳

Guinan, P., and Bostrom, R. P. "Development of Computer-Based Information Systems: A Communication Framework." *Data Base,* Spring 1986.

Hayes-Roth, F. *Building Expert Systems.* Reading, Mass.: Addison-Wesley Publishing, 1984.

Hindin, H. J., and Rauch-Hindin, W. B. "Real-Time Systems." *Systems & Software,* January 1983.

Horwitt, E. "DSS: Effective Relief for Frustrated Management." *Business Computer Systems,* July 1984.

House, W. C., Ed. *Decision Support Systems.* Princeton, NJ: Petrocelli Books, 1983.

Joseph, E. "A Knowledge-Based Era." *Computerworld,* January 11, 1982.

Kaiman, R. A., and Erickson, E. E. "From EDP to MIS to DSS." *Mid-South Business Journal,* January 1982.

Kanter, J. *Management-Oriented Management Information Systems,* third ed. Englewood Cliffs, NJ: Prentice-Hall, 1984.

Keen, P. G. W. "Adaptive Design for Decision Support Systems." *Data Base,* Numbers 1/2, Fall 1980.

King, J. L., and Kraemer, K. L. "Evolution and Organizational Information Systems: An Assessment of Nolan's Stage Model." *Communications of the ACM,* May 1984.

Kitchener, A. "The Impact of Technology on the Information Systems and Operations Research Professions." *Interfaces,* May-June 1986.

Knapp, E. M. "What's Best for Graphics—Mainframes or Micros?" *Computerworld Focus,* April 17, 1985.

Kopcych, T. "Evolution of the MIS Function." *Infosystems,* April 1986.

Leavitt, D. "More Than End-User Tools, 4GLs Add to Productivity." *Software News,* April 1986.

Lecht, C. P. "Users Trail Galloping Progress of Technology." *Computerworld,* April 15, 1985.

Lennon, R. J. "Unraveling the Meaning of DSS." *Computerworld,* May 23, 1983.

Linder, J. C. "Avoiding Information Systems Failures." *Infosystems,* October 1984.

Lipner, L. D. "Tomorrow's Information Demands Could Bowl You Over." *Business Software Review,* May 1986.

Lipton, R. "How Much Is Your Data Worth?" *Business Computer Systems,* August 1984.

Livingston, D. "A System to Grow With." *Datamation,* October 1, 1985. ✗

Major, M. J. "Plugging Into the Computer, Decision Support for Managers." *Modern Office Technology,* November 1983.

Marke, E. N. "Will We Manage Technology or Will Technology Manage Us?" *Information Management,* July 1984.

McFarlan, F. W., and McKenney, J. L. "The Information Archipelago—Governing the New World." *Harvard Business Review,* July-August 1983. ✝

———. "The Information Archipelago—Plotting a Course." *Harvard Business Review,* January-February 1983. ✝

———. "The Information Archipelago—Maps and Bridges." *Harvard Business Review,* September-October 1982. ✝

McLeod, R. Jr., *Management Information Systems.* third ed. Chicago: SRA, Inc., 1986.

Meade, J. "Information Strategies Finally Hits the Charts." *Information Week,* April 8, 1985.

Meads, J. A. "Friendly or Frivolous?" *Datamation,* April 1, 1985. ✶

Mikita, R. "Toward a Strategic Info Center." *Computer Decisions,* December 22, 1985.

Millar, V. E. "Decision-Oriented Information." *Datamation,* January 1984. ✶

Minicucci, R. "DSS: Computer Wizardy for the Executive." *Today's Office,* June 1983.

Morey, R. C. "Estimating and Improving the Quality of Information in a MIS." *Communications of the ACM,* May 1982.

Morgan, H. "The Microcomputer and Decision Support." *Computerworld,* August 19, 1985.

Naylor, T. H. "Decision Support Systems or Whatever Happened to MIS?" *Interfaces,* August 1982.

Nekoranik, A. "Personal Computers: A Data Center Dilemma." *Infosystems,* March 1986.

Orman, L. "Fighting Information Pollution with Decision Support Systems." *Journal of Management Information Systems,* Fall 1984.

Paller, A. "Executive Support Systems Put Corporate Data Base at Top Managers' Fingertips with Touch of a Button." *Computerworld,* March 25, 1985.

Paradice, D. B., and Courtney, J. F., Jr. "Controlling Bias in User Assertions in Expert Decision Support Systems." *Journal of Management Information Systems,* Summer 1986.

Pearson, W. H. "Information: Using It As a Profitable, Strategic Asset." *Management Information Systems Week,* August 28, 1982.

Pekar, P. P. "Planning in the 80s." *Managerial Planning,* March-April 1981.

Petre, P. "How to Keep Customers Happy Captives." *Fortune,* September 2, 1985. ✗

Pomerantz, D. "Managing Information in the Eighties." *Today's Office,* February 1983.

Porter, M. E., and Millar, V. E. "How Information Gives You Competitive Advantage." *Harvard Business Review,* July-August 1985. ✝

Rhodes, W. L., Jr. "The Information Center: Harvesting the Potential." *Infosystems,* November 1985.

Riemann, B. C. "Decision Support Systems: Strategic Management Tools for the Eighties." *Business Horizons,* September-October 1985.

Rittersbach, G. H. "The 'Computer-Illiterate' Executive." *Financial Executive,* January 1982.

Roman, D. R. "MIS on the Attack." *Computer Decisions,* February 26, 1985.

———. "Executives Who Love Their Personal Computers." *Computer Decisions,* January 1983.

Rosenberg, N. V., and Frost, J. "Look to Future Needs When Introducing PCs." *Office Systems,* May 1986.

Schultz, B. "Business Prepares to Embrace MIS." *Computerworld,* December 28, 1981–January 4, 1982.

———. "Data as a Corporate Resource." *Computerworld,* December 28, 1981.

Schutzer, D. *Artificial Intelligence: An Application-Oriented Approach.* New York: Van Nostrand Reinhold, 1986.

Shoor, R. "Micro Managers: New Skills & Problems." *Infosystems,* January 1986.

———. "The New Breed of Executive Information Users." *Infosystems,* June 1986.

Slack, G. "The Paperless Chase." *PC World,* January 1986.

Snyders, J. "The Written Word Is Passe!" *Infosystems,* April 1985.

Sontarelli, M. B. "A View from the Top, Executives Look to the Future of DSS." *Software News,* August 1983.

Stone, J. "'Credibility Gap' Undermines User Confidence." *Computerworld,* April 8, 1985.

Strossmann, P. "Information Payoff." *Computerworld,* February 11, 1985.

Summer, M. "Organization and Management of the Information Center." *Journal of Systems Management,* November 1985.

Thierauf, R. J. *Decision Support Systems for Effective Planning and Control—A Case Study Approach.* Englewood Cliffs, NJ: Prentice-Hall, 1982.

Vacca, J. R. "Life, Liberty, and the Pursuit of Decision Support." *Information Center,* September 1986.

Vincent, D. R. "Information as Corporate Asset." *Computerworld,* September 26, 1983.

Wetherbe, J. C. *Executive's Guide to Computer-Based Information Systems.* Englewood Cliffs, NJ: Prentice-Hall, 1983.

———. "MIS—Steps to Success." *Datamation,* July 1983.

White, L. "Florida Power and Light Turns on with Graphics." *Computerworld Focus,* April 17, 1985.

Wilcox, D. L. "The Pluses and Minuses of Graphics on Micros." *Computerworld Focus,* April 17, 1985.

Wiley, J. M. "Making DDP and Centralized Nets Compatible." *Data Communications,* March 1983.

Young, J. "Simplicity is Key to Productivity." *Computerworld Focus,* February 19, 1986.

Young, T. R. "Beyond Elemental Literacy." *Datamation,* October 15, 1985.

PART TWO

Decision Making Underlying Effective Management Information Systems

Effective decision making provides the underlying framework for new management information systems. Hence, in chapter 3, problem-finding and problem-solving approaches that are used in decision making are discussed along with the quantitative models available to assist in these approaches.

CHAPTER 3

Decision-Making Approach to Effective Management Information Systems

ISSUES

What are the essential elements of the decision-making process?

What are the important differences between a quantitative and qualitative approach to decision making?

What are the principal differences between the problem-solving and problem-finding approaches used in decision making?

What impact have mathematical and statistical models made on decision making?

What is the relationship of behavioral models to effective decision making?

How important is managerial decision making in the effective practice of management information systems?

INTRODUCTION TO DECISION MAKING

No matter how the process of management is viewed, it is fundamentally one of *decision making*. Management functions involve evaluating, selecting, and initiating courses of action. The manager makes decisions in establishing objectives. Equally important, the manager makes planning, organizing, directing, and controlling decisions. Generally, major emphasis is placed on planning and control decisions. *Planning* requires that the manager evaluate and select from among alternatives for achieving desired organization objectives as they are integrated within short- to long-range plans. Similarly, *control* is heavily decision oriented, because many decisions have to be made to keep organization activities in line with predetermined plans.

    Because decision making is at the center of the functions comprising the management process, it follows that management information systems should also provide an effective approach to assist the manager and operating personnel in making good decisions. From this perspective, this chapter examines various ways of viewing decision making. Initially, the decision-making process is defined, followed by a discussion of ways to view the decision-making process. This background serves as an introduction to two approaches to problem solving: the quantitative-centered approach and the decision-centered approach. Next, the problem-finding approaches used in decision making are discussed. Additionally, quantitative and statistical models as well as behavioral models as they relate to management information systems are explored. Finally, the effective practice of computer modeling by the manager is discussed.

DECISION-MAKING PROCESS

The development of what some management writers call the "decision-making school" of management was given impetus and structure by Herbert Simon. He viewed decision making as synonymous with managing and suggested that activities involving decision making account for a large part of the manager's job. Peter Drucker popularized decision theory at about the same time. He predicted that managerial emphasis for the next two decades would center on understanding decision making. In retrospect, this prediction has

DECISION MAKING
UNDERLYING
EFFECTIVE
MANAGEMENT
INFORMATION
SYSTEMS

been partially fulfilled. Attention has focused on *problem solving* using quantitative decision-making models of operations research (OR), that is, management science (MS) within a computerized MIS environment. The main emphasis is on integrating mathematical and statistical decision-making models in effective management information systems.

More recently, a new direction in decision making is taking place. It is an emphasis on *problem finding,* which precedes problem solving. The rationale for a problem-finding approach to decision making is the recognition that changes are occurring so rapidly that it is impossible for the decision maker, working alone, to evaluate all factors for an effective decision. A group of people, backed up by the computer, can solve a quantitative problem mathematically or statistically in a matter of minutes and hours instead of the days, weeks, or months that a manual approach would require. Similarly, a group of people can solve a quantitative problem much faster and with a better solution than can an individual working alone. Hence, it is helpful to discuss a framework for decision making from a broad perspective before considering the problem-solving and problem-finding approaches.

Decision-Making Process Defined

A definition of decision-making activity is often taken for granted. It is associated with making a choice among alternatives. As Fishburn states:[1]

> Solving the decision model consists of finding a strategy for action, the expected relative value of which is at least as great as the expected value of any other strategy in a specified set. The prescriptive criterion of a strategy will be maximization of the decision maker's total expected relative value.

From a management viewpoint, Churchman says, ''The manager is the man who decides among alternative choices. He must decide which choice he believes will lead to a certain desired objective or set of objectives.''[2] Herbert Simon suggests that managers divide their time among three activities:[3]

1. finding occasions for making a decision
2. finding possible courses of action
3. choosing among courses of action

He further described these activities as the principal phases of decision making. They are set forth in some detail later in the chapter.

Based upon the foregoing definitions, decision making is the process by which the decision maker moves from a current position to the position in which he or she wants to be. The essential ingredients in this general definition are (1) that the decision maker has several alternatives, and (2) that a

---

[1]P. C. Fishburn, *Decision and Value Theory,* New York: John Wiley & Sons, 1964, p. 11.

[2]C. West Churchman, *Challenge to Reason,* New York: McGraw-Hill, 1968, p. 17.

[3]Herbert A. Simon, *The New Science of Management Decision,* New York: Harper & Row, 1960, p. 1.

choice involves a comparison between these alternatives and the evaluation of their outcomes. From the context of a manager's view, the *decision-making process* can be defined as:

DECISION-MAKING
APPROACH TO
EFFECTIVE
MANAGEMENT
INFORMATION
SYSTEMS

> A series of steps that start with an analysis of the information and ultimately culminate in a resolution—a selection from the several available alternatives and verification of this selected alternative (now and at some time in the future) to solve the problem under study.

The real essence of this definition will be apparent in the master case study in this text.

DECISION MAKING FROM TWO PERSPECTIVES

Fundamentally, the decision-making process can be viewed from two major perspectives: (1) the quantitative approach and (2) the qualitative approach. Within a quantitative framework, the goal is to determine specific values for all parameters of the problem and solve for a specific value or a range of values. In contrast, a qualitative framework does not attempt to quantify factors, but rather to state them in general terms and solve the problem on that basis. Due to the importance of both for decision making, they are presented below in both normative (quantitative) and descriptive (qualitative) terms.

One way of describing decision making is with the two general types of decision models in use: (1) normative and (2) descriptive. The *normative* framework describes the traditional situation in which a decision maker faces a known set of alternatives and selects a course of action by a rational decision process. The *descriptive* framework incorporates adaptive or learning features, and the act of choice spans many dimensions of behavior, rational as well as nonrational.

Normative (Quantitative) Framework   *uses numbers*

At the center of this framework is the concept of rationality. *Normative* models show how a consistent decision maker acts to be successful. Decision procedures are followed that will optimize such items as output, income, revenue, costs, or utility. A rational individual makes a choice on the basis of:[4]

1. a known set of relevant alternatives with corresponding outcomes
2. an established rule or set of relations that produces a preferred ordering of alternatives
3. the maximization of something such as money, goods, or some form of utility

The major features of a typical decision structure are (a) the strategies of the decision maker, (b) the states of nature, and (c) the outcomes (i.e.,

---

[4]Marcus Alexis and Charles Z. Wilson, *Organization Decision Making*, Englewood Cliffs, NJ: Prentice-Hall, 1967, p. 150.

FIGURE 3.1
Typical decision matrix
showing the possible
outcomes (O_{nm}) or
payoffs for combined
strategy (S_n) and a state
of nature N_m).

	States of Nature			
Strategies	N_1	N_2	$\bullet\bullet\bullet$	N_m
S_1	O_{11}	O_{12}	$\bullet\bullet\bullet$	O_{1m}
S_2	O_{21}	O_{22}	$\bullet\bullet\bullet$	O_{2m}
$\bullet$	$\bullet$	$\bullet$	$\bullet\bullet\bullet$	$\bullet$
$\bullet$	$\bullet$	$\bullet$	$\bullet\bullet\bullet$	$\bullet$
$\bullet$	$\bullet$	$\bullet$	$\bullet\bullet\bullet$	$\bullet$
S_n	O_{n1}	O_{n2}	$\bullet\bullet\bullet$	O_{nm}

payoffs).[5] A typical decision matrix is illustrated in figure 3.1. In this matrix, strategies refer to the alternatives available to the decision maker, and the states of nature represent possible economic conditions occurring in the future, such as good, average, and bad economic times. The outcomes represent the payoffs given a certain strategy and certain economic conditions. Overall, the values developed for potential payoffs are of great importance to the decision maker since a large positive value, such as profits, is preferable to a negative value, such as a loss.

Descriptive (Qualitative) Framework

In the normative decision model, the decision maker is influenced by personal values, the time available for the decision, uncertainty of the outcomes, the importance of the decision, and comparable items. In the descriptive model, the decision maker can be characterized as passing through three time periods.[6]

PERIOD 1. The individual starts out with an idealized goal structure. He defines one or more action goals as a first approximation of the "ideal goal" in the structure. The action goals may be considered representative of the decision maker's "aspiration level."

PERIOD 2. The individual engages in search activity and defines a limited number of outcomes and alternatives. He does not attempt to establish the relationships rigorously. His analysis proceeds from loosely defined rules of approximation. The alternatives discovered establish a starting point for further search toward a solution.

PERIOD 3. The limited alternatives are searched to find a satisfactory solution, as contrasted with an optimal one. "Satisfactory" is defined in terms of the aspiration level or action goals.

[5]Robert J. Thierauf, Robert C. Klekamp, and Marcia L. Ruwe, *Management Science: A Model Formulation Approach with Computer Applications,* Columbus, OH: Charles E. Merrill Publishing Company, 1985, chapter 7: Decision Analysis.

[6]Alexis and Wilson, p. 16.

DECISION-MAKING
APPROACH TO
EFFECTIVE
MANAGEMENT
INFORMATION
SYSTEMS

Descriptive decision models allow the human capacities of the decision maker to be given some measure of recognition. They bring to bear the totality of forces—external and internal to the decision maker—influencing a decision. While normative decision models are generally the most valuable for recurring decisions, descriptive decision models are usually the most significant for one-time, nonrecurring decisions.

PROBLEM-SOLVING APPROACHES USED IN DECISION MAKING

A survey of the literature in many disciplines reveals a great number of approaches to solving problems. Rather than try to explore and compare most of them, two approaches germane to effective MIS are presented below. The first one is a *quantitative approach;* the second is a *decision-centered approach.* The first is oriented more toward the normative framework set forth above for solving structured problems facing managers. The accent is on utilizing mathematical models that optimize performance (i.e., maximize profits, minimize costs, etc.) for one or more functional areas of an organization. In contrast, the emphasis of the second approach to decision making is on solving poorly structured problems, using the descriptive framework described above. The best approach for solving a problem is dictated by the problem to be solved.

Because the second approach encourages the integration of the manager's capabilities with those of a computerized mathematical model, it enhances the quality of the final decision. The human–machine interface allows the decision maker to retain control throughout the entire problem-solving process. From this view, creativity is an important part of decision-making activities. The individual's intuition, judgment, and experience are helpful in understanding reactions in the environment to any decision made. Of equal importance is a systematic approach that forces the decision maker to evaluate the facts critically before reaching a final decision.

Quantitative-Centered Approach

The quantitative-centered approach to problem solving is essentially an extension of the scientific method. The scientific method, originally formulated by Francis Bacon in the sixteenth century and elaborated by John Stuart Mill in the nineteenth, demands these traditional steps: (1) observation, (2) defining the problem, (3) formulating a hypothesis, (4) experimentation, and (5) verification. This method, altered to accommodate the ever-changing business environment, includes sixth and seventh steps: the utilization of sensitivity analysis and the establishment of proper controls over the final answer. The seven steps are discussed below.[7]

[7]Thierauf, Klekamp, and Ruwe, *Management Science,* chapter 1.

DECISION MAKING
UNDERLYING
EFFECTIVE
MANAGEMENT
INFORMATION
SYSTEMS

STEP 1: *OBSERVATION.* The first step starts with observation of the phenomena surrounding the problem—the facts, opinions, symptoms, etc. Observation may be a casual glance or a concentrated, detailed, and lengthy study, depending on the requirements of the problem. Observation identifies the problems. The capable manager is always alert and sensitive to the presence of problems. He or she must be certain that the basic or real problem has been identified, not just its symptoms. After recognizing a problem, the manager should begin to work—calling in outside help if necessary—to solve the problem. In either case, the conditions surrounding the problem will be observed. This permits the manager or the problem-solving group to become thoroughly acquainted with the detailed aspects of the real problem as opposed to its symptoms.

STEP 2: *DEFINING THE REAL PROBLEM.* Defining the real problem means ignoring the symptoms and defining the actual problem that is impeding the accomplishment of one or more desired objectives. To define the actual problem, the manager should deepen his or her knowledge by discussing the matter with knowledgeable people. Because defining the real problem can be a difficult task, it behooves the manager to investigate as completely as possible all the relevant factors surrounding the problem. Taking this enlarged view, a thorough analysis of all the factors with all the appropriate parties should lead to a definition of the real problem.

STEP 3: *DEVELOPING ALTERNATIVE SOLUTIONS.* The third step in this problem-solving approach is to develop alternative courses of action, which are tentative solutions to the real problem. The alternative courses of action can take the form of mathematical models that can be developed to accommodate the real-world problem. They are generally computer-oriented for a final solution. As each model is developed, deficiencies may become apparent if the model's behavior is inconsistent with that of the modeled problem. Thus, certain models which looked promising from the outset may have to be discarded. Instead of half a dozen models, the choice might be narrowed to one, two, or three.

STEP 4: *SELECTING THE OPTIMUM SOLUTION USING EXPERIMENTATION.* Once the number of alternative models or tentative solutions has been narrowed, those remaining are evaluated in order to select the optimum one. If the resulting solution fits one of the standard mathematical or statistical models (as described in a later section), then a solution may be obtained by it. On the other hand, if the mathematical relationships of the model are too complex for the *standard* techniques, a *custom-made* model is required. Thus, the selection of the appropriate model using experimentation depends upon the nature and complexity of the problem under investigation.

STEP 5: *VERIFICATION OF THE OPTIMUM SOLUTION THROUGH IMPLEMENTATION.* In the fifth step, verification involves most or all of the target population (as defined in statistics). This step is necessary because reaction of

DECISION-MAKING
APPROACH TO
EFFECTIVE
MANAGEMENT
INFORMATION
SYSTEMS

competitors, consumer buying traits, and comparable factors observed in the limited sample during the development of alternative courses of action (and eventually, therefore, the selection of the optimum solution) may not really be representative of the target population. In order to verify the optimum model or solution, it must be translated into a set of operating procedures that can be understood and applied by the personnel who will be responsible for their use. Major or minor changes must be specified and implemented.

Dual operations, sometimes called *parallel operations,* are needed to test the efficiency of the solution against the prior one. Initially, one phase or section is converted in order to highlight any shortcomings of the model (solution). This process can be very trying, since one or more factors which were initially determined to be insignificant and thus ignored later may be found to be critical. The dynamics of the business world can cause this to happen overnight. Moreover, the resistance of operating personnel to changes can cause additional problems.

STEP 6: *UTILIZING SENSITIVITY ANALYSIS.* Going beyond the verification of the optimum solution through implementation, the next important step of the quantitative approach is the utilization of sensitivity analysis. *Sensitivity analysis* is a way of observing output changes while varying inputs to determine their relative impact on the model's performance. In essence, it is helpful to know how "sensitive" the solution is to changes in the values of certain factors—that is, key parameters. For example, in a typical investment decision problem, estimates are made for future cash flows, interest rates, market competition, and prices. It is important to know what impact on the final solution will result from a change in one of these factors.

STEP 7: *ESTABLISHING PROPER CONTROLS OVER THE SOLUTION.* Once action has been recommended and implemented and the results have been interpreted, the seventh and final step establishes controls over the solution. A solution remains an optimum one as long as the factors retain their original relationships. The solution goes out of control when the factors and/or one or more of the relationships have changed significantly. The importance of the change depends on the cost of changing the present solution as opposed to the deviation under the changed conditions from the true optimum solution. To establish control over the model (solution), it is necessary to establish a monitoring system, preferably as part of an MIS that will permit *feedback* to the managers who are responsible and accountable. Continuous monitoring through feedback provides a means for modifying the solution as external–internal conditions change over time. If changes are necessary, a study should be initiated, starting with the first step. It is obvious that making good decisions requires a continuing effort, since business organizations are operating in a dynamic economy, not a static one.

The seven steps are seldom, if ever, conducted in a particular order since there is usually a constant interplay between them. For example, an exact and precise formulation of the problem is not completed until the project is almost

81

DECISION MAKING
UNDERLYING
EFFECTIVE
MANAGEMENT
INFORMATION
SYSTEMS

finished. However, these seven steps provide a conceptual framework for dealing with a complex problem. The methodology certainly gives direction to one's thinking, as some more general method might not. In figure 3.2, these quantitative-centered problem-solving steps are restated.

ILLUSTRATION OF THE QUANTITATIVE-CENTERED APPROACH. To understand this approach to problem solving, consider the problem of allocating production facilities in a typical manufacturing firm. Typical symptoms encountered (Step 1) were late shipments to customers, high overtime costs in production departments, and low profitability of certain customer orders. After a thorough analysis of all the symptoms affecting the allocation of production facilities, the real problem underlying these difficulties was determined to be (Step 2) the improper allocation of these facilities to meet specific delivery dates.

To develop alternative solutions (Step 3), standard mathematical and statistical techniques were reviewed to solve for the proper allocation of production. Custom-made models were discussed for possible use as well. Using experimentation, a standard mathematical technique, linear programming, was selected (Step 4). Not only was linear programming a logical fit to solve the problem, but, more importantly, it was currently available from the computer vendor.

Verifying the optimum solution through implementation (Step 5) centered on linear programming to solve for the proper allocation of production resources. Reliable results were obtained by running the linear programming model over a two-year period, thereby justifying its applicability to the current situation. Similarly, sensitivity analysis was employed to determine which input changes affect the solution (Step 6). Finally, the need for establishing proper controls over the solution was addressed (Step 7). This took the form of monitoring late shipments to customers, reviewing overtime by production departments, and reviewing profitability on customer orders. For the most part, these control functions were computerized for controlling the solution. Fundamentally, this illustration is a relatively well-structured problem that is solvable by quantifying the important parameters. Because many problems solved in an MIS environment are not so well structured, there is need to go further and look at another approach: the decision-centered approach.

Decision-Centered Approach

In the preceding approach to problem solving, most managers try to choose the best of "optimal" alternatives, that is, one that balances the costs, benefits, and uncertainties best and is therefore most likely to achieve the most satisfactory results. Optimizing a decision means making the best choice available to the organization at a given time. In practice, however, the manager may lack important information affecting the decision, may be under pressure to act quickly and with apparent decisiveness, or may have overlooked alternatives in the early stages of the problem-solving process. These limitations restrict decision making and, thereby, result in *satisficing.* The word "satis-

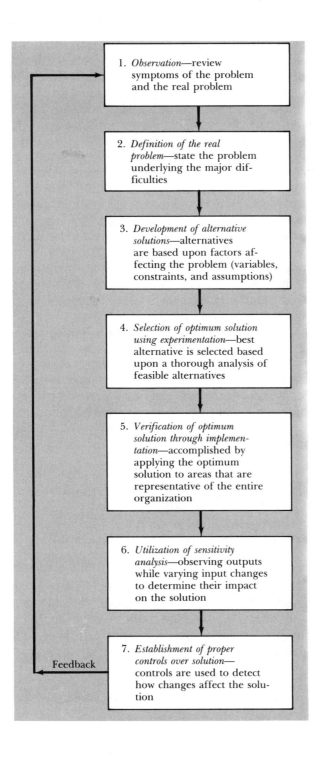

1. *Observation*—review symptoms of the problem and the real problem

2. *Definition of the real problem*—state the problem underlying the major difficulties

3. *Development of alternative solutions*—alternatives are based upon factors affecting the problem (variables, constraints, and assumptions)

4. *Selection of optimum solution using experimentation*—best alternative is selected based upon a thorough analysis of feasible alternatives

5. *Verification of optimum solution through implementation*—accomplished by applying the optimum solution to areas that are representative of the entire organization

6. *Utilization of sensitivity analysis*—observing outputs while varying input changes to determine their impact on the solution

7. *Establishment of proper controls over solution*—controls are used to detect how changes affect the solution

Feedback

FIGURE 3.2
Seven steps in the quantitative-centered approach to problem solving.

DECISION MAKING
UNDERLYING
EFFECTIVE
MANAGEMENT
INFORMATION
SYSTEMS

ficing'' means finding and selecting a satisfactory alternative—as opposed to the best one—that achieves a minimally acceptable solution.[8] Thus, James March and Herbert Simon have made a valid point in coining the term. They go on to say that managers should not select the first satisfactory alternative developed, but take the time to develop other good satisficing alternatives.

An essential part of satisficing is the concept of *bounded rationality.* Because managers often make decisions without knowing all the alternatives available to them and their possible consequences, there is a limit to how logical or rational their decision can be. In organizational life, managers make the most logical decisions they can, limited by their inadequate information and by their individual ability to utilize that information, thereby resulting in bounded rationality.[9] With bounded rationality, rather than make the best or ideal decision, managers more realistically settle for a decision that will satisfice rather than optimize.

This satisficing approach does not mean that managers should give up trying to make the best possible decisions. Rather, it simply means that they recognize at some point it is too expensive, time-consuming, and difficult to acquire additional information or attempt to analyze it. For example, it is more practical for a finance manager to try to decide what must be done in order to earn an acceptable level of profits than to try to maximize potential profits. It is virtually impossible for managers to make perfect decisions since they have neither the mental capacity, time, or information to do so.

In light of the realities of the business world, Herbert Simon's three steps of problem solving are applicable.[10] To them we have appended two more steps, seeking a more complete decision-centered approach to decision making, and a more valid comparison to the quantitative approach set forth above.

STEP 1: *INTELLIGENCE.* This initial step is concerned with searching the environment for conditions calling for decision (i.e., problem recognition). It is basically a data-gathering phase in which the manager seeks information so as to more clearly define the problem and provide some input to the solution process.

STEP 2: *DESIGN.* The second comprises inventing, developing, and analyzing possible courses of action. It involves manipulation of the data obtained to develop various alternative solutions to the problem. As the data are assembled and manipulated, the manager's perception of the problem is used to provide input in the development of alternatives.

STEP 3: *CHOICE.* In this step, the task is to evaluate alternatives. This phase of the problem-solving process also requires selecting the best choice from

---

[8]James G. March and Herbert A. Simon, *Organizations,* New York: John Wiley & Sons, 1958.

[9]Herbert A. Simon, *Models of Man: Social and Rational,* New York: John Wiley & Sons, 1957.

[10]Herbert A. Simon, *The New Science of Management Decisions,* New York: Harper & Row, 1960, pp. 2–3.

DECISION-MAKING
APPROACH TO
EFFECTIVE
MANAGEMENT
INFORMATION
SYSTEMS

among the alternatives developed in the design phase. The choice may be made from a satisficing, or even from an optimizing, perspective.

STEP 4: *IMPLEMENTATION.* The fourth step puts the chosen solution into effect. In essence, the alternative selected in the prior step is placed into operation for better or for worse. If a good alternative has been selected, the results should be favorable; if a poor alternative has been implemented, the results reflect it.

STEP 5: *CONTROL.* The fifth step is monitoring the outcome and making necessary adjustments. In essence, the last step feeds back to the first step—namely, intelligence—by recognizing any new problem that has arisen and needs to be solved.

The foregoing steps are summarized in figure 3.3. Although the steps are similar to figure 3.2 (a quantitative-centered approach to problem solving), they differ basically in that the emphasis is on satisficing versus optimizing.

ILLUSTRATION OF THE DECISION-CENTERED APPROACH. To illustrate this approach, the following problem is used. In a portfolio management system (PMS), there are functions (computerized histograms, scatter plots, and the like, that graphically display security and/or portfolio information) that allow the portfolio manager to scan the accounts under his or her direction, in order to identify portfolios containing a particular type of investment that may no longer satisfy the objectives of the client (Step 1). Using these functions, the manager can assess the extent of the problem and obtain data to be used in the design phase.

PMS functions that allow the manager to examine alternative investments for accounts identified in the intelligence phase provide the means to develop alternatives for the necessary changes in investment strategy (Step 2). In turn, PMS functions that permit the manager to evaluate the impact of investment alternatives on individual portfolios—and then select the best alternative—support the choice phase of reaching a decision (Step 3).

Next, the portfolio manager acquires the appropriate investments to meet the objectives of the desired investment strategy (Step 4). In addition, the manager must exercise control over investments held in institutional and individual portfolios (Step 5). Changes in investors' needs, newer investment opportunities, and so forth generally signal the need to start the problem-solving process anew. As illustrated in figure 3.3, this refers to feedback regarding the portfolio management system.

Overall Relationship of the Two Problem-Solving Approaches

In essence, a quantitative-centered approach concentrates on mathematical and statistical models that are computer oriented to explore the innumerable possible outcomes in a structured problem environment, searching for an optimal answer to one "What if?" question. In contrast, the decision-centered approach allows the manager or operating personnel to be at the center of

85

DECISION MAKING
UNDERLYING
EFFECTIVE
MANAGEMENT
INFORMATION
SYSTEMS

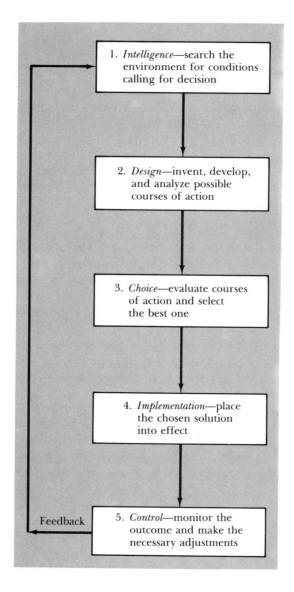

FIGURE 3.3
Five steps in the
decision-centered
approach to problem
solving.

the decision-making process by asking a number of "What if?" questions
(rather than concentrating on a single question as in the quantitative
approach) as the structure dictates to solve a poorly structured problem. To
explore all of the possibilities within such an environment and compare them
on the same basis for an optimum answer would be too costly and time consuming, using a quantitative-centered approach. The use of satisficing, then,
is necessary in such an environment. In a similar vein, to try to explore all of
the possibilities of a long string of "What if?" questions in a structured problem environment would also incur high costs and extreme time demands on
the part of the decision maker. Again, there is need for satisficing in such
situations. If the problem structures are more difficult than those posed by a

DECISION-MAKING
APPROACH TO
EFFECTIVE
MANAGEMENT
INFORMATION
SYSTEMS

well-structured environment, the decision-centered approach would be a more logical solution than the quantitative-centered approach.

In summary, the two approaches to decision making recognize the difficulties of assessing the real world accurately. If a structured problem within the business environment is simple to complex, and if the manager or operating personnel are allowed to have control over decision making, it may well be that a quantitative-centered approach is best for that problem. On the other hand, if the problem is poorly structured, generally it is best to use the decision-centered approach. In essence, the attendant circumstances should be surveyed when searching for the appropriate tack.

PROBLEM-FINDING APPROACHES USED IN DECISION MAKING

The current business literature abounds with examples of techniques, quantitative or otherwise, to solve specific problems. Typically, one reads: "Consider the problem . . . " But the really important questions are never discussed, such as "How did the decision maker come to know this problem?" and "How does the decision maker know that the problem is important enough to be solved?" Because the problem-solving process (i.e., quantitative- and decision-centered approaches) does not resolve these questions, there is need for a problem-finding process to address these important organization questions and similar ones. This subject is discussed below.

In the prior approaches to the problem-solving process, the accent has been on "an analytical technique," which is currently the main thrust of many management information systems. However, there is need to go a step further for truly effective MIS by utilizing *logical-analytical thinking*. Logical-analytical thinking goes beyond analyzing the present problems of an organization that are found in the problem-solving process. Its goal is to identify future problems and their impact on the organization today and tomorrow. Additionally, logical-analytical thinking addresses future problems as actually being opportunities in disguise. If the decision maker has identified future problems, the individual has identified one or more opportunities. Based upon the following two views, the problem-finding process can be separated into a *problem-centered approach* and an *opportunity-centered approach*.

With the problem-centered approach, logical-analytical thinking is used to examine the environment with the idea of looking out into the future and exploring problems that will affect the organization now or at some time in the future. Essentially, the process is one of going out into the future and determining important problems (i.e., problem finding) and bringing these problems back to the present time to examine their cause-and-effect relationships. The problem-centered approach includes dividing problems into their component parts, employing operational decision rules when deemed necessary, utilizing the language of numbers to quantify the parameters surrounding the problem, and searching for convergence, that is, for an answer. The main thrust, then, is on *logical-analytical thinking* that will identify future problems

87

DECISION MAKING
UNDERLYING
EFFECTIVE
MANAGEMENT
INFORMATION
SYSTEMS

having a great impact on the organization not only today, but also in the future.

In the opportunity-centered approach, there is also need for logical-analytical thinking. However, the perspective is somewhat different in that the main focus is on identifying opportunities for the organization to pursue that generally come from problems uncovered. The decision maker needs to change an organizational liability into an organization asset; that is, identify problems that can result in important opportunities for the organization. For example, the remnants (which are a nuisance to most manufacturers because of disposal) from the production process of some product being contemplated for sale can be reprocessed and sold as a finished product or sold to another manufacturer as input to their production process. Thus, what was considered to be scrapped materials for a new product is found to be valuable raw materials for input to other products. From this view, the opportunity-centered approach identifies important opportunities that are often overlooked since the problem-solving process has been employed by the decision maker. The decision maker, by taking off his or her "blinders," can by logical-analytical thinking look inside the problem and examine it thoroughly in order to identify opportunities that are typically overlooked by the traditional approach to problem solving. Additionally, the opportunity-centered approach need not always be related to future problems. Rather, it can center on current opportunities that are identified by top management and/or the corporate planning staff. From this perspective, specific opportunities can be addressed directly by organizational members at the higher levels of management.

Problem-Centered Approach

Because the steps for the problem-centered approach to the problem-finding process are not currently found in the business literature, there is a need to develop them here. The problem-centered approach consists of four steps, plus the solution and implementation phases from the quantitative-centered approach or the decision-centered approach.

STEP 1: *GENERATION.* This is the most important step in problem search. It focuses on probing for potential problems that might exist out in the future that have a great impact on the organization. Initially, the analysis is "forward looking" because this is a search for future problems. Once these problems are identified, the analysis becomes "backward looking" since there is need to evaluate the cause-and-effect relationships of each problem and its possible effects on the organization currently. Each problem is examined as to how it affects planning—from short range to long range. In addition, it may be necessary to look at each problem in different economic climates: good, average, and bad.

The best approach to identifying important problems at the highest level, for example, is to utilize the well-known *brainstorming* approach for a problem-finding group. Generally, top management and their staff, along with members from the corporate planning staff, meet periodically to "brainstorm" future organizational problems. In a typical session for this problem-finding group, all important organization problems are recorded. An analysis is performed that yields the important aspects of each problem. That is, the original question concerning the *problem as given* and the subsequent spontaneous ideas are all written down. When participants' minds have cleared, they concentrate on reformulations which are produced from the collected material and a choice of one or more is made before continuing with questions in sequence concerning the *problem as understood.* (As noted above, the analysis which initially is "forward looking" becomes "backward looking.") This can be repeated until all aspects have been considered. Rather complex problems may need other creativity techniques in order to be approached from an unexpected, new angle.

DECISION-MAKING
APPROACH TO
EFFECTIVE
MANAGEMENT
INFORMATION
SYSTEMS

STEP 2: *EVALUATION.* After the problem-generation phase, problems are classified as being valid or invalid for managerial concern. Because many of these problems will occur in the future—the next two to ten years—the question can be asked, "Which problem or problems should be undertaken for solution?" To answer this question, there is need to evaluate what impact the solution of a problem has on the organization, such as in terms of net profit (before federal income taxes) and return on investment. In other cases, consideration might be given to other important areas of an organization such as impact on the company's sales and customer service.

In most situations, a cost/benefit analysis must be performed to determine what impact solving the problem has on the financial aspects of the organization today and tomorrow. This task can be relegated to the corporate planning staff to determine those problems that are of valid concern for managerial action. The problems generated in Step 1, then, are evaluated in terms of benefits versus costs, thereby becoming the basis for validation in the next step.

STEP 3: *VALIDATION.* Building upon the prior step of problem evaluation, actual problems are selected as being worthy of managerial concern for today and tomorrow. The validation for solving these problems is generally backed up by a cost/benefit analysis. If such an analysis is not available or too difficult or costly to develop, it may be necessary to use alternative means, such as the consensus of the majority of this problem-finding group, to substantiate the selection as an important problem to be solved. Like in Step 1—the problem-generation phase—a brainstorming approach may be necessary "to get a handle" on problems that cannot be quantified.

For example, to determine what problems should be validated and solved, the problem-finding group meets again and reviews the recommendations of the corporate planning staff. For the most part, the staff has prioritized the important problems to be solved. It is up to the problem-finding group to pass judgment on them. As noted above, some of the problems cannot be resolved in terms of a cost/benefit analysis. Input from the corporate planning staff is generally necessary to finalize the prioritized list for implementation.

DECISION MAKING
UNDERLYING
EFFECTIVE
MANAGEMENT
INFORMATION
SYSTEMS

STEP 4: *ESTABLISH BOUNDARIES.* Once the problems have been validated per the above step, each problem must be described, or defined, within its boundaries. This ensures that areas which the problem might touch will be included in the problem-finding process. The net result is some "fine tuning" so that the problem's appropriate boundaries will be considered in its solution. Typically, to establish realistic boundaries, the problem-finding group must have a good knowledge of the future (good, average, or poor economic conditions), a clear description of performance that a solution must fulfill, and a clear idea of what to expect from solving the problem. These areas must be as clear and accurate as possible, because when the problem is badly defined, the solution is generally of no value to management. The GIGO (Garbage-In, Garbage-Out) principle of data processing is found in such cases.

STEPS 5 AND 6: *SOLUTION.* The solution to the problem-centered approach can take one of two directions. One is the use of Step 3 (development of alternative solutions) and Step 4 (selection of optimum solution) in the quantitative-centered approach. The other is the use of Step 2 (design) and Step 3 (choice) in the decision-centered approach. The appropriate approach is dictated by the type of future problems being solved. In either case, the solution lies in solving future problems before they actually occur. The goal is to practice "management by perception" versus the "management by exception" that is traditionally found in the problem-solving process.

STEPS 7, 8, AND 9: *IMPLEMENTATION.* In these final steps of the problem-centered approach, the solution implementation steps for the problem-solving process are usable. Fundamentally, these steps are quite similar for the quantitative-centered approach and the decision-centered approach. In addition to implementation and sensitivity analysis (if deemed necessary), there is need to establish control over the solution in order to detect how changing times are affecting it.

The foregoing steps are normally taken in the order given due to the uncertainty of the future. These steps are set forth in figure 3.4. Overall, these steps provide the underlying structure for the problem-centered approach to decision making.

ILLUSTRATION OF THE PROBLEM-CENTERED APPROACH. The following situation illustrates the problem-centered approach. A company's president wants the corporate planning staff to examine its operations from an overview, long-term standpoint—up to five years. In view of this mandate, problem generation (Step 1) centers on a probe for potential problems that could arise in future years. Of great importance to the corporate planning staff is the evaluation of the company's forthcoming products over the next five years. A brainstorming approach regarding future sales potential pinpoints that the company is depending too heavily on variations of the present products rather than developing new products. As a result, the company will be losing its market share, especially in the fourth and fifth years. As a result of lost market share, administrative overhead as well as many manufacturing and

DECISION-MAKING
APPROACH TO
EFFECTIVE
MANAGEMENT
INFORMATION
SYSTEMS

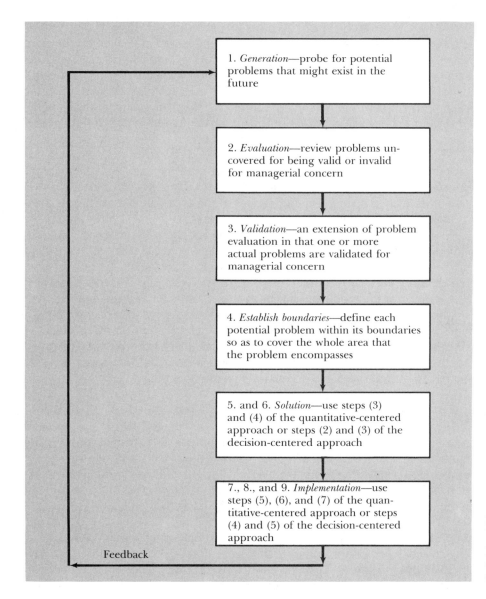

1. *Generation*—probe for potential problems that might exist in the future

2. *Evaluation*—review problems uncovered for being valid or invalid for managerial concern

3. *Validation*—an extension of problem evaluation in that one or more actual problems are validated for managerial concern

4. *Establish boundaries*—define each potential problem within its boundaries so as to cover the whole area that the problem encompasses

5. and 6. *Solution*—use steps (3) and (4) of the quantitative-centered approach or steps (2) and (3) of the decision-centered approach

7., 8., and 9. *Implementation*—use steps (5), (6), and (7) of the quantitative-centered approach or steps (4) and (5) of the decision-centered approach

Feedback

FIGURE 3.4
Nine steps in the problem-centered approach to problem finding.

marketing expenses will be higher than normal due to reduced sales volume. Other problems will arise from the current expansion of capacity at manufacturing plants and expanding the current sales force. Additionally, the problem of improving service to meet competition plus many others can be projected over the next five years.

All of these problems are evaluated thoroughly by the corporate planning staff during problem evaluation (Step 2) as being valid or invalid for management's concern. In addition, each problem needs to be viewed from the standpoint of benefits to be derived from its solution versus costs incurred to solve it.

DECISION MAKING
UNDERLYING
EFFECTIVE
MANAGEMENT
INFORMATION
SYSTEMS

In the next step (3) of the problem-centered approach, the important problems encountered by the corporate planning staff are validated for managerial concern. The benefits to be derived are examined in more detail for accuracy and completeness, as are the costs that would be incurred. A cost/benefit analysis for solving each problem, then, quantifies the magnitude of each problem confronting the corporate planners. For example, the benefits of relying too heavily on variation of the present product line over the next five years for sales revenue are related to costs incurred for these sales. In addition, other factors that cannot be quantified should be included with the cost/benefit analysis. An example is level of customer service, which is very difficult to quantify. Typically, several major problems will be validated by the corporate planning staff. The major ones in the areas of marketing, manufacturing, and overhead have been identified above.

In the next step—establishing boundaries (Step 4)—each of the problems is described within its normal limits as determined by the corporate planning staff. For the manufacturing problem, boundaries might be restricted to the United States for manufacturing locations, versus several other countries.

Now that the problems have been adequately explored and defined, their solutions revert back to either the quantitative-centered approach or a decision-centered approach. Due to the semistructured nature of the problem—caused by the long-term time frame over five years—the decision-centered approach is generally used. However, the attendant circumstances must be examined to determine the appropriate solution method.

Opportunity-Centered Approach

Like the first approach in the problem-finding process, no formal steps for the opportunity-centered approach have been developed to date. However, recommended approaches are given below. They entail three steps plus the addition of the solution and implementation phases from the quantitative-centered approach or the decision-centered approach.

STEP 1: *EXPLORATION.* This initial step examines the internal and external environment for opportunities that comes from problems uncovered. The focus is directed away from the short range to the medium range and long range. Fundamentally, corporate planning tries to determine what opportunities are presented by the problems uncovered for the future. Like in the prior approach, the analysis is initially forward-looking in that there is a search for future problems. Once the problems have been identified, they are examined to identify opportunities for improving the company's operations whether they be in sales, profits, or otherwise. From this perspective, the concept of opportunities has a "positive" connotation, while the concept of problems has a "negative" meaning. As in the problem-centered approach, brainstorming is generally used by top management and the corporate planning staff.

STEP 2: *SELECTION.* Once opportunities have been identified, the next step is to determine what opportunities (one or more) should be explored by top

DECISION-MAKING
APPROACH TO
EFFECTIVE
MANAGEMENT
INFORMATION
SYSTEMS

management and the corporate planning staff. The selection process should focus on those opportunities that relate to a company's *critical success factors,* i.e., those factors that are critical to its success. Typically, these factors include price, sales promotion, customer service, product mix, inventory turnover, cost control, and quality dealers. (A detailed discussion of critical success factors is given in chapter 11). In turn, the interrelationships of the critical success factors and the company's goals and objectives are discussed for further clarification. But more important, this discussion determines what opportunities should be pursued by the company, thereby identifying them in a clear and meaningful way. Moreover, it takes into consideration all the key facts that bear on important company opportunities. Where deemed necessary, a cost/benefit analysis can be used to determine what opportunities are more important than others in terms of how they affect the company's future profits.

STEP 3: *EXAMINE BOUNDARIES.* In this next step, the environment is surveyed for identified opportunities before pursuing an opportunity solution. Due to the nature of some opportunities, the boundaries may be quite wide; that is, they extend outside the company and are related to emerging and established organizations and industries. Typically, greater opportunities exist when boundaries are extended rather than within very narrow boundaries. Thus, it behooves top management and their corporate planning staff to examine the boundaries surrounding all opportunities from a narrow to a very large perspective. The net result is that the proper boundaries are used in the solution and implementation of the opportunity.

STEPS 4 AND 5: *SOLUTION.* As with the problem-centered approach, the solution to the opportunity-centered approach can take one of two directions: the quantitative-centered approach, or the decision-centered approach. Fundamentally, current problem-solving approaches require that the decision maker pick the best solution from the set of feasible ones. An opportunity solution, then, requires that the decision maker pick the best opportunity from the set of feasible opportunities under study. As with the previous problem-centered approach, the main emphasis is on practicing "management by perception."

STEPS 6, 7, AND 8: *IMPLEMENTATION.* For these last steps in the opportunity-centered approach, the implementation steps for the problem-solving process are used. More specifically, the opportunity is implemented as well as monitored, thereby effecting the necessary adjustments to changing times.

The above steps are set forth in figure 3.5. As is illustrated, these opportunity-centered approach steps are related to those for the problem-centered approach. Both approaches provide for feedback.

AN EXAMPLE OF THE OPPORTUNITY-CENTERED APPROACH. To demonstrate this approach, consider a company that is manufacturing and selling products for the home market. It has an aggressive long-term strategy of add-

DECISION MAKING
UNDERLYING
EFFECTIVE
MANAGEMENT
INFORMATION
SYSTEMS

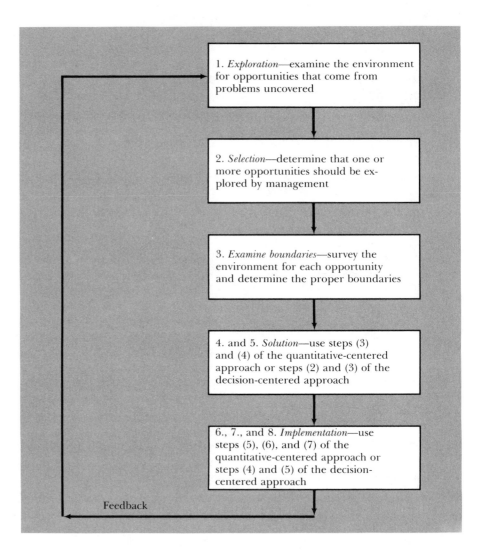

FIGURE 3.5
Eight steps in the opportunity-centered approach to problem finding.

ing new sales offices (approximately two per year) around the country where population growth warrants. Based upon this strategy, projections were made by the corporate planning staff to determine if this was a viable approach over the next five years. Due to shifting population trends, some northern and midwest cities can no longer support sales offices. Thus, a major problem was identified in specific areas of the country—a problem that needs to be addressed today.

Although the foregoing analysis did not give solutions, it did identify the need for corporate management to join with the corporate planning staff in an extensive planning effort in order to determine what opportunities exist for the sales office problem. Opportunities were explored by using a brainstorming approach. Important opportunities were identified, such as expand-

DECISION-MAKING
APPROACH TO
EFFECTIVE
MANAGEMENT
INFORMATION
SYSTEMS

ing the company's product line so that these marginal sales offices could remain open, and performing the customer field service from the sales office rather than relying on outside service companies. Another opportunity took the form of working with another company having a similar problem and merging with it. Overall, the net result was exploration (Step 1)—examining the environment for opportunities that come from the problems uncovered.

To resolve opportunity selection (Step 2), top management and their corporate planning staff directed their efforts initially at identifying those factors that are critical to the company's success, that is, the critical success factors. They were identified as: (1) effective sales promotion, (2) reliability of products in the customer's home, (3) high-quality customer service, (4) fast inventory turnover, and (5) effective cost control over manufacturing and service operations. Based upon these factors, the sales office situation is linked directly or indirectly to all of the above factors. To select the opportunity to follow, it was decided to use a cost/benefit analysis approach that included considering intangible factors related to the sales offices. The net result was that the company decided to explore the feasibility of working with or merging with another company that is experiencing a similar sales office problem in the future.

In examining boundaries (Step 3) for the opportunity of maintaining profitable sales offices, a relationship with another company in the same industry or dissimilar industries could be explored. Also, consideration should be given only to those firms that operate throughout the United States.

Now that the opportunity has been adequately identified, a good answer to the various ways of resolving this opportunity reverts back to either the quantitative-centered approach or a decision-centered approach. Due to the structure and long-term nature of the problem, the decision-centered approach is generally a logical choice. If other opportunities were identified to be solved, perhaps the quantitative-centered approach might be more appropriate. The solution to the opportunity and its implementation represents the final steps in this opportunity-centered approach.

Overall Relationship of the Two Problem-Finding Approaches

The main thrust of the problem-centered approach is on identifying future problems and determining appropriate solutions today to minimize their impact on the organization. In contrast, the opportunity-centered approach goes a step further by not only identifying future problems, but also determining what opportunities exist that can be used to overcome these problems. This viewpoint is very positive. The major goal is *improving* operations as opposed to focusing exclusively on finding where operations *can go wrong* in the future.

For both approaches, standard and custom-made mathematical/statistical models are employed to support the problem-finding process. Typically, there is a great reliance on heuristic methods (i.e., rules of thumb, covered in the next section), because not all variables can be identified and defined, and those that are cannot always be quantified. Numerous "What if?" questions

DECISION MAKING
UNDERLYING
EFFECTIVE
MANAGEMENT
INFORMATION
SYSTEMS

as they arise in the normal course of using either approach can be answered in an interactive mode using quantitative models. Regardless of the problem structure, answers can be given today that both pinpoint future problems and opportunities and determine their impact on the functional areas to which they are related. In summary, quantitative models are a great help to top management, along with the corporate planning staff, in getting an overview of where the company stands today and tomorrow as well as showing specific interrelationships of functional areas. Failure to deploy appropriate quantitative models may result in the implementation of corporate strategy that will produce less than desired results.

DECISION MAKING USING MATHEMATICAL AND STATISTICAL MODELS

Within the foregoing approaches to decision making, the utilization of mathematical and statistical models of operations research or management science enables the manager to view a problem from a new viewpoint, not available with older methods of analysis. It permits the manager to supplement his or her subjective feelings—intuition, hunches, judgment—with the objective findings of the mathematical or statistical model in order to make better managerial decisions. As noted previously, the quality of the managerial decision-making process improves, and the manager is freed from spending too much time on the formulation and solution of current problems. The individual can investigate new problems that arise and previously ignored poorly structured problems.

Overview of Mathematical and Statistical Models

The successful marriage of computerized systems with mathematical and statistical models has produced a rapid growth in the number of quantitative techniques for solving business problems. The number is still increasing as more techniques are developed for new business applications. Problems that can be successfully solved are not restricted to one functional area of the firm, but often involve the entire firm. The categories of mathematical and statistical models that have been used to solve business problems are set forth in figure 3.6. These models are applicable to well-structured problems, except for *heuristic methods,* which can solve even poorly structured problems. A problem is said to be well structured if the relationships between the variables and the objective function are known and if computational procedures exist for determining the values of the variables that optimize the objective. A problem is said to be poorly structured when it does not satisfy these conditions.

No attempt is made in figure 3.6 to describe each mathematical or statistical model in great detail; however, those models that are used in the text's master case study—on the XYZ Corporation—are so noted. Further information on these models can be found in chapters 11 through 15 of this book.

Models Focus on Problem as Technique Is Secondary

DECISION-MAKING
APPROACH TO
EFFECTIVE
MANAGEMENT
INFORMATION
SYSTEMS

One of the major contributions of quantitative models has been in the area of problem definition. A quantitative approach helps to clarify problems, separate symptoms from sources, and to enhance a broader view so that alternative solutions can be developed and an optimum one chosen. Increasingly, however, it has been the experience of practicing managers that the technical analysts, rather than aiding in problem definition, tend to define "the problem" in terms of the techniques available. Often the only techniques considered are those that the analyst is familiar with, a dangerous bias foreseen many years ago by Russell L. Ackoff and Patrick Rivett, when they wrote:[11]

> . . . they [the OR people] should appreciate the primacy of the problem rather than of the technique. The task of OR is to develop techniques for existing problems. The task is not, repeat not, to search for problems to fit existing techniques.

In a much-cited case, they give the example of the manager of a large office building whose tenants complained about having to wait too long for an elevator. The manager hired a firm of consulting engineers, who saw the problem as one of slow elevators and applied the appropriate techniques and produced a set of alternative solutions for speeding up the elevator service. But the manager, dissatisfied with the engineers' proposals because they were either too costly or failed to yield enough reduction in waiting time, mentioned the problem to a psychologist. The psychologist perceived the problem as one of boredom, not slow elevators, and suggested placing mirrors on the elevator banks to provide a diversion for those waiting. The complaints stopped.

This analyst's tendency to find the "right" solution to the "wrong" problem usually results in the solution's not being implemented. An obvious, though neglected, solution to this dilemma is for the manager and the technical analyst to spend sufficient time with each other examining and discussing the situation with mutual respect. The analyst must understand the decision-making process well enough to get what has been described as "an adequate solution to a major problem (rather) than an elegant solution to a trivial one."

The manager, on the other hand, should consider receptively the analyst's recommendations, recognizing that "objectivity" and technical skills are being provided in search of insights and alternatives. Familiarity with the proposed techniques will aid the manager in evaluating their applicability, advantages, and limitations. But most important, straightforward communication about the problem and about the manager's own preconceptions and judgments must be shared.

---

[11]Russell L. Ackoff and Patrick Rivett, *A Manager's Guide to Operations Research*, New York: John Wiley & Sons, 1963, p. 77.

Allocation

Allocation, sometimes called resource allocation, is applicable to problems dealing with limited resources. When there are a number of activities to be performed, alternative ways of doing them, and limited resources of facilities for performing each activity in the most effective way, a business is facing an allocation problem. The approach to such a problem is to combine activities and resources so that overall efficiency is maximized—that is, profit is maximized or cost is minimized. This process is known as "mathematical programming." When the constraints and the objective function (maximize profits or minimize costs) are expressed as linear equations, it is called "linear programming." Its use as an advertising allocation method is illustrated in chapter 12. Also, its use as a production mix problem in chapter 13 is another example of this category. If any of the constraints or the objective function is nonlinear, the technique is called "nonlinear programming."

Assignment

Assignment problems call for the assignment of a number of jobs to the same number of resources. The desired assignment is one that will result in the greatest overall benefit to the organization. This type of problem becomes more complex if some of the jobs require more than one resource and if the resources can be used for more than one job. Typical problems are those of scheduling jobs on machines or assigning tasks to people for minimum overall cost or time.

Combined Methods

Combined methods for well structured and poorly structured problems indicate one of the future directions that mathematical and statistical models will take for solving complex problems. Several of the standard techniques plus other custom-made models are combined to produce a new tool for managers. For example, a production control system usually includes some combination of inventory allocations and waiting-line models. Although the usual procedure for solving combined processes consists of solving them one at a time in some logical sequence, operations researchers must initially combine the models (where there are interrelationships) for an optimal solution. An excellent example of combined methods is venture analysis, which allows for planning the entire life cycle of a product—set forth in chapter 12.

Competition

Competition models are used by business to develop advertising strategies, pricing policies, and timing for the introduction of new products. Statistical decision theory (probability) is an essential part of game theory to evaluate strategies. Because each competitor has many possible alternative courses of action, the problem is to determine the best method for making specific choices during

FIGURE 3.6   Mathematical and statistical models that have been successfully used to solve a wide range of business problems.

Models Successfully Employed by Managers

Because a sophisticated model does not in itself guarantee an optimum solution to a problem, the manager must know enough to judge confidently whether the model is appropriate to the problem at hand, and whether it is giving the right information for making decisions. Today, managers must have

the game. Another type of competition model follows Markov analysis, which is illustrated in chapter 15. Markov analysis is a method of analyzing the current movement of certain variables in order to predict their future movement.

Decision Theory

The essential characteristic of decision theory is that the consequences of courses of action are not known with certainty. In these instances, probabilities are used. Decision theory is used in competitive-type problems, such as bidding and establishing pricing policies, and in some marketing problems. An example is the revision of probabilities used in quality control. In a similar manner, decision trees are helpful in solving problems under uncertainty.

Dynamic Programming

Dynamic programming is a relatively recent approach to problem solving in which decisions have to be made sequentially. Instead of optimizing each decision as it occurs, dynamic programming takes into account the effect of current decisions on future periods and adjusts every decision to yield the best overall performance. Models of this type are especially suitable for processes that extend over a number of time periods. The method consists of a search for the optimal combination of decisions to be made in all periods and requires the manipulation of large amounts of information. Hence, the computer is almost always indispensable. Examples are truck-routing problems, production-line problems, and the replacement of machines or facilities.

Heuristic Methods

Heuristic methods denote learning or self-adapting systems for poorly structured problems. A *heuristic* is any rule for selecting an item from a set. The selected item may or may not have any desirable mathematical properties. Examples of heuristics are the "first-in, first-out" rule of inventory, shortest operation in job shop scheduling, and seniority rules in personnel management. In essence, rules of thumb are used to explore the most likely paths and to make educated guesses in reaching a solution. This method replaces checking all the alternatives to find the best answer—a characteristic of most approaches for well structured problems.

Inventory   *Economic Order in Quantity*

Inventory models, which are basically concerned with two decisions—how much to order at one time and when to order—center on keeping total inventory costs at a minimum. Carrying costs, ordering costs, and out-of-stock costs of inventory are determined so that a cost effectiveness model can be employed to find an appropriate balance between costs and shortages. Lowest cost

FIGURE 3.6   (continued)

the ability to recognize the right model for the right time and the right place if they are to solve the problems at hand. Thus, managers should learn what the various quantitative models are designed to do and the limits of their capabilities. They must be able to understand what the mathematical specialist is attempting to achieve by a particular analysis and to discuss the appropriateness of alternative procedures. Similarly, they must fully understand the con-

decision rules for inventory can be obtained by algebra, calculus, probability, and simulation methods. The appropriate technique to use depends upon the attendant circumstances.

Queuing

Queuing models, sometimes called waiting-line theory, explore uniform or random arrivals at a servicing or processing facility of limited capacity. The objective of this model is to determine the optimum number of personnel or facilities necessary to service arriving customers when considering the cost of service and the cost of waiting or congestion. Waiting lines are applicable not only to customers, shop personnel, and airplanes, but also to problems such as inventory.

Replacement

Replacement problems generally involve two types of items: those that degenerate over a period of time and those that fail after a certain amount of time. The first group consists of the organization's fixed assets, such as machines and equipment, while the second group contains inexpensive items, such as vacuum tubes and tires. Solutions to high-cost-item problems are obtained by the use of calculus and specialized programming methods. Indifference or breakeven analysis provides another method for solving equipment selection and replacement problems. Statistical sampling and probability are used to replace low-cost items as they fail or at specified intervals.

Routing

Routing models are concerned with selecting a route from a point of origin, through each city (intermediate point) on a trip, and back to the starting point in the shortest distance in terms of time or cost. The routing model has been applied to production in such a way that the number of models or items produced is analogous to cities. Change-over production costs correspond to the cost of travel between cities.

Search

Search theory makes use of prior experience and information in order to narrow down the areas that have the attributes of the desired objective. It has been applied to problems dealing with the storage and retrieval of information and the search pattern of customers in stores, as well as to other problems, such as exploration and quality control systems.

Sequencing

Sequencing models, sometimes referred to as network models, involve determining an optimal sequence for a set of jobs or events or the best sequence for servicing customers in order to

FIGURE 3.6   (continued)

trollable and uncontrollable variables a model can and cannot consider, and be able to evaluate whether the relationships among the variables are realistic. Management cannot use an analytical tool wisely unless they fully comprehend what the underlying assumptions of the model are, what the analysis achieves, how its conclusions are to be adapted to changing circumstances, and the weight of intangibles.

minimize total time and cost. Sequencing problems are basically ones dealing with coordination of a large number of different tasks. Specific tasks must be performed in a certain order to complete a single project. Current techniques to handle sequencing problems include PERT (Program Evaluation and Review Technique)/time and PERT/cost. They are currently being applied to research and development, construction, new product planning, and similar areas. Other sequencing problems, such as machine scheduling, are solved by using heuristic methods and simulation.

Simulation

Simulation techniques are used as an alternative to direct analysis of problems. Generally, a simulation business model takes little computer time. In less than an hour, a computer can evaluate several years of operations involving very complex simulation models. For example, in the simulation of a distribution system, the computer is instructed to simulate events such as shipments, customer orders, and inventory receipts. Consequences such as costs, inventory levels, and stockouts are then tabulated. In a short time, operation of a fifty-warehouse distribution system involving thousands of items can be evaluated on a computer. An example of simulation applied to corporate financial planning is given in chapter 11 and an example of a work force simulator is set forth in chapter 15.

Statistical Techniques

Some of the most commonly applied statistical techniques in operations research include input/output analysis, testing of hypotheses, control charts, exponential smoothing, correlation, and analysis of variance. All these methods are very useful for dealing with uncertainty, errors, samplings, estimation, and predictions. In chapter 12 statistical techniques are applied to forecasting, while in chapter 13 they are applied to quality control. As with many of the preceding methods, the particular circumstances dictate what statistical technique should be applied.

Transportation

The transportation problem is concerned with the most efficient shipping schedule for materials or products that must be moved from one location to another. There are often excess products at the origins and deficiencies at the destination points. What is required to solve the problem is a calculation of the minimum cost or time requirement. The whole field of physical distribution, in which transportation is the only or the major cost element, lends itself to this approach. Linear programming and similar quantitative techniques can be employed to solve this kind of problem.

FIGURE 3.6   (continued)

Furthermore, quantitative models impose a discipline that may at first be troublesome to managers. Not only must the problem be defined exactly and reduced to a conceptual framework, but the relevant factors must be clearly identified, and assumptions about all the ways each bear on ultimate business decisions must be spelled out. Similarly, data must be selected to test theories. Although management has been undertaking these activities in general terms for years, a mathematical or a statistical approach requires that the relevant variables, factors, constraints, and assumptions be defined precisely rather

DECISION MAKING
UNDERLYING
EFFECTIVE
MANAGEMENT
INFORMATION
SYSTEMS

than in general terms. This precision demands a more thorough understanding of operations than was previously the case.

Additionally, managers must develop an ability to spot patterns in data outputs that suggest hypotheses worthy of further exploration. If they attempt to reduce decision making to a mechanical routine based on computer output, they will miss the very patterns that forewarn them of changes, which it is their responsibility to exploit. However, if significant patterns can be spotted, this information will enable managers to at least "meet" the competition and, at times, "beat" it.

In summary, the use of mathematical and statistical models by managers, coupled with intuition, judgment, and experience as well as creativity within the framework of the problem-finding or problem-solving approaches (depending upon the circumstances), will result in decisions more finely tuned to realities. While computer-oriented mathematical/statistical analyses are capable of handling routine managerial decision making, the same may not be true for poorly structured problems. In either case, the ultimate responsibility still lies with the managers.

DECISION MAKING IN THE NEWER MIS ENVIRONMENTS

Needless to say, effective management information systems can comprehend the foregoing approaches used in decision-making and their use of mathematical and statistical models. The important criterion is simply whether the problem is well or poorly structured. The latest thrust in systems—distributed data processing systems, decision support systems, and expert systems—can make great use of the problem-solving and problem-finding approaches to decision making plus mathematical and statistical models. Because of the importance of each type of system, their use of these techniques and models to improve the decision-making process is explored below.

Distributed Data Processing Systems

Regardless of the type of distributed processing network in place, the ability to employ decision-making approaches using mathematical and statistical models should not be restricted to only one part of an organization, or to only certain managerial or professional groups. Instead, the capabilities should be distributed to whoever needs these systems. Without widespread access, the power of advanced distributed processing systems may go untapped, as they typically have in the past. In a DDP environment, the decision maker should have access to powerful computing capabilities that can be used without the help of technical intermediaries.

Going one step further, the *ideal* distributed data processing system should not be a "system" at all, in the strict sense of the term. Rather, it should be a highly adaptive support environment for decision making that can be easily used by professionals to design prototypes suited to each specific

DECISION-MAKING
APPROACH TO
EFFECTIVE
MANAGEMENT
INFORMATION
SYSTEMS

decision-making task. This adaptive approach allows quick design changes if the original design does not closely match the user's information needs. Thus, widely distributed computers with the foregoing capabilities assist organization personnel in gathering, manipulating, and presenting accurate, updated information in ways that will enhance the decision-making process.

Decision Support Systems

Within the context of DSS, typical problem areas faced by today's managers include the uncertain economic climate, a changing international marketplace, and a myriad of governmental regulations. The role of both the MIS and DSS is to provide support to managers working within these constraints, seeking to achieve organization goals. But the two types of systems differ. Traditional MIS takes a long lead time, deals with repetitive problems, and uses internal data. DSS, in contrast, is both structured and unstructured, uses both internal and external data sources, is interactive, answers "What if?" questions, and is flexible and timely.

To highlight the differences between "traditional" MIS and DSS, consider the following example. If a manager from a functional area comes to the MIS manager and asks for assistance, that individual would not be very pleased with a response requiring many stages of systems development and a long time before the assistance is rendered. One conclusion that could be drawn is that the typical traditional large-scale MIS does not always do an adequate job in satisfying the immediate needs of managers. The decision support system is oriented toward alleviating just these shortcomings. As noted in the preceding chapter, the main thrust of DSS lies in supporting the decision maker throughout the entire problem-solving process—from problem definition to final solution. Hence, the manager interfaces now (not at some time in the future as in traditional MIS) with the DSS in evaluating a number of alternatives, from among which he or she chooses the answer to the problem under study.

In essence, an effective DSS environment allows managers and support personnel (and some operating personnel) to deal with the computer directly. The single greatest and most enduring problem with traditional MIS has been their inflexibility, their inability to allow persons who actually need important information to deal directly with computers. In addition, an unfortunate and long-standing DP tradition has been that skilled technicians (i.e., systems analysts and programmers) must be intimately involved in designing systems for organization personnel. Too often, these technicians did not thoroughly understand how, why, and by whom these systems would be used. Particularly, because of the intuitive nature of the decision-making process, it is essential that managers and their support personnel interface directly with the computer—using the DSS to support their approach to resolving problems. The approach may include the quantitative-centered approach or the decision-centered approach for problem solving and the problem-centered approach or the opportunity-centered approach for problem finding along with the use of mathematical and statistical models. In this way, organization personnel can

103

DECISION MAKING
UNDERLYING
EFFECTIVE
MANAGEMENT
INFORMATION
SYSTEMS

solve their own problems by circumventing the MIS department. However, where deemed necessary, they should draw upon the technical expertise of MIS or operations research (MS) personnel for best results in decision making.

Expert Systems for Business

A synthesis of the preceding approach indicates that DSS is designed to assist organization personnel in decision making. Closer examination, however, reveals some differences. While decision support systems can model routine decisions that are understood well enough to be specified in quantitative models and nonprocedurally programmed, they are incapable of modeling expert decisions because such decisions are not fully understood. In addition, expert systems employ unique programming techniques to model their systems. The production system (as explored in the prior chapter) has thus far proved to be the best programming method of expert knowledge for decision making. This knowledge is usually contained in a set of *If-Then* rules. These rules are processed in a strict order of deduction or induction inference. They are typically invoked by a pattern match with specific features of the task environment. For example, the pattern in a rule's premise is matched with client data to see if the rule applies to this particular client. Because uncertainty is often present in expert judgments, expert systems allow conclusions to be reached with less than complete certainty.

In light of the foregoing, decision support systems are concerned with answering recurring or ad hoc "What if?" questions, while expert systems for business center on the evaluation of *If-Then* conditions that result in giving expert advice. Although this difference is substantial, they are viewed as complementary to decision making, that is, one builds upon the other. Inasmuch as information is produced by a review of "What if?" analysis over time with DSS, this information can be embedded in a knowledge base in terms of *If-Then* rules for giving advice within an expert system environment. Hence, decision support systems can produce information needed by organizational personnel to answer current operating needs, while expert systems provide organizational personnel with advice based upon knowledge about the subject domain that has been gathered over time.

USING BEHAVIORAL SCIENCE MODELS TO EFFECT CHANGE

Behavioral science models have their place in effective management information systems just as do quantitative and statistical models. However, they are used from a different perspective. Basically, quantitative and statistical approaches are used in assisting managerial and support personnel in improving the quality of their final decisions. The end result is that profits can be improved, costs can be reduced, customer service can be improved, and so forth. These models, then, can have a decided impact on the bottom line. In contrast, behavioral science models tend to have a more qualitative impact on the decision process or task. They may or may not directly reduce costs, and it can be equally difficult to identify their impact on profits and performance. However, behavioral science models are designed to change the human element so that the important features of effective MIS can be realized. From this viewpoint, behavioral science models complement mathematical and statistical models.

DECISION-MAKING
APPROACH TO
EFFECTIVE
MANAGEMENT
INFORMATION
SYSTEMS

Lewin-Schein Model

A basic framework for discussing behavioral and organizational change has been set forth by K. Lewin and E. Schein.[12] They view change as a three-stage process. For a change program to be effective, each of the following stages must be internalized by the individual:

STAGE 1: *UNFREEZING.* In this initial stage, an environment for change is created and some type of reason (or pressure if deemed necessary) for change is applied to bring about a change in the individual's attitudes and/or habits. The unfreezing stage is critical to the change process since inadequate acceptance of change can prevent movement toward a desired state.

For example, consider the implementation efforts of a portfolio management system (PMS) where the unfreezing period stretches over an extended period of time. Sufficient unfreezing occurs as client acceptance of the MIS approaches the desired level. Additionally, unfreezing occurs in the support personnel, who were not the primary targets for change.

STAGE 2: *MOVING.* In the movement stage, attitudes and/or habits are moved toward a desired state.

In the PMS example, the movement should occur in the direction envisioned by the designers for those using PMS to manage investment portfolios. Also, support personnel come to rely on PMS for account maintenance and customer relations activities. The actual process of changing attitudes occurs for both portfolio managers and their support personnel.

STAGE 3: *REFREEZING.* In the refreezing stage, attitudes and/or habits are refrozen in the desired state, to be unfrozen again when the next change process occurs.

In the PMS example, the refreezing occurs in the decision-making environment of portfolio managers. This environment has moved to an optimal or prescribed state. Further attempts to implement change toward a desired state would require another round of unfreezing and movement of attitudes and habits.

Within the foregoing framework, change needs to be backed by top management. But more important, change needs to be self-motivated. Individuals who take responsibility for the change must be committed to the pro-

[12]E. H. Schein, "Management Development as a Process of Influence," *Industrial Management Review,* vol. 2, no. 2, Spring 1961.

DECISION MAKING
UNDERLYING
EFFECTIVE
MANAGEMENT
INFORMATION
SYSTEMS

gram or the desired change will not be effected. Also, there must be an accommodating environment that is supportive of the change. Hence, there are important implications for designing and installing effective MIS.

To be meaningful, the change must be truly complete and integral to the organization—as it were, *embedded* in it. This may necessitate extensive training and even the assignment of systems support personnel within the user department for a period of time. In addition, change is not complete until the MIS is an essential part of the organization's planning/control process. Overall, the dynamics of the Lewin-Schein model are indeed complex and far reaching. However, if this approach to undertaking change for a management information system is implemented properly, the results can be extremely rewarding for all parties.

Kolb-Frohman Model

The Kolb-Frohman model of the consulting process in organizational development extends the Lewin-Schein model. As with the prior model, the Kolb-Frohman involves working through a series of stages—presented in terms of a consultant's actions.[13] Although MIS analysts in an organization are generally internal staff specialists, they are generally thought to be—at least from a manager's viewpoint—outside consultants. From this perspective, their strategies for action can be viewed according to the Kolb-Frohman model as follows:

STEP 1: *SCOUTING.* This initial step involves matching the capabilities of the consultant (i.e., systems analyst) with the needs of the client-organization. The consultant must avoid predefining the problem in terms of any favorite methodology.

STEP 2: *ENTRY.* In this second step, entry involves ensuring legitimacy for action: defining the problem situation, the nature of a solution, the criteria for evaluation, and the allocation of responsibilities and resources, even if only at a general level. MIS analysts should define the criteria for success—those key indicators that can be used to measure progress and accomplishment. Just as important is a discussion of the analysts' roles as facilitators as well as builders of a climate and commitment for change. The goal is to avoid people problems by stressing trust, mutual understanding, mutual support for each other's style and needs, and realistic expectations of the new management information system.

STEP 3: *DIAGNOSIS.* Scouting and the processes of entry involve preliminary diagnostic activity that brings about readiness for change. In step 3, the

---

[13]D. A. Kolb and A. L. Frohman, "An Organizational Development Approach to Consulting," *Sloan Management Review*, vol. 12, no. 1, Fall 1970.

DECISION-MAKING
APPROACH TO
EFFECTIVE
MANAGEMENT
INFORMATION
SYSTEMS

forces that impede movement toward current goals and the forces that facilitate such movement must be identified. The MIS analyst has the responsibility for helping the client to interpret the causes of the problems and the implications for change. The analyst needs to determine the restraints that keep organization personnel from trying to get things done in the most effective and economical manner.

STEP 4: *PLANNING.* Having acquired a diagnostic sensitivity to "where the client is" and "what the operating problems are," the client is ready for the planning phase—the fourth step. Here it is essential to start with setting meaningful MIS goals as a basis for sound planning. The planning process helps to answer the questions of what, who, and how. The MIS analyst has access to knowledge about answers to these proverbial questions for planning purposes.

STEP 5: *ACTION.* In step 5, the payoff comes in the successful implementation of action to accomplish the goals set in planning. A key function of the MIS analyst is the skill development necessary for increasing the probability that the action will be successful rather than unsuccessful. Within an MIS environment, the analyst can introduce skill-development activities (refer to the Lewin-Schein model). Likewise, the analyst needs to ensure the presence of an optimal focus on work and the needed support of organization personnel.

STEP 6: *EVALUATION.* In this step, appropriate procedures to elicit *feedback* about progress and to involve the necessary persons in the assessment of this feedback is crucial. This continuing assessment of consequences (the real meaning of evaluation) may save considerable time and cost. Because the MIS analyst is in touch with day-to-day operations, he or she is able to secure feedback about the change process directly. Finally, feedback is helpful only if it results in appropriate changes where they were deemed necessary.

STEP 7: *TERMINATION.* An important part of every consultation relationship is to have some plan for a healthy, mutually satisfying termination of the working relationship. With a management information system, it is complete only when it is self-sustaining and is able to accommodate routine changes as they occur in everyday operations. Implied in this is the successful implementation of the refreezing stage (again to the Lewin-Schein model).

As indicated previously, the Kolb-Frohman model assumes the unfreezing-moving-refreezing stages of change. In essence, the MIS analyst is a change agent or a facilitator of organizational change in terms of effective MIS. Because there are no absolute rules for successful implementation, the change agent must be able to diagnose the situation and identify relevant factors. One factor may be critical in one situation but not in another. The responsibility for sorting out the factors is the job of the change agent—the MIS analyst.

107

In the previous sections of the chapter, the focus has been on the effective use of mathematical and statistical models for decision making to help an organization move from the present position to a more desirable position in the future. To effect this change, the typical manager must possess certain prerequisites for successful use of computer modeling. The following factors are important: (1) a knowledge of quantitative techniques and MIS technology, (2) an understanding of how the computer model will be used, (3) a sense of need for the model and proprietorship over the model, and (4) an ability to use the model output in an effective manner.

Regarding the first factor, familiarity with quantitative methods—such as goal programming and venture analysis—enables the manager to recognize the problems to which these methods can be applied, to formulate the model in general terms, and to recognize the terminology, applications, and limitations of quantitative techniques. The knowledge of the technology of computers, in this context, means an awareness of computer programming and computer information storage and retrieval systems. Finally, the technology of computer modeling means a knowledge of how models can be implemented on computers for interactive decision making.

In regard to the second factor—an understanding of how the computer model will be used—a manager does not rely on the model to make a decision, but rather to help explore and understand the complex environment in which the individual is operating. It is important that this notion be understood by managers, for it has significant implications for how the model should be built and for reasonable expectations about what a model can do.

The third factor—a sense of need for the model and proprietorship over the model—relates to having a perceived need for the model. This need results from the manager's frustration with current available information or from a lack of knowledge about the problem he or she is facing. Sometimes it results from a desire to emulate others who are known to have an information system or model that is considered useful. Similarly, the manager must feel that the model uses his or her assumptions, designed according to his or her specifications, for a particular problem. This implies that the manager must be deeply involved in model building—something many managers tend to avoid since it is very time consuming. And yet many failures of models can be attributed to managers' attitudes that they can get something for nothing and that systems analysts can read their minds and build just the appropriate model.

The fourth and final factor—an ability to use the model output effectively—is the most important of all from a successful MIS standpoint. Whether or not the manager is going to perform the technical work of actually programming the computer, collecting data, and running the model is not the real test of successful computer modeling. Rather, the focus is on the application of the output to the problem at hand. In this manner, the real problem

DECISION-MAKING
APPROACH TO
EFFECTIVE
MANAGEMENT
INFORMATION
SYSTEMS

is solved (as opposed to dealing with a mere symptom of the problem) and organizational performance improved.

Overall, the first of the above prerequisites is *technological*—the need to know the computer, as well as mathematical methodology. The other three can be called *managerial* prerequisites; that is, they would apply equally well to any innovation. Hence, successful utilization of computer modeling by the manager focuses on both technical and managerial prerequisites.

CHAPTER SUMMARY

As emphasized throughout the chapter, decision making is at the center of the functions comprising the management process. Similarly, it is an integral part of effective management information systems. The manager has several approaches to decision making. First, the quantitative-centered approach is useful for solving well-structured problems. In contrast, the second one—the decision-centered approach, which incorporates the best features of the normative and descriptive framework with creativity—is helpful for solving poorly structured problems. This approach allows a human–machine interface, whereby the manager maintains control throughout the decision-making process. Third, the problem-centered approach centers on identifying future problems and bringing them back to the present time for solution. Closely related to this approach is a fourth, the opportunity-centered approach, which is a method for identifying future opportunities. In actuality, these opportunities are the opposite side of future problems that are identified for solution.

These four approaches to decision making allow managers and their support personnel to employ mathematical and statistical models at any phase of the problem-solving or problem-finding process. As new "What if?" questions are raised, other models or the same ones can be brought into play for solving the problem. However, before these models can be employed within an MIS environment, there may be need for changes in the attitudes and habits of organization personnel. This can be accomplished by using behavioral science models. From this perspective, the systems analysts need to function as change agents. Tact and diplomacy are required of systems analysts for best results.

QUESTIONS

1. Explain what is meant by the following statement: "Decision making is the primary task of management."
2. What is wrong with using only experience, hunches, judgment, and intuition in reaching a final decision? Explain thoroughly.
3. Why don't systems analysts always understand or relate to management's needs and decision processes?

109

DECISION MAKING
UNDERLYING
EFFECTIVE
MANAGEMENT
INFORMATION
SYSTEMS

4. Distinguish between the quantitative-centered approach for problem solving and the decision-centered approach.

5. Distinguish between the problem-centered approach for problem finding and the opportunity-centered approach.

6. What determines whether the problem-solving process or the problem-finding process will be used by a manager?

7. What mathematical and statistical models have been developed to solve:
   a. well-structured problems?
   b. poorly structured problems?

8. How important are mathematical and statistical models in effective MIS?

9. Contrast the behavioral science models of Lewin-Schein and Kolb-Frohman for effecting change.

10. What is the relationship of mathematical and statistical models, as well as behavioral science models, to effective MIS?

PROBLEMS

11. Since decision making can be viewed from two basic perspectives, i.e., normative (quantitative) and descriptive (qualitative) points of view, give three business examples of normative decision making. Do the same for descriptive decision making. Is it possible that one of your examples could have included both the normative and descriptive elements of decision making? Explain thoroughly.

12. For well-structured problems, seven steps were given for a quantitative-centered approach to problem solving (refer to figure 3.2), along with a sample application. Similarly, for poorly structured problems, five steps were set forth for the decision-centered approach to problem solving (refer to figure 3.3) plus a sample application. Apply these two approaches to a problem from your own business experience.

13. For future poorly structured problems, nine steps were given for a problem-centered approach to problem finding (refer to figure 3.4) along with a sample application. Similarly, for future poorly structured problems that have identifiable opportunities, eight steps were given for an opportunity-centered approach to problem finding (refer to figure 3.5) along with a sample application. Apply these two approaches to a poorly structured problem from your own business experience.

14. Behavioral science models as discussed in the chapter were viewed from the standpoint of changing the human element so that the essential features of effective MIS can be realized. They included the Lewin-Schein model and the Kolb-Frohman model. Using a typical business behavioral problem with which you are familiar, apply these models to the problem. Show how the behavioral models are alike and how they are different when applied to the sample problem. Is one better than the other for the sample problem used?

PROJECTS

15. For the Tilton Company of 3,000 employees, the systems group started work on a complete marketing, forecasting, production, inventory, and personnel MIS.

DECISION-MAKING
APPROACH TO
EFFECTIVE
MANAGEMENT
INFORMATION
SYSTEMS

They are working closely with the managers from the functional areas on the design of the new MIS. To assist in the development of the new management information system, suggest what mathematical and statistical models can be used in managerial decision making. Appropriate mathematical and statistical models are to be stated for each functional area, and interrelationships of these models for the functional areas are to be identified. To assist in showing the interrelationships, a block diagram that represents the information flow should be developed using mathematical and statistical models.

16. Not too many years ago, a combined methods technique called *venture analysis* was developed for evaluating the life cycle of a new product. By using this combined methods approach, DuPont modeled a material for shoes—called Corfam—for analysis on a computer. The variables which had to be aggregated in some cases included the following: market size, selling price, consumer buying habits, advertising, reaction of competition, manufacturer costs, cutting yields, substitute products (e.g., leather), shoe market segments, profit margins, sales and administrative expenses, capital investment, and return on capital. Using these variables plus others if deemed necessary, develop a block diagram that represents a model of the new venture for DuPont. Include in your diagram the interaction between the external and the internal factors affecting Corfam. Also indicate the appropriate inputs and the resulting outputs from using the venture analysis model.

17. The Contemporary Lumber Company grows timber and sells twenty classes of lumber—from soft to hard woods. The new manager of management information systems plans to take a quantitative approach to decision making. He notes that most trees require planting twenty to twenty-five years in advance of cutting. Just recently, by meeting regularly with top management, he has been able to formulate the requirements for future markets, future products, land to be used, and location of processing plants. Based upon the information compiled to date, draft a letter to the new manager of MIS that will assist him in making use of the information gathered from top-level executives. Include in your answer potential well-structured quantitative techniques that can be used, the advantages of taking a specific quantitative approach, and the use of cost/benefit analysis. Also, consider the use of poorly structured quantitative techniques as well as other information that you feel would be useful in zeroing in on the appropriate technique(s) for utilizing the information gathered on the company's present and future plans.

BIBLIOGRAPHY

Adelman, L. "Real-Time Computer Support for Decision Analysis in a Group Setting: Another Class of Decision Support Systems." *Interfaces*, March-April 1984.

Aggarwal, R., and Khera, I. "Using Management Science Models: A Critique for Planners." *Managerial Planning*, January-February 1980.

Altier, W. J. "Objectivity: The Critical Element." *Business Horizons*, November-December 1982.

Anthony, R. M. *Planning and Control Systems: A*

Framework for Analysis. Boston: Harvard University Graduate School of Business Administration, 1965.

Basadur, M.; Graen, G. B.; and Green, S. G. "Training in Creative Problem Solving: Effects on Ideation and Problem Finding and Solving in an Industrial Research Organization." *Organization Behavior and Human Performance, 30,* 1982.

Bonczek, R. H.; Holsapple, C. W.; and Winston, A.

B. "The Evolving Role of Models in Decision Support Systems." *Decision Sciences,* vol. 11, 1980.

Clift, P. E. "Modeling Business Problems: How to Get Started." *Computer Decisions,* August 1981.

Davis, K. R. "The Process of Problem Finding: A Production-Marketing Example." *Interfaces,* November 1977.

Dery, D., and Mock, T. J. "Information Support Systems for Problem Solving." *Decision Support Systems,* April 1985.

De Sanctis, G., and Gallupe, B. "Group Decision Support Systems: A New Frontier." *Data Base,* Winter 1985.

Drucker, P. F. "How to Make People Decisions." *Harvard Business Review,* July-August 1985.

Due, R. T. "Predicting Results with Statistics." *Datamation,* May 1980.

Economides, S., and Cohen, M. "Microcomputer-Based Decision Support Systems Aid Managers in Evaluating Alternatives." *Industrial Engineering,* September 1985.

Evans, J. R. "Creative Thinking and Innovative Education in the Decision Sciences." *Decision Sciences,* vol. 17, 1986.

Ford, C. N. "Manage by Decisions, Not by Objectives." *Business Horizons,* February 1980.

Freeman, M., and Mulkowsky, G. "Implementation of Quantitative Techniques: A Managerial Perspective." *Management Review,* July 1979.

Getzels, J. W. "Problem Finding and the Inventiveness of Solutions." *The Journal of Creative Behavior,* vol. 1, 1975.

Gladstein, D. L., and Reilly, W. P. "Group Decision Making Under Threat: The Tycoon Game." *Academy of Management Journal,* September 1985.

Goslar, M. D.; Green, G. I.; and Hughes, T. H. "Decision Support Systems: An Empirical Assessment for Decision Making." *Decision Sciences,* vol. 17, 1986.

Graham, R. J. "Problem and Opportunity Identification in Management Science." *Interfaces,* August 1976.

Greenberger, M. "A Way of Thinking About Model Analysis." *Interfaces,* April 1980.

Grove, A. S. "Decisions, Decisions." *Computerworld,* September 19, 1983.

Grudnitski, G. "Eliciting Decision-Makers' Information Requirements: Application of Rep Test Methodology." *Journal of Management Information Systems,* Summer 1984.

Henderson, J. C., and Nutt, P. C. "The Influence of Decision Style on Decision Making Behavior." *Management Science,* April 1980.

Herrman, J. "Savin Takes the Guesswork Out of Decision Making." *Management Technology,* January 1984.

Hickok, R. S. "Looking to the Future: A Key to Success." *Journal of Accountancy,* March 1984.

Houghton, A. D. "Creative Thinking Aids Documentation Focus." *Software News,* March 1984.

Huber, G. P. "The Nature of Organizational Decision Making and the Design of Decision Support Systems." *MIS Quarterly,* June 1981.

Isenberg, D. J. "How Senior Managers Think." *Harvard Business Review,* November-December 1984.

Jelassi, M. T.; Jarke, M.; and Stohr, E. A. "Designing a Generalized Multiple Criteria Decision Support System." *Journal of Management Information Systems,* Spring 1985.

Keen, P. G. W.; and Scott Morton, M. S. *Decision Support Systems: An Organizational Perspective.* Reading, MA: Addison-Wesley Publishing Company, 1978.

Kiechel, W., III. "Getting Creative." *Fortune,* July 25, 1983.

King, R. H., and Love, R. R., Jr. "Coordinating Decisions for Increased Profits." *Interfaces,* December 1980.

Kowalkowski, F. F., and McElyea, L. M. "Plugging DSS into the Information Center." *Software News,* December 1984.

Landry, M.; Pascot, D.; and Briolat, D. "Can DSS Evolve Without Changing Our View of the Concept of 'Problem'?" *Decision Support Systems,* January 1985.

Lasden, M. "Computer-Aided Decision Making." *Computer Decisions,* November 1982.

———. "Enriching the Decision-Making Process." *Computer Decisions,* November 1983.

———. "Intuition: The Voice of Success?" *Computer Decisions,* February 26, 1985.

———. "Facing Down Groupthink." *Computer Decisions,* May 6, 1986.

Leary, E. J. "Decision Support Systems Aid in Management of Operations, Resources and Financing." *Industrial Engineering,* September 1985.

Levitt, T. "A Heretical View of Management Science." *Fortune,* December 18, 1978.

MacCrimmon, K. R., and Wehrung, D. A. *The Management of Uncertainty, Taking Risks.* New York: The Free Press, 1986.

Magnet, M. "How Top Managers Make a Company's Toughest Decisions." *Fortune,* March 18, 1985.

———. "Who Needs a Trend-Spotter?" *Fortune,* December 9, 1985.

Maidique, M. A. "Point of View: The New Management Thinkers." *California Management Review,* Fall 1983.

Martin, A. P. *Think Proactive: New Insights into Decision-Making.* New York: The Professional Development Institute, 1984.

Millar, V. E. "Decision-Oriented Information." *Datamation,* January 1984.

Minch, R. P., and Sanders, G. L. "Computerized Information Systems Supporting Multicriteria Decision Making." *Decision Sciences,* vol. 17, 1986.

Neumann, S., and Hadass, M. "DSS and Strategic Decisions." *California Management Review,* Spring 1980.

Polilli, S. "Micro-Based DSS Bring Decision-Making to the Desktop." *Micro Manager,* November 1984.

Porter, M. E., and Millar, V. E. "How Information Gives You Competitive Advantage." *Harvard Business Review,* July-August 1985.

Pounds, W. F. "The Process of Problem Finding." *Industrial Management Review,* September 1971.

Quintelier, G. L. M. "A Technique for Problem Finding and Market Introduction." *Research Management,* September 1978.

Roach, J. M. "Simon Says . . . Decision Making Is a 'Satisficing' Experience." *Management Review,* January 1979.

Rosenman, B. B. "Problems of Quantitative Models in Large Management Information Systems." *Interfaces,* April 1980.

Rubenstein, M. F. *Tools for Thinking and Problem Solving.* Englewood Cliffs, NJ: Prentice-Hall, 1986.

Sanderson, M. "Successful Problem Finding." *Journal of Systems Management,* October 1974.

Smithers, T. "Maps of the Mind: New Pathways to Decision-Making." *Business Horizons,* December 1980.

Snyders, J. "Decision Making Made Easier." *Infosystems,* August 1984.

Thierauf, R. J.; Klekamp, R. C.; and Geeding, D. W. *Management Principles and Practices: A Contingency and Questionnaire Approach.* Santa Barbara, CA: Wiley/Hamilton, 1977.

Thierauf, R. J.; Klekamp, R. C.; and Ruwe, M. L. *Management Science—A Model Formulation Approach with Computer Applications.* Columbus, OH: Charles E. Merrill Publishing Company, 1985.

Wakin, E. "Decisions, Decisions: How Top Executives Make Them." *Today's Office,* September 1982.

———. "Brainstorming: It's Raining Ideas." *Today's Office,* January 1985.

Watkins, P. R. "Perceived Information Structures: Implications for Decision Support System Design." *Decision Science,* vol. 13, 1982.

———. "Preference Mapping of Perceived Information Structure: Implications for Decision Support Systems Design." *Decision Sciences,* vol. 15, 1984.

Weber, E. S. "Systems to Think With: A Response to 'A Vision for Decision Support Systems.'" *Journal of Management Information Systems,* Spring 1986.

Wedley, W. C., and Field, R. H. G. "A Predecision Support System." *Academy of Management Review,* vol. 9, no. 4, 1984.

White, C. S. "Problem Solving: The Neglected First Step." *Management Review,* January 1983.

PART THREE

Computer Hardware and Software for Effective Management Information Systems

In chapter 4 computer hardware found in typical MIS installations is illustrated and discussed. Chapter 5 focuses on the software that assists organization personnel in answering "What if?" questions. Emphasis is placed on packages available from software vendors.

CHAPTER 4

Computer Hardware for Effective Management Information Systems

ISSUES

What are the key factors in evaluating computer hardware for an efficiently run management information system?

What influence have personal computers and minicomputers had on improving the effectiveness of MIS?

What impact have intelligent terminals and graphic systems devices had on management information systems?

How important is a data base management system in supporting an effective management information system?

How necessary is a data communications network in a widely dispersed MIS processing mode?

How can computer graphics be used as a tool for improving management productivity?

OUTLINE

INTRODUCTION TO COMPUTER HARDWARE

Although the essential components of an effective management information system are the main thrust of this chapter, an important theme underlies computer hardware. The theme is that the management information system must be tailored to meet the needs of the user—that is, the manager and support personnel—rather than tailored to the capabilities of the hardware. User considerations must always come first. This important point was partially ignored in previous information systems. However, managerial considerations built into the computer hardware constitute a most important factor in effective MIS.

Initially in this chapter, key factors in evaluating computer hardware are discussed. Typical computer systems ranging from small-scale to large-scale are illustrated. Next, computer hardware that provides an interface with the manager or support personnel is reviewed: microcomputers, intelligent terminals, graphic devices, and other input and output computer devices. Due to the great importance of data storage devices, they are described, along with a data base management system approach to coordinating and controlling on-line data elements. The linkage between terminals and one or more computer systems (with attached data bases), called data communications networks, is discussed. Typical computer equipment used in effective MIS is presented, including management workstations and management decision rooms. Finally, the use of computer graphics to improve managerial productivity is set forth.

EVALUATION OF COMPUTER HARDWARE

In order for management and support personnel to make use of *terminals* physically dispersed in an organization, it is necessary to have the terminals communicate via a *data communications network* to the *computer system.* In turn, the computer system will normally access the *data base* for stored programs, software packages, and appropriate data elements. Hence, computer hardware under the guidance of some type of software provides the means for a human–machine interface in an MIS environment. Due to the importance of computer hardware, its essential components are discussed at some length in the chapter. For a typical company to obtain the proper hardware, an evaluation of requirements is needed. Hence, before examining current computer

COMPUTER
HARDWARE AND
SOFTWARE FOR
EFFECTIVE
MANAGEMENT
INFORMATION
SYSTEMS

systems and their peripheral devices, key factors in evaluating computer hardware are set forth.

Key Factors in Evaluating Computer Hardware

The computer hardware of a management information system comprises four components: (1) the central processing unit (CPU), which controls the other computer system parts; (2) data storage files, which hold business information; (3) operator workstations where users enter, verify, and update data; and (4) a printer, which gives a permanent record of the data files or transactions. Depending on the company's needs, the management information system may have multiple workstations, printers, or data storage units plus other peripheral units. Due to the importance of these four components, key factors in evaluating them are offered below.

CENTRAL PROCESSING UNIT (CPU).   Even though system CPUs are fast enough to handle any business function required, it is advisable to acquire a CPU with more memory capability than needed initially, so the system can be expanded as the company grows. A memory protection capability is important, whether there are multiple users or a need to limit access of pertinent information to authorized personnel. Also, some CPUs require a special physical environment in order to operate effectively; this can be a hidden cost, affecting budget considerations.

DATA STORAGE FILES.   The most important consideration for a mass storage unit is its capacity. The capacity selected should be based on the amount of information stored now as well as projected growth. Vendors can give record size estimates to help determine storage requirements. On-line data storage files are usually available in three forms: diskettes (floppy disks), hard disks, and magnetic tapes. Diskette storage, used for small volumes of data, is measured in "thousands of characters of information," or kilobytes (KB). Hard disks and magnetic tapes, which hold large volumes of data, are measured in "megabytes" (millions of characters of information, or MB). In general, a management information system should offer a broad enough range of mass storage capabilities that the company will not outgrow the hardware. Removable disks, diskettes, and magnetic tape units make data backup and copying simple and inexpensive if they are part of the initial system configuration. Incompatibility problems are reduced if all mass storage units are from a single vendor.

OPERATOR WORKSTATIONS.   The criteria here are operator-comfort features that reduce physical strain, such as swivel and tilt screens, movable keyboards, and brightness controls. If a workstation requires a specially designed desk or table, it is necessary to check for hidden costs.

PRINTERS.   Two types of printers are available with computer systems. The type and speed needed is best determined by the frequency and amount of printed transaction copies required. *Character* printers print one character at a time, and *line* printers print an entire line at a time. Character printers are

COMPUTER
HARDWARE FOR
EFFECTIVE
MANAGEMENT
INFORMATION
SYSTEMS

slower but less expensive than line printers and may produce higher quality output. Line printers are used for high-speed report production. Ideally, the vendor should offer a variety of printers; that is, different speeds and types, so that the one that best meets the specific requirements can be selected. There should be a range of character features—upper- and lower-case letters, underscore, and punctuation marks generally improve report quality and readability. Also, the system should allow the printer and the operator workstations to operate simultaneously. Sometimes, printers are used as workstations, providing printed output instead of video. Printer workstations are slower and are usually used in specialized applications requiring immediate documentation.

An evaluation of these factors will ensure that the most important criteria have been considered in acquiring the appropriate hardware for the management information system.

CURRENT COMPUTER SYSTEMS FOR MIS

Depending upon the type of MIS processing environment, a combination of microcomputers, minicomputers, small-scale computers, medium-scale computers, and large-scale computers is generally used. Microcomputers are normally used for specific business applications to assist managers and their support personnel. Minicomputers and small-scale computers normally produce management reports for use at the local level, support their own local and remote satellite terminals, and perform high-speed communications with a host processor within a distributed MIS environment if deemed necessary. In price and performance, minicomputers and small-scale computers cover a broad range. At the other end of the computing continuum we find medium-scale and large-scale computer systems. The capabilities of these larger systems, which far exceed those of the smaller computer system, are discussed shortly.

Microcomputers (Personal Computers)

The microcomputer (personal computer) has made tremendous inroads not only in the home market, but also as an integral part of an effective management information system. It was first popularly marketed by Apple Computer, Inc., in June 1977. A newer version, the Apple III computer, is illustrated in figure 4.1.

The most popular microcomputer today is the IBM Personal Computer, illustrated in figure 4.2. The IBM model consists of a slightly modified typewriter keyboard attached to a box along with a display screen (or a TV monitor). Standard memory is 64KB, expandable to 640KB. It is contained in the box along with one or two records that can be used to read in programs or stored data.

A number of programs are available for the IBM PC, such as the Personal Decision Series (PDS). Six programs, or Editions, are available and can be bought individually, depending on the user's needs. The first one, DATA Edi-

FIGURE 4.1
A typical micro-computer or personal computer available for use in an MIS environment—Apple III Personal Computer. (Courtesy Apple Computer, Inc.)

FIGURE 4.2
The IBM Personal Computer (Micro-computer). (Courtesy IBM)

COMPUTER
HARDWARE FOR
EFFECTIVE
MANAGEMENT
INFORMATION
SYSTEMS

tion, is a flexible data base manager that organizes information and takes it from a variety of sources. When the HOST ATTACHMENT Edition is used, valuable information from an inside source—the central computer—can be obtained without having to be re-entered. By adding PLANS+, the user can answer "What if?" questions with a financial model or spreadsheet that can remember how the answers were arrived at. Numbers can be translated into different shapes, sizes, and colors by using GRAPHS. Documents can be customized by making layout and type style decisions with REPORTS+. Finally, WORDS provides the user with an easy-to-learn word processing program.

Although the IBM PC is common in business, its capabilities have been surpassed with the introduction of the IBM Personal Computer AT and XT. The AT is illustrated in figure 4.3. The XT has an extended data storage capacity of 10.7 million bytes, or characters of information—considerably more than the IBM PC. The greatly enlarged memory is achieved through a so-called hard disk storage device built into the XT model. IBM PC owners previously could achieve such memory capacities only by attaching hard disk devices. The XT model has optional memory expansion units to raise storage capacity to more than 20 million bytes, equivalent to 10,000 double-spaced typewritten pages of text, or up to 200,000 names and addresses, in one place.

FIGURE 4.3
Another typical microcomputer—the IBM Personal Computer AT. (Courtesy IBM)

COMPUTER
HARDWARE AND
SOFTWARE FOR
EFFECTIVE
MANAGEMENT
INFORMATION
SYSTEMS

THE MICRO-MAINFRAME CONNECTION.   Before exploring the capabilities of typical mainframes, it is helpful to understand the microcomputer and mainframe connection. Organizational personnel acquire microcomputers not on the basis of cost justification and productivity increases, but rather on the basis of doing better work, especially increasing the quality of decision making. At the outset, they are mainly concerned with four application areas: spreadsheets, word processing, data base (for screen-driven applications as well as creating simple ad hoc lists), and simple business graphics. They can get by quite satisfactorily without accessing mainframes, minis, or other micros. But once users become familiar with these initial applications, they begin to see good reasons to make contact with the outside.

Currently, the only significant kind of micro-mainframe interconnection is mainframe terminal *emulation.* A user who wants to access the applications available on the corporate mainframe does not want a mainframe terminal sitting beside the personal computer on his or her desk. So the individual installs some mainframe terminal emulation hardware and software and logs onto a mainframe just as if using a "dumb" terminal. Most of the emulation uses elementary asynchronous protocols, although with difficulty more complex bisynchronous protocols are commonly beginning to be installed.

When a close look is taken at the reasons for emulation, it turns out that there are three main applications. The first is access to mainframe timesharing. Many large companies already have personal computing facilities in place on their mainframes. Perhaps the best known examples of mainframe personal computing are financial planning packages, such as IFPS, and end-user-oriented file management systems, such as FOCUS. (These fourth-generation languages are explored in the next chapter.)

Second, there is access to external proprietary data bases, such as Dow Jones and DIALOG (discussed in this chapter). With their wealth of current information, these can be excellent research tools. They can also be very useful for non-business purposes. Communication in this case has normally been implemented using asynchronous terminals, so here the micro-mainframe communication is done using modems, dial-up lines, and asynchronous protocols.

The third and last kind of terminal emulation involves turnkey systems developed in-house. Information system departments have spent many years and millions of dollars building applications fundamental to the running of the corporation. Many of these have interactive facilities consisting of menu-driven formatted screens. Transaction processing implementations of accounts payable and receivable, general ledger, and payroll/personnel systems are the mainstays.

Overall, these three applications contain much of interest. Users reason that because micros look like mainframe terminals, they should be capable of accessing mainframe applications. Unlike access to mainframe personal computing facilities, however, for which the user interface is typically line-oriented, these transaction processing systems depend heavily on the processing of complete screens of information at a time. Thus, in timesharing applications, terminal communications are normally based on IBM 3270-type bisynchronous protocols rather than the asynchronous protocols.

Minicomputers and Small-Scale Computer Systems

Exceeding the capabilities of microcomputers are those of minicomputers and small-scale computer systems. Though they differ widely in their architecture, data formats, peripheral equipment, and software, today's minicomputers and small-scale computer systems typically consist of a keyboard and CRT for data entry (cards, floppy disks, or cassettes may also be used), a processor that starts with about 128KB of memory, a disk for file storage, and a serial printer with a speed of about 30 characters per second. From there, the only way to go is upward to more memory, additional peripheral devices, faster printers, and so forth.

The small business computer market is served by distinct types of vendors. The first type is represented by "Fortune 500" companies, such as Burroughs, Control Data, Honeywell, IBM, NCR, and Sperry Univac,[1] all of which have vast production lines and resources. For these firms, the small business computer is just one of a broad line of products (although in the case of Burroughs and NCR, minicomputers and small business computers account for a sizable portion of their total corporate revenues). A second group consists of specialized minicomputer manufacturers, such as Basic/Four Corporation, Computer Automation, Data 100, Data General, Digital Equipment Corporation, Four Phase Systems, General Automation, Harris, Hewlett-Packard, Interdata, Microdata, Prime Computer, Wang, and others. They address this segment of the marketplace with a package consisting of a minicomputer and associated peripherals, usually accompanied by some applications software. Most minicomputer vendors also offer assemblers and compilers for users who want to do their own programming.

MINICOMPUTER SYSTEMS. A typical minicomputer system is the Hewlett-Packard HP 3000 Series 44, pictured in figure 4.4. Not only is this system useful within an MIS operating mode, it is also an important link in a *distributed*

---

[1]Burroughs and Sperry Univac merged in late 1986 to form Unisys.

COMPUTER
HARDWARE AND
SOFTWARE FOR
EFFECTIVE
MANAGEMENT
INFORMATION
SYSTEMS

processing network. Specifically, paper-tape readers, magnetic tapes, and magnetic disks can operate on line with the system processor (system console) for processing current data. In a similar manner, card readers, line printers, and terminals can be linked with the system processor through the communications processor for local processing. Also, data can be communicated to and from another computer system—for example, an IBM computer. This interactive HP system can service local DP needs, fulfill the on-line needs of local and remote users, and meet the requirements of regional or central headquarters in an MIS distributed processing network. Another popular minicomputer system is the Digital Equipment Corporation's (DEC) VAX 11/750 system, illustrated in figure 4.5.

SMALL-SCALE COMPUTER SYSTEMS. There is a wide range of minicomputers to select from, and the same can be said for small-scale computer systems. Many of these are oriented toward distributed data processing within an MIS environment. The IBM 8100, for example, is such a system. It includes a choice of two processors, a storage unit, a display station, a magnetic tape

FIGURE 4.5
Another typical
minicomputer system—
DEC VAX 11/750
System. (Courtesy
Digital Equipment
Corporation)

FIGURE 4.6
A typical small-scale
computer system for
use in an MIS
environment—IBM
Model 8100
Information System.
(Courtesy IBM)

FIGURE 4.7
Another typical small-
scale computer
system—Unisys System
80 small business
computer system.
(Courtesy Unisys)

unit, and a line printer. In a large organization, the new system can be linked
to an IBM mainframe as well as to other 8100s as part of a cooperative network processing plan. With the Distributed Processing Control Executive, DP
personnel at headquarters can assemble and distribute programs to 8100 locations to provide greater productivity and consistency throughout the organization. On the other hand, with the Distributed Processing Programming Executive, programs can be prepared locally using high-level languages, or with a
special 8100 capability called Development Management System. This application development aid enables users to define screen formats, enter data or
access files on the spot, and develop entire programs without the assistance

COMPUTER
HARDWARE AND
SOFTWARE FOR
EFFECTIVE
MANAGEMENT
INFORMATION
SYSTEMS

of programming professionals. Thus, the 8100 goes beyond the capabilities of many previous small-scale computer systems. Shown in figure 4.6 is the IBM 8100 Information System. Also illustrated is another small-scale computer system, the Unisys System 80 (figure 4.7). The System 80 is designed to satisfy a wide range of MIS requirements.

Medium- and Large-Scale Computer Systems

In terms of medium- to large-scale computer systems, the "Fortune 500" manufacturers mentioned above have almost the entire market to themselves. As in the past, IBM still leads this segment of the mainframe business. In addition, these large mainframes are useful in supporting a "war room" environment (discussed in a later section).

MEDIUM-SCALE COMPUTER SYSTEMS.   A current offering widely used for management information systems is the IBM 4361 illustrated in figure 4.8. The 4361 provides for the attachment of a wide range of peripheral devices. It may be used in an environment where it is the single processor, or as a complementary computer within a multisystem installation, or as a member of a complex of machines located in multiple sites. A 4361 then, along with appropriate hardware components, can be the main processing source or part of a large-scale processing facility within an MIS environment.

FIGURE 4.8   A typical medium-scale computer system found in an MIS environment—IBM 4361. (Courtesy IBM)

LARGE-SCALE COMPUTER SYSTEMS. An example of a large-scale computer system is the IBM 3090 Model 200 (figure 4.9). It is designed to operate as a central headquarters mainframe for medium- and large-size companies. The "dyadic" design of the complex includes two processors that have their own assigned set of channels, but share main memory and operate under a single control program. A typical 3090 complex would include two processors, a processor controller, power unit, coolant distribution unit, systems and operator consoles, 32 data channels, and 64 million characters of main memory. With these hardware capabilities, a computer system can easily handle the complex needs of a large management information system.

COMPUTER
HARDWARE FOR
EFFECTIVE
MANAGEMENT
INFORMATION
SYSTEMS

CURRENT INPUT/OUTPUT TERMINAL DEVICES FOR MIS

Not only microcomputers are used as input/output devices; a number of other terminal devices can provide input and output to a system. First, we focus on the use of intelligent and graphic terminals. Then the more traditional input

FIGURE 4.9 A typical large-scale computer system for use in an MIS environment—IBM 3090 Model 200 Processor Complex. (Courtesy IBM)

COMPUTER
HARDWARE AND
SOFTWARE FOR
EFFECTIVE
MANAGEMENT
INFORMATION
SYSTEMS

and output devices are described briefly. This orderly presentation serves to place current I/O equipment advances in their proper perspective within an MIS environment.

Intelligent Terminals

Distinguishing features of intelligent terminals are built-in memory and control functions for programming. Within a programmed environment, they can stand alone or be configured in a cluster, sharing any or all of the power storage, printers, and sometimes communications of the computer. The cathode-ray tube (CRT) is the most common display technology for these terminals. The trend today is for programmed intelligent terminals to perform multiple functions, such as data entry, data retrieval, inquiry/response, and monitoring and control. This trend, along with the extensive utilization of microcomputers, is expected to continue as offices become more automated.

Generally, an intelligent terminal must have—as a minimum—the following characteristics: self-contained storage, random access memory, user interaction with the terminal itself, stored program capability, processing capability at the terminal through a user-written program, capability of on-line communications with another intelligent terminal, human-oriented input (such as keyboard), and human-oriented output (such as printer or a CRT). These characteristics are found in the typical intelligent terminals explored below.

TYPICAL INTELLIGENT TERMINALS. An example of an intelligent terminal, figure 4.10, is the Unisys UTS (Universal Terminal System) 40 programmable terminal. Being a general-purpose intelligent terminal, its primary benefits are programmability, peripheral sharing, keyboard control of peripherals, data editing, and screen control. The microprocessor, acting as a general-purpose computer, controls operation of the terminal by executing the programmed logic. Maximum system memory size is 65KB. The UTS has the Screen Management System (SMS 40), which provides a set of control routines to support programs written in the MAC/80 language. The availability of these routines greatly simplifies programming of common functions, such as screen formatting, input validation, and I/O functions. SMS 40 also provides various arithmetic and editing capabilities, all of which are loadable as separate modules.

Another example of an intelligent terminal is the IBM 5280, shown in figure 4.11. The system is designed to be used by employees working with the information that needs to be processed, not by data processing professionals. The 5280 can be hooked up to most major IBM computer systems. A representative 5280 configuration consists of a programmable keyboard/display station with a main storage capacity of 64KB, two diskette drives that accommodate 1.2MB of information each, a 120 character-per-second serial printer, and a communications adapter. Available with the 5280 is a line printer.

COMPUTER
HARDWARE FOR
EFFECTIVE
MANAGEMENT
INFORMATION
SYSTEMS

FIGURE 4.10
An example of an intelligent terminal— the Unisys UTS (Universal Terminal System) 40 programmable terminal. (Courtesy Unisys)

Graphic Terminals

The need for business graphics has been caused largely by the advent of the so-called "information explosion." As computing technology has advanced and the ability to process and display information has steadily grown, users (managers and their support personnel) have found themselves inundated in a rising tide of computer-generated facts and figures. So great, in fact, has the flood of information—and accompanying paper documents—become that no

129

COMPUTER
HARDWARE AND
SOFTWARE FOR
EFFECTIVE
MANAGEMENT
INFORMATION
SYSTEMS

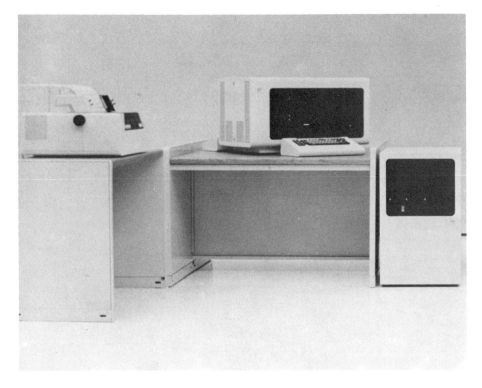

FIGURE 4.11
Another example of an intelligent terminal—IBM 5280 Intelligent Terminal. (Courtesy IBM)

manager can possibly hope to review it all. The end result is that many managers are finding themselves faced with a growing sea of irrelevant facts and are increasingly unable to extract the key financial information they need.

COMPUTER GRAPHICS IN AN MIS ENVIRONMENT. Within an MIS environment, computer graphics promise to bring the information explosion at least partially under control by allowing managers to distill quickly the essence of large amounts of business data and by reducing greatly the mass of financial reports and other paper with which managers are forced to contend. An effective computer graphics system, especially one that displays its data in color, can condense reams of printout into a few readily understandable graphs and charts.

Generally, "at a glance" graphical presentations of information allow managers to start their thinking processes quickly. The usual method—also the slower method—involves a lot of reading. A "picture" may tell a manager immediately what he or she wants to know. The information in this visual aid might otherwise be buried in stacks of computer-generated reports. As another alternative, the manager may view graphs of concern on a display screen and also generate a paper printout of graphical data to ponder later. Whatever the choice, computer-prepared graphics are very effective for supporting decision making in an MIS environment.

As a starting point, if the manager already has a terminal that displays

COMPUTER
HARDWARE FOR
EFFECTIVE
MANAGEMENT
INFORMATION
SYSTEMS

alphanumeric information, the same terminal (CRT or printer) might be modified into a simple graphics unit. Newer types of display terminals and printers (to be explored below), however, have become available for producing alphanumerics and graphics. The addition of color permits users to pick out exceptions to trends even more rapidly than with graphics seen in black and white. Also, a number of display terminals can provide three-dimensional representations.

TYPICAL COLOR GRAPHIC TERMINALS. In figure 4.12, the IBM 3279 Color Display Station is illustrated, which can produce high-quality color displays. Also shown is the IBM 3287 Printer (four-color). The 3279 can present information in many graphic forms, such as bar and pie charts, line graphs, diagrams, and maps. Such color displays can emphasize and simplify information in many ways. For example, they can present sales or financial data, pinpoint inventory shortages or approaching deadlines, and clarify many business situations. This color display terminal can be used with current IBM computers.

Currently, the IBM 3287 can utilize a three-dimensional-presentation-graphics facility/matrix math editor. This is an interactive facility intended to enhance many business-oriented color-graphics applications. The facility includes a full screen matrix math editor which allows the user to enter, manipulate, and perform arithmetic operations on columns and rows of data. In addition, the user may perform limited regression analyses and moving average calculations on the data to create comparative values for color graphic presentation. The user may customize the three-dimensional graph with selections of color; shading patterns; annotations; figure types; legends; pitch, depth, and height control; and other options to produce a customized three-dimensional chart.

Going beyond terminals aimed primarily at the business marketplace, other color graphic terminals are aimed at the engineering and scientific market. For example, the Tektronic color terminal—Model 4027A is illustrated in figure 4.13—can use any eight colors at once or define up to 120 color patterns. Additionally, output can be reproduced in gray scale on a video copier or plotted in color on an easy-to-use plotter.

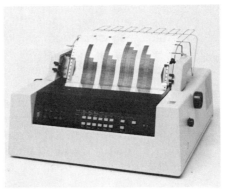

FIGURE 4.12
A color graphic terminal—the IBM 3279 Color Display Station with the IBM 3287 Printer. (Courtesy IBM)

  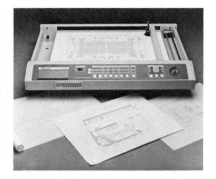

FIGURE 4.13 Another example of a color graphic terminal—the Tektronic 4027A Color Graphic Terminal can be used to reproduce in gray scale on a video copier or plot in color on a plotter. (Courtesy Tektronix, Inc.)

Other Input Devices

In addition to the foregoing intelligent and graphic terminal devices and microcomputers that are used as input devices, several methods are available for capturing data from originating documents and sources. Of the data entry devices (to be explored briefly below), the keypunch method has been the most widely used. However, data punching directly onto magnetic disks has rapidly replaced keypunch machines because it saves time and expense.

The more common input methods are:

□ *Card punches and verifiers*—were the most common methods of converting source data into punched cards and verifying the same data. Due to their limited storage and file handling problems, newer forms of data entry have replaced card punches and verifiers.

□ *Key-to-tape systems*—allow a complete record to be key entered and verified before it is released to magnetic tape. Since each unit stands alone, a disadvantage is that tapes must be gathered and merged before computer processing can occur.

□ *Key-to-disk systems*—permit data to be recorded and verified on magnetic disks before transferring completed batches to magnetic tape for computer processing. Of the current input methods of data entry, this one has experienced wide acceptance because there are fewer steps than with prior input methods.

□ *Key-to-floppy-disk systems*—allow data to be recorded on diskettes rather than on magnetic disks; this too has experienced wide acceptance.

□ *Distributed data entry systems*—center on single or multiple data entry units distributed at various company locations. This important current trend in data entry utilizes single or multiple data entry units. Since input is captured on either tape or disk, it is communicated in an on-line or off-line mode as input to the computer system. Addition-

132

COMPUTER
HARDWARE FOR
EFFECTIVE
MANAGEMENT
INFORMATION
SYSTEMS

ally, this data entry approach brings flexibility to an organization's data entry operations.

□ *Optical character readers*—read source documents via optical fonts. It is possible to read pencil marks on preprinted forms, a wide variety of type fonts, and hand-printed characters.

□ *Point-of-sale devices*—provide a convenient way for retail stores to capture input data. In turn, these data are converted into a machine-processable form for computer processing.

□ *Data collection systems*—allow the collection of input data, either on-line or off-line, for controlling manufacturing activities. Data collection devices are located throughout the production area.

Overall, a wide range of input methods are available. For best results, systems design personnel should be knowledgeable about the latest developments in this area.

Other Output Devices

Not only can intelligent and graphic terminals serve as input devices, they are also capable of being used as output devices. Many types of systems output can be incorporated into a management information system. Because computer hardware and peripheral devices produce a variety of output quickly, it is essential for an organization's MIS systems analysts to know the capabilities of this equipment. Otherwise, the appropriate technology and developments relative to the forms of output will be missing from the management information system.

Output from computerized management information systems can take a variety of forms. The most common ones follow.

□ *Printed output*—centers on high-speed printers to produce listings, invoices, summaries, etc., along with management reports and exception reports. Although speeds can range up to 18,000 lines a minute for the very fastest printers, most computer printers range from several hundred up to 3,000 lines per minute in printing continuous forms.

□ *Microfilm or microfiche output*—allows output to be stored on microfilm where a sheet of microfiche can hold from one hundred to three hundred pages. By employing microfilm output, the physical size of output is reduced, and output is produced faster. Computer output can be up to thirty times faster than the typical several hundred lines-a-minute printer.

□ *Audio response unit*—allows the computer system to answer inquiries regarding the data stored on line. It consists of a message handling unit, touch-tone telephone units, and standard telephone lines for an on-line mode. The audio response unit has a vocabulary of up to three hundred words tailored to the user's needs.

□ *Plotter output*—is used to represent graphics of pictorial data in place

133

COMPUTER
HARDWARE AND
SOFTWARE FOR
EFFECTIVE
MANAGEMENT
INFORMATION
SYSTEMS

of extensive numeric or alphabetic listings. Automatic graph plotters are utilized where graphic or pictorial presentation of computer data is meaningful and easier to use than extensive numeric or alphabetic listings. They are indispensable when the volume of graphic presentation required is uneconomical or impossible to produce manually.

□ *Turnaround document output*—is produced as output by a computer system which, in turn, serves as input to the computer system at a later date. A good example is the punch card enclosed with a customer's monthly telephone bill. This card is returned with the customer's payment which, in turn, serves as input to the computer system.

□ *Data storage devices*—magnetic disk, magnetic tape, and mass storage. Due to their importance, they are discussed separately below.

As with input methods, a number of outputs are available for use in any management information system. The attendant circumstances must be analyzed to determine which one or ones are needed for effective MIS.

Summary—Current Input/Output Terminal Devices for MIS

In addition to the use of *microcomputers* as input/output devices, the following represent the major types of terminal devices:

Intelligent Terminals—are capable of performing certain editing and validating functions. The chief advantage of intelligent terminals is the capability to bypass many of the input processing procedures of traditional methods, thereby providing a direct link with the computer in an interactive mode.

Graphic Terminals—are capable of displaying data in color and condensing reams of printed materials into a few readily understandable graphs and charts. It is a meaningful way to support management in decision making.

Other Input Devices—include card punches and verifiers, key-to-tape systems, key-to-disk systems, key-to-floppy-disk systems, distributed data entry systems, optical character readers, point-of-sale devices, and data collection systems.

Other Output Devices—encompass printed output, microfilm or microfiche output, audio response units, plotter output, turnaround document output, and data storage devices.

DATA STORAGE DEVICES

Currently, most types of data storage can be categorized as off-line storage or on-line storage. *Off-line storage* refers to data stored off line; that is, not under the direction of the computer. These data files can be used as input for a computer system to permit the updating and retrieval of information, or they can be used to produce management reports from the MIS. Generally, data that need to be referenced periodically, usually weekly or less frequently, are good candidates for off-line storage.

In contrast, *on-line storage* refers to data under the direct control of the computer. Where there is a need to refer to data frequently, on-line storage is employed. Common examples are inventory updating and accounts receivable retrieval. On-line data files are commonly referred to as an organization's *data base,* where information is centrally located in one or several data bases. However, with distributed processing within an MIS environment, data files are presently referred to as *distributed data bases* because many data bases are scattered throughout an organization's operations.

Although storage can be identified as off-line or on-line, another way of viewing the subject is in terms of how the data are accessed; that is, must the data be accessed (while under the direct control of the computer) in a sequential or random order? If data must be accessed in a *sequential* manner, the most popular type of data storage is the utilization of magnetic tape files. In contrast, if the data can be accessed directly (i.e., if stored data can be accessed randomly as needed), the method is referred to as *direct access* file storage. Popular types of direct access storage are magnetic disk and mass storage.

Magnetic Tape Units

Currently, equipment manufacturers have a variety of magnetic tape units compatible with their own computer lines. They differ basically in two ways: the speed in reading or writing data on tape and the data density (number of bits, digits, or characters per inch) of the tape. For example, the IBM 3420 magnetic tape unit (Models 3 and 8) reads and writes data at densities up to 6,250 bits per inch on 0.5-inch magnetic tape. It is under the control of the 3803 control, where several tape drives can be combined (figure 4.14).

The *major advantages* of magnetic tape files are their fast input/output processing speeds and their capability of storing large amounts of data on a small piece of tape. A single reel of tape can hold the equivalent of many thousands of punched cards. The *principal shortcoming* of magnetic tape is that data must be stored and processed in a sequential manner. For certain business applications that are processed periodically, this presents no major problem. However, because of the need for timely management information in an interactive mode, there is no time to search one or more magnetic tapes for an answer. Thus, this data file method is outmoded for an increasingly large number of MIS applications that require data to be accessed in a very short time.

Magnetic Disk Units

To answer "What if?" questions on a timely basis, stored data must be immediately accessible to the computer system. For this mode of operation, the data base must be on-line. Exactly what management information must be available on an immediate basis should have been determined as part of the requirements for the data base structure. Generally, important data required by the system are stored on line in data access file devices, while less impor-

COMPUTER
HARDWARE AND
SOFTWARE FOR
EFFECTIVE
MANAGEMENT
INFORMATION
SYSTEMS

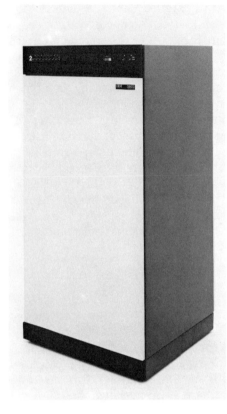

FIGURE 4.14
The IBM 3803 tape
control and IBM 3420
magnetic tape unit.
(Courtesy IBM)

tant data should be stored in another, low-cost storage medium, such as magnetic tape files.

Data stored on line must be thoroughly evaluated in terms of:

□ the amount of space needed for storing important data records in the data base
□ the time required to find and retrieve a data record
□ the time needed to transfer the proper record from the terminal devices to the main computer memory, as well as from the computer to the device after the record has been processed.

An intensive review and analysis of these factors is necessary to evaluate online direct access file storage requirements within an MIS environment. Hence, storage capabilities, speeds, and transfer rates are of utmost importance when stating equipment specifications.

Typical data storage devices are illustrated in figure 4.15. The IBM 3370 (shown as *a*) is a direct access storage device for the current IBM processing systems (4300 series). The storage medium and read/write heads are enclosed in a head/disk assembly that is an integral part of the disk drive. A fixed block data recording technique is incorporated in the 3370. This provides for recording data in permanent, preformatted 512-byte blocks on the disk surface. Fixed block architecture also permits efficient utilization of the disk surface

(a)

(b)

FIGURE 4.15
(a) The IBM 3370 and
(b) the IBM 3380
Direct Access Storage
devices. (Courtesy IBM)

COMPUTER
HARDWARE AND
SOFTWARE FOR
EFFECTIVE
MANAGEMENT
INFORMATION
SYSTEMS

for data and simpler, more flexible system attachment. Another direct access storage device (shown in *b*) is the double capacity IBM 3380. It is intended for large-scale computers. It can be also attached to the IBM 4300 series (certain models). More than 5 billion characters of data can be stored for direct on-line access. It should be noted that many other data storage devices are available from a wide range of equipment manufacturers. An intensive analysis of data storage devices is a study unto itself.

Important advantages of the magnetic disk are that any item of data is as quickly obtainable as any other, and that it is possible to skip over unwanted data. Another decided advantage over magnetic tape is its ability to process transactions without previously sorting the data. Also, several different but related data may be stored on disk files, thereby allowing a transaction to be processed on line against these files at the same time. For example, a customer order can be processed on line against the credit check, inventory, accounts receivable, and sales analysis files. In essence, magnetic disks are best for random access operations where input data are not arranged in any particular sequence before they are written on the disk. This direct accessibility plus the vast storage capability and relatively fast transfer rate have made this type of file widely used in computerized management information systems. A *principal disadvantage* of magnetic disk files is their higher cost over magnetic tape files. In addition, if the magnetic disks are removable, it is necessary to insert the proper disk pack(s) when processing is required. However, for those data files that are updated based upon continuous operations, this is not a disadvantage.

MICROCOMPUTER FILE STORAGE TODAY AND TOMORROW. The preceding description of magnetic disk units focused on on-line storage for computer mainframes. In contrast, there is a wide range of storage devices available on microcomputers. An examination of them is beyond the scope of this text; however, reference is made to their current and future directions. As micros advance in processing power, they must be supported by matching disk (floppy and hard) and backup storage devices. With microprocessor power approaching 1 million instructions per second and RAM exceeding 1MB, disk storage capacity must increase and access times must decrease to maximize throughput.

With the new desktop generation will come a reduction in physical size. History shows micro disk storage evolves first as a form-factor change at the floppy disk level, followed later by a hard disk of the same size—witness the 8-inch to 5¼-inch changeover a few years ago. This pattern is now well developed with 3½-inch floppy drives, leading initially to companion hard disks in the 10MB to 20MB range. With all of this comes price pressure, high-volume manufacturing, and stringent reliability requirements. Microcomputer file storage, like most computer hardware, is driven by economics and not by technology. The price of microcomputer data storage determines its penetration into a computer price range. Historically, mass storage devices have constituted 20 percent to 30 percent of the total system cost across most price ranges. As hard disk drives come down in price, more of them will appear in low-priced microcomputer systems.

Summary—Data Storage Devices

Magnetic tape units—Speed of transfer rates are very fast for either input or output. For certain business applications which are processed periodically, magnetic tape files offer the most economical method for storage and processing.

Magnetic disk units—Speed of data transfer rates is high, while the average search time is much slower. Magnetic disks have the ability to process transactions without first sorting the data, a decided advantage over magnetic tape. This feature of direct accessibility, a vast storage capability, and relatively fast transfer rate have made disk files widely used.

COMPUTER
HARDWARE FOR
EFFECTIVE
MANAGEMENT
INFORMATION
SYSTEMS

DATA BASE MANAGEMENT SYSTEMS

With on-line data base elements available for immediate processing using direct access file storage devices, some method is needed to control the data base. One method of maintaining a large, complex data base and managing relationships among the data base elements is to employ a data base management system (DBMS).

Typically, the reach of a data base management system extends beyond the individual file management systems, such as inventory files and accounts receivable files of the past, to an entire data base (or data bases), consisting of corporate planning, marketing, manufacturing, accounting, personnel, and other data elements. Furthermore, a DBMS allows *procedure independence* of the data base of a large number of data elements. This means that the programmer does not have to describe the data file in detail, as is the case with procedure-oriented languages like COBOL and FORTRAN, but rather only specify what is to be done in a *data management language.*

Essential Characteristics of DBMS

The relationship between the application program and the data base in a DBMS environment is illustrated in figure 4.16. The "data description component" analyzes each requirement of the application program, then transfers control to the "data manipulation component," which retrieves the needed data elements from the data base. In this manner, a data base management system reduces coding time and improves efficiency by allowing the programmer to use a catalog of file definitions for storing and accessing data efficiently. Thus, much of the efficiency of a DBMS is the procedure independence of the data base for producing the desired output report.

Typically, a data base management system (based upon controlled activ-ities as shown in figure 4.16) has the following characteristics:

- *operating environment independence*—capability to run on many computers with certain types of operating systems
- *user-oriented*—provision for an English-like language which enables the user to consider logical entities in place of physical entities, such as hardware and system software

139

COMPUTER
HARDWARE AND
SOFTWARE FOR
EFFECTIVE
MANAGEMENT
INFORMATION
SYSTEMS

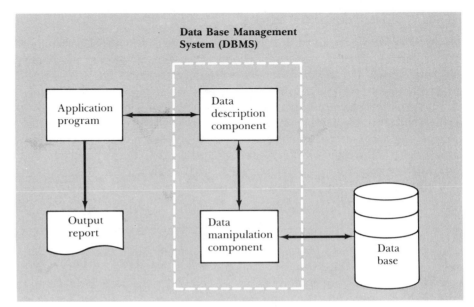

FIGURE 4.16
The relationship
between the application
program and the data
base in a data base
management system
(DBMS) environment.

□ *data base independence from application programs*—use of a data base language and "call" commands from the application program

□ *security features*—provision for controlling data base access and direction of the data base elements

Advantages and Disadvantages of DBMS

Inasmuch as a typical management information system normally includes a data base management system, its advantages should be considered. First, DBMS is not only effective for generating and maintaining a wide variety of routine management and operating reports, but also adaptable to meeting the new requirements of management to answer a myriad of "What if?" questions. The latter capability means data base management systems will be important aids to managers seeking to explore and understand new relationships among various data elements.

Second, data elements can be structured in a manner more suitable to their application, allowing retrieval with minimum of effort. Third, DBMS keeps redundancy of data elements to a minimum, since one data file serves many users. As a result of this "single record" concept, a transaction is entered once for all users. The DBMS also allows two or more files to be updated with the entry of a single transaction. Fourth, application programs are independent of the changes in the data base, so that their maintenance is kept to a minimum. Fifth, DBMS provides data protection not only for accessing one data base record at a time, but also for preventing data base access by unauthorized personnel.

Although the foregoing provide excellent advantages to DBMS users, the initial investment of system personnel time as well as software and equipment

COMPUTER
HARDWARE FOR
EFFECTIVE
MANAGEMENT
INFORMATION
SYSTEMS

costs can be high; however, increasing experience with data base management systems is reducing these costs. Another disadvantage of DBMS is that incorrect transaction data tend to precipitate additional problems and errors throughout the system. Therefore, various tests should be incorporated to catch errors before information is stored. These input tests, such as limit checks and reasonableness tests, will be treated in chapter 9 (Effective Control of MIS). Overall, these disadvantages of DBMS can be greatly minimized if the management information system is properly designed using the appropriate data base organization model.

Three Organization Models for DBMS

Although vendors offer a variety of data base management systems, programs that provide for the creation, access, and maintenance of data to aid organizations in the effective management of data bases fall into three categories:

1. hierarchical
2. network
3. relational

Each of these organization models for DBMS is discussed briefly.

A *hierarchical data base* uses a tree structure to distinguish relationships between records in a file. Every data item or field is "owned" by a higher ranking item, and access to it must be routed through that hierarchy. In other words, items are arranged according to a parent/child relationship whereby each parent may have many children, but each child may have only one parent. A fixed relationship between the data elements in the hierarchy is established, and data are retrieved by the data base management system moving along the hierarchy in a manner dependent on the request from the user. This model is illustrated in figure 4.17(a).

A *network data base system* establishes individual files for each major element of data. "Pointers" in the records are used to link these elements together. Pointers are the disk addresses where each record in a file is stored. In effect, the network model allows "children" to be related to many "parents" and very general interdependencies can be expressed. As such, a network data base tends to be more flexible than a hierarchical data base. This second organization model is shown in figure 4.17(b).

A *relational data base management system* is simply a collection of two-dimensional tables (called relations) with no repeating group. In the tables, the rows constitute records and columns constitute fields. The term "relational" comes from the clearly defined relations that the data within a field have, which orders the records in the data base. For example, numeric fields can be ordered from least to greatest, alphabetic fields can be in alphabetical order, and so forth. An example of this third organization model is in figure 4.17(c).

The relational model, which is the current trend in DBMS models, offers many advantages over hierarchical and network models. It is based on a logical rather than a physical structure and shows the relationships between various

141

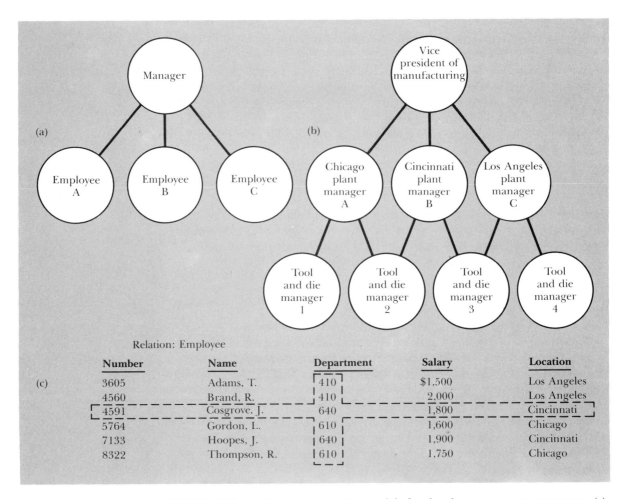

FIGURE 4.17   Three organization models for data base management systems: (a) hierarchical, (b) network, and (c) relational.

items. Data are represented in tabular form and new relations can be created. Searching is generally faster than within the other schemes, modification is more straightforward, and the clarity and visibility of the data base are improved.

Software for DBMS

The newer software for DBMS is based on a flexible row-and-table format; that is, the relational organization model. Generally speaking, the relational data base approach is appropriate for all applications—from the simplest ones built by end users to high-volume applications involving millions of transactions per day. Because software developers and programmers find the relational DBMS far easier to use, they are using it to reduce the monumental applications backlogs found in most MIS departments currently. In fact, many relational data base vendors report productivity improvements on the order of about five to ten times over hierarchical systems. Relational DBMS is appealing because hierarchical and network systems require in-depth knowledge of how to navigate the data base structure with programming languages and of how to use the system's indices. A relational system does not require this knowledge. It allows the user to access information without having to go through a particular program to find data entered for that program. The user does not need to understand how the data are arranged within the data base. The query language itself contains all of that information; thus, a query, in effect, automatically searches out data.

A relational DBMS also processes records one set at a time. The computer will search for and identify all members of the sought-after set; for example, all past due accounts. By contrast, hierarchical DBMSs examine each record and identify whether it is past due. If it is not, the system goes to the next record. If overdue, the system sends out a notice. In addition to these time- and money-saving attributes, the relational DBMS has a formal theoretical foundation, which provides rules for structure, maintenance, and integrity (preserving the data against unauthorized changes). More important, organizations can add new data fields, build new access paths, and split tables without disturbing other programs or data stored in the data base. A listing of typical data base management systems for all types of computer systems, including microcomputers, is in figure 4.18.

Until a few years ago, most organizations installed hierarchical and network DBMSs at considerable cost and with much difficulty. Most of these systems remain in place and will be used for years to come. A principal reason for this is IBM's intention to support its dominant hierarchical DBMS—Information Management System (IMS)—with its new relational data base, DB2, and its new version of its query language, SQL/DS. Even though so many advantages to relational systems exist that it appears they will quickly drive the other methods out, some vendors, analysts, and users do not prefer them. Hence, the older DBMS systems will continue for years to come.

External On-Line Data Bases

Going beyond the development and use of DBMSs for controlling internal data, a new industry has emerged addressing external on-line data bases to assist the manager in planning and controlling operations. Large banks of information are processed, stored, and delivered electronically. What is provided is not so much additional information (most of it has been around in printed form for a long time), but an improvement in the ease with which information can be retrieved. Hence, users of financial planning and statistical packages are being provided with information that has been germane to the problems being studied for solution.

Currently, the field is crowded with competing companies. Consider just the traditional publishers of financial data. Dow Jones & Company already has several offerings available via computer terminal, including a package that

COMPUTER
HARDWARE AND
SOFTWARE FOR
EFFECTIVE
MANAGEMENT
INFORMATION
SYSTEMS

Vendor	Package
Advanced Data Management	DRS
Applied Data Research	Datacom/DB
Battelle Software	Basis and Basis-DM
Cincom Systems	Total, TIS, and Ultra
Computer Associates Int'l.	CA-Universe Release 2.1
Computer Corporation of America	Model 204
Contel Information Systems	RTFile
CRI	Relate/3000
Cullinet Software	IDMS and IDMS/R
D&B Computing Services	Nomad2
Database Systems	Transact and Facts
Economic Sciences	EMS
Exact Systems & Programming	DNA-4
Henco Software	Info
Infodata Systems	Inquire
Information Builders	Focus and PC/Focus
Logica	Rapport
Logical Software	Logix
Management Decision Systems	Express
Mathematica Products Group	Ramis II
McDonnell Douglas Information Services Group	Magnum
On-Line Software Int'l.	Freestyle
Oracle	Oracle
Pro-IV	PRO-IV
Relational Database Systems	Informix
Relational Technology	Ingres
Rexcom	Rexcom D and Rexcom E
SAS Institute	System 2000
Scientific Info. Retrieval	Sir/DBMS
Signal Technology	Omnibase
Software AG	Adabas Natural
Software House	System 1022 and System 1032
Systemhouse	Minisis
Tominy	Data Base Plus
United Software Systems	Clio

FIGURE 4.18
A listing of typical data base management systems for all types of computer systems, including micro-computers.

allows an investor to learn the value of his or her portfolio every five minutes. Dun & Bradstreet sells on-line some of the printed information that was formerly distributed by mail. McGraw Hill owns Data Resources Inc., probably the pre-eminent company in the on-line information field. Other companies with multiple on-line data base offerings include ABC, Boeing, Chase Manhattan, Citicorp, Control Data, General Electric, G.T.E., Lockheed, Mead, Time Inc., and Xerox. A sample listing of offerings, together with vendors and producers, is shown in figure 4.19.

DIALOG. One of the most widely used of all on-line data bases by busi-

Data Base	Description	Producer	Vendor
Disclosure Online	Extracts from SEC filings of over 12,000 publicly held companies	Disclosure, Inc.	Lockheed Corp.; Mead Corp.
Dow Jones News/ Retrieval Service	Complete and abridged articles from the *Wall Street Journal, Barron's,* and the Dow Jones News Service; price quotations on stocks, bonds, options, and mutual funds	Dow Jones & Company	Dow Jones & Company Bunker Ramo Corp.; Telerate Systems, Inc.; General Telephone & Electronics
EBIS	Contains detailed records on firms that account for 90 percent of all sales of products and services in the United States	Economic Information Systems, Inc.	Control Data CYBERNET Services
Environline	Abstracts of literature on the environment from special reports, conference proceedings, and 8,000 international journals	Environment Information Center, Inc.	Lockheed Corp.; System Development Corp.
LEXIS	The full text of state and federal court decisions, statutes, regulations, etc.	Mead Corporation	Mead Corp.
New York Times Information Bank	Abstracts of the *New York Times,* 13 other newspapers, and over 40 magazines	New York Times Company	Mead Corp.
NTIS	Citations and abstracts of unrestricted technical reports from federally sponsored R&D projects	U.S. National Technical Information Service (Commerce Department)	Lockheed Corp.; System Development Corp.; Bibliographical Retrieval Services, Inc.
Petroleum Data System	Geological and production data on every gas and oil field or reservoir in the United States, Canada, and the outer continental shelf	University of Oklahoma, under contract to the U.S. Geological Society	General Electric Information Services Company
PROMT	Citations and abstracts on new products, technology, markets, etc. from over 2,000 U.S. and foreign publications	Predicasts, Inc.	Lockheed Corp.; System Development Corp.

FIGURE 4.19   Typical on-line data bases available from vendors.

COMPUTER
HARDWARE AND
SOFTWARE FOR
EFFECTIVE
MANAGEMENT
INFORMATION
SYSTEMS

ness, government, and education is DIALOG. The DIALOG Information Retrieval Service gives the user immediate access to the world's largest and most comprehensive computer storehouse of information. No matter what is needed, useful answers can be found among the more than 60 million references, abstracts, or statistical series from published material that can be searched on line with DIALOG. With an inexpensive terminal or personal computer (connected via the telephone), the user searches quickly for the desired information, describing the topic in his or her own words and using simple English commands to get the wanted results. No programming knowledge is needed to access over 150 DIALOG data bases that cover all the major disciplines—science, chemistry, technology, medicine, law, business, finance, social sciences, humanities, the arts, public affairs, and general news. With this breadth of coverage, the user has assurance that, no matter what information is needed, DIALOG has a data base that can help find the answer.

The types of information DIALOG provides include:

- Descriptions of published articles from popular magazines and professional/trade journals, government and industrial reports, conference papers, newspaper stories, patents, and books. The user is provided with title, author, publisher, subject headings, and usually a summary/abstract of the contents.
- Hard business data on products, single companies, or entire industries, including detailed financial information and both current and older business news.
- Directory-type information on businesses, associations, and foundations, giving officers, addresses, and business objectives.
- Statistical time series (domestic and international) drawn from several sources, including the U.S. Bureau of Labor Statistics.

DIALOG's computers help the user find information faster and more precisely than a typical manual search through library catalogs or printed indexes. With DIALOG, the use is not limited to searching only key words of subject headings. The individual may search any combination of words or phrases in the title and abstract as well as subject indexing terms. This provides the capability to retrieve information using newly-coined terms, personal names, or phrases—none of which may be listed in a printed index. In addition, the user can search and combine various types of information, for example:

- two or more separate ideas (e.g., houses and energy conservation)
- *and* the name of a particular journal in a certain year
- *or* a particular author, or citation of a particular author's article or report
- *or* a given language or a specified type of publication
- *or* any combination of the above

Such information can help the manager make key decisions, increase productivity, and save thousands of dollars. The cost of DIALOG is low. A typical search in a single data base averages ten minutes for experienced searchers and 15 minutes for beginners. Depending upon the data base, that search would cost approximately $5.25. That same search done manually could take several hours, days, or longer and not be as comprehensive.

Within an MIS environment, some of the terminal devices will not be linked directly to the local computer. They are instead connected to the central computer. For example, the mathematical and statistical packages used for supporting managerial decision-making are stored only at the home office. Because a conversational mode is generally required throughout the problem-solving process, the managers and their staff located at distant points from the home office may need to utilize these packages as well as specific data stored on the central data base for finalizing decisions. Hence, in this typical example, there is need for a data communications network that allows authorized organization personnel throughout the system to utilize specific MIS capabilities that may be at one central location.

Depending on the time requirements of organizational personnel in a data communications network, computer access can be on a "permanent" (leased lines) or on an "as required" (dial-up arrangement) basis. The terminal specifications determine the type of lines (*simplex* allows one-way transmission of data; *half-duplex* carries data in both directions, but permits the transmission of data in only one direction at a time; and *full-duplex* can transmit data in both directions simultaneously) and the speed of the lines (*narrowband* transmits data more slowly than that needed for voice transmission; *voiceband* transmits data at the rate of voice transmission; and *broadband* transmits data much faster than the rate of voice transmission). Because each terminal has a certain rated speed, it is possible to determine the lines required to transfer data from the terminal to the centralized computer. Moreover, a data communications network that allows transfer of information to and from management and their support personnel must be developed within the required time limits and at a low cost.

The type of equipment needed to connect the transmission lines to the main computer requires extensive study. There are many types of units available, each with different characteristics. Knowledge of the communication lines required for the management information system is prerequisite to specifying the number and types of communication-line control units that are needed. Each unit has a maximum number of lines it can handle as well as a maximum speed of any line. Thus, a feasibility study of communication equipment and lines should be undertaken to minimize costs.

Types of Data Communications Lines

The two major components involved in the transfer of data are communications channels and terminals. The interconnection of these channels and terminals and a computer(s) forms a network whose purpose is to receive, process, and transfer information. As illustrated in figure 4.20, several different

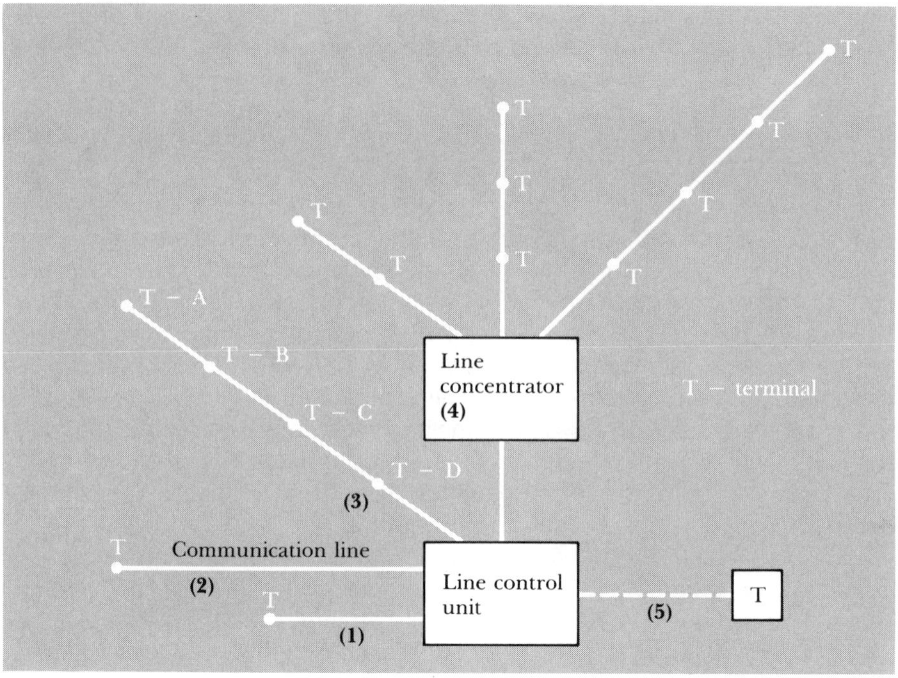

COMPUTER
HARDWARE AND
SOFTWARE FOR
EFFECTIVE
MANAGEMENT
INFORMATION
SYSTEMS

FIGURE 4.20

A data communications network that utilizes several different types of lines within an MIS environment.

types of lines can be employed in a data communications network. Lines (1) and (2) are examples of point-to-point transmission; that is, any connection between two terminals or between a terminal and a computer. Line (3) is a multipoint line that contains more than one terminal station on one communication line. Note that the connection between T–A and T–B is a point-to-point connection. Line (4) consists of three lines (multipoint) entering a line concentrator.

A line concentrator is a hardware device that accepts data from many low-speed, low-activity stations and transfers the data to the computer at much higher speeds. It also can receive data from the computer at a faster rate than it sends to terminals by storing data temporarily in its own buffer memory. The purpose of this device is to make the communication process more efficient between terminals and the computer(s) and to reduce overall communication network costs.

The last line (5) is a dial-up line that is used with the telephone. When a telephone connection is made, the terminal is connected directly to the computer. After the data transmission is completed, the terminal is disconnected from the computer. This data communications approach is used for terminals with limited data transmission requirements. It keeps line costs to a minimum because the user is charged only for the duration of the connection, which is not the case with lines (1) through (4).

The line control unit in figure 4.20 can be utilized as a simple data exchange unit or a multiplexer. Operating in a simple data exchange mode, it allows changing data transmission from one direction to another—say for half-duplex lines. As a multiplexer, it can be connected to a computer for handling simplex, half-duplex, and full-duplex lines, or it can be a stand-alone unit, working as a special-purpose computer. The maximum rate at which lines are able to transfer data to and from the computer is dependent upon the service provided—that is, narrowband, voiceband, broadband, or some other service. For a balanced approach, the speed at which a terminal device is able to transmit information should be equal to the speed of the line.

COMPUTER
HARDWARE FOR
EFFECTIVE
MANAGEMENT
INFORMATION
SYSTEMS

Types of Equipment

Referring again to line (2) in figure 4.20, information may pass through several types of communications equipment before it reaches its destination. The required equipment is illustrated in figure 4.21. It should be noted that the same equipment is required for any of the multipoint lines in figure 4.20.

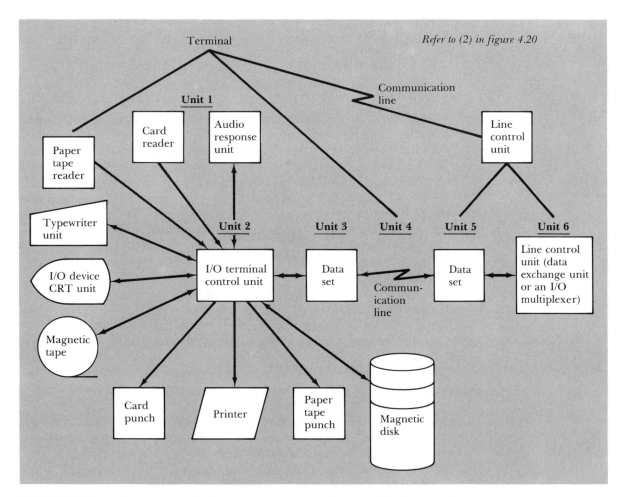

FIGURE 4.21 Data communications equipment needed to transfer data to and from remote locations.

COMPUTER
HARDWARE AND
SOFTWARE FOR
EFFECTIVE
MANAGEMENT
INFORMATION
SYSTEMS

In figure 4.21, unit 1 can be almost any type of input device or I/O device as illustrated. It is the originating point of data or the transferring point of information. The terminal control unit, or unit 2, accepts and stores input data (the reverse of the procedure for forwarding output information) temporarily by means of a buffering device so that its speed is compatible with the communication facility. The data set (modulator—unit 3) converts bits into signals that can be transmitted over communication lines (unit 4). The data set (demodulator—unit 5) receives signals over the communication facility and converts the signals into bits. Unit 6—the line control unit—controls and coordinates the flow of information to and from the computer.

As pointed out above, unit 6 serves as a data exchange or a multiplexer for the control of information to and from the various terminals. Polling is a common technique employed to coordinate and control on-line flows of data. The system interrogates each station on each line and asks if there are data to be transferred to the computer from input terminals, and if the terminal is able to receive information for the output terminals. It should be noted that polling and/or the transferring of data can take place simultaneously on each communication line.

Local Area Networks (LANs)

The basic approach of the above data communications networks centered on connecting computers and their peripheral devices at far distances from one another. In contrast, local area networks (LANs) meet the increasingly vital need to interconnect computers, terminals, word processors, fascimile, and other office machines within a building, campus, or metropolitan area. A local area network may be designed to support only one vendor's terminal equipment, or it may be designed for multivendor support. Network logic may be embedded in the terminal equipment, in bus/network interface units, or in central controllers.

Local area networks rely on two main methods for transmitting information: analog technology and digital. Analog signals are waves of voltage or current amplitude. Information is transmitted in analog transmissions by varying either the amplitude or the frequency of the continuous waves. Cable television is an example of analog technology. In the Cable TV (CATV) network, several frequencies are transmitted over the same cable. The end user tunes into any of the frequencies, selecting a specific signal, or channel. Because a broad range of analog frequencies can be transmitted over a single cable, this type of system is coded as "broadband." Broadband systems permit a variety of terminals/devices to share a cable by assigning frequencies (or addresses) to each one. This approach permits the simultaneous transmission of a variety of signals or channels on a single cable. The Ethernet system developed by Xerox is based on the use of analog transmission.

Digital signals, in contrast to analog signals, do not vary. They have only two forms: on or off. The signals produced by turning on a current are known as bits, the smallest "pieces" of information that can be transmitted. In digital technology, individual bits of information are sent at an established rate (bits

COMPUTER
HARDWARE FOR
EFFECTIVE
MANAGEMENT
INFORMATION
SYSTEMS

per second, or bps). Patterns of these bits are used to represent numbers, characters, system commands, etc. In digital transmission, several signals can share a single cable via time sharing. Systems that use digital transmission techniques are called ''baseband.'' Each terminal or device in a baseband system is assigned a specific time slot in which to transmit information (generally in thousandths or millionths of a second). Only one terminal is permitted to transmit during any given time slot.

PRINCIPAL NETWORK CONFIGURATIONS. As illustrated in figure 4.22, four principal network configurations are used in LANs. They are:

- □ *Star*—A star configuration connects end-users' workstations point-to-point to a master computer or controller. The end points can be intelligent or non-intelligent terminals/devices and can be data-, text-, or even voice-oriented. Since all end-user devices must be connected to

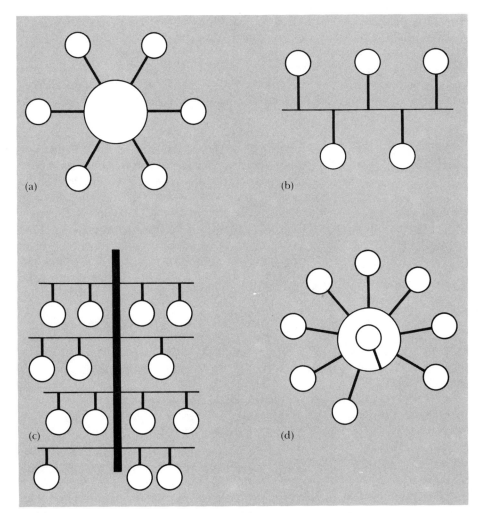

FIGURE 4.22
Four principal network configurations used in local area networks: (a) star, (b) bus, (c) tree, and (d) ring.

COMPUTER
HARDWARE AND
SOFTWARE FOR
EFFECTIVE
MANAGEMENT
INFORMATION
SYSTEMS

it, the central control unit requires a great deal of cable. All transmissions must pass through the central control area to be passed along to a receiving device. The star configuration is the least effective option for a LAN, since failure of the central control area knocks out the system.

☐ *Bus*—This configuration is not centralized like a star, since the system has defined end points that can be added to. All devices are connected directly to the main bus line. A signal originating at a terminal or processor propagates away in both directions along the bus line. Each connected device "listens" for its address on the bus. Recognizing its address, it accepts the data transmitted. Otherwise, it ignores the transmitted data. Control of a bus network resides in each individual terminal.

☐ *Tree*—The tree configuration offers an expanded version of the bus configuration. By turning the bus to a vertical position and extending its branches, we now have a tree. End user terminals are spaced along a central "line." Workstations communicate with devices called "servers" that provide electronic mail, disk storage, and printer facilities.

☐ *Ring*—Also known as "round robin," the ring approach is based on token passing (a slot in the communications program) logically implemented on a bus. Essentially, the ring is a continuous path without defined ends. Signals pass around the ring and are pushed along by each device as they pass.

BENEFITS OF LANs.   The important benefits of LANs are efficiency and monetary savings. In any office where access to a common store of information is necessary, floppy disks can be passed back and forth. However, this can be tedious. Files must be repeatedly updated—three, four, or even more times a day—if the users are not to have outdated information. Copying and reading the updates not only takes time, but can also, if done frequently, damage the disks and lead to lost data. LANs, by contrast, offer instant access to a given set of files for anyone working within the network. The latest data incorporated into those files are constantly and quickly available from the hard disks that are integral to any LAN. Reading large files from a hard disk is much faster than reading the same files from floppies.

The savings resulting from LANs can be traced largely to the sharing of such peripherals as plotters and printers, particularly, expensive laser printers. A laser printer, under-utilized when linked to a single microcomputer, suddenly becomes cost-effective when coupled with half a dozen of them, or so it would seem. However, where long lines of cabling are required, this approach makes the network considerably less cost-effective.

The latest twist in low-cost LANs is the P.B.X. connection. The private branch exchange (P.B.X.) and the interoffice branch exchange (I.B.X.) have joined the mainstream of today's information technology by going digital. As digital systems they go above and beyond providing the traditional telephone functions to supporting point-to-point asynchronous circuit service. A local area network can be used to connect various computers to the P.B.X. installed in an office for telephone communication. The per-unit expense of the LAN is then reduced to the price of a short cable to connect each computer to a handset—a savings of thousands of dollars in wiring costs alone over the expense of the standard hardware LAN—plus the price of the software. Not as fast as a full-scale hardware LAN, such a P.B.X. connection still has surprisingly fine performance.

TYPICAL COMPUTER EQUIPMENT IN AN MIS ENVIRONMENT

The preceding sections of the chapter have illustrated a wide range of computer equipment and systems. Computer hardware is needed not only for implementing effective information systems, but also for powering the newer MIS environments. In distributed data processing, an extremely broad range of computers and related peripheral devices can be used at various levels in a widely dispersed organization. Although decision support systems can also operate in a DDP mode, they emphasize using a terminal device (i.e., a management workstation), where the manager and support personnel can interface directly with the computer. This is the approach taken in the presentation below.

Local-Centralized Equipment in a DDP Environment

To illustrate the utilization of computer hardware in a DDP environment, let's say a manufacturer of consumer goods has implemented a complete distributed system. The system includes these areas: sales, research and development, and manufacturing—shown in figure 4.23. The hardware configuration is a star network (depicted previously in chapter 2). The network provides the mechanism for communicating between the central computer and the outlying minicomputers. Data that originate at a lower level generally must pass through another level before their summary contents are communicated to the central site. Where deemed necessary, detailed and summary data are forwarded to the appropriate functional area from the central processing level. In essence, the central processor acts as a receiver of data and a communicator of information for the appropriate application. To illustrate the functioning of the distributed data processing system, three typical functional areas are described briefly.

Sales offices that perform sales order processing are widely dispersed. They need to access current inventory information and shipping data. Because individual telephone lines to a central computer are expensive, a communications network is used to reduce line costs. It contains terminal concentrators at the regional centers to send data over high-speed lines to the central system. Processed sales information can be communicated back to the offices—to terminals or disk storage for later off-line printing, depending on the needs of the sales offices. However, at the highest level, weekly sales data (budget versus actual) are processed on Saturday and are available on Monday morning for evaluation by sales managers at headquarters. The ability of the

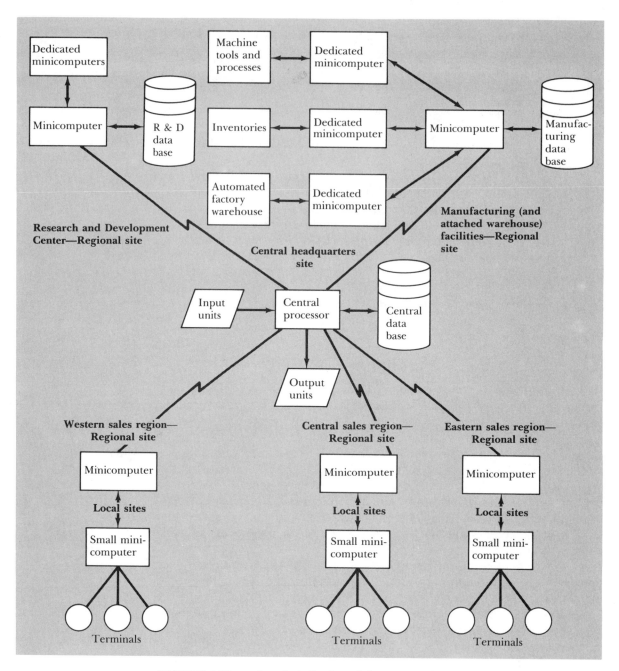

FIGURE 4.23 A typical distributed data processing system (in a star network) for a manufacturing company using minicomputers and a central processor.

distributed network to provide timely sales reports gives the company an idea where to focus its current sales efforts.

Scientists in the company's research and development center work on laboratory experiments and gather data for analysis. Each lab uses a dedicated minicomputer that includes a console terminal. Scientists use the terminal to edit, compile, and transmit data and programs for storage and execution. The output from these dedicated minis is communicated to the larger sized mini-computer for processing. In turn, the output is returned to the dedicated minis. When large scientific programs are run, the larger minicomputer is used. In all cases, information on R & D projects at scheduled intervals is forwarded to central headquarters for periodic evaluation. In this manner, management has control over the time and cost of R & D projects.

The manufacturing plant, which has automated its plant operations, con-trols raw material input, manufacturing machinery, and operations of an auto-mated warehouse (attached to factory) for storing finished goods. Because management wants access to current inventories and stock levels, these tasks are assigned to a dedicated minicomputer. Also, the real-time process control system monitors via a dedicated mini the actual manufacturing operations, and it is linked to a supervisory system that controls the overall parts flow. In turn, the supervisor computer (large-sized minicomputer) sends critical man-ufacturing operational data for management control to the central headquar-ters site. Lastly, a dedicated minicomputer is used to monitor the automated factory warehouse operations.

The implementation of the above hardware requires the development of a coherent plan for connecting its regional and central computing sites into a single network. Such a plan is indispensable if the organization expects to eliminate its hardware incompatibilities and permit effective communication between hardware supplied by different vendors. It is also necessary for hav-ing adequate DDP systems controls. One of DDP's major challenges during the 1980s will be to interconnect the hodgepodge of incompatible mini- and microcomputers and terminals that the typical large system user has amassed in the past. But to surmount that hurdle, the organization must *plan* its inter-facing hardware requirements. Otherwise, control over the DDP system will prove to be impossible.

Management Workstation in a DSS Environment

Distributed data processing focuses on the use of a wide range of computers and peripheral devices at various levels of an organization. A decision support system may also operate in such a mode. However, in a typical DSS, the inter-face between the computer and the decision maker is some type of manage-ment workstation. Made possible by the continuing improvements in process-ing, storage, communications, and like items, a management work-station—like that shown in figure 4.24—is designed to support all or most of the infor-mation-handling needs of a typical decision maker. It integrates electronic mail, data, text, and image-handling modules which are currently supported by separate devices such as telephones, calculators, typewriters, and copiers.

COMPUTER
HARDWARE FOR
EFFECTIVE
MANAGEMENT
INFORMATION
SYSTEMS

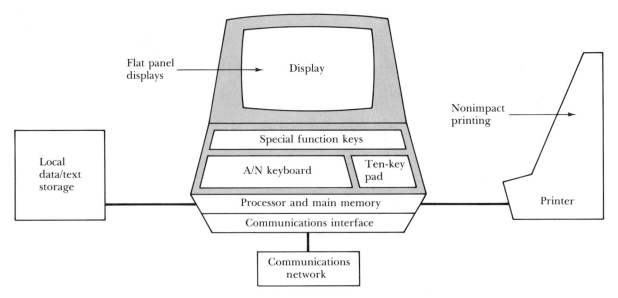

FIGURE 4.24 A typical management workstation using multifunction components as found in a DSS environment.

Modular in design, it incorporates the necessary hardware and software features to satisfy varying end user requirements for information storage and retrieval, text preparation, mathematical and statistical calculations, and interfaces to internal and external communications systems.

The hardware necessary to provide these capabilities includes a variety of separate components. Generally, they include: an output display for soft copy, a mini/microprocessor for processing, internal storage for applications and operating software, a printer or at least access to a conveniently located shared printer for hard copy, at least limited graphics output capability for soft or hard copy, communications capability with a computer and data base for accessing and storing important data, and capability of utilizing mathematical and statistical models for solving simple to complex problems. These hardware components of a typical multifunction management control station adequately meet the requirements for supporting decision making in a DSS environment. Current manufacturers of such stations include Apple Computer, DEC, Grid, IBM, Tandy, and Wang.

To support decision making adequately, the management workstation should have the following capabilities. First, it should present information in ways that are familiar to managers and permit quick analysis of the information being presented. Good representations not only stimulate managerial insights and facilitate analysis, but also can be used to generate new requests to the computer. For example, by selecting points on a graph or locations on a map, a manager can request more detailed information. Once representations have been chosen, the second capability comes into play; namely, a set of *easy-to-use operators* (shown as special function keys in figure 4.24) that can be invoked to prepare and transform the representations. Simple commands that select data to be graphed, call up sales figures in a tabular format, or run a model to generate and display possible production schedules are examples. Single, meaningful key words or phrases, such as TOTAL SALES or RUN SCHEDULER, or selections from "menus" of operations are used to simplify operations. The purpose of such operators is to generate results useful to the manager.

COMPUTER
HARDWARE FOR
EFFECTIVE
MANAGEMENT
INFORMATION
SYSTEMS

To save these results, and to retain the method of obtaining them, a DSS should provide a third capability—a memory that acts like scratch paper in developing intermediate results and like a file drawer in retaining useful results. To make the representations, operators, and memories useful, there is need for the fourth capability—the interactive processing mode. The manager must be able to control what is being processed on line by being able to select or change the colors of a graph, the format of a table, or the place where subtotals appear in a report. Control over ongoing operations also means letting the manager pick the order in which operations are performed and making them easy to select. The ability to be interactive, then, allows a quick response to commands and easy availability where decisions are made, such as in a manager's office.

Computer Equipment in "Management War Rooms"

The preceding computer equipment and systems are extremely useful in supporting managerial decision making. However, when viewing the support of management decision making from a broad perspective, some of the above computer systems can best be used in conjunction with a "management war room." In such an environment, large display screens show many types of planning and control information in graphic form (refer to figure 4.25). Whether this environment to support decision making is called by another name (e.g., a "decision support room" or a "management control center") is purely academic. Its importance lies in its ability to call up a wide range of management information. Instead of searching manual files and cluttering up the manager's office with paperwork, executives can obtain the required information immediately in a conference-room type of environment. They can, for example, obtain sales figures for any time period together with comparable figures for previous periods. Current production schedules, the number of pending orders, status of back orders, amounts of accounts receivable and payable, profit analysis by periods and products, equipment utilization, and divisional performance factors are other types of information that are readily available. In a similar manner, a host of strategic and operational planning information can be retrieved from the data base and presented as is or combined with other information in graphic form for supporting management decisions.

BENEFITS OF MANAGEMENT WAR ROOMS. The benefits from a management war room are many for effective management information systems. Data will always be current, accurate, and in a form well-suited for fast eval-

COMPUTER
HARDWARE AND
SOFTWARE FOR
EFFECTIVE
MANAGEMENT
INFORMATION
SYSTEMS

FIGURE 4.25
Typical "management
war room" that is
helpful to managers for
supporting their
decisions. (Courtesy
Intelligence Interlink
Corporation)

uation. Graphs, charts, indexes, and the like on the large display screen will keep the *quantity* of information to a minimum, thereby increasing management's understanding. Pages and pages of tabular information can be condensed into one projected display picture. Exception reporting will reduce the amount of data for possible viewing. The use of computer-generated displays will further reduce the need for paper reporting. The speed and simplification of reporting will allow the executive considerable time for supporting managerial tasks and decisions.

Current management war rooms are designed to assist management at all levels. More specifically, they can focus on operational and tactical applications, helpful to meet the needs of lower and middle management, respectively, for the short run. Additionally, they are useful to top management in the support of planning decisions—evaluating new products over their life cycle, allocating available factory capacity most efficiently throughout the organization, and setting long-range plans and objectives for the organization. The utilization of management war rooms allows managers to "get a handle" on present and future operations that they can plan and control. In essence, managers—from the lowest to the highest level—can "put their heads together" and develop appropriate plans, strategies, programs, and policies to support organization objectives.

For the most part, discussions of productivity to date have ignored the productivity of higher-level managers. Most of the attention has focused on robots on the assembly line or the implementation of the electronic "paperless" office; that is, on increasing the productivity of individual workers at the lower levels of the organization. However, when viewed from a strictly financial perspective, the productivity of labor and clerical workers is only one element in achieving corporate productivity. The financial community measures productivity in terms of return on stockholders' equity, return on capital, and other financial tests. If the management of an organization decides to launch a new product which the customer will not buy, it is irrelevant whether the workers actually assembling the product are performing their jobs efficiently. Having the right product at the right time, however, has a much greater impact on corporate productivity than gaining an incremental improvement in labor or clerical productivity.

Because a manager makes decisions and not products per se, his or her productivity is measured by the quality and timeliness of those decisions. Accepting the fact that management decision making is at least as important to corporate productivity as the automation of lower-level work leads to the conclusion that management productivity is worthy of a great deal of time, attention, and money. As stressed from the outset of this text, the key to decision making is information, and the key to good managerial decision making is good information. The problem with past information systems was that there were plenty of data, but the data became information only when they were gainfully employed in supporting decision making. Unfortunately, many computer specialists in the past—and some are still guilty today—confused information with data. This results in managers being literally buried in data while simultaneously forced to make important decisions in a relative vacuum of pertinent information.

To overcome this prevalent problem, managers need to see important trends and relationships in widely disparate data in the form of computer graphics. For graphic representations to accomplish anything, whether generated manually or electronically, they must communicate relationships—contrasts, comparisons, and trends. These are important elements of which decisions are made. The right kind of graphics system overcomes the inability of tabular data to represent relationships.

The output of computer graphics is quite helpful to the manager and support personnel in another way. Many times, the manager must go before a high-level committee and present the analysis for the decision reached. Computer graphics allow the individual to present it in any number of ways: pie charts, bar charts, graphs, or three-dimensional images; on a black-and-white or color terminal; and on paper, overhead transparencies, or 35-mm slides. In terms of cost and time effectiveness, the old "send it to the art department"

159

COMPUTER
HARDWARE AND
SOFTWARE FOR
EFFECTIVE
MANAGEMENT
INFORMATION
SYSTEMS

method has become archaic. Instead of managers having to convene, adjourn, and reconvene meetings while graphics materials go to and from the art department for modifications, current interactive computer graphics systems enable the user to manipulate images on a CRT screen until they are ready to be produced as hard-copy output. The cost savings, particularly if the output media are 35-mm slides, can be substantial, and the savings in management time are obvious. In summary, computer graphics are an important means to improve management productivity and, at the same time, support managerial decision making.

CHAPTER SUMMARY

In this chapter, we emphasized the essential components of computer hardware in a typical management information system. Besides looking at microcomputers and minicomputers, typical small-, medium-, and large-scale computer systems were described. Special note was made of the use of intelligent terminals to speed up the flow of transactional processing. The use of computer graphic devices was highlighted for supporting the manager in effective decision making. These instruments, plus the other input devices, output devices, data storage devices, data base management systems, and data communications networks, comprise the essential hardware components of a computer system for MIS. The appropriate combination of computer peripherals to acquire is an integral part of an MIS feasibility study. This orderly presentation of computer hardware for effective MIS sets the stage for the subject matter for the next chapter—computer software.

QUESTIONS

1. What key factors should be used in evaluating the computer and peripheral equipment an organization should obtain for a management information system?
2. How important are microcomputers (personal computers) to effective MIS?
3. What hardware components are found in a typical management information system for a small- to medium-sized organization?
4. How important are intelligent terminals and color graphic devices within an MIS environment? Explain thoroughly.
5. **a.** What DP activities in a management information system make use of sequential file storage?
   b. What DP activities in an MIS make use of direct access file storage?
6. What is the current direction in data storage devices for microcomputers?
7. **a.** What is the function of a data base management system as an integral part of a management information system?
   b. What is the current direction of data base management systems? Why?
8. **a.** What is the function of a data communications network as an integral part of an MIS?
   b. How important are local area networks currently? Explain.

160

COMPUTER
HARDWARE FOR
EFFECTIVE
MANAGEMENT
INFORMATION
SYSTEMS

9. Distinguish between a management workstation and a management control center.

10. As one computer professional once stated, "I think the problem with past management information systems in many companies has been that they're overwhelming as far as managers are concerned. They have to go through reams of reports and try to determine for themselves what are the most critical pieces of information contained in the reports so that they can take the necessary action and correct any problems that have arisen." Explain what is meant by this statement. How can an effective management information system overcome this past problem?

PROBLEMS

11. In this chapter, various equipment devices were discussed from the viewpoint of being "user friendly." State at least five factors that are indicative of user-friendly equipment and your reasons for selecting them.

12. Describe how information generated by intelligent terminals, graphic system devices, and personal computers can be used by an effective management information system. More specifically, describe how output from these types of devices would assist a marketing manager in the planning and control of her sales quotas. In a similar manner, describe how information from these devices would help an accounting manager in the preparation of annual operating budgets.

13. The usefulness of a data base and a data base management system (DBMS) was demonstrated in the chapter for an effective management information system. Show how the use of a data base along with a DBMS is helpful to a typical personnel manager or a purchasing agent. In addition, state what type of managerial reports could be extracted now from the data base to answer "What if?" questions as they arise in the normal course of business.

14. At the end of the chapter, reference was made to the fact that computer graphics can be used to improve management productivity. Demonstrate how the use of computer graphics can assist a typical executive vice-president in improving overall organizational productivity. In like manner, show how the use of computer graphics can assist the vice president of office administration in improving the productivity of administrative and office operations. In both cases, state typical "What if?" questions that pertain to productivity.

PROJECTS

15. The RC Corporation has a number of printing devices located throughout its warehousing operations that print orders processed by the sales order processing section at central headquarters. The printers operate at a rate of 100 lines per minute. The MIS manager notes that they operate too slowly, thereby resulting in the need to operate them on a second shift. Because a number of alternative speeds and manufacturers of printers exist, what factors should be evaluated before purchasing new printers? In addition, consideration should be given to the type of management information system that can be used to replace the present centralized management information system. From this perspective, is the present approach to sales order processing ideal for the corporation? Write a memorandum to the

COMPUTER
HARDWARE AND
SOFTWARE FOR
EFFECTIVE
MANAGEMENT
INFORMATION
SYSTEMS

MIS manager stating your conclusions along with a recommendation to improve sales order processing operations.

16. The Newcomb Corporation is a medium-sized, widely dispersed organization operating in twenty states. Currently, the MIS manager is considering new hardware that will assist in upgrading the present information system to a decision support system. The initial goal is to obtain hardware that will support top- and middle-management in decision making. Write a memorandum to the MIS manager stating at least three types of equipment that can be used within a DSS environment. Additionally, state why these devices were selected over others.

17. North American Airlines is a regional airline operating in the United States. Like most airlines, it is a very closely coupled operation that has a lot of time interdependencies. It needs to keep track of customer reservations on an on-line real-time basis, maintain flight surveillance, control maintenance and spare parts inventories, plan flights, bill credit customers, etc. The continual development of a more effective management information system to accomplish the foregoing tasks, with an eye to the basic objectives of the airline, not only requires a more careful determination of total system objectives, but also requires the use of the latest advances in computer hardware. In light of these factors, state which latest hardware developments (as set forth in the chapter) would prove useful to airline managers for realizing more fully stated organization objectives—improving customer service, increasing profitability, and improving productivity of available organization resources. Write a memorandum to the MIS manager stating your hardware recommendations.

18. Tri-State Electronics Company, which has a large warehouse in Columbus, Ohio, sells electronic parts and TV tubes to 60 retailers in Ohio, Kentucky, and Indiana. Once a day, the warehousing manager sends a truck on a circuit throughout the three-state area to make deliveries. Each truck returns five days later. The warehousing manager is wondering if he can develop a management information system to minimize inventories in both his warehouse and his customers' stores as well as to reduce the number of trips the trucks are making. Could he use a commercial carrier or carriers more economically? Could he install a data communications network that ties directly with its 60 retailers to speed deliveries? Could he resort to a better method for forecasting the products desired by the retailers? Develop a proposal for acquiring computer hardware and peripherals that will help the warehouse manager do a better job of matching retailer needs to the company's inventory levels, as well as improve customer service. Likewise, consider improving company profits and overall company productivity.

BIBLIOGRAPHY

Appleton, D. S. "The Technology of Data Integration." *Datamation*, November 1, 1985. ✗

Austin, S. "New On-Line Choices for Business." *Business Computer Systems*, April 1985.

Baker, J. "SQL: A New Standard." *Computerworld Focus*, February 19, 1986.

Bateman, S. "How to Buy the Right Database." *Compute*, July 1985.

Beach, L. G. "Data Base Management Systems." *Information Management*, December 1984.

Beaver, J. E. "Building Up Your Personal Computers." *Computer Decisions*, February 1984.

————. "Portable Computers: Light as a Feather." *Computer Decisions*, November 1984.

————. "New Options for Data Crunching." *Computer Decisions*, December 1984.

Bender, E. "Desktop Computing." *Computerworld,* December 30, 1985–January 6, 1986.

Benoit, E., and Bernstein, A. "Graphic Detail." *Business Computer Systems,* April 1984.

Bernhard, R. "Data Terminals." *Systems & Software,* December 1983.

Bernstein, A. "Decision Support Graphics Draw Better Bottom Line." *Business Computer Systems,* August 1985.

Betts, K. S. "Building the Executive Workstation." *Modern Office Technology,* March 1985.

Billadeau, T. R. "The PC Evolves to a Useful Workstation." *Mini-Micro Systems,* December 1983.

Blanning, R. W. "A Relational Framework for Join Implementation in Model Management." *Decision Support Systems,* January 1985.

Bolger, C., Jr. "Using Teleconferencing As a Management Information Tool." *The Office,* November 1983.

Booker, E. "Computers Help You Win the Game." *Computer Decisions,* September 15, 1984.

Borrell, J. "Users Get More For Less in Graphics Terminals." *Mini-Micro Systems,* November 1985.

Bowerman, R. "Relational Database Systems for Micros." *Datamation,* August 1983.

Brennan, J. J., and Molloy, M. K. "Microcomputers." *Interfaces,* February 1983.

Bromson, R. S. "Put Contracts Under the Glass." *Computer Decisions,* November 5, 1985.

Brown, A. S. "Cost Keys Switch to Micro DBMS." *Micro Manager,* July 1984.

Brown, M. D. "Mainframe Business Graphics." *Datamation,* May 1, 1984.

Bryan, S. W. "Building a Better DBMS." *PC Products,* April 1986.

Burns, P. "The Personal Computing Syndrome." *Infosystems,* February 1985.

Calkins, M. "Multiple-User PCs Are Finding a Niche." *Systems & Software,* October 1984.

Carr, R. "The Dawn of the Universal Workstation." *Computer Decisions,* March 15, 1984.

Cashin, J. "Solutions Are Evolving in PC-Mainframe Linkups." *Software News,* May 1986.

Chester, J. A. "Dialing for Data with Multifunction Workstations." *Infosystems,* June 1985.

————. "Demystifying Relational Data Base Management Systems." *Infosystems,* October 1985.

Chorafas, D. N. *Management Workstations for Greater Productivity.* New York: McGraw Hill, 1985.

Christoff, K. A. "You Don't Need a DBMS to 'Do Data Base.'" *Infosystems,* January 1985.

Clark, T. "Needed: Graphics Standards." *Computerworld,* April 22, 1985.

Codd, E. F. "Is Your DBMS Really Relational?" *Computerworld,* October 14, 1985.

————. "Does Your DBMS Run by the Rules?" *Computerworld,* October 21, 1985.

Colby, W. "The Graphics Triangle." *Infosystems,* August 1985.

————. "The Human Connection." *Infosystems,* September 1985.

Cooper, M. S. "Micro-Based Business Graphics." *Datamation,* May 1, 1984.

Courtney, J. F., Jr., and Jensen, R. L. "Teaching DSS with DBMS." *Data Base,* Spring 1981.

Cowen, R. *Teleconferencing, Maximizing Human Potential.* Reston, VA: Reston Publishing Company, 1984.

Cross, T. B. "Teleconferencing, When You Absolutely, Positively Have to Be There." *The DEC Professional,* May 1984.

Curtice, R. M., and Casey, W. "Database: What's In Store?" *Datamation,* December 1, 1985.

Curtice, R. M., and Jones, P. E., Jr. "Database: The Bedrock of Business." *Datamation,* June 15, 1984.

Data Decisions. "Micros at Big Firms: A Survey." *Datamation,* November 1983.

Date, C. J. "How Relational Systems Perform." *Computerworld,* February 23, 1984.

DeSanctis, G., and Gallupe, B. "Group Decision Support System: A New Frontier." *Data Base,* Winter 1985.

Dobberstein, M. "IBM: The Drive Behind the Disks." *Computer Decisions,* December 3, 1985.

Downward, J. G. "The VAX Professional Workstation." *The DEC Professional,* September 1984.

Edwards, C. *Developing Microcomputer-Based Business Systems.* Englewood Cliffs, NJ: Prentice-Hall, 1983.

Estrin, J., and Cheney, K. "Managing Local Area Networks Effectively." *Data Communications,* January 1986.

Farin, J., and Nazariv, A. "DBMS Basics." *Infosystems,* June 1986.

Feldman, S. "Touch Terminals Feel Way Into New Markets." *Systems & Software,* July 1983.

————. "Touch Panels—Getting a Feel for the Technology." *Systems & Software,* October 1983.

Ferris, D. "The Micro–Mainframe Connection." *Datamation,* November 1983.

Freedman, D. H. "Is the Micro–Mainframe Link Connecting with MIS?" *Infosystems,* February 1984.

Friend, D. "Graphics for Managers: The Distributed Approach." *Datamation,* July 1982.

————. "The New Promise of Graphic Information Systems." *Financial Executive,* October 1982.

Garnto, C., and Watson H. J. "An Investigation of Database Requirements for Institutional and Ad Hoc DSS."*Data Base,* Summer 1985.

Gillin, P. "Users Told Both Micros, Mainframes Need DSS," *Computerworld,* October 17, 1983.

Giuliana, V. E., and Winnig, M. "Computer Conferencing." *Today's Office,* September 1984.

Glossbrenner, A. "Getting the Most Out of On-line Information Services, Part I." *Lotus,* September 1985.

————. "Getting the Most Out of On-line Information Services, Part II." *Lotus,* October 1985.

Gold, J. "The Well-Tempered Workstation." *Computer Decisions,* June 18, 1985.

————. "The Art of Low-Cost Graphics." *Computer Decisions,* July 30, 1985.

————. "Micro DBMS to Suit." *Computer Decisions,* September 24, 1985.

Good, P. "How to Make It a Success, Micro/Mainframe Marriage." *Business Software Review,* September 1986.

Greenberg, K. "The Shape of Things to Come." *PC World,* January 1986.

Guertin, E. A. "Top Management: Data Base Management Systems Bring Organizational Expertise to the Minicomputer Environment." *Digital Review,* June 1985.

Guttman, M. K. "Multi-User Micros." *Computers and Electronics,* February 1985.

Hammer, M. "The Battle for the Desktop." *Datamation,* July 1, 1984.

Hart, R. "It's Time to Put Your PC Into a Color-Graphics Mode." *Office Systems,* February 1986.

Horwitt, E. "Making Data Go the Distance." *Business Computer Systems,* September 1983.

————. "Making Connections." *Business Computer Systems,* February 1984.

House, W. C. *Interactive Computer Graphics Systems,* Princeton, NJ: Petrocelli Books, 1982.

Jarke, M., and Shalev, J. "A Database Architecture for Supporting Business Transactions." *Journal of Management Information Systems,* Summer 1984.

Jaworski, J. "Mass Storage Market Stages a Comeback." *Mini-Micro Systems,* June 1986.

Johansen, R., and Bullen, C. "What to Expect from Teleconferencing." *Harvard Business Review,* March–April 1984.

Juris, R. "Micros Ease Backlog Blues." *Computer Decisions,* May 6, 1986.

Kalowski, N. "The Marriage of Video and Computer Graphics." *Computerworld,* May 13, 1985.

Karasik, M. S. "Selecting A Small Business Computer." *Harvard Business Review,* January–February 1984.

Kelleher, K., and Cross, T. B. *Teleconferencing.* Englewood Cliffs, NJ: Prentice-Hall, 1985.

Kenealy, P. "Product Profile: Graphics Workstations." *Mini-Micro Systems,* July 1983.

Kiechel, W., III. "Why Executives Don't Compute." *Fortune,* November 14, 1983.

Kroenke, D. M. *Database Processing: Fundamentals, Design, Implementation.* Palo Alto, CA: SRA, 1983.

Kull, D. "Group Decision: Can Computers Help?" *Computer Decisions,* May 1982.

————. "Matching Workstations to Executive Styles." *Computer Decisions,* October 1984.

————. "Getting the Most from Disk Storage" *Computer Decisions,* November 19, 1985.

————. "Dispersed Data, One DBMS." *Computer Decisions,* February 25, 1986.

————. "Database Machines Come of Age." *Computer Decisions,* June 17, 1986.

Lacob, M. "Do You Need a Data Czar?" *Computer Decisions,* March 11, 1986.

Lasden, M. "Make Room for Executive Workstations." *Computer Decisions,* December 1982.

Leavitt, D. "Growth May Not Be Explosive but DBMS Still a Good Bet." *Software News,* July 1985.

Lee, R. M. "Database Inferencing for Decision Support." *Decision Support Systems,* January 1985.

Lehman, J. A. "Microcomputer Use of Mainframe Data Base." *Journal of Systems Management,* January 1986.

Li, L. "Ready When You Are." *Business Computer Systems,* August 1984.

————. "Mastering Mass Storage." *Business Computer Systems,* December 1984.

Lipton, R. "Getting Rid of Data Redundancy." *Business Computer Systems,* December 1984.

Lusa, J. M. "Just Graph It Fast!" *Infosystems,* February 1983.

Maier, D. "Capturing More Meaning in Databases." *Journal of Management Information Systems,* Summer 1984.

Major, M. "DSS Embraces New Environments." *Software News,* September 1985.

Mantelman, L. "IBM's Personal Computer: A Great Communicator." *Data Communications,* December 1985.

McCartney, L. "Teleconferencing Comes Down to Earth." *Datamation,* January 1982.

McClellan, S. T. "The End of the Hardware Era." *Datamation,* May 1, 1984.

McCormick, J. H. "Controlling the Data Exchange." *Infosystems,* March 1983.

McLeod, J. "Graphics Software." *Systems & Software,* July 1983.

Meador, C. L., Kean, P. G. W., and Guyote, M. I. "Personal Computers and Distributed Decision Support." *Computerworld,* May 7, 1984.

Meads, J. A. "The Graphics Standards Battle." *Datamation,* May 1, 1984.

Miller, F. W. "Are Multifunction Terminals Disguised Desk-Top Computers?" *Infosystems,* January 1983.

————. "Packing the Disks with More Data." *Infosystems,* July 1983.

Moskowitz, R. A., "IBM's PC at: Overload or Overkill?" *Computer Decisions,* October 22, 1985.

Myers, D. "DP Managers Say DSS Needed to Tie Together: Corporate Micros." *Computerworld,* October 17, 1983.

Nie, E. "Reaching Decisions with Micro-to-Mainframe DSS." *Micro Manager,* November 1984.

Olson, M. H. "Do You Telecommute?" *Datamation,* October 15, 1985.

Opper, S., and Boomstein, A. D. "Corporations Conquer Distance." *Computer Decisions,* November 15, 1984.

Ossa, E. W. "Selecting a DBMS: Match Every Application's Demands to Product's Capabilities." *Computerworld,* June 24, 1985.

Paller, A. "Executive Support Systems Put Computer Data Base at Top Managers' Fingertips with Touch of a Button." *Computerworld,* March 15, 1985.

Perry, R. L. "Relational DBMS Takes Off." *Computer Decisions,* February 12, 1985.

Polis, R. "Administering Contracts and Managing Vendors: The Path to Successful Procurement." *Infosystems,* November 1985.

Rae, S. G. "Stretching Your Hardware Dollar." *Business Software Review,* September 1986.

Regan, H. J. "Micros for DSS Fueling Opportunities, Problems." *Computerworld,* February 13, 1984.

Roman, D. R. "Executives Who Love Their Personal Computers." *Computer Decisions,* January 1983.

————. "Building Up Your Personal Computers." *Computer Decisions,* March 1984.

Romeny, M. B., and Stocks, K. D. "How to Buy a Small Computer System." *Journal of Accountancy,* July 1985.

Rothstein, M. "Graphics Information Systems With Desk-Top Computers." *Information Management,* November 1984.

Shinn, R. "Color Graphics." *Systems & Software,* July 1983.

————. "Workstations, Desktop Terminals Take on Communications." *Systems & Software* October 1983.

Simpson, D. "Micro-Winchesters Save Money, Space and Watts." *Mini-Micro Systems,* October 1985.

Siragusa, G. "The Executive Workstation—Fancy Phone or Productivity Tool." *Administrative Management,* February 1986.

Smith, G. W., Jr. "Graphic Answers at Your Fingertips." *Software News,* April 1983.

Snyders, J. "Let's Talk DBMS." *Infosystems,* December 1984.

Stamps, D. "The New Generation of Workstations." *Micro Manager,* June 1984.

————. "Micro Database Programs: Growing in Sophistication." *Micro Manager,* July 1984.

Stewart, D. "Computer Conferences Come to Order." *Business Computer Systems,* April 1985.

Sullivan, K. "Professional Computers as Office Work Stations." *The Office,* May 1984.

————. "Database Management Software: What Are the Choices?" *Micro Manager,* July 1984.

Sumner, M. "A Workstation Case Study." *Datamation,* February 15, 1986.

Talsky, G. R. "Small Businesses Bolster PC Sales." *Mini-Micro Systems,* June 1986.

Teorey, T. J., and Fry, J. P. *Design of Database Structures.* Englewood Cliffs, NJ: Prentice-Hall, 1982.

Thiel, C. T. "Teleconferencing—A New Medium for Your Message." *Infosystems,* April 1984.

Tucker, M. "Database Integration Shakes Mini Market." *Mini-Micro Systems,* April 1986.

Ungaro, C. "Teleconferencing Focuses on a New Era." *Data Communications,* September 1982.

Uttal, B. "Linking Computers to Help Managers Manage." *Fortune,* December 26, 1983.

Van Rensselaer, C. "Global, Shared, Local." *Datamation,* March 15, 1985.

Vinberg, A. "Device-Intelligent Graphics Software." *Mini-Micro Systems,* July 1982.

Vinberg, A., and George, J. E. "Computer Graphics and the Business Executive—The New Management Team." *Computer Graphics and Applications,* January 1981.

Walsh, M. E. "Unscrambling the Kaleidoscope: A Look at IBM's PC." *Infosystems,* February 1985.

Warren, C. "PC Compatibles Become Faster, More Adaptable." *Mini-Micro Systems,* March 1986.

————. "Databases Manage Network Environments." *Mini-Micro Systems,* May 1986.

Washam, G. I. "Design Trade-Offs in a Multifunction Graphic Terminal." *Mini-Micro Systems,* November 1983.

Watkins, N. "Micro Networks: Integrating PC Users and MIS." *Infosystems,* May 1986.

Weizer, N., and Withington, F. "IBM: Mainframes in 1990." *Datamation,* January 1, 1985.

Whieldon, D. "On-the-Job Terminals." *Computer Decisions,* November 5, 1985.

Wilcox, D. L. "Business Graphics on Micros: Plus & Minus." *Computerworld,* April 17, 1985.

Yonda, M. "Negotiating Computer Contracts." *Computerworld Focus,* February 19, 1986.

Young, L. H. "The Age of Intelligent Workstations." *Infosystems,* June 1985.

Young, T. R. "Who Works at Workstations?" *Datamation,* April 1983.

CHAPTER 5

Computer Software for Effective Management Information Systems

ISSUES

Why is there a trend away from internally written custom computer programs toward externally marketed software packages?

What guidelines should be followed when evaluating computer software packages?

What are the essential elements of custom-made computer programs written by company programmers?

What typical electronic spreadsheets, financial planning languages, and statistical packages are available today?

What is the relationship between electronic spreadsheets, financial planning languages, and statistical packages and effective MIS?

What is an effective way to integrate computer hardware and software with managers' needs?

OUTLINE

INTRODUCTION TO COMPUTER SOFTWARE

EVALUATION OF COMPUTER SOFTWARE
    Purchased Versus Custom-Made Software
    Sources of Computer Software Packages
    Guidelines in Evaluating Computer Software
      Packages

CUSTOM-MADE COMPUTER PROGRAMS—
WRITTEN BY COMPANY PROGRAMMERS
    Program Development
    System Level Testing

SOFTWARE PACKAGES—AVAILABLE FROM
OUTSIDE SOURCES
    Rationale for Popularity of Electronic
      Spreadsheets
    Answering Recurring and Ad Hoc "What if?"
      Questions
    Research on Programming Languages

POPULAR SOFTWARE PACKAGES CURRENTLY
AVAILABLE
    SuperCalc 3

INTRODUCTION TO COMPUTER SOFTWARE

The increased complexities of today's constantly changing economic and business situations have necessitated a much more thorough analysis and evaluation of strategies prior to making crucial decisions. In addition to the traditional variables concerning competition, profitability, costs, and so forth, managers need to consider externally imposed factors that are difficult (if not impossible) to predict and control, such as energy consumption, resource shortages, uncertain money markets, declining productivity, and regulatory restrictions. Even though many of these factors are interrelated and tend to move in trends together, their combined influence greatly increases the level of difficulty in effectively evaluating the information inputs to organization activities. In light of such complexities, this chapter looks at computer software as a way of adjusting to meet these changing times.

Initially, we look at the key factors in evaluating computer software, followed by the tradeoffs of acquiring computer software from the outside versus writing it within the organization. Although a cost/benefit analysis might indicate the need to go outside, there is still need for custom-made computer programs—the next matter for discussion. In the second part of the chapter, software packages available from outside vendors are discussed from the standpoint of answering "What if?" questions. Because managers and their staff cannot, for the most part, specify in advance what they want from programmers and model builders, a means out of this dilemma is offered in terms of electronic spreadsheets, financial planning languages, and statistical packages. In essence, the chapter describes an effective approach whereby top managers and their support personnel are able to ask and answer pressing standard questions as well as ad hoc "What if?" questions confronting them.

EVALUATION OF COMPUTER SOFTWARE

Just as there are a number of guidelines to assist in evaluating computer hardware, similar criteria exist for computer hardware. *Custom-made* computer programs (written by company programmers) are just one way to assist the manager in decision making. The more promising approach is the use of pur-

168

chased software packages (written by outside sources) whereby the manager can be at the center of the decision-making process. The goal is an ability to answer a whole series of recurring and ad hoc "What if?" questions as they arise in the normal course of business. This important development in computer software is a prerequisite to effective management information systems.

Purchased Versus Custom-Made Software

Today, the amount spent on computer software in an MIS environment is inversely related to hardware purchases. As hardware costs continue to fall, software costs—as a component of the total cost equation—tend to escalate. Equipping computers with flexible, easy-to-use application software is going to be an even greater problem in the future than it is today, for two reasons. Applications are becoming more complex, and application software must be truly easy for the unschooled user to employ.

Many user companies—especially the small-system users—do not have the capabilities to develop their own software programs. Even companies that have such capability may find that the costs involved in the internal development of software programs are prohibitive. This is partially due to the shortage of trained software development personnel, which is forcing companies to pay very high salaries for qualified personnel. As a result of this problem, demand increases for "off-the-shelf" software. The move to buy or use software developed by specialized software and service firms will accelerate. It will be wasteful—even impractical in terms of dollars and lead time—for user organizations to develop software that already exists and can be easily tailored for specific user needs.

When software is purchased off the shelf, the user receives several benefits. These include the choice of a variety of offerings, reduced risk by buying the expertise and experience of the vendor, and curtailment of expenses by buying a software package that includes maintenance. In the future, business users will reap even more benefits from packaged software because many vendors are starting to direct more attention as well as research and development expenditures to this area. Because users are computerizing more and more applications as the cost of hardware comes down, more and more sophisticated software products are in demand. Currently, many software packages are offered by vendors. Typical software packages are covered in some depth in this chapter.

Sources of Computer Software Packages

Today, there are five sources of computer software packages. They are: (1) computer manufacturers, (2) software houses, (3) software brokers, (4) time-sharing companies, and (5) user groups and individual users. Until the 1970s, IBM and other manufacturers provided software free in order to sell machines. When IBM unbundled and began to charge for its software, the whole software industry received a boost. Now a large part of a computer manufactur-

169

COMPUTER
HARDWARE AND
SOFTWARE FOR
EFFECTIVE
MANAGEMENT
INFORMATION
SYSTEMS

er's revenue comes from software designed for specific applications by internal employees, by field employees, and by customers.

Sources in the second category, software houses, are moving away from contract programming, which was once their lifeblood, to the development and mass distribution of packages. The best-selling packages have been extremely profitable. Some of these packages were created by small companies formed by people with a good deal of knowledge about a particular application area. These small organizations generally have excellent products. In contrast, because creating software is a cottage industry, software brokers have found a place in the market. Moreover, most new, small software corporations cannot handle worldwide marketing and do not want to be bothered with the administrative chores that success can bring. A software broker, like a book publisher, handles sales, service, and administration, and pays royalties to the software creators.

Timesharing organizations make software available via teleprocessing. This type of access to software is becoming cheaper and easier because public data networks are spreading. Lastly, user groups are playing an important role in facilitating information exchange and making programs available to members. Since user groups vary considerably, when a company obtains a package or program from a user group or individual user, it should research such details as support, documentation, quality of product, and characteristics that affect maintenance. Also, some individual users who have developed an excellent application keep it proprietary; others sell it.

Guidelines in Evaluating Computer Software Packages

In order to make an intelligent and controlled acquisition, the following guidelines should be used in evaluating computer software packages. The *first* guideline is on the basic functions: input, processing, and output must be clearly defined. Equally important is a thorough evaluation of interfaces with other systems. *Second,* the purchaser should gather information from DP publications, user groups, and buyers' reference guides, which are helpful in the evaluation process.

Third, a detailed evaluation and comparison of those products that seem to fit the company's needs must be performed, based on these questions:

- ☑ Does the package fit the requirements as specified in the detailed evaluation?
- ☑ Will the package run on the present computer (i.e., microcomputer and/or mainframe)?
- ☑ Is the package flexible? Can the input forms or reports be changed to meet the company's changing requirements?
- ☑ Does the package have the performance capabilities needed? If the package can only just handle the current workload, then beware.
- ☑ How difficult is it to install the package? What changes will have to be made in the existing system? There is nothing wrong with having to modify a package, but get a commitment from the vendor as to how much support it will give during this phase.

- Is the package easy to use?
- Is there adequate documentation?
- What support will be provided? Support should be received during the installation phase—system, operational, and user. Will bugs be fixed free of charge? Will new releases of the software be received as modifications and improvements are made?
- What is the operational status of the package? Where was it written, when, by whom, and for what user?

Fourth, there should be a provision that allows one to talk to other users. Potential vendors should be asked for lists of customers that can be called. If the vendor refuses, it should be stricken from the list. *Fifth,* if possible, benchmark tests should be conducted to test the application on the user's computer. *Sixth* and last, the contract should be studied. The temptation to sign the vendor's standard agreement should be avoided. If possible the company's lawyer should be consulted. If the potential user is willing to take the time to follow these procedures, he or she will be satisfied. In turn, the user will gain or increase others' confidence and trust in satisfying important MIS processing needs.

CUSTOM-MADE COMPUTER PROGRAMS—WRITTEN BY COMPANY PROGRAMMERS

Although the main thrust of management information systems is no longer on the development of custom-made computer programs, there is still some need for such programs today. This is particularly true when periodic reports are needed to plan and control ongoing organizational activities. Because custom-made programs provide the essential framework for effective MIS, they are discussed below from the standpoint of program development and system level testing.

Program Development

Program development is the process of taking a set of program specifications (input, processing requirements, and output) and converting it into a tested and documented computer program. The activities in program development include:

1. finalizing program design
2. developing program code and debug
3. testing the program
4. reviewing program code for adherence to standards
5. documenting the program

Each is discussed below.

FINALIZING PROGRAM DESIGN. The first step in developing a custom-made computer program is to review its specifications for clarity and com-

COMPUTER
HARDWARE AND
SOFTWARE FOR
EFFECTIVE
MANAGEMENT
INFORMATION
SYSTEMS

pleteness. Programmers should review the program's input, processing, and output with the implementation project manager and/or the system users. The review should be sufficiently detailed so that the programmer, the project manager, and the system user agree on what the computer program is to accomplish. The project manager should comment on any special programming techniques that might be useful; the system user can caution the programmer about unusual processing conditions that might arise. Both the project manager and the system user should offer suggestions on how to test the program. Overall, handling this first step well can make the remaining steps easier.

DEVELOPING PROGRAM CODE AND DEBUG. A modular approach used in a "structured programming" framework should be employed to make the job of programming and debugging easier. *Modular programming* is a technique in which the logical parts of a problem are divided into a series of individual routines so that each routine may be programmed independently. Access to the individual routines is controlled by a single routine, commonly known as the "mainline program" in a batch-processing mode. The mainline program governs the flow of data to the proper processing routines, as depicted in figure 5.1.

In a modular programming approach, a program consists of several modules, each of which is generally limited to 50 to 200 machine language instructions, or 1 to 6 pages of coding. A *program module* is defined as a closed subroutine to which control is passed by a *calling program* (mainline program routine) and which, when it completes its processing, returns control to the calling program. Decisions may be made in a module that will cause a change in the flow of the system, but the module will not actually execute the branching; it will communicate the decision to the calling program to execute the branching. The creation of a modular design is relatively easy because a computer problem consists of functional DP modules. The actual processing in the

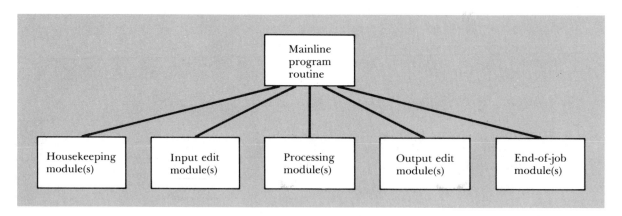

FIGURE 5.1   An overview of modular programming—batch-processing mode.

modules is a function of the relationship between data elements and results from the analysis. The only functions actually programmed are the data processing functions at the bottom ends of the branches, because they are the building blocks that make up the higher-level functions.

To illustrate the modular programming concept (batch-processing mode), figure 5.2 depicts a typical weekly payroll program broken down into eleven modules. These individual modules are separate tasks that vary in size and complexity. For example, the highest level module, module 1 (process weekly employee payroll file), represents the solution to the weekly payroll program. Each module of the next level (modules 2 through 6) and succeeding levels (modules 7 and 8, and modules 9 through 11) solves one of the tasks to be performed in order to process the program. Within this sample programming project, four programmers handle several modules within the same program. Each programmer is responsible for coding and testing his or her own modules, and the lead programmer supervises and is responsible for final program testing (figure 5.3).

So far we have described only one approach to modular programming—that in which every transfer of control is made in a mainline program. However, for an interactive environment, a more important approach exists. For the sake of speed and efficiency, each module controls the program flow by

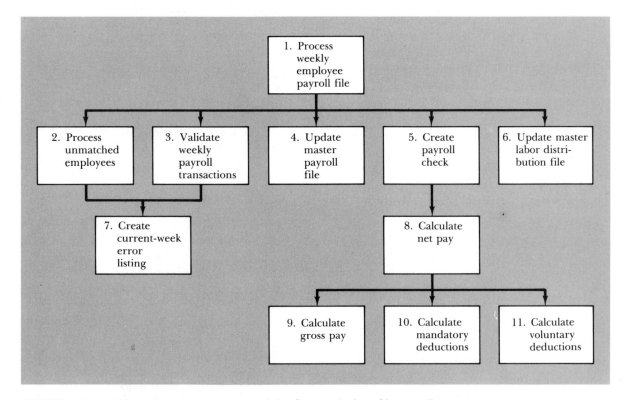

FIGURE 5.2 The major programming modules for a typical weekly payroll program.

COMPUTER
HARDWARE AND
SOFTWARE FOR
EFFECTIVE
MANAGEMENT
INFORMATION
SYSTEMS

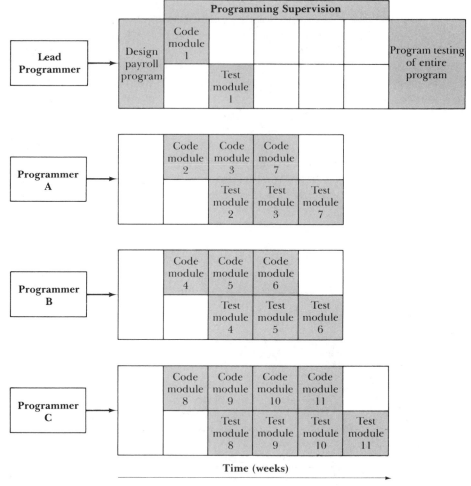

FIGURE 5.3
The organization of
modular programming
for a typical weekly
payroll program, as
depicted in figure 5.2.

ordering an RTCP (real-time control program) to call in another module. The RTCP is not a mainline program because it functions as a housekeeper and does not control the logical system flow. This is, then, a type of modular programming in which the flow continues on a smooth path through a chain of modules, rather than flowing in and out of the mainline control program.

The benefit of a modular design is that it accommodates changes occurring after the system design phase (coding, testing, learning, operating, and maintaining the system). Given that both fundamental system logic and specific procedures invariably change throughout the system, modularity enhances the identification of these changes and therefore the control of the system evaluation. The modular design approach helps the programming staff to build an interactive operating environment—including the necessary batch functions—that is efficient and capable of being maintained.

The process of *debugging* a program refers to correcting programming language syntax and diagnostic errors so that the program "compiles cleanly."

A *clean compile* means that the program can be successfully converted from the source code written by the programmer into machine language instructions. Once the programmer achieves a clean compile, the program is ready for testing.

Debugging can be a tedious task. It consists of four steps: inputting the source program to the compiler, letting the compiler find errors in the program, correcting lines of code that are in error, and resubmitting the corrected source program as input to the compiler. Usually, this process must be repeated a half dozen or more times using a *batch* compiler. The length of time required to debug a program can be shortened considerably by the use of an *interactive* compiler. The interactive compiler checks the source program and displays any errors on a CRT or prints them on a typewriter unit. The programmer corrects the indicated errors and initiates the interactive compiler as often as necessary until all errors are corrected. The interactive compiler allows the programmer to debug a program in a few hours, as opposed to several days using a batch compiler.

TESTING THE PROGRAM.   A careful and thorough testing of each program is imperative to the successful installation of any system. Approximately 30 to 50 percent of the resources required for program development should be allocated to program testing. The programmer should plan the testing to be performed, including testing all possible exceptions. The test plan should require the execution of all standard processing logic. Lastly, the program test plan should be discussed with the project manager and/or system users.

A log of test results and all conditions successfully tested should be kept. The log will prove invaluable in answering the inevitable question, "Did you ever test for this condition?"

Software packages are available that allow interactive testing of batch processing programs. They can greatly reduce the length of time required for testing. Interactive testing allows the programmer to monitor each step required to process a program input. If a problem in program logic flow is discovered, the programmer can stop the execution of the program, correct the problem, and have the program resume processing at that point just prior to the interruption.

REVIEWING PROGRAM CODE FOR ADHERENCE TO STANDARDS.   One of the preparatory steps of the system implementation phase is to set standards for program coding. It is necessary to review each program to ensure the standards being met; ideally, someone who is not directly connected to the implementation team should review it so that the quality of the system and adherence to standards are evaluated objectively without concern for project schedule and budget. It is recommended that this evaluation occur long before the programmer has a clean compile. Because less than half of the total program development effort is complete at this stage, the programmer is much more receptive to constructive criticism and more open to changes. A second review should be scheduled sometime during the program testing stage to ensure that suggestions have been followed.

175

COMPUTER
HARDWARE AND
SOFTWARE FOR
EFFECTIVE
MANAGEMENT
INFORMATION
SYSTEMS

DOCUMENTING THE PROGRAM. The best program documentation is the program itself. Each program should contain an initial paragraph of comments describing the basic input, processing, and output of the program, as well as any assumptions or limitations concerning the program. The program itself should be heavily annotated; each module should have an introductory paragraph of comments. The program itself should be written in a clean and concise manner, with particular emphasis on implementing future program changes as deemed necessary. Overall, there must be an insistence on the development of programs that will be easy to maintain.

THE RELATIONSHIP OF MODULAR PROGRAMMING TO STRUCTURED PROGRAMMING. Modular programming provides the underlying framework for structured programming. Fundamentally, a *structured program* consists of a series of program modules. The program structuring governs the transfer between different parts of the program of their contents (the modules). From this perspective, structured programming can be defined as a discipline of organizing and coding a computer program that makes it easily understood and modified. Its fundamental goal is "simplifying the control paths" within a program to minimize program errors. In a similar manner, structured programming maximizes the ease with which errors are corrected and modifications made.

Much of programming complexity arises when a program contains many jumps (GO TO's) to other parts of the program; that is, jumps made both forward and backward in the code. These jumps make it hard to follow the program logic. Similarly, it is difficult to ensure at any given point of the program what conditions are present. Furthermore, as a program undergoes changes during its development, the complexity of the program can grow at an alarming rate. In some cases, new coding is added because the programmer cannot find a program code that performs the desired operation, is not sure how the coding works, or is afraid to disturb the existing code.

In a structured programming environment, any program function can be performed using one of three control structures: (1) sequence, (2) selection, and (3) repetition. Any kind of processing, any combination of decisions, or any sort of logic can be accommodated with one or a combination of these control structures. Each structure has a simple, single point of transfer of control into the structure, and a single point of transfer out of the structure. These structures can be combined to form a program that is very simple in that control flows from top to bottom or from beginning to end. Thus, structured programming reduces a program's complexity and increases its clarity during the programming and testing phases and later during program maintenance.

System Level Testing

System level testing must be conducted before any system is installed. It involves: (1) preparing realistic test data in accordance with the system test plan, (2) processing the test data using the new equipment, (3) thorough checking of the results of all system tests, and (4) reviewing the results with the future users, operators, and support personnel. System level testing is an excellent time for training employees in operating and maintaining the new system. Typically, it requires 25 to 35 percent of the total implementation effort.

One of the most effective ways to perform system level testing is to perform parallel operations with the existing system. *Parallel operations* consist of feeding both systems the same input data and comparing data files and output results. Despite the fact that the individual programs were tested, related conditions and combinations of conditions are likely to occur that were not envisioned. Last-minute changes in computer programs are necessary to accommodate these new conditions.

For an interactive MIS project, the process of running dual operations for both new and old systems is more difficult than it is for a batch-processing system, because the new system has no true counterpart in the old system. One procedure for testing the new interactive system is to have several remote input/output terminals connected on line which are operated by supervisory personnel, backed up by other personnel operating on the old system. The outputs are checked for compatibility, and appropriate corrections are made to the on-line computer programs. Once this segment of the new system has proven satisfactory, the entire terminal network can be placed into operation for this one area. Additional sections of the system can be added by testing in this manner until all programs are operational.

During parallel operations, the mistakes detected are often not those of the new system, but those of the old. Such differences should be reconciled as far as economically feasible. Those responsible for comparing the two systems should clearly establish that the remaining deficiencies are caused by the old system. A poor checking job at this point can result in complaints later from customers, top management, salespersons, and others. Again, it is the responsibility of the MIS manager and assistants to satisfy themselves that adequate time for dual operations has been allowed for each functional area changed.

SOFTWARE PACKAGES—AVAILABLE FROM OUTSIDE SOURCES

To cope with the fast-changing world, effective management information systems have been developed for "getting a handle on" changes. They allow the manager's intellectual resources to be coupled with the capabilities of a computer. Management information systems for a manager, as an example, can be said to enhance the faculties of memory and reasoning. Together with a data base management system, they give the manager the ability to retrieve information in such a way that meaningful patterns and correlations may be discerned. Seen in this light, they augment a person's memory. In like manner, this system can be seen as extensions of an executive's reasoning powers. Models of the business environment help a manager envision possibilities for

COMPUTER
HARDWARE AND
SOFTWARE FOR
EFFECTIVE
MANAGEMENT
INFORMATION
SYSTEMS

the future, foresee consequences, and identify and select alternative solutions. Effective management information systems contain elements of both data base management and modeling, although typically one element is dominant in a particular situation.

To assist the manager in this modeling process while using data bases, several important developments have taken place over the past several years. These include the development of electronic spreadsheets, financial planning languages, and statistical packages. Due to their importance, each of these is discussed in the next section of the chapter. First, however, other items relevant to software packages are discussed.

Rationale for Popularity of Electronic Spreadsheets

Background on electronic spreadsheets is set forth first before we look at programming languages that are financially or statistically oriented. Today, as in the past, the tremendous growth of microcomputers can be attributed to electronic spreadsheets. The question can be asked: "Why have business people embraced spreadsheets so heartily?" The reason is that ledger-sheet analysis is a singularly tedious, repetitive, and error-prone task. Consider the following scenario: A manager of a relatively large company must submit a report that projects income for the next five years. The manager must assume values for sales revenues, overhead costs, interest rates, repeat business, and cost of materials. The support staff of the manager makes a ledger sheet containing all the information and submits it to the company's controller, who asks that the repeat business be assumed at 80 percent instead of 75 percent. The staff must then recalculate all the ledger values that have been affected by this one change in the repeat-business category. Manually recalculating the effects of this single change is so arduous and time-consuming that very few managers allow their staff to make more than two assumptions per category.

A spreadsheet program, however, transforms a microcomputer screen into a huge ledger sheet. By simulating the rows and columns of a ledger sheet, the program lets a user work with a large number of interrelated values. When a user changes a given value on the spreadsheet, the program automatically recalculates any affected values in seconds. The program not only makes managers' projections less time-consuming and more accurate, but also encourages them to ask more "What if?" questions and to make more complex assumptions. Although originally intended for accountants, spreadsheet programs are now being used by nearly everyone with a microcomputer who needs to recalculate figures. Spreadsheet programs are used to produce budgets, action and profit plans, and sales forecasts. They also help produce income statements, cash-flow projections, currency conversions, expense reports, and job-cost analyses.

Answering Recurring and Ad Hoc "What if?" Questions

In the electronic spreadsheets, financial planning languages, and statistical packages that follow, great emphasis is placed on "What if?" type of questions; that is, "What if we change this variable; what impact will it have on our final solution?" To visualize typical "What if?" questions, consider the following two examples. "*What* happens to net income *if* the initial total market is only 6,000 units but grows at a 5% quarterly rate for the next five years?" and "*What* happens to net income *if* the new union contract goes into effect and the labor rate is increased by $0.10 per unit and the selling price is increased by $0.05 per unit in the second year?" In the first example, the goal is determining the net income (solution) over the next five years based upon known sales income; that is, only one variable changes. In the second example, the net income (solution) is related to two variables: labor rate and selling price.

By no means do "What if?" questions relate to the company's finances only. "What if?" questions can be asked for most functional areas of a manufacturing- or a service-oriented organization. The capability to ask numerous "What if?" questions that have a direct impact on the organization and to answer them through a human–machine interface goes a long way toward improving overall organizational performance. More examples of typical "What if?" questions will be found in the section to follow.

Research on Programming Languages

A most important innovation to assist the manager in computer-based modeling is that of financial planning languages. These programming languages enable non-MIS personnel (i.e., the manager and operating personnel) to become competent in building and solving models in an interactive, exploratory manner. The ways in which such a planning language are used were indicated by one survey of clients.[1] Among the results was the finding that 44 percent of the models were actually built by middle- or upper-level managers. By contrast, middle- and upper-level managers performed only 21 percent and 9 percent, respectively, of the "What if?" analyses. Apparently, managers want to be involved in the building of their models; but once a model has credibility, they turn the mechanics of using a terminal over to a staff assistant. The key persons actually performing "What if?" analyses tend to be intermediaries, such as MBA assistants and support personnel, after the model has been aligned with the thinking processes of the executive.

In other research, the larger users of financial models were found to be in the manufacturing sector, followed by banking and finance.[2] In addition, the larger the sales of the corporation, the more likely the company would be using a financial model. Corporate planning is the single largest user group, followed by finance. The modeling application most frequently used is cash flow analysis in such areas as cash from operations, short-term investments and debt structure, accounts payable, and inventories. Other typical uses include pro-forma financial reports and financial forecasts, investment analy-

[1]Gerald R. Wagner, "Enhancing Creativity in Strategic Planning through Computer Systems," *Managerial Planning*, July–August 1979, pp. 15 and 16.

[2]Juergen Hahn, "Management Warms Up to Modeling Languages," *Infosystems*, July 1980, p. 46.

179

COMPUTER
HARDWARE AND
SOFTWARE FOR
EFFECTIVE
MANAGEMENT
INFORMATION
SYSTEMS

sis, profit planning, sales forecasts, budgeting, merger and acquisition, and project models. Multinational firms frequently use the international network of time-sharing vendors for consolidation of financial data. The most important modeling techniques identified by users include ''What if?'' analyses, financial ratio analysis, sensitivity analysis, return on investment analysis, and forecasting and regression techniques.

Basically, financial planning languages are high-level computer programming languages designed to excel in a certain class of applications that include financial planning and analysis, strategic planning, budgeting, modeling, business simulations, and the like. Actually, they are quite useful in handling any problems whose answer is likely to end up in a row-and-column format, or whose complex nature reflects logic and data manipulation, as opposed to high-volume transaction processing.

POPULAR SOFTWARE PACKAGES AVAILABLE CURRENTLY

For software packages to provide decision-making support for the manager, they must resemble the business person's vocabulary and allow the manager's thought processes to respond to changing times. Furthermore, they must react in sufficient time to allow the person's attention to remain focused on the problem under study. It is from this view that popular software packages—electronic spreadsheets, financial planning languages, and statistical packages—are presented below.

SuperCalc 3

SuperCalc 3 is an electronic spreadsheet designed to run on any microcomputer that uses the CP/M operating system. It is similar in speed and simplicity to VisiCalc, the first and most popular electronic spreadsheet, which is no longer being marketed. With SuperCalc 3, microcomputer operators can make personal or professional financial forecasts, create a balance sheet, project sales and inventory, schedule personnel, or perform a multitude of other tasks. SuperCalc 3 provides the user with the following functions: (1) each row or column of the worksheet can have individual format specifications; (2) each cell, row, or column can have separate numeric formats and justifications; (3) row and column labels can be any length; (4) all formulas can be displayed simultaneously; and (5) current values and formulas can be displayed, printed, or stored. A computer-naive user can construct a completely integrated accounting system with SuperCalc's aid. SuperCalc 3 can integrate any portion of any previous worksheet into the current one.

To illustrate SuperCalc 3 in the area of accounting, the subroutine BALANCE provides the basic format for a balance sheet and permits the easy insertion of various amounts of assets, liabilities, and net worth. The user can expand or modify it as required to meet individual needs. Another subroutine in accounting, BRKEVN, aids in exploring possibilities of break-even analysis. It permits the entry of various fixed costs, variable costs, discount rates, and retail prices to determine the break-even point and various levels of profit. As can be seen, electronic spreadsheet subroutines can be employed to solve for answering "What if?" questions.

Lotus 1-2-3

Lotus 1-2-3 (Release 2) integrates spreadsheet processing, file management, business graphics, and limited text editing into one software package for a microcomputer. It has a spreadsheet capacity of 8,192 rows by 256 columns. When the program is first loaded, the screen display looks similar to that of any other spreadsheet program, but differences exist. The software uses a two-line menu throughout. The *first* line displays editing formulas and labels before they are entered onto the spreadsheet. The *second* line shows full-word command choices. In addition, a *third* line briefly explains the commands. Commands are invoked either by moving the cursor to the desired choice and pressing the Enter key or by typing the first character of the command name. The third line explains the command on which the cursor is positioned. It is often a list of the command choices at the next level in the menu hierarchy.

Within an MIS context, the program has many interesting spreadsheet features. It is possible to repeat a series of "What if?" questions with a single command. For example, in a model in which projected profit is a function of interest rate, 1-2-3 can take a table of alternative interest rate values and automatically generate the corresponding table of profit estimates. This capability is particularly convenient when used with the business graphics package, which can plot profit against interest rate.

Another interesting feature is the capability to store sequences of 40 pre-programmed commands. These sequences can be used for something simple; for instance, for entering a certain formula or label at several points on the spreadsheet. Or they can perform complex functions, like setting up one's own menu to simplify operations for a relatively unskilled user. For instance, one could set up a menu with five choices: READ, CONSOLIDATE, PRINT, GRAPH, and SAVE. The preprogrammed command sequences associated with each choice would take care of specifying file names, printer and graphics set-up commands, and so forth. These custom menus and programs will require some expertise, but they enable novice users to run custom applications easily.

As previously indicated, 1-2-3 has a subsystem for manipulating files. Fundamentally, file management is a conceptual extension of the spreadsheet idea. A file, like a spreadsheet, is a rectangular array, with a row for each record and column for each field. In fact, many file management functions are possible with spreadsheet programs which do not purport to be more than spreadsheets. They can be used to set up a file with numeric and character fields, and records can be updated, added, deleted, sorted, printed, and so on. However, 1-2-3 has made several file-oriented extensions. For example, a file can be up to 8,191 records or rows. (Headings take up at least one row.) A fast, two-key field sort, search, and extract command is also provided.

The criteria to be used in searching for and extracting records are stored

COMPUTER
HARDWARE AND
SOFTWARE FOR
EFFECTIVE
MANAGEMENT
INFORMATION
SYSTEMS

right on the worksheet. If one had a file with baseball players' batting statistics, one could search for things like all players who had more than 150 hits and 30 home runs. Once records satisfying search criteria are found, they may be highlighted one at a time, moved to a separate area on the spreadsheet (creating another subfile), or deleted from the file. Lastly, the graphics package generates bar charts (stacked or side-by-side), pie charts, or line graphs. Data to be graphed are placed on a spreadsheet, and menu commands are entered to specify the graph type, axes labels and scaling, and the like. Common microcomputer spreadsheets are listed in figure 5.4.

EXAMPLES OF LOTUS 1-2-3. Due to the popularity of Lotus 1-2-3, it is demonstrated in this chapter as well as in the master case study of Chapters 10 through 15. As a starting point, two examples using this electronic spreadsheet are given below. In addition, there are end-of-chapter exercises, which

Software Package	Vendor
CalcStar	MicroPro International Corporation
COPE	Antech Inc.
Context MBA	Context Management Systems
Corporate MBA	Context Management Systems
Data-Vue	Berman Associates Inc.
Enable	The Software Group
ExecuPLAN II	Vector Graphic Inc.
FlashCalc	VisiCorp
InterCalc	Schuchardt Software Systems
Lotus 1-2-3	Lotus Development Corporation
Magic Worksheet	Structured Systems Group
MicroFORESIGHT	Information Systems of America
Multiplan	Microsoft Corporation
MyCalc	Software Toolworks Inc.
PeachCalc	Peachtree Software Inc.
PFS:Plan	Software Publishing Corporation
Planner Calc	Comshare
PLAN 80	Business Planning Systems
ProCalc	Software Products International
Report Manager	Datamension Corporation
Scratch Pad Plus	SuperSoft Inc.
SMART Spreadsheet	Innovative Software
SuperCalc 3	Sorcim/Information Unlimited Software
Symphony	Lotus Development Corporation
Timberline Spreadsheet	Timberline Systems Inc.
TMP/CALC	The United Software Company
20/20	Access Technology
UniCalc	Lifeboat Associates
VisiCalc IV (Apple)	VisiCorp
Wedge	Systems Plus Inc.

FIGURE 5.4
A listing of current microcomputer spreadsheets.

build upon the material presented. In this manner, the reader will have an opportunity to solve typical real-world problems using a microcomputer. A diskette is provided for all programs to solve end-of-chapter problems.

FINANCIAL STATEMENT ANALYSIS

In the first example of Lotus 1-2-3, a typical company needs to develop financial statement analysis for the next two years based upon the current (base) year. Its current sales are $1.2 million, increasing at 20 percent per year. Selling and general and administrative expenses are 40 percent and 30 percent, respectively, of sales. A long-term loan of $100,000 is currently outstanding, with interest being paid at 10¼ percent annually. The current federal income tax rate is 46 percent. Based upon the data as input, the financial results before and after federal income taxes are shown in figure 5.5 for the current year and the next two years. An analysis of profit before federal income taxes indicates that growth is 29.2 percent in the first year and 29.4 percent in the second year over the first year.

Financial Statement Analysis

		Base Year	First Year	Second Year
Base Sales	$1,200,000	$1,200,000	$1,200,000	$1,440,000
Annual Growth	20.00%	0	240,000	288,000
Total Sales		$1,200,000	$1,440,000	$1,728,000
Expenses:				
Selling	40.00%	$480,000	$576,000	$691,200
Gen. & Admin.	30.00%	360,000	432,000	518,400
Long Term Loan	$100,000			
Interest At	10.25%	10,250	10,250	10,250
Total Expenses		$850,250	$1,018,250	$1,219,850
Profit Before Federal Income Tax		$349,750	$421,750	$508,150
Federal Income Tax	46.00%	160,885	194,005	233,749
Profit After Federal Income Tax		$188,865	$227,745	$274,401

FIGURE 5.5 Financial statement analysis over a three-year period using Lotus 1-2-3.

Part - A

Sales	Actual Base Year	Assumptions		
		Year 1	Year 2	Year 3
Unit Growth Low		10%	10%	10%
Unit Growth High		18%	15%	15%
Sales Price Growth-Low		4%	4%	4%
Sales Price Growth-High		9%	10%	10%
Low Growth Projections				
Units	200,000	220,000	242,000	266,200
Price	$2.50	$2.60	$2.70	$2.81
High Growth Projections				
Units	200,000	236,000	271,400	312,110
Price	$2.50	$2.73	$3.00	$3.30
Cost of Goods Sold % of Sales	65%			
Commission Fixed	$25,000			
Commission Variable	5%			
Admin. Exp. Fixed	$10,000			
Admin. Exp. Variable	3%			
Tax Rate	46%			
Div. Growth Rate	2.5%			
Outstanding Shares	40,000	40,000	40,000	55,000

Part – B

Projections Based on Lower Growth Rates for Units and Selling Price
----

	Actual	Projected		
	Base Year	Year 1	Year 2	Year 3
Sales Rev.	$500,000	$572,000	$653,400	$748,022
Cost of Goods Sold	325,000	371,800	424,710	486,214
Gross Profit	$175,000	$200,200	$228,690	$261,808
Commissions	50,000	53,600	57,670	62,401
Admin. Exps.	25,000	27,160	29,602	32,441
Income Before Fed. Income Tax	$100,000	$119,440	$141,418	$166,966
Fed. Income Tax	46,000	54,942	65,052	76,804
Net Income for Year	$54,000	$64,498	$76,366	$90,162
Dividends	$30,000	$30,750	$31,519	$32,307
Begining Year Retained Earnings	$100,000	$124,000	$157,748	$202,595
Year End Retained Earnings	$124,000	$157,748	$202,595	$260,450
Earnings per Share	$1.35	$1.61	$1.91	$1.64

FIGURE 5.6 Financial forecasts using Lotus 1-2-3 that consider best-case and worst-case scenarios: (a) the assumptions are the framework upon which the spreadsheet is built and (b) a three-year financial forecast for worst-case business conditions.

FINANCIAL FORECASTS

To illustrate the development of financial forecasts using Lotus 1-2-3, consider the R J Corporation, a typical growth company. Top management is facing a major problem. They are applying for a loan to finance an expansion,

COMPUTER
HARDWARE AND
SOFTWARE FOR
EFFECTIVE
MANAGEMENT
INFORMATION
SYSTEMS

yet their corporation lacks the historical financial data necessary for a statistical analysis of earnings. The solution is straightforward; that is, using a spreadsheet program to construct a future earnings forecast that combines present market conditions with management's best guesses about the future.

The data-gathering process is started by polling the corporation's managers for number estimates and market assumptions. In the spreadsheet model, there is almost complete consensus among managers on all assumptions other than unit sales and selling price. The importance of unit sales and selling-price growth, coupled with the range of estimates received, makes the use of multiple projections prudent. Consequently, the model will provide best-case and worst-case scenario forecasts.

As figure 5-6 (a) illustrates, the model incorporates assumptions for several variables. These include growth factors for unit sales as well as selling price for the next three years. Also, the actual cost of goods sold, sales commissions, administrative expenses, tax and dividend growth rates, and the number of shares of stock outstanding are shown in the illustration. The best approach to building this model is to isolate all assumptions from the formulas used in calculating model results. Assumptions are thus grouped into an assumption block in the upper half of the spreadsheet. This scheme provides on-line documentation of the model, allows assumptions to be revised easily, and eliminates the danger of destroying a formula when altering an assumption. A best-case and worst-case estimate is included in the assumption block to enable the creation of multiple projections. Growth rates for unit sales and selling price can differ year to year.

Using the estimates based upon the assumptions, managers can create the projected income statements with actual figures for the current (base) year and for the next three years. Low-growth projections for unit sales and selling price are used in the model shown, since it represents a worst-case forecast. These results are shown in figure 5.6 (b).

IFPS

The Interactive Financial Planning System (IFPS) is an English-language software package designed to provide decision and planning support for managers. Fundamentally, it allows planning as a natural extension of the manager's normal thought processes. Developed by the EXECUCOM Systems Corporation, IFPS supports problem-solving through building easily understood models of business situations. A flexible, human-oriented command structure permits instantaneous reporting, immediate answers to "What if?" questions, sensitivity and impact analysis, and the incorporation of risk analysis through the quantification of uncertainty. The command structure is designed so that complex requirements may be satisfied by using a set of compact, straightforward statements. IFPS has elaborate reporting capabilities and a rich variety of options for producing and exploring model outputs. A list of its features is found in figure 5.7.

Based upon first-hand experience with clients, EXECUCOM has found evi-

- English-like language
- Built-in "What if?" capabilities
- Built-in goal seeking
- Risk analysis (Monte Carlo)
- Automatic report generation
- Personalized reports
- Hierarchical modeling
- Comprehensive editor
- Adapts to any organization structure
- Automatic simultaneous solutions (optional)
- Plot capability
- Template models and data files
- Consolidation
- User can build own special functions and subroutines
- Financial, statistical, and mathematical functions
- Interface to existing data bases
- Supported by dedicated professionals
- Active R & D effort to identify and implement enhancements
- Quickly produces useful and meaningful results
- Command file feature for automated procedures involving several models and files

{ Characteristics of IFPS

FIGURE 5.7
Important features of the Interactive Financial Planning System (IFPS).

dence of increasing management productivity using IFPS in areas associated with corporate planning and decision making. This is particularly true where top management gets directly involved in the model-building process using IFPS. The result is that there is a description of the problem to be solved—not the creation of a set of data processing procedures. IFPS can be thought of as a helpful "administrative assistant." In addition, improved communication with other staff levels and functions is one of the most frequently quoted benefits. The value of IFPS has been demonstrated through years of actual use in a wide variety of corporate, governmental, and academic settings.

IFPS SUBSYSTEMS. The IFPS package consists of six basic subsystems. They are listed below.

- The *executive subsystem* is used to specify all permanent (i.e., unchanging) files, list the models and reports, combine models, consolidate models and data files, call other subsystems, and save compiled modules.
- The *modeling language subsystem* creates and edits models. This subsystem is used to ask "What if?" questions and perform goal structuring and risk analysis.

{ Subsystems

187

COMPUTER
HARDWARE AND
SOFTWARE FOR
EFFECTIVE
MANAGEMENT
INFORMATION
SYSTEMS

□ The *report generator* allows special report definitions to be created or edited. This subsystem enables the user to customize reports with special titles or column formats.

□ The *data file subsystem* allows the user to create, edit, or maintain IFPS data files. Data files are files used to hold variable data for general-use models and to allow multi-unit consolidations and hierarchical models.

□ *Command files* are permanent files on which IFPS commands and directives are stored. These stored commands are executed by a single IFPS executive (i.e., master) command, facilitating applications that require a long series of commands. These files are created and edited in the command file subsystem.

□ The *plot subsystem* allows the user to generate graphic output from a model on a terminal or a line printer. Built-in specifications allow the user to generate plots with a single command or to use the plot command language to control the size of the graph, the plotting of characters, and the axes.

IFPS PROPERTIES. Three fundamental properties of IFPS make it a helpful tool for top management and its corporate planning staff. *First,* the modeling language and command structure allow the user to describe the problem with no interruption of normal thought processes. The natural language orientation means that the user does not need to learn a new vocabulary. The language approach implies that commands are interpreted consistently and in contexts familiar to everyday use.

Second, IFPS is a language for modeling rather than programming. Another way of stating this principle is to say that IFPS utilizes a nonprocedural approach to problem description. This means that the order of statements in an IFPS model is immaterial because the entire body is a description (model) of a problem, not a set of statements executed in order to solve the problem. As an example of this, consider the statements:

```
TOTAL EXPENSES = SELLING EXPENSES + OTHER EXPENSES
SELLING EXPENSES = 6000
OTHER EXPENSES = 4000
```

In a procedural language, the result of this set of statements is:

```
TOTAL EXPENSES       0
SELLING EXPENSES 6000
OTHER EXPENSES   4000
```

This result occurs because the statements are computed sequentially (procedurally) and the program has no mechanism for referring to statements after TOTAL EXPENSES. In IFPS, the following values are obtained:

```
TOTAL EXPENSES   10000
SELLING EXPENSES  6000
OTHER EXPENSES    4000
```

These statements model a problem. The values obtained are exactly those that are expected. From the user's viewpoint, this means that it is no longer necessary to modify thought processes to fit the solution vehicle. The solution vehicle is modified to fit thought processes.

Finally, the *third* key property of IFPS is that the solution can be viewed as a matrix of numbers:

IFPS is the means by which the relationships between rows and columns (or cells) are expressed. The interpretation of the rows and columns is up to the user. A traditional interpretation is that of the spreadsheet, with rows being line items and columns being time periods. It is important to note that any other interpretation is equally valid. IFPS is flexible enough to adapt to the needs of almost every user.

USING IFPS.   To use IFPS, the user describes the model with the appropriate language for the system. This is accomplished by entering a series of statements defining the source of data for rows and columns and how they are to be manipulated computationally. The user may call special subroutines, insert commas, define computations between lines or columns, establish conditional computations, utilize a broad range of forecasting functions, and perform risk analysis and other measurement functions.

The IFPS expression permits six comparison operators: less than, less than or equal to, equal to, greater than, greater than or equal to, not equal to, and the two logical operators "and" and "or." One of four modeling language commands can be used to calculate and solve the model: Solve, Genreport, Goal Seeking, and Monte Carlo. Any of them may be used with the "What if?" facility to perform sensitivity analysis. Extensive diagnostic error messages and a diagnostic command called Analyze assist users in setting up models and system relationships.

EXAMPLES OF IFPS.   To visualize how easy it is to use corporate planning software designed for interactive use, an example of "What if?" planning is shown in figure 5.8. The manager first describes the problem in the language of the business world, such as "I wish to describe my projected statement of income over the next five years. I estimate sales to be $400,000 in the first year and increase 12 percent annually thereafter. Gross profit will be sales less

189

COMPUTER
HARDWARE AND
SOFTWARE FOR
EFFECTIVE
MANAGEMENT
INFORMATION
SYSTEMS

Step 1. Statement of the problem in a financial modeling language.

```
MODEL INCOME STATEMENT VERSION
 10   COLUMNS YEAR 1–YEAR 5
 20   SALES = 400000, 1.12 * PREVIOUS SALES
 30   GROSS PROFIT = SALES – COST OF GOODS SOLD
 40   COST OF GOODS SOLD = .60 * SALES
 50   TOTAL EXPENSES = FIXED EXPENSES + INTEREST PAID
 60   FIXED EXPENSES = 25000, 1.08 * PREVIOUS FIXED EXPENSES
 70   DEBT LEVEL = 80000
 80   INTEREST PAID = .0925 * DEBT LEVEL
 90   TAX LIABILITY = .48 * PROFIT BEFORE FEDERAL INCOME TAX
100   PROFIT BEFORE FEDERAL INCOME TAX = GROSS PROFIT –
      TOTAL EXPENSES
110   NET INCOME = PROFIT BEFORE FEDERAL INCOME TAX –
      FEDERAL INCOME TAX LIABILITY
END OF MODEL
```

Step 2. Solve the problem.

```
? SOLVE
ENTER SOLVE OPTIONS
? ALL
```

	YEAR 1	YEAR 2	YEAR 3	YEAR 4	YEAR 5
SALES	400,000	448,000	501,760	561,971	629,408
GROSS PROFIT	160,000	179,200	200,704	224,788	251,763
COSTS OF GOODS SOLD	240,000	268,800	301,056	337,183	377,645
TOTAL EXPENSES	32,400	34,400	36,560	38,893	41,412
FIXED EXPENSES	25,000	27,000	29,160	31,493	34,012
DEBT LEVEL	80,000	80,000	80,000	80,000	80,000
INTEREST PAID	7,400	7,400	7,400	7,400	7,400
TAX LIABILITY	61,248	69,504	78,789	89,230	109,968
PROFIT BEFORE FEDERAL INCOME TAX	127,600	144,800	164,144	185,896	210,351
NET INCOME	66,352	75,296	85,355	96,666	109,382

FIGURE 5.8   An example of "What if?" corporate planning using a financial planning language. (Courtesy EXECUCOM Systems Corporation)

costs of goods sold, which is 60 percent of sales. Total expenses include fixed expenses (at $25,000 in the first year, increasing with inflation at 8 percent per year) and interest paid on a long-term debt of $80,000 at 9¼ percent. The federal income tax liability is 48 percent of profit before tax. What is the net income projected to be each year?" The foregoing statements are shown as step 1 in figure 5.8 for a financial planning language.

Next (step 2 in figure 5.8), the problem is solved based upon the computerized model that was developed in step 1. In step 3, there is a change of cost of goods sold from 60 to 70 percent to determine what impact this one variable has on net income through the next five years. This step represents a

Step 3. Query: "What if my cost of goods sold approximates 70 percent of sales? How does this affect my net income?"

```
? WHAT IF
WHAT IF CASE 1
ENTER STATEMENTS
? COST OF GOODS SOLD = .70 * SALES
? SOLVE
ENTER SOLVE OPTIONS
? ALL
***** WHAT IF CASE 1 *****
1 WHAT IF STATEMENTS PROCESSED
```

	YEAR 1	YEAR 2	YEAR 3	YEAR 4	YEAR 5
SALES	400,000	448,000	501,760	561,971	629,408
GROSS PROFIT	120,000	134,400	150,528	168,591	188,822
COSTS OF GOODS SOLD	280,000	313,600	351,232	393,380	440,585
TOTAL EXPENSES	32,400	34,400	36,560	38,893	41,412
FIXED EXPENSES	25,000	27,000	29,160	31,493	34,012
DEBT LEVEL	80,000	80,000	80,000	80,000	80,000
INTEREST PAID	7,400	7,400	7,400	7,400	7,400
TAX LIABILITY	42,048	48,000	54,705	62,255	70,757
PROFIT BEFORE FEDERAL INCOME TAX	87,600	100,000	113,968	129,699	147,410
NET INCOME	45,552	52,000	59,263	67,443	76,653

Step 4. Query: "What level of sales do I have to generate to produce a net income of $70,000 in the first year and increasing by 15 percent per year after that?"

```
? GOAL SEEKING
GOAL SEEKING CASE 1
ENTER NAME OF VARIABLE TO BE ADJUSTED TO ACHIEVE PERFORMANCE
? SALES
ENTER COMPUTATIONAL STATEMENT OF PERFORMANCE
? NET INCOME = 70000, 1.15 * PREVIOUS NET INCOME
***** GOAL SEEKING CASE 1 *****
```

	YEAR 1	YEAR 2	YEAR 3	YEAR 4	YEAR 5
SALES	417,538	473,019	536,472	609,065	692,138

```
ENTER SOLVE OPTIONS
? ALL
```

	YEAR 1	YEAR 2	YEAR 3	YEAR 4	YEAR 5
SALES	417,538	473,019	536,472	609,065	692,138
GROSS PROFIT	167,015	189,208	214,589	243,626	276,855
COSTS OF GOODS SOLD	250,523	283,812	321,883	365,439	415,283
TOTAL EXPENSES	32,400	34,400	36,560	38,893	41,412
FIXED EXPENSES	25,000	27,000	29,160	31,493	34,012
DEBT LEVEL	80,000	80,000	80,000	80,000	80,000
INTEREST PAID	7,400	7,400	7,400	7,400	7,400
TAX LIABILITY	64,615	74,300	85,454	98,272	113,013
PROFIT BEFORE FEDERAL INCOME TAX	134,615	154,808	178,029	204,733	235,443
NET INCOME	70,000	80,500	92,575	106,461	122,430

FIGURE 5.8　　(continued)

COMPUTER
HARDWARE AND
SOFTWARE FOR
EFFECTIVE
MANAGEMENT
INFORMATION
SYSTEMS

typical case of "What if?"—that is, if one change is made in the computer model, what impact will it have on the bottom line?

From a reverse viewpoint of the "What if?" approach, the goal-seeking capability allows "backwards" solution of the problem; that is, the user is able to set a goal for a certain variable—net income in this case—and adjust another variable—sales in this case—to achieve that (net income) goal. In figure 5.8, step 4 asks what level of sales are necessary to produce a desired level of net income of $70,000 in the first year and to increase that sum by 15 percent per year thereafter. This goal-seeking approach results in the final output shown in figure 5.8.

In this example, there is no need to rely on a systems specialist, as in the past, to translate the problem into a computer programming language or to schedule the task into the computer's job stream. The ability to ask "What if?" questions, to perform goal seeking, and to quantify uncertainties and recognize the sensitivity of results to varying assumptions stimulates creative and analytical thought. The process provides a common ground for communication. Since the corporate planner is using the tools directly, he or she is making higher quality decisions on a more timely basis.

IFPS APPLICATIONS. Going beyond the income statement applications set forth above, common IFPS applications include balance sheets, cash flow projections, spreadsheets, forecasting, lease versus purchase, risk analysis, market strategies, R & D project selection, strategic planning, mergers, acquisitions, profit planning, budgeting, plant expansion, real estate evaluation, municipal planning, make or buy, capital budgeting, cost estimation, and others. In addition, applications will be demonstrated in chapter 11 on corporate planning for the XYZ Corporation.

EXPRESS

As with the previous financial planning languages, EXPRESS can be used in a number of environmental settings, such as strategic planning, portfolio analysis, projecting financial evaluations, and system planning. Fundamentally, EXPRESS is a comprehensive, totally integrated information analysis language specifically designed to support financial and planning professionals. Based on the English language, it is easy to use and integrates all of the software components essential to support a dynamic planning environment. Such an environment includes data base management, ad hoc and formal reporting, preprogrammed financial and statistical routines, color graphics, and extensive financial modeling capabilities.

With EXPRESS's large data base capability, the user need not go to many sources for data to solve a problem, which can result in inconsistent data. Rather, the user has consistent historical data with this MIS generator. In addition, EXPRESS has graphical and statistical capabilities along with features like deseasonalization (adjusting data to take out regular seasonality patterns—most economic data factors are deseasonalized) and correlation abilities (determining if and how two variables are related).

SAS

SAS (Statistical Analysis System) is a software system for statistical analysis, data management, and report writing. It is used by statisticians, marketing researchers, biologists, auditors, social scientists, business executives, medical researchers, computer performance analysts, and many others.

SAS PROCEDURES. The statistical procedures in SAS are easy to use. The user never needs to specify the number of levels in a given factor. Nor must one state how many observations there are. SAS offers more than 75 statistical procedures. Among these procedures are a wide range of superior statistical capabilities including means, frequency, regression, analysis of variance, categorical data analysis, multivariate analysis, discriminant analysis, clustering, and scoring. If descriptive statistics for large data sets are desired, the SUMMARY procedure provides statistics for all possible subgroup combinations in just one pass of the data. No sorting is required. To describe a variable's distribution—percentiles, frequencies, stem-and-leaf plots—the UNIVARIATE procedure is employed. Means, totals, standard deviations, and many other descriptive statistics for variables or for groups of observations are available with the MEANS procedure.

For example, you can find the average bonus paid to employees with just two statements:

```
PROC MEANS;
VAR BONUS;
```

MEANS, as well as other SAS procedures, can also create one or more new data sets containing results for later use in the same job. The GLM (General Linear Model) procedure is used to perform linear and multiple regression analysis, analysis of variance and covariance, and multivariate analyses of variance. Market researchers find the FUNCAT procedure useful for analyzing multidimensional contingency tables. Also, customized analyses can be performed with SAS's MATRIX procedure. These are just a few of the statistical procedures in SAS.

Going beyond the standard procedures mentioned above, SAS/ETS provides an expanded set of tools for time series, forecasting, modeling, and flexible row-and-column financial reporting. For example, the COMPUTAB procedure organizes data into a tabular form commonly used in business and research, and prints row-and-column reports like balance sheets and income statements. COMPUTAB is more than a formatting tool; it allows the user to program new variables, accumulate totals, and compute new functions of totals. For example, an SAS data set, as shown below, can be used to produce the report in figure 5.9.

OBS	TYPE	DATE	SALES	RETDIS	TCOS	SELLING	RANDD	GENERAL	ADMIN	DEPREC	OTHER	TAXES
1	BUDGET	JAN8	4600	300	2200	480	110	500	210	14	−8	510
2	BUDGET	FEB8	4700	330	2300	500	110	500	200	14	0	480
3	BUDGET	MAR8	4800	360	2600	500	120	600	250	15	2	520
4	ACTUAL	JAN8	4900	505	2100	430	130	410	200	14	−8	500
5	ACTUAL	FEB8	5100	480	2400	510	110	390	230	15	2	490

COMPUTER
HARDWARE AND
SOFTWARE FOR
EFFECTIVE
MANAGEMENT
INFORMATION
SYSTEMS

```
                      PRO FORMA INCOME STATEMENT
                       XYZ COMPUTER SERVICES, INC
                            BUDGET ANALYSIS
                          AMOUNTS IN THOUSANDS

  ---- CURRENT MONTH ----                              ---- YEAR TO DATE -----
  BUDGET  ACTUAL    %                                  BUDGET  ACTUAL    %
  ------  ------  -------                              ------  ------  -------

  4,700   5,100   108.51   GROSS SALES                 9,300  10,000   107.53
    330     480   145.45   LESS RETURNS & DISCOUNTS       630     985   156.35
  ------  ------  -------                              ------  ------  -------
  4,370   4,620   105.72      NET SALES                8,670   9,015   103.98

  2,300   2,400   104.35   TOTAL COST OF SALES         4,500   4,500   100.00

  2,070   2,220   107.25      GROSS PROFIT             4,170   4,515   108.27

                            OPERATING EXPENSES:
    500     510   102.00      SELLING                    980     940    95.92
    110     110   100.00      R & D                      220     240   109.09
    500     390    78.00      GENERAL                  1,000     800    80.00
    200     230   115.00      ADMINISTRATIVE             410     430   104.88
     14      15   107.14      DEPRECIATION                28      29   103.57
  ------  ------  -------                              ------  ------  -------
  1,324   1,255    94.79                               2,638   2,439    92.46
  ------  ------  -------                              ------  ------  -------
    746     965   129.36   OPERATING INCOME           1,532   2,076   135.51
              2            OTHER INCOME/-EXPENSE          -8      -6    75.00
  ------  ------  -------                              ------  ------  -------
    746     967   129.62   TAXABLE INCOME             1,524   2,070   135.83
    480     490   102.08   INCOME TAXES                 990     990   100.00
  ------  ------  -------                              ------  ------  -------
    266     477   179.32      NET INCOME                534   1,080   202.25
  ======  ======  =======                             ======  ======  =======
```

FIGURE 5.9
Pro-forma income
statement. (Courtesy
SAS Institute, Inc)

SAS/GRAPH. Another important feature of the system is SAS/GRAPH, which provides device-intelligent color graphics. With just a few statements to control colors and patterns, tedious income statements, pricing schedules, and performance reports can be turned into meaningful charts and plots.

For example, the statements below use an SAS data set containing financial information for a typical corporation to produce a star chart in SAS:

```
PROC CHART;
    STAR MONTH/SUMVAR = INCOME MIDPOINTS = 'JAN' 'FEB' 'MAR'
        'APR' 'MAY' 'JUN' 'JUL' 'AUG' 'SEP' 'OCT' 'NOV' 'DEC';
    TITLE INCOME BY MONTH;
```

But by changing the procedure name to GCHART, adding FILL = SOLID to the STAR statement, and taking advantage of SAS/GRAPH's TITLE statement, a display can be produced.

STATPRO

While the preceding SAS package is designed for computer mainframes, STATPRO is a multipurpose statistics and graphics data base system designed specifically for a microcomputer; that is, the personal computer. Data analysts, researchers, and business professionals will notice the simplicity of this comprehensive program since STATPRO requires no previous computer experience and no special command language. Simple, single keystrokes allow the user to access all of the data manipulation, statistics, and graphics power of the system.

STATPRO's strength is its user-friendly, menu-driven data base. Unlike command-driven mainframe systems, one can easily learn to enter and edit, manipulate, transform, and print out data. STATPRO's searching capabilities allow these functions to be performed on all data, or on any subset of data. Transformations and over 600 conversions are available. The results of these transformations can be placed in the same field or into any other field in STATPRO's data base.

The statistics component of STATPRO contains a multitude of procedures grouped in the following modules: *descriptive* (such as cross tabulation and contingency analysis), *regression* (such as linear, non-linear, stepwise and multiple regressions), *analysis of variance* (such as single and nested classifications), *time series* (such as moving averages and multistage least squares), and *multivariate* (such as discriminant functions and multiple contingency). With STATPRO graphics, the results of the statistical analyses can be plotted, including scatter, triangle, regression, and box plots as well as pie charts, histograms, and dendograms. In addition, STATPRO documentation includes an

Software Package	Vendor
Accent R	National Information Systems
ADS/Online	Cullinet Software
ASCENT	Control Data Corporation
CA-Universe	Computer Associates International
CUFFS	Cuffs Planning and Models, Ltd.
Easytrieve Plus	Pansophic Systems
EMPIRE	Applied Data Research
EXPRESS	Information Resources
FCS-EPS	Thorn EMI Computer
FOCUS	Information Builders
FORESIGHT	United Computing Systems, Inc.
IDEAL	Applied Data Research
IFPS	EXECUCOM Systems Corporation
IMPACT	MDCR, Inc.
INQUIRE	Infodata Systems
MANTIS	Cincom Systems
NATURAL	Software AG
NOMAD2	D&B Computing Services
RAMIS II	Martin Marietta Data Systems
SAM	Decision Sciences Corporation
SAS	SAS Institute, Inc.
SIMPLAN	SIMPLAN Systems, Inc.
SPSS-X	SPSS
STATPRO	Wadsworth Professional Software
STATSII	Compuserve
System W	Comshare
Xerox Business Management System	Xerox Computer Services

FIGURE 5.10
Current financial planning languages and statistical packages.

COMPUTER
HARDWARE AND
SOFTWARE FOR
EFFECTIVE
MANAGEMENT
INFORMATION
SYSTEMS

introductory tutorial that "walks" the user through the major features of each of the components of the STATPRO workstation and familiarizes the user with the self-documenting nature of the software.

A listing of common financial planning languages and statistical packages is shown in figure 5.10. The software packages set forth in this chapter plus similar widely used applications are included.

IMPORTANT DIRECTIONS IN THE NEWER MIS ENVIRONMENTS

In the previous sections of the chapter, both custom-made computer programs and ready-made software packages to provide the desired output for effective MIS were discussed. In the new systems environments—distributed data processing systems, decision support systems, and expert systems—these packages are also necessary. The newer MIS operating modes not only build upon them but accent newer directions of their own. Because of their importance, typical new thrusts for these systems are set forth below.

Multidimensional Spreadsheets in MIS

As described in a prior section, the spreadsheet is the software component that allows the technically unsophisticated business user to put the microcomputer immediately to work. Now newer developments, including the addition of a third dimension to the familiar row-and-column format, give the spreadsheet an even larger role in the integration of corporate information for managers. Typically, a manager describes the elements of the problem and their mathematical relationships in cells on the spreadsheet. In turn, the spreadsheet directs the micro to get the job done. The addition of the third dimension extends this power to cover problems of much greater complexity, allowing the spreadsheet to replace even more difficult programming tasks.

The third dimension can be thought of as a series of spreadsheet pages, one atop another. Besides being able to specify relationships between elements on one page, as with a two-dimensional spreadsheet, the user can also relate elements on different pages. Consider a simple spreadsheet application for tallying expense accounts. A different column represents each day of the week and a weekly total; rows represent costs for travel, food, lodging, and a daily total. The C column might represent Monday activity, for example; the 4 row, food expenditures. The individual would enter his or her outlay for Monday's meals in cell C4. Suppose there were a stack of these spreadsheets from several employees, with the pages numbered consecutively from 2 to 6, and a blank sheet, numbered 1, on top. Cells on the blank page can be specified to receive totals from the pages beneath. Cell 1C4, for example, meaning page 1, column C, row 4, can receive the total of cells 2C4 to 6C4; that is, the total of the Monday food expenses for all employees as specified on pages 2 through 6.

Such front-to-back computation lends itself to consolidation of similar spreadsheets maintained by different employees or offices. Financial consolidations, in which the ledgers for various divisions are combined in the corporate books, are a natural application for the three-dimensional spreadsheet. However, the front-to-back relationships and computations are not limited to corresponding cells on the different spreadsheet pages. A cell on any given page can receive information from any cells on any other pages. An application for tracking advances for employee expenses might be set up on a spreadsheet, for example. That page might then exchange information with the expense account spreadsheets. This is a fairly simple illustration of the concept. Two typical three-dimensional spreadsheets are Boeing Calc (from Boeing Computer Services) and Megacalc (from Mega Group). Both products allow spreadsheets with thousands of rows, columns, and pages.

Video Teleconferencing in Distributed Data Processing

To assist in more effective management over distributed data processing operations, video teleconferencing is available for organizations that are widely dispersed throughout the country. The list of intangible benefits of using video teleconferencing is long. It includes such items as better decision making, better organization during meetings, a time-saving approach, and session brevity. For example, not only does a coast-to-coast teleconference save travel dollars, it also saves at least two days in travel time, which in some cases is worth a lot more than airplane fare, hotel costs, and the general aggravation for those who hate to travel. Interestingly, many of these intangible benefits apply not only to long-distance meetings, but also to local ones (say, within 50 miles) as well. An important side benefit of teleconferencing is the capability to hold meetings that otherwise may never have been held.

It is not always necessary to own a viewing room to take advantage of video teleconferencing. Several vendors (and some users) have been offering public rooms or sharing their private rooms. The public room concept, which was pioneered by AT&T, is offered under the name of Picturephone Meeting Service (PMS). (AT&T's original Picturephone service is well over a decade old.) Offered from a number of public rooms, PMS service can be rented on an hourly basis. Currently, AT&T has the service available in 42 cities. Besides its public PMS, the telephone company also installs private rooms that will be compatible with public ones. A user could build private rooms in some of its company's key locations while using public facilities elsewhere. Another organization in this business, the American Satellite Company, has a teleconferencing rental offering that obviates a large initial user investment.

Although video teleconferencing is basically hardware, it is designed to be used as a business tool to assist managers in overseeing dispersed operations. Referring to the above Picturephone Meeting Service of AT&T, the meeting room is equipped for audio-visual demonstrations in addition to transmitting and receiving color TV images. Likewise, slides, transparencies, and hard copy can be transmitted. The users can draw on a blackboard or use

197

COMPUTER
HARDWARE AND
SOFTWARE FOR
EFFECTIVE
MANAGEMENT
INFORMATION
SYSTEMS

charts. Additionally, the meeting can be recorded on videotape. Hence, managers and support staff can make a complete presentation on any subject, like the demonstration of new products and packaging.

A video conference can provide an exchange of ideas between management of dispersed operations. The goal may be a free exchange of potential answers to specific "What if?" questions as they arise in the normal course of conversation. This interaction of managers and support staff at points distant from one another may signal the need to develop specific computer programs using procedural or nonprocedural languages for answering the questions posed. At the next video teleconferencing meeting, a presentation can be made that focuses on potential answers to important "What if?" questions posed earlier. Thus, the video teleconferencing method is an excellent vehicle for increasing managers' involvement both in the planning and control of their functional areas and in the tie-in with overall organization goals and operations.

Computer Graphics in Decision Support Systems

As pointed out earlier in the chapter, the use of financial planning languages and statistical packages has become part of an effective MIS. Similarly, they are integral to decision support systems where the current focus is on using computer graphics to evaluate alternative courses of action. Computer graphics essentially provides the creative interface between people and machines. Traditionally, people had to learn computer languages. Today, the computer can "talk" in people language (converting the output to pictures and words). By the same token, the computer can understand typical human inputs—through the use of an input device to enable the computer to understand what people want it to do. A user can now take advantage of computer power without being a specialist by choosing from among a large number of software packages. This is the primary reason for the tremendous growth in computer graphics usage in decision support systems.

Answers to "What if?" questions are enhanced by computer graphics. For a business situation in which a series of data are used to see what results emerge under a certain set of conditions, results can be plotted. Interactively, the set of conditions can be changed and the new output plotted. Needless to say, a whole series of business problems benefit from graphic solutions—project planning, break-even curves, and learning curves, to name but a few. A picture is often worth a thousand words . . . or a thousand lines of printout . . . or ten minutes of discussion. The eye is able to discern patterns easier than it can see individual numbers from a computer printout, which enables the user to absorb a tremendous amount of information if shown graphically. Overall, decision support systems make great use of computer graphics, resulting in a blend of hardware and software. They allow organization personnel to build models and speculate with their computers using graphic output on how hypothetical decisions might translate into reality based upon specific "What if?" questions.

Utilization of Natural-Language Systems

With the recent advances in computer programming languages, current fifth-generation languages, commonly referred to as *natural-language systems,* are supplementary to fourth-generation languages. Natural-language systems allow computer users to converse with their machines in English rather than rigid programming-language commands. They allow users to enter commands in conversational English, the same way they would make a request of any co-worker or subordinate.

An important advantage of natural languages over prior languages is that the same command can be worded several ways. For example, suppose the user tells the computer to get the BiPi Division's sales for this year, but accidentally mistypes the input, uses slang, or omits words. Conventional languages will not respond. With a natural language, however, the computer will not be confused by errors. Natural-language programs take the user's input and translate it into computer code. The computer will, then, execute the instructions.

A limited number of natural-language programs are available for computer mainframes and microcomputers. But before long, the market will be flooded with software—particularly as mainframe-software vendors redo natural languages for microcomputers. A typical natural-language program, INTELLECT, is discussed below.

INTELLECT. INTELLECT is a true English-language query system. It employs the technology of artificial intelligence to understand even the complex pronoun references and incomplete sentences that one uses in conversational English. Executives can access data themselves—more easily than ever before—without learning any jargon or "computerese." INTELLECT is not just for simple "What if?" type questions. The system can combine information from several files to respond to a query, so that a request does not have to be confined to a single file. A user can compare different sets of data with one question, as when comparing actual sales figures with projections.

INTELLECT can handle questions, such as: "Give me the sales managers with salary plus commissions, plus bonuses, minus deductions greater than $30,000." By defining words and phrases in a *lexicon,* the query system understands each user's vocabulary, linguistic style, and external view of the data base. The lexicon can be expanded easily; it takes literally seconds to add new words, definitions, or synonyms. For new users, "lexicon managers" receive four-day training on developing and maintaining the dictionary. Defining the lexicon for specific applications is something users do themselves. INTELLECT handles pronoun references and partial or ungrammatical sentences. When faced with overly complex, ambiguous phrases or words not found in its lexicon, INTELLECT asks the user for clarification. Sample dialogue demonstrates how the same question may be phrased differently, but understood by INTELLECT: "How many clerical people work for the company? Count the clerical people. How many employees are clerical? Give me the number of employees

COMPUTER
HARDWARE AND
SOFTWARE FOR
EFFECTIVE
MANAGEMENT
INFORMATION
SYSTEMS

in clerical. Clerical count." INTELLECT interprets all these requests into: "Count the employees within the clerical group."

INTELLECT's ability to understand English is so unique that IBM and leading software companies have arranged to integrate it into their product lines. Currently, it is marketed by Cullinet Software under the name "On-Line English." Management Decision Systems offer INTELLECT as "ELI-English Language Interface." InSci markets INTELLECT with their human resources package as "GRS EXEC." INTELLECT also interfaces directly to leading data bases, such as ADABAS, IDMS, and VSAM, as well as with sequential files.

EFFECTIVE MIS PRACTICE—INTEGRATION OF THE MICROCOMPUTER WITH THE MANAGER

The use of management information systems for keeping management abreast of the status quo is fairly well established. Their use, however, to evaluate that status relative to meeting and beating competition in the future, and to examine the financial and operating impacts of both controllable and uncontrollable future scenarios, is not so well developed. To state it another way, MIS as a decision-support tool is not widespread.

Why not? In some cases, the manager has operated successfully in the past without such capabilities and does not see a need to attain them. The change of pace of business conditions today is rapidly rendering this position untenable. Even where the need is recognized, though, the difficulty of meeting the need can seem to outweigh the benefit—the problem might appear to be unsolvable.

What has made the problem seem so difficult to solve? Computer power has been scarce—not because the computer itself is a scarce resource, but because people who understand both the problems and the solutions are scarce. The manager understands the problem, the systems analyst attempts to understand the problem, and the programmer understands the solution but not always the problem. The communication required among these people—manager, systems analyst, and programmer—to forge an information system has been the real scarcity. How can management make use of the computer to alleviate its needs without suffering the costs, confusion, and frustrations that have plagued the migration of the computer into the executive suite?

The answer is somewhat obvious. Simplify access to the computer so that systems analysts and programmers are not needed every step of the way. Managers and staff should be able to explain their needs to the computer directly, without intermediaries, and without having to become systems analysts and programmers themselves. To a great extent, this can be accomplished by selective applications of microcomputer software packages. These packages are designed for the nonstructured work and informational needs of management; they can directly support managerial decision making in the areas of planning and control without requiring the assistance of computer specialists.

Because problems, explanations, and the responses needed by management often occur on short notice, managers have been conditioned by experience with the difficulty of getting answers from the computer (i.e., from the DP function) to the point of not even considering a computer solution of many frequent needs. Today's MIS manager is indeed faced almost daily with the problem of having many more requests and requirements from the organization's user community than can be met by his or her capability. The most frustrating requests are for single-use, complex analysis reports. Certainly, a part of the problem may be due to gaps in the technology or state of the art. However, for the most part it is not the state of the art per se, but the state of the art as it exists within the organization, typically the cost/benefit factors involved with meeting the requirement. Most often, the difficulty is simply a lack of available manpower within a given time frame for solution. In my experience, the majority of data processing organizations are simply operating below budgeted staff, and have been for several years due to a shortage of qualified personnel.

To overcome this difficulty, financial planning languages and statistical packages now can provide users the ability to satisfy a significant percent of their own requests, requests that are presently going unanswered or being addressed at the expense of considerable skilled manpower—a precious commodity. The technical support function and the hardware may also be overburdened, but a system which utilizes the language of the business world requires virtually no technical support on a microcomputer by the MIS organization. It is common to hear users in non-DP management talk about the structure of the language they use and how easy it is for people with limited programming capabilities to tie into such systems and comfortably interact with a certain software package.

Overall, decision-making support tools, such as the numerous financial planning systems set forth in the chapter, should be viewed in a very positive light; that is, as a means of lessening a high percentage of user requests for mainframe time and as a means of encouraging managers to reconsider the microcomputer as a solution to needs that might have been considered inappropriate in the past. With a flexible, human-oriented command structure permitting instantaneous reporting, answers to "What if?" questions and such options as goal seeking and risk analysis capabilities using financial planning languages and statistical packages allow the MIS function to provide a higher level of service with minimal investment in hardware and software resources.

CHAPTER SUMMARY

Initially, the chapter focused on the current trend toward the use of software packages from outside sources. This was followed by a discussion of the essentials of writing custom-made computer programs—a traditional approach to computer programming. However, from the point of view of assisting the manager in decision making, the advisability of using "off the shelf" electronic spreadsheets, financial planning languages, and statistical packages (by which answers to ad hoc "What if?" questions can be obtained)

COMPUTER
HARDWARE AND
SOFTWARE FOR
EFFECTIVE
MANAGEMENT
INFORMATION
SYSTEMS

was stressed. A discussion of their intricacies made up the main content of the remainder of the chapter, The field of computer-assisted software is destined for dramatic developments. Further increases in user awareness of the benefits to be gained from thorough analysis of decision-making situations, heightened availability and affordability of the hardware/software configurations needed to support interactive planning activities, and increased uncertainty in the world of business will all combine to provide the necessary thrust for additional product growth. Electronic spreadsheets, financial planning languages, and statistical packages, then, are certain to become an indispensable part of the repertoire of computer tools available to managers and their staff.

The main theme of this chapter on computer software—as well as the prior one on computer hardware—is that the microcomputer or the mainframe, from a management perspective, is something more than sophisticated electronic gadgetry. Its general capabilities in processing information can provide the manager and his or her staff with a useful tool for evaluating the company's present position as well as projecting future positions. It places the manager at the center of the decision-making process when examining alternatives for action. It is from this point of view that computer software and hardware must be successfully integrated for effective management information systems.

QUESTIONS

1. What impact has the shortage of qualified software development professionals had on small-, medium-, and large-sized organizations?

2. What are the benefits of purchasing software packages from outside sources as opposed to writing your own programs?

3. **a.** What are the principal sources for acquiring computer software packages?
   b. What might be another source of computer software packages in the future?

4. State two other guidelines for evaluating computer software packages not given in the chapter.

5. What are the steps involved in program development?

6. Underlying the current trend toward structured programming is the modularity concept. Explain what it is.

7. How important is systems level testing when implementing effective management information systems?

8. What is the rationale for the popularity of electronic spreadsheets such as Lotus 1-2-3?

9. What are the essential elements of Lotus 1-2-3?

10. How are statistical packages different from financial planning languages; that is, in what ways are they different?

11. **a.** What are the essential features of English-based programming languages?
    b. What are the essential benefits of English-based programming languages from the standpoint of the user?

12. Distinguish between the following functions of financial planning systems: asking "What if?" questions and goal seeking.

13. What advantages to managers and their staff are found in newer management information systems using software packages that are not found in older information systems?

14. Currently, the trend is away from internally written custom-made computer programs toward externally marketed software packages. Although this is basically true of small-sized MIS departments, what can be said for large MIS departments in the "Fortune 500"? Should they develop all of their own in-house software rather than go to the outside, considering their vast resources? Whether yes or no, state your rationale.

15. Suppose you were on the corporate planning staff of a medium-sized company. When would you use Lotus 1-2-3 and when would you use a financial planning language (such as IFPS and EXPRESS) or a statistical package (like SAS and STAT-PRO) for the following business applications: (a) comparison of company sales to industry sales, (b) preparation of yearly budgets, (c) calculations for potential mergers or acquisitions, (d) risk analysis of capital projects, (e) selection of research and development projects, (f) make versus buy decisions, and (g) projection of cash flow? Wherever applicable, indicate where more than one software package can be used for the specific business application.

16. Many of the financial planning languages, like IFPS and EXPRESS, can perform a series of commands, ranging from "What if?" to "goal seeking." Give four business examples of using the "What if?" command and four examples of using the "goal seeking" command. Also, give two examples where the two commands can be used together in a decision support system environment to assist a typical business manager in answering pressing business questions confronting the firm on a day-to-day basis.

17. The Arnold Company, which manufactures space heaters for the home market, is currently evaluating electronic spreadsheets for use in corporate planning, i.e., the development of flexible budgets. These spreadsheets include SuperCalc 3, Lotus 1-2-3, and the latest multidimensional spreadsheets. To help the assistant to the MIS manager in determining which spreadsheet to purchase, develop a list of six major criteria for evaluating the desirability of acquiring one software package versus others.

18. The Regis Corporation—a firm specializing in small household appliances—is contemplating the use of either Lotus 1-2-3, another financial planning language, or a statistical package to answer a series of "What if?" questions it faces in its current budget plans. Because of the wide range of software packages available currently, the MIS manager is undertaking a feasibility study to determine which package should be purchased or leased. To assist the MIS manager, develop a list of ten criteria that could be employed to evaluate the desirability of acquiring one software package versus another. Also, state whether the criteria are major or minor and your reasons for saying so.

COMPUTER
HARDWARE AND
SOFTWARE FOR
EFFECTIVE
MANAGEMENT
INFORMATION
SYSTEMS

19. The Holcomb Corporation is a national organization specializing in the sale of industrial products to large manufacturers. Due to the fast-changing times confronting the corporation, the executive vice president has asked the MIS vice president to investigate the feasibility of using teleconferencing. This technique could tie together the corporation's five manufacturing plants scattered throughout the country. To assist the MIS vice president, develop a list of eight criteria that are useful to evaluate the desirability of utilizing teleconferencing. Additionally, state whether these criteria are major or minor and your reasons for doing so.

Retrieval of Worksheet File (i.e., Program) from the Lotus 1-2-3 Template Disk

To utilize the Lotus 1-2-3 template disk supplied with this text, the Lotus 1-2-3 system disk must be initially loaded into the main memory of the microcomputer (personal computer). The template disk for the twelve Lotus 1-2-3 programs is then loaded into the microcomputer. To retrieve the appropriate worksheet file (i.e., program), first choose "1-2-3" from the menu. The screen instructs the user to depress any key to continue. After a key is depressed, the system displays a "blank" worksheet. Next, depress the backslash (/) key. A command menu appears at the top of the screen. To retrieve the desired worksheet file (i.e., program 1, 2, 3, etc.) depress the "F" file key, which causes a new menu to be displayed. Finally, depress the "R" (retrieve) key and select the appropriate program by typing in the program name or moving the cursor to the appropriate file (program) and pressing the return/enter key. At this point, the user has accessed the desired worksheet file, which is available for completing the end-of-chapter exercises. The variables which are subject to change are highlighted on the screen for the user. The preceding procedures, then, form the basis for the retrieval of a worksheet file from the Lotus 1-2-3 template disk.

LOTUS 1-2-3 EXERCISES AND PROGRAMS

20. The RT Corporation is engaged in selling services for the home market. It is expanding these services such that sales revenues are expected to increase at the rate of 10 percent per year over the next two years. Currently, its sales revenues are $3.0 million. Its selling expenses are 49 percent of sales, and its general and administrative expenses are 30 percent of sales. Also, a long-term loan of $100,000 is currently outstanding with interest paid at 11 percent per annum. RT pays a federal income tax of 46 percent. What is the net profit after federal income taxes for the next two years? What would be the net profit after federal income taxes if the selling expenses were 45 percent of sales? Use the program provided on the Lotus 1-2-3 diskette or as given in the program found for this section.

21. The Kirby Company, a small manufacturer of cooling equipment, is currently having a difficult time meeting its yearly profit objectives. Due to this difficulty, management has decided to employ financial statement analysis this year in developing its proposed budgets. More specifically, the company desires to start with a sales level of $1.6 million, and have that increase by 10 percent per year for two more years. There is a long-term loan outstanding of $100,000 with interest being paid at 10¼ percent per annum. Total manufacturing and selling expenses are 70 percent of sales, and general and administrative expenses are 18 percent of sales.

Using a federal income tax rate of 46 percent, what is the net profit after federal income taxes for the next two years? Use the program provided on the Lotus 1-2-3 diskette or as given in the program found for this section.

22. In the chapter, reference was made to the R J Corporation—figure 5.6—for financial forecasts using Lotus 1-2-3 that consider best-case and worst-case scenarios. In part (b) of this figure, projections were based on lower growth rates (worst-case scenario) for units and selling price. Inasmuch as the best-case scenario was not developed, develop this condition based upon the assumptions given in part (a) of this figure. Is there a substantial difference between the earnings per share for the projected years of the best-case scenario versus the worst-case scenario? If there is a substantial difference (20 percent or more) between the two, what approach would you recommend to resolve the differences such that the figures are realistic for the projected years? Use the program provided on the Lotus 1-2-3 diskette or as given in the program found in this section.

23. The top management of the Cromer Corporation, a manufacturer of electrical industrial products, has decided that the corporation's product line needs to be expanded. In order to do so, it will be necessary to finance a loan. However, before approaching the local banks, top management feels that it must develop projected financial information for the next three years that it can present. The financial assumptions that were put together for the corporation and approved by top management are as follows:

	Current Year	Projected Years		
	Base	First	Second	Third
Unit sales growth—low	—	4%	5%	5%
Unit sales growth—high	—	10%	10%	10%
Sales price increase—low	—	3%	4%	4%
Sales price increase—high	—	6%	6%	7%
Units—low and high	2,000,000			
Selling price—low and high	$10.00			
Variable costs—cost of goods sold	60%			
Commissions—fixed	$1,000,000			
—variable	6%			
Administrative exp—fixed	$400,000			
—variable	3%			
Federal income tax rate	46%			
Dividend growth rate	3.5%			
Outstanding shares	400,000			
Dividends	$1,000,000			
Retained earnings—beginning of year	$2,000,000			

Using the data provided above, develop the projected income statement and earnings per share for the next three years (based upon low and high growth rates) along with the actual figures for the current year. Use the program provided on the Lotus 1-2-3 diskette or as given in the program for this section.

LOTUS 1-2-3 PROGRAM—FINANCIAL STATEMENT ANALYSIS (PROGRAM 1)

```
D1:  'Financial Statement Analysis       C19:  (CO) U 100000
D2:  '-----------------------------      A20:  '   Interest At
D4:  "Base Year                          C20:  (P2) U 0.1025
F4:  "First Year                         D20:  (,0)  ($C$19)*($C$20)
H4:  'Second Year                        F20:  (,0)  ($C$19)*($C$20)
D5:  ' ----------                        H20:  (,0)  ($C$19)*($C$20)
F5:  ' ----------                        D21:  (CO) ' ----------
H5:  ' ----------                        F21:  (CO) ' ----------
A7:  'Base Sales                         H21:  (CO) ' ----------
C7:  (CO) U 1200000                      A22:  'Total Expenses
D7:  (CO) ($C$7)                         D22:  (CO) @SUM(D15..D20)
F7:  (CO) ($D$11)                        F22:  (CO) @SUM(F15..F20)
H7:  (CO) ($F$11)                        H22:  (CO) @SUM(H15..H20)
A9:  '   Annual Growth                   D23:  (CO) ' ----------
C9:  (P2) U 0.2                          F23:  (CO) ' ----------
D9:  (,0) 0                              H23:  (CO) ' ----------
F9:  (,0)  (D11)*($C$9)                  A24:  'Profit Before Federal
H9:  (,0)  (F11)*($C$9)                  A25:  '  Income Tax
D10: (CO) ' ----------                   D25:  (CO) +D11-D22
F10: (CO) ' ----------                   F25:  (CO) +F11-F22
H10: (CO) ' ----------                   H25:  (CO) +H11-H22
A11: '   Total Sales                     A27:  'Federal Income Tax
D11: (CO)  (D7)+(D9)                     C27:  (P2) U 0.46
F11: (CO)  (F7)+(F9)                     D27:  (,0)  (D25)*($C$27)
H11: (CO)  (H7)+(H9)                     F27:  (,0)  (F25)*($C$27)
A13: 'Expenses:                          H27:  (,0)  (H25)*($C$27)
A15: '  Selling                          D28:  (CO) ' ----------
C15: (P2) U 0.4                          F28:  (CO) ' ----------
D15: (CO)  (D11)*($C$15)                 H28:  (CO) ' ----------
F15: (CO)  (F11)*($C$15)                 A29:  'Profit After Federal
H15: (CO)  (H11)*($C$15)                 A30:  '  Income Tax
A17: '  Gen. & Admin.                    D30:  (CO) +D25-D27
C17: (P2) U 0.3                          F30:  (CO) +F25-F27
D17: (,0)  (D11)*($C$17)                 H30:  (CO) +H25-H27
F17: (,0)  (F11)*($C$17)                 D31:  (CO) U ' ==========
H17: (,0)  (H11)*($C$17)                 F31:  (CO) U ' ==========
A19: '  Long Term Loan                   H31:  (CO) U ' ==========
```

```
A1:   'Part - A
B3:   ^Actual
D3:   '     Assumptions
B4:   ^-------
C4:   '     ---------------------------------------
A6:   'Sales
B6:   ^Base Year
C6:   "Year 1
D6:   "Year 2
E6:   "Year 3
A8:   'Unit Growth
A9:   '  Low
C9:   (P0) U 0.1
D9:   (P0) U 0.1
E9:   (P0) U 0.1
A11:  'Unit Growth
A12:  '  High
C12:  (P0) U 0.18
D12:  (P0) U 0.15
E12:  (P0) U 0.15
A14:  'Sales Price
A15:  '  Growth-Low
C15:  (P0) U 0.04
D15:  (P0) U 0.04
E15:  (P0) U 0.04
A17:  'Sales Price
A18:  '  Growth-High
C18:  (P0) U 0.09
D18:  (P0) U 0.1
E18:  (P0) U 0.1
A20:  'Low Growth
A21:  '  Projections
A23:  '  Units
B23:  (,0) U 200000
C23:  (,0) @ROUND(B23*(1+C9),0)
D23:  (,0) @ROUND(C23*(1+D9),0)
E23:  (,0) @ROUND(D23*(1+E9),0)
A24:  '  Price
B24:  (C2) U 2.5
C24:  (C2) @ROUND(B24*(1+C15),2)
D24:  (C2) @ROUND(C24*(1+D15),2)
E24:  (C2) @ROUND(D24*(1+E15),2)
A26:  'High Growth
A27:  '  Projections
A29:  '  Units
B29:  (,0) U 200000
C29:  (,0) @ROUND(B29*(1+C12),0)
D29:  (,0) @ROUND(C29*(1+D12),0)
E29:  (,0) @ROUND(D29*(1+E12),0)
A30:  '  Price
B30:  (C2) U 2.5
C30:  (C2) @ROUND(B30*(1+C18),2)
D30:  (C2) @ROUND(C30*(1+D18),2)
E30:  (C2) @ROUND(D30*(1+E18),2)
A32:  'Cost of
A33:  '  Goods Sold
```

```
A34: '   % of Sales
B34: (P0)  U 0.65
A36: 'Commission
A37: '   Fixed
B37: (C0)  U 25000
A39: 'Commission
A40: '   Variable
B40: (P0)  U 0.05
A42: 'Admin. Exp.
A43: '   Fixed
B43: (C0)  U 10000
A45: 'Admin. Exp.
A46: '   Variable
B46: (P0)  U 0.03
A48: 'Tax Rate
B48: (P0)  U 0.46
A50: 'Div. Growth
A51: '   Rate
B51: (P1)  U 0.025
A53: 'Outstanding
A54: '   Shares
B54: (,0)  U 40000
C54: (,0)  U 40000
D54: (,0)  U 40000
E54: (,0)  U 55000
A60: '****************************************************************************
A62: 'Part - B
A64: 'Projections Based on Lower Growth Rates for Units and Selling Price
A65: '----------------------------------------------------------------------
B67: ^Actual
D67: '         Projected
B68: ^-------
C68: '   ----------------------------------------
B69: ^Base Year
C69: "Year 1
D69: "Year 2
E69: "Year 3
A71: 'Sales Rev.
B71: (C0)  U @ROUND(B23*B24,0)
C71: (C0)  U @ROUND(C23*C24,0)
D71: (C0)  U @ROUND(D23*D24,0)
E71: (C0)  U @ROUND(E23*E24,0)
A73: 'Cost of
A74: 'Goods Sold
B74: (,0)  @ROUND(B71*$B$34,0)
C74: (,0)  @ROUND(C71*$B$34,0)
D74: (,0)  @ROUND(D71*$B$34,0)
E74: (,0)  @ROUND(E71*$B$34,0)
A76: '  Gross
B76: "---------
C76: "---------
D76: "---------
E76: "---------
A77: '  Profit
B77: (C0)  +B71-B74
C77: (C0)  +C71-C74
```

```
D77:  (C0) +D71-D74
E77:  (C0) +E71-E74
A79:  'Commissions
B79:  (,0) @ROUND($B37+($B$40*B71),0)
C79:  (,0) @ROUND($B37+($B$40*C71),0)
D79:  (,0) @ROUND($B37+($B$40*D71),0)
E79:  (,0) @ROUND($B37+($B$40*E71),0)
A81:  'Admin. Exps.
B81:  (,0) @ROUND($B$43+($B$46*B71),0)
C81:  (,0) @ROUND($B$43+($B$46*C71),0)
D81:  (,0) @ROUND($B$43+($B$46*D71),0)
E81:  (,0) @ROUND($B$43+($B$46*E71),0)
B82:  "---------
C82:  "---------
D82:  "---------
E82:  "---------
A83:  '  Income Before
A84:  '  Fed. Income
A85:  '  Tax
B85:  (C0) +B77-(B79+B81)
C85:  (C0) +C77-(C79+C81)
D85:  (C0) +D77-(D79+D81)
E85:  (C0) +E77-(E79+E81)
A87:  'Fed. Income
A88:  '  Tax
B88:  (,0) @ROUND($B$48*B85,0)
C88:  (,0) @ROUND($B$48*C85,0)
D88:  (,0) @ROUND($B$48*D85,0)
E88:  (,0) @ROUND($B$48*E85,0)
B89:  "---------
C89:  "---------
D89:  "---------
E89:  "---------
A90:  '    Net Income
A91:  '    for Year
B91:  (C0) +B85-B88
C91:  (C0) +C85-C88
D91:  (C0) +D85-D88
E91:  (C0) +E85-E88
A93:  'Dividends
B93:  (C0) U 30000
C93:  (C0) @ROUND(B93*(1+$B$51),0)
D93:  (C0) @ROUND(C93*(1+$B$51),0)
E93:  (C0) @ROUND(D93*(1+$B$51),0)
A95:  'Begining Year
A96:  '  Retained
A97:  '  Earnings
B97:  (C0) U 100000
C97:  (C0) (B101)
D97:  (C0) (C101)
E97:  (C0) (D101)
A99:  'Year End
A100: '  Retained
A101: '  Earnings
B101: (C0) (B97)+(B91)-(B93)
C101: (C0) (C97)+(C91)-(C93)
```

```
D101: (C0) (D97)+(D91)-(D93)
E101: (C0) (E97)+(E91)-(E93)
A103: 'Earnings per
A104: 'Share
B104: (C2) +B91/B54
C104: (C2) +C91/C54
D104: (C2) +D91/D54
E104: (C2) +E91/E54
```

BIBLIOGRAPHY

Abbey, S. G. "COBOL Dumped." *Datamation,* January 1984.

Alesandrini, K. "Graphics: A Two-Edged Sword." *PC Magazine,* June 11, 1985.

Anderson, J. J. *Business Computing with Lotus 1-2-3.* Englewood Cliffs, NJ: Prentice-Hall, 1986.

Anderson, L., and Welch, D. "Application Generator Speeds Development." *Mini-Micro Systems,* November 1985.

Arvai, E. S. "Software Selection Takes Teamwork." *Today's Office,* October 1985.

Austin, S. "New On-Line Choices for Business." *Business Computer Systems,* April 1985.

Beeler, J. "Programming Productivity." *Computerworld,* December 30, 1981–January 6, 1986.

Bender, E. "The House That 1-2-3 Built." *Computerworld,* July 15, 1985.

Benoit, E. "The Financial Shape of Things to Come." *Business Computer Systems,* September 1983.

————. "Financial Modelers Add Might to Minis." *Business Computer Systems,* October 1983.

Benoit, E., and Bernstein, A. "Graphic Detail." *Business Computer Systems,* April 1984.

Bernknopf, J. "4GLs Without Philosophy." *Information Center,* June 1986.

Bernstein, A. "Decision Support Graphics Draw a Better Bottom Line." *Business Computer Systems,* August 1985.

Blissmer, R. H. "Micro Software Promotes Ease of Use." *Mini-Micro Systems,* June 1985.

Bond, G. "Now Appearing on the Wide Screen . . ." *Business Computer Systems,* August 1983.

Borgmann, M. "Visual Information Systems: New Hope for Decision Makers." *Computerworld Focus,* April 17, 1985.

Briggs, W. G. "An Evaluation of DSS Packages." *Computerworld,* March 1, 1982.

Brown, M. D. "Mainframe Business Graphics." *Datamation,* May 1, 1984.

Brown, S. "Presto! Mainframe Computing Gets Personal." *Computer Decisions,* June 1984.

Bruce, P., and Pederson, S. M. *The Software Develop-ment Project, Planning and Management.* New York: John Wiley & Sons, 1982.

Bryan, S. W. "SPSS/PC Does Almost Anything with Statistics." *Business Computer Systems,* June 1985.

Bryant, S. F. "Integrated Software Gives You Functions Within Functions." *Computer Decisions,* September 1984.

Casella, P. "Simply Spreadsheets." *PC Products,* August 1985.

Christoff, K. A. "Building a Fourth-Generation Environment." *Datamation,* August 1985.

Cobb, R. "Fourth-Generation Languages: From Backwater to Mainstream." *Computerworld,* October 14, 1985.

Cobb, R. H. "In Praise of 4GLS." *Datamation,* July 15, 1985.

Colby, W. "A Picture Is Worth a Thousand Printouts." *Infosystems,* May 1984.

Cook, R. "Graphics Hit the Big Time." *Computer Decisions,* July 15, 1985.

Cullum, R. L. "Interactive Development." *Datamation,* February 15, 1985.

Data Decisions. "End Users Rate Applications Software." *Datamation,* March 1983.

Data Decisions. "System Software Survey." *Datamation,* December 1983.

Davidson, J. P. "Speeding Your Professional Reading." *Computer Decisions,* July 30, 1985.

Denise, R. M. "Technology for the Executive Thinker." *Datamation,* August 1983.

Desmond, J. "Window to MIS: Graphics Focuses Business Picture." *Software News,* April 1986.

Dickson, G. W.; DeSanctis, G.; and McBride, D. J. "Understanding the Effectiveness of Computer Graphics for Decision Support: A Cumulative Experimental Approach." *Communications of the ACM,* January 1986.

Durell, W. "The Politics of Data." *Computerworld,* September 9, 1985.

Ferrarini, E. "Doing Research with an On-Line Library." *Business Computer Systems,* February 1983.

————. "All the Data You Will Ever Need." *Business Computer Systems,* October 1983.

————. "Direct Connections for Software Selections." *Business Computer Systems,* February 1984.

Ferris, D. "Spreadsheets vs. Financial Planning Packages." *Software News,* April 1983.

Gardner, E. S., Jr. "Making Graphics Talk." *Lotus,* December 1985.

Giddings, R. V. "Accommodating Uncertainty in Software Design." *Communications of the ACM,* May 1984.

Glossbrenner, A. "Getting the Most of On-Line Information Services, Part 1." *Lotus,* September 1985.

————. "Getting the Most of On-Line Information Services, Part II." *Lotus,* October 1985.

Gold, J. "The Art of Low-Cost Graphics." *Computer Decisions,* July 30, 1985.

Grammas, G. W. "Software Productivity as a Strategic Variable." *Interfaces,* May–June 1985.

Grant, F. J. "Twenty-First Century Software." *Datamation,* April 1, 1985.

————. "The Downside of 4GLS." *Datamation,* July 15, 1985.

Gremillion, L. L., and Pyburn, P. "Breaking The System Development Bottleneck." *Harvard Business Review,* March–April 1983.

Guinier, D. "Interactive Language Analysis." *The VAX Professional,* August 1985.

Handelman, S. A. "Pitfalls of Acquiring Software." *Infosystems,* September 1983.

Harris, C. E. "Negotiating Software Contracts." *Datamation,* July 15, 1985.

Harris, L. "The Materials, Languages for End Users." *Computerworld,* February 15, 1985.

Hart, R. "It's Time to Put Your PC Into a Color-Graphics Mode." *Office Systems,* February 1986.

Hayen, R. L. "Design Strategy for Nonprocedural Languages." *Journal of Systems Management,* June 1983.

Hessinger, P. R. "Strategies for Implementing Fourth-Generation Software." *Computerworld,* February 20, 1984.

Hirsch, A. "New Spread-Sheet Packages Do More Than Model." *Mini-Micro Systems,* June 1983.

Hodil, E. D., and Richardson, G. L. "New Faces for Old Systems." *Computer Decisions,* July 15, 1985.

Horton, L. "Users Find a Tool to Manage Themselves." *Software News,* May 1985.

Horwitt, E. "Creating Your Own Solutions." *Business Computer Systems,* June 1983.

————. "Up from Spreadsheets." *Business Computer Systems,* June 1985.

Jenkins, A. M. "Surveying the Software Generator Market." *Datamation,* September 1, 1985.

Jones, C. "How Not to Measure Programming Productivity." *Computerworld,* January 13, 1986.

Jones, E. "Risk Analysis with 1-2-3." *Lotus,* July 1985.

Katzan, H., Jr. *Invitation to MAPPER.* Hasbrouck Heights, NJ: Hayden Publishing Company, 1984.

Knapp, E. M. "What's Best for Graphics—Mainframe or Micros?" *Computerworld Focus,* April 17, 1985.

Krakow, I. H. "Integrated Software Sweeps: More Than a Numbers Game." *Business Computer Systems,* February 1984.

Kull, D. "Nonprocedural Languages, Bringing Up the Fourth Generation." *Computer Decisions,* December 1983.

————. "Software—What's Ahead, Interview with James Martin." *Computer Decisions,* November 1984.

————. "Getting the Information Out." *Computer Decisions,* April 23, 1985.

————. "Anatomy of a 4GL Disaster." *Computer Decisions,* February 11, 1986.

————. "Decision Support with 20/20 Foresight." *Computer Decisions,* May 6, 1986.

Langlois, A. "A DSS Leads to a Corporate Micro Strategy." *Software News,* December 1983.

Leavitt, D. "Making Financial Packages Become Integrated Systems." *Software News,* July 5, 1982.

————. "Many 'Decision Support Systems' Aren't." *Software News,* November 1, 1982.

————. "More Than End-User Tools, 4 GLs Add to Productivity." *Software News,* April 1986.

Lehman, J. A.; Vogel, D.; and Dickson, G. "Business Graphics Trends." *Datamation,* November 15, 1984.

Lipton, R. "PC/FOCUS Bring Mainframe DBMS Power to Micros." *Business Computer Systems,* January 1985.

Major, M. "In Graphics, It's Clear the Market is Booming." *Software News,* January 1985.

——. "DSS Embraces New Environments." *Software News,* September 1985.

Martin, J. *Application Development Without Programmers.* Englewood Cliffs, NJ: Prentice-Hall, 1982.

Martin, J., and McClure, C. "The Latest Look in Programmer Productivity Tools." *Business Software Review,* May 1986.

Mayo, K. "How Business Buys Software." *Business Computer Systems,* November 1984.

McCartney, L. "Teleconferencing Comes Down to Earth." *Datamation,* January 1983.

McCusher, T. "New Wrinkles in the Software Market." *Software News,* November 1983.

McKibbin, W. L. "On the Road to Instant Information." *Infosystems,* September 1983.

Meade, J. "Computer Graphics Finally Hit the Charts." *Information Week,* April 8, 1985.

Mellman, G. S. "Fourth-Generation Languages: The Friendly Micro-Mainframe Connection." *Today's Office,* July 1985.

Miller, B. B. "Fourth-Generation Language for the Personal Computer." *The Office,* February 1985.

Miller, F. W. "Micro Software Enters 'Second Generation'." *Infosystems,* March 1983.

Mimno, P. "4GL, Power to the User, Part One." *Computerworld,* April 8, 1985.

——. "4GL, Power from the Products, Part Two." *Computerworld,* April 15, 1985.

Minicucci, R. "DSS: Computer Wizardry for the Executive." *Today's Office,* June 1983.

Monk, J. T., and Landis, K. M. "PC or Mac? Software's the Key." *Business Computer Systems,* September 1984.

Morison, R. "4GLs vs. COBOL." *Computerworld,* August 2, 1985.

Munro, J. "Reducing the Cost for Finer Graphics." *Systems & Software,* November 1984.

Nee, E. "Reaching Decisions with Micro-to-Mainframe DSS." *Micro Manager,* November 1984.

Needle, D. "Why Not Add Graphics . . . " *Personal Computing,* August 1985.

Norman, M., and Muriel, A. "Writing Simple Program Generators: A Case Study in Building Productivity Tools." *Journal of Management Information Systems,* Summer 1984.

O'Leary, M. "Electronic Directories." *Datamation,* October 15, 1984.

Osgood, W. R., and Curtin, D. P. *Preparing Your Business Plan with Symphony.* Englewood Cliffs, NJ: Prentice-Hall, 1985.

Parks, M. "Boost Programmer Productivity with Software Tools." *Data Communications,* January 1982.

Perry, R. L. "The Latest Revolution in Financial-Modeling Software, Part I." *Computer Decisions,* October 1984.

——. "The Latest Revolution in Financial-Modeling Software, Part II." *Computer Decisions,* November 1984.

Poppel, H. "New Partners in Information." *Computerworld,* May 6, 1985.

Praytor, E. "How to Work with Your Applications Software Vendor." *Business Software Review,* September 1986.

Press, L. I. "Friendly 1-2-3: Spreadsheets and More." *Business Computer Systems,* June 1983.

Quinones, W. "Finding Better Software for Your Business." *Business Computer Systems,* November 1982.

——. "Cashing In on Custom Programs." *Business Computer Systems,* September 1983.

Reimann, B. C., and Waren, A. D. "User-Oriented Criteria for the Selection of DSS Software." *Communications of the ACM,* February 1985.

Riley, B. "Who Copes with the Graphics Deluge?" *Computerworld Focus,* April 17, 1985.

Roman, D. "MIS/DP Trapped Behind Backlogs." *Computer Decisions,* September 1984.

——. "Presentation Graphics: Producing a Hit Show." *Computer Decisions,* September 1984.

Rosenthal, M., and Loftin, R. "PC Software Integration." *Datamation,* June 15, 1985.

Rubin, C. "The Coming of Age of 'Smart' Software." *Personal Computing,* May 1984.

Ruggera, M. "Four Tools to Build System Synergy." *Computerworld,* October 31, 1983.

Santarelli, M-B. "How Far Should Integrated Software Go?" *Software News,* November 1985.

Scott, J. E. *Introduction to Interactive Computer Graphics.* New York: John Wiley & Sons, 1981.

Seligman, D. "Life Will Be Different When We're All On-Line." *Fortune,* February 4, 1985.

Seymour, J. "Electronic Spreadsheets: A Fortuitous Accident." *Today's Office,* March 1985.

————. "Building a Desktop Modelling/Forecasting System." *Today's Office,* November 1984.

————. "Twelve Steps to Better Spreadsheets." *Today's Office,* March 1985.

————. "Integrating Software: How Tight Is the Bond?" *Today's Office,* September 1985.

Sheil, B. "Power Tools for Programmers." *Datamation,* February 1983.

Simondi, D. "Which Is Best? Don't Gamble on a DSS." *Software News,* August 1982.

Snyders, J. "Generators Do the Trick." *Computer Decisions,* June 1982.

————. "The Master Managers: Dictionaries and Librarians." *Computer Decisions,* May 1983.

————. "Online Essentials: Dictionaries and Librarians." *Computer Decisions,* February 1984.

————. "In Search of a 4th Generation Language." *Infosystems,* October 1984.

————. "Illustrate and Educate With Graphics Software." *Infosystems*, April 1986.

Spezzano, C. "Decision Support Software." *Popular Computing,* October 1985.

Stahl, B. "Friendly Mainframe Software Guides Users Toward Productivity." *Computerworld,* February 3, 1986.

Stein, D. "The Calc Wars." *Business Computer Systems,* September 1982.

————. "Software Renaissance a Boon for Business." *Business Computer Systems,* January 1983.

Stevens, L. "Getting Data in Plain English." *Computer Decisions,* April 22, 1986.

Stiefel, M. L., and Simpson, D. R. "Minicomputer Spreadsheets Take Advantage of Hardware Capabilities." *Mini-Micro Systems,* September 1983.

Sussman, P. N. "Evaluating Decision Support Software." *Datamation,* October 15, 1984.

Thiel, C. T. "The 'Big Boom' in Computer Graphics." *Infosystems,* May 1982.

————. "New Packages Spark Change." *Infosystems,* July 1983.

————. "Software of the Future." *Infosystems,* September 1983.

Thierauf, R. J. *Decision Support Systems for Effective Planning and Control—A Case Study Approach.* Englewood Cliffs, NJ: Prentice-Hall, 1982.

Thompson, G. M. P. "Packaged Software: Purchase or Perish." *The Financial Executive,* January 1983.

Tinnirello, P. "Making a Sensible 4GL Selection." *Computer Decisions,* July 30, 1985.

Trivette, D. B. "Putting Lotus Financial Functions to Work." *Lotus,* November 1985.

Uttal, B. "The Best Software for Executives." *Fortune,* December 26, 1983.

Walden, J. "A New Formula for Spreadsheets." *Business Computer Systems,* October 1984.

Warner, J. "How to Shop for Graphics Software Tools." *Infosystems,* October 1984.

Wasserman, A. J., and Gutz, S. "The Future of Programming." *Communications of the ACM,* March 1982.

Watson, H. H., and Christy, D. P. "University Support Programs Offered by Vendors of DSS Generators." *Communications of the ACM,* December 1982.

Whieldon, D. "Computer Graphics: Art Serves Business." *Computer Decisions,* May 1984.

White, L. "Florida Power and Light Turns on with Graphics." *Computerworld Focus,* April 17, 1985.

————. "Lotus Busters!" *Computerworld Focus,* February 19, 1986.

Wilcox, D. L. "The Pluses and Minuses of Graphics on Micros." *Computerworld Focus,* April 17, 1985.

Withington, F. G. "The Golden Age of Packaged Software." *Datamation,* December 1980.

Yonda, M. M. "Putting on a Good Show with Computer Graphics." *The Office,* March 1985.

Zachmann, W. F. "Statistics by 'Statpro'." *Software News,* March 1985.

Zakevsky, M. M. "Easing into the Fourth Generation." *Management Information Systems Week,* July 31, 1985.

PART FOUR

Development, Implementation, and Control of Effective Management Information Systems

The underlying structure needed to develop effective management information systems using the newer structured methodologies and computerized system tools is based on a systems approach, the subject matter of chapter 6. The important steps in the analysis and design of management information systems are set forth in chapter 7. This is followed by equipment selection and the implementation of MIS in chapter 8. Finally, in chapter 9, the types of control over management information systems are highlighted to detect processing irregularities and to prevent computer crime.

CHAPTER 6

Systems Approach to Effective Management Information Systems

ISSUES

How important is the tie-in of the major subsystems with their component parts in the systems approach to MIS?

What are the principal ways of depicting the data processing flow in a typical organization?

How good are data flow diagrams and Warnier-Orr diagrams when analyzing and designing a new management information system?

How important are computerized analysis and design packages in developing an effective MIS environment?

How important is prototyping in the development of new management information systems?

What common pitfalls are to be avoided in developing a new MIS?

INTRODUCTION TO THE SYSTEMS APPROACH

In the past, systems analysis and design tools have included system flow-charts, hierarchy diagrams, and narratives. As management information systems have increased in complexity, these techniques have been refined to create a common understanding between systems analysts and users. To meet system software requirements, the concept of structured programming was developed about 1969, credited primarily to Edsger Dijkstra. Further developments in hierarchical design, largely due to H. Mills of IBM, are known as HIPO (Hierarchical Input-Process-Output). Fundamentally, hierarchical design is a process whereby a system is specified in terms of a "top-down" structure.

While the foregoing work was being undertaken at IBM in the early 1970s, J. Warnier of Honeywell-Bull of France developed data structure techniques for systems analysis and design. This work was published in French, which delayed its immediate implementation in the United States. The data structure techniques use a hierarchical approach that begins with the system data output, determines the data needed to produce the output, and iterates this approach until the basic elements of input data are determined. Given the data structure, the program can be developed in a straightforward manner. Continuing in the mid-1970s, functional decomposition techniques were pioneered by L. Constantine and E. Yourdon of Yourdon, Inc., and by D. Ross of SofTech. As will be demonstrated in the chapter, functional decomposition also uses a hierarchical approach. Basically, it begins with a "system function" and successively decomposes this function into subfunctions.

Based mainly upon these developments, a group of structured design methods for implementing effective management information systems are available today for use by systems analysts. Due to their importance, they are the central focus of this chapter after we introduce the systems approach and the traditional flowchart tools. Toward the end of the chapter, computerized (microcomputer and mainframe) approaches to structured design methods are examined, followed by a discussion of prototyping new systems design. The chapter concludes with ways of improving a management information system.

THE SYSTEMS APPROACH

As stated previously, information produced by a management information system is an asset, a sixth resource of the organization. Even though it may be undervalued and underused, information is an essential part of the systems approach to management information systems. Hence, the generation of important managerial information is the rationale for an MIS and is the basis for understanding the systems approach to effective MIS today.

DEVELOPMENT,
IMPLEMENTATION,
AND CONTROL OF
EFFECTIVE
MANAGEMENT
INFORMATION
SYSTEMS

Before exploring the systems approach, it is helpful to define it as it relates to effective MIS. Basically, the *systems approach* is a discipline or mode of thought that can be applied to analyzing, designing, and implementing an organized flow of management information. It is based on the premise that the total organization is a system. It starts with an understanding of how the organization relates to its external and internal environment when striving to meet predetermined organization goals and objectives. It recognizes the importance of management in making decisions affecting the resources of the organization, and thereby achieving organization goals and objectives. The systems approach is concerned not only with the information flow for decision making in an organization, but also with the physical flow of materials. It is concerned with how the subsystems of the functional areas interact in information and material flows. In essence, the systems approach provides the manager as well as the systems analyst with an overview of the essentials of a system—from the highest level to the lowest level. It shows how the system can be used to obtain important information to aid organizational personnel in effective decision making.

In an effective systems approach, there is need to go outside the organization so that relevant data describing the external environment are used. Similarly, there is need to include those internal environmental factors that influence the system. An important part of examining the internal factors is determining the degree of coordination in the subsystems of the functional areas. To effect the desired level of coordination, it is necessary for the organization goals and objectives to be compatible with these subsystems. In figure 6.1, the external and internal environmental factors, along with organization goals and objectives, are illustrated.

Using organization goals and objectives (based upon a solid understanding of the external and internal environments) as a starting point, management directs and oversees the management information system as well as the company's transformation process, as shown in figure 6.1 for a typical manufacturing company. The *management information system*—viewed in this light—is a system that has subsystems or component parts integral to the functional areas that interface with each other. As data pass through these interfaces, the system converts input (i.e., data) into information that can be used for decision making in a timely and meaningful way for managerial personnel and, in many cases, for operating personnel as well. (This is shown in figure 6.1 as output: reports, summaries, etc.) In turn, the output provides information for management in making decisions affecting the inputs: data and resources. In addition, the management information system interfaces with the *transformation process,* which converts input resources into desired finished products. The end results of the transformation process are the products desired by the company's customers. (The interface of the management information system with the transformation process is also depicted in figure 6.1.) Overall, the foregoing process represents a systems approach to MIS because it stresses the conversion of data into useful information for managerial decision making and its relationship to the transformation process.

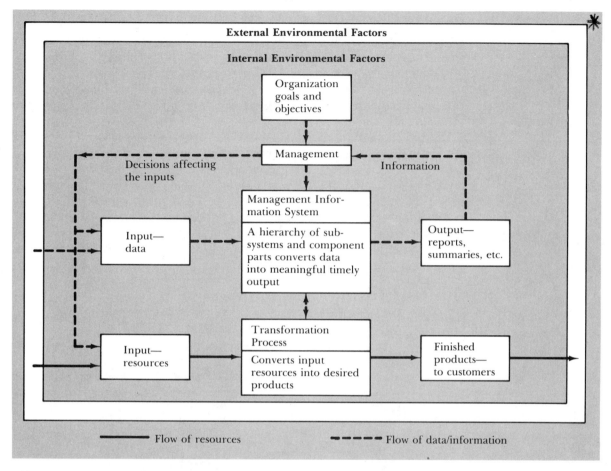

FIGURE 6.1   A systems approach stresses the importance of information in the decision-making process and its relationship to the transformation process.

Building upon the foregoing assumptions, the systems approach for effective MIS is also concerned with breaking down the management information system into its major subsystems. These include corporate planning, marketing, manufacturing, accounting, and personnel. Next, these subsystems are subdivided into their component parts. The end result of this approach is that the system is ultimately stated in terms of its essential elements, which form the building blocks or modules of the system. This iterative process of subdividing the system components provides a basis for functional decomposition of the present system. But more importantly, the building blocks can be evaluated and serve as a basis for designing the system. Thus, the systems approach provides an excellent analysis vehicle for "getting a handle on" a system without losing sight of important information, as well as a design method for building a new system that gives management meaningful, timely information.

219

DEVELOPMENT,
IMPLEMENTATION,
AND CONTROL OF
EFFECTIVE
MANAGEMENT
INFORMATION
SYSTEMS

Applying the Systems Approach for Effective MIS

The systems approach to an effective MIS environment stresses the need ultimately to answer managerial questions, and thereby provide the basis for
effective decisions. Fundamentally, decision-making capabilities are incorporated into the framework of the MIS. Decision makers receive important information as determined by the MIS (as shown in figure 6.2), from which they
recommend courses of action.

The decision-making component may take a variety of forms. For example, it may be a mathematical model using a micro or mainframe approach
that uses specific information to recommend decision alternatives. The decision-making component of the MIS should have the flexibility to handle a variety of decision problems. For the most part, there must be on-line interactive
capabilities. The user can ask various questions and receive sufficiently quick
indications of the potential effects of these modifications. This interactive
approach provides the projected report information, and shows how these
questions affect the recommended decisions.

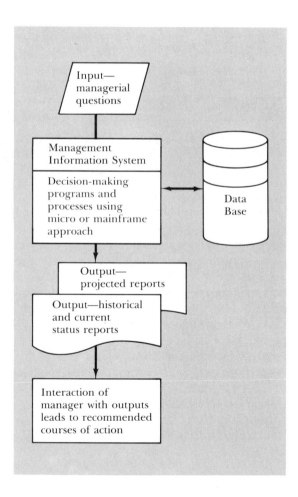

FIGURE 6.2
Within an effective MIS
environment, infor-
mation—i.e., answers
to managerial questions
in the form of output—
is used by the manager
to recommend courses
of action.

It should be recognized that decision making ultimately rests with management. The MIS output is not attempting to impose a decision or claim an absolute optimal decision for the problem. The results are meant only to provide recommendations to managers. Overall, the decision maker must evaluate the MIS recommendations, incorporate his or her management skills and judgment, and then make the final managerial decisions.

Because the systems approach calls for an orderly approach to the analysis and design of management information systems, traditional flowcharting and structured design tools are presented in the next sections of the chapter. The type of project dictates which method(s) are appropriate.

Relationship of the Systems Approach to Information Centers

Just as the systems approach should be applied to the development and implementation of a management information system, so it should be applied to the systems developed by users under the guidance of information centers. As you will recall from chapter 2, typically information centers are controlled by MIS managers. Although systems analysts and programmers staff information centers, MIS managers can play a key role in the acquisition of user software packages and related training. From a systems approach perspective, this takes the form of assisting the user not only within the confines of micro hardware and software, but beyond. More specifically, this takes the form of a micro–mainframe link for data essential to users.

Functional managers do not have easy access to the large volumes of current data required by the models they build. In fact, one response to the growing number of micros is the increase in computing cycles on mainframes resulting from micro data needs. Usually, an extract from a data base is needed for modeling efforts. Thus, the information center under the guidance of the MIS manager must provide a link to get current information from the center's data bases into the models. As an example, higher-level management can then pull together departmental models into a corporate budget with the knowledge that consistent assumptions and values have been used. The end result is an integrated systems approach for the betterment of the entire organization.

TRADITIONAL SYSTEM FLOWCHARTING

Before examining current structured design tools, it is helpful to set forth the traditional approach to systems and design. Fundamentally, this centers on utilizing system flowcharts. Because of the wide usage of flowcharts today, their essentials are set forth below, followed by what constitutes a system flowchart.

A *flowchart* allows for a better understanding of existing or proposed methods, procedures, and systems. It is defined as a graphical representation of the definition, analysis, or solution of a problem using symbols to represent operations, data flows, equipment, and the like. In essence, it is a diagram-

DEVELOPMENT,
IMPLEMENTATION,
AND CONTROL OF
EFFECTIVE
MANAGEMENT
INFORMATION
SYSTEMS

matic representation of a series of events. A computerized management information system requires a visual display of accurate and detailed end-to-end activities. The flow of data and paper work, from the input stage through the intermediate stages (including complex computer programs) to the final outputs, must be explicitly detailed for effective communication. Otherwise, the logical flow of data processing activities is difficult to follow.

It has been said that a picture is worth a thousand words. A flowchart is a valuable picture of some part of an MIS. From this view, a flowchart:

□ _aids understanding_. A flowchart shows explicitly what is happening and in what order, and has the capability to illustrate gaps in procedures and overlaps in system activities. It is much easier to comprehend what is occurring with diagrams than with a written description. When one diagrams on paper the logic involved in a DP procedure, errors and omissions stand out.

□ _communicates effectively_. The flowchart can communicate the interworkings of a new method, procedure, or system or other interested parties. Likewise, it is a succinct presentation of data flow to management and operating personnel for controlling organization activities. Hence, an important value of the flowchart is communicating to personnel other than its originator.

□ _becomes a permanent record_. Another value of flowcharts is their existence as a permanent record that does not depend on oral communication. Since the chart is written, it can be used for reviews for accuracy and completeness. It also provides a basis for analyzing and comparing present and proposed systems so that efficiency, cost, timeliness, and other relevant factors may be improved.

Standard Flowchart Symbols

Over the years, a concerted effort has been made to standardize flowcharting symbols. The rationale for standardization is that thereby anyone can interpret accurately the work of another. This is particularly important today because of the high job mobility of systems personnel; the person preparing the flowchart today may not be the one interpreting it tomorrow. If standard flowcharting symbols are used, the amount of confusion about the exact meaning intended is kept to a minimum. Thus, standardized flowchart symbols have been developed by the United States of America Standards Institute (USASI) and the International Standards Organization (the international counterpart of USASI).

Standard flowchart symbols that indicate the type of operations to be performed by computer and related equipment are either general or specialized. A template, like the one pictured in figure 6.3, aids in drawing those symbols. Generally, these standard symbols can be grouped into three main categories: basic, input/output (I/O) and file, and processing. This classification and typical payroll examples are illustrated in figures 6.4 through 6.6.

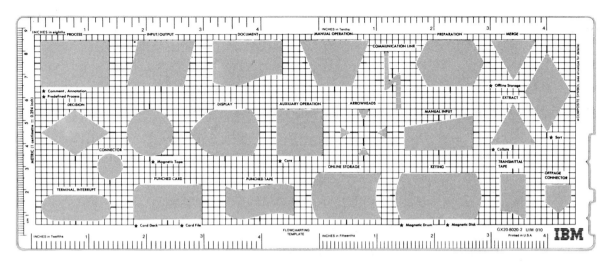

FIGURE 6.3   A template for drawing standard flowchart symbols.

No matter what combination of flowchart symbols is used, flowcharts are constructed to follow our natural tendency to read from left to right and top to bottom. At times, it is desirable to deviate from this pattern in order to achieve symmetry and to emphasize important points. *Solid flowlines* are drawn to indicate the direction of the flow, whereas *dashed flowlines* depict a transfer of information and annotated information. In either case, flowlines can be drawn horizontally, vertically, or diagonally, as needed, for a meaningful flowchart.

System Flowcharts

System flowcharts, sometimes referred to as *procedural flowcharts,* show the sequence of major activities that normally comprise a complete operation. They are generally prepared to assist all organizational personnel—and in particular, the systems analyst—in understanding some specific data processing operation as well as in obtaining an overview of the operation itself. Before a system flowchart can be drawn, the area under study must be clearly defined. Questions relating to the type and number of inputs (source documents), exceptions, transactions, files, and reports must be answered. Further questions refer to the relationship of the area under study to other functions and parts of the system, the timeliness of data, and source(s) of various data. Answers to these typical questions provide the necessary information for the initial system flowchart.

RAW MATERIALS INVENTORY ILLUSTRATION.   A typical system flowchart is found in figure 6.7, depicting computerized raw material procedures. This flowchart indicates that current transactions are processed as they occur.

223

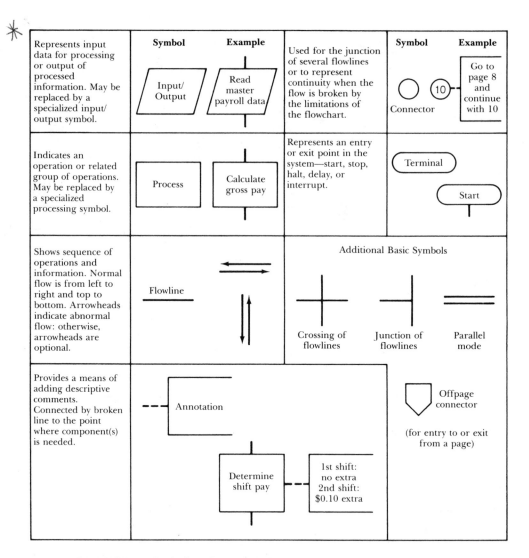

Represents input data for processing or output of processed information. May be replaced by a specialized input/output symbol.	**Symbol**	**Example**	Used for the junction of several flowlines or to represent continuity when the flow is broken by the limitations of the flowchart.	**Symbol**	**Example**
	Input/Output	Read master payroll data		Connector ○ ⑩	Go to page 8 and continue with 10
Indicates an operation or related group of operations. May be replaced by a specialized processing symbol.	Process	Calculate gross pay	Represents an entry or exit point in the system—start, stop, halt, delay, or interrupt.	Terminal Start	
Shows sequence of operations and information. Normal flow is from left to right and top to bottom. Arrowheads indicate abnormal flow: otherwise, arrowheads are optional.	Flowline		Additional Basic Symbols Crossing of flowlines · Junction of flowlines · Parallel mode		
Provides a means of adding descriptive comments. Connected by broken line to the point where component(s) is needed.	Annotation Determine shift pay	1st shift: no extra 2nd shift: $0.10 extra	Offpage connector (for entry to or exit from a page)		

FIGURE 6.4   Basic flowchart symbols and illustrated payroll examples.

These include raw material receipts from vendors, physical inventory count changes (physical inventory counting is performed on a rotating basis for counting raw materials once a month), and miscellaneous adjustments based on spoilage, scrappage, obsolescence, shrinkage, and similar items. Additionally, purchase requisitions for raw materials are entered as the basis for automatic purchasing of raw materials on line. Daily reports are printed to signal excess inventory and certain inventory errors that result from on-line activities. In essence, this approach to raw materials allows inquiry into the system at any time for updated managerial information that is critical to maintaining continuous manufacturing operations.

Numerous examples of other system flowcharts are found in part five—

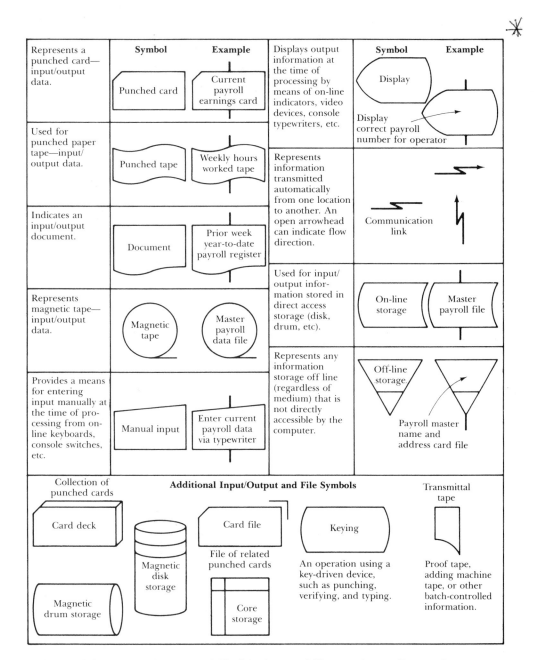

FIGURE 6.5   Input/output and file flowchart and illustrated payroll examples.

Major Subsystems of an Effective Management Information System. The chapters on the major subsystems (corporate planning, marketing, manufacturing, accounting and finance, and personnel) of the XYZ Corporation depict the flow of input data into the systems and the resulting output in the form of meaningful and timely managerial information.

225

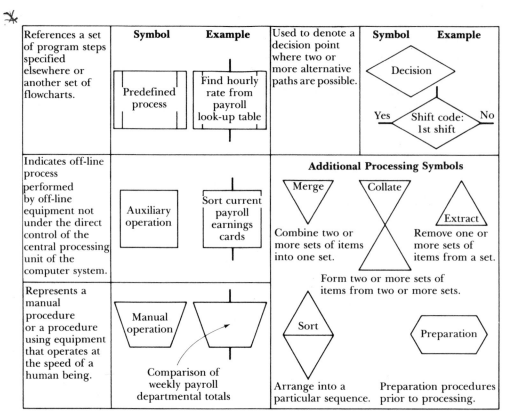

FIGURE 6.6   Processing flowchart symbols and illustrated payroll examples.

Summary—Traditional System Flowcharting

Flowcharts are pictorial representations of data flow. They aid in understanding what is happening, serve as effective communicators to those using them, and become permanent records. There are three major categories of *standard flowchart symbols.*

1. Basic symbols
   - input/output
   - process
   - flowline
   - annotation
   - connector
   - terminal
2. Input/output and file symbols
   - punched card
   - punched tape
   - document
   - magnetic tape
   - manual input
   - display
   - communication link
   - on-line storage
   - off-line storage
3. Processing symbols
   - predefined process
   - auxiliary operation
   - manual operation
   - decision

226

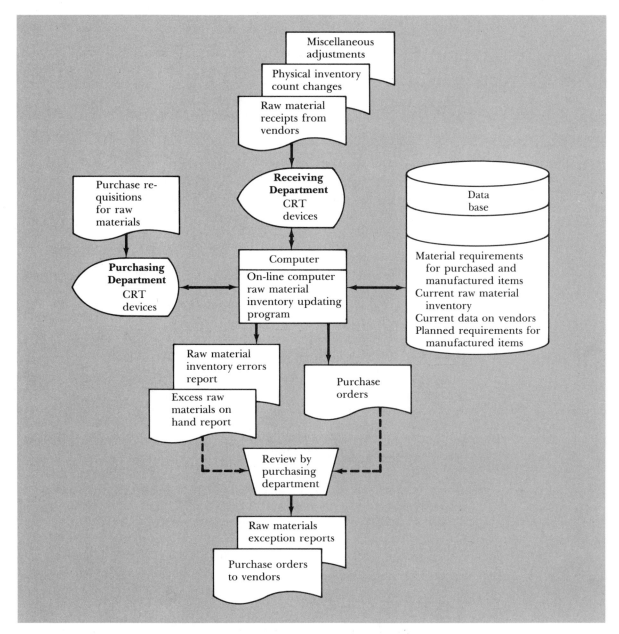

FIGURE 6.7   System flowchart for processing raw materials.

A *system flowchart* or *procedural flowchart* depicts the flow of data through the major parts of a system with a minimum of detail. For the most part, it shows where input enters the system, how it is processed and controlled, and how it leaves the system to storage and/or output.

To improve systems analysis and design in terms of logical flow, new structured design tools are currently available. They apply many of the structured design concepts that have been so successful in the area of programming to logical systems design. In general, the goal of structured methodologies using these tools is to ensure that all persons affiliated with the systems design project gain full understanding of the system, its data structures, and processes. Within this framework, there is an attempt to reduce time and errors in later systems development phases and build a system that meets user needs. Hence, structured methodologies using a logical approach to systems design should result in more complete and accurate systems. Fundamentally, the key tasks in these structured design methods are describing the current work system being investigated in functional terms—exactly what it does, not how it does it—and then stating the requirements of a new system to perform these functions more effectively.

Typical current structured design tools that emphasize top-down design approaches are (1) data flow diagrams (DFD) and (2) Warnier-Orr diagrams (WOD). These design tools are covered in some detail below.

Data Flow Diagrams

Although system flowcharts have been and still are widely used in computerized management information systems, they are not the ideal design tool. The flow of the system may not be obvious to the reviewer. Most systems analysts do not label the lines that connect the blocks of the diagram. The reviewer has to guess the actions of the transform (i.e., the changing of data) and guess what data are moving from block to block. In addition, system flowcharts do not show clearly the separation of various subsystems. To overcome these limitations, several design techniques for representing systems have come into use. One is the data flow diagram (DFD), which comes the closest to the system flowchart.

TWO APPROACHES TO DATA FLOW DIAGRAMS. There are two major schools on data flow diagrams: Yourdon and IST (Improved Systems Techniques, a division of McAuto). They differ somewhat; however, they are much more like than different.

The first item of note about them is their simple vocabulary of symbols. Both use a square for a data source or a destination. A source or destination is something outside of the control of the system—the "real world." Both use a line with an arrowhead to show the flow of data in the system. Yourdon uses a circle for a data transform, whereas IST uses a rectangle with rounded corners. A data transform can be a program, a subsystem, a manual operation, or anything that changes the data. The goal of DFDs is to illustrate in terms of abstracts rather than in terms of actual software or methods to be used. Yourdon uses a labeled straight line for a data store; IST uses a long, thin,

228

open-ended rectangle. A data store is a file, a data base, a paper record, or anything else that holds data for pickup or deposit by a transform.

As illustrated in figure 6.8, IST has a special template that can be used to draw its DFDs. Although many symbols are shown, actually there are only four basic DFD symbols as described above. They are reiterated in figure 6.9 along with appropriate payroll examples (same approach used in figures 6.4 through 6.6 for system flowcharts). These four symbols enable systems analysts to draw a picture of the system without committing themselves to how it will be implemented.

In contrast, Yourdon diagrams can be made with almost any stock circle template (refer to figure 6.3). Which method to choose is generally a matter of preference, but experience with both methods shows that the IST diagrams tend to be drawn in a squared-off style. The Yourdon circles lead to freer arcs, and the final drawing looks more casual. The author prefers the IST rectangles because they hold lettering more easily, which is especially helpful in a publication.

DATA FLOW DIAGRAMS AND RULES. Both IST and Yourdon label everything. Even more importantly, the labels mean something. The transforms are labeled with an identifier in the top part of the rectangle or bubble (if applicable) and a description below. Some hints for writing a description: it should be a verb and an object since the subject is the transform; it should be a short, complete item; and it should be exact.

The data flow arrows are labeled. The name of the data or a description of them is given. This can be a subtle point. For example, an edit routine can have "raw data" come into it and "verified data" come out of it. The edit has transformed the data by changing their state. Verified data can be used for things that raw data cannot. Also, the data stores are labeled. IST uses an

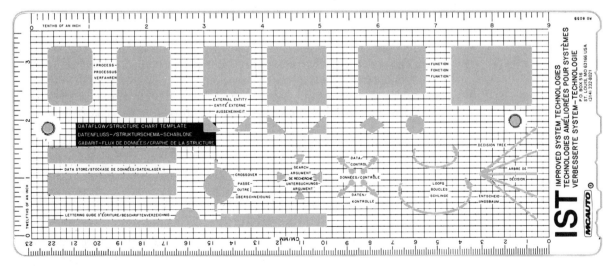

FIGURE 6.8 A template for drawing data flow diagrams (DFDs).

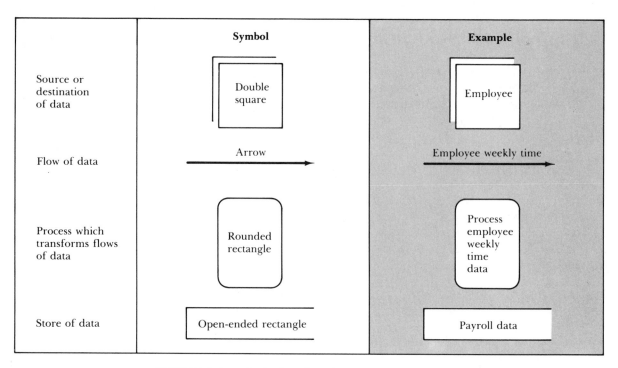

	Symbol	Example
Source or destination of data	Double square	Employee
Flow of data	Arrow	Employee weekly time
Process which transforms flows of data	Rounded rectangle	Process employee weekly time data
Store of data	Open-ended rectangle	Payroll data

FIGURE 6.9   Basic data flow diagram symbols and illustrated payroll examples.

identifier (if applicable) in addition to the description, while Yourdon uses only a description.

The major rules for data flow diagrams (regulating sources, destinations, data flows, transforms, and subdiagrams) are set forth in figure 6.10. A thorough understanding of these rules indicates that they are the product of logical thinking. They make sense and are simple and easy to use.

The best way to think of a data flow diagram is as a pipe or electrical circuit diagram for data. Not every flow has to have data in it at all times, but no data can move anywhere outside of the path shown. Data might be continuous, they might come in bursts, or they might come in pulses. The transforms can be viewed as integrated circuit chips or circuit cards. At one level, they can be viewed as a single unit; they can, however, be decomposed into circuits in themselves. This ability to decompose a diagram in finer and finer DFDs is quite important. It allows the user to follow the top-down structured programming philosophy.

As shown in figure 6.11, data flow diagrams can be decomposed into lower-level diagrams, each of which is a complete network of more elementary modules. This process of functional decomposition can continue with more lower-level diagrams until the lowest-level modules specify the origin and use of every data element in the system. The data flow diagrams should be supported by a *system glossary*. This document contains detailed infor-

DATA FLOW DIAGRAM RULES

Sources and Destinations

□ A source cannot leak data directly to a data store.

□ A data store cannot pass data directly to a destination. In both cases, the data have to go through a transform to give the system control over itself.

Data Flows

□ A data flow into a data store assumes that the transform can also take data out.

□ Data flow out of a data store is presumed to be read-only.

□ Data cannot flow from one store to another without a transform.

Transforms

□ One cannot get output without input. Any transform that is producing output by itself should be a source.

□ One cannot have only input to a transform. In effect, this is a black hole: why bother with it? It probably should be a data destination.

Subdiagrams

□ Each subsystem must be a rectangle or bubble on the next-higher-level diagram.

□ The number of data flows in and out of the corresponding rectangle or bubble at the higher levels must match the data flows at the lower levels in number and direction of flow.

FIGURE 6.10 Data flow diagrams rules regarding sources, destinations, data flows, transforms, and subdiagrams.

mation about data sources, data flows, transformation processes, and data storage.

Data flow diagrams[1] are illustrated in part five of the text for the XYZ Corporation. There they are used to depict the data processing flow among that firm's various subsystems—corporate planning, marketing, manufacturing, accounting and finance, and personnel.

RAW MATERIALS INVENTORY ILLUSTRATION. An earlier example of raw materials inventory was given in the section on system flowcharts. The data flow diagram for the same subsystem is set forth in figure 6.12. A comparison with the previous system flowchart (figure 6.7) indicates a more complete picture of raw materials receipts and changes, along with a clearer picture of the resulting flow. In a similar manner, more details concerning the flow of raw materials requisitions are included. Thus, many details missing from a system flowchart are shown using the DFD method.

[1]For more information on data flow diagrams, consult Chris Gane and Trish Sarson, *Structured Systems Analysis: Tools and Techniques* (Englewood Cliffs, N.J.: Prentice-Hall, 1979). Also refer to Tom De Marco, *Structured Analysis and System Specification* (Englewood Cliffs, N.J.: Prentice-Hall [A Yourdon Book], 1979).

231

DEVELOPMENT,
IMPLEMENTATION,
AND CONTROL OF
EFFECTIVE
MANAGEMENT
INFORMATION
SYSTEMS

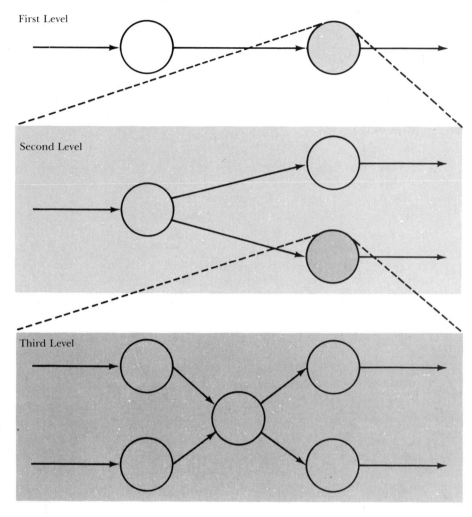

FIGURE 6.11 A hierarchy, or leveled set, of data flow diagrams whereby higher-level data flow diagrams can be decomposed into lower-level DFDs. Each lower-level diagram represents a complete network of more elementary modules.

Warnier-Orr Diagrams

Another structured method utilizes Warnier-Orr diagrams. They are a formal method of successively decomposing processes into subprocesses. These processes can be either data elements, activities, or functions. All the items of a particular functional decomposition must be of the same type. The diagram flows top-down, left-right, and uses the bracket as its major symbol. It provides a sequence of events and allows for a single sequence, the repetition of a process, or a decision between performing two processes.

DEVELOPING THE DIAGRAM. In figure 6.13 the system name is listed to the left of the bracket and the processes (i.e., steps) which make up the system are listed top-down to the right of the bracket. As illustrated, the system is first decomposed into three processes and then into their subprocesses. The symbol (1, *N*) means that a specific step is to be performed *N* times (Process

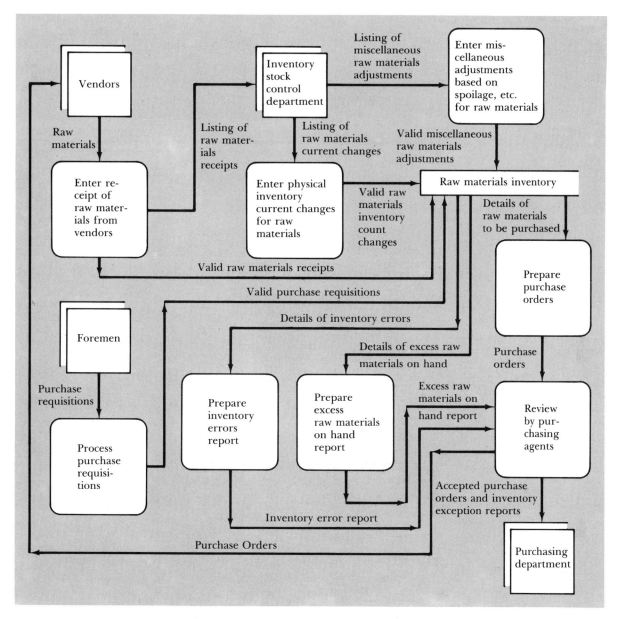

FIGURE 6.12 Data flow diagram for processing raw materials (as set forth previously in figure 6.7 in a system flowchart).

3) while the symbol ⊕ symbolizes a decision (either Process 21 or Process 22 is to be performed). Otherwise, all other steps are performed one at a time in top-down order. Process 1, per the illustration, which centers on Processes 11, 12, and 13, is performed first. Process 2 follows, which focuses on Processes 21 or 22 being performed. Finally, Process 3 is performed N times, which means that Processes 31, 32, and 33 are performed in order N times.

DEVELOPMENT,
IMPLEMENTATION,
AND CONTROL OF
EFFECTIVE
MANAGEMENT
INFORMATION
SYSTEMS

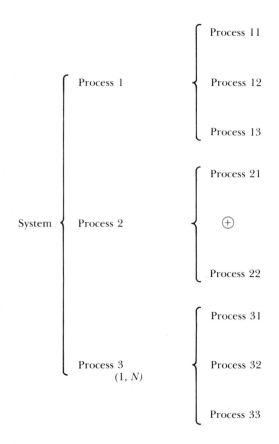

FIGURE 6.13
A Warnier-Orr diagram
illustrating
decomposition of
structure.

If the systems analyst desires further detail (beyond that shown in figure 6.13), each step can be subdivided further by placing a bracket to the right of the process step and listing the subtasks. The systems analyst can continue to decompose, that is, subdivide, to whatever level is desired by following this approach.

As noted previously, the sample illustration is divided into three processes and three subprocesses. In turn, the data flow sequence was described. To assist the reader in getting a better idea of the data flow, the process is defined further in figure 6.14. The use of sequencing, logic, and repetition is represented by dotted lines. The arrowhead indicates the direction of data flow.

Warnier-Orr diagrams can be used in a variety of contexts other than describing system activities. They have been used to define system outputs and inputs, to define data bases, to plan projects, and to design computer programs, since they can be used as a hierarchical notational tool. Although these diagrams describe the logical activities and data within a system, they do not indicate relationships to data bases (and vice versa), nor do they indicate activity relationships.

When relating this structured methodology to system flowcharts, it can be shown that for any flowchart there is an equivalent Warnier-Orr diagram.

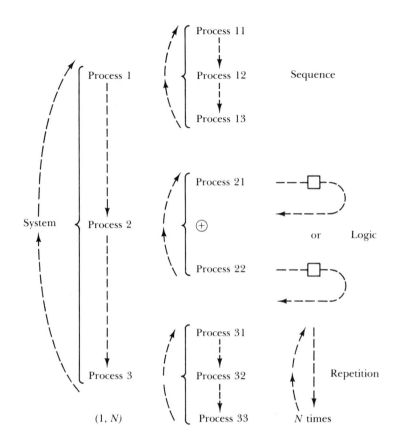

FIGURE 6.14
Warnier-Orr diagram illustrating the data flow for sequence, logic, and repetitive processes.

However, Warnier-Orr diagrams have two important advantages over system flowcharts. The first is the ease with which one can communicate by using these diagrams. The second advantage is the transparency of the structure of the problem and the natural way in which the structure is presented. Thus, Warnier-Orr diagrams can communicate the essentials of a system without losing the reader in a myriad of detail.

RAW MATERIALS INVENTORY ILLUSTRATION. Referring to the earlier illustrations of our example in system flowcharts (figure 6.7) and data flow diagrams (figure 6.12), the first item to the left in figure 6.15 is the raw material inventory system. The system is then broken down into three major processes. The right side of the first major process (processing raw materials receipt) is further decomposed into counting raw materials received and entering raw materials received. Counting raw materials is decomposed twice further: storage in inventory stock control department, and entering of physical inventory records. Similarly, entering raw materials received is decomposed twice: addition to raw materials inventory, and checking for excess raw materials on hand. Just as the first major process was decomposed, so was the second major process, processing requisitions for raw materials, and the third, processing physical inventory count changes. One final item should be

235

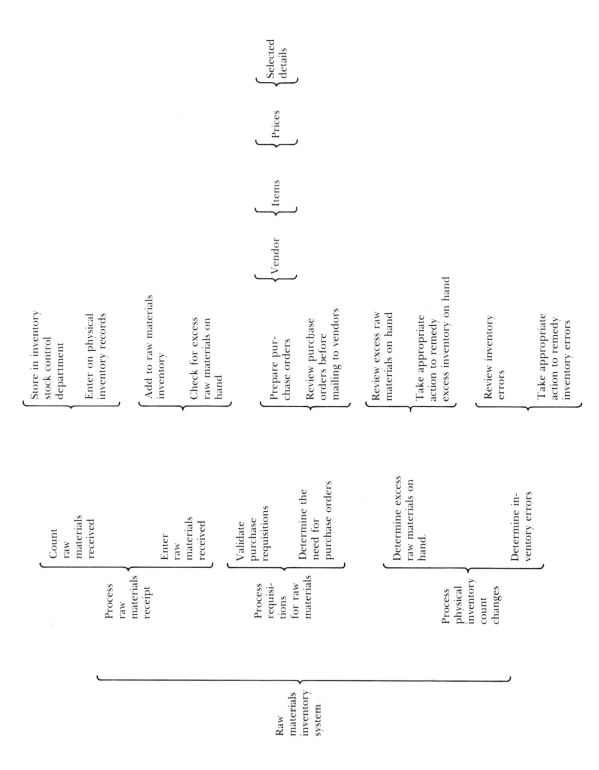

FIGURE 6.15 A Warnier-Orr diagram for processing raw materials (as set forth previously in figures 6.7 and 6.12).

noted. Any time a document is to be output, the data required on the document are listed to its right. Referring to the figure, purchase orders entail vendor, items, prices, and selected details to be printed on the order.

Summary—Structured Design Tools

Data Flow Diagrams (DFD) show the detailed flow of data within a system. They are useful in portraying a "snapshot" of some part of a system. The four common symbols used are:

- □ double square—source or destination of data
- □ arrow—flow of data
- □ rounded rectangle or circle—process which transforms flows of data
- □ open-ended rectangle—store of data

In its simplest form (based on these four symbols), a DFD consists of a rounded rectangle or a circle representing a transformation process with arrows connecting the rounded rectangles or the circles to illustrate the process flow. In addition, DFD incorporates the use of a square to represent outside entities which interact with the system and an open-sided rectangle to denote data storage, that is, some type of data file. All these symbols are tied together by arrows to show the data flow from the entities to processes to storage, and so forth. The rounded rectangle or the circle notes that a transformation takes place, but does not describe how.

The rules regarding data flow diagrams relate to:

- □ sources and destinations
- □ data flows
- □ transforms
- □ subdiagrams

These rules are based upon logical thinking.

Warnier-Orr Diagrams (WOD) are used in both the system and programming design phases for representing hierarchies. The diagram flows top-down, left to right, and utilizes the bracket as its major symbol. These diagrams allow for further functional decomposition for greater detail. The system name is listed to the left of the bracket. The processes (i.e., the steps) that make up the system are listed top-down to the right of the bracket.

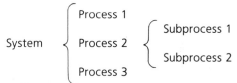

If the systems analyst desires further detail, each process may be subdivided further by placing a bracket to the right of the process and listing the subprocesses. The systems analyst can continue to decompose to the level desired following these same rules. The diagram allows for a single repetition of pro-

237

cesses (following the processes top-down), multiple repetition using the (1, N) statement, and decision-making choices between performing two processes.

COMPARISON OF TRADITIONAL AND CURRENT STRUCTURED SYSTEMS ANALYSIS AND DESIGN TOOLS

Now that the traditional and structured tools of systems analysis and design have been described and illustrated, a comparison will be helpful. Fundamentally, the motivation for the development of the newer structured tools was the addition of discipline to the development of a new management information system. From this perspective, both the systems analyst and user are working within a more structured environment that encourages a functional decomposition approach that starts at the top and goes down to the lowest level. Breaking down the system into its components (modules) not only provides both the systems analyst and the user with the desired level of detail, but also enables them to examine levels and components more critically than with traditional approaches.

Perhaps the most important benefit of the new structured tools is improved systems analyst–user communication that comes from the development of a shared logical model of the new MIS. The system must be understood by both parties to provide proper system inputs, processing, and outputs as well as to ensure that all system requirements are defined accurately and completely. Past experience with information systems installations shows that systems analysts and users conceptualize situations differently. The failure to establish a semantic bridge between these different views helps to explain many past information system failures. A related issue is the maintainability and the ease of modification of the system logical model. A process can be added or deleted without requiring diagram restructuring as compared to previous flowcharting.

Because the newer structured tools are mechanisms for building a logical model of the new MIS, the systems analyst and user can settle on a single mutually satisfactory viewpoint using the vocabulary and set of symbols of the technique. Both groups can productively discuss the form as well as the transformation of the system as they relate to the shared logical model. In short, they can communicate to a degree impossible with previous system flowcharts. Users can also become more involved in the structured systems design due to their increased understanding of the new MIS.

Closely related to communication is the amount of training required for understanding. With structured tools, there are few rules to understand and few symbols to memorize, and the diagrams are constructed in English in a top-down manner. In contrast, traditional flowcharts have many symbols and rules governing their use. As a consequence, more training time is required. Without this training time, the communicability of the system is low.

As will be noted in the next chapter, systems analysts begin analysis and design by working with users of the new system to identify the tasks the system must perform. The analysts then devise a plan to produce a system that meets users' requirements. This may sound easy, but it is the point at which problems often arise. Because users' ambiguous English statements must be translated twice—first by systems analysts who shape them into workable plans and second by programmers who then transform these plans into syntactically precise computer languages—the resulting outcome may not reflect the original intention.

To assist in making the translation more precise, systems analysts have been working to create formal approaches to design that provide a framework for interpretation. These methodologies aim to help the systems analysts cover all the essential points in their analyses, and then to help them develop designs that are complete, accurate, and easy for systems analysts to implement. Recent research has produced a variety of tools that automate much of the designer's work, enforce a methodology's standards, and ease the translation of plans into programs. Some of the newer tools allow systems analysts to create diagrams and manage documents—two important functions for converting concepts into specifications. The newest products, which automatically translate design specifications into executable code, allow analysts and users to pass their instructions directly to the computer. And project-management packages, which help development teams allocate resources and plot their work schedules, make the entire design life cycle more efficient. These functions are integrated in some packages.

Microcomputer Systems Analysis and Design Packages

Action Diagrammer, from Database Design, Inc., is an example of an entry-level microcomputer package that runs on the IBM PC. As its name suggests, it automates the production of action diagrams. These diagrams allow the software designer to move from the general to the particular when identifying and explaining a system's components. The designer builds an action diagram by inserting levels of detail into a list of statements that describe the system in broad terms. Vertical brackets enclosing listed statements of operations represent program modules and indicate the system's basic structure. By adding modules and nesting brackets to embellish earlier ideas, the systems analyst can move from a system sketch to executable code. At the most detailed level, Action Diagrammer generates control statements for a variety of third- and fourth-generation languages.

Somewhat more complex than Action Diagrammer are tools built around data flow diagrams that help users and analysts visualize the systems they are building. As shown earlier in the chapter, data flow diagrams use boxes, circles, and other symbols to represent processes and data files. Arrows con-

DEVELOPMENT,
IMPLEMENTATION,
AND CONTROL OF
EFFECTIVE
MANAGEMENT
INFORMATION
SYSTEMS

necting the symbols show how the data flow among them. Like action diagrams, data flow diagrams can depict various levels of detail of a system. For example, at the highest level, the entry of an order might be shown as a procedure in a distribution system. The next lower level would show the procedures that comprise order entry and the flow of information among them.

Detailed, written descriptions of processes, data, and their relationships are the specifications from which the programmers—or code generators—work. These must be maintained as separate documentation, which when done manually requires a prodigious clerical effort. Most systems analysts would be grateful if the design tools built around data flow diagrams provided only graphic support, relieving them from the tedious task of drawing diagrams by hand. But the tools have an even more important function: they manage written documentation and provide some verification of the design's logic. As an example, Design 1, offered by Arthur Andersen & Company, independently or as a component of Method 1 is a personal-computer package that manages documentation. It has a system dictionary that cross-references related documentation entries. The package reports on the system-wide impact of design changes, points out processes that have been referenced but not described, and performs other checks on the design's logic. It also allows systems analysts to develop input forms and report prototypes that simulate how the system will finally operate.

Another package, Structure(s) (designed by Ken Orr and Associates), creates structured data flow diagrams and manages detailed documentation on the IBM PC AT and XT as well as IBM mainframes. The vendor's code generator produces COBOL code from the completed design. Still another microcomputer package is Excelerator, a design tool from Intech that runs on the IBM PC XT. It provides graphics for creating data flow diagrams and diagrams that depict a system's file structures. This package, shown in figure 6.16, also facilitates the designing of reports and data entry screens. Documentation is cross-referenced and keyed to the diagrams. By placing the cursor on a diagram symbol and pressing a button, the designer can call up either another diagram that shows the element in greater detail or the associated documentation. The system also produces a variety of reports that help the designer verify the design's consistency. These and other microcomputer system analysis and design tools are shown in figure 6.17.

Mainframe Systems Analysis and Design Packages

Microcomputers are fine when systems analysts communicate one-on-one with users. But they pose a problem when many analysts on a large project try to communicate with each other. Because only one systems analyst at a time can use a microcomputer, system design teams using stand-alone equipment for large projects must either share disks or communicate via local-area networks. They also need a system for managing design changes and tracking design versions.

Addressing this situation are systems analysis and design tools for multiple users. Maestro, a design and development tool from Four-Phase Systems,

FIGURE 6.16
Excelerator is a design
tool that runs on the
IBM PC XT for
creating data flow
diagrams and diagrams
that depict a system's
file structures.
(Courtesy Index
Technology
Corporation,
Cambridge,
Massachusetts)

for example, provides and enforces a structured methodology. It allows an organization to define the elements necessary for various types of documentation, then prompts analysts to include all of them. Systems analysts describe their systems with *pseudocode*—highly formatted English statements that adhere to Maestro's methodology. A menu at the bottom of the screen helps analysts formulate the pseudocode. Maestro then produces charts that depict the system. The package also generates much of the third-generation code (in most cases COBOL) needed to make the system run. The original pseudocode appears as notations embedded in the program.

Pride-ASDM from M. Bryce & Associates is a mainframe package that emphasizes logical design (descriptions of what the user wants a system to do) over physical design (how the tasks are to be done). Analysis begins with descriptions of desired outputs, such as the frequency of a report, required response times, and the information to be included. Pride-ASDM automatically analyzes these elements, groups related items into subsystems, and determines which data must be input or stored and which procedures performed

241

Vendor	Package	Requirements
AGS Management Systems	SDM/Structured	Methodology
	SDM/70	Methodology
	ISDM	IBM PC
Arthur Andersen	Honeywell	Honeywell DPS 8
	Middleware and Dictionary Systems	DPS 6
	Method/1	Methodology with IBM PC component
	Design/1	IBM PC and PC XT
M. Bryce & Associates	Pride-ASDM	Wide range of minis and mainframes
	Pride-SDM	Methodology
	PMC^2	Wide range of minis and mainframes
Database Design	Action Diagrammer	IBM PC
	Data Designer	IBM mainframes
	Hierarchical Design Aid	Same systems
	Information Planner	Same systems
Deltacom	Prism	IBM PC; IBM mainframes
Higher Order Software	Use.It	DEC VAX
IBM	Plancode/1	IBM mainframes
	Generalized CICS	IBM mainframes
Intech	Excelerator	IBM PC and PC XT
ISDOS	PSL/PSA	Wide range of minis and mainframes
	PSA-SA	IBM PC and compatibles
McDonnell Douglas Automation	Stradis	IBM mainframes
	DFD Draw	IBM PC
Management & Computer Services	Systemacs	Methodology
	Estimacs	IBM PC XT, Apple II Plus, IIe
National Systems	Trac I	IBM PC, DEC VAX
	Trac II	IBM PC, DEC VAX
Ken Orr & Assoc.	Structure(s)	IBM S/38, IBM mainframes and PCMs
	Structure(s)/PC	IBM PC XT, PC AT

FIGURE 6.17
Computerized approach to systems analysis and design tools—microcomputers and mainframes.

Shawware	SDDA	IBM S/34, S/36
Synerlogic	Act/1	IBM mainframes
Visible Systems	Visible Analyst	IBM PC, PC XT, PC AT

FIGURE 6.17
(continued)

to produce the desired results. The analyst sees several iterations of design changes, noting the effects each decision has on the system. The automated analysis also checks the design's consistency to guarantee, for example, that it does not contain inputs that are never used. Only when the logical design satisfies users does the systems analyst begin to develop detailed specifications for each subsystem.

Another mainframe package, Problem Statement Language/Problem Statement Analyzer (PSL/PSA), from ISDOS, allows systems analysts of detailed systems models to define a large variety of "objects" which, unlike data flow diagrams, include both processes and files and their relationships. The PSA section of the package performs rigorous checks on a design's validity. PSA also creates extensive documentation and automatically checks the consistency of work done by the members of large development teams.

For projects that require high reliability, Use.It (from Higher Order Software) takes a different approach to systems design. Based on complex mathematical formulas, Use.It provides specifications that are mathematically provable. As a result, codes generated from these specifications are free of errors in logic. These mainframe systems analysis and design tools and others are set forth in figure 6.17.

PROTOTYPING NEW SYSTEMS DESIGN

Beyond the prior design approaches is another one called *prototyping.* Under current methodology of the system development process (i.e., the traditional life cycle approach or the structured development approach, explained in the next chapter), the management information system comes to its final state prior to implementation. This represents the first and only complete specification of the new system. Unfortunately, it is available too late in the cycle to permit a thorough evaluation early enough to preclude costly systems redefinitions.

To overcome this problem, prototyping may be appropriate. A "prototype" is defined as the model after which anything is formed. The term prototyping, then, refers to making a full-scale working product, but one not intended for fielding (implementing). It is intended to be the basis for the system to be fielded. In practice, users provide general system specifications while working with systems analysts, who develop the prototype. The users, then, try it out and systems analysts modify the system as needed to meet the users' detailed specifications. In some cases, the users accomplish the proto-

DEVELOPMENT,
IMPLEMENTATION,
AND CONTROL OF
EFFECTIVE
MANAGEMENT
INFORMATION
SYSTEMS

typing process on their own. Prototyping sometimes can be viewed from another perspective, in which the prototype turns out to be the final product that will be fielded. However, it should be fielded with the full expectation that many changes will follow.

The Prototyping Process as Practiced Today

Currently, many large companies, such as Procter & Gamble and RCA, employ prototyping to great advantage in developing new management information systems, especially large and complex ones. Prototypes also are widely used in decision support systems that evolve over time.

For these companies, the prototype process consists of the following items:

1. The software prototype is a live, working system and not just an idea on paper. Therefore, it can be evaluated by the designer and/or the eventual end users through actual use. It performs work; it does not just simulate it.

2. The prototype may become the actual production system, or it may be replaced by a conventionally coded production system. Thus, the prototype may or may not be discarded.

3. The prototype's purpose is to test assumptions about users' requirements and/or a system design architecture, and/or perhaps even test the logic of a program.

4. The prototype is created quickly—often within hours, days, or weeks—rather than over months or years. In the past, many people felt that software prototyping was impractical because it could not be performed quickly. With only conventional programming methods available, companies would not accept developing two versions of a system. So MIS departments had to create their production systems "right" the first time around. But now some programmers are making innovative use of various types of software tools to get prototypes up and running quickly—tools such as the data management systems (DMS). DMS generally involves the use of a data base management system, plus retrieval facilities for queries and reports, selection, and sorting features.

5. The prototype is relatively inexpensive to build, less expensive than coding in a conventional high-level language. Software tools make prototyping less expensive because they create most, if not all, of the code.

6. Prototyping is an iterative process. It begins with a simple prototype that performs only a few of the basic functions in question. These functions need not be performed elegantly or efficiently. But it is expected that, through use of the prototype, systems analysts or end users will discover new requirements and refinements which will then be incorporated in the next version. In essence, it is a trial and error process in which one builds a version of the prototype, uses it, evaluates it, then revises it or starts over on a new version. Each version

performs more of the desired functions, in an increasingly efficient manner.

When prototyping is used in new systems design, generally in-depth user interviewing is not important. This is because user specifications are no longer based on how well the systems analyst interprets the users' spoken requirements. Rather, the specifications are based on the demonstrated working prototype. Furthermore, the systems analyst does not need to uncover all requirements at the beginning, since each version of the prototype helps the user refine the essential requirements and identify missing ones.

In addition, different system procedures are utilized in prototyping. In a conventional system development process, user requirements are defined in a specification document, which is then approved by the user. Only after that phase is completed does the design of the new system begin. On the other hand, requirements and design evolve together in prototyping. The development of the prototype deals with both the requirements from the users' view and the design from the systems analysts' view. Hence, the user and the systems analyst are more in agreement throughout the prototyping process than they are in a conventional system development process.

Prototyping and Programming

Prototyping can also help in programming. A software prototype is a scaled-down version of the final program that focuses on the functions the user requires. It is studied by user and programmer to see if it meets specified requirements, needs additional options, and can be modified to meet future business changes. The real software package built is then modeled on this prototype. Although this prototype may cost thousands, users will save hundreds of thousands of dollars since the major cost in software development begins after the initial software is completed. This is particularly true where a large part of the cost of software (i.e., 60 percent) is in the area of program maintenance. In other words, after the software is delivered, a large percentage of the code must be rewritten to fit requirements that were never specified properly. In addition, still more code must be rewritten as users' needs change. Typically, the cost of changing a software system after building it is many times the cost of developing it. Thus, prototyping can save considerable time and expense over the traditional approach to programming.

EFFECTIVE MIS PRACTICE—IMPROVING A MANAGEMENT INFORMATION SYSTEM

Although there are a number of effective design tools for assisting the systems analysts, non-system-related problems may limit the use of a new MIS. Typically, the management information system is underutilized and poorly organized because management lacks understanding of its purpose or product. William T. Spencer, president of Citicorp, succinctly defined the ideal function of an MIS as producing "exactly enough of the most relevant information at

DEVELOPMENT,
IMPLEMENTATION,
AND CONTROL OF
EFFECTIVE
MANAGEMENT
INFORMATION
SYSTEMS

precisely the right moment to produce an infallible management decision and at the least possible cost."[2] For MIS to be effective, it must be tailored to fit a company's managerial philosophy, long- and short-term goals, internal structure, budget, and, most importantly, its existing communications network. In fact, several years and a substantial investment using newer design methodologies may be spent in making the system truly responsive to user needs.

Several common pitfalls in the operation of an MIS can either effectively sabotage an existing system or hinder the development of a new one. Here are four pitfalls, followed by suggestions on how to avoid them.[3]

First, there may be inactivity at the highest levels of management. Some top executives may fear committing themselves to the development and use of a management information system. They may feel that they would be locking themselves and the company into a decision-making process they are uncomfortable with or unaccustomed to. Or they may be skeptical that the system can provide them with valid information. Frequently, management will procrastinate or transfer the decision to a subordinate who is unqualified either to develop or administer an MIS.

Unfortunately, the result will be an inadequately functioning system viewed with increasing suspicion by executives who feel their original doubts have been justified. The more inadequately the system functions, the graver management's misgivings become, and the less support any improvement plans are given, until the MIS is ignored or abandoned. Obviously, then, it is essential that the company's top executives become intimately involved with both the design and operation of the MIS.

Second, goals and needs can be insufficiently defined. Unless the kind of information the company will require from the MIS is defined at the outset, the system cannot respond accurately or relevantly. Top-level executives, as well as department managers, must identify clearly the types of information they expect to derive from the system. This process is especially vital since false assumptions about the benefits and potential of an MIS can lead later to frustration and disappointment.

Third, management can be ignorant of the problems that may be created by the human response to the system. An MIS is a cooperative effort involving both technology and psychology. Because each organization has its own particular psychological nuances, the system must be designed to accommodate them and still permit the most efficient operation. Such factors as employee aspirations, job satisfaction, work attitudes, and human interaction must be taken into account. An adjustment period during which executives are permitted to explore and become comfortable with the system will pay off handsomely later in increased cooperation and enthusiasm. Along these same lines, the MIS must be viewed at all times as a tool and not the ultimate decision maker. Complete reliance on MIS information without consideration of human judgment can result in an unpleasant, nonproductive business environment.

[2]Mitchell B. Salmere, "How to Improve a Management Information System," *Infosystems,* November 1981, p. 90.

[3]Ibid, pp. 90 and 91.

Fourth, inflexibility can be a problem. An MIS may be highly efficient at the beginning, but unless flexibility is built in, the system may quickly become antiquated and unresponsive. Potential changes in growth stages, communications systems, and data processing resources must be allowed for and expected. An ongoing review of the system's performance should be conducted along with a thorough, yearly evaluation by all who have access to and rely on the system, particularly top executives. This will prevent it from becoming too rigid and too complex before it is too late.

Because each MIS is as unique as the organization it serves, one company's approach may be unworkable elsewhere. These general suggestions, however, are guidelines that can be adapted to a specific need. The information provided by an effectively operating MIS can be combined with human intelligence, intuition, and judgment to become an extremely valuable tool for any manager.

CHAPTER SUMMARY

The chapter opened with a discussion of the systems approach to effective MIS, followed by the essentials of system flowcharting. Fundamentally, the top-down approach provides the underlying framework for most of the structured design methodology set forth in the chapter. The structured design methods—data flow diagrams (DFD) and Warnier-Orr diagrams (WOD) along with their computerized packages—offer greater opportunities for improving systems productivity than is possible with traditional design methodologies such as system flowcharting. Similarly, prototyping new systems is another method for not only improving productivity, but also ensuring that the user gets the system wanted now rather than later, or possibly never. Using newer design methodologies of management information systems, then, is essential to improving overall organizational productivity.

Before the implementation of the newer design methodologies, management must realize the benefits that the new (existing and off-the-shelf) technologies offer. To do this, management must organize itself, that is, its resources (including information), to meet what will surely be even greater demands in the future. The "winners" of tomorrow will be those organizations that can react quickly with an effective MIS in a rapidly changing environment. It takes a great effort to acquire the "fleetness of foot" needed to organize information that meets user needs not only today, but also tomorrow.

QUESTIONS

1. **a.** Define the systems approach to effective MIS.
   b. How important is this approach for the implementation of effective MIS?
2. **a.** What are the values of system flowcharts?
   b. What are the shortcomings of system flowcharts?

DEVELOPMENT,
IMPLEMENTATION,
AND CONTROL OF
EFFECTIVE
MANAGEMENT
INFORMATION
SYSTEMS

3. What important concept underlies structured design tools? Explain.

4. **a.** Contrast data flow diagrams and system flowcharts.
   b. What is the importance of data flow decision rules?

5. **a.** Contrast data flow diagrams and Warnier-Orr diagrams.
   b. Are both applicable to designing management information systems for small, medium, and large organizations?

6. **a.** How important are the newer computerized systems analysis and design packages in improving the productivity of systems analysts and programmers?
   b. Are mainframe systems analysis and design packages better than microcomputer packages? Why or why not?

7. Of the methods given in the chapter, is there one best structured design method for small-size companies? For medium-size companies? For large-size companies?

8. How is prototyping different from the standard system development process (i.e., a life-cycle approach to new management information systems)?

PROBLEMS

9. The systems approach to effective MIS is forward looking in that it looks to the present and the future as a means of controlling operations. This is opposed to the traditional approach that is backward looking, i.e., that uses historical facts and depends on feedback after measurement of the output. Relating the traditional approach to order processing, show how it can be improved by using the systems approach. Similarly, illustrate how the traditional approach to inventory control can be improved by using the systems approach.

10. In the chapter, several flowcharting methods were given for illustrating the flow of data and their input (i.e., information) from one step, operation, etc., to another. These included system flowcharts, data flow diagrams, and Warnier-Orr diagrams. When these techniques are used, describe specifically how knowledge about the flow of planning and control information can benefit typical business managers and their support personnel. In turn, contrast how these techniques are useful to typical management information systems managers and their support personnel. Also, describe how information derived from these flowcharting techniques would assist in the planning and control of specific sales plans or specific budgets for a typical business manager as opposed to a typical systems project manager.

11. The manager of information systems consulting for a CPA firm uses Action Programmer, a microcomputer-based systems analysis and design package, in strategic planning for systems and in analyzing and describing organizational structures. She finds the package's ability to "expand and contract" levels of detail particularly useful when she explains a system's structure to users. "A designer can choose the level of detail appropriate to his or her audience." she says. "A designer might use more general information to formulate policy with top executives, then introduce additional details when discussing implementation with managers." In light of these capabilities of this microcomputer package, list three advantages over a noncomputer approach. Do you see any disadvantage with the microcomputer package approach?

12. A senior systems specialist uses Excelerator to help users understand a new manufacturing resource-planning package his employer is installing. Rather than

design a system from the ground up, the systems specialist used the tool to describe both the existing, primarily manual system and the new system. The technique provides users with "before and after" pictures of the firm's manufacturing resource-planning system. Because the specialist is able to experiment with changes in quick succession, it is easier to refine ideas—a big plus when the individual and users work out ideas together at the IBM PC. "I was used to the scribble-and-erase technique," the systems specialist says. "With Excelerator, I can complete a design in a fraction of the time it would take to do it manually." Do you agree or disagree with his comments? Why or why not?

13. At the end of the chapter, the use of prototyping as a new systems design technique was given. Because prototyping is essentially a full-scale working model of the real system, give two prototyping examples where users can modify the system as needed to meet the user's detailed specifications. From another viewpoint, cite two examples where the prototype turns out to be the final product which will be fielded. It should be noted that the prototype fielded may require many or few changes as deemed necessary over time.

PROJECTS

14. To effect more efficient and economical order processing, the Corning Company has updated their old computerized system to a new management information system. Daily, customer orders are received via mail and serve as input to the system. Orders, after they are batched and control totals are established, are forwarded to the data-entry section for recording and verifying onto magnetic disk. Next, the computer sorts the transactions (items to be shipped) by customer number (first computer run). An error listing is produced along with control totals (for checking with the beginning control totals), and a transaction file (by customer number sequence) is produced. In turn, this file provides the necessary input for the combined inventory updating and billing run (second computer run). In addition to updating inventory files for items shipped, the customer master shipping orders are printed along with control totals for comparison with the first totals of customer orders established.

Based upon the foregoing facts, prepare a system flowchart, a data flow diagram, or a Warnier-Orr diagram to illustrate the flow of inputs and outputs from the first computer run to the second computer run. Also, show the balancing of control totals where deemed necessary.

15. To assist marketing management in getting greater control over their salespeople, the Grosse Company has decided to install a new management information system. Fundamentally, a weekly master charge magnetic disk file which has been previously sorted by customer account number provides input for the computerized sales report run. The weekly and year-to-date (YTD) customer sales master disk files are updated and a weekly and year-to-date sales report by customer is printed (first computer run). The aforementioned file is then sorted by salesperson number and written on a magnetic disk file (second computer run) which, in turn, provides necessary input for printing a weekly and year-to-date report by salesperson (third computer run). The totals of the third run are then compared to the weekly and year-to-date sales report by customer.

Based upon the foregoing factors, prepare a system flowchart, a data flow diagram, or a Warnier-Orr diagram that depicts the flow of inputs and outputs for

DEVELOPMENT,
IMPLEMENTATION,
AND CONTROL OF
EFFECTIVE
MANAGEMENT
INFORMATION
SYSTEMS

the three computer runs. Also, show the balancing of control totals where deemed necessary.

16. The International Electrical Corporation manufactures and sells a wide variety of electrical devices around the world. Through its sales agencies, it supplies more than 500 independent dealers from company-owned warehouses. Intense competition both at home and abroad has made management very aware of the need for a better MIS, directed toward on-line information. An MIS project is currently being undertaken. The new management information system must tie the following to headquarters: (a) independent dealers (to provide sales reports), (b) company-owned warehouses (to provide inventory, shipping, and receiving information), (c) sales agencies (to provide sales reports and inventory information), and (d) factories (to provide information on production, inventory, and shipping). Needless to say, the development of an MIS for such a world-wide corporation requires considerable planning and design work prior to undertaking the actual implementation.

Due to the complexity of the design effort, the MIS manager has decided to utilize a functional decomposition approach for breaking the design aspects into manageable parts. Since you have been assigned to assist the manager, you are to use a functional decomposition design technique. Relationships between the dealers, warehouses, agencies, and factories, then, are to be shown along with the appropriate information needed by these organizational units.

BIBLIOGRAPHY

Adamski, L. "Prototyping." *Computerworld,* May 6, 1985.

Ahituv, N., and Neumann, S. *Principles of Information Systems for Management.* Dubuque, IA: William C. Brown, 1982.

Alavi, M. "An Assessment of the Prototyping Approach to Information Systems Development." *Communications of the ACM,* June 1984.

————. "The Evolution of Information Systems Development Approach: Some Field Observations." *Data Base,* Spring 1984.

Appleton, D. S. "Data-Driven Prototyping." *Datamation,* November 1983.

Bernstein, A. "Shortcut to System Design." *Business Computer Systems,* June 1985.

Boar, B. H. *Application Prototyping, A Requirements Definition Strategy for the 80s.* New York: John Wiley & Sons, 1984.

————. "Prototyping." *Computerworld,* September 12, 1984.

Bowman, B.,; Davis, G.,; and Wetherbe, J. "Modeling for MIS." *Datamation,* July 1981.

Cheney, P. H.; Mann, R. I.; and Amoroso, D. L. "Organizational Factors Affecting the Success of End-User Computing." *Journal of Management Information Systems,* Summer 1986.

Connell, J., and Brice, L. "Rapid Prototyping." *Datamation,* August 15, 1984.

Conner, D. A. "Applications Systems Development Methodologies." *Computerworld,* February 28, 1982.

Couger, J. D.; Cotter, M. A.; and Knapp, R. W. *Advanced System Development/Feasibility Techniques,* sec. ed. New York: John Wiley & Sons, 1982.

Davis, W. S. *Tools and Techniques for Structured Systems Analysis and Design.* Reading, MA: Addison-Wesley Publishing Company, 1983.

DeMarco, T. *Structured Analysis and System Specification.* Englewood Cliffs, NJ: Prentice-Hall, 1979.

Earl, M. J. "Prototype Systems for Accounting Information and Control." *Data Base,* Winter-Spring 1982.

Edwards, P. "The Designing Mind." *Datamation,* September 15, 1985.

Forest, R. B. "Top-Down Interview Design." *Infosystems,* February 1982.

Frenkel, K. A. "Toward Automating the Software-Development Cycle." *Communications of the ACM,* June 1985.

Friend, D. "Color Graphics Information Systems Boost Productivity." *Mini-Micro Systems,* May 1980.

———. "Can Graphics Raise Executive Productivity?" *Software News,* October 5, 1981.

Gane, C., and Sarson, T. *Structured Systems Analysis: Tools and Techniques.* Englewood Cliffs, NJ: Prentice-Hall, 1979.

Gremillion, L. L., and Pyburn, P. "Breaking the Systems Development Bottleneck." *Harvard Business Review,* March-April 1983. ✳

Grupe, F. "Tips for Better Worksheet Documentation." *Lotus,* August 1985.

Guimaraes, T. "A Study of Application Program Development Techniques." *Communications of the ACM,* May 1985.

Hodil, E. D., and Richardson, G. L. "New Faces for Old Systems." *Computer Decisions,* July 15, 1985.

Johnson, J. R. "A Prototypical Success Story." *Datamation,* November 1983. ✳

Jokiel, R. A. "Pitfalls to Avoid in Prototyping New Applications." *Management Information System Week,* September 8, 1986.

Katz, B. "Building a Three Dimensional Work Breakdown Structure." *Data Base,* Summer 1985.

King, D. "Current Methodologies in Structured Design." *Computerworld,* October 12, 1981.

Klein, M. "Information Politics." *Datamation,* August 1, 1985. ✳

Koffler, R. "A Scientific Approach to Human Engineering." *Computerworld,* February 10, 1986.

Kull, D. "Tooling for Design." *Computer Decisions,* February 12, 1985.

Lantz, K. E. *The Prototyping Methodology.* Englewood Cliffs, NJ: Prentice-Hall, 1986.

Leavitt, D. "The Proper Design Tools Can Bring Improved Productivity." *Software News,* February 1985.

———. "Application Development Systems Help Get Systematic." *Software News,* March 1985.

———. "Finding the Right Niche in Programmer Productivity Tools." *Software News,* May 1985.

———. "Optimizers Aren't Just for Execution Any More." *Software News,* December 1985.

———. "Design Tools: The Real Starting Point." *Software News,* February 1986.

———. "Application Development Systems Mean Speed, Quality." *Software News,* March 1986.

Martin, J. *An Information Systems Manifesto.* Englewood Cliffs, NJ: Prentice-Hall, 1984.

Martin, J., and McClure, C. *Diagramming Techniques for Analysts and Programmers.* Englewood Cliffs, NJ: Prentice-Hall, 1985.

Mason, R. E. A., and Carey, T. T. "Prototyping Interactive Information Systems." *Communications of the ACM,* May 1983.

Meirovitz, E., and Goldberg, D. "Programmers: Do It With Tools." *The DEC Professional,* January 1986.

Messerich, P. "Prototyping Gives Users More Enthusiasm." *Computerworld,* May 28, 1984.

O'Dell, P. "Development Methods Meld." *Computer Decisions,* March 25, 1986.

Orr, K. T. *Structured Systems Development.* New York: Yourdon, 1977.

———. *Structured Systems Design.* New York: Yourdon, 1978.

———. "Systems Methodologies for the 80s." *Infosystems,* June 1981.

———. *Structured Requirements Definition.* Topeka, KS: Ken Orr and Associates, 1981.

Pages-Jones, M. *The Practical Guide to Structured Systems Design.* New York: Yourdon, 1980.

Panzl, D. J. "A Method for Evaluating Software Development Techniques." *The Journal of Systems and Software,* June 1981.

Parikh, G. "Structured Maintenance, The Warnier/Orr Way." *Computerworld,* September 21, 1981.

Rhodes, W. L. "Information Systems Management, A Hybrid Blossoms." *Infosystems,* January 1981.

Ruprecht, M. M. "Is Your Organization Ready for Systems Integration?" *Office Systems,* April 1986.

Salmere, M. B. "How to Improve a Management Information System." *Infosystems,* November 1981.

Samid, G. "Modified Top-Down Design." *Datamation,* November 1981. ✳

Scharer, L. L. "General Problem-Solving Methods Will Ease Your Move to Prototyping, If You Use Them." *Computerworld,* May 28, 1984.

Seagle, J. P., and Belardo, S. "The Feature Chart: A Tool for Communicating the Analysis for a Decision Support System." *Information and Management,* vol. 10, no. 1, 1986.

Sheil, B. "Power Tools for Programmers." *Datamation,* February 1983. ✳

Shneiderman, B. "How to Design with the User in Mind." *Datamation,* February 1983. ✳

Smith, W. "Alternative Approaches for Successful Prototyping." *Computerworld,* September 16, 1985.

Teague, L. C., and Pidgeon, C. W. *Structured Analysis Methods for Computer Information Systems.* Chicago: SRA, Inc., 1984.

Thierauf, R. J. *Decision Support Systems for Effective Planning and Control—A Case Study Approach.* Englewood Cliffs, NJ: Prentice-Hall, 1982.

———. *Systems Analysis and Design—A Case Study Approach,* sec. ed. Columbus, OH: Charles E. Merrill Publishing Company, 1986.

Townsend, D. F. "Systems Analysis: Key to the Future." *Datamation,* October 1980. ✳

Troy, D. A., and Zweben, S. H. "Measuring the Quality of Structured Designs." *The Journal of Systems and Software,* June 1981.

Vessey, I., and Weber, R. "Structured Tools and Conditional Logic: An Empirical Investigation." *Communications of the ACM,* January 1986.

Vignone, A. F. "Beyond Structured Design, Designing with Data Models." *Computerworld,* July 20, 1981.

Walsh, R. J. "System Development Methodology," *The DEC Professional,* Part I, January 1983; Part II, May 1983; Part IIIa, July 1983; Part IIIb, September 1983; Part IV, November 1983; and Part V, May 1984.

Weinberg, V. *Structured Analysis.* Englewood Cliffs, NJ: Prentice-Hall, 1980.

Whieldon, D. "Prototyping: Shortcut to Applications." *Computer Decisions,* June 1984.

Witten, I. H., and Bromwell, B. "A System for Interactive Viewing of Structured Documents." *Communications of the ACM,* March 1985.

Young, T. R. "Superior Prototype." *Datamation,* May 15, 1984. ✳

Yourdon, E. *Managing the Structured Techniques.* New York: Yourdon, 1979.

Yourdon, E., and Constantine, L. L. *Structured Design, Fundamentals of a Discipline of Computer Program and Systems Design.* Englewood Cliffs, NJ: Prentice-Hall, 1979.

CHAPTER 7

Analysis and Design of Management Information Systems

ISSUES

What guidelines should be followed for successful development of management information systems?

What are the phases in the development of management information systems, and what is the primary objective of each phase?

What important activities are performed during the systems analysis phase?

How are MIS alternatives identified and evaluated?

What are the essential contents of the exploratory survey report issued to top management?

What practical approach to systems design should be followed without reservation?

OUTLINE

INTRODUCTION TO ANALYSIS AND DESIGN OF MANAGEMENT INFORMATION SYSTEMS

During the 1980s and beyond, computers will evolve into utilities consisting of a number of specialized nodes and terminals in a DDP network. Low communication costs and standardized communications protocol will open the door for greater resource sharing, allowing even the nontechnical person to take advantage of a computer's processing power. Additionally, as hardware prices fall, the continuing influx of microcomputers is even now making some relatively new systems obsolete. Overall, future MIS will only further emphasize the need for an MIS development process that recognizes the shortening life cycles of new computers and systems.

Initially in this chapter, guidelines in the MIS development process are outlined, followed by discussion of the systems analysis phase. The result of such analysis is an examination of the benefits and costs of the present system to determine whether new system alternatives would prove beneficial. A detailed investigation of these important matters is contained in the exploratory survey report to top management. The feasibility (or infeasibility) of applying newer systems equipment and procedures is established. Next, systems design is explored. The underlying theme is that the management information system must be tailored to meet the needs of the user rather than the capabilities of the hardware. This becomes particularly evident in the final part of the chapter—the "effective MIS practice" section—where the proper relationship of the MIS staff to the users and operating personnel is explored.

GUIDELINES FOR SUCCESSFUL MIS DEVELOPMENT

To overcome problems experienced in the development of MIS, appropriate general implementation guidelines are offered. More specifically, these guidelines point out the need to:

- involve top management in the overall planning phase as well as in the succeeding phases of an MIS project.
- provide adequate presystem planning for getting started on an MIS project.
- involve the appropriate functional managers and their support personnel in the detailed aspects of the MIS project.
- obtain the assistance of the data base administrator to facilitate the proper planning of MIS data as well as operational data.

254

◩ recruit qualified MIS personnel from within or outside the organization to undertake the MIS project.

◩ provide the capability to extend the management information system into functional areas.

These guidelines attack only the major problems hindering the successful development of MIS.

Going beyond these general guidelines, the management information systems specialist's role needs to be given the proper perspective—that is, viewing the work being done as solving the business problems of the user and not just those of data processing. Hence, the following guidelines to ensure that the user's needs are considered first are provided.

◩ Ensure that the management information system being built is truly molded to meet user objectives, not just self-serving interests of the MIS staff.

◩ Ensure that the MIS staff does not assume responsibility for building the system by themselves. This means insisting on meaningful involvement by management—and corporate management, as well, if the system extends to multiple functions.

◩ Ensure that the required user involvement is agreed upon before any work on the MIS takes place.

◩ Ensure that the user both understands and accepts full responsibility and commitment toward the ultimate success of the MIS project.

◩ Ensure that the user involvement is active, not passive, and maintained throughout the development of the MIS. The dominant thrust in the definition of user requirements and system objectives must emanate from the user and not the management information systems staff.

◩ Ensure that schedules are realistic and accurately reflect not only the MIS staff's ability, but also that of the user to participate in development and absorb and use the new MIS. But once the schedules are set, adhere to commitments.

◩ Ensure that the MIS staff understands the importance of observing commitments, though not at the expense of system quality, so that there are no surprises.

◩ Ensure that the user management is constantly informed about the MIS project, that the communication channels are open at all times, and that all communication between the MIS staff and the user is clear.

Sacrifice the foregoing guidelines, and the end result is usually a DP-oriented system, rather than a user-oriented one.

MIS DEVELOPMENT PROCESS

The major phases of the MIS development process (i.e., of developing a new management information system) are set forth in table 7.1. Another name for this development process is the *life cycle approach* to systems. Later in the

TABLE 7.1 Phases in the development of a management information system.

Phase	Overall Objective
Feasibility study:	Determine the *appropriateness* of making a systems change.
Systems analysis	Define *what* the system must do.
Systems design	Define *how* the system will work.
Equipment selection	Select *appropriate* hardware/software.
Systems implementation	Provide the user with a *fully* operational system.
Periodic review	Insure the system *continues* to meet the user's needs effectively.

chapter, the traditional life cycle approach and a structured approach are compared. Both approaches use the phases set forth in table 7.1. These phases are, for the most part, the subject matter for this chapter and the next. Due to the importance of getting started correctly on an MIS project, first a clear statement of the overall objectives is formulated. Each phase of the development process must have well-defined objectives. At the end of each phase, progress toward meeting the objectives must be evaluated. The development process should not continue until the objectives of all prior phases have been met. Table 7.1 illustrates one way of separating the development process into distinct phases. This approach has been used successfully over the years to develop large-, medium-, and small-scale systems.

The MIS development process based on phases has several advantages. It allows management to make incremental (phase-by-phase) commitments rather than one total commitment of resources. At the end of each phase, the go/no-go decision can be reevaluated and plans adjusted based on information gained. It allows specialists to be assigned for each phase. (Different skills are more important to systems analysis than to systems implementation.) It forces a higher degree of thoroughness throughout the project and reduces the possibility that a key user requirement or important hardware constraint will be overlooked. Finally, it offers greater flexibility in designing for change and eventual termination of the system.

FEASIBILITY STUDY OF A NEW MIS

To understand the importance of a feasibility study, it is helpful to examine it from these perspectives:

- Why is the feasibility study undertaken?
- Who conducts the feasibility study?
- What is the scope of the feasibility study?
- How much time should be spent on the feasibility study?

However, before doing so, we will first look at a microcomputer versus a mainframe approach to a feasibility study for helpful context.

Microcomputer Versus Mainframe Approach to a Feasibility Study

The feasibility study of a new MIS applies both to a computer mainframe system and to the installation of a number of micros. Typically, when computer mainframe systems are constructed, an overall systems analysis precedes the detailed design, equipment selection, and implementation phases. In the microcomputer world, some think that because the micro systems are so small and simple these phases are not necessary. However, with today's microcomputers and their communications capabilities, a micro-based system can be as complicated as a mainframe system. This is especially true when new nodes are continually installed in the network for maintenance and further development. New functions are added when external requirements change and as user needs warrant. Hence, the approach set forth in this chapter for systems analysis and design, as well as equipment selection and system implementation of the next chapter, applies equally to both micro-based and computer mainframe systems.

Why Is the Feasibility Study Undertaken?

The primary purpose of a feasibility study, as noted in table 7.1, is to determine the appropriateness of making a change to a functional area of the organization. The MIS feasibility study is usually triggered by one or more of the following reasons:

- There is an opportunity to *provide better information to management.* For example, the manufacturing manager demands more accurate sales forecasts to allow better production planning.
- There is an opportunity to make a change that will result in *improved profitability*—increased sales or decreased costs. For example, upgrading the current manual payroll operation to a computerized system will result in less clerical effort and lower personnel costs.
- There is a need to modernize or replace an old system to *ensure adequate control.* For example, the 15-year-old accounts payable system may be replaced because it is no longer reliable.
- There is a need to make a change in order to *meet a new corporate or government requirement.* For example, the personnel system must be modified to produce reports required by new EEOC or OSHA requirements.

Who Conducts the Feasibility Study?

Any of the above needs may lead to a feasibility study that may, in turn, lead to modification of the present management information system or development of a new MIS. Generally, someone from the organization most directly affected initiates the feasibility study by calling the problem to the attention of the appropriate manager(s).

257

DEVELOPMENT,
IMPLEMENTATION,
AND CONTROL OF
EFFECTIVE
MANAGEMENT
INFORMATION
SYSTEMS

A highly successful organizational model during the systems analysis phase of major feasibility is presented in table 7.2. This model consists of three groups: (1) the executive steering committee, (2) the user review group, and (3) the project team. For small- to medium-sized feasibility studies without inter-organization issues, the executive steering committee may be unnecessary, and the user review group may consist of only one or two others besides the project manager.

Members of the *executive steering committee* include middle- to high-level managers of any organization groups that will use or be affected by the new system. The chairperson of the committee might be the highest level manager from the organization that will achieve the major benefits of the new system. For example, if a new inventory control system is to be examined, the vice-president of physical distribution might be the chairperson; other members might be the vice-presidents of manufacturing, marketing, and accounting. As with all committees, the effectiveness is inversely proportional to the number of members: in other words, keep the committee small.

The executive steering committee typically has these responsibilities:

- to ensure appropriate personnel are assigned to the user review group and project team.
- to resolve issues that cut across organizational units.
- to review key decisions of the user review group and project team to ensure that they are consistent with long-range company objectives.
- to ensure that the scope of the study is broad enough to allow accomplishment of company objectives in an effective manner.

TABLE 7.2   Organization for the systems analysis phase of a major feasibility study.

Executive Steering Committee	User Review Group	Project Team
Leader: High-level manager of organizational unit that will use the new system.	**Leader:** Immediate manager of organizational unit that will use the new system.	**Leader:** Project manager.
Members: High-level managers from other organizational units that will be affected by the system.	**Members:** Project manager and managers from other organizational units that will be affected by the system.	**Members:** Systems analysts, programmers, experienced users of current system, and consultants.
Role: Set overall objectives; resolve inter-organizational issues; and review key decisions of project team/user review group.	**Role:** Approve system specifications and recommendations of the study; identify system benefits; and identify tasks that must be performed by systems users, prioritize work, and assign personnel.	**Role:** Develop systems specifications—what the system must do—and document the conclusions and recommendations of the systems analysis and design phases.
Meeting frequency: Quarterly.	**Meeting frequency:** Monthly and as deemed appropriate.	**Meeting frequency:** As deemed appropriate.

☑ to enhance credibility and support the user review group and project team.

The *user review group* includes the project manager and the lower- to middle-level managers of the organization units that will use or be affected by the new system. This will ensure that appropriate attention is given to details—file conversion, training, user manuals, parallel testing, and operational procedures. Frequently, the immediate manager of the system user group is appointed chairperson of the review group. Again, it is important to keep the group small. Often, there is a rotating membership—only managers from areas of the business currently being studied are included. As the systems analysis phase moves from one area to another, a previous member of the committee is dropped and a new member is selected from the new area under study.

The user review group typically has the following responsibilities:

☑ to participate in developing system specifications, with final approval/ rejection responsibility.
☑ to identify benefits associated with the new system.
☑ to identify tasks for people from the organizational units that will use or be affected by the new system.
☑ to prioritize this work and schedule it into the ongoing daily work load associated with the current operation.
☑ to assign personnel and manage the work.

The *project team* includes the computer technical experts (systems analysts and programmers), people from the system user organization unit familiar with the current system, and people who will be affected by changes in the current system. The noncomputer people on the project team should bring a background of in-depth experience, an interest in working on details, and a desire to help improve the current system. The project manager must be able to bring such a group of people together and help them to work together productively. The project manager is often chosen from the computer area because the individual has previous experience in leading such groups, but many successful projects have been led by noncomputer personnel.

The project team has the following responsibilities:

☑ defining the user requirements for the system as clearly, accurately, and completely as possible; requirements are subject to final approval by the user review group.
☑ defining how the system will do what the user wants.
☑ documenting the conclusions and final recommendations of the system analysis phase.

What Is the Scope of the Feasibility Study?

Typically, the executive steering committee initially defines the scope of the feasibility study. This top-level group might ask the project team and user review group to restrict their activities to a single functional area, or to

DEVELOPMENT,
IMPLEMENTATION,
AND CONTROL OF
EFFECTIVE
MANAGEMENT
INFORMATION
SYSTEMS

include the entire organization. Or the scope might be somewhere between these two extremes.

An outside consultant(s) may be engaged to help in this initial stage. As the project team and the user review group get into the details of the study, it may be necessary for the consultant to suggest modification to the scope of the study.

SELECTION OF DESIRED OBJECTIVES. Once the scope has been set by the executive steering committee, the next step is to identify the overall objectives to be met. The formulation of objectives is a joint effort among the executive steering committee, the user review group, and the project team. Selecting objectives forces management to think seriously about the organization's future and brings to light problems that might otherwise be overlooked. It provides the project team with a framework from which to operate, since the constraints and limitations under which the system must function are clear. Experience has indicated that a feasibility study will go much more smoothly when it begins with a formal statement of objectives.

Objectives desired by management can take several directions. The objective can be cost savings, in which case both tangible and intangible benefits must be considered for the evaluation to be complete and realistic. Other objectives can emphasize faster and more timely information for supporting management decisions—an approach that really aims at cost reduction as well as faster service. Ideally, a new system will meet as many objectives as possible.

It is advisable to state the objectives in writing. A written memorandum by the executive steering committee ensures the accomplishment of what was originally intended and reduces the risk of going off on a tangent. A carefully laid-out plan indicates where the study will cut across organizational lines and where authority is needed for changes in systems, methods, procedures, forms, reports, or organization.

How Much Time Should Be Spent on the Feasibility Study?

An important item in a feasibility study is the preparation of a time schedule for the entire systems study. Such a study may take a long time, ranging from many months to several years. Experience has shown that the tendency is to underestimate the time element of the feasibility study as well as other succeeding steps. The time factor is a function of the objectives to be met and the resources to be committed. For a successful study, depth and thoroughness are important; the time factor is secondary.

Another question to consider is, "What is the potential payoff?" If the potential payoff is small, it is unwise to spend a considerable amount of time on the feasibility study.

When developing a time schedule, the user review group and project team determine the amount of work in each step of the systems change and what personnel and skills will be needed. Consideration must also be given to the following areas: training, programming, program testing, delivery of equipment, physical requirements and installation of the equipment, files development, delivery of new forms and supplies, and conversion activities. The foregoing includes the major items that must be included in a realistic schedule.

FEEDBACK ON THE MIS PROJECT. Those responsible for scheduling must both prepare a realistic time table and always be in a position to report whether the study is ahead, behind, or on schedule. In turn, the project team and user review group issue reports periodically to the executive steering committee on the project status. Included in the reports should be information that is critical to the study, such as bottlenecks and delays. Use of the "exception principle"[1] is always appropriate.

SCHEDULING THE MIS PROJECT

For a feasibility study, an integral part of the activities is the preparation of a time schedule for the entire MIS project. Generally, the development and installation of a major MIS takes place over several years. Experience has shown a tendency in most projects to underestimate the time. If time gets telescoped, an optimum decision for the organization's information needs will probably not be made.

When developing a time schedule, the project team must determine the amount of work involved in each step of the system change and the personnel and skills resources needed. Consideration must also be given to the areas of training, programming, program testing, equipment delivery, physical requirements and installation of the equipment, file development, delivery of new forms and supplies, and conversion activities.

The member of the project team responsible for scheduling should not only prepare a realistic time table, but also be in a position at all times to report whether the study is ahead of, behind, or on schedule. The project manager of the project team should issue reports periodically to the executive steering committee and the user review group on the status of the project. Included in the reports should be problem areas, delays, and other information critical to the study. Utilization of the "exception principle" in progress reports is needed to control the project when employing a Gantt chart or a PERT/time network (as discussed below).

The activities of a management information system project should be scheduled in sufficient detail so that each important milestone can be planned and controlled. Even though uncertainty may exist for some activities, accurate times should be developed. Generally, past experience can be utilized as a starting point in scheduling.

The scheduler must determine appropriate starting dates for each activity. Analysis of allotted periods generally indicates whether organization per-

---

[1]The "exception principle" refers to highlighting for investigation those items that have exceeded limits by a specified amount. If necessary, action is undertaken to correct ongoing deficiencies.

DEVELOPMENT,
IMPLEMENTATION,
AND CONTROL OF
EFFECTIVE
MANAGEMENT
INFORMATION
SYSTEMS

sonnel have ample time to complete all the necessary tasks, especially in light of the equipment delivery date; overtime and additional personnel may be required at certain periods to meet the delivery date. The capability today to foresee a problem is a great help to the project team in planning and controlling the project.

Gantt Chart

The *Gantt chart* was first formulated by Henry L. Gantt as a means of controlling the production of war materials. It is currently used in scheduling projects from the first major phases to the last. It can also be used for the various phases of a systems study; that is, for systems analysis, systems design, equipment selection, and/or system implementation. The complexity of the project determines what phase or phases should be charted.

GANTT CHART COMPONENTS. Within a Gantt bar chart, the horizontal axis is used to depict time, with activities listed vertically in the left-hand column. Ordinarily, the chart is used to compare planned performance against actual performance. Comparison of the planned and actual times indicates whether the system project is ahead, behind, or on schedule. As illustrated in figure 7.1, the solid line is the scheduled event and the dotted line is the completed event. In this illustration only the introductory investigation phase has been completed to date for systems analysis. As of March 1, the project is on schedule.

Another way of depicting the various events is to utilize colored lines or bars. The scheduled events, for example, would appear in one color; the actual

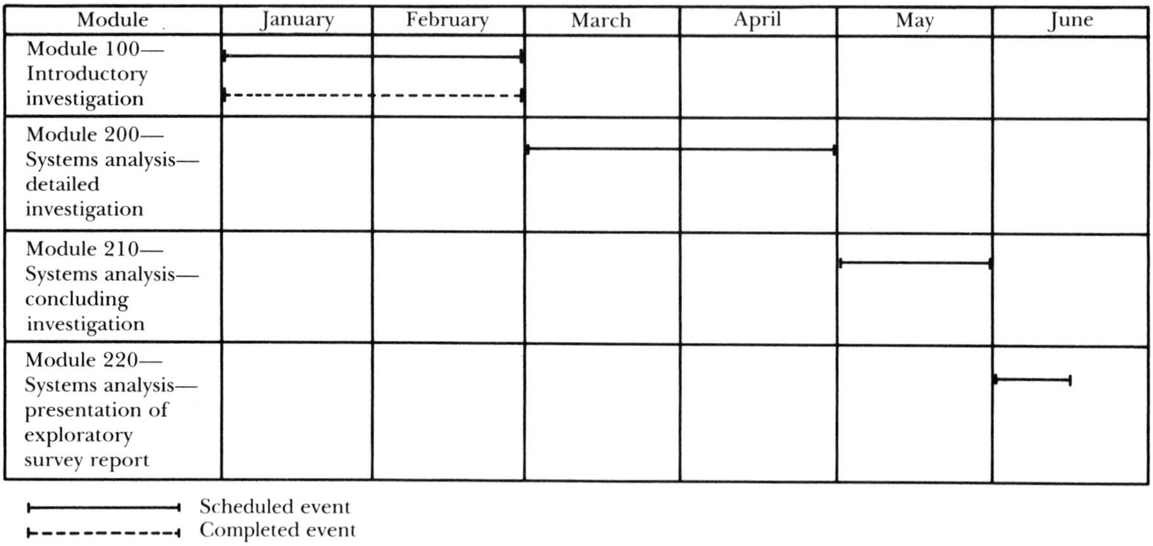

Module	January	February	March	April	May	June
Module 100— Introductory investigation	⊢—————	—————⊣				
Module 200— Systems analysis— detailed investigation			⊢—————	—————⊣		
Module 210— Systems analysis— concluding investigation					⊢—————⊣	
Module 220— Systems analysis— presentation of exploratory survey report						⊢———⊣

⊢————————⊣ Scheduled event
⊢----------⊣ Completed event

FIGURE 7.1   Typical Gantt chart for scheduling the introductory investigation and the systems analysis phase of an MIS project.

times achieved are added in another color as the various activities are accomplished. In this manner, a visual review of the chart will reveal the current status of the project.

An important advantage of this bar chart over other time-charting techniques is its simplicity. Managers are accustomed to working with charts; in relatively simple projects, they can comprehend a schedule and its status easily from a Gantt chart. However, the Gantt chart fails to show the relationship between one event and another. This shortcoming is not found in PERT/time networks discussed below.

PERT/Time Network

PERT, an acronym for Performance Evaluation and Review Technique, is a method of minimizing trouble spots, such as delays and interruptions, by determining critical activities before they occur so that various parts of a larger job can be coordinated. It is basically a *planning* and *control* technique that uses a network to complete a predetermined project on schedule. This technique helps facilitate the communications function by reporting potential problems before they happen. In effect, a PERT/time network is useful to an MIS project manager in appraising those critical factors and considerations that bear heavily on a system project.

CONSTRUCTING THE PERT/TIME NETWORK. A PERT network (such as the one illustrated in figure 7.2) shows some differences from a Gantt chart. The first to be considered is terminology. A *PERT network* is concerned with developing a logical sequence of those activities that are undertaken to carry out the project and the interrelationships of these activities over time. The term *activity* (job) is defined as one work step in the total project and is represented

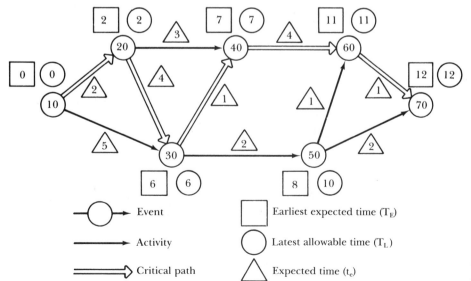

FIGURE 7.2
PERT/time network depicting the critical path and the earliest expected and latest allowable times.

DEVELOPMENT,
IMPLEMENTATION,
AND CONTROL OF
EFFECTIVE
MANAGEMENT
INFORMATION
SYSTEMS

by an arrow. The tail of the arrow represents the beginning of the activity and the head represents its completion. The length, shape, or position of the arrow is unimportant. The important thing is the way the activities, represented by arrows, are linked together in a time sequence for an operational network.

In constructing an arrow diagram, the user should think through the activities required and their respective time relationships. This can be accomplished by developing a list of the project's activities. In a very complex project, initially it may not seem possible to list all of the activities. However, additional activities will come to light as the arrow diagram is developed. Next, the user should determine the logical order of the activities, that is, how does one activity fit in with others? Does a particular job precede or follow, or is it concurrent with another activity? Finally, it is necessary to draw the arrow diagram to show how the activities are interrelated over time. The user should watch for activities that are too large or too small. It is possible that a large activity can be treated as more than one activity or that many small activities can be combined into a single activity.

The starting and ending points of activities, shown in figure 7.2 as circled numbers, are called *events* (nodes). Events are points in time, as contrasted with activities which have a time length or duration. Events are numbered serially from start to finish of a project. The general rule for numbering is that no event can be numbered until all preceding events have been numbered. Referring to figure 7.2, this means that no event can be numbered until we have first numbered the tail of the arrow whose head points to that event. The number at the head of an arrow is of course always larger than that at its tail.

The term *network* relates to the way activities and events are combined together, resulting in a diagram. Within the network in figure 7.2, we can see that event 10 is the network-beginning event, while event 70 is the network-ending event. Upon inspection of event 40, we notice that activities 20–40 and 30–40 lead to it, which means that event 40 is the ending event for these two activities. The same type of reasoning can be applied to the other activities in the PERT network.

METHODOLOGY OF PERT. The methodology of a PERT/time network is shown in figure 7.3. The first step centers on calculating expected times. The time within the triangles (as illustrated in figure 7.2) represents expected time (t_e), which is calculated by the formula[2]

$$t_e = \frac{a + 4m + b}{6}$$

where a equals the most optimistic time, m equals the most likely time, and b equals the most pessimistic time. The values developed from the formula have proven to be more accurate than those from any other method, but can

---

[2]The expected value is the midpoint of a beta distribution. As such, it states that there is a 50:50 chance that the activity will be completed by the calculated time.

Step 1—Calculate Expected Times   Calculate the expected time (t_e) for each activity by inserting three time estimates—optimistic (a), most likely (m), and pessimistic (b)—in the following equation:

$$t_e = \frac{a + 4m + b}{6}$$

As each t_e is calculated, it is entered on the network (shown in a triangle above or below the appropriate activity arrow).

Step 2—Determine Earliest Expected and Latest Allowable Times   Determine earliest expected times (T_E—shown in squares above the appropriate events) by adding the expected times, starting with the first event and going from left to right. However, when an event has two or more activities flowing into it, take the *maximum* time.

Determine latest allowable times (T_L—shown in circles above the appropriate events) by subtracting the expected times, starting with the last event and going from right to left. However, when an event has two or more activities flowing out of it, take the *minimum* time.

Step 3—Locate Critical Path(s)   Locate the critical path(s) by determining the longest time path(s) throughout the network. This is accomplished by observing the events on the critical path—their earliest expected times are equal to their latest allowable times.

Step 4—Calculate Slack   Calculate the amount of slack for each activity by taking the time difference between the latest allowable time (T_L) and the earliest expected time (T_E) for the same event, applying the following equation:

$$S = T_L - T_E$$

Step 5—Evaluate PERT Network   Evaluate the PERT network from an overview standpoint. If total time is unsatisfactory, realign resources, add personnel from noncritical activities, pay overtime, and use comparable schemes to improve completion dates throughout the project. Redo the PERT network employing the preceding steps. Any "trading off" of foregoing items will generally necessitate a recomputation of network times.

FIGURE 7.3   Methodology of a PERT/time network.

be adjusted based on the firm's past experience. Those appearing in figure 7.2 were calculated on this basis.

In the second step of figure 7.3, the earliest expected times (T_E) and the latest allowable times (T_L) are calculated and are shown in the boxes and circles above the events, respectively. In the third step, the *critical path* is determined. This is the longest time path or paths throughout the network, represented by those events where the earliest expected and latest allowable times are equal. An examination of figure 7.2 indicates that the critical path is as follows; 10–20–30–40–60–70. The double lines shown in the illustration represent the critical path. Any delays in starting or completing times on this path will delay the end completion date.

In the fourth step in the PERT/time network, the *slack* is calculated. The time difference between the latest allowable time and the earliest expected time represents slack (extra) time available for each activity within the project.

DEVELOPMENT,
IMPLEMENTATION,
AND CONTROL OF
EFFECTIVE
MANAGEMENT
INFORMATION
SYSTEMS

As noted above, where the earliest and latest allowable times are equal, the event is on the critical path. In a PERT network, dummy arrows (dotted lines) do not represent activities, but rather connect related events in the network that have no time estimates. (This condition is not illustrated in figure 7.2.)

Once the network has been drawn, all time values calculated (t_e, T_E, and T_L, and slack), and the critical path(s) determined, the real job of PERT has actually just begun. This is where *sensitivity analysis* plays an important role in the fifth and final step of figure 7.3. Certain activities whose times have been estimated may have no effect on the critical path even if they fall behind schedule. However, other estimated timed activities may be on the critical path or may become critical at a later date. The results of all these initial path activities must be assessed. As time passes, adjustments and revisions of the original plans may be necessary to assure that the PERT network is completed by a scheduled end date.

If overall times are unsatisfactory, several methods of adjustment are available to the user, one being the interchanging of workers, machines, and materials (if they are comparable) from the noncritical path(s) to the critical path(s). Another network adjustment is reducing the technical specifications of the project.

If activities can be rearranged, it may be possible to speed up the completion of the project. The overlapping of concurrent activities may be available to the user. Moreover, the use of overtime provides additional flexibility for network replanning and adjustment. Thus, the user has several alternatives available for adjusting the critical path(s) in order to improve completion dates throughout the project. Generally, any "trading off" of resources and revision in standards or specifications will necessitate a recomputation of times—expected, earliest expected, latest allowable, slack, and critical path(s).

It is not realistic to assume that the PERT/time method can be maintained manually for complex system projects. In light of this problem, software packages are available from equipment and software vendors to permit monitoring of current critical paths and available slack times. Typically, a computer approach is used weekly to update and control project activities for a two-year project. Failure to make use of a computerized PERT software package means that MIS personnel are not being used in the most productive manner.

SYSTEMS ANALYSIS FOR EFFECTIVE MIS

The purpose of systems analysis is to define what the new system must do. Three major activities are performed in systems analysis. First, the existing system is studied to answer the question, "What if we do nothing?"—in other words, the existing system with no changes is a possible solution. The strengths, weaknesses, and costs associated with the current system must be defined to serve as a benchmark for evaluation of other alternatives. Second, other alternatives are identified and evaluated. Third, an exploratory survey report is issued that states the conclusions of the systems analysis phase and recommends what should be done during the rest of the feasibility study.

Traditional System Life Cycle Approach Versus Structured System Life Cycle Approach

Before setting forth the details of systems analysis, a brief review of what constitutes a traditional system life cycle approach versus a structured system life cycle approach is beneficial. When a systems analyst undertakes a detailed analysis of the present information system, he or she prepares detailed, complete system flowcharts or similar charting technique(s). System flowcharts that have been prepared in the past (as found in the systems and procedures manuals) generally serve as a starting point in systems analysis. Essentially, system flowcharts describe the *physical structure* of the current information system. Their main purpose is to describe the physical characteristics of the current information system, whether manual, automated, or a combination. They emphasize the type of equipment (batch or interactive), kinds of inputs (punched card, magnetic tape, magnetic disk, floppy disk, etc.), types of storage (on-line and off-line), and like items. Although the current physical system refers to these items, its major focus is on end results; that is, its use by organizational personnel in various departments. The existing system is studied in great detail because many of its current capabilities and data items will be needed in the new system. Overall, system flowcharts or similar charting technique(s) center on physical flow through the present information system.

As with the traditional system life cycle approach, the initial step in the structured system life cycle approach is preparing system flowcharts (including the flowcharts presently available from the systems and procedures manuals) in order to depict the *physical structure* of the current information system. Once the physical structure is developed, the next phase is to describe the *logical process* involved. That the current information system involves punched cards, magnetic tape, and comparable media which must be sorted and interpreted before processing is usually irrelevant. The systems analyst must describe the current information system in terms of the logic of its data without mentioning that it is contained on punched cards, magnetic tapes, etc. Thus, the systems analyst understands the logical data flow in the present information system.

In applying this approach to understanding the present information system, the systems analyst needs to perform a logical analysis from the highest level to the lowest level. This approach brings structure to the analysis process in a top-down manner, permitting *functional decomposition* to whatever level of detail is required. In the process, data flow diagrams or comparable diagramming methods are used to ensure clarity and ease of understanding. Thus, combining logical flows of data and their logical processes with functional decomposition provides an underlying framework for *structured systems analysis*.

Due to space limitations, we will demonstrate only the structured sys-

267

DEVELOPMENT,
IMPLEMENTATION,
AND CONTROL OF
EFFECTIVE
MANAGEMENT
INFORMATION
SYSTEMS

tem life cycle approach. Refer to the end-of-chapter bibliography for a structured approach to systems analysis or to a current text by the author.[3]

Studying the Present System

Systems analysts, organization personnel from the functional areas, and other appropriate personnel are usually split into teams to investigate each area under study. The study should concentrate on identifying the strengths, weaknesses, and costs associated with the current system. No area should be excluded unless it is unrelated to the desired objectives. The *physical system* analysis should be comprehensive and include these areas:

- *A review of historical facts* to identify the major turning points and milestones that have influenced the organization over time. Current and future plans should also be examined.
- *An analysis of inputs* to identify where source documents are used to capture originating data. An understanding of the nature of the document, what is contained in it, who prepared it, where it was initiated, when it was completed, and its distribution is important since outputs from one area are inputs for others. A sample list of input records for the major functional areas of a manufacturing firm are found in table 7.3.
- *A review of methods and procedures* to understand the relationship between inputs, files, and outputs. The series of procedural steps by which MIS operations are accomplished can be examined to determine what action is required, who must do it, and when it must be done.
- *A review of files maintained* to understand the number and size of files maintained by departments, where they are located, who uses them, the amount of time it takes to refer to a file, and the number of times they are referenced. The maintenance of files is a function of their value versus cost of storage and must satisfy legal requirements.
- *An analysis of outputs* to determine how well present reports are meeting the organization's needs. The questions of what information is needed and why, who needs it, and when and where it is needed must be answered; additional questions on the sequence of the data, how often the form is used, how long it is kept on file, and the like must be investigated. A typical list of outputs for the functional areas of a manufacturing firm are shown in table 7.3.
- *A review of internal controls* to indicate control points critical to maintaining efficient MIS operations. Locating these control points allows one to visualize the essential parts and the overall framework of a system.
- *An analysis of present personnel requirements* to classify present personnel by type, skill, and pay scale; these data are obtained from personnel records, monthly reports, and interviews. Every effort should

---

[3]Robert J. Thierauf, *Systems Analysis and Design, A Case Study Approach,* sec. ed., Columbus, OH: Charles E. Merrill Publishing Company, 1986.

TABLE 7.3 Sample inputs and outputs for the major functional areas of a typical manufacturing company.

Functional Area	Sample Inputs	Sample Outputs
Corporate planning	Product forecasts, planned production facilities, financial analyses and ratios, and manpower planning forecasts	Projected sources and applications of funds, projected short- to long-range financial statements, flexible budgets, and budget exception reports
Marketing	Sales quotations, sales reps' reports, sales forecasts, sales invoices, listing of customers, advertising budget, and customer credit information	Marketing sales analyses, sales by products and product lines, comparisons of company to industry sales, monthly actual versus budgets, and salesperson commissions reports
Manufacturing	Production orders, receiving reports, shipping reports, purchase orders, time cards, stock records, stock requisitions, personnel records, and time standards	Production control reports, production shipping schedules, inventory control reports, quality control reports, spoilage and scrap analyses, departmental actuals versus budgets, and factory turnover analyses
Accounting and Finance	Vendor invoices, weekly time cards, cash receipts, fixed asset records, tax returns, stockholder listings, and insurance records	Cash flow analyses, checks and earnings statements, sales registers, customer invoices, monthly balance sheets and income statements, capital project studies, and aging of accounts
Personnel	New personnel data, skill inventory changes, personnel search entries, and wage and salary data	Skill inventory listings by employees, wage and salary administration reports, salary curves by job classifications, seniority listings, and salary surveys

DEVELOPMENT,
IMPLEMENTATION,
AND CONTROL OF
EFFECTIVE
MANAGEMENT
INFORMATION
SYSTEMS

be made to understand thoroughly this most important element of MIS operations since these same people will normally be involved in the new system.

□ *A review of present work volumes* to identify average and peak work loads, as well as periodic totals. Where work volumes are low and processing procedures complex, the feasibility of applying new computer and peripheral equipment is unlikely. On the other hand, where large work volumes require straightforward processing, the chances of using new equipment are very high. Additionally, work volume analysis is helpful to determine whether a particular workstation is a control, storage, or terminal point in a system.

□ *A review of other requirements and considerations* to help locate important items that may be critical to the present system. Items such as the effects of exceptions and errors on the present system, seasonal or other cyclical characteristics, current production facilities, and present financial resources should be investigated if critical to current operations.

Once the physical system has been documented, the next step in the structured approach is to develop the *logical* system. This entails using *data flow diagrams* to trace the origin of input data through each phase of processing and communication, into files, and finally out of files for desired outputs—many in the form of reports. The diagramming of the present operations not only organizes the facts, but also helps disclose gaps and duplication in the data gathered. It allows a thorough logical comprehension of the numerous details and related problems in the present operation. In essence, the knowledge gathered to date is brought altogether in a logical and meaningful relationship for the project team and user review group.

The help and advice of operating personnel and first-line supervisors will be invaluable throughout the process of studying the current system. It is imperative that the project team relate to the problems and frustrations of existing system users because (1) it will give the project team more insight into the actual operation of the current system, and (2) it will help elicit positive reaction to proposed system changes.

PRESENT SYSTEM COSTS AND BENEFITS. A major reason for reviewing the present operation is to determine its costs. Present system benefits can also be identified. Benefits include the present level of service to customers, the value of reports, return on investment, rate of profit, ability of the present system to grow with the organization, and increased inventory turnover. Many of these benefits can be measured precisely while others are intangible and require subjective evaluation.

Proposing MIS Alternatives

Before feasible MIS alternatives are developed, proposed system specifications (user requirements) must be clearly defined. These specifications, which pertain to each functional area of the feasibility study, are determined from the desired objectives set forth initially in the study and information gained during the study of the current system. Likewise, consideration is given to the strengths and the shortcomings of the existing system. Required system specifications, which must be clearly defined and in conformity with the study's objectives, might include such items as:

- □ input data from original source documents for processing by the management information system
- □ methods and procedures that show the relationship of input data to files and files to outputs of the management information system
- □ files to be maintained with automated MIS equipment or otherwise
- □ outputs to be produced, with emphasis on managerial reports that utilize the "exception principle"
- □ work volumes and timing considerations for present and future periods, including peak periods

A starting point for compiling these specifications is a clear statement of the cause of the current system weaknesses, after which it is possible to infer appropriate solutions—what outputs, inputs, and files are required and what methods and procedures must be employed for each alternative. Future workloads of the new system must be defined for inputs, files, and outputs in terms of average and peak loads, cycles, and trends. This information is developed for each MIS alternative, but not to the same depth as was undertaken to understand the present system. Otherwise, such an effort would increase the time and personnel requirements of the study beyond its intended scope and budget.

FLEXIBLE SYSTEM REQUIREMENTS FOR DEVELOPING MIS ALTERNATIVES. The requirements of the new management information system may appear on the surface to be fixed; a closer examination often reveals their flexibility. For example, the original objectives set forth in the study may state that certain computer files or a common data base must be updated once a day, whereas the best solution may be an interactive computer system where files or common data bases are updated as actual transactions occur. This approach is within the constraints initially set forth and introduces a new way of maintaining files. With this in mind, it is possible to design a number of different systems with varying features, costs, and benefits. In many cases, additional MIS alternatives can be investigated and analyzed when flexible system requirements are considered. The project team must clearly communicate with the user review group any time it seems appropriate to modify an original requirement. Changes must be clearly documented and approved.

CONSULTANT'S ROLE IN DEVELOPING AND SELECTING AN MIS ALTERNATIVE. Outside consultant(s) can be of great value to the project team. The consultant's knowledge can narrow down the number of promising solutions. Too often, a project team focuses in on a specific system alternative that should have been discarded initially as infeasible. Also, the consultant can

DEVELOPMENT,
IMPLEMENTATION,
AND CONTROL OF
EFFECTIVE
MANAGEMENT
INFORMATION
SYSTEMS

point out the shortcomings of a certain approach that may have been pushed strongly by certain individuals. The consultant can act with the project team and user review group to resolve potential conflicts. The consultant's objectivity can enhance the organization's chances of developing viable MIS alternatives and selecting the best choice.

COST AND TANGIBLE BENEFITS OF EACH MIS ALTERNATIVE. The next step after developing feasible MIS alternatives is to determine the anticipated savings and incremental costs for each. The difference between the estimated savings and estimated incremental costs represents the estimated net savings (losses) to the organization before federal income taxes.

Estimated savings, sometimes called *cost displacement,* include: reduction in the number of personnel; sale or elimination of some equipment; reduced repairs, maintenance, insurance, and personal property taxes; lower cost rental and utilities; and elimination or reduction of outside processing costs.

Incremental costs are segregated into two categories, one-time and operating. Major *one-time costs* relate to development of the system: for the feasibility study, systems design, training of programming and operating personnel, programming and testing of programs for the new system, parallel operations where the old and the new systems operate concurrently, file conversion, site preparation, conversion activities from existing system to new system, and other equipment and supplies. *Operating costs* include monthly rental or depreciation of computer and related equipment; maintenance of equipment; wages and salaries, payroll taxes, and fringe benefits of personnel; program maintenance; forms and supplies of computer and related equipment; and miscellaneous additional costs.

Savings and cost projections for the present system and system alternatives are typically made for a 3- to 7-year period. The rationale is this: If a computer is selected, it will not be processing on a daily basis for about a year from the day of equipment selection (the final step of the feasibility study). Also, the equipment must be able to handle the organization's workload for at least three years.

Accurate savings and costs projections are of great importance in selecting the appropriate system alternative. The need for accurate projections strongly suggests the need for the accounting department's assistance. Many times, the best way to increase the accuracy of the projections is for an outside consultant to work with the project team in their preparation and review.

When computing the estimated savings and incremental costs, the trend of growth or cutback in the organization's workload should be analyzed and projected. These data can then be used to project savings and costs, similar to the sample analysis found in table 7.4. In this feasibility study for alternative #4, consideration has been given to high future costs due to large work volume and inflation.

DISCOUNTED CASH FLOW
Since projected savings and costs in a feasibility study are in the future, the difference between the two sums after federal income taxes should be

TABLE 7.4   A sample analysis of MIS alternative #4.

THE ARGO COMPANY: MIS ALTERNATIVE #4

Estimated Net Savings on a Rental Basis over Five Years

| | Years from start of system implementation | | | | | Five-year total |
	1	2	3	4	5	
Estimated savings						
Reduction in personnel	$120,200	$400,500	$440,300	$490,500	$540,500	$1,992,000
Sale of equipment	150,000					150,000
Rental (space) savings	25,000	51,000	54,500	58,000	61,800	250,300
Elimination of rental equipment	2,050	4,380	4,690	5,000	5,300	21,420
Other savings	3,000	3,060	3,210	3,370	3,540	16,180
TOTAL	$300,250	$458,940	$502,700	$556,870	$611,140	$2,429,900
Estimated one-time costs						
Feasibility study	$75,000					$75,000
Training	50,000					50,000
Systems and programming	255,500					255,500
Master file conversion	262,500					262,500
Other conversion costs	95,500					95,500
Site preparation	55,400					55,400
Other one-time costs	2,300					2,300
TOTAL	$796,200					$796,200
Estimated operating costs						
Equipment rental	$110,000	$120,800	$127,400	$134,100	$141,000	$633,300
Additional personnel	34,000	60,700	62,300	63,400	64,600	285,000
Program maintenance	20,000	30,700	32,200	33,800	36,000	152,700
Forms and supplies	10,000	21,500	23,000	24,500	26,000	105,000
Other operating costs	4,400	12,400	12,800	13,290	17,600	60,490
TOTAL	$178,400	$246,100	$257,700	$269,090	$285,200	$1,236,490
NET SAVINGS (losses) before federal income taxes	$(674,350)	$212,840	$245,000	$287,780	$325,940	$397,210

DEVELOPMENT,
IMPLEMENTATION,
AND CONTROL OF
EFFECTIVE
MANAGEMENT
INFORMATION
SYSTEMS

discounted back to the present time to account for the time value of money. This also provides a sound economic comparative analysis of alternatives. Such an analysis is shown for system alternative #4 in table 7.5. Notice that the net savings—after federal income taxes of $214,494 over the five-year period (anticipated life of the system), when discounted at 20 percent—show a negative amount of $1,312 for this alternative. This alternative should not be undertaken if the cutoff point for capital investments is 20 percent.

INTANGIBLE BENEFITS FOR EACH MIS ALTERNATIVE. A number of intangible benefits or qualitative factors may be uncovered by studying the potential contributions of the new MIS to the organization's activities and problems. A listing of such factors is found in figure 7.4. These factors may ultimately lead to an increase in revenues or a decrease in operating costs. There is not a strong, directly traceable relationship between achieving these benefits and improved profitability.

Submitting Exploratory Survey Report to Top Management

At the conclusion of the studies just mentioned, ample information has been accumulated by the project team and the user review group to make a final recommendation to top management. The exploratory survey report should be prepared by the project team, approved by the user review group, and directed to the executive steering committee. It may be financially oriented since large sums of money may be involved. Generally, the approval of the recommendation must come from the executive steering committee before any further steps are taken.

The contents of this report must be as objective as possible so that the best MIS alternative is selected. Consideration must be given to a fundamental principle underlying information systems, which is that a computer-oriented system is in far better position to absorb growth in volume with a slight increase in operating costs than are other systems. Comparable principles

TABLE 7.5   A sample analysis of MIS alternative #4.

THE ARGO COMPANY: MIS ALTERNATIVE #4

Discounted Cash Flow—20 Percent Return after Federal Income Taxes on a Rental Basis over a Five-Year Period

Year	Net savings (losses) before federal income taxes (table 7.4)	Federal income tax at 46 per cent rate	Net savings (losses) after federal income taxes	At 20 percent Present value of $1,000	At 20 percent Present value of net savings (losses)
1	$(674,350)	$(310,201)	$(364,149)	.833	$(303,336)
2	212,840	97,906	114,934	.694	79,764
3	245,000	112,700	132,300	.579	76,602
4	287,780	132,379	155,401	.482	74,903
5	325,940	149.932	176,008	.402	70,755
Totals	$397,210	$182,716	$214,494		$(1,312)

Improved customer service through better techniques to anticipate customer requirements, resulting in fewer lost sales, less overtime in the plant for rush orders, and so forth.

Better support of decision-making capability in the areas of marketing, manufacturing, finance, purchasing, personnel, engineering, and research and development through more timely and informative reports.

More effective use of management time for planning, organizing, directing, and controlling because of the availability of timely data and information.

Ability to handle more customers faster with more automatic processing equipment.

Closer control over capital investments and expenses through comparisons with budgets, standards, or forecasts.

Improved scheduling and production control, resulting in more efficeient employment of personnel and machines.

Greater accuracy, speed, and reliability in information handling and MIS operations.

Better control of credit through more frequent aging of accounts receivables and analyses of credit data.

Reversal of trend to higher hiring and training costs arising from the difficulties in filling clerical jobs.

Improved promotional efforts to attract new customers and retain present ones.

Enhanced stature in the business community as a progressive and forward-looking organization.

FIGURE 7.4
Feasibility study—intangible benefits to consider for a new management information system.

should be embodied in the system recommended for a constructive report to management.

FEASIBILITY OR INFEASIBILITY OF APPLYING MANAGEMENT INFORMATION SYSTEMS. The study of implementing a new management information system is difficult when numerous alternatives are available. Comparing only the tangible benefits shown in table 7.6, only alternatives #1 and #2 appear attractive. However, when the intangible benefits are included, the remaining four alternatives become promising. Thus, the feasibility of applying newer MIS equipment and techniques has been established. The question, then, is to determine which proposal is best when all critical factors are appraised.

Since the project team's primary job is to recommend the best alternative, it must weigh quantitative and qualitative factors with emphasis on the organization's growth pattern and future problems. A specific organization's circumstances must be analyzed for an accurate conclusion.

TABLE 7.6   Matrix table for appraising feasible MIS alternatives.

Table Name: Feasibility Study—Exploratory Survey

| MATRIX TABLE | | Date: July 2, 198–
 Preparer: R. J. Thierauf | | | | | |

CRITERIA FOR EVALUATION	1	2	Alternative 3	4	5	6
Tangible benefits						
Meets return on investment criteria—20% after taxes*	Y	Y	N	N	N	N
Reduced order processing costs	Y	Y	Y	Y	Y	Y
Lower investment in inventory	Y	Y	Y	Y	Y	Y
Lower future cash requirements	N	N	Y	Y	Y	Y
Intangible benefits						
Improved customer service	N	N	Y	Y	Y	Y
Improved promotional efforts	N	N	N	Y	Y	Y
Ability to handle more customers faster	N	N	N	Y	Y	Y
Better decision-making ability	Y	Y	Y	Y	Y	Y
Better use of management's time	N	N	N	Y	Y	Y
Improved scheduling and production control	Y	Y	Y	Y	Y	Y
Closer control over capital investments	N	N	Y	Y	Y	Y
Handle more volume at lower costs	N	N	Y	Y	Y	Y
More accuracy and reliability of data	Y	Y	Y	Y	Y	Y
SYSTEM FEATURES						
Uses a new batch processing system	X	X	X	—	—	—
Uses an interactive processing system	—	—	—	X	X	X
Substantial changes of inputs and outputs	X	X	X	X	X	X
Need for new files	X	X	X	X	X	X
Moderate revision of methods and procedures	X	X	X	—	—	—
Major revision of methods and procedures	—	—	—	X	X	X
Employ outside consultants	—	—	—	X	X	X
Recruit new information systems personnel	X	X	X	X	X	X
Reevaluate benefits of system alternative	—	—	X	X	X	X

Other Information
*1—22%, 2—20%, 3—19%, 4—19%, 5—18%, 6—18%

In the example, an examination of table 7.6 indicates that alternatives #4 through #6 are best. In terms of tangible and intangible benefits, more affirmative answers for an interactive information system exist than for a newer batch-processing information system. The returns on investment are generally comparable. Which alternatives, then—#4, #5, or #6—should be implemented? On the surface, all three have about the same benefits, except that alternative #4 utilizes intelligent and color graphic terminals. Conversion today to these terminals will mean no or minimal conversion costs in the future for this area. With this added advantage in mind, the project team believes that future cost savings justify accepting a lower return. Its recommendation to the executive steering committee is now clear.

1. Scope and objectives of the study.
2. Overview of the existing system, noting its weaknesses and problems.
3. Adequate description of the recommended MIS alternative, indicating its tangible and intangible benefits, its superiority in eliminating or reducing the deficiencies of the present system, and its general impact on the organization.
4. Financial data on the recommended MIS alternative. (Refer to tables 7.4 and 7.5.)
5. Reference to other feasible MIS alternatives which were investigated, giving reasons for their final rejection. Matrix table (refer to table 7.6) should be included.
6. Financial data on system alternatives that were not selected. (Refer to tables 7.4 and 7.5.)
7. Schedule of funds required for specific periods of time during system implementation.
8. List of additional personnel needed to implement the new system and personnel requirements during conversion.
9. Accurate time schedule for the remainder of the MIS project.
10. Other special factors and considerations.

FIGURE 7.5
Suggested format for a final exploratory survey report to top management.

When the project team and the user review group agree on a particular system, a comprehensive report must be prepared. A suggested format for the final exploratory survey report is depicted in figure 7.5. The report gives management an opportunity to examine the data and appraise the validity and merit of the recommendation and provides a sound basis for constructive criticism of the MIS project.

Considerable time, effort, and cost during systems analysis may result in concluding the infeasibility of newer computer and peripheral equipment and of methods and procedures. Sometimes this conclusion may be caused by inappropriately limiting the initial scope of the study to areas where technological progress has been slow or nonexistent or areas that do not lend themselves to newer equipment. (When an opportunity exists for technical improvement, a broader approach is usually desirable.) This possibility can be minimized with the help of an outside consultant or experienced user in setting the initial scope of the study.

Summary—Systems Analysis for Effective MIS

STUDY THE PRESENT SYSTEM. Systems analysis, being a detailed survey of the present physical system, involves a comprehensive investigation of these areas under the supervision of the feasibility study manager:

- □ review of historical facts
- □ analysis of inputs

DEVELOPMENT,
IMPLEMENTATION,
AND CONTROL OF
EFFECTIVE
MANAGEMENT
INFORMATION
SYSTEMS

□ review of methods and procedures
□ review of files maintained
□ analysis of outputs
□ review of internal controls
□ analysis of present personnel requirements
□ review of present work volumes
□ review of other requirements and considerations

Next, we will use data flow diagrams to analyze the *logical* flow of the present system.

PROPOSE MIS ALTERNATIVES.   A most important task of the project team is to develop feasible MIS alternatives. An integral part of each alternative is developing projections of savings, costs, and tangible benefits. Likewise, consideration is given to intangible benefits. A thorough analysis of these facts by both the project team and the user review group finally leads to the recommendation of the best MIS alternative.

SUBMIT EXPLORATORY SURVEY REPORT TO TOP MANAGEMENT.   Once the project team and the user review group have selected an MIS alternative, an exploratory survey report to the executive steering committee is prepared that states this recommendation. This report must provide an adequate description of the selected MIS alternative, particularly in financial terms and in comparison to other alternatives.

SYSTEMS DESIGN FOR EFFECTIVE MIS

The MIS project manager and the participants who draw up the exploratory survey report generally undertake the design of the recommended MIS alternative. If additional systems personnel are required, they should be enlisted. The participation and cooperation of all functional areas, represented by department personnel, is the key to successful implementation. It is much easier to design the system to accommodate their constructive suggestions than to redesign it at a later date. Too many installations have faced this embarrassing situation, only because appropriate departmental personnel were not given an opportunity to evaluate the system design as it progressed.

Traditional System Life Cycle Approach Versus Structured System Life Cycle Approach

In the traditional approach to systems design, the systems analyst undertakes a detailed design of the new system using system flowcharts or similar charting techniques based upon the information in the MIS exploratory survey report. The result is a physical structure of the new system. (A comparable physical structure was set forth during the systems analysis phase.) These flowcharts describe the physical attributes of the newly designed system whether they be manual, automated, or a combination of the two. They include the types of equipment (batch or interactive), kinds of inputs (punched card, magnetic tape, magnetic disk, floppy disk, etc.), kinds of outputs (reports, documents, stored data, etc.), types of storage (on-line or off-line), and similar items. Overall, the physical flow is highlighted, and the comparable logical flow is ignored. In addition, because there is often little or no interface with users, systems analysts often design a system that they like, disregarding the users' needs. Hence, the physical system as designed using the traditional system life cycle approach is not only less than "user friendly," but also cannot be maintained economically after installation.

In contrast, the overall design methodology for the structured system life cycle approach starts with the information in the MIS exploratory survey report, in particular, the outputs. Using the information contained in this report for the selected MIS alternative, the new system's *logical structure* using a hierarchical set of data flow diagrams (i.e., functional decomposition) is modeled. The design is concerned with identifying the proper hierarchy of modules—and the interfaces between these modules—to implement the system specifications for the outputs, the data base, methods, procedures, data communications, inputs, and internal control. The design of the logical structure of the selected MIS alternative must describe the data flow for the new management information system, without deciding whether it will be an on-line data base, a serial magnetic tape file, or a stack of index cards. Similarly, the design must describe the functional activities of the new MIS without mentioning partitions, job steps, and other physical aspects.

The logical design of an MIS and its related systems must always be decomposed using *modularity* or the *building block* concept. Functional decomposition involves identifying all of the major systems that become the major modules of functional areas to be designed. At this point, all of the major modules are identified in a first-level data flow diagram. Since they are the highest-level functions, they are the beginning of a functional breakdown of an MIS into its parts, applying the process iteratively from the top down. The resulting analysis is represented by a high-level data flow diagram, wherein major modules at the top are successively broken down into separate data processing modules, which are represented in lower-level data flow diagrams. Based upon the logical structure, the *physical structure* of the new MIS is developed. Developing the physical structure requires a fair amount of expertise, since both the systems analysts and users decide how the data should be handled. Also, both groups should specify newer methods and equipment so that the new MIS is structured using the latest computer environments. This includes use of microcomputers and computer graphics along with electronic spreadsheets and fourth-generation languages. Hence, the resulting physical structure should represent the new MIS that will be implemented.

Due to space limitations, only the structured approach is presented below. Refer to the end-of-chapter bibliography or the previous referenced text by the author for a full explanation of the structured approach.

DEVELOPMENT,
IMPLEMENTATION,
AND CONTROL OF
EFFECTIVE
MANAGEMENT
INFORMATION
SYSTEMS

Is the report necessary to plan, organize, direct, or control organizational activities?

What would be the effect if operating personnel got more or less information?

How would work be affected if the report was received less frequently or not at all?

Is all information contained in the report used?

Can data on this report be obtained from another source?

How long is the report kept before being discarded?

Is the report concise and easy to understand?

How many people refer to it?

Are other reports prepared from pertinent data on the report?

Does the use of the data justify the preparation cost of the report?

Is the report flexible enough to meet changes in the company's operating conditions?

Is the report passed to someone higher or lower in the organizational structure?

When and where is the report filed?

FIGURE 7.6
Systems design—
questions to test the
validity of a report.

Determining New MIS Requirements

The systems design team begins by reviewing data on the present system and information contained in the exploratory survey report—in particular, the new management information system recommendation and its requirements. Key features of the new logical system that must be determined include:

- *New policies consistent with organization objectives* to reduce the complexity and the number of exceptions in the system. Examples are simplifying pricing and discount policies to conform to organization objectives.
- *Output needs* determined by user's requirements. Information users should work with systems designers so that the format, detail and degree of accuracy, and the frequency of the report can be specified. Questions that relate to testing the validity of a report are set forth in figure 7.6.
- *Data file maintenance,* or the amount of data to be contained in on-line and off-line files. Efficient systems design dictates keeping storage data at a minimum.
- *Planned inputs* to capture source data initially in a processible form.

Time constraints on the inputs and variations in input volume are important considerations.

□ *New methods and procedures* to produce output given certain inputs and data files. Operational procedures should be tested for practicality. In addition, methods and procedures must be compatible among functional areas or activities. Questions for testing the validity of any procedure are listed in figure 7.7.

□ *Internal controls,* or checks established at control points to ensure that what has been processed is accurate. Likewise, established internal controls focus on making certain that no one person has full responsibility over an entire operation. This should be apparent in such areas as cash and payroll since one person with complete responsibility can too easily defraud an organization.

Designing the New Management Information System

Determining the above requirements is concurrent with designing the *logical* flow of the new system. The structured design of a system involves many decisions about each of its parts—outputs desired, files to be maintained, planned inputs, and data processing methods and procedures that link inputs with out-

---

Can the procedure be improved to more fully realize organizational objectives?

Are all steps in the procedure necessary?

Is it possible to simplify or even eliminate the procedure by modifying existing company policies, departmental structures, practices of other departments, or similar considerations?

Does the procedure route the document through too many operations and/or departments?

Can the procedure be performed in a faster and a more economical manner?

Is the cost of the procedure greater than its value to the organization?

Are all of the forms used in the procedure necessary? Can some be combined?

Does duplication of work exist in the procedure?

Are the steps in a logical sequence for the greatest efficiency in the procedure?

Are there parts of the procedure that functionally belong to another activity?

Is the new procedure really essential to the organization's operations?

FIGURE 7.7
Systems design—
considerations for new
procedures.

DEVELOPMENT,
IMPLEMENTATION,
AND CONTROL OF
EFFECTIVE
MANAGEMENT
INFORMATION
SYSTEMS

puts. An integral part of logical systems design work is answering questions like those in figures 7.6 and 7.7 for new reports and procedures.

MODULAR (BUILDING BLOCK) CONCEPT.   Using a design methodology such as a structured design tool (as set forth in chapter 6), the logical design of a new system should be approached with modularity in mind. All system requirements are incorporated into a functional block diagram. Starting with the highest, each function is broken down into individual subfunctions, applying the process iteratively from the top down. The resulting analysis can be represented by an inverted tree diagram in which major functions at the top are successively broken into separate functions in the lower branches.

As the breakdown continues, two important phenomena can be observed: some branches are beginning to terminate (they do not lend themselves to further breakdown), and some of the functions are turning up in more than one place (duplicated modules). When the breakdown is complete, a thorough functional analysis is obtained even though the system has not

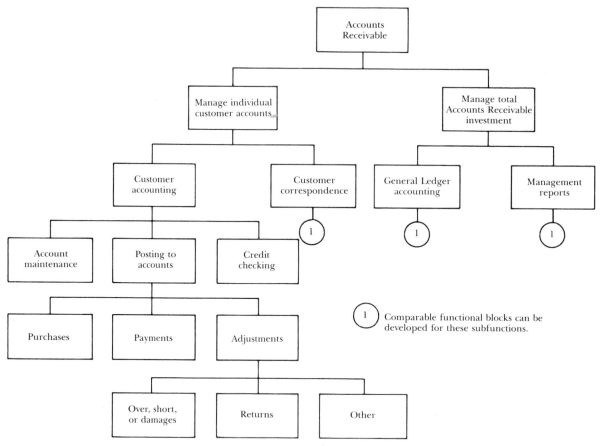

FIGURE 7.8   Partial functional block diagram of a typical accounts receivable system.

been fully designed. An analyst often finds alternative ways to break a function down into its component parts. Much time is spent on changing and filling in details considered unimportant on an earlier pass. Time spent here now is worthwhile, however, since this step forms the heart of the new system. A functional block diagram of an accounts receivable system is shown in figure 7.8.

When the functional analysis is complete, the systems analyst creates a logical system structure for the functional modules that will operate in whatever constraints are imposed. This modular approach allows the complexity of an overall system to be reduced, since many of the duplicated modules are eliminated. It also provides excellent documentation that will facilitate modification or updating of the system in the future.

STEPS IN STRUCTURED SYSTEMS DESIGN.   The structured systems design steps that should be effectively managed are noted in figure 7.9. The first two steps—determining and designing the logical system—have been treated. The remaining steps treat the structured method for resolving the final systems design. Data flow diagrams are drawn to appraise the merits of logical system alternatives with appropriate organization personnel. Since as many logical systems designs as possible are considered, some will be obviously more appealing than others and should be investigated further. Alternative

---

Determine logical outputs, files, inputs, and their basic contents.

Devise many logical systems design possibilities through a modular (building block) or similar approach, including detailed methods and procedures; consider internal controls and other parts of the system.

Prepare data flow diagrams showing the logical relationships of inputs, files, methods, procedures, and outputs for the various MIS alternatives.

Review logical systems design MIS alternatives with appropriate personnel.

Select the more promising logical MIS alternatives with the aid of properly designated personnel.

Select the best logical systems design from among the promising MIS alternatives that best meets the study's requirements.

Prepare physical system specifications for the recommended systems design and systems flowcharts. Relate the systems design to other appropriate parts of the management information system.

Compare the tangible and intangible benefits of the promising MIS alternative in the final exploratory survey report. Cost factors, volumes, and requirements for equipment and personnel should be carefully analyzed to check the report's validity.

Document the final physical design for bid invitations to equipment manufacturers.

FIGURE 7.9
Systems design—steps for one of the organization's functional areas.

DEVELOPMENT,
IMPLEMENTATION,
AND CONTROL OF
EFFECTIVE
MANAGEMENT
INFORMATION
SYSTEMS

MIS designs not covered in the original survey report are evaluated before selecting a final logical one; this permits a comprehensive review of all other promising system alternatives that come to light when the creative talents of the systems analysts are employed to their fullest.

Next, the *physical* system specifications are prepared using system flowcharts. They are compared to information in the exploratory survey report to top management to ensure that the final system meets pre-determined criteria. Finally, the new MIS is documented.

HUMAN FACTORS.   The foregoing requirements for a new physical system are not complete until the human factors in all areas are considered. For example, in coding and data representation, research indicates that while a machine can read documents numbered ''A4B'' as easily as those coded ''AB4'', a human being cannot. Systems analysts must consider the human element as well as procedures, data, and machines before finalizing any design. When tradeoffs are necessary, people should be given preference over machines.

Further, a system's results should be easily comprehensible to anyone who uses them. This requirement applies equally to employees and customers. If employees can understand what the system requires from them and, at the same time, the system is helpful to them, the end result can only be improved operating efficiency. If a customer can easily understand and process the invoices rendered, then improved customer relations will result. Less time and money will be spent dealing with customer and employee inquiries.

EQUIPMENT CONSIDERATIONS.   As shown in the final step of Figure 7.9, documentation must be prepared for bid invitations to equipment manufacturers. Equipment for the new system should be identified in general terms. However, to design a system with only one equipment manufacturer in mind is restrictive, reduces the potential of the system, and often reduces the ultimate success of the systems project. Equipment is important at this stage, but only in terms of class and type of equipment. This area is covered in depth in the next chapter.

EXCEPTION REPORTING ON SYSTEMS DESIGN.   Once the final physical design has been defined, any significant deviations from the findings of the exploratory survey report must be reported to the executive steering committee. It is the function of these top managers to make a final decision on the feasibility of applying the recommended management information system under changed conditions. In this manner, the systems design evolves from the system proposed in the exploratory survey report.

Designing Considerations for Newer MIS Environments

The preceding steps in systems design for effective management information systems must be supplemented with specific design considerations when the system is to be operated in a distributed data processing environment. Similarly, special design considerations to accommodate a decision support system and expert systems should be discussed. Because they differ, these considerations are set forth separately.

DESIGN CRITERIA FOR EFFECTIVE DISTRIBUTED DP SYSTEMS.   First of all, the procedures designed for an effective distributed data processing system are just as important as the hardware technologies used. The interplay of the data throughout the organization—through local, regional, and central sites—depends very much on the way they enter the system, how they are analyzed and manipulated, and how they move from one system to another. Because much of the singularity of this processing depends on labor content, a distributed data processing system should either displace or support labor content, with the net result of being cost effective.

Building upon this premise, accurate and efficient data handling at local and higher levels requires measurement. The systems analyst must insist that a vendor provide a clear methodology on how to measure performance at every level—from the data-entry phase at the local level to computation at the central site. Such measurements are critical for determining cost allocations at the local and higher levels.

An effective network design must be a function of the DDP system and not any individual operator, group of operators, or departments. By definition, a distributed system is used by all types of personnel in various environments. Thus, control of the quality, accuracy, and completeness of the entire network system is paramount. Such an approach leads to overall optimization of the entire DDP environment, as opposed to letting one person, group, or department exercise control over the new system requirements.

Lastly, productivity must be "designed into" the distributed system. This is not a natural by-product. The goal is to improve each person's performance, no matter where he or she is located. Otherwise, there may be little real economic justification for a distributed data processing system. Overall, the implementation of the foregoing design criteria for distributed data processing will go a long way toward realizing its benefits and controlling costs.

DESIGN CRITERIA FOR EFFECTIVE DECISION SUPPORT SYSTEMS.   Specific design criteria are applicable both to effective DDP systems and decision support systems. However, DSS criteria differ due to DSS's essential nature. From the nature of the systems development process—the life cycle approach presented in this chapter—comes a need to restructure, update, or expand system activities periodically to current practice, which is unrelated to system maintenance and error elimination functions. Without such updating, the system's usefulness could decline rapidly. The frequency of these operations for a decision support system is normally shorter than for a management information system. A typical MIS is changed about every 3 to 5 years to handle new requirements, equipment, and so forth, but a decision support system can be changed every few months, possibly every few weeks, particularly during the early phases of implementation and use. The demand for design flexibility, then, is an important criterion for effective DSS. Moreover, this need is

DEVELOPMENT,
IMPLEMENTATION,
AND CONTROL OF
EFFECTIVE
MANAGEMENT
INFORMATION
SYSTEMS

consistent with an important characteristic of DSS set forth earlier in the text (particularly in chapter 2)—namely, the adaptability of the system to changing times to answer "What if?" questions as they arise in the normal course of business.

To better understand this important point about design flexibility, consider this difference: A traditional management information system is report-oriented, in the sense that data are extracted, manipulated, and summarized into predefined formats—often on a periodic basis—for the purposes of managerial review in reporting exceptions, deviations, and the like from standards, historical reports, and similar items. Now, although decision support systems subsume portions of an MIS, especially the summarization, manipulation, and extraction capabilities, the procedures for DSS design by systems analysts are more loosely defined, thereby permitting the user to select on an ad hoc basis the frequency and, to a certain degree, the contents of the reports. From this perspective, DSS is not prespecified as in MIS design but rather is aperiodic. Hence, systems analysts must recognize decision support systems that are ad hoc. The user possibly cannot provide functional design specifications. A semi-structured or an unstructured decision environment, for example, may indicate a lack of necessary knowledge about the work environment to lay out specific procedures and requirements. Or, perhaps there is a feeling that a statement about the work to be performed possibly can never be specified. Hence, in many cases for specific functional areas of decision support systems where the future of a new system is undefined, the final design may be left up to the user as the individual develops new "What if?" questions in a semi- or unstructured environment.

DESIGN CRITERIA FOR EFFECTIVE BUSINESS EXPERT SYSTEMS. The design criteria for effective expert systems in business differ substantially from those for distributed data processing systems and decision support systems. Design activities for developing expert systems center on selecting the appropriate development tools, developing the knowledge base, and then prototyping, developing, and verifying the new expert system. Currently available from outside vendors are development tools or "shells" for building expert systems. These shells are somewhat analogous to electronic spreadsheets or fourth-generation languages used in DSS development. Essentially, they are expert system "building blocks." They include a knowledge editor for constructing the knowledge base and an inference engine that describes how to use the knowledge to reach conclusions and solve problems. Developing an expert system around a prefabricated shell takes far less time than doing it from scratch with a programming language such as LISP or PROLOG. However, what is to be accomplished by the expert system will dictate which approach is best—an off-the-shelf approach or a custom-made approach.

The use of development tools (i.e., off-the-shelf shells) allows a company to develop expert systems without having years of programming experience in LISP or PROLOG. While these tools cannot extract information from human experts and will not replace knowledge engineers, they do make it easier to build expert systems. It is the function of the feasibility study to select the appropriate development tool(s) for the expert system project. Similarly, it is up to the expert system project leader to make sure that the outlays for these development tools are within the cost constraints of the exploratory survey report to top management. Typically, costs tend to get out of hand if they are not closely supervised.

Documenting the New MIS

An important part of the structured systems design is preparing final data flow diagrams and system flowcharts for the recommended management information system, without specifying the actual equipment. Accuracy, simplicity, and ease of understanding are the essential components since nontechnical personnel may be reviewing and evaluating them.

Since all data compiled on the new system will be needed for submitting bid invitations to equipment manufacturers and preparing program flowcharts, detailed documentation is needed for the following: data origination and communications, planned inputs, files to be maintained (common data base), methods and procedures, output needs, and special requirements of the system. Also included in the bid invitation are data flow diagrams and system flowcharts depicting the interrelationships of the various parts to the entire system and those showing each area under study. Without this documentation, the feasibility study group is vulnerable since data can be easily forgotten and personnel associated with the development of the systems design can leave.

To prepare program flowcharts for later coding, appropriate logic must be developed. Block diagrams or program flowcharts can be prepared to document the new system, and decision tables can show the details of the programming effort required during systems implementation. The development of system documentation should be supervised by information systems management throughout the entire MIS project to ensure accuracy, completeness, and ease of understanding.

Summary—Systems Design for Effective MIS

DETERMINE NEW MIS REQUIREMENTS.   Systems design, or devising new system approaches, centers on determining the requirements for a new system. This initial step in logical systems design for effective MIS takes into account the information compiled to date on the present system, as well as that contained in the exploratory survey report to top management. After systems analysts have reviewed appropriate data, they must specify the following:

- new policies consistent with organization objectives
- output needs
- data files to be maintained
- planned inputs
- new methods and procedures
- internal control considerations

287

DEVELOPMENT,
IMPLEMENTATION,
AND CONTROL OF
EFFECTIVE
MANAGEMENT
INFORMATION
SYSTEMS

DESIGN THE NEW SYSTEM. It is recommended that a structured approach to systems design be undertaken initially during this critical phase. Recommended is a structured design tool that uses the *modular* or *building block* approach wherein major system functions are successful separated logically into distinct minor functions. When the functional analysis is complete, the systems analyst creates a physical structure for the functional modules that can operate within whatever hardware constraints are imposed. The net result of the structured approach is that duplicated modules—i.e., MIS tasks—are eliminated, and the complexity of the overall system is reduced.

DOCUMENT THE NEW SYSTEM. An important last step in designing a new system is preparing data flow diagrams and system flowcharts. Likewise, documentation is needed for those items determined during the systems design phase (refer to the listing above). Throughout the entire systems project, there must be proper documentation.

EFFECTIVE MIS PRACTICE—RELATIONSHIP OF THE MIS STAFF TO USERS AND OPERATIONS

In the design of an effective management information system, there should be a recognition that the MIS function is in charge of the organization's most valuable resource—information. One need only ask the question: "How many companies could function without MIS?" to gain the necessary perspective of its proper importance and role in an organization.

To help foster this critical viewpoint, the MIS staff of a project should:

- ensure that user goals are clearly defined and stated by the user and clearly understood by the project team before proposing any system solutions.
- never do anything that may undermine the user involvement. Always foster it.
- during the front-end phases of the system life cycle, serve as the stimulus for ideas from the user. Credit for ideas should never be a concern. When the creative solutions come forth from the user, then the system will be regarded by the user as his own, not someone else's.
- as the systems design evolves, ensure that it is effective not from the DP viewpoint (such as ease of implementation by DP at the expense of ease of use by the user), but rather from that of the users served by the new system.
- ensure that no shortcuts are taken to get the system done in a hurry. And always ensure that the system works according to approved specifications and that it has been comprehensively tested even if it means delays. The development process must be phased and orderly.
- limit the computerese to communication between colleagues. Confidence should not be gained by "snowjobs" that prove oneself the expert, but rather by showing an understanding of the user's problems, concerns, and objectives.

288

In addressing the role of MIS, it is not enough only to examine the relationship between the user and the MIS management and/or MIS development staff. The DP function also includes interactions with operating personnel. Their role is overlooked all too often. Everyday MIS operations are the equivalent of production in manufacturing. Once the system has been implemented, it is the operations responsibility to run the system on a regular basis and get the outputs delivered to the users on time. It should be recognized that when an MIS is placed into a production mode, the user typically interfaces with operations staff rather than with the original project team. Operations does *not*, however, have much if anything to do with the design of the MIS. Operations simply follows instructions that have been laid out for them, albeit through close coordination among the project team, the user, and their own departmental management.

CHAPTER SUMMARY

The importance of the first part of the feasibility study, namely systems analysis, cannot be overemphasized: an intensive analysis of the present system is necessary to assess its strong points and shortcomings. There is no need to duplicate the problems of the present system in the new MIS. Likewise, the strengths of the present system may be carried over into the new one without redesign.

Once the present system has been analyzed, promising and feasible management information systems are evaluated. This permits the project team to recommend the best system under the circumstances to the executive steering committee. A quick and unsophisticated undertaking will result generally in the selection and implementation of a mediocre management information system. The need for a thorough systems analysis, then, is important to the organization's future success and provides a basis for preparing a comprehensive report to top management regarding the feasibility or infeasibility of applying newer equipment and procedures.

Creative systems analysts draw upon intuition, experience, and inventive talents to develop promising MIS alternatives, each of which is analyzed by a group of systems and functional area personnel to determine its benefits and resulting impact on the organization. The most promising MIS alternative is then designed and documented. The basis for selection is the successful accomplishment of organization objectives and the attainment of quantitative and qualitative factors set forth in the exploratory survey report.

QUESTIONS

1. State at least two more guidelines for successful MIS development not given in the chapter.
2. How important is user involvement in the development of a successful management information system?

DEVELOPMENT,
IMPLEMENTATION,
AND CONTROL OF
EFFECTIVE
MANAGEMENT
INFORMATION
SYSTEMS

3. What are the essential elements of a feasibility study?

4. If you were assembling an ideal project team and a user review group for a typical manufacturing firm that is implementing a new cost accounting system, who would be the members?

5. What part of the detailed investigation of the present system is most important from a managerial viewpoint?

6. What problems are associated with calculating the net savings after federal income taxes for feasible MIS alternatives?

7. a. What questions must the systems analyst answer if the present system is to be improved?

   b. What questions must the management information systems manager answer if the present system is to be improved?

8. Why have an MIS exploratory survey report? Why not, instead, divert this cost to procuring newer equipment to effect a systems change?

9. What questions must a systems analyst ask when designing a management information system?

10. What is the relationship between reporting requirements and file design?

11. What are the typical structured steps a systems analyst should follow when designing a new management information system?

12. For the most part, initial estimates of MIS benefits are too high and estimates of costs too low. Why is this so? What can be done to change this condition?

PROBLEMS

13. In the chapter, the traditional life cycle approach to systems analysis and design was contrasted to the structured life cycle approach. Based upon the information given, state an overall approach for both life cycle approaches such that the physical and/or logical structures are included in your answer. In addition, state why one approach is preferable to the other from the systems analyst's and user's viewpoints.

14. In the chapter, intangible benefits to consider for a new management information system were given. For a typical service-oriented organization, develop your own list of eight important intangible benefits. Reference can be made to figure 7.4 as well as your own experience. Give your rationale for the inclusion of these particular intangibles in the listing.

15. In the design of an effective management information system, internal controls should be built into the system; that is, it is necessary to ensure that what has been processed is accurate. Likewise, internal controls should focus on making sure that no one person has full responsibility over an entire operation. In the area of accounts receivable for a service-oriented firm or a manufacturing-oriented firm, set forth a list of internal controls that should be an integral part of the final systems design. Include in your answer controls which assure that the proper account has been posted versus only making sure that the grand totals are correct. Also, include those controls that are necessary to ensure that the outstanding accounts receivable balances—current and old—are truly correct as to their amounts.

16. The North Company is in the process of initiating a feasibility study for a new management information system. To help the MIS manager's assistant in controlling the study, a PERT (Program Evaluation and Review Technique) time approach was used. Appropriate time estimates were developed for systems analysis, systems design, and equipment selection, and an appropriate time network was produced. However, as the MIS feasibility study progressed, actual expenditures of time and money exceeded initial plans at an appalling rate. The following questions can be raised about the use of PERT. Why was PERT ineffective during the feasibility study phase? What factors contributed to cost overruns? And what can be done now to ensure that the same problems will not crop up again during the systems implementation phase? In view of the limited facts given, write a letter to the MIS manager stating what factors might have caused this unfortunate situation to occur. Also, offer recommendations to improve the situation so that the same problems will not occur in the systems implementation phase.

17. The Roberts Company, which is switching from a batch-oriented system to an interactive-oriented management information system, conducted a study to evaluate the feasibility of making the transition. This project centers currently on the first step of the feasibility study—in particular, the financial aspects of the exploratory survey. In the exploratory survey report to the MIS executive steering committee, financial data on five feasible system alternatives were developed. The data below were used in calculating the net savings (losses) before federal income taxes for MIS system alternative #1. The company expects a 20 percent return after federal income taxes, discounted back to the present time.

Estimated savings—first year, $120,000

Estimated savings—second year, $300,000

Estimated savings—third, fourth, and fifth years, add 7 percent to each previous year

Estimated one-time costs—first year, $450,000

Estimated additional operating costs—first year, $110,000

Estimated additional operating costs—second year, $140,000

Estimated additional operating costs—third, fourth, and fifth years, add 7 percent to the previous year

Federal income tax rate—48 percent

Present value of $1 at 20 percent—first year, .833

Present value of $1 at 20 percent—second year, .694

Present value of $1 at 20 percent—third year, .579

Present value of $1 at 20 percent—fourth year, .482

Present value of $1 at 20 percent—fifth year, .402

Based upon these facts, determine whether or not the company should study the intangible benefits if the present value of net savings at 20 percent for system alternative #1 is negative after considering all tangible benefits. Assume five-year savings and costs projections that start after the completion of the feasibility study.

18. The Bender Company is switching from a batch-oriented to an interactive-oriented management information system. This project centers on the first step of a fea-

DEVELOPMENT,
IMPLEMENTATION,
AND CONTROL OF
EFFECTIVE
MANAGEMENT
INFORMATION
SYSTEMS

sibility study, namely, the analysis of feasible MIS alternatives, which is an integral part of the final exploratory survey report to top management. The MIS feasibility study group, in conjunction with the MIS executive steering committee, has decided to utilize a matrix table to select the MIS alternative that best meets the needs of the company. The MIS feasibility study group of the Bender Company has developed the following criteria (tangible and intangible benefits) and system features for evaluation. After several meetings, both groups have agreed upon the number of feasible MIS alternatives, which is five. A "Y" answer indicates that the feasible system has this important benefit or system while an "N" answer indicates the opposite.

			Alternatives			
Benefits—Tangible and Intangible		**1**	**2**	**3**	**4**	**5**
T	Meets established return on investment (20%)*	N	N	Y	Y	Y
I	Improves managerial decision making at the highest levels of management	N	N	N	N	Y
I	Improves managerial decision making at the middle levels of management	N	Y	Y	Y	Y
I	Improves managerial decision making at the lower level of management	Y	Y	Y	Y	Y
I	Improves marketability of products	Y	Y	Y	Y	Y
I	Improves customer service	N	N	Y	Y	Y
	Improves cash flow	Y	N	N	Y	Y
	Lowers the amount of accounts receivable outstanding	N	N	N	Y	Y
T	Lowers the amount invested in inventory	N	N	N	Y	Y
T	Lowers order processing costs	N	N	N	Y	Y
I	Lowers production costs	Y	Y	N	Y	Y
I	Improves production scheduling and control	N	Y	Y	Y	Y
I	Improves control over capital investments	Y	Y	Y	Y	Y
I	Improves accuracy and reliability of data	N	Y	Y	Y	Y
I	Improves decision-making ability for well structured problems	Y	Y	Y	Y	Y
I	Improves decision-making ability for poorly structured problems	N	N	N	N	Y
	System Features					
	Uses a batch-processing system	Y	Y	N	N	N
	Uses an interactive-processing system	N	N	Y	Y	Y
	Uses intelligent terminals	N	N	Y	Y	Y
	Uses graphic terminals	N	N	N	N	Y
	Uses a data base management system	N	N	Y	Y	Y
	Uses a distributed data processing system approach	N	N	N	Y	Y
	Uses a decision support system approach	N	N	N	N	Y
	Employs outside consultants	N	N	Y	Y	Y

*1—18%, 2—19%, 3—21%, 4—22%, 5—20%

Using the foregoing criteria—i.e., benefits and system features—prepare a matrix table that not only separates the tangible benefits from the intangible ones, but also uses them along with system features to determine which one of the MIS alternatives should be selected for implementation. The maximum number of benefits and system features that can accrue to the firm is the basis for selecting one MIS alternative.

BIBLIOGRAPHY

Adamski, L. "Prototyping." *Computerworld,* May 6, 1985.

Ahn, T., and Grudnitski, G. "Conceptual Perspectives on Key Factors in DSS Development: A Systems Approach." *Journal of Management Information Systems,* Summer 1985.

Alavi, M. "An Assessment of the Prototyping Approach to Information Systems Development." *Communications of the ACM,* June 1984.

Alavi, M., and Henderson, J. C. "An Evolutionary Strategy for Implementing a Decision Support System." *Management Science,* November 1981.

Alavi, M., and Weiss, I. R. "Managing the Risks Associated with End-User Computing." *Journal of Management Information Systems,* Winter 1985–86.

Alexander, D. J. "Planning and Building a DSS." *Datamation,* March 15, 1986.

Appleton, D. S. "Very Large Projects." *Datamation,* January 15, 1986.

Axelrod, C. W. "Getting a Clear Picture of Costs & Benefits." *Computerworld,* May 7, 1982.

—————. "The New Economics of Computers." *Infosystems,* June 1985.

Baroudi, J. J., and Ginzberg, M. J. "Impact of the Technology Environment on Programmer/Analyst Job Outcomes." *Communications of the ACM,* June 1986.

Batiste, J. L., and Jung, J. T. "Requirements, Needs, and Priorities: A Structured Approach for Determining MIS Project Definitions." *MIS Quarterly,* December 1984.

Beaver, J. E. "Breaking Down Old Barriers." *Computer Decisions,* April 22, 1986.

Benoit, E. "Those Hidden Costs." *Business Computer Systems,* January 1985.

Bernstein, A., "File Conversion Simplified." *Business Computer Systems,* May 1985.

—————. "Shortcut to Systems Design." *Business Computer Systems,* June 1985.

Boar, B. H. "Prototyping." *Computerworld,* September 12, 1983.

—————. *Application Prototyping.* New York: John Wiley & Sons, 1984.

Bonczek, R.; Holsapple, C.; and Whinston, A. B. "Development Tools for Decision Support Systems." *Computerworld,* September 14, 1981.

Bromberg, H. "In Search of Productivity." *Datamation,* August 15, 1984.

Brown, P. "Managing Software Development." *Datamation,* April 15, 1986.

Burch, B. M. "Are We Automating the Problem or the Process?" *Information Management,* December 1984.

Burch, J. S. "Adaptation of Information Systems Building Blocks to Design Forces." *Journal of Management Information Systems,* Summer 1986.

Buss, M. D. J. "How to Rank Computer Projects." *Harvard Business Review,* January-February 1983.

Carlson, E. "An Approach for Designing Decision Support Systems." *Data Base,* Winter 1979.

Celko, J. "There's Movement, But Is There Progress?" *Software News,* May 1985.

Connell, J., and Brice, L. "Rapid Prototyping." *Datamation,* August 15, 1984.

Conor, D. A. "Application System Development Methodologies." *Computerworld,* February 28, 1982.

Cook, R. "Automated Tools Are Backlog Breakers." *Computer Decisions,* April 23, 1985.

Cozette, C. "Everyone Needs a Backlog." *Infosystems,* April 1986.

Cronan, T. P. "Applications System Development: A Communication Model for Business Users and DP Personnel." *Data Base,* Fall 1984.

Cullum, R. L. "Iterative Development." *Datamation,* February 15, 1985.

De, P., and Sen, A. "Logical Data Base Design in Decision Support Systems." *Journal of Systems Management,* May 1981.

DeMarco, T. *Structured Analysis and System Specification.* Englewood Cliffs, NJ: Prentice-Hall, 1979.

Denise, R. M. "Technology for the Executive Thinker." *Datamation*, August 1983. ✳

DeSanctis, G., and Courtney, J. F. "Toward Friendly MIS Implementation." *Communications of the ACM*, October 1983.

Dilworth, J. B.; Ford, R. C.; Ginter, P. M.; and Rucks, A. C. "Centralized Project Management." *Journal of Systems Management*, August 1985.

Doll, W. "Avenues for Top Management Involvement in Successful MIS Development." *MIS Quarterly*, March 1985.

Doll, W. J., and Ahmed, M. V., "Objectives for System Planning." *Journal of Systems Management*, December 1984.

Drury, D. H. "An Evaluation of Data Processing Committees." *Mis Quarterly*, December 1984.

Earl, M. J. "Prototype Systems for Accounting Information and Control." *Data Base*, Winter-Spring 1982.

Frank, W. L. "Structured vs. Prototyping Methodology." *Computerworld*, August 15, 1983.

Franz, C. R. "User Leadership in the System Development Life Cycle: A Contingency Model." *Journal of Management Information Systems*, Fall 1985.

Frenkel, K. A. "Toward Automating the Software-Development Cycle." *Communications of the ACM*, June 1985.

Fronk, W. C. "You Can Increase the Worth of Feasibility Studies." *Infosystems*, September 1981.

Furge, S., and Mau, D. H. "Fourth-Generation Application Development." *Information Center*, June 1986.

Gane, C., and Sarson, T. *Structured Systems Analysis: Tools and Techniques*. Englewood Cliffs, NJ: Prentice-Hall, 1979.

Gildersleeve, T. R. *Data Processing Project Management*. New York: Van Nostrand Reinhold, 1985.

Gold, J. "Models of Inefficiency, Demons of Productivity." *Computer Decisions*, May 20, 1986.

Good, P. "Get Your Projects Under Control." *Business Software Review*, April 1986.

Graham, R. J. *Project Management, Combining Technical and Behavioral Approaches for Effective Implementation*. New York: Van Nostrand Reinhold, 1985.

Greer, W. R., Jr. "Value Added Criterion for Decision Support System Development." *Journal of Systems Management*, May 1980.

Gremillion, L. L. "Managing the Implementation of Standardized Computer Based System." *MIS Quarterly*, December 1980.

Gremillion, L.L., and Pyburn, P. "Breaking the Systems Development Bottleneck." *Harvard Business Review*, March-April 1983. ✳

————. "Justifying Decision Support and Office Automated Systems." *Journal of Management Information Systems*, Summer 1985.

Guinan, P. J., and Bostrom, R. P. "Development of Computer-Based Information Systems: A Communication Framework." *Data Base*, Spring 1986.

Hansen, J. V.; McKell, L. J.; and Heitger, L. E. "ISMS: Computer-Aided Analysis for Design of Decision Support Systems." *Management Science*, November 1979.

Hedburg, B., and Jonsson, S. "Designing Semiconfusing Information Systems for Changing Environments." *Data Base*, Winter-Spring 1982.

Hedrick, R. T. "Improving Productivity at Northern Trust." *Datamation*, May 15, 1986. ✳

Henderson, J. C., and Schilling, D. A. "Design and Implementation of Decision Support Systems in the Public Sector." *MIS Quarterly*, June 1985.

Hogue, J. T., "Decision Support Systems and the Traditional Computer Information System Function: An Examination of Relationships during DSS Application." *Journal of Management Information Systems*, Summer 1985.

Hogue, J. T., and Watson, H. J. "Management's Role in the Approval and Administration of Decision Support Systems." *MIS Quarterly*, June 1983.

Horton, L. "Could Project Management Be the Next Super Product?" *Software News*, May 1985.

————. "Users Find a Tool to Manage Themselves." *Software News*, May 1985.

Huber, G. P. "Cognitive Style as a Basis for MIS and DSS Designs: Much Ado About Nothing?" *Management Science*, May 1983.

————. "The Nature of Organizational Decision Making and the Design of Decision Support Systems." *MIS Quarterly,* June 1983.

Johnson, J. R. "A Prototypical Success Story." *Datamation,* November 1983. ✗

Jones, C. "How Not to Measure Programming Quality." *Computerworld,* January 20, 1986.

Juris, R. "Automater, Automate Thyself." *Computer Decisions,* February 25, 1986.

Karten, N. "REMark: MIS in Eclipse." *PC World,* June 1986.

Keen, P. G. W. "Adaptive Design for Decision Support Systems." *Data Base,* Nos. 1 and 2, Fall 1980.

————. "Value Analysis: Justifying Decision Support Systems." *MIS Quarterly,* March 1981.

————. "A Walk Through Decision Support." *Computerworld,* January 14, 1985.

Kempf, T. "End-User Training; Self-Teaching Methods Are Maturing." *ISOWorld,* February 7, 1983.

Kendall, K. E., and Kendall, J. E. "Observing Organizational Environments: A System Approach for Information Analysts." *MIS Quarterly,* March 1981.

King, D. "Current Methodologies in Structured Design." *Computerworld,* October 12, 1981.

Klein, G.; Konsynski, B.; and Beck, P. O. "A Linear Representation for Model Management in a DSS." *Journal of Management Information Systems,* Fall 1985.

Kolodziej, S. "Gaining Control of Maintenance." *Computerworld Focus,* February 19, 1986.

Kull, D. "Tooling up for Design." *Computer Decisions,* February, 12, 1985.

————. "Designs on Development." *Computer Decisions,* April 9, 1985.

Leavitt, D. "The Proper Design Tools Can Bring Improved Productivity." *Software News,* February 1985.

————. "Application Development Systems Help Get Systematic." *Software News,* March 1985.

————. "Design Tools: The Real Starting Point." *Software News,* February 1986.

————. "Application Development Systems Mean Speed, Quality." *Software News,* March 1986.

Lee, A. F. "Why Prototyping Works." *Infosystems,* March 1985.

Leighton, R. T. "Decision Support Systems." *Journal of Systems Management,* February 1981.

Leventhal, N. S. "Systems Designing—What Is Wrong?" *Management Information Systems Week,* March 10, 1986.

Lindgren, R. K. "Justifying a Decision Support System." *Data Management,* May 1981.

Litecky, C. R. "Intangibles in Cost/Benefit Analysis." *Journal of Systems Management,* February 1981.

Locander, N. B.; Napier, H. H.; and Scamell, R. W. "A Team Approach to Managing the Development of a Decision Support System." *MIS Quarterly,* March 1979.

Lorentzen, R., and Tinnirello, P. "Application Development, A Guide Through the Maze of Tools and Methods." *Computerworld,* February 24, 1986.

Lucas, H. C., Jr. *The Analysis, Design, and Implementation of Information Systems.* New York: McGraw-Hill Book Company, 1981.

Mahmood, M. A.; Courtney, J. F.; and Burns, J. R. "Environmental Factors Affecting Decision Support System Design." *Data Base,* Summer 1983.

Martin, J. *Application Development Without Programming.* Englewood Cliffs, NJ: Prentice-Hall, 1983.

————. *System Design from Provably Correct Constructs.* Englewood Cliffs, NJ: Prentice-Hall, 1985.

Martin, J., and McClure C. "The Latest Look in Programmer Productivity Tools." *Business Software Review,* May 1986.

Martin, M. P. "Determining Information Requirements for DSS." *Journal of Systems Management,* December 1982.

Mason, R. E. A., and Carey, T. T. "Prototyping Interactive Information Systems." *Communications of the ACM,* May 1983.

Mazzucchelli, L. "Structured Analysis Can Streamline Software Design." *Computerworld,* December 9, 1985.

Meador, C. L., and Mezger, R. A. "Selecting an End User Programming Language DSS Development." *MIS Quarterly,* December 1984.

Menkus, B. "Practical Considerations in Decision Support Systems Design." *Journal of Systems Development,* June 1983.

Meyer, N. D. "Implementing Technology: The Quest for Support." *Data Communications,* Mid-September 1983.

Miller, F. W. "Secrets of Successful Bridge Builders." *Infosystems,* December 1982.

Mills, J. A. "A Pragmatic View of the System Architect." *Communications of the ACM,* July 1985.

Monk, J. T., and Landis, K. M. "Gaining Control of Time and Resources." *Business Computer Systems,* October 1984.

Moore, J. H., and Chang, M. G. "Design of Decision Support Systems." *Data Base,* Nos. 1 and 2, Fall 1980.

Naumann, J. D., and Jenkins, M. A. "Prototyping: The New Paradigm for System Development." *MIS Quarterly,* September 1982.

Nichols, J. M. "User Involvement: What Kind, How Much, and When?" *Journal of Systems Management,* March 1985.

O'Dell, P. "Design: Do-It-Yourself System." *Computer Decisions,* May 7, 1985.

————. "Development Methods Meld." *Computer Decisions,* March 25, 1986.

Paulson, R. D. "The Chief Executive as Change Agent." *Management Review,* February 1982.

Ramsgard, W. C. *Making Systems Work, the Psychology of Business Systems.* New York: John Wiley & Sons, 1977.

Rau, K. "Accounting for Computers, When Management Asks, Can You Answer?" *Computerworld,* October 21, 1985.

Reimann, B. C. "Decision Support Systems: Strategic Management Tools for the Eighties." *Business Horizons,* September-October 1985.

Rifkin, G. "DP as a Profit Center." *Computerworld,* February 10, 1986.

Rockhold, A. G. "MIS Feels Pressure of ROI Cost/Benefit Analysis." *Infosystems,* July 1982.

Rosenberg, M., "The Craft of Project Management," *Business Computer Systems,* September 1985.

Rowe, L. A. "Tools for Developing OLTP Applications." *Datamation,* August 1, 1985. ✳

Ruggera, M. "Four Tools to Build System Synergy." *Computerworld,* October 31, 1983.

Schoman, K. E., Jr. "The Case of the Applications Backlog." *Datamation,* November 1, 1984. ✳

Senn, J. A. *Analysis and Design of Information Systems.* New York: McGraw-Hill Book Company, 1984.

Shaw, D. L. "A Total System Approach." *Infosystems,* November 1984.

Shneiderman, B. "How to Design with the User in Mind." *Datamation,* April 1982. ✳

Snyder, C. A., and Cox, J. F. "A Dynamic Systems Development Life-Cycle Approach: A Project Management Information System." *Journal of Management Information Systems,* Spring 1986.

Snyders, J. "Programmer Aids: Boosting Productivity." *Computer Decisions,* March 1983.

————. "The Benefits of Programmer Productivity Software." *Infosystems,* June 1985.

Spadaro, D. "Project Evaluation Made Simple." *Datamation,* November 1, 1985. ✳

Stahl, B. "Friendly Mainframe Software Guides Users Toward Productivity." *Computerworld,* February 3, 1986.

Strauss, P. "Managing Information Systems for Payback and Planning." *Data Communications,* Mid-September 1983.

Sweet, F. "Managing Data-Driven Development." *Datamation,* June 15, 1986. ✳

Symonds, K. "Introducing the Decision Support System." *Management Accounting,* December 1981.

Tharrington, J. M. "The Science of MIS Planning." *Infosystems,* June 1985.

Thierauf, R. J. *Decision Support Systems for Effective Planning and Control—A Case Study Approach.* Englewood Cliffs, NJ: Prentice-Hall, 1982.

————. *Systems Analysis and Design—A Case Study Approach,* sec. ed. Columbus, OH: Charles E. Merrill Publishing Company, 1986.

Troy, D. A., and Zweben, S. H. "Measuring the Quality of Structural Designs." *The Journal of Systems and Software,* June 1981.

Tucker, M. "Software Tools Shrink Development Time." *Mini-Micro Systems,* June 1986.

Vacca, J. R. "Can the Prototype Do the Job?" *Information Center,* June 1986.

Venkatakrisnan, V. "The Information Cycle." *Datamation,* September 1983. ✳

Verity, J. W. "Empowering Programmers." *Datamation,* August 15, 1985. ✳

Vierek, R. K. "Decision Support Systems: A MIS Manager's Perspective." *MIS Quarterly,* December 1981.

Volkema, R. J. "Problem Formulation in Planning and Design." *Management Science,* June 1983.

Ward, P. T. *Systems Development Without Pain: A User's Guide to Modeling Organizational Patterns.* New York: Yourdon, 1984.

Watkins, P. R. "Perceived Information Structure: Implications for Decision Support System Design." *Decision Sciences,* January 1982.

Weiss, E. "The Next Wave of User Documentation." *Computerworld,* September 9, 1985.

Whieldon, D. "Steering Committees: A Teamwork Approach." *Computer Decisions,* September 15, 1983.

————. "Prototyping: Shortcut to Applications." *Computer Decisions,* June 1984.

Wybolt, N. "Step by Step." *The DEC Professional,* May 1986.

Yadav, S. B. "Determining an Organization's Information Requirements: A State of the Art Survey." *Data Base,* Spring 1983.

Young, J. F. "Right-Brained Decision Support Systems." *Data Base,* Summer 1983.

Zachmann, W. F. *Keys to Enhancing System Development Productivity.* New York: AMACOM, 1981.

Zalud, B. "Decision Support Systems—Push End User in Design/Build Stage." *Data Management,* January 1981.

Zells, L. "A Practical Approach to a Project Expectations Document." *Computerworld,* August 29, 1983.

Zmud, R. "Management of Large Software Development Efforts." *MIS Quarterly,* June 1980.

Zvegintzov, N. "Front-End Programming Environments." *Datamation,* August 15, 1984.

CHAPTER 8

Equipment Selection and Implementation of Management Information Systems

This chapter builds on the previous one. Initially, the key factors in evaluating hardware and software vendors are explored. The underlying theme is that the vendor must be able to meet the equipment needs of the MIS. Next, the chapter looks at equipment selection. In addition to the traditional material about bid invitations, we discuss the bargaining process with equipment vendors. This latter emphasis highlights the need to get the best equipment for the least cost.

This background sets the stage for enumerating the major steps of systems implementation, namely, the detailed steps of preparatory work and operation of the new system. Systems implementation becomes more of a team effort since user, systems, and operations personnel are involved in a wide range of MIS activities. This team will not only schedule the new system, advise on personnel selection and training, and assist in the preparatory work of the new MIS, but also do whatever is necessary to assist in the operation of a new system. Additionally, a periodic review of new system approaches should be undertaken to determine the feasibility of starting the MIS development process anew.

KEY FACTORS IN EVALUATING VENDORS

Before exploring the major stages of the equipment selection process in an MIS project study, it is helpful to look at the key factors in evaluating equipment vendors, both of microcomputers and mainframes. Due to the emergence of a great many hardware and software vendors over a very short period of time, the MIS manager and assistant should visit the vendors' offices, talk with their personnel, and get a feel for the organization. The following vendor evaluation criteria assist in analyzing vendors in some detail. Particularly, the criteria help one examine the vendor's background, support, and plans for the future. The vendor should:

- □ possess long-range plans for support of the product
- □ possess a good corporate reputation for reliability
- □ reflect financial stability
- □ possess a high credibility rating in the industry
- □ provide a staff with in-depth industrial knowledge and background
- □ possess an intimate knowledge of their product
- □ be totally committed to the support of the product
- □ be easily accessible and available to clientele
- □ provide an effective implementation program
- □ provide additional services as needed to support the product
- □ maintain effective communication with users
- □ encourage user interaction and involvement
- □ provide for a well-defined maintenance plan

DEVELOPMENT,
IMPLEMENTATION,
AND CONTROL OF
EFFECTIVE
MANAGEMENT
INFORMATION
SYSTEMS

An incorrect evaluation of the foregoing key factors could harm the systems function for years to come. What are the savings from improved planning, control, and accountability? What are the benefits of being associated with users using the same approach to design and management? What are the savings in training and good communications, to name but two areas? There are no clear-cut answers to these questions since each installation is unique. What benefits one installation may not benefit another. Hence, the MIS manager must be actively involved in the vendor evaluation process for best results, both for hardware and software.

Users versus MIS

Although the foregoing key factors have been the mainstay in vendor evaluation, the days when the MIS department had the first, last, and only word in acquiring equipment are gone. As users discovered the personal computer and departmental computing, vendors found they could sell around MIS. When users become aware of the importance of information, vendors found opportunities to sell over MIS. However, MIS is regaining its former position as a business-oriented architect of information policy. In most cases, it is winning new support from users and senior management alike. The job of MIS managers will be much easier if vendors understand and support the goal of a rational, corporate-wide approach to information management and office automation. For one thing, vendors can be MIS allies in gaining support from impatient departments. For another, manufacturers can concentrate on the hardware, software, and communications tools that provide the long-term, integrated solutions that MIS seeks.

EQUIPMENT SELECTION PROCESS

Equipment selection should be undertaken by the MIS study group after systems design is complete. Basic steps are to determine equipment manufacturers, submit bid invitations to manufacturers, evaluate manufacturers' proposals, and select equipment manufacturer(s).

Determining Equipment Manufacturers

Before submitting necessary data to equipment manufacturers, their representatives should be contacted and invited to an orientation meeting on the proposed new system. During the meeting, they should be instructed about the areas to be converted, general problems that will be encountered, approximate present and future volumes, and other pertinent data. Each manufacturer should indicate in writing whether it wishes to receive a bid invitation so that the preparation of a packet of specifications, data flow diagrams, program flowcharts,decision tables, and comparable material will not be wasted on a firm with no interest in bidding on the system.

Most organizations undertaking a management information systems project have some type of computer equipment under consideration based on the exploratory survey report. Since they have computer and related peripheral equipment salespersons calling at various times, they have had previous contact with most of the manufacturers. Hence, the determination of appropriate equipment manufacturers generally presents no problem to the MIS study group.

Submitting Bid Invitations to Manufacturers

After letters of intent are on file from equipment manufacturers, the company submits bid invitations to interested suppliers. The preferred approach is to mail the same set of data to all competing manufacturers. This permits bids to be placed on an unbiased basis, informs the manufacturers what requirements they must meet, minimizes questions, and allows a valid basis for comparison of equipment. The manufacturers will probably need additional information and assistance from the prospective customer as they progress with the preparation of their proposals. Generally, one person from the MIS study group will perform this consultative function for a specific manufacturer.

With this approach, the respective manufacturers should have ample information to familiarize themselves with the company and its peculiar information systems problems. Their proposals should show clearly how the equipment will meet the customer's needs. If the specifications lack clear definition from the beginning, the bid invitations will come back as proposals with standard approaches that are applicable to any and all potential customers, and the organization's preliminary work will have been a waste of time. The equipment manufacturers cannot prepare proposals tailored specifically for a particular customer if the data contained in the bid invitation are deficient. It is of utmost importance for MIS management to see that data submitted to manufacturers are as complete and self-explanatory as possible.

NEW SYSTEMS SPECIFICATIONS. Much of the material needed for the bid invitation can be taken directly from the exploratory survey report and developed during systems design. The contents of the bid invitation include

    I. general company information
    II. future management information systems plans
    III. new system specifications
    IV. new data flow diagrams
    V. data requested of each manufacturer

Each topic is detailed in figure 8.1.

Sections I and II should be brief to focus attention on the remaining parts of the invitation. Data necessary for a thorough study are contained in Sections III and IV and will form the basis of the manufacturer's proposal. Section III contains 5 essential parts: planned inputs, methods and procedures for handling data, files to be maintained, output needs, and other requirements and considerations for the new system. Material developed for Section IV was discussed in the prior chapter; if the design was properly documented, most

I. General Company Information

A. Description of the company and its activities
B. Overview of present MIS equipment and applications
C. Unusual information system exceptions and problems
D. Other important general information

II. Future Management Information Systems Plans

A. List of areas encompassed by the new system
B. Target date for installation
C. Deadline for submitting proposals
D. Equipment decision table by the company
E. Criteria for analyzing and comparing manufacturers' proposals

III. New System Specifications

A. Planned inputs:
   1. Where data originate within the system
   2. Name and content of input data, such as documents and forms
   3. Hourly rates of input data
   4. Volume of inputs, including high and low points

B. Methods and procedures for handling data:
   1. Transmission of local and distant data
   2. Types of transactions handled
   3. Computations and logical decisions required
   4. New data generation within the system
   5. Control points to test accuracy of data and eliminate processing of fraudulent data

C. Files to be maintained:
   1. Specify on-line and off-line storage
   2. Name and contents of files to be maintained
   3. Methods and procedures for updating files
   4. Size of files to be maintained

D. Output needs:
   1. Name and content of output, such as reports and summaries
   2. Timely distribution of output data
   3. Hourly rates of output data
   4. Volume and outputs, including high and low points

E. Other requirements and considerations:
   1. Policy changes to conform with new system
   2. Compatibility of common data processing language
   3. Special internal controls
   4. Ability to handle company's future growth

FIGURE 8.1 Contents of a bid invitation to an equipment manufacturer.

    5. Equipment cost ceiling (whether lease or purchase)

    6. Additional special requirements and considerations

IV. New Data Flow Diagrams

A. Brief description of the systems approach for each functional area under study

B. Data flow diagrams for each area

C. Data flow diagrams to show interrelationships between functional areas

D. Data flow diagrams showing overview of the new system

V. Data Requested of Each Manufacturer

A. Processing time for each area

B. Proposed computer hardware:
1. Basic equipment and components—capabilities and technical features
2. Peripheral equipment—capabilities and technical features
3. Expansion capability of MIS equipment (modular concept)
4. Purchase price and monthly rental figures on one-, two-, and three-shift bases for basic and peripheral equipment
5. Alternative purchase and lease option plan (third-party leasing)
6. Estimated delivery and installation data
7. Number of magnetic tapes and/or disk packs and their cost
8. Equipment cancellation terms

C. Site preparation and installation requirements:
1. Amount of space needed
2. Electrical power, air conditioning, and humidity control requirements
3. Flooring and enclosure requirements

D. Extent of manufacturer's assistance:
1. Manufacturer's personnel installation—cost and duration of assistance
2. Availability and location of programming classes
3. Possibility of on-site training classes
4. Availability of procedure-oriented languages, compilers, programming aids, and program libraries
5. Nearest testing facilities and available shifts
6. Duration of free equipment time for compiling and testing programs

E. Maintenance service to be provided

F. Equipment support for emergency processing

G. Other pertinent information

FIGURE 8.1   (continued)

DEVELOPMENT,
IMPLEMENTATION,
AND CONTROL OF
EFFECTIVE
MANAGEMENT
INFORMATION
SYSTEMS

material can be used without change. Data flow diagrams will provide an over-view of the system and its subsystems.

Data to be stated in each manufacturer's proposal are listed in the final section of the bid invitation. Specifying in advance what the proposals should contain ensures that comparable information for a final evaluation will be forthcoming.

CONFERENCES WITH MANUFACTURERS. Even though bid invitations specify the numerous details of the new system, legitimate questions will be raised by the various equipment companies. Many will reflect possible modification of some areas to take advantage of the equipment's special features. Conferences between the manufacturer and the potential customer, then, can prove beneficial to both parties.

Evaluating Manufacturers' Proposals

The manufacturers should be given a reasonable amount of time to prepare their proposals; 60 days is often adequate, although large and advanced systems may take longer. The customer receives several copies for review, followed by an oral presentation. After this procedure has been followed by all competing manufacturers, the MIS study group, in conjunction with the management information systems manager, is prepared to evaluate the information in the various proposals.

GENERAL EQUIPMENT CRITERIA FOR MANAGEMENT INFORMATION SYSTEMS. Many general criteria can be developed for evaluating a manufacturer's proposal. They include:

□ *Extent of automation proposed* refers to the amount of new MIS equipment proposed for the new system, ranging from micros to large-scale minis. This criterion gives the study group an overview of what is being advocated by each equipment manufacturer.

□ *Throughput performance* relates to the amount of data that can be processed by the computer system within a specific time period. In view of the difficulties with running computer programs—malfunctions of the computer's components, paper jams, error stops, input/output units out of cards, etc.—most experienced MIS managers add 50 percent to the manufacturer's time estimates. To test the validity of time estimates, a *benchmark* problem approach can be employed, which consists of selecting a representative job or group of jobs to be performed by the new system, and then requesting results from the vendor.

□ *Type of equipment* addresses the make, model, and quantity of basic and related peripheral equipment, as well as their capabilities, operating characteristics, and technical features. Data on internal memory, operating speeds, storage capacity, and hardware controls are a part of the manufacturer's proposals on computers and related equipment.

EQUIPMENT
SELECTION AND
IMPLEMENTATION OF
MANAGEMENT
INFORMATION
SYSTEMS

- *Rental, purchase, or other basis* refers to the methods of acquiring MIS equipment. They currently include outright purchase, option to buy, rental, third-party leasing, and financial lessor (leased with borrowed money). Generally, total rental charges are high since manufacturers write off the costs of equipment over relatively short periods so that the capital recovery portion of the monthly lease is high. They also have to include cost factors to cover the possibility of having to lease the equipment to others. For these reasons, third-party leases and financial lessors are widely used today. Overall, the decision to purchase or lease is based on many factors, such as the availability of capital funds, obsolescence of equipment, and the usage factor.
- *Delivery of equipment* relates to the delivery date. It must allow ample time to test the equipment on the user's premises. Delivery dates run from several weeks to several years. This is normally contingent upon the manufacturer, the type of hardware, and the order date.
- *Manufacturer's assistance* is the amount and type of assistance expected from the equipment manufacturers. Assistance includes: programmers, systems analysts, and engineers to implement the new system; training schools for the client's managers, programmers, and operators; software packages to simplify programming; and equipment for program testing prior to the installation. (Service for MIS education and systems engineering are normally billed separately to the user.)
- *Availability and quality of software* concerns software to support the hardware. Software includes: third-, fourth-, and fifth-generation programming languages for business and scientific applications; program packages for reading and punching cards, reading and writing magnetic tapes, sort and merge routines, and others; compilers to assist in writing the final programs' routines, to aid the computer operator during program debugging, and to handle successive programs during production runs; and routine programs for handling specialized problems. The availability of reliable software reduces the user's time and expense, since the MIS staff can work at a reasonably high level of programming efficiency.
- *Maintenance contracts* are normally provided free under a rental contract, but not when the equipment is purchased. For small equipment installation, the maintenance function will be performed from the manufacturer's sales office. For large machine systems, the manufacturer may assign maintenance personnel to one or more systems.
- *Other considerations* include the ability to handle exceptions and unusual items, nearness to compatible machines for processing data on an emergency basis, overtime costs, and similar items.

SPECIFIC EQUIPMENT CRITERIA FOR DISTRIBUTED DATA PROCESSING SYSTEMS. In addition to these general criteria for evaluating equipment proposed by a manufacturer, the equipment criteria that are peculiar to distributed data processing systems must be identified because a wide range of

DEVELOPMENT,
IMPLEMENTATION,
AND CONTROL OF
EFFECTIVE
MANAGEMENT
INFORMATION
SYSTEMS

equipment is available to undertake DDP. More importantly, however, because a small distributed data processing system in one area of an organization may eventually be extended nationwide, there is added incentive to develop such a list. In view of these factors, the following equipment criteria are offered:

- *Capability of incorporating newer DDP equipment* as it comes to the market, so that the lowest-cost equipment can be integrated into the distributed data processing system to minimize costs.
- *Successful integration of current usable equipment with newer DDP equipment*—if deemed appropriate—so that disruption of operations can be minimized, and the DDP system can be more effective in meeting users' needs.
- *Capability of performing operations at the appropriate level;* that is, allowing the user to perform processing at the local, regional, and central sites with the DDP equipment.
- *Integration of equipment within the DDP network* such that the network operates as efficiently as possible while allowing adequate control over the network of distributed data processing system.
- *Capability of improving local autonomy of data processing operations* such that operational activities and exception items peculiar to one operational system can be easily accommodated.

Based upon these criteria, perhaps the most important factors in choosing distributed equipment are those that relate to all hardware. They are *flexibility* to meet almost any DDP requirement for an organization and *expandability* of the equipment to meet expansion needs. As lower-cost devices become even more reasonable in the future, an organization should be able to take advantage of these buys. Also, the expense to replace, change, and maintain a distributed data processing system might well become greater than the value of the system hardware itself. Hence, an effective distributed data processing system should be flexible and expandable to take advantage of newer, lower-cost equipment and, at the same time, be sensitive to the benefits and costs of converting to the newer equipment.

SPECIFIC EQUIPMENT CRITERIA FOR DECISION SUPPORT SYSTEMS.   Just as specific equipment criteria fit DDP systems, the same can be said for decision support systems. DSS criteria emphasize equipment that assists the decision maker throughout the problem-solving process. In essence, they help the decision maker interface with the computer. Typical criteria are:

- *Greater accessibility for the decision maker* in the use of computer power, due to simplified programming and implementation.
- *Use of management workstations* that can interface with the decision maker throughout the problem-solving process.
- *Availability of color graphic devices* to plot trends, exceptions, and similar items for decision making.
- *Availability of high-quality DSS software* to support the decision

maker, including mathematical and statistical packages as well as non-procedural languages.

□ *Capability of DSS hardware to interface with other computer systems* so that all of the systems are compatible.

EQUIPMENT
SELECTION AND
IMPLEMENTATION OF
MANAGEMENT
INFORMATION
SYSTEMS

The acquisition of appropriate equipment for decision support systems enhances the capabilities and effectiveness of decision makers. Thus, it can increase the productivity of managers and support personnel at all organization levels in various departments. Appropriate DSS hardware can effectively extend the organization's present MIS staff by reducing its workload. It can bring the organization even closer to bridging the chasms still separating the traditional MIS world.

SPECIFIC EQUIPMENT CRITERIA FOR EXPERT SYSTEMS. Going beyond previous equipment considerations for DDP and DSS, the criteria for expert systems take a slightly different direction. The emphasis is on procuring specific hardware built for developing and implementing expert systems *only*. Typical criteria are:

□ *Capability of acquiring new hardware* specifically designed for expert systems that support the use of AI programming languages, like LISP and PROLOG, to implement these systems.
□ *Use of AI workstations* that facilitate the development of expert system programs.
□ *Availability of color graphics* to assist in making expert system decisions.
□ *Capability of expert system hardware to interface* with other computer systems.
□ *Availability of high-quality expert system shells* to allow the programmer to produce low-cost and easy-to-use expert systems.

Within the framework of these criteria, one must also try to acquire hardware that can meet the company's future as well as current needs. Too often, hardware is purchased without regard to the future. Typically, after the first expert systems are developed—which tend to be straightforward—expert system development is undertaken that is considerably more complex. The net result is that the wrong hardware was acquired. Since this is relatively new territory for MIS, consideration for the long term should be given in acquiring expert system hardware.

SOFTWARE CONSIDERATIONS. In the preceding specifications of general and specific equipment criteria for the various information systems, reference was made to the availability and quality of software. Although software can be purchased from computer manufacturers, sometimes it does not meet the needs of the newer information systems. Hence, it may be necessary to inquire about software available from sources other than computer manufacturers.

307

DEVELOPMENT,
IMPLEMENTATION,
AND CONTROL OF
EFFECTIVE
MANAGEMENT
INFORMATION
SYSTEMS

Whether computer manufacturers or software vendors are used, several questions must be asked. They include:

□ *How much does the fully operational product cost?* What options are offered, at what cost, and how are they installed? Getting a clear statement initially on the options—particularly on the cost of desirable options if they are incorporated into the delivered package versus how much the same options would cost if tacked on after installation—is extremely important.

□ *Is there a trial period?* Some vendors customarily allow their software to be installed at a prospective purchaser's site for trial use. A nominal pre-acquisition investment could short-circuit many future problems by helping the user to decide on options, training, and other costly variables.

□ *What are the costs for installation assistance and training?* Costs tend to vary from one vendor to another.

□ *What are the documentation costs? How are updates covered?* Update costs are usually bundled into the maintenance fee, although updates can often be purchased separately if the purchaser does not take a maintenance contract.

□ *What is the cost of a maintenance contract?* The fee is generally about 10 percent of the then-current one-time license fee of the package, beginning in the second year. Because fees are being pressured upward toward the 15 percent level, a fixed rate at the front end of an agreement—rather than letting the rate float at the vendor's discretion—should be contracted.

□ *How are the enhancements handled?* The difference between a genuine enhancement and a "fix" should be clarified. Enhancements for a fee are optional; fixes are usually free as long as the user has not tampered with the package. Also, the user should make sure that the full price of the package can be credited against the next major version of the package.

Answers to the preceding questions provide the potential purchaser with a good idea of software acquisition costs. However, several other factors can influence both the acquisition and the ongoing costs of software. Some selected questions that should be asked are:

□ *What discounts apply to multiple acquisitions* for installations at the same site or at different sites of the same company?

□ *Is the source code available?* Given the source code and perhaps a couple of other listings, the purchaser knows as much about a package as the vendor. The vendor invariably charges a one-time fee for the code, and the purchaser usually then assumes all maintenance responsibilities.

□ *What arrangements have been made for ongoing maintenance if the vendor goes out of business?* The answer to this question and the next question should be tied back to the availability of the source code.

EQUIPMENT
SELECTION AND
IMPLEMENTATION OF
MANAGEMENT
INFORMATION
SYSTEMS

□ *What are the charges for custom modifications?* These are invariably expensive, but possibly beneficial in the long run if the modifications substantially improve the package's utility to the purchaser.

□ *What penalties can be levied* on the vendor for late delivery or nonperformance?

□ *What notification period* is required or what penalty is incurred if a leased or rented package is removed before the contract expires?

□ *What support guarantees* are provided if an older version of the package is retained?

As with the first set of questions, answers to this second set help the purchaser determine the feasibility of acquiring the appropriate software.

COMPLIANCE WITH TERMS OF BID INVITATION.   One last consideration is how well each manufacturer (or software vendor if applicable) has complied with the terms of the bid invitation. This involves completeness, clarity, accuracy, and responsiveness. Does each proposal cover all points set forth in the bid invitation, especially if it involved a distributed data processing approach or a decision support system? Is the proposal clear in every respect? Are all estimates of time and cost for peak, medium, and low workloads accurate? Does the proposal reflect a proper understanding of the bid? The manufacturer's failure in any one of these points could indicate a weakness and potential problems in the future. Final equipment evaluation, then, should include compliance with the original bid terms.

Selecting Equipment Manufacturer(s)

Selection of the equipment manufacturer(s) is a difficult task for the MIS study group. The selection process is much easier if the equipment proposed is virtually identical; the choice is normally based on the cost. But this is generally not possible since equipment features will vary. Various methods have been developed for evaluating and selecting from among dissimilar equipment. Often discussion with other customers of the vendor and/or consultants will yield useful information. Other methods include the matrix table and the weighting method, which are discussed below.

MATRIX TABLE FOR EVALUATION PROCESS.   One method of evaluation is the use of a table, as shown in table 8.1. A matrix table for a final evaluation defines the important criteria in compact notation and permits an objective evaluation, since the values have been determined before receipt of the manufacturer's proposals. In the illustration, the highest possible score is one hundred points for each of the five competing manufacturers. A value of 10 points is deducted for each ''no'' answer of a major criterion, and 5 points is deducted for each minor criterion. Each major criterion has long-range effects on profits and return on investment, so the deduction of 10 points indicates greater importance attached to this particular item. Values for another organization might be different. For the study currently under evaluation, this is a

309

TABLE 8.1   Criteria to select equipment manufacturer.

MATRIX TABLE					
Table Name: Selection of Equipment Manufacturer					
	Date: October 3, 198–				
	Preparer: R. J. Thierauf				

	Alternative				
CONDITION	**1**	**2**	**3**	**4**	**5**
Major criteria					
Low-cost throughput performance	Y	Y	Y	Y	N
Expandability of equipment	Y	Y	Y	N	Y
Low monthly rental	N	Y	Y	Y	Y
Dependable and efficient software	Y	Y	Y	Y	Y
Equipment backup in local area	N	Y	N	Y	Y
Availability of operating personnel	Y	Y	Y	Y	Y
Minor criteria					
High degree of automation proposed	Y	Y	Y	N	Y
Availability of equipment when needed	Y	Y	N	Y	Y
Capable of meeting installation requirements	Y	Y	Y	Y	Y
Adequate programming assistance	N	N	Y	Y	N
Good quality training offered	Y	Y	Y	Y	N
Equipment for initial compiling and testing	N	Y	Y	Y	N
Adequate equipment maintenance	Y	N	Y	Y	Y
Compliance with terms of bid invitation	Y	Y	Y	N	Y
ACTION					
Subtract 10 points for each no (N) answer of a major criterion	X	X	X	X	X
Subtract 5 points for each no (N) answer of a minor criterion	X	X	X	X	X

Other Information

Total points = 100 (6 major criteria × 10 points + 8 minor criteria × 5 points = 100)
Competitor's total points: 1—70, 2—90, 3—85, 4—80, 5—75

realistic and precise approach in making this final decision for an interactive management information system. Thus, equipment manufacturer #2 with the highest score of 90 should be selected to receive the equipment contract.

WEIGHTING METHOD FOR EVALUATION PROCESS.   Another approach is the weighting method. It consists of assigning different weighting factors to each criterion and giving each manufacturer a score for each weighting factor. In most cases, the score is lower than the absolute value of the weighting factor. The values of all criteria are totaled for each manufacturer. As with matrix tables, the competitor with the highest score is selected.

Summary—Equipment Selection Process

The four major aspects of equipment selection are:

1. *Determine equipment manufacturers.* This is the process of determining which manufacturers should receive bid invitations.

2. *Submit bid invitations to manufacturers.* Bid invitations should include:
   - □ general company information—overview of company and MIS operations
   - □ future management information systems plans—areas to be implemented, completion dates, and so forth
   - □ new system specifications—planned inputs, data-handling methods and procedures, files to be maintained, output needs, and other important items
   - □ new data flow diagrams—one for each functional area to be implemented plus an overview of the proposed system
   - □ data requested of each manufacturer—proposed computer hardware and processing times, site preparation requirements, manufacturer's assistance, and other similar information
3. *Evaluate manufacturer's proposals.* The criteria that can be developed for evaluation purposes include:
   - □ extent of automation proposed
   - □ throughput performance
   - □ type of equipment
   - □ rental, purchase, or other basis
   - □ equipment delivery
   - □ manufacturer's assistance
   - □ availability and quality of software
   - □ maintenance contracts
   - □ other considerations
4. *Select equipment manufacturer(s).* The task of the selection process is relative easy if the equipment proposed is identical. If the equipment proposals are somewhat dissimilar, the selection process can be difficult. Whether the proposals are somewhat alike or totally different, the dilemma can be resolved through a matrix table or the weighting method. The manufacturer(s) scoring the highest number of points is (are) selected.

BARGAINING ON EQUIPMENT CONTRACTS

Bargaining on equipment contracts is an important activity of MIS management. When sitting down at the bargaining table, the manager should recognize that his or her objectives are to maximize contractual protection and minimize total systems expense. Based upon these objectives, there are several guidelines that apply. First, even if the manager and the vendor have established a personal relationship—and the manager may be friendly with the vendor personnel, after years of working together—all the points agreed upon should be stipulated in the written contract. Too often, the MIS manager forgets that personal relationships—and personnel—come and go, particularly in the management information systems area; as personnel and relationships change, the actual parties to the contract remain legally obligated. Only the written contract can be upheld in court.

DEVELOPMENT,
IMPLEMENTATION,
AND CONTROL OF
EFFECTIVE
MANAGEMENT
INFORMATION
SYSTEMS

The manager should make it clear that the vendor's promised performance, software specifications, and other specific claims will be included in the contract. This approach has added benefit during the equipment selection phase, since vendors tend to submit accurate proposals when they know these will be reflected in the contract. Specifically, to ensure thorough user protection, the contract should spell out such basics as the degree of systems support to be supplied by the vendor, and the type of input and output devices desired, including specifications for print quality, format, and delivery schedules. The contract should also call for disaster backup, including any security and safeguard specifications to be provided.

This kind of "nuts and bolts" contractual checklist should be augmented by larger protective considerations. If the vendor suddenly introduces a new, more powerful system than the one the user has purchased, the user should be able to switch over to it or upgrade without having to revise software or change peripheral devices. Similarly, the user should benefit from any price cuts the manufacturer announces within a specified period. This protection should extend at least through the date the equipment is actually accepted and should continue ideally for the duration of any warranty period. Currently, when many manufacturers are continually slashing prices, this critical point may be overlooked.

Negotiating such contract protection is relatively easy, and managers will do well as long as they are aware of all the ways in which the company should be covered. Financial bargaining is a far more complicated matter and requires another guideline. The unsuspecting information systems manager can be burned, particularly if the individual opts to acquire the vendor's whole package—everything from hardware and peripherals to maintenance and software—or accepts pricing figures at face value. Purchasing everything in one neatly wrapped package is appealing because it is the easiest way to buy a system. But the user who is more concerned with cost than convenience might well break that package down and analyze each component to determine if everything the vendor offers is really needed. For example, a recently proposed package included a completely new set of peripheral devices. They were not necessary, because the user's existing equipment functioned perfectly well with the new computer. By evaluating this element of the package independently and eventually eliminating it from the purchase, the information systems manager saved several hundred thousand dollars. Overall, each part of the package should be made to stand on its own merit against competitive bids. By shopping around for elements of a package that can be found elsewhere in the market—items like peripherals, programming and systems support, software, and financing—the MIS manager can often cut costs. In fact, a vendor sometimes charges more for an item that is tied into a package than if sold independently.

Signing an Equipment Contract

Signing the equipment contract by a top-level executive who has been the guiding force brings the feasibility study to a formal close. However, before the official signing, the executive is well-advised to submit the contract to a lawyer for interpretation and the addition of user-protecting addendums.

The task of systems implementation is generally a major undertaking, especially if a number of organizational units are involved. This results in a great need for implementation planning for the MIS manager. A logical starting point for this type of planning involves knowledge of the following areas: personnel needs, programming, documentation, controls, equipment selected, physical requirements, and conversion activities. An understanding of these areas establishes the specific tasks that must be undertaken and the relationships among them. Also, knowledge of the problems and exceptions is needed. This background permits detailed planning of the various tasks that must be incorporated into a schedule with specific deadlines. The scheduling method should follow the natural flow of work to be undertaken. The usual questions of who, what, where, when, how, and why must be answered in developing the schedule. Implementation planning should include a method for reviewing completed and uncompleted tasks so that it can be a control tool for the entire systems project.

The major steps of MIS implementation are *preparatory work* of the new system and *operation* of the new system. These basic elements and their related subcomponents are discussed below. However, first it is helpful to set forth a desirable approach to implementation from a behavioral viewpoint, that is, "working with and through people" effectively.

MANAGEMENT BY OBJECTIVE (MBO) PROGRAM. Typically, organization personnel involved in a systems conversion perceive their jobs as a set of duties and responsibilities, with job performance measured in terms of the effectiveness and efficiency with which those duties are carried out. However, within the confines of an MBO program, they participate in the definition of the goals and objectives of the job. Job performance then is measured by the progress made toward achieving those goals. The emphasis shifts from functions to objectives during systems implementation. The success of management by objective, then, is based on its ability to convert organization objectives into personal goals.

Fundamentally, management by objective is a method by which organization members jointly establish the organization's goals. Each member, with assistance from his or her superior, defines his or her own area of responsibility and sets objectives that state expected results clearly. The persons involved develop organization performance measurements that are guides for managing and serve as standards for evaluation. MBO has four steps:

1. *Set objectives.* "Key result" areas are identified with respective performance criteria to serve as standards for measuring results.

313

DEVELOPMENT,
IMPLEMENTATION,
AND CONTROL OF
EFFECTIVE
MANAGEMENT
INFORMATION
SYSTEMS

2. *Develop action plans.* All activities with specific date(s) for accomplishing results are defined and scheduled.
3. *Conduct periodic reviews.* A control mechanism is established for monitoring activities so that periodic reviews can be performed through the feedback of essential information.
4. *Appraise annual performance.* Final results are evaluated by an annual performance appraisal program which, itself, renews the MBO process.

In addition to reviewing and evaluating what has been accomplished, performance appraisal forms the basis for beginning the MBO process anew. The process of completing this year's program is also the starting point for next year. Whether for an individual or an organizational unit, the appraisal process is very similar. Mutually agreed-on objectives for which individuals are responsible are reviewed. Actual results are measured against predetermined standards. Any significant deviations that require further attention by the accountable individual are noted for review and correction.

Preparatory Work of New MIS

The preparatory work that must be accomplished and managed before the new management information system can operate on a day-to-day basis includes these points:

□ *Scheduling the installation* should be done in sufficient detail so that each important activity can be identified and assigned appropriate starting and completion dates. For complex installations, the use of a PERT chart is recommended to ensure that the relationship among activities is considered.
□ *Selecting qualified personnel* for systems implementation and the ongoing system operations is a shared responsibility. The management information systems manager may have the authority and responsibility for staffing the program team; management from the user organization may select staff for system operations. If qualified personnel cannot be found within the organization. It may be necessary to train personnel or to look outside.
□ *Training personnel* to operate the new system complements formal training with on-the-job training. Management also must have a good grasp of what the MIS is, who can use it, and how to control it. Otherwise, there is great potential for system misuse.
□ *Realigning personnel* relates to reassigning personnel prior to conversion to the new system. During systems implementation, both the new and old systems run in parallel in order to check the new system. Hence, personnel realignment begins on a massive scale when converting the functional areas set forth in the feasibility study.
□ *Determining physical requirements and alterations* is important to implement the new system. Alterations may be needed to handle new inputs, data files, and outputs. New methods and procedures may require physical modifications to many departments.

EQUIPMENT
SELECTION AND
IMPLEMENTATION OF
MANAGEMENT
INFORMATION
SYSTEMS

□ *Testing and accepting the new equipment* refers to manufacturer-supplied diagnostic routines to test the major equipment components. A common method is to use field service programs capable of testing the various hardware components. This method should be supplemented with company-developed tests.

□ *Programming and testing* is necessary for computer programs, equipment, methods, and procedures. The detailed steps for developing a batch-processing computer program as well as an interactive-processing computer program were set forth in chapter 5.

□ *Converting files* from one medium to another must be done before programming and testing is completed. Thus, a great need exists for adequate control, such as record count controls and control totals, during conversion.

MANAGING TIME OF SOFTWARE DEVELOPMENT PROJECTS. In the areas of computer programming and testing, MIS managers frequently make two incorrect assumptions about software development: that people and time are interchangeable, and that productivity levels are relatively constant for all software projects within the same organization. The first assumption is that the development time can be determined arbitrarily by management simply by setting the number of people on the project.

For large programs, people and time are not interchangeable. Fred Brooks (past manager of the IBM 360 operating system project) described this phenomenon so graphically that a variant of it has become known as Brooks' law: "Adding people to a late project only makes it later." The reason should be clear. As the number people on a project increases arithmetically, the number of human interactions increases geometrically. More and more time must be spent on human communication and less and less on productive work. The only way to avoid the inevitability is to reduce the number of people who must interact and thereby stretch out the time. However, reduction should be limited because of risks of personnel turnover and system obsolescence.

MIS managers arrive at the second false assumption by taking some overall productivity figures from previous projects that they think are similar. However, they do not examine closely the major characteristics of the similarity. An estimate of total computer program source statements to be written is divided by the productivity figures to give an effort-year estimate. For example, assume a system of 100,000 source statements is to be completed and that productivity is 2,000 source statements per effort-year, by analogy with a previous project. Thus, the development effort equals 100,000 divided by 2,000, or 50 effort-years.

Experience shows that productivity is not constant. Rather, it is a complex function of the effort, time, and technology applied to the task. Productivity cannot be improved without changing these factors. It is not unusual for a group of programmers to achieve a productivity of, say, 5,000 or more source statements per effort-year on a small, relatively simple business application, yet only 1,000 to 3,000 source statements per effort-year on a large real-time system. WIth this kind of variation in productivity, it is little wonder that estimates based on the constant productivity assumption are not reliable.

DEVELOPMENT,
IMPLEMENTATION,
AND CONTROL OF
EFFECTIVE
MANAGEMENT
INFORMATION
SYSTEMS

A COMPUTER MAINFRAME APPROACH VERSUS A MICROCOMPUTER APPROACH. The foregoing preparatory work for a new MIS is applicable to a computer mainframe-based MIS. It generally requires a relatively long time period, perhaps a year or more. In contrast, the preparatory work of a microcomputer-based MIS takes a different direction. The focus is on utilizing the resources of the company's information center. Although there is a widespread feeling that microcomputers and their applications are easily self-taught, many good employees are not capable of doing so for simple to complex programs. Three methods are available to train employees: (1) via vendors, (2) via consultants, and (3) in house.

Vendor training is usually low in cost. In fact, in most cases, it costs nothing. Unfortunately, "you get what you pay for" and that is precisely the case with vendor training. An important problem using this approach is that when employees have a question, they have no one to consult for answers, only a manual. Another problem is that no adequate follow-up is available since no one is directly overseeing the training.

Like vendor training, consultant training has its advantages and disadvantages. The principal advantage of consultant training is that managers do not have to use the company's resources to instruct employees. However, consultant training is costly. Second, once the training is over, it is lost forever unless someone records it.

In contrast, in-house training offers several distinct advantages. First, it is cheaper than consultant training. Second, it is more reliable than using vendor training. Third, it allows the company to tailor training to the needs of the company. Fourth, it is instructor intensive. Fifth, and last, it can be upgraded to the abilities and needs of each employee. From this perspective, in-house training is the recommended microcomputer approach when treating the preparatory phase for users.

Operation of New MIS

Once programs have been written and tested, considerable work remains to integrate successfully all the components into a system. Even though the programs have been systems tested, there is no way of knowing that the system will really operate correctly without duplicating the actual flow of work with all its exceptions and timing considerations. The best way to ensure that the new system will work is to complete the following activities:

- run parallel operations
- convert to new system
- provide for necessary changes
- schedule equipment and personnel
- develop alternative plans in case of equipment failure

RUN PARALLEL OPERATIONS. Parallel operations consist of feeding both the old and new systems the same input data and comparing files and output results. Even though the best possible systems testing was undertaken during the preparatory work phase, related conditions and combinations of conditions are likely to occur that were not envisioned. Last-minute computer program changes are generally necessary to accommodate these new conditions.

EQUIPMENT
SELECTION AND
IMPLEMENTATION OF
MANAGEMENT
INFORMATION
SYSTEMS

The systems implementation project team must keep the entire organization informed about parallel operations and other conversion activities. This can be accomplished via a series of bulletins that start at the inception of the feasibility study. Department personnel should be informed when systems implementation is to start and what specific activities will be required of them. They should be informed before the actual date of conversion activities so that potential problems can be identified and corrected. Time spent instructing personnel on parallel operations or conversion activities is well worth it.

During parallel operations, differences in results are often not caused by problems in the new system, but in the old. These differences should be reconciled as far as it is economically feasible. Those responsible for comparing the two systems should establish clearly that the remaining deficiencies are caused by the old system. A poor checking job at this point can cause undue harm later when complaints are received from customers, top management, salespersons, departments, and other parties. It is extremely inconvenient to return to the old system if significant errors appear later in the new system. It is the responsibility of the systems implementation team to satisfy themselves that adequate time for dual operations has been undertaken for each functional area changed.

When implementing an interactive management information system, the process of running dual operations on the new and old systems is more difficult than for a comparable batch-processing system. The problem is that the new system has no true counterpart in the old. One procedure for testing the new interactive system is to have several remote input/output terminals connected on line and to have them operated by supervised personnel who are backed up by other personnel operating the old system. The outputs are checked for compatibility and appropriate corrections are made to the on-line computer program. Once this segment of the new system has proven satisfactory, the entire terminal network can be placed into operation for this one area. Additional sections of the system can be added by testing in this manner until all programs are operational.

CONVERT TO NEW SYSTEM. After files have been converted and the new system's reliability has been proven for a given functional area, daily processing can be shifted from the existing system to the new one.

A cutoff point is established so that all files and other data requirements can be updated to that point. All transactions initiated after this time are processed on the new system. The systems implementation team should be available to assist and answer any questions. The old system should be operated for a short time longer in case of new system failure during conversion.

PROVIDE FOR NECESSARY CHANGES. Both programming and operational procedures should be completely documented for the new management infor-

DEVELOPMENT,
IMPLEMENTATION,
AND CONTROL OF
EFFECTIVE
MANAGEMENT
INFORMATION
SYSTEMS

mation system before any parallel or conversion activities can start. Information on inputs, files, methods, procedures, outputs, and internal controls must be set forth in *clear, concise,* and *understandable* terms for the system users. Written operating procedures must be supplemented by oral communication during training sessions; many more questions will arise during the conversion activities. Having qualified systems personnel in the conversion area to communicate and coordinate new developments as they occur is a must. Likewise, revisions to operating procedures should be issued as quickly as possible.

Once the new system has been completely converted, the systems implementation team should check with all supervisory personnel about their areas. In every new installation, minor adjustments can be expected. The system as initially designed should be flexible enough to accommodate changes. Channels of communication should be open between the systems implementation team and all supervisory personnel so that modifications can be initiated as conditions change. There is no need to get locked into a rigid system when it is more beneficial to make necessary changes.

SCHEDULE EQUIPMENT AND PERSONNEL. Scheduling operations of a new system is a difficult task for the MIS manager. As individuals become more familiar with the new system, the job becomes more routine. The objectives of scheduling that relate to both personnel and equipment are in figure 8.2.

Schedules should be set up by the MIS manager together with department managers of the operating units serviced by the equipment. The master schedule for next month should provide sufficient computer time to handle production runs that occur daily, weekly, semimonthly, monthly, or on some other periodic basis. Daily schedules should be prepared in accordance with the master schedules. They should include time for reruns (if necessary), program compiling and testing, special nonrecurring reports, and other programs. In all cases, schedules should be as realistic as possible.

Scheduling an interactive system is more difficult than a batch-processing system. Even though the "executive program" handles the allotted time for each random inquiry of the system, the total response time for these inquiries may vary from a few seconds to several minutes. The time to assign remote batch programs under these conditions is a problem since the number of interruptions is generally unknown.

FIGURE 8.2
Objectives of
scheduling equipment
and personnel.

Maximize use of personnel and machines.

Meet deadlines for reports and desired outputs.

Increase productivity of personnel by including time for training.

Facilitate the planning of proposed new applications for new and/or existing equipment.

Reduce conflicts between several jobs waiting for the same piece of equipment.

There is an alternative approach to this problem. It is to assign a block of time each day for operation of remote input/output consoles. If this arrangement is not feasible, the MIS manager must rely on experience. When total random and sequential demands are not high, the machine will have sufficient capacity to complete all scheduled work even though batch-processing runs will be stretched out by random system inquiries.

Just as equipment must be scheduled for maximum use, so must operators. It is imperative that personnel who enter input data and handle output data be included in the data processing schedule. Otherwise, data may not be available when the equipment needs it for processing. Effective supervision of personnel enhances compliance with established procedures and scheduled deadlines.

DEVELOP ALTERNATIVE PLANS IN CASE OF EQUIPMENT FAILURE. Alternative processing plans must be employed in case of equipment failure. It does not matter who or what caused it to happen; the fact is that the system is down. Priority must be given to critical jobs, such as billing, payroll, and inventory. Critical jobs can be performed manually until the equipment is functioning again. For obvious reasons, the preferred method is using identical hardware at another location. The failure of an interactive system for any length of time may mean loss of data for certain areas, such as inventory and sales analysis. There is not sufficient time to enter all the information necessary to update the files, say for one week. A better plan is simply establishing a cutoff date and starting from there.

Documentation of alternative plans is the responsibility of the management information systems manager and should be part of the company's systems and procedures manual. It should state explicitly what the critical jobs are, how they are to be handled in case of equipment failure (use identical equipment at another location, manual methods, or some other data processing method), where compatible equipment is located (including service bureaus), who will be responsible for each area during downtime, and what deadlines must be met during the emergency. A written manual of procedures will help expedite the unfavorable situation. Otherwise, panic will cause the least efficient method to be used when time is of the essence.

A COMPUTER MAINFRAME APPROACH VERSUS A MICROCOMPUTER APPROACH. The foregoing activities—running parallel operations, converting to the new system, providing for necessary changes, scheduling equipment and personnel, and developing alternative plans in case of equipment failure—are essential to implementing a new MIS. Implementation thus requires a wide range of activities. In contrast, implementing a microcomputer-based MIS is quite different in that the accent is on one small area; generally one micro, possibly more than one. Hence, implementation takes a different direction. Typically, the current goal of micro-based MIS is integrating electronic spreadsheets or fourth-generation programming languages with word processing, graphics, a data base management system, and the like. In addition, implementation can include a micro-to-mainframe link. Regardless of

DEVELOPMENT,
IMPLEMENTATION,
AND CONTROL OF
EFFECTIVE
MANAGEMENT
INFORMATION
SYSTEMS

the specifics of the implementation, users require simplicity and support to use the product to its fullest potential. To assist in future implementations of micro approaches, currently software vendors are responding to users of information centers by designing new software packages that help MIS departments make greater contributions to fulfilling their goals.

Summary—Implementation of Management Information Systems

Implementation of the new management information system begins after the formal signing of the equipment contract.

Preparatory work must be undertaken before day-to-day operation of the new system can begin. It includes:

- scheduling the installation
- selecting qualified personnel
- training personnel
- realigning personnel
- determining physical requirements and alterations
- testing and accepting the new equipment
- programming and testing
- converting files

Operation focuses on day-to-day running of the new system. Even though computer programs and operational procedures have been tested, there is no way of duplicating actual operations with all their exceptions and irregularities except by following these steps:

- *Run parallel operations.* Feed both systems (old and new) the same input data for comparison of updated files and output results.
- *Convert to the new system.* After files have been converted and the new system's reliability proven, shift one area from the existing system to the new one.
- *Provide for necessary changes.* Make those minor program and system adjustments deemed necessary for improving operations.
- *Schedule equipment and personnel.* Establish daily equipment schedules that involve organization personnel to operate the equipment efficiently.
- *Develop alternative plans in case of equipment failure.* Give preference to critical jobs during equipment downtime.

REPRESENTATIVE IMPLEMENTATION PROBLEMS.   Throughout the implementation process, numerous problems can plague the MIS project. Sample problems, and representative ways to overcome them to increase the chances of a successful MIS implementation, follow:

- *Lack of clearly defined MIS objectives for implementation.* An absolutely essential starting point for implementation is an MIS plan based upon clearly defined MIS objectives.
- *Lack of a clear-cut implementation plan from the beginning.* If MIS objectives are clearly defined, the next logical step is the development

of a clear-cut implementation plan to accomplish the predetermined objectives.

□ *Ineffective leadership of the MIS project during the implementation phase.* To overcome this typical problem, experienced leaders should be selected over inexperienced MIS personnel for critical implementation activities.

□ *Inadequate training of operations personnel to undertake the implementation phase.* This problem is generally solvable by making it mandatory for implementation personnel to attend MIS training during working hours versus optional attendance.

□ *Failure to enlist the help of special skills in selected areas of the implementation process.* The MIS person in charge should utilize the implementation plan as a guide to determine when and where specialized skills are needed rather than ignoring the need for them.

This list centers heavily on "people problems." Failure to consider the human element can foil the best-laid plans in implementing a management information system.

PREPARATION OF USER DOCUMENTATION. A successful user documentation program requires goals and procedures for creating and updating documentation. Specific goals include:

□ a simplified, yet comprehensive, method for creating and updating documentation.

□ a standards manual whose format and organization would be a model for documentation to be developed by project teams.

□ A standard approach to documenting all systems.

In a typical MIS installation, documentation provides information covering the user, systems analysis, systems design, programming, implementation, and operations. Rather than create a separate manual for each, one should put together a single master manual that incorporates all the data pertinent to these areas. Utility manuals, including only those items useful to user departments and computer operations, are also prepared.

The documentation group begins its work under the direction of the MIS manager. They collect all the items of information that are the nucleus of the documentation. Next, the group evaluates the items collected, combining similar ones, eliminating others, and deciding which ones could best be consolidated on preprinted forms (knowledge of forms design is desirable here). When the list of required items is reduced to a workable size, the applicability of each item to the basic information areas (user, systems analysis, systems design, programming, implementation, and operations) is decided.

To assist the documentation group, a list of required items is formalized on preprinted documentation checklists, which are tailored to the individual needs of the organization. The checklist should:

□ identify all documentation requirements of a system.

□ serve as an index or table of contents for the system documentation throughout all stages of development.

DEVELOPMENT,
IMPLEMENTATION,
AND CONTROL OF
EFFECTIVE
MANAGEMENT
INFORMATION
SYSTEMS

□ show what items are required before approval for the system can be sought.

□ serve as a reminder of what is completed and what is not, allowing documenters to pick up where they left off.

□ eliminate the possibility of duplication when an item applies to more than one area.

After all items on the checklist have been accounted for by the documenter, they are turned over to the documentation group in rough draft form. It is advisable to include a cover sheet supplying the submitter's name, phone extension, and the (critical) completion deadline.

Following a review for accuracy, completeness, and finalization of forms, data flow diagrams, systems flowcharts, etc. by the documentation group the user documentation manual can be prepared. In turn, the required number of manuals are distributed to appropriate users. One back-up copy should be stored in a documentation library. This process assures a successful documentation program for any organization.

PERIODIC REVIEW OF NEW SYSTEM APPROACHES

After the system is installed, the MIS manager and system users should review the tangible and intangible system benefits set forth in the exploratory survey report. The purpose of this review is to verify that these benefits are, in fact, being achieved. Discussions with managers of operating units being serviced will determine how well the new system is performing. Tangible benefits, such as clerical reduction and lower inventory, and intangible benefits of improved customer service and more managerial information, are open to constructive criticism. Typical comments will be along the following lines: certain areas have been improved significantly, some are about the same, and others are not as good as before. The task of the management information systems section, then, is to make the necessary adjustments to accomplish the quantitative and qualitative goals of the feasibility study. It may take from several months to a year or more to effect the changes. Changes may include reprogramming the most frequently used programs for greater efficiency.

As time passes, the workload for the present management information system increases. Factors that previously were not problems can become significant. Can the equipment run longer hours or should additional equipment be obtained? Can modification of methods and procedures be made to reduce processing time and cost? Can noncritical processing be shifted to another time? How does the time differential affect the staffing of a real-time system operating throughout the continental United States? Answers to these questions must be evaluated by the MIS department through a periodic review of the existing system. The ultimate aim of such an investigation is system improvements. In essence, it may be necessary to undertake a feasibility study periodically in order to devise an optimum system for changed operating conditions.

From another perspective, periodic reviews of new systems approaches extend beyond those discussed above. They include a complete evaluation of controls over the management information system. They include general controls (relating to all MIS activities) and application controls (relating to specific MIS tasks). Due to the importance of these MIS controls, they are discussed at some length in chapter 9.

EQUIPMENT
SELECTION AND
IMPLEMENTATION OF
MANAGEMENT
INFORMATION
SYSTEMS

EFFECTIVE MIS PRACTICE—PURCHASE VERSUS LEASE DECISION CHECKLIST

The effective practice of implementing MIS includes not only the selection of the appropriate equipment vendor(s), but also determining whether to purchase or lease for the selected equipment. Incidentally, for the most part, the distinction between rent and lease has been lessened in recent rears. Historically, a vendor would offer a choice of renting (which included maintenance) or purchasing. The rental period was usually one year with month-to-month extensions. If the user wished to find a less expensive method, a third-party lessor would be used. This lease arrangement involved a much longer commitment and reduced the user's freedom to upgrade or make other changes. Today, most vendors offer a variety of lease plans of varying lengths, costs, and specifications. For this reason, our purchase versus lease decision checklist in figure 8.3 considers only lease and purchase, since today rent and lease are considered synonymous.

The proper method to use in examining the economies of purchase versus lease is a discounted-after-tax cash flow analysis. This method takes into account the effect of taxes, the amount of cash flow, the timing of the cash flows, and the time value of money. The result of such an analysis is, for each acquisition method, a dollar figure which represents the predicted cash to be expended throughout the useful life of the equipment. The method of acquisition which requires the least cash outflow is usually the most financially attractive.

The use of cash flow for evaluating equipment vendors and determining answers to figure 8.3 (checklist for purchasing or leasing) assist the MIS manager in reaching a final decision. It may well turn out that only one or two factors are important, such as high interest rates and/or the role of equipment obsolescence. Overall, the attendant circumstances must be surveyed for a conclusive answer.

CHAPTER SUMMARY

The final step of the feasibility study is the selection of equipment. Bid invitations describing important aspects of the new system provide the basis for manufacturers' proposals. Proposals are then compared for selected criteria which have been assigned specific numerical values. The manufacturer rated highest is awarded the contract. The ultimate responsibility for determining equipment and the layout planning necessary for its installation, however, lies not with the manufacturer but with the MIS manager.

PURCHASE VERSUS LEASE DECISION CHECKLIST

General Considerations

What is the life expectancy of the equipment?

What is the cost of money?

What is the effective federal income tax rate?

What is the company's discount rate?

What factors are most important in the company's overall considerations?

Purchase Considerations

When is the next generation due for release, i.e., the rate of equipment obsolescence?

Will it materially affect the company?

Are manuals, training, and service available?

Is there an adequate pool of programming talent available?

Are applications sufficiently stable to permit a long, useful life?

Will the system be updated to reflect current engineering modifications at no cost?

What are the maintenance costs?

What deprecation method is to be used?

Are there personal property taxes involved?

What is the investment tax credit?

What will be the resale value at the end of the useful life?

What interest rate will the company pay?

What are the company's plans regarding mergers or acquisitions?

Lease Considerations

Who assumes shipping costs of the equipment?

Who assumes installation costs of the equipment?

Who pays the personal property taxes?

Is maintenance of equipment included?

Who assumes responsibility for systems integration and checkout?

Who will provide systems engineering services, and what will they cost?

Are all penalties explicitly stated?

Will the lessor agree to a no-substitution clause?

Is the upwards expansion clause a solid commitment, or is it an "if available" conditional statement?

How much, if any, of the investment tax credit can you claim?

Will you have a single long-term lease or short-term renewals?

How long is the lease period?

Can it be extended?

What portion of rents apply to purchase?

What will the purchase price be when you decide to exercise the purchase option?

Who pays the personal property taxes?

Which method of depreciation will be used?

Will the company utilize the investment tax credit?

What is the estimated salvage value?

FIGURE 8.3   A purchase versus lease decision checklist for making a decision on new computer equipment.

Systems implementation begins after the formal signing of the equipment contract. It involves two steps—preparatory work and operation of the new system. The number of operating personnel outside the MIS group increases substantially and the organization will incur high costs during the systems conversion. Programming and testing, the mainstay of the preparatory work phase, are time-consuming and costly; advanced programming techniques and programming languages can help in developing computer programs and reducing programming costs. Once a program has reached the operational stage, parallel operations should be initiated to check for abnormal conditions that might have not been present during program and systems testing. This phase culminates in conversion of all activities for daily operation. Consideration must be given to alternative plans in case of unforeseen difficulties during conversion or later.

Periodic review of the management information system—examining new system approaches, new equipment, and cost factors—should follow the installation. Many times, an evaluation of the existing MIS may signal the need for a new feasibility study to permit system changes that reflect the existing business environment. In essence, the systems project life cycle must be initiated again by the MIS manager.

QUESTIONS

1. Give at least five key factors in selecting equipment for a management information system.
2. Are there are any problems associated with having various computer manufacturers draw up the new MIS specifications for an organization and then submitting bids on this basis?
3. What steps should the MIS manager follow in determining what microcomputers or computer mainframes and peripheral equipment an organization could procure?
4. What are the most important factors in selecting computer equipment?
5. **a.** What are the most important factors to consider when purchasing equipment?
   b. What are the most important factors to consider when leasing equipment?
6. How important is the bargaining process in negotiating equipment contracts?
7. **a.** What programming difficulties can be experienced by the programming staff during the preparatory work phase?
   b. Explain how each can be resolved by the MIS manager.
8. How important are parallel operations to a simple and a complex computer program?
9. Why should the MIS manager review the management information system periodically for improvements? Explain.

PROBLEMS

10. In figure 8.1, the content of a bid invitation to an equipment manufacturer was given for the implementation of an effective management information system. The major sections were as follows: I, general company information; II, future

DEVELOPMENT,
IMPLEMENTATION,
AND CONTROL OF
EFFECTIVE
MANAGEMENT
INFORMATION
SYSTEMS

management information systems plans; III, new system specifications; IV, new data flow diagrams; and V, data requested by each manufacturer. Suppose the implementation of a distributed information system was the focus of the bid invitation. What additional information should be added to the contents of the bid invitation? Similarly, if an organization was undertaking the implementation of a newer information system operating in a decision support system mode, what additional information would be required in the contents of the bid invitation? In both cases, set forth appropriate items for each of the foregoing five sections.

11. In the second half of the chapter, the accent was on the preparatory work phases as well as the operation phases of a new management information system. If the new information system will be operating in a distributed data processing mode, what additional implementation factors should be taken into consideration for both preparatory and operation phases? In a similar manner, if the new information system is to function in a decision support system environment, what other implementation factors should be considered for both preparatory and operation phases? In both situations, itemize the important factors for the implementation phase.

12. The last item discussed in the chapter was the need for a periodic review of new system approaches. What typical questions could be asked by the MIS manager of a service-oriented firm to determine whether or not there is need for a new feasibility study of the present management information system? Also, would the questions be different from those of a manufacturing-oriented company?

PROJECTS

13. To convert to the present interactive management information system, the MIS manager of the Regis Company undertook an exhaustive study of current equipment available. After determining those equipment manufacturers who were interested in bidding, invitations were submitted to five vendors. Several methods were considered to evaluate the manufacturers' proposals. After a lengthy discussion, the MIS executive steering committee and MIS feasibility study group decided to utilize a matrix table to select the equipment manufacturer. The completion of this activity brings the feasibility study to a formal close for the Regis Company.

The MIS feasibility study group has developed criteria for selecting the appropriate equipment manufacturer before mailing bid invitations. Each major criterion will be valued at 10 points and each minor criterion at 5 points. These criteria were reviewed and approved by the executive steering committee. Based upon the five manufacturers' proposals for an interactive management information system, the MIS feasibility study group has determined the following evaluation. An X mark in the table on page 327 indicates that the competing firm has received a value of 10 or 5 points for the specific criterion listed.

Using these criteria, prepare a matrix table that determines which equipment manufacturer should be selected to receive the computer equipment contract.

14. The MIS manager of the Eaton Company, with the assistance of the MIS feasibility study group, has utilized a matrix table to select the appropriate equipment manufacturer(s). However, together they have determined that two manufacturers have the same largest number of total points for the acquisition of new computer equipment and related peripherals. Due to this tie condition, they have decided

EQUIPMENT
SELECTION AND
IMPLEMENTATION OF
MANAGEMENT
INFORMATION
SYSTEMS

Major Criteria	Equipment Manufacturer				
	1	2	3	4	5
Low-cost throughout performance	X		X	X	X
High degree of automation proposed	X	X	X		
Low monthly rental cost	X		X	X	X
Programming assistance availability		X	X	X	X
Dependable and efficient software	X	X	X	X	X
Backup equipment availability		X	X	X	X
Good reputation for meeting commitments	X	X	X	X	X
Compliance with terms of bid invitation	X	X	X		X
Minor Criteria					
Availability of equipment		X		X	X
Acceptable quality of training	X	X	X	X	
Adequate equipment maintenance	X	X	X	X	X
Free programming assistance				X	

to investigate the purchase versus the lease criterion to determine which manufacturer should get the contract. The following list of purchase/lease factors (taken from figure 8.3) has been determined to be crucial:

□ How long is the lease period?
□ Can it be extended?
□ What portion of rents apply to purchase?
□ What will the purchase price be when you decide to exercise the purchase option?
□ Who pays the personal property taxes?
□ Which method of depreciation will be used?
□ Will the company utilize the investment tax credit?
□ What is the estimated salvage value?

In addition to the foregoing, give five other purchase/lease factors that are critical in the selection of one manufacturer versus the other for the installation of an effective management information system. If the information system is to be operated in a distributed data processing mode, state three other factors that might influence the purchase or lease of the equipment. Similarly, if the information system is to utilize a decision support system mode, state three additional factors that are critical to the purchase/lease decision. In all three situations, prepare the list of purchase/lease factors such that the list is ordered from the most important to the least important, so as to assist the MIS manager and the feasibility study group in selecting the best of the two equipment manufacturers.

15. The Beta Corporation, which manufactures 40 products, has 30 sales offices located throughout the United States with an average of six salespersons in each office. Every week, the sales reports in each office are manually tabulated. They show sales according to the salesperson, product, and customer. In turn, the reports are mailed to corporate headquarters, where they are combined manually. The results are then typed and given to top management as well as marketing managers. While top management studies the reports, marketing management analyzes them and forecasts sales for next three months. However, by the time management receives the reports, they are from three to four weeks old.

In order to overcome the problem of untimely reports, a new system has been designed in which daily sales by salesperson, product, and customer are sent over

DEVELOPMENT,
IMPLEMENTATION,
AND CONTROL OF
EFFECTIVE
MANAGEMENT
INFORMATION
SYSTEMS

a data communication line from each sales office to corporate headquarters. The computer will then compile and analyze the data and forecast sales. Since the systems project has been approved by management, the assistant to the MIS manager is now ready to specify detailed plans for implementation. Based upon all the foregoing factors, develop a detailed plan for implementation that is usable by the MIS manager. Include in your plan the preparatory work and operation work phases of the new management information system.

BIBLIOGRAPHY

Abdel-Hamid, T. K., and Madnick, S. E. "The Dynamics of Software Project Scheduling." *Communications of the ACM*, May 1983.

Alavi, M., and Henderson, J. C. "An Evolutionary Strategy for Implementing a Decision Support System." *Management Science*, November 1981.

Allen, L. "Who Are the End Users?" *Computerworld*, November 19, 1984.

Argyis, C. "Organizational Learning and Management Information Systems." *Data Base*, Winter-Spring 1982.

Artis, H. P. "The Maturation of Capacity Planning." *Datamation*, December 15, 1985.

Beaver, J. E. "Fitness Programs for Your Data Center." *Computer Decisions*, September 15, 1984.

Boctor, W., and Cohen, K. I. "On-Line Transaction Processing." *Computerworld*, March 12, 1984.

Boehm, B. W. "Keeping a Lid on Software Costs." *Computerworld*, January 18, 1982.

Bradley, J. H. "Why Tolerate Untested Programs?" *Computerworld*, October 10, 1983.

Bramson, R. S. "Pub Contracts Under the Glass." *Computer Decisions*, November 5, 1985.

Brandon, D. H., and Segelstein, S. *Data Processing Contracts: Structuring, Contents, and Negotiation.* New York: Van Nostrand Reinhold, 1978.

Cook, R. "Automated Tools are Backlog Breakers." *Computer Decisions*, April 23, 1985.

Cozette, C. "Everyone Needs a Backlog." *Infosystems*, April 1981.

Cronan, T. P. "Application System Development: A Communication Model for Business Users and DP Personnel." *Data Base*, Fall 1984.

DeBord, W. A., and Siebel, J. D. "Training MIS Users Through Simulation." *Management Accounting*, January 1982.

DePree, R. W. "The Long and Short of Schedules." *Datamation*, June 15, 1984.

DeSanctis, G., and Courtney, J. F. "Toward Friendly MIS User Implementation." *Communications of the ACM*, October 1983.

Ewers, J., and Vessey, I. "The Systems Development Dilemma, A Programming Perspective." *MIS Quarterly*, June 1981.

Freedman, D. H. "Are Vendors Backing MIS?" *Communications of the ACM*, October 1983.

Ginzberg, M. J. "Early Diagnosis of MIS Implementation Failure: Promising Results and Unanswered Questions." *Management Science*, April 1981.

————. "Key Recurrent Issues in the MIS Implementation Process." *MIS Quarterly*, June 1981.

Greer, W. R., Jr. "Added Criterion for Decision Support System Development." *Journal of Systems Management*, May 1980.

Grochow, J. M. "Software, When and How to Modify Packages." *Computerworld*, March 12, 1984.

Harris, C. E. "Negotiating Software Contracts." *Datamation*, July 15, 1985.

Healy, R. "A Call for Mainframe Software Standards." *Computerworld*, July 1, 1985.

Held, G. "Tax Options and New Equipment: Buy Versus Lease." *Data Communications*, Mid-September 1983.

Hilliard, B. L. "Techniques for Negotiating a Computer System Acquisition." *Computers in Accounting*, July/August 1985.

Hughes, C. G. "To Lease or To Buy?" *Business Computer Systems*, February 1984.

Kaiser, K., and Srinivason, A. "User-Analyst Difference: An Empirical Investigation of Attitudes

Related to Systems Development." *Academy of Management Journal*, September 1982.

Kapur, G. "Software Maintenance." *Computerworld*, September 26, 1983.

Karasik, M. S. "Selecting a Small Computer." *Harvard Business Review*. January-February 1984.

Kleim, R. L. "In-House Training for Microcomputer Users." *Administrative Management*, December 1985.

Leavitt, D. "Setting the Stage for Improved Programmer Productivity." *Software News*, January 1985.

Markus, M. L. "Power, Politics, and MIS Implementation." *Communications of the ACM*, June 1983.

Mathews, R. S. "Comparison Measurement of DP Shops at Heart of PARS." *Data Management*, May 1980.

Mazzucchelli, L "Structured Analysis Can Streamline Software Design." *Computerworld*, December 9, 1985.

McKibbin, W. L. "Managing the Large Programming Project." *Infosystems*, March 1984.

Meador, C. L., and Mezger, R. A. "Selecting an End User Programming Language for DSS Development." *MIS Quarterly*, December 1984.

Meyer, N. D. "Implementing Technology: The Quest for Support." *Data Communications*, Mid-September 1983.

Miller, D. M. "Technical Documentation Comes of Age." *Information Management*, March 1985.

Mullen, J. W. "Keeping Data Centers on Track." *Computer Decisions*, April 9, 1985.

Nichols, M. L. "A Behavioral Analysis for Planning MIS Implementation." *MIS Quarterly*, March 1981.

Nolan, R. L. "Managing Information Systems by Committee." *Harvard Business Review*, July-August 1982.

Peterson, R. O. "Maintenance Isn't Maintenance Anymore." *Computerworld*, October 22, 1985.

Polis, R. "The Path to Successful Procurement." *Infosystems*, November 1985.

————. "Administering Contracts and Managing Vendors: The Path to Successful Procurement." *Infosystems*, November 1985.

Prutch, S. F. "In Praise of Operations Managers." *Datamation*, June 15, 1984.

Raysman, R., and Brown, P. "Don't Rush to Court When Your Computer Fails." *Harvard Business Review*, January-February 1984.

Richardson, G. L.; Butler, C. W.; and Hadil, E. D. "Mending Crazy Quilt Systems." *Datamation*, May 15, 1984.

Rifkin, G. "DP As a Profit Center." *Computerworld*, February 10, 1985.

Riley, W. B. "Program Documentation." *Systems & Software*, July 1983.

Roman, D. "MIS/DP Trapped Behind Backlogs." *Computer Decisions*, March 25, 1986.

Romberg, F. A., and Thomas, A. B. "Reusable Code, Reliable Software." *Computerworld*, March 26, 1984.

Rowe, L. A. "Tools for Developing OLTP Applications." *Datamation*, August 1, 1985.

Schoman, K. E., Jr. "The Case of the Applications Backlog." *Datamation*, August 1, 1985.

Schuff, F. "Developing System Code." *Computerworld*, June 11, 1984.

Schultz, B. "Systems Implementation Said 'Deterministic'." *Computerworld*, June 21, 1982.

Shafer, D. "Software: Slowing Time's March." *Computer Decisions*, January 29, 1985.

Sheil, B. A. "The Psychological Study of Programming." *Computing Surveys*, March 1981.

Stix, G. "User Vs. Vendor: To Sue or Settle." *Computer Decisions*, March 1985.

Thackray, J. "You Can't Play If You Don't Know How." *Datamation*, October 1982.

Thierauf, R. J. *Systems Analysis and Design—A Case Study Approach*, sec. ed. Columbus, OH: Charles E. Merrill Publishing Company, 1986.

Thierauf, R. J., and Reynolds, G. W. *Effective Information Systems Management*. Columbus, OH: Charles E. Merrill Publishing Company, 1982.

Verity, J. W. "Empowering Programmer." *Datamation*, August 15, 1985.

Walsh, R. "How to Contract Your DP Project." *The DEC Professional*, January 1985; February 1985.

Weiss, E. "The Next Wave of User Documentation." *Computerworld*, September 9, 1985.

————. "Smoothing Conversions." *Computer Decisions,* March 12, 1985.

Whieldon, D., and Synders, J. "How to Avoid Outgrowing Your System." *Computer Decisions,* May 1980.

Wood, L, and Leavitt, D. "Breaking the Application Logjam." *Computer Decisions,* March 26, 1985.

Yonda, M. "Negotiating Computer Contracts." *Computerworld,* February 19, 1986.

Zvegintzov, N. "Front-End Programming Environments." *Datamation,* August 15, 1984.

CHAPTER 9

Effective Control of Management Information Systems

INTRODUCTION TO CONTROL OF MANAGEMENT INFORMATION SYSTEMS

As noted throughout the book, changes in MIS technology have occurred concurrently with the expansion of both management and nonmanagement information needs and government requirements. Not only has the number of computerized management information systems multiplied, but new capabilities and user applications also have continually been developed and refined. These advances have had many implications for MIS management, especially in auditing and control procedures. A great need exists for effective control over management information systems.

A starting point for effective control of management information systems is setting forth appropriate standards of performance for the MIS development process and the operations area. Maintaining effective standards requires continuous effort by the MIS manager and staff, due to changes in the organization's needs and the introduction of new technology. Successful MIS management depends on appropriate standards to meet its goals. Furthermore, measuring the impact of standards is necessary to determine whether they remain effective. From this perspective, the chapter initially sets forth standards that play a significant role in MIS development and MIS operations. Next, internal controls are discussed from both overview and accounting viewpoints. General and applications controls are outlined and discussed. *General controls* are related to the management information systems department, its systems and program procedures, built-in hardware and system software, computer center, and security. *Application controls* relate to input, processing, output, data base, and data communication. In turn, these controls provide the underlying framework for a comprehensive MIS questionnaire. Research results using the questionnaire are reported.

Lastly, the computer disaster uncovered in Equity Funding is explored. Conditions that are conducive to computer manipulation are presented as a warning to MIS management: if these conditions are present in their organization, correction is urgently needed. Also, the most common internal audit practices are set forth in order to enlighten management concerning what organizations are doing to evaluate their management information systems. Recommendations are made to use the talents of auditors to increase the effectiveness of internal controls across the entire organization.

The justification for MIS organization is to provide services to the user. The manager must see that these services are developed in an appropriate manner, delivered at an acceptable cost, and operated effectively. Standards define such key aspects of services provided to the user as:

- □ what the service includes
- □ how the service will be developed
- □ how the service will be evaluated
- □ who will provide the service and how

Standards serve as an important means of communicating management and user expectations. The manager's planning, organizing, directing, and controlling activities will be greatly aided by these improved communications. The effort required to develop, maintain, and enforce useful standards will pay further benefits in essential areas of management concern, as shown in figure 9.1, including resource planning, quality assurance, cost reduction, and performance evaluation. Each of these areas is covered shortly in this chapter.

STANDARDS FOR CONTROL OVER THE MIS
DEVELOPMENT PROCESS

Standards for the MIS development process can be the single most effective productivity tool of the MIS manager. Through the application of appropriate standards, the resources (personnel time, computer time, and so forth) required to develop and install a system can be greatly reduced. However, management can neither approach the process of standards definition casually nor blindly follow the standards laid down by predecessors. The economic

Resource Planning. Management must develop realistic project or operation schedules, budgets, and staffing plans. The use of valid standards allows determination of the resources necessary for each task associated with a given project or operation.

Quality Assurance. Standards help to ensure that a management/user specified level of quality is obtained for services provided by the information systems organization.

Cost Reduction. Standards provide guidelines for others to follow in accomplishing some task. They help specify how the task should be performed based on the careful analysis of past experience, thereby helping others to avoid less effective ways.

Performance Evaluation. Standards help define a basis of comparing individual performance vs. management/user expectations.

FIGURE 9.1
Typical areas of management concern for developing standards.

DEVELOPMENT,
IMPLEMENTATION,
AND CONTROL OF
EFFECTIVE
MANAGEMENT
INFORMATION
SYSTEMS

tradeoff between initial design and implementation cost and the ongoing costs of maintenance activities and future system enhancements must be examined. Also, management must be sensitive to the changing needs of the organization and the introduction of new technology. This section will summarize the value of standards for management information systems development and outline some typical standards applied in many systems development activities.

THE VALUE OF STANDARDS. The value of standards in the development and documentation of management information systems becomes obvious when one considers these facts:

1. In the typical MIS organization, 50 to 75 percent of the total systems development resources are spent on maintaining and enhancing of existing information systems. Good systems documentation and adherence to a few standards during the development of the system will dramatically reduce the maintenance and enhancement required.
2. Adding new features to existing systems costs proportionally more than the original development effort (on a cost-per-line-of-code basis). Poor system documentation and inflexible systems design are the primary problems.
3. Due to the above factors and the increase in demand for management information systems, the typical MIS organization has a backlog of more than one year of new development work. Each month that goes by without implementation of the new systems results in lost benefits or missed opportunities for the potential system users.
4. Not only does the MIS organization have a high turnover rate—currently 25 percent per year—but also the system user organization experiences personnel turnover. Good system documentation is absolutely essential to ensure that the system can continue to be supported and operated in such a dynamic environment. Poor system documentation plus high turnover can quickly lead to chaos.

Typical Standards for Control

Before expanding on typical standards in areas of management concern (refer to figure 9.1) for system development, it is helpful to discuss major guidelines in setting standards for system development activities:

1. Different standards are appropriate for different types of systems. Factors to be considered in applying standards must include whether the system is batch or interactive, what type of hardware might be used, the nature of the application (cash, inventory, or personnel data), the frequency of operation (daily, on demand, weekly, monthly), and the project schedule and budget.
2. Standards usually fall into one of three categories: (a) absolute requirements that must be met, (b) negotiable requirements that may or may not be necessary, and (c) recommended practices that would be useful to follow, but are not mandatory.

3. The system developers must understand what standards they are expected to meet prior to beginning system development.

The following sections provide typical examples of how system development standards might be applied. Four specific areas of management concern for applying these standards are resource planning, quality assurance, cost reduction, and performance evaluation.

RESOURCE PLANNING.   The typical MIS organization has a backlog of 12 to 24 months and is continually struggling to prioritize projects. The most important resource planning the organization can do is to make correct decisions on which resources should be committed and at what level of effort. Effectiveness and response can be greatly improved by establishing project prioritization standards that are fair and that work.

Most prioritization schemes classify each project into the appropriate priority and charge system development expenses back to the eventual user. A typical priority classification for project implementation is described below:

□ Management information systems projects that will enable the organization to meet a government requirement will have highest priority. For example, when the maximum FICA taxable amount and tax rate change, it is necessary to change payroll system programs. These projects are assigned the very highest priority (usually #1) because it is a legal requirement that the correct FICA be withheld from each person's paycheck. This example is illustrated in table 9.1 along with another #1 item.

□ Measurable benefit projects that will result in a net increase in profits or decrease in operating expenses are very attractive projects. Among these priority #2 projects, those with the highest projected rate of

TABLE 9.1   Sample project priority list for a management information systems organization.

Priority level	Rank	Project description	Justification
1	1	Change the maximum FICA taxable amount and tax rate in the payroll system	Government requirement
1	2	Modify all accounting related systems to enable them to report all taxable information for the current acquisition of XYZ Company	Government requirement
2	3	Develop new system to print an exception list of all customer shipments that violated distribution management's newly defined shipping guidelines	Measurable benefit, rate of return = 75 percent
2	4	Develop new system to reduce the clerical effort in the partially computerized accounts receivable department	Measurable benefit, rate of return = 25 percent
3	5	Correct inaccurate sales reps' totals on monthly report	Intangible benefit

DEVELOPMENT,
IMPLEMENTATION,
AND CONTROL OF
EFFECTIVE
MANAGEMENT
INFORMATION
SYSTEMS

return are undertaken first. In determining the rate of return on a project, it is important to account for all costs, especially salaries, benefits, and other overhead items associated with MIS personnel working on the project. Table 9.1 has two examples of #2 projects.

□ Most projects are #3 projects or intangible benefit projects. Their prioritization is difficult at best. Management must discuss the relative merits of one project versus another with the personnel requesting them. A policy of charging system users the full development cost will ensure that requesters are aware of the costs and can evaluate whether the costs are offset by the intangible benefits. If the intangible benefits do not offset the costs, the project should not be undertaken. An example of a #3 project is also shown in table 9.1.

QUALITY ASSURANCE.   Quality assurance standards, the second area of management concern, ensure that a level of quality, agreed upon by MIS management and the user, is obtained for software developed. Two practical ways to provide quality assurance are:

□ Have the system development team and users define the criteria for successful completion of the system development effort *prior to* starting the effort. The criteria for success should be documented and approved by both groups; this leads to a clear statement of what the users are expecting of the system development team, gets issues out in the open before they become a problem, and is an excellent "joining up" exercise that brings the two groups closer together. A typical list of criteria for successful completion of a project is found in figure 9.2.

□ Establish quality assurance checkpoints throughout the system devel-

FIGURE 9.2
Example of criteria for successful completion of a system development effort.

The system must be ready to go by June 30. From this date, two months will be allowed for system user training, so that by September 1 the system must be completely operational by the user.

Total system development cost through installation and user turnover point on September 1 will not exceed $350,000.

The system must reduce the error rate from 1 error per 10 records to less than 1 error per 100,000 records.

No more than 20 hours per week of system user personnel time will be required to prepare all necessary system input.

No more than 4 hours per week of system user personnel time will be required to check all outputs, correct errors, and distribute output.

The system output will be available by 9 AM the morning after submitting input.

opment life-cycle. The checkpoints should be scheduled and defined so that each party knows what will be evaluated at each checkpoint and what constitutes acceptable quality. Quality assurance should be designed to focus on system documentation so that the system can be maintained and changed easily. User instructions should be designed so that the system can be operated correctly. Flexibility and capacity for expansion should be built into the systems design and program coding.

COST REDUCTION. In the third area of management concern, three basic standards can help reduce system development costs.

- Identify clearly the tasks that must be performed during each phase of the system development life cycle. This will ensure that all the "right things" are done and that completion of each phase represents a thorough and complete job of all that should be done at this time. An example of the tasks associated with the definition of system requirements is found in figure 9.3.
- Use modular units of software code as building blocks in a wide variety of applications. For example, the processing logic to update a sequential file can be designed so that it is applicable to an employee file, customer file, and so forth. Going one step further, skeleton code can be written to conform to the basic processing logic for this generalized update routine; programming productivity can be increased by using the same skeleton code on all updates; only a minor amount of new code is necessary to meet the specific needs of a particular application. Perhaps as much as 80 percent of the code for the update can be generalized, compiled, debugged, documented, and stored away for easy access and use as a building block for future systems.
- Enable the system developer to have easy access, perhaps through a CRT, to all material pertinent to system development. Almost all mature MIS organizations have a wealth of good reference material— manuals, standards, project-related memos, written procedures—that are useful to development personnel. Unfortunately, this information

---

Examine whether new policies are consistent with organization objectives.

Define output needs.

Define data base structure.

Define new methods and procedures.

Define inputs.

Assess potential for common input representation.

Define internal controls.

Define system performance requirements.

FIGURE 9.3 Tasks in the systems design phase—determining system requirements.

DEVELOPMENT,
IMPLEMENTATION,
AND CONTROL OF
EFFECTIVE
MANAGEMENT
INFORMATION
SYSTEMS

is usually not well organized or available when needed; therefore it is not used. The key to effective use of reference materials is knowing what information is available and having ready access to that information at the right time.

PERFORMANCE EVALUATION.   The last area of management concern is performance evaluation; system development personnel should be evaluated primarily on three factors.

□ Are the systems they develop acceptable to users? This evaluation can be made in a straightforward and objective manner if the developers and users agree to the criteria for a successful project before starting it.

□ Is the system development effort completed within budget? Provided all costs are tracked accurately, this performance evaluation factor can be determined quickly.

□ Is the system development effort completed on schedule? This can be a very difficult question to answer if the developers and users have not agreed upon a definition of completion. Is completion when the first successful production run is made, when the users are fully trained and can operate the system successfully on their own, or at some other time? Thus, definition of the project completion criteria should not be overlooked.

ENFORCING STANDARDS.   The best way to enforce any standards is to be sure they are clearly understood by those expected to meet them and are recognized as meaningful, useful, and fair. Of course, follow-up is necessary to evaluate compliance of the development team to the standards. This follow-up can be performed at the scheduled quality assurance checkpoints throughout the system development life cycle.

Management must be prepared to periodically review standards. Inappropriate standards must be identified and changed or discarded. Active participation by MIS management in the quality assurance review process will make sure this goal is met.

STANDARDS FOR CONTROL OVER MIS OPERATIONS

The operations department of the MIS organization resembles a custom job shop. The "customers" are the system users, and the "customer orders" are the sets of data or service requests they submit. The operations department "fills the customer orders" by providing the information or data processing service requested. If management accepts this philosophy of a data processing services department, then they must be very sensitive to the two key considerations of every service organization:

□ What are the demands of the system user, both current and future?
□ How can these demands be met most cost-effectively?

The operations department will set many standards to ensure that proper emphasis is given to finding an answer to both these questions and then making sure the solution is implemented. Although there are many areas in which operations standards may be set, this section will concentrate only on operations department service levels.

Operations Department Service Levels

If the operations department views itself as a true service organization, it should have a continual performance review process to ensure that it is meeting current and future service needs in a cost-effective manner. The performance review process should include the activities discussed below.

EVALUATING HOW EFFECTIVELY AND EFFICIENTLY CURRENT SERVICE NEEDS ARE BEING MET. The services provided by the operations department should be reviewed to identify current problems. This review should reach into all aspects of operations: input processing and procedures, the staging of jobs, the distribution of output, and the relationship with users. Users of the services, as well as MIS management and other MIS personnel, should be solicited for their ideas of problem areas and opportunities for improvement. A special effort should be made to identify specific service needs that are not being met. Such a review by a typical operations department will yield at least a dozen opportunities for improvement, many of which will be fairly easy and will yield immediate benefits. Also, standard service goals for key services should be set and performance against these standards tracked. Typical kinds of service goals might be: 90 percent of all interactive system responses within five seconds, system unavailable no more than one hour per month, and 95 percent of all batch job outputs available to users within six hours after job submission.

A typical service goal chart is shown in figure 9.4 for the foregoing service goals. The top chart (a) shows the interactive system response time performance. The 90 percent response time is plotted day-by-day; the horizontal line represents the goal of five seconds. The middle chart (b) shows system unavailability performance. The hours per month that the system was "down" is shown for each month; the horizontal line represents the acceptable level of unavailability—one hour per month. The bottom chart (c) illustrates the turnaround time for batch program runs. The elapsed time from job submission to available output (turnaround time) is plotted day-by-day; the horizontal line is the goal of 6 hours turnaround time for 95 percent of all batch jobs.

MEASURING CURRENT RESOURCE USAGE AND DETERMINING THE CURRENT EXCESS CAPACITY. It is necessary to maintain fairly accurate measurements of all major resource usage in the operations department. The number of operation shifts, hours per shift, and people per shift should be determined. On what activities do these people spend their time? Many hardware and software monitoring devices exist to measure the use of the CPU, main memory, printers, card readers, tape drives, disk drives, channels, and

339

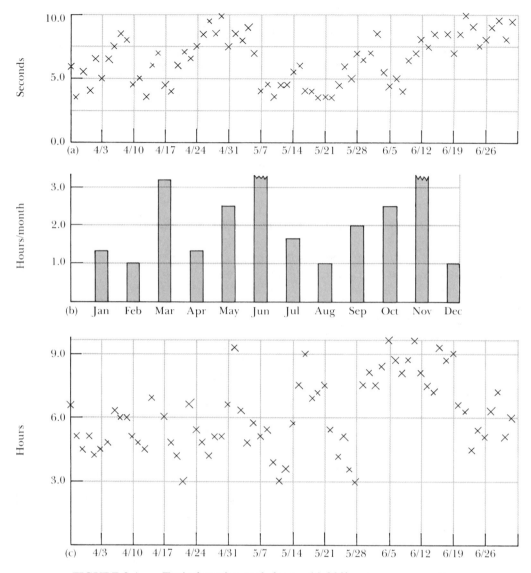

FIGURE 9.4   Typical service goal chart—(a) 90% system response time goal of 5 seconds, (b) system unavailability goal of 1 hour per month, and (c) 95% batch job turnaround time goal of six hours.

the like. Many operations departments have a performance group that uses such monitors to help get the best performance from current equipment and recommend hardware and software upgrades.

DETERMINING FUTURE SERVICE NEEDS AND PERFORMING RESOURCE PLANNING TO MEET THESE NEEDS.   The long lead times associated with obtaining equipment, rapid business growth putting heavier-than-anticipated work loads on all areas of the organization, and the difficulty in obtaining funds at a reasonable interest rate all are reasons why successful resource planning requires thinking ahead three to five years. This requires excellent communication with users and system development personnel to be aware of what applications are likely to come on-line within the planning horizon. It also requires keeping abreast of new equipment and technology as it is being developed. Having completed the previous two activities in this section, the operations department has a clear picture of where things stand today; this activity will provide them with a picture (albeit somewhat fuzzy) of what the future holds. It then takes good transition management to move from where the operations department is today to where it should be three to five years hence.

THE NATURE OF INTERNAL CONTROLS

Due to the value of internal controls, MIS management must ensure that the proper management information system controls have been included and are operational. The "Statement on Auditing Standards" (SAS) No. 1, issued by the American Institute of Certified Public Accountants (AICPA), defines internal controls.[1]

> Internal controls, in the broad sense, include . . . controls which may be characterized as either accounting or administrative, as follows:
> *Administrative control* includes, but is not limited to, the plan of organization and the procedures and records that are concerned with the decision processes leading to management's authorization of transactions. Such authorization is a management function directly associated with the responsibility for achieving the objectives of the organization and is the starting point for establishing accounting control of transactions.
> *Accounting control* comprises the plan of organization and the procedures and records that are concerned with the safeguarding of assets and the reliability of financial records and consequently are designed to provide reasonable assurance that:
> a. Transactions are executed in accordance with management's general or specific authorization.
> b. Transactions are recorded as necessary (1) to permit preparation of financial statements in conformity with generally accepted accounting principles or any other criteria applicable to such statements and (2) to maintain accountability for assets.
> c. Access to assets is permitted only in accordance with management's authorization.
> d. The recorded accountability for assets is compared with the existing assets at reasonable intervals and appropriate action is taken with respect to any differences.

The foregoing definitions are not necessarily mutually exclusive. Some of the procedures and records comprehended in accounting control may also be involved in administrative controls. For example, sales and cost records clas-

[1]*Statement on Auditing Standards (SAS) No. 1.* New York: AICPA, 1973, sections 320.10 and 320.27–29. © 1973 by the American Institute of Certified Public Accountants, Inc.

DEVELOPMENT,
IMPLEMENTATION,
AND CONTROL OF
EFFECTIVE
MANAGEMENT
INFORMATION
SYSTEMS

sified by products may be used for accounting control purposes and also in making management decisions concerning unit price or other aspects of operations.

A comprehensive system of internal controls extends beyond the finance and accounting functions; it includes promoting operational efficiency in the MIS and control over operating programs and procedures. In fact, all information under the control of the management information systems manager should incorporate internal controls.

Ideally, internal controls are integrated as an essential part of the methods and procedures in processing an organization's activities. The self-correcting mechanism of the system allows MIS personnel to take appropriate action when errors, mistakes, or equipment malfunctions arise. In such a system, the amount of internal and external auditing is kept to a minimum. The adequacy of internal controls, then, has a direct bearing on the amount of auditing required and serves as a measure of the system's effectiveness in following prescribed procedures.

In addition, effective internal controls are required to ensure conformance to the Foreign Corrupt Practices Act of 1977. This act made bribes to foreign officials by U.S. companies a criminal offense and established the Internal Accounting Control Standards. It requires that internal controls be sufficient to provide reasonable assurances in four specified objectives:

1. all transactions are authorized
2. all transactions are recorded
3. access to equipment and data is controlled
4. data produced are correct and verifiable

The Act is enforced by the Securities and Exchange Commission, which requires documentation of the system of internal controls. Those who have the power to control the direction, management, and policies of a company and who are found to have willfully violated the internal control provisions are subject to a $10,000 fine and/or five years in prison.

MIS QUESTIONNAIRE TO EVALUATE INTERNAL CONTROLS

To apply the foregoing internal controls, internal and external auditors must augment the normal audit of the company's accounting and financial records. This addition takes the form of an MIS audit which includes computer application systems development, computer service center operations, and controls internal to computer application programs. Emphasis shifts from the evaluation and verification of processing results—data files, records, and reports—to the evaluation and verification of controls that ensure the continuing accuracy and reliability of processing results. This emphasis results in new internal audit approaches and techniques, an extension of traditional internal audit responsibilities, as MIS management seeks assurance that computer application systems are accurate and reliable. In light of this trend, a questionnaire is generally employed to evaluate systems controls.

The *first* purpose of such a questionnaire is to help internal and external auditors as well as consultants perform a comprehensive audit of the organization's MIS. The questionnaire focuses on appraising the accomplishment of MIS objectives in the areas of systems, programming, and operations; the ability of MIS management to perform their assigned functions of planning, organizing, directing, and controlling in their assigned areas; and the adequacy of MIS managerial decisions and actions in moving toward stated objectives. Hence, its questions appraise the management of MIS resources.

Going beyond an appraisal of managerial capabilities, a *second* purpose is to appraise the adequacy of controls over MIS operations and their operating procedures. The questionnaire also informs management of operating problems that need to be corrected for greater efficiency and economy of operations. Within this framework, MIS personnel, operating policies, computer facilities, and the operating environment are reviewed in terms of their contribution (or lack of contribution) to operating efficiency or cost savings. A secondary purpose of the management information questionnaire, then, is evaluating the efficiency of operational activities.

Including both the managerial and operational aspects provides a logical framework for a thorough and comprehensive evaluation of any information system. Evaluating both aspects leads to improved operations in most areas. In addition, because managerial and operational activities complement and supplement one another, they should be treated accordingly.

Using this combined approach, the same question can be asked from two perspectives. For example, in the area of operational activities, What are working conditions like in the computer room? Would one enjoy working under these conditions? A look around the computer room for any capital equipment extras might just provide the answer. Quiet, comfortable air conditioning and sophisticated, machine-protecting fire prevention equipment (not sprinklers on the ceiling) make the data center more pleasant and safe. But of even greater significance from the standpoint of managerial activities, the presence of these extras indicates a concern and commitment on the part of management which probably extends to other areas more difficult to measure, such as staffing, policies, funding, and training. The physical layout of the equipment in the computer room is indicative of how much thought went into the design of other aspects under management's direction.

How to Use the MIS Questionnaire

The management information systems questionnaire[2] does not give answers, it simply asks questions. If the questions are all answered "yes," the function or area under investigation is operating as desired. If there are some "no" answers, it is experiencing difficulty, and the negative answers must be expanded upon in writing. If the question does not apply, the "N.A." (not applicable) column is checked. The questionnaire serves as a tool to analyze current MIS activities. But more importantly, it allows the consultants or audi-

[2]Refer to Robert J. Thierauf and George W. Reynolds, *Effective Information Systems Management,* Columbus, OH: Charles E. Merrill Publishing Company, 1982, Chapter 13.

DEVELOPMENT,
IMPLEMENTATION,
AND CONTROL OF
EFFECTIVE
MANAGEMENT
INFORMATION
SYSTEMS

tors to *synthesize* those elements causing difficulties and deficiencies. The capability to assess all negative answers helps separate real problems from symptoms.

Once the auditors or consultants have diagnosed the real problems and their attendant difficulties and deficiencies, they are ready to assess the level of performance for the function or area being investigated. Many times, performance is far below expectations. Subsequent recommendations provide a basis for an oral presentation and a written report to improve operations.

TYPES OF CONTROLS FOUND IN MIS QUESTIONNAIRE

Certain controls that relate to all MIS activities are called *general controls*. In contrast, those that relate to specific MIS tasks are called *application controls*. Both classes of controls form the MIS questionnaire. Due to the importance of each, they are treated separately below.

General Controls for MIS

According to the American Institute of Certified Public Accountants, "General controls comprise (a) the plan of organization and operation of the EDP activity, (b) the procedures for documenting, reviewing, testing, and approving systems or programs and changes thereto, (c) controls built into the equipment by the manufacturer (commonly referred to as 'hardware controls'), (d) controls over access to equipment and data files, and (e) other data and procedural controls affecting overall EDP operations."[3] This five-part breakdown is explained below in the author's words; however, the content remains largely unchanged. The types of general controls, then, for management information systems are:

1. MIS department controls
2. system and program procedures controls
3. built-in hardware and system software controls
4. computer center controls
5. security controls

The relationships among general controls are illustrated in figure 9.5.

1. MIS DEPARTMENT CONTROLS. The first of the general controls, as noted above, focuses on the plan of organization and operation of the department. It looks at the normal management functions undertaken by MIS managers—planning, organizing, directing, and controlling activities relating to overall MIS department objectives. The key areas are master plans and related

[3]*Statement on Auditing Standards (SAS) No. 3, The Effects of EDP on the Auditor's Study and Evaluation of Internal Controls;* New York: AICPA, 1974, p.3, para. 7. Also refer to *Statement on Auditing Standards (SAS) No. 9, The Effect of an Internal Audit Function on the Scope of the Independent Auditor's Examination;* New York: AICPA, 1976. © by the American Institute of Certified Public Accountants, Inc.

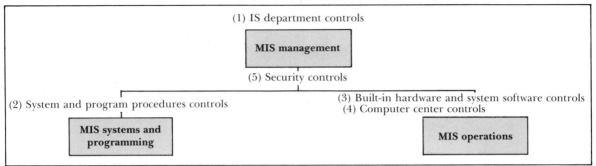

GENERAL CONTROLS

(1) IS department controls

MIS management

(5) Security controls

(2) System and program procedures controls

(3) Built-in hardware and system software controls
(4) Computer center controls

MIS systems and programming

MIS operations

FIGURE 9.5   Relationship of general system controls to the management information system department.

controls, contingency control plans, organization structure controls, personnel standards, performance standards, and performance appraisal.

2. SYSTEM AND PROGRAM PROCEDURES CONTROLS.   Procedures must be designed to control the review of systems and programs, as well as subsequent changes. Of great importance is the degree of documentation practiced by the department. Too often, this important aspect is ignored by systems and programming personnel in favor of more challenging MIS tasks. Poor internal controls in MIS methods and procedures are a reflection on the department's management. Basic categories of system and program procedures controls, then, cover methods and procedures, systems and programming procedures, procedures via the review process, changes, and documentation.

3. BUILT-IN HARDWARE AND SYSTEM SOFTWARE CONTROLS.   Built-in hardware and system software controls are incorporated by the manufacturer to check the reliability of the computer equipment and its operating system. Typically, they include parity checks, duplication checks, echo checks, dual heads, overflow and sign checks, firmware controls, and operating system controls.

4. COMPUTER CENTER CONTROLS.   As a rule, anyone who is not involved in operations or systems programming should be escorted at all times in the computer room. This includes presidents, directors, and applications programmers. Typical computer center controls cover access to computers, computer operators, tape and disk library, and computer maintenance.

5. SECURITY CONTROLS.   Basically, security controls cover contingencies not adequately encompassed by other controls. They must be standardized for daily operations or operational difficulties and inconsistent corrective action will result. Most computer installations have security controls covering programs, equipment log, fire protection, and media protection.

DEVELOPMENT,
IMPLEMENTATION,
AND CONTROL OF
EFFECTIVE
MANAGEMENT
INFORMATION
SYSTEMS

Research on General Controls for MIS

In research conducted by the author on general controls, the number of "no" answers in the first part of the two-part MIS questionnaire for the above five control areas was calculated. The number of "no" answers is indicative of the degree of control or lack thereof over MIS operations for nine large corporations and nine small companies. The percentage (from the highest to lowest) were calculated as follows (for both large corporations and small companies):[4]

1. Information system department controls	24.6%
5. Security controls	21.6%
2. System and program procedures controls	19.5%
4. Computer center controls	13.3%
3. Built-in hardware and software controls	5.8%

It was found that the order of the five parts is the same for large corporations and small companies although their percentages differ. The average percentage of "no" answers to the total questions is 18.8 percent for all organizations. The percentage for large corporations is 13.5, and the percentage for and small companies 24.0. Overall, large corporations seem to have fewer problems than small companies. When the two groups are compared, the number of "no" answers for small companies is about 1.8 times that of large corporations.

These research data provided a starting point for uncovering the problem areas confronting a typical management information system. Based upon the "no" answers to questions in the first part of the two-part questionnaire, the information systems professionals participating in this research project synthesized the problems confronting this MIS area. The major problems in their order of importance are:[5]

1. Lack of proper documentation of standards and procedures
2. Lack of short- to long-range plans for information systems
3. Lack of security protection measures
4. Lack of an independent third party to review IS operations
5. Lack of a contingency recovery program

These major problems were mentioned seven to thirteen times out of a possible eighteen for the nine large corporations and the nine small companies. In addition, eleven other problems (moderate and minor) were identified based upon the research results. These ranged from lack of control over computer center operations to lack of control over new or about-to-be discharged IS personnel. For additional information on these problems and other areas, refer to the cited source by the author.

[4]Robert J. Thierauf, *A Manager's Complete Guide to Effective Information Systems—A Questionnaire Approach.* New York: The Free Press (A Division of Macmillan Company), 1983, p. 76.

[5]Ibid, p. 95.

Application Controls for MIS

Complementary and supplementary to general controls are application controls. While general controls are related to organization factors, personnel, and equipment, application controls focus on the systems aspects of an information system. For the MIS and programming manager, no design job is complete without adequate internal controls. The systems analyst should make certain that the final design allows no one person full responsibility over an entire operation; the clearest example is in payroll where one person with complete responsibility can defraud an organization. Built-in checkpoints ensure that what has been processed agrees with predetermined totals. To a degree, these controls relieve the manager of detailed checking and reviewing.

Referring again to the AICPA's Statement on Auditing Standards No.3, "Application controls relate to specific tasks performed by EDP. Their function is to provide reasonable assurance that the recording, processing, and reporting of data are properly performed. There is considerable choice in the particular procedures and records used to effect application controls. Application controls often are categorized as 'input controls,' 'processing controls,' and 'output controls'."[6] This breakdown can be expanded to include other application controls deemed appropriate for the time. Thus, the types of application controls can be segregated as

1. input controls
2. processing controls
3. output controls
4. data base controls
5. data communication controls

This breakdown is illustrated in figure 9.6.

It should be noted that internal and external auditors also have a special interest in system controls. Similarly, stockholders, creditors, and the government want assurance that processed data are reliable when transmitted from one source to another. Control points for checking the accuracy of processed information and the distribution of control over one specific area are vital for effective control.

1. INPUT CONTROLS. Control of input is defined as the procedural controls necessary to handle data prior to computer processing. Input data must be handled very carefully since they are the most probable source of errors in the entire management information system. If errors are created anywhere between the origination point and input into the computer equipment, they will be carried forward throughout the entire system. To keep errors to a minimum, the following procedural controls over input data for a computer installation should be used: verification methods, input control totals, and external labels.

[6]*Statement on Auditing Standards (SAS) No. 3*, op. cit., pp. 3–4, para. 8.

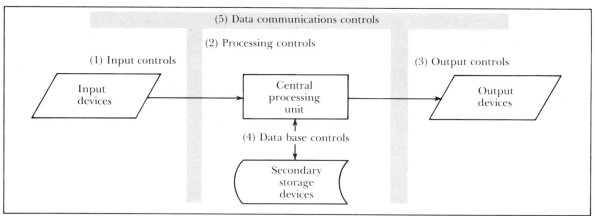

FIGURE 9.6   Relationship of application system controls to a computer system—batch or interactive processing mode.

2. PROCESSING CONTROLS.   A high degree of programmed controls is always advisable on the computer since undetected errors can have serious, far-reaching consequences. Programmed control procedures should be included as a part of the computer's internally stored instructions. The extent of control implemented depends upon the increased costs in programming and machine time versus the resulting increased accuracy. In addition to this consideration, the extent of computer-programmed controls includes the programming ability of the MIS section, the requirements of the particular run, and the capabilities of the equipment. Since most computer applications are slowed by the speeds of input/output units, the central processor has generally more than sufficient time to perform the necessary control checks. Therefore, the number of programmed controls depends upon the amount of program memory available. If sufficient space is available, the programmer should include as many controls as is necessary. They can be classified as validation checks and tests, computer control totals, internal labels, and error routines.

3. OUTPUT CONTROLS.   The role of the computer as a control center is further accentuated when output controls are present. Whereas input controls ensure that all data are processed, output controls assure that results are reliable. They promote operational efficiency within the computer area over programs, processed data files, and machine operations. Output controls also ensure that no unauthorized alterations have been made to data under computer control. They can be classified as output control totals, control by exception, and control over operator intervention.

4. DATA BASE CONTROLS.   Just as computer-programmed controls are essential for an effective management information system, the same can be said for data base controls. Without adequate controls in this area, important data items found in on- and off-line files can be lost or destroyed. If loss or destruction occurs, recovery procedures must be undertaken to recreate essential data items. Through the use of the foregoing programmed controls, the systems analyst can help ensure, to a large degree, that file data are not destroyed during regular processing. However, there is still need for additional controls over factors relating to file processing and storage, including supervisory protection programs, file record controls, and physical safeguard controls.

5. DATA COMMUNICATION CONTROLS.   The foregoing MIS controls are generally applicable to all systems, whether they use batch or interactive processing. However, data communication controls are necessary for a two-way flow of information in an interactive environment. In fact, these systems create many problems not found in stand-alone batch-processing systems. How can confidential data be made accessible to only authorized personnel? What happens to data in the system when the computer is down for repairs? How can accuracy be assured with interactive processing? Generally, controls will be dictated by such factors as the requirements of the system, the equipment itself, and security specifications. The areas set forth below are not all-encompassing, but do represent control requirements found in a typical data communication system. They include: on-line processing controls, data protection controls, and diagnostic controls.

Research on Application Controls for MIS

Related to the research on general controls is that on application controls conducted by the author. The number of "no" answers in the second part of the two-part MIS questionnaire was determined. The number of "no" answers, as in the previous research results, is an indication of the degree of control or lack thereof over MIS operations for three large corporations and three small companies. (These organizations differ from those set forth in the prior research.) The percentages, from the highest to the lowest, were tabulated as follows for both large corporations and small companies:[7]

1.	Input controls	21.8%
3.	Output controls	19.0%
2.	Processing controls	15.2%
4.	Data base controls	13.7%
5.	Data communication controls	10.5%

The order of the five parts is *not* the same for large and small companies. However, they approximate the above ranking. Looking at the preceding research results from a broader viewpoint, the average percentage of "no" answers of the total questions is 15.9 percent. When viewing the percentages for large corporations versus small companies, a different picture emerges.

[7]Robert J. Thierauf, op. cit., p. 121.

DEVELOPMENT,
IMPLEMENTATION,
AND CONTROL OF
EFFECTIVE
MANAGEMENT
INFORMATION
SYSTEMS

The percentage for large is 12.6 percent; for small, 19.3 percent. The point in the prior section on research results of general controls—that large corporations experience fewer problems than small companies—also applies to application controls. To place this point in perspective, the ratio of "no" answers for small companies is approximately 1.6 to 1 when compared to large corporations.

The preceding research provides a starting point in determining the problems confronting an MIS. The IS participants in this research used the "no" answers in the second part of the questionnaire to determine the problems confronting MIS operations. The major problems encountered, in order of importance, are:[8]

1. Lack of an independent third party to review IS operations
2. Lack of control over input data
3. Lack of training programs for new and experienced IS personnel
4. Lack of a data base administrator (DBA)
5. Lack of proper documentation on standards and procedures

The foregoing major problems were noted three to five times out of six for three large corporations and three small companies. Additionally, six other problems (moderate and minor) were identified by the research. These include lack of security protection measures over the system and lack of communication in the IS area. For additional information, refer to the prior reference under general controls.

SECURITY OVER MANAGEMENT INFORMATION SYSTEMS

As illustrated by the foregoing results, security is an important issue confronting management information systems. The Data Processing Management Association (DPMA) recently conducted a survey of 1,000 data processing executives in Fortune 1000 companies and found that only two percent of discovered computer abuses were reported to the police or other authorities.[9] More unsettling, perhaps, is that the survey found only two percent of the reported abuses were perpetrated by people outside the firm: the vast majority were committed by a firm's own employees. The survey also revealed that while the hacker (a non-authorized person who gains access to the firm's computer and/or data base) and the occasional spectacular case of fraud tended to receive the most notice, the majority of computer abuses were far more mundane. Misuse of computer services made up nearly half of all the incidents reported in the DPMA survey. Misuse could be anything from game-playing or using the computer for personal work to diverting funds or altering records. Program abuse—copying or changing programs—was the next most prevalent area (24 percent). Data abuse—diverting information to unauthorized

[8]Ibid, p. 134.

[9]Sam Dickey, "Is Getting In Getting Out of Control?" *Today's Office,* September 1985, p. 30.

individuals—was third (22 percent) and hardware abuse—damaging or stealing computer equipment—was last (5 percent). According to the survey, motivation for internal abuse was fairly evenly divided: ignorance of proper professional conduct accounted for 27 percent, misguided playfulness was 26 percent, personal gain was 25 percent, and maliciousness or revenge was 22 percent.

DPMA also found that technical people (programmers, systems analysts, machine operators, data-entry clerks, etc.) were the most common perpetrators of computer crimes. An obvious reason is their nearness to the computer system. They work with it every day and have the requisite knowledge. But there may be more to it. The technology expert's attitude also plays a part since his or her attitude goes back to an education that focuses on gamemanship and problem solving. When a technical person looks at a situation, the individual tends to see the problem-solving aspects, not the moral, social, or legal aspects. This ties into the fact that many security breaches in computer systems are not motivated by monetary gain, but simply by the challenge of gaining access to a firm's data base. A company is vulnerable to this sort of interference if its data base is on-line and can be accessed via a local area network or a telephone. However, the situation is exacerbated if the system is controlled and operated by technical personnel who are not directly involved with the business of the organization and have no interest in the information they handle.

The indifference with which technical staff members sometimes approach an organization's information resources is often matched—or caused—by management's lack of attention to these employees. Too often, management does not understand the role technical personnel play in attaining a company's business goals. This can result in employee alienation and the erosion of loyalty and respect for an employer or its assets. Ultimately, the responsibility for security over computer systems rests with management. It is management's task to control the use of and access to information and to establish standards—understood and followed by all—that motivate employees to respect and protect information. It is from this perspective that security over computer mainframes and microcomputers within an MIS environment is presented below.

Security Over Computer Mainframes

Past and current well-publicized events have deepened management's concern for the security of their computer mainframes. Since these events have focused on terminals or microcomputers accessing hardware in a distant city via telephone, the immediate concern is commercial networks or dial-in access. While commercial networks do present exposures, the greater risk is unsupervised dial-in. There are numerous ways to control dial-in ports effectively. If dial-in traffic is low and the computer mainframe is always attended by an operator when dial-in is allowed, it may be practical to have dial-in ports set up to preclude "direct dial." That is, the operator must authenticate the caller and make the connection. For many operations, this is an effective solu-

DEVELOPMENT,
IMPLEMENTATION,
AND CONTROL OF
EFFECTIVE
MANAGEMENT
INFORMATION
SYSTEMS

tion at a modest cost. However, this method is ineffective in a moderate- or high-traffic situation and leaves room for error or deception.

When the system being accessed by dial-in lines has effective controls, direct connection (i.e., the caller reaching an auto-answer modem that makes direct connection to the computer without any operator intervention) can be acceptable. The most important consideration in this process is proper user identification and authentication. When attempts to thwart or penetrate this process are detected, specific predetermined actions can be automatically set in motion. For example, after a specified number of unsuccessful attempts to present a valid identification code is reached, the lines should be disconnected and disabled automatically. Also, the identification code should be suspended from further use. Sessions of properly authenticated users should be automatically terminated if they exceed a specified number of violations. Serious consideration should be given to automatic suspension. To a reasonable degree, this approach ensures system integrity and effectively precludes penetration via brute force—repeated attempts to present a valid identification code and authentication. It will not prevent someone from "finding" a company's computer and inconveniencing the company by keeping lines busy or making repeated attempts to penetrate.

If a company wishes to avoid this problem, and the dial-in traffic is heavy or access to an unsupervised computer is allowed, several devices are now available for use. They all share one characteristic: they operate independently of the computer and consume none of its resources. Such a solution is vendor- and model-independent because security is maintained on the communication line to the computer. Typically, a device is placed on the telephone line, either before or after the modem. If the device is in front, the fact that a caller has reached a computer is unknown until the security requirements have been satisfied. The modem issues the carrier tone associated with a computer. If this tone is hidden until security screening is complete, it is impossible to "find" the computer by calling every number in a designated area and listening for the carrier tone.

Other features of such devices include the requirement that the caller furnish a security code. Variations occur according to product and can commence prior to security code presentation. There may or may not be a prompting for the code. Options vary in how the code is presented; the most common is via "touch-tone." Assuming a valid code is presented, some devices then immediately make the connection (pass-through authentication) whereas others require the caller to hang up. The device then calls the caller back at a predetermined number. Once the caller answers, the device may require a second security code before a connection to the computer is made. This is referred to as *call-back authentication*. The ability to record and report attempted (and denied) accesses varies greatly. Features that include hard-copy logs of all activity, specific time limits, port selection, line capacity (number), speed and whether interfacing hardware restrictions (modems) exist, vary among products.

Additional security devices/techniques are not as complete nor as cost effective as those discussed. When access to the computer is via commercial network, the first line of defense is to use all the security controls it offers, followed by placing other software controls as deemed necessary. Unfortunately, the use of hardware enhancements in most instances is cost prohibitive. The marketplace today offers numerous alternatives to establish a secure processing environment while maintaining the accessibility necessary to conduct business. New devices and software are emerging with increasing frequency. Because data processing is always evolving, it is entirely possible for risks to increase without any changes in one's own environment. It is incumbent upon the users of computing resources to analyze their exposures and implement necessary controls to offset the risks.

Security Over Microcomputers

In addition to being required for computer mainframes, security over micro-computers is essential. Typically, security and microcomputing do not seem to mix. "Securing" a microcomputer risks making it a bureaucratic burden rather than a tool to increase employee productivity. Yet expensive equipment and sensitive data must be protected. Security procedures and employee awareness can solve the micro-security problem. If most of the micros in a company are used only to raise employee productivity, the best security provisions are those administered with a "light touch." However, when micros store sensitive corporate data, security becomes critical, particularly when mainframe data are accessible.

In light of the problem, different types of security devices are available for controlling actual use of the micros. One is Stopper (from Secure Systems Technology). This effective lock controls access to computer power since it appears to be part of the original equipment. SST Keeper—used in conjunction with Stopper—restricts users from gaining access to the equipment's inner hardware. However, physically securing the micros is only the first step in their defense. Often, in the business environment, it is impractical to frequently turn the equipment on and off. Software controls are more appropriate. A great variety of software-control products now available have a common element: they all use some form of encryption. Two are briefly noted below. *Encryption* is a method of scrambling data before thet are sent. After being received, the data must be unscrambled by *decryption* so that they are usable.

Softlock (from Computer Security Investigation) begins by securing the operating system. To "boot" the system, the user must supply the correct password. This control cannot be bypassed. If an incorrect password is presented three times in succession, the system locks. To be accessed, the system must be rebooted and the correct password entered. Softlock also supports an encryption routine that is rapid and virtually painless. No keys are needed and the routine knows whether it must encrypt or decrypt the file. To protect a file, the user calls up the "SoftEncr" program and enters the file's name. The password is not the encryption key; rather, it is the key to the file that contains the encryption key. Both the password and the encryption key are encrypted. The password may be changed daily or even more frequently with-

DEVELOPMENT,
IMPLEMENTATION,
AND CONTROL OF
EFFECTIVE
MANAGEMENT
INFORMATION
SYSTEMS

out jeopardizing any previously encrypted files. Softlock can be installed on several systems using the same encryption key but different passwords.

In contrast, P/C Privacy (from McTel) does not require installation other than copying the three programs supplied. It is easy to use. To protect a file, the user enters "Encrypt" and the name of the file to be protected, the name of the file after it is protected, and the key to be used to protect it. When encryption is completed, the unprotected file remains intact. In addition, decryption is available; that is, it is like encryption using the Decrypt program.

THE MIS MANAGER AND COMPUTER CRIME

The Equity Funding debacle, like all disasters caused by human actions, offers useful lessons. The dimensions of the Equity Funding disaster and its general causes were revealed within a few weeks in the spring of 1973. In March of that year, press reports questioned the integrity of the consolidated financial statements and other records and reports of the apparently successful Equity Funding Corporation of America (EFCA) and its subsidiaries, including Equity Funding Life Insurance Company (EFLIC). Within a month (on April 4), the parent company filed a petition of bankruptcy. It appeared by then that a fraud of substantial proportion had been carried out over several years by certain officers and employees of the Equity Funding companies. The result of the fraud was to present to investors, creditors, and regulators a picture of ever-increasing earnings and assets and to stimulate an active market in the securities of the parent corporation. It was now apparent that much of the reported earnings and assets were false. EFCA's publicly held securities, with a previous market value in the hundreds of millions of dollars, became virtually worthless overnight.

The Equity Funding collapse brought on a host of legal proceedings. In addition to bankruptcy, there have been investigations by insurance regulatory agencies of several states, the Securities and Exchange Commission, and other federal agencies. Grand jury investigations have resulted in the indictment (and in some cases, conviction) of corporate officers and employees, the indictment of certain auditors, disciplinary proceedings by the New York Stock Exchange, and scores of civil lawsuits.

A number of questions are raised by such a disaster. In addition to criminal culpability and civil liability, the questions involve the sufficiency of regulatory procedures affecting publicly owned companies, including life insurance companies, and the adequacy of prevailing assumptions about the responsibilities of various kinds of professions and occupations—accountants, lawyers, actuaries, investment bankers, and security analysts—in relation to enterprises like Equity Funding. The integrity of MIS management and their staff is essentially open to question.

The demise of Equity Funding represents the tip of an iceberg that must be understood by MIS managers. With or without high-level management prodding, the MIS manager must make security planning and implementation a priority because the stakes are enormous. Some decisions could easily involve tens of millions of dollars. In view of this awesome responsibility, the MIS manager should not be making such decisions personally, but should be passing on assessments of the hazards, the costs of security measure, and recommended actions. It is up to higher management to decide the level of permitted risk—the tradeoffs—to assure that it is acceptably low and at reasonable cost. They must be convinced that, in the event of failure, recovery is still possible and relatively efficient. In addition to primary security concerns— survival of the organization and preventing the destruction of major corporate assets—attention should be given to the integrity, accuracy, and validity of the organization's information system, the prevention of large-scale computer-related fraud, and needed privacy of proprietary data.

Conditions Conducive to Computer Crime

MIS management must work hard to manage the risk of computer crime. That risk is highest in those systems that affect the cash flow of the company (payroll, accounts payable, and billing) or that guard important assets of the company (inventory and accounts receivable). If any of the following conditions are present, that risk is heightened:

- low employee morale and little loyalty toward the company
- no separation of sensitive job functions, such as authorization of payment and issuance of check
- little attention paid by management to the risk of computer crime, saying "that couldn't happen here"
- access to computer files or computer programs not tightly controlled
- no record of who has access to computer files or computer programs

An analysis finding these conditions indicates that MIS management is very lax in promoting effective control over personnel and operations. In such an environment, the perpetrators find it easy to obtain all the information they need about a system for their fraudulent acts. In fact, the elements of challenge and game playing are found in such situations. In some cases, claims by MIS managers that their computer systems are safe and cannot be penetrated encourage eager programmers who look at the intellectual challenge of pitting their minds against the computer. These people usually become frustrated with their success unless there is some way they can take credit publicly for their achievements. One perpetrator who claims to have gained over one million dollars from his deeds said that aside from making money rapidly, his motive was to see how far he could go with his crime before he stopped and informed his victim of his acts. He was confident that the victim could not find evidence of his act even if he confessed.

In the United States, the FBI estimates that the average amount stolen in a bank holdup is $3,200 and from embezzlement, $23,500. In contrast, the average amount for computer crime is $500,000.[10] Thus, the message is clear

---

[10]Lois Paul. "Exec Warns Computer Crime Already Here." *Computerworld*, July 6, 1981, p. 25.

DEVELOPMENT,
IMPLEMENTATION,
AND CONTROL OF
EFFECTIVE
MANAGEMENT
INFORMATION
SYSTEMS

to MIS management. The need for evaluating systems controls by qualified auditors and consultants is overwhelming.

Special Conditions Conducive to Computer Crime in the Newer MIS Environments

In addition to the foregoing conditions applicable to computer crime within a centralized processing mode, there are other problems applicable to distributed data processing systems and decision support systems. Because newer MIS environments have special control problems conducive to computer crime, they are discussed separately below. It should be noted that expert systems are not included below since their nature does not center on daily processing of business activities, but rather on giving advice to organization personnel.

DISTRIBUTED DATA PROCESSING SYSTEMS. As noted previously, the decision to distribute a large number of small computers of various types at the local and regional levels allows many organizational personnel to do their own processing. Certainly there is a place for small computers that fit the needs of many users dispersed throughout the organization. But while the use of small computers is often cost-effective and often meets many user needs, control over data cannot be ignored.

To understand what data should be protected in a widely dispersed organization, it is necessary to divide data into two categories. In the first category is data of limited use and no empirical value, including those facts used by an individual or a single department to pose and address specific questions. Once these questions have been answered, the data have no further value and need not be retained. Other examples include physical distribution studies, market forecasts, and mathematical modeling projects. Because of the limited use and constantly changing nature of the output, these data—albeit important—do not represent information that must be protected and secured against computer crime.

Data that must be protected against computer crime fall into the second category—data, for example, that are used as input for order, customer, or marketing information. Because of their organization-wide significance, these facts must be protected. General ledger, accounts payable, stockholders' records, and inventory information are further examples of "organizational data." Thus, the MIS department particularly needs to exercise caution where organizational data are used (i.e., analyzed, manipulated, and reported).

How can MIS management extend necessary processing power to those who need it, yet assure protection of the organization against computer crime? One approach is to make interactive service available. For example, by providing a capability such as IBM's Conversational Monitoring System (CMS), a full range of the organization's data can be made available to dispersed users, yet be secured. Copies of the existing data can be provided to users, removing the requirement in many instances to rekey data. In addition, the power of the large mainframe and huge disk capacity can be provided for any processing too large for a minicomputer.

Using CMS or a similar product, the MIS department can provide computer power, copies of data, and technical assistance when required, and at the same time maintain control over the data. Dispersed users, at the same time, have the ability to get their jobs done on an independent basis.

In sum, MIS management should not "fight" distributed processing due to the special problems of control over data. Small computers of varying types are an appropriate solution to many problems, although they are no panacea. MIS management, if it is to be successful, must be responsive to the needs of the organization. Producing information that will drive the organization must be the MIS goal. However, in the process of delivering that information, the ongoing viability of the organization must not be placed in jeopardy through inadequate protection of its data—particularly to be avoided are conditions that can lead to computer crime.

DECISION SUPPORT SYSTEMS.   Beyond the problems of widely distributed data processing systems are certain other special control problems associated with decision support systems. More specifically, there is a seemingly uncontrolled mix of computer hardware brands with a resulting diverse mixture of operating systems requiring an even greater mix of software for implementing DSS. For the most part, this wide range of hardware (and software) renders the various brands incompatible with each other. To overcome this problem, it is highly recommended that an extensive organization-wide feasibility study be undertaken. It should determine how best the introduction of new hardware (and software) for DSS can be implemented; moreover, the study should show how control over the equipment can be better realized.

An integral part of the proliferation of computer hardware is the problem of dealing with the management workstation itself (chapter 4 offers a description). Because each workstation has its own storage space plus the capability to access other data files, one important problem centers on several organization personnel working with the same set of data. Although the solution might be to keep data in one or more centrally located data bases (as typically found in a distributed data processing system) in situations where organization personnel make copies to reformat, manipulate, and so forth, such an arrangement may not be very practical for the user.

To overcome this problem, integration of the management workstation with software within a master MIS plan is a way to ensure that data are compatible at some point in time. It is recognized that data file storage of management workstations are updated at different times. However, when the updating occurs, the use of data from a source that has been planned for in advance by MIS finally results in compatibility of data at the management workstation. This contrasts with an unplanned approach, where data come from a wide variety of sources that never tie in with each other. There the lack of control of input data results in a myriad of different answers to the same problems posed by different managers (at various locations) using management workstations. This incompatibility of data can even allow the user to alter critical data files, thereby resulting in conditions that are conducive to computer crime.

CURRENT AUDIT PRACTICES TO DETECT COMPUTER CRIME

Internal auditors, like external auditors, are increasingly involved in evaluating controls for computer application systems. This is a result of their relative independence in reviewing internal controls in user areas as well as in information processing. It is important to note, however, that although auditors can be used effectively in reviewing systems controls and in making control recommendations, the responsibility for these controls properly resides with the MIS manager and the user groups responsible for preparing and processing transactions, record-keeping, and resulting management reports. The role of the internal and external auditors is to judge the adequacy of controls and to recommend control improvements. Responsibility to implement and maintain appropriate controls resides with the MIS function and user organizations.

In fulfilling their tasks, auditors of computerized operations are confronting a number of challenges. Among them are:

- changing input data in a variety of ways before they become output
- the comparative invisibility of data, records, and transactions
- centralized or aggregated activities or transactions
- resequencing the steps of traditional procedures
- integrating processing functions, which frequently has the side effect of eliminating formerly available audit trails
- creating new applications in company operations
- the problem of supporting systems of far greater complexity than traditional manual operations
- the proliferation of microcomputers throughout the company

Today's typical organization frequently depends on the operation of its computer systems for its ability to conduct business. This places a high priority on the auditing and control functions.

The recognition that computer technology is a source of problems and challenges to the auditors should not obscure the fact that the same computer technology can serve as a considerable aid to auditability and control. The computer is a powerful device for accomplishing its intended tasks of computing, data communications, process control, and so forth; it is also an ideal instrument for keeping records and producing information about its own activities and the nature of its work. Such records as statistics and analyses about its own activities can often be compiled concurrently with the main task it performs. If these capabilities of computers can be exploited by the auditors, they can be very powerful and useful tools for their work.

From this viewpoint, computer programs have been designed to do major audit analyses that otherwise would be performed manually. Based upon The Institute of Internal Auditors' SAC (Systems Auditability and Control) Study, 28 practices used by internal auditors were identified in performing their audit tasks.[11] These practices included techniques for compliance and substantive testing plus practices for managing and participating in the development phase of data processing applications. Thirteen of these audit practices were found to be used in both the auditing of developments and modifications and the auditing of production systems (like daily production runs). These 13 practices are listed in table 9.2, along with a brief description of the practice and percentage of use information. An inspection of this table indicates that generalized audit software, manual tracing and mapping routines, test data method, parallel operations, and tagged transactions are the most widely used audit practices for production systems. It should be noted that these internal auditing methods are also widely used by external auditors. In reference to the first audit practice in table 9.2, a number of generalized audit software packages are available. These are set forth in figure 9.7 on page 362.

Use of Auditors to Prevent Computer Crime

Although the foregoing computer audit practices are widely used by auditors to detect computer fraud, problems, and irregularities, it should be pointed out that users, including users of micros, are responsible for establishing requirements for controls within the computer processing phase of an application system. In turn, MIS management typically is responsible for designing and implementing the controls governing automated phases of computer application systems and the controls governing other phases of MIS activities. In many situations, controls in these two areas reflect accounting and financial reporting control objectives. Unfortunately, controls are often established to meet the needs of various stages of manual and computer processing without being evaluated in the context of the total computer application system and its associated control objectives.

In view of these difficulties, users and management must look beyond themselves to those individuals whose sole task is to evaluate the degree of systems controls: the internal auditors. Hence, management looks to the internal auditors to evaluate and verify the effectiveness of internal controls across the entire organization where computer crimes can be easily undertaken. Four things must occur, however, before the internal staff can be effective:

- Top management must ensure that the proper auditability mandate is established for the organization.
- MIS personnel must pay close attention to building in adequate controls for computerized applications.
- Internal auditors must be involved in systems design and subsequent audits of computerized applications.
- Internal auditors must gain sufficient information systems knowledge to meet their new responsibilities.

[11]William E. Perry and Henry C. Warner. "Systems Auditability: Friend or Foe?" *The Journal of Accountancy,* February 1978, p. 58. © 1978 by William E. Perry and Henry C. Warner.

TABLE 9.2   Thirteen most common computer audit practices of internal auditors.

EDP audit practice	Description of practice	Percentage of survey respondents that used each practice in the audit of	
		Developments and modifications*	Production Systems*
Generalized audit software	A set of computer programs that have the capability to process computer data files under the control of input parameters supplied by the internal auditor	12.5	32.6
Manual tracing and mapping routines	Manual analysis of program language and logic to determine patterns of usage	22.9	31.2
Test data method (e.g., test-decking)	Verifies processing accuracy of computer application systems by executing these systems using specially prepared sets of input data designed to produce pre-established results	27.1	26.6
Parallel operation	Use of one or more special computer programs to process "live" data through test programs	32.2	23.1
Tagged transactions	Flagging transactions in "live" operations for later review	12.0	20.9
Snapshot	Picture-taking of selected transactions through the flow of transactions	10.0	18.4
Systems performance monitoring and analysis (e.g., SMF, SCERT)	A feature of the computer operating system software or a separate program that provides the means for gathering and recording information to be used for evaluating systems usage	8.2	15.8

If any of the four is missing, auditability and control will remain elusive.

In summary, MIS management must not abdicate its responsibility for systems controls, but rather must involve users as well as internal auditors in building in the necessary controls at the design stage. This is opposed to the "add-on approach" currently employed by many organizations. The involvement of the audit control functions in all phases of information systems is absolutely necessary and proper in today's more complex DP environment, especially in light of increasing computer crimes. The growth of data communications to connect facilities at remote locations in a DDP environment is one example of how new technology has complicated the control of computer crimes, not to mention normal DP problems and irregularities.

TABLE 9.2   (continued)

EDP audit practice	Description of practice	Percentage of survey respondents that used each practice in the audit of	
		Developments and modifications*	Production Systems*
Program source code comparison	Comparison of two copies of a program made at different times to verify that program change and maintenance procedures are being followed correctly	9.6	14.5
Control flowcharting	Technique provides the documentation necessary to explain the system of control	8.3	9.0
Program object code comparison	Same as program source code comparison except the comparison is performed after program compilation	4.7	8.9
Integrated test facility (mini or dummy company)	Uses auditor-developed fictitious or dummy entity within the framework of the regular application processing cycle	4.2	5.0
Modeling (simulation)	A procedure to compare estimates of expected values to actual values to identify potentially important differences	9.5	7.6
Automatic tracing and mapping routines	Computer analysis of source language and logic to determine if any program segments are not being utilized	3.6	3.9
Other		6.5	10.5

*Percentages are based on actual repsonses to the SAC project mail survey, weighted to reflect the probable response distribution of all orgnizations in the sampling frame. The organizations in this sample represent the approximately 3,000 largest (nongovernment) U.S. organizations with computer systems.

SOURCE: William E. Perry and Henry C. Warner, "Systems Auditability: Friend or Foe?" *The Journal of Accountancy*, February 1978, p. 58. © 1978 by William E. Perry and Henry C. Warner.

EFFECTIVE MIS PRACTICE—APPLICATION OF QUESTIONNAIRE TO SECURITY

The executive vice president of the R & G Company just finished reading an article on computer fraud. The article mentioned the Equity Funding Corporation of America, which had revealed some gaping holes in computer security and control methods. Officials at Equity had used the corporation's computer to create false insurance policies and to inflate the apparent financial status of their corporation. The fall of Equity Funding and a number of related scandals in other organizations made it clear to R & G's executive vice president that there is a real threat to the company from inside the computer center.

□ *Unitech Audit & Control Reporting System (U/ACR)* is designed for use by systems development, computer operations, and internal audit personnel. It eliminates manual balancing, reduces programming effort, enhances internal control, and improves data integrity.

□ *Panaudit Plus* is used by financial, operational, and DP auditors to test and report on data stored in computer files. It allows auditors to extend the reliability and scope of an audit while increasing the auditors' independence. The system consists of general, statistical, and specialized routines.

□ *Audex 100 system* performs functions such as reading and extracting certain fields on data files; comparing data fields; sequence checking, sorting, and merging data; and printing, adding, and performing calculations. Routines can be selected and linked together to perform a desired procedure. Users can, for example, extract, add, and print control totals. This system was originally developed for internal use by Arthur Andersen & Company.

□ *Auditpak II* of Coopers & Lybrand requires the user to indicate the logic needed for the audit objectives by completing an Auditpak II questionnaire, which is processed to produce a diagnostic-free COBOL program. With this package, the auditor can address certain control concerns unachievable through manual performance.

□ *TSI International's Audit Analyzer* is designed to provide computer-assisted auditing tools and techniques for the DP financial and operational auditing areas. With this package, an auditor can access, retrieve, manipulate, and present audit data in a timely manner. Information can be sampled to conform to established audit objectives and requirements.

□ *Computer Audit Retrieval System (CARS)* allows the auditor to extract computer-based information that meets audit specifications. CARS can be used to audit more than twenty different operating environments, including Burroughs, Control Data, Data General, DEC, Hewlett-Packard, Honeywell, and IBM. Only one syntax must be learned. The CARS Audit Library, which functions as a system dictionary, incorporates audit and report-generating routines, and accommodates additional user-written routines. These routines are invoked through function definitions for selecting data and operations as well as report formatting. Once this information is known, CARS then generates its own COBOL code.

□ *Dylakor's Dyl-Audit* is a generalized auditing, file management, information-handling, and report-generating software system. Dyl-Audit uses free-form, English-language statements. Programmers can use the program to generate variable test data, take snapshots of files for analysis, or generate letters for preprinted forms.

FIGURE 9.7
A listing of current generalized audit software packages.

Thus, he reasoned, systems personnel, with their highly specialized knowledge and skills and their easy access to operating hardware and software, can rob or defraud the company and go undetected for months, possibly indefinitely.

In light of the possibility of computer theft, fraud, and the like in the information systems area, he called in outside auditors. While meeting with them, he stressed the need for going beyond the normal audit and spending a minimum of one week in doing interim review work on the computer department alone. Although this extended the scope of the regular audit, the executive vice president felt that money spent investigating this area in great detail would benefit the company, particularly since the company manufactures and sells consumer products which can be easily sold on the outside.

The outside auditors brought in MIS consultants from their staff. Being accustomed to reviewing computer systems in depth, they used the entire MIS questionnaire.[12] After a thorough review of the computer system, the outside MIS consultants concluded that most controls were operating as intended, with the exception of security controls. Due to major problems in this area, two subsections on security controls are set forth in figure 9.8. Although additional subsections from this section plus other sections of the questionnaire could have been included, since some answers were negative, evaluation of the questions in figure 9.8 sufficiently highlights important ongoing deficiencies in the operation.

In answer to question 2 under program control, computer programs and supporting materials maintained in the tape and disk library are accessible to all company personnel, thereby allowing anyone to access a program and alter it. Similarly, according to question 3, the computer department is deficient in its method of handling changes to the computer run log.

Referring to question 1 under equipment log, although a daily equipment log is maintained, no one checks to make sure that all computer time is accounted for. Thus, in many cases available computer time is unexplained. The "no" answers to questions 4 and 5 indicate that the internal auditors have too great a workload to do an adequate job of reviewing the management information systems controls.

Recommendations to Improve Security

Overall, the main thrust of the negative answers in figure 9.8 is that managerial control over computer security leaves a lot to be desired. This was the essential content of the verbal presentation that the outside MIS consultants made to the executive vice-president. As one computer person said, "In the area of security controls, things are loose as a goose." To rectify this problem, their first recommendation was to improve managerial controls over computer processing time as well as the programs themselves. In the current situation, a programmer could obtain a program (on magnetic tape), alter it using the computer, and return it—and no one would be the wiser. This

---

[12]See prior reference on MIS questionnaire.

QUESTIONNAIRE 1: General Controls of Information Systems

	Yes	No	N.A.
V. Security Controls			
B. Program Control			
1. Are computer programs duplicated on magnetic tape or disk and stored in a safe storage area as back-up for emergency conditions?	X		
2. Are computer programs stored in a safe location where they are controlled by a tape and disk librarian?		X[1]	
3. Does each program have a computer run book that is available to the console operator for meeting any contingency during the processing of the program?		X[2]	
4. Does an independent third party periodically conduct a surprise audit of computer programs to make sure they serve their intended purposes?		X[3]	
C. Equipment Log			
1. Is a daily equipment log prepared so that computer operating time can be monitored?		X[4]	
2. Does the equipment log contain			
a. program identification?	X		
b. start time?	X		
c. stop time?	X		
d. production time?	X		
e. test time?	X		
f. down time?	X		
g. unusual conditions?	X		
3. If there is an installed computer device for recording time, does the internal auditor periodically check the equipment log time against this time usage for falsification of computer time?			X
4. Does the internal auditor periodically check the equipment log (when the run was completed) against the library record (when the program tape or disk was returned) for time discrepancies?		X[5]	
5. Is a copy of the computer console typewriter output delivered to the internal auditor at the end of each day? (If possible, the auditor should initial the printout at the start of his or her workday.)		X[6]	

[1]Computer programs and supporting materials maintained in the tape and disk library are available to computer personnel without written authorization.

[2]There is a computer run for each program available to the console operator. However, there is no control over changes to the computer run book, nor over who initiates them.

[3]Because this is the first audit of computer programs, there have been no surprise audits in the past.

[4]Although daily logs of computer time are maintained, they are incomplete since computer operators and programmers testing programs fail to log in and out at all times.

[5]Due to the workload of the internal auditors, there is no time to check the equipment log against the library record, even periodically.

[6]Again, due to the workload of the internal auditors, there is no attempt to check the computer console typewriter output.

FIGURE 9.8   Section V. (B. and C.) of Questionnaire 1, answered.

allows computer personnel to steal the company blind by altering payroll, inventory, and other programs.

An important recommendation is to hire a computer tape and disk records librarian to monitor and maintain the computer records library and issue computer programs and supporting materials to authorized personnel only. In this manner, a complete record is kept of what programs are used, by whom, and at what time. If there is any question regarding the altering of computer programs and related materials, the individual can be identified. Additionally, the MIS consultants suggested that the systems and programming manager establish effective controls over computer run books and changes to them. In this manner, computer operators will have up-to-date instructions for meeting any emergency condition.

Another recommendation is for proper maintenance of daily equipment logs. The outside consultants recommended that the internal auditors have the responsibility of reviewing this log time sheet for irregularities. A typical example of a computer irregularity is testing a computer program that has proved to be operational for a long time.

Additional recommendations were presented based upon problems found in other sections of the MIS questionnaire. However, the foregoing represent the typical security problems encountered in the engagement and recommendations to overcome them.

CHAPTER SUMMARY

Initially, this chapter focused on developing standards for management information systems controls. Two important areas were discussed at some length. First, typical system *development* standards center on helping management control resource planning, quality assurance, cost reduction, and performance evaluation. Second, system *operation* standards focus on service levels and costs to users and the need for protecting and securing computer systems and their data. Thus, standards control not only the creative work of analysts and programmers, but also the daily DP activities of the computer center.

Next, the nature of internal controls was discussed, including accounting control and administrative control. This discussion provided a background for introducing a two-part questionnaire to explore the specifics of general and application controls for management information systems. Many concepts and techniques throughout the text have been captured in these management information system controls. Thus, they provide a convenient way of synthesizing the important essentials of what constitutes an effective management information system.

In the final part of the chapter, the relationship of the MIS manager to computer crime was explored, with particular attention to conditions that make an installation prone to computer crime. An understanding of these conditions and of current audit practices to detect irregularities is essential for the manager. In like manner, auditors can assist in designing and evaluating systems controls to minimize crime. As was demonstrated under "effective

MIS practice," the MIS questionnaire should be looked upon as an additional tool for the MIS manager to analyze department effectiveness in planning, organizing, directing, and controlling.

QUESTIONS

1. How important are standards for controlling management information systems?
2. Name four typical areas of management concern for developing standards. Name additional areas not set forth in the chapter.
3. Do the same standards apply to all MIS development efforts? Explain.
4. **a.** Define the term *internal controls* and explain their essential components.
   b. Who is interested in internal controls? Why?
5. Is there such a thing as too much control over management information systems? Explain.
6. What two purposes are served by the MIS questionnaire for system controls?
7. What is the best use of the MIS questionnaire for system controls?
8. **a.** What are the essential components of general controls for management information systems?
   b. What are the essential components of application controls for management information systems?
9. **a.** Distinguish between input controls and output controls.
   b. Distinguish between batch-processing controls and interactive-processing controls.
10. Compare the research results on general control to application controls. How are they alike and how are they different?
11. What effect do MIS controls have on the audit function?
12. What impact has the Equity Funding disaster had on typical management information system controls?
13. What conditions frequently indicate computer fraud, theft, and the like?
14. What software audit approaches are available to auditors and consultants to assess the effectiveness of a management information system?
15. What can the MIS manager do to improve the effectiveness of systems controls?

PROBLEMS

16. In the chapter, controls that relate to all MIS activities were identified as *general controls*. The major categories of general controls were given as: (1) MIS department controls, (2) systems and program procedures controls, (3) built-in hardware and system software controls, (4) computer center controls, and (5) security controls. Using the second category—systems and program procedures controls—develop a list of ten questions to test the adequacy of control over systems and programming procedures.
17. In the chapter, controls that relate to specific MIS tasks were termed to be *application controls*. The major categories of application controls were set forth as: (1) input controls, (2) processing controls, (3) output controls, (4) data base controls,

and (5) data communication controls. Using the second category—processing controls—develop a list of ten questions to test the adequacy of controls over a batch processing mode. Also, develop a comparable list for an interactive processing mode.

18. Suppose that you have been asked to undertake an audit of the computer center for a medium-sized company—a manufacturer of forty products. How would the scope of the audit differ from that of a large company, such as General Motors or General Electric; that is, how would it differ in complexity and comprehensiveness? Include in your answer such items as the scope of the audit, personnel requirements, and timing considerations to complete the audit.

PROJECTS

19. The Argo Company is audited by a national CPA firm. When the company was using an integrated management information system (batch processing), the outside auditors criticized its handling of inventory. Now the company has implemented an interactive management information system, and the MIS vice-president wonders what problems may be incurred in inventory. Under the old system, the problems encountered by the company in this area were considered substantial by the outside auditors. In the past, many of the physical inventory counts differed substantially from the perpetual figures. With an interactive MIS, just about anyone can alter (add or subtract) the inventory data, since numerous on-line CRT terminals and micros are available for use. Even if entry was restricted to certain personnel, the vice-president is wondering about routine errors that would never be caught since they are handled directly by the computer and not by company personnel.

In view of these difficulties, the MIS vice-president has requested that you supply specific answers to the inventory problem and, in particular, the type of controls necessary to keep inventory errors to a minimum. Write a memorandum stating your recommendations on inventory control.

20. The accounts receivable problems encountered by the Cosco Company were considered to be substantial, based upon a review by outside auditors under the present integrated management information system (batch-processing oriented). In the past, many charges, payments, and adjustments were posted to the wrong accounts, although the details of the accounts agreed in total. With the anticipated installation of an interactive management information system, more company personnel will be working with the on-line accounts receivable file. The vice-president of management information systems is wondering whether the number of errors will increase under the changed conditions.

The vice-president of management information systems has requested that you supply specific answers to the problems in the area of accounts receivable. Specifically, he wants controls that will minimize accounts receivable problems and incorrect postings to the accounts receivable on-line file. Write a memorandum stating your recommendations to overcome these problems.

21. The Sabin Company's business has depended upon developing new products, getting them into production, and then getting them to the market place before being met by extreme competition. Once the products are on the market, its major problem, according to the president, is keeping the products profitable by controlling them. Because no formal procedures exist for control over its new and

DEVELOPMENT,
IMPLEMENTATION,
AND CONTROL OF
EFFECTIVE
MANAGEMENT
INFORMATION
SYSTEMS

existing products, the president is wondering what can be done to ensure that adequate controls exist over its products after they have been marketed.

You are to write a memorandum to the president specifying the controls that should be initiated to ensure that controls are adequate, since the products are highly marketable on the outside by its employees. Also, you should specify what control conditions are conducive to computer crime in terms of MIS personnel. In effect, the main thrust of your memo to the president is assurance that new and existing products can be tightly controlled against theft, alteration of their records, and similar problems, so that the company can remain profitable.

BIBLIOGRAPHY

Ackerman, A. F., and Buckley, F. J. "Software Standards Take Shape." *Datamation,* October 1983.

Atkins, W. "Jesse James at the Terminal." *Harvard Business Review,* July-August 1985.

Baab, J. G.; Paroby, S. M.; and Marquard, W. H. "A Three Dimensional Look at Computer Fraud." *Financial Executive,* October 1984.

Bailey, A. D.; Gerlach, J.; McAfee, R. P.; and Whinston, A. B. "Internal Accounting Controls in the Office of the Future." *Computer,* May 1981.

——. "White-Collar Crime." *Computerworld,* December 26, 1983, and January 2, 1984.

Baker, R. H. "Lining Up Computer Crooks." *Micro Communications,* May 1985.

Batt, R. "Measurement Held Integral Part of MIS." *Computerworld,* June 21, 1982.

Beach, L. M. "Data and Information Controls." *Information Management,* January 1985.

Becker, H. B. "Data Network Security: Everyone's Problem." *Data Communications,* September 1980.

Bequai, A. *How to Prevent Computer Crime—A Guide for Managers.* New York: John Wiley & Sons, 1983.

——. "Management Must Learn to Cope With Computer Crime." *The Office,* August 1984.

——. "Information Security: Guidelines for Obtaining." *Computers and People,* November-December 1985.

Berman, A. "Evaluating On-Line Computer Security." *Data Communications,* July 1983.

Blakeney, S. "Computer Crime, A Worldwide Concern." *Computerworld,* December 26, 1983, and January 2, 1984.

Bloom Becker, J. "Playpens and Cookie Jars: An Invitation to Computer Crime." *Computerworld,* May 4, 1981.

Boger, D. C., and Lyons, N. R. "The Organization of the Software Quality-Assurance Process." *Data Base,* Winter 1985.

Brill, A. E. "Why Data Processing Managers Fear EDP Audits." *Infosystems,* August 1982.

Buss, M. D., and Salerno, L. M. "Common Sense and Computer Security." *Harvard Business Review,* March-April 1984.

Campbell, R. P. "Locking Up the Mainframe." *Computerworld,* October 10, 1983, and October 17, 1983.

Carmichael, D. R. "Internal Accounting Control—It's the Law." *The Journal of Accountancy,* May 1980.

Computer Services Executive Committee, *The Auditor's Study and Evaluation of Internal Control in EDP Systems.* New York: American Institute of Certified Public Accountants, 1977.

Connell, J., and Brice, L. "Practical Quality Assurance." *Datamation,* March 11, 1985.

Cooper, R. A. "Evaluating the Need and Worth of Data Cryptography." *Data Communications,* September 1980.

Cottrell, P., and Weiss, B. D. "Third-Party Liability Insurance: Protection in Case of Computer Error." *Computerworld,* April 2, 1984.

Courtney, R. H., Jr. "Computer Security: The Menace Is Human Error." *The Office,* March 1984.

Craig, R. "The Test's the Thing." *Computer Decisions,* August 13, 1985.

Diesen, J. "DP Auditing: A Team Effort." *Computer Decisions,* February 25, 1985.

Dietz, L. D. "Computer Security: Not Just for Mainframes." *Mini-Micro Systems,* June 1982.

Dodge, F. "Security Implications of the Micro-Mainframe Connection." *Software News,* April 1985.

Dugan, E. "Disaster Recovery Planning: Crisis Doesn't Equal Catastrophe." *Computerworld,* January 27, 1986.

Durham, S. J. "Callback Modems Mean Security and Savings." *Data Communications,* April 1985.

Farmer, D. F. "Confessions of an Auditor." *Datamation,* July 1983. ✶ ✓ •

Fidlow, D. "A Comprehensive Approach to Network Security." *Data Communications,* April 1985.

Fogler, R. A., and Sanderson, G. R. "A Control Framework for Distributed Computer Systems." *The Internal Auditor,* October 1983.

Foster, E. "Computer Insurance, Are You Protected?" *Personal Computing,* August 1985.

Friedman, B. A. "Taking a Byte Out of Organized Crime." *Infosystems,* August 1984.

Gardner, J. E. "How to Assemble a Comprehensive Disaster Recovery Plan." *Computerworld,* November 25, 1985.

Gish, J. "'Salting' the Password." *Infosystems,* April 1985.

Halper, S. "Coopers & Lybrand: Early Developer of Micro-Based Auditing and Accounting Software." *Micro Manager,* October 1984.

Hansen, J. V. "Audit Considerations in Distributed Processing Systems." *Communications of the ACM,* August 1983.

Harrison, B. "Plan for the Worst." *Infosystems,* June 1982.

Hertog, J. F. "Information & Control Systems: Roadblock or Bridge to Renewal?" *Data Base,* Winter-Spring 1982.

Horwitt, E. "Protecting Your Network Data." *Business Computer Systems,* July 1985.

Howe, E. "Coping with Computer Criminals." *Datamation,* January 1982. ✶ ✓ •

Hsiao, D. K.; Kerr, D. S.; and Madnick, S. E. *Computer Security,* New York: Academic Press, 1979.

Johnston, R. E. "How to Select and Implement a Data Security Product." *Infosystems,* Part 1, January 1984; Part 2, February 1984; and Part 3, March 1984.

——. "Foiling the Micro Pirate." *Infosystems,* May 1985.

——. "Protection on the PC." *Infosystems,* June 1985.

Kaunitz, J., and Ekert, L. V. "Audit Trail Compact for Database Recovery." *Communications of the ACM,* July 1984.

Kellerher, J. "Computer Security: A Double Threat." *Business Computer Systems,* October 1982.

Klein, P. "Experts Say Users Must Demand Security." *Information Systems News,* May 19, 1980.

Koch, H. S. "Online Computer Auditing Through Continuous and Intermittent Simulation." *MIS Quarterly,* March 1981.

Krauss, L. I., and MacGahan, A. *Computer Fraud and Countermeasures.* Englewood Cliffs, NJ: Prentice-Hall, 1979.

Lancaster, H., and Hill, G. "Fraud at Wells Fargo Depended on Avoiding Computer's Red Flags." *The Wall Street Journal,* February 26, 1981. ✶

Landwehr, C. E. "Formal Models for Computer Security." *Computing Surveys,* September 1981.

Litecky, C. R., and Rittenberg, L. E. "The External Auditor's Review of Computer Controls." *Communications of the ACM,* May 1981.

Martin, T. A. "Security Is Unlike Other Types of DP Planning." *Software News,* November 1985.

Mautz, R. K., and White, B. J. "Internal Control—A Management View." *Financial Executive,* June 1979.

McKibbin, W. L. "Who Gets the Blame for Computer Crime?" *Infosystems,* July 1983.

Merten, A. G., and Severance, D. G. "Data Processing Control: A State-of-the-Art Survey of Attitudes and Concerns of DP Executives." *MIS Quarterly,* June 1981.

Miles, M. "Disaster Recovery Update." *Computer Decisions,* July 1980.

——. "DP Disaster: Ready or Not." *Computer Decisions,* September 1984.

Miller, J. E. "Avoiding Security Blunders." *Infosystems,* May 1985.

Miskiewicz, J. "DP Security: A Delicate Balance." *Computer Decisions,* April 23, 1985.

Morton, C. "Buying EDP Auditing Software: You Gotta Shop Around." *Business Software Review,* September 1986.

Moulton, R. T. "Network Security." *Datamation,* July 1983.

Murray, J. P. "The Question of Data Control." *Computerworld,* January 11, 1982.

———. "Contingency Planning." *Computerworld,* May 10, 1982.

Mylott, T. R., III. "Computer Security and the Threats from Within." *The Office,* March 1985.

Naib, F. "Technical Review Exposes Weaknesses of Micro Systems." *Computerworld,* December 16, 1985.

Nesbit, I. S. "On Thin Ice: Micros and Data Integrity." *Datamation,* November 1, 1985.

Page, J., and Hooper, P. "Internal Control in Computer Systems." *Financial Executive,* June 1982.

Parker, D. B. *Fighting Computer Crime.* New York: Charles Scribner's Sons, 1983.

Parker, D. B., and Nycum, S. H. "Computer Crime" *Communications of the ACM,* April 1984.

Paulk, M. C. "Security and VAX/VMS, Discover the World of System Security—Its Pluses and Minuses." *The DEC Professional,* December 1984.

Podolsky, J. L. "The Quest for Quality." *Datamation,* March 1, 1985.

Pomerantz, D. "Wanted: Data Security." *Today's Office,* March 1984.

Popek, G. J., and Kline, C. S. "Encryption and Secure Computer Networks." *Computing Surveys,* December 1979.

Porter, T., and Perry, W. E. *Controls and Auditing,* third ed. Computer Security Institute, 1981.

Post, D. W. "Armed Against Calamity." *Business Computer Systems,* April 1984.

Pressman, G. L. "The Issue Is Stealing." *Modern Office Technology,* February 1985.

Reid, G. L. "Decentralizing Data Security." *Datamation,* December 1, 1984.

Rhodes, B. "Micro Security That Makes Sense." *Computer Security,* May 7, 1985.

Ritz, J. R. "A Practical Approach to Catastrophe Planning." *Infosystems,* February 1986.

Romney, M. B.; Albrecht, W.; and Cherrington, D. J. "Auditors and the Detection of Fraud." *The Journal of Accountancy,* May 1980.

Roussey, R. S. "Microcomputers and the Auditor." *Journal of Accountancy,* December 1983.

Shannon, T. C. "Standing Guard." *Digital Review,* April 1986.

Srinivasan, C. A. and Dascher, P. E. "Computer Security and Integrity: Problems and Prospects." *Infosystems,* May 1981.

Stamm, S. L. "Assuring Quality Quality Assurance." *Datamation,* March 1981.

Thierauf, R. J. *Management Auditing, A Questionnaire Approach.* New York: American Management Association, 1980.

———. *Systems Analysis and Design—A Case Study Approach,* sec. ed. Columbus, OH: Charles E. Merrill Publishing Company, 1986.

Thierauf, R. J., and Reynolds, G. W. *Effective Information Systems Management.* Columbus, OH: Charles E. Merrill Publishing Company, 1982.

Troy, G. "Thwarting the Hackers." *Datamation,* July 1, 1984.

Uhl, M. "Crime on Line." *Business Computer Systems,* February 1984.

Vacca, J. "Information Quality Analysis." *Infosystems,* December 1985.

Vohs, D. "The Financial Executive's Role in Computer Security." *Financial Executive,* April 1981.

Wallach, G. "Controls Prevent Computer Negligence and Fraud." *Journal of Systems Management,* May 1983.

Ware, W. H. "Information Systems Security." *Communications of the ACM,* April 1984.

Whalen, J. D. "A False Sense of Security." *Infosystems,* August 1983.

White, C. E., Jr. "The Microcomputer as an Audit Tool." *Journal of Accountancy,* December 1983.

Will, H. J. "ACL: A Language Specific for Auditors." *Communications of the ACM,* May 1983.

Wong, R. "One-Time Passwords Fortify System Security." *Computerworld,* December 23, 1985.

Zimmerman, J. S. "Is Your Computer Insecure?" *Datamation,* May 15, 1985.

———. "PC Security: So What's New?" *Datamation,* November 1, 1985.

Zipp, E. "More Security Tips for VMS System Managers." *Digital Review,* April 1985.

Zipp, E., and Shannon, T. C. "Restricted Access." *Digital Review,* April 1986.

PART FIVE

Major Subsystems of an Effective Management Information System

An overview of an effective management information system for the XYZ Corporation is found in chapter 10. In succeeding chapters, the major subsystems for this corporation are fully presented. Initially, chapter 11 focuses on corporate planning in all its dimensions from the long-range to the short. This is followed by the major MIS operations for marketing in chapter 12. Similarly, the essentials of an effective MIS in manufacturing—in chapter 13—and in accounting and finance—in chapter 14—are examined. Solving MIS needs of the personnel area in chapter 15 concludes this discussion of what constitutes a typical effective management information system.

CHAPTER 10

Overview of an Effective Management Information System—XYZ Corporation

ISSUES

What is the distinction between industrial organizations and service organizations?

What type of MIS organization structure is found in the XYZ Corporation?

What type of data communications network is necessary for the XYZ Corporation to operate in a distributed processing mode?

What is the function of microcomputers for management and operating personnel?

How important are distributed data bases for an effective management information system operating in a DDP environment?

What are the major subsystems of a typical industrial organization, such as the XYZ Corporation?

What shortcomings of the previous system have been overcome with the present effective management information system?

How can the employment of Lotus 1-2-3 and IFPS assist management in performing their activities?

OUTLINE

NEW MIS—ELIMINATING PREVIOUS SYSTEM
SHORTCOMINGS
EFFECTIVE MIS PRACTICE—ESTABLISHING
AN INFORMATION CENTER AT CORPORATE
HEADQUARTERS
    Employing Current Information System Tools
    Break-even Analysis Using Lotus 1-2-3

CHAPTER SUMMARY
QUESTIONS, PROBLEMS, AND PROJECTS
LOTUS 1-2-3 EXERCISES AND PROGRAM
BIBLIOGRAPHY

INTRODUCTION TO MASTER CASE STUDY: THE XYZ CORPORATION

In this, the last part of the text, focus is on overall and detailed aspects of an effective management information system. Throughout chapters 10 through 15, the XYZ Corporation—a typical industrial organization—exemplifies the essentials of a typical management information system. The MIS illustrated uses distributed data processing. It also incorporates many characteristics found in decision support systems. Within this broad framework, the theory underlying effective MIS can be demonstrated in actual practice. This approach assists the reader in understanding what constitutes an up-to-date, effective management information system.

    First, the basic types of business organizations are discussed, followed by an overview of the XYZ Corporation, including its central headquarters, manufacturing facilities, and warehouses. This overview includes important information on the corporation organization structure, the MIS organization structure, the data communications network, the distributed data bases, and the use of microcomputers. Next, the major subsystems of the XYZ Corporation are introduced. Such a presentation specifies not only the essential activities of each subsystem, but the relationships among subsystems. This introduction to the text's master case study is helpful as background for the detailed design of each major subsystem that follows in the forthcoming chapters. The net result is a comprehensive look at a typical effective management information system. Also, the shortcomings of the previous information system are discussed together with the ways they have been overcome in the new, effective management information system. Lastly, the establishment of an information center at corporate headquarters is discussed, along with the employment of Lotus 1-2-3 and IFPS.

INDUSTRIAL VERSUS SERVICE ORGANIZATIONS

The distinctive feature of industrial organizations is the manufacture of some type of product(s). They can be defined as organizations of *men* (i.e., people), *materials,* and *machinery* that are backed by *money* and under *management* control to produce, sell, and distribute goods. Utilizing this definition, the industrial organization is typically more complex in terms of organization structure than the service organization. The most important subsystems (business functions) for a typical industrial organization include corporate planning, marketing, manufacturing, accounting, finance, and personnel. In this chapter, these subsystems form the basis for obtaining an overview of the XYZ Corporation.

While industrial organizations are oriented toward the production of goods, other business organizations are involved in the sale and distribution of goods and services. Typically, such organizations include retailers, wholesalers, distributors, and utilities. In addition, another type of service organization is the "governmental organization," which includes federal, state, county, and city governments, as well as education institutions. Both governmental and educational organizations are normally concerned with providing some type of service(s).

Of the many subsystems found in industrial organizations, the *basic* ones include marketing, manufacturing, and finance. Although these are basic for a manufacturing company like the XYZ Corporation, they may not be basic for other types of organizations, in particular, service organizations. The basic subsystems of a department store are considered to be marketing, purchasing, and finance. For a railroad, they are traffic, maintenance, and finance. Additional *complementary* subsystems are necessary, similar to those found in industrial organizations. In contrast, the basic functions found in a university are education and research, supported by complementary functions. Thus, an organization's objectives will determine its basic and complementary subsystems.

XYZ CORPORATION—AN OVERVIEW

The XYZ Corporation is a company specializing in the manufacture of small electrical appliances for the home market. Sales are currently over $140 million per year and are projected to be about $200 to $210 million in five years. Its product line of 30 products can be categorized into five basic groups. Variations of these basic products are for specific customers whose requirements differ owing to the markets they serve. For large orders, products are shipped directly to retailers from XYZ's manufacturing plants. All other orders are shipped from its warehouses to the many retailers. Ten percent of the corporation's dollar volume is represented by direct shipments from the plants, and 90 percent is represented by shipments through the warehouses.

Corporation Organization Structure

Corporate headquarters are in Cincinnati; manufacturing plants are in Chicago, St. Louis, and Los Angeles. Wherever a manufacturing plant is located, a warehouse is attached. The present employment level of the entire organization is approximately 3,000 employees.

As shown in the organization chart (figure 10.1), the president and chief executive officer reports to the board of directors and is assisted by the corporate planning staff. The executive vice president, in turn, reports to the pres-

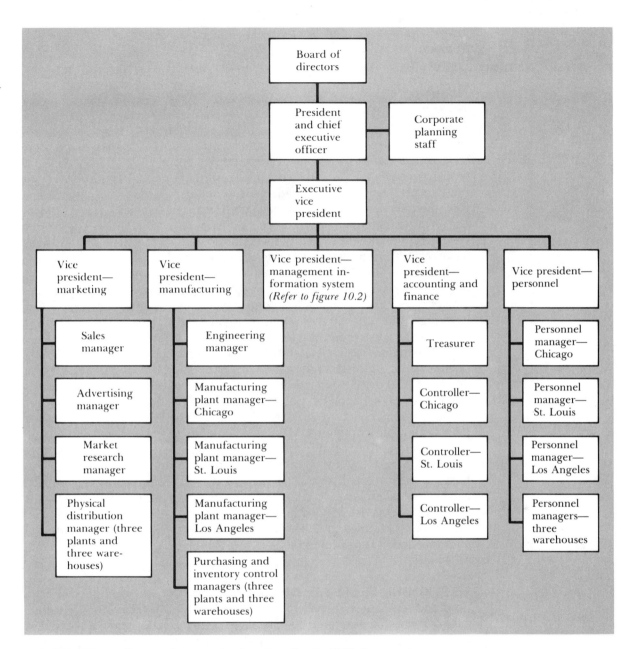

FIGURE 10.1 Corporation organization chart for the XYZ Corporation.

ident. In a similar manner, five vice presidents (marketing, manufacturing, management information system, accounting and finance, and personnel) report to the executive vice president. Various corporate headquarters managers, plant managers, and warehouse managers report to their respective vice presidents. Overall, the corporation organization structure represents a logical framework for achieving the desired objectives of the XYZ Corporation.

MIS Organization Structure

The XYZ Corporation has progressed through a series of data processing systems. Presently, the corporation uses MIS in a distributed data processing environment that has interactive processing capabilities. Its MIS organization chart for the DDP processing mode is illustrated in figure 10.2. The systems and programming director and the computer operations director report directly to the vice president of the management information system. On the systems side, the new systems projects manager and the maintenance projects manager report to the systems and programming director. From an operational viewpoint, the CRT terminal managers, the computer managers, and the internal auditor (from the accounting department) report to the computer operations director. The CRT terminal managers control operators of on-line CRT and hard-copy units at corporate headquarters, the plants, and the warehouses. The computer managers control the computer operators and service personnel. Thus, the interactive capabilities of the system involve equipment that must be supervised for effective control.

In addition to the systems and programming director and computer operations director is an information center director, who reports to the vice president of the MIS. This individual is assisted by systems analysts and programmers who are knowledgeable about the use of microcomputers from the user's standpoint. Accent is placed on assisting end users in developing their own systems and programs. The use of word processing, electronic spreadsheets, and fourth-generation programming languages is the mainstay of end-user tools provided. Although this approach is appropriate for many straightforward applications that assist end users, it is not feasible for medium- and large-scale MIS projects. As discussed in chapter 7, a feasibility study (systems analysis, systems design, and equipment selection, along with system implementation) is required to undertake an MIS project. To illustrate the time and effort needed, it is helpful to relate briefly the relationship of systems personnel to users.

RELATIONSHIP OF MIS PERSONNEL TO USERS. Although the specific positions and levels of systems work are clearly set forth (figure 10.2), an MIS project cannot be delegated completely to systems analysts who are asked to find "the answer." The corporation's management must work closely with systems analysts to create an awareness of value systems and premises used in planning and decision making. Top management must exert leadership, and operating managers must actively cooperate with MIS personnel in order to form an effective team to implement an effective MIS. Only when managers get involved, cooperate with MIS personnel, and relate their problems to the computer's capabilities can objectives be fully realized for the XYZ Corporation. Similarly, the systems analysts need to communicate and work with the operating people on the detailed methods and procedures of the new system.

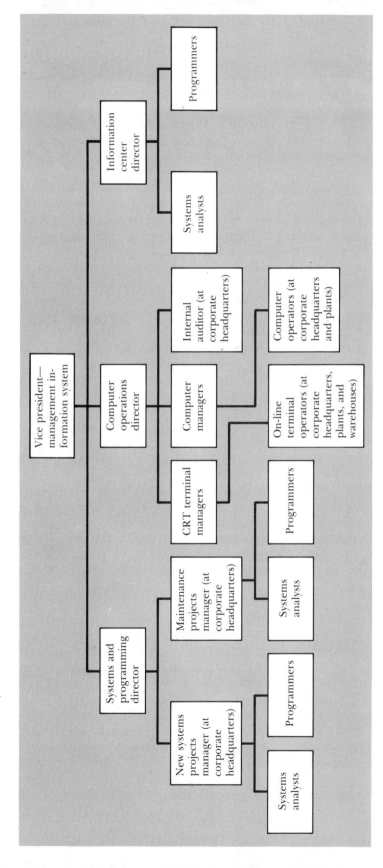

FIGURE 10.2 MIS organization chart (operating in a distributed data processing environment) for the XYZ Corporation.

This is necessary in order to determine how exceptions and problems are to be handled. Also, cooperation is needed to evaluate realistically the decision-making process at the local and central headquarters levels and the information flow necessary for that process. Systems analysts and programmers must work with people above, below, and at the same level for effective results, because managers and operating personnel generally will accept only methods and procedures that they fully comprehend.

Data Communications Network

Currently, the XYZ Corporation's computer system integrates satellite mini-computers at each of the three manufacturing plants (including the attached warehouses) with a centralized computer system. An examination of figure 10.3 indicates that a hierarchical (tree) network is utilized by the corporation. Essentially, the central or host computer employs a data communications network processor for controlling all input from the three satellite minicomputers. At each of the plants (with attached warehouses) CRT terminals and microcomputers have been installed for sales order processing, accounting, manufacturing, inventory, purchasing, physical distribution, and personnel. In addition, there are a number of microcomputers in the other functional areas at corporate headquarters and the plants. The use of these CRT terminals (some of which have printers) and microcomputers in an effective MIS environment is the subject matter for the master case study.

The data communications network (as shown in figure 10.3) for a distributed operating environment is a full duplex system that links all of the corporation's plants, including warehouses, to the corporate headquarters in Cincinnati. The full duplex communication channels can transmit information in both directions simultaneously. All communications from and to corporate headquarters are fully dedicated lines; that is, it is not necessary to telephone in order to reserve a communication line from the plants, including warehouses, to corporate headquarters or vice versa. This approach for relaying information back and forth simplifies data communications for the data communications network processor.

Distributed Data Bases

In this distributed processing environment, a data base management system (DBMS) is used because it is designed for high-volume, on-line transaction processing and efficient, interactive remote querying and reporting. It uses a common language for defining, managing, and directing data and provides a standard user interface that is simple and logical. A common file description governs the structure of all data, but is independent of that structure. In effect, the DBMS gives organizational personnel timely access to vital information and provides data integrity protection, security, and automatic recovery and restart.

For an effective management information system, distributed data bases are a must. They provide lower management and their staff with the opera-

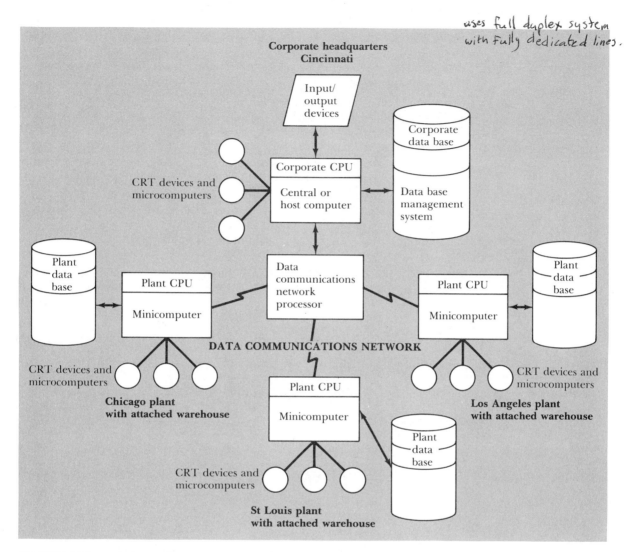

uses full duplex system with fully dedicated lines.

FIGURE 10.3   A data communications network using a hierarchical (i.e., tree) approach—XYZ Corporation.

tional information needed to plan and control daily, weekly, and monthly operations. In turn, these data are summarized for use by middle management for planning and control over a longer time frame. In many cases, the data are communicated to the home office in Cincinnati for use by middle as well as top management. Thus, distributed data bases are a means of helping management to carry out their managerial functions of planning and control.

Microcomputers for Managers and Operating Personnel

Closely related to distributed data bases is the utilization of microcomputers both to assist management and their staff in answering routine questions about operations, and to answer ad hoc "What if?" questions. Microcomputers enable managers to employ concepts underlying a decision support system environment. DSS is of profound benefit to the corporation's managers since they can learn *without* doing (i.e., simulate experience), thereby saving thousands to millions of dollars in wasted efforts. The "What if?" facilities of DSS give them an understanding of the sensitivity of a particular decision outcome to variations in a number of input values in a way not feasible without a microcomputer.

The managers of the XYZ Corporation are finding that DSS is a competitive necessity, both internally and externally for outside competition. Similarly, the XYZ Corporation is finding that managers perform better when aided by DSS and have the competitive edge over their peers. When DSS clarifies a decision process so that the process can be replicated, decision making can move down in the corporation, freeing time at higher levels.

MICROCOMPUTER TO MAINFRAME LINK. As shown in figure 10.4a, microcomputers can be quite helpful to the corporation's managers and their

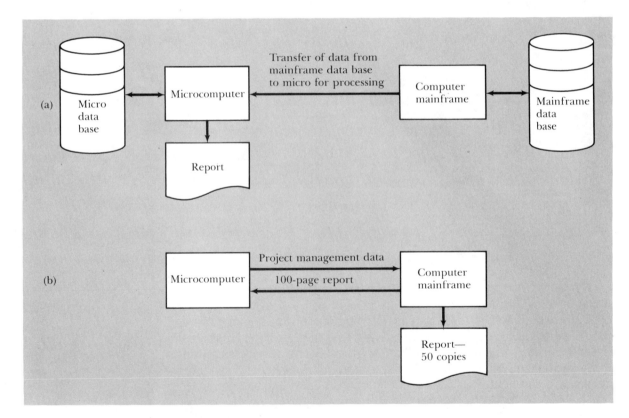

FIGURE 10.4   Utilization of microcomputers by managers and their staff (a) to provide transfer of data from mainframe data base to microcomputer for processing, i.e., the data base is used for downloading to the microcomputer and (b) to provide the mainframe with the ability to share expensive peripherals with a microcomputer, i.e., sharing peripherals with microcomputer users.

OVERVIEW OF AN
EFFECTIVE
MANAGEMENT
INFORMATION
SYSTEM—XYZ
CORPORATION

staff, who use them for data base downloading. Within a DSS operating mode, managers can query the mainframe data base for information on corporate personnel, budget, expenses, and so forth, incorporate it into a word processing document, a spreadsheet or a barchart, and send the result to a vice president—or display it at an important meeting. In contrast, as illustrated in figure 10.4b, a mainframe enables managers and their staff to share expensive peripherals. A manager can do a final edit of a 100-page report using a microcomputer word processing program; then send it, via mainframe, to a high-speed printer that turns out 50 copies in time for a meeting the next day. A project manager, for example, compiles scheduling data on the next stage of a job and sends it on to the mainframe where a project management program uses a graphics plotter to create a PERT chart.

Although microcomputers are widely used in DSS, their widest use today in the XYZ Corporation, like most organizations, is as a front-end processor. At the corporate headquarters and plants, microcomputers function as front-end processor/data entry stations to a mainframe. For example, the foremen at a plant could store the hours their employees worked on the microcomputer's disk storage. In turn, they could upload the data weekly to the plant minicomputer, where a general ledger program consolidates data from several plant departments into the general ledger and financial reports and prints checks for employees. Such an approach is illustrated in figure 10.5

OVERCOMING PROBLEMS IN THE MICROCOMPUTER TO MAINFRAME LINK.   As is currently the case with other organizations, the XYZ Corporation's link from computer mainframes to IBM PCs contains a series of obstacles. Commercial micro-to-mainframe products are available, but many leave a communication gap that only a programmer can bridge. In view of these facts, the XYZ Corporation has chosen one of the two basic methods of physically connecting microcomputers and mainframes. It uses the asynchronous approach; that is, a modem connected to ordinary dial-up telephone lines. Asynchronous dial-up can support transmission speeds of up to 2400 baud. The advantages of this method are lower cost and ease of installation. The lines already in the corporation's central headquarters or plants can be used.

Once the microcomputers and mainframe have been linked physically,

Modem connected to ordinary dial up telephone lines. Use file transfer package.

FIGURE 10.5   Utilization of microcomputers by operating personnel to provide transfer of data from microcomputers to mainframe data base for processing, i.e., the microcomputer is used as a front-end processor.

the user must decide on how the microcomputers are to get in touch with the mainframe. The file-transfer package Smartcom (from Hayes Microcomputer Products, Inc.) is used, permitting the microcomputer to request a particular file from the mainframe, download it, and store it in a local floppy or its hard disk.

Another problem XYZ Corporation faces, like other corporations, is that many mainframe programs were designed for data processing professionals, not non-technical managers and operating personnel. Fortunately, most popular mainframe data base management and decision support systems are linked to report generators and/or data query programs. Such is the case with IFPS, which is employed by the XYZ Corporation. This fourth-generation language can extract from a mainframe data base according to user specifications ("give me sales figures for products 100, 200, and 300 for January and February").

In summary, microcomputer-to-mainframe link problems are addressed and solved by the MIS department as they arise. These fundamental problems have arisen in other organizations. These solutions are then used by the XYZ Corporation to fulfill the needs of managers and operating personnel.

XYZ CORPORATION—MAJOR SUBSYSTEMS

From an overview standpoint, the XYZ Corporation can be described as a *materials flow company*. Purchased materials and manufactured materials of stock flow into the various stages of the production process. As they do, the materials take on a variety of forms and shapes until they become finished goods. Next, the finished products flow through the distribution system, either directly via direct shipments or indirectly through corporation-owned warehouses, until they reach the customer. Thus, in this materials-flow concept, several of the corporation's subsystems are involved: purchasing, inventory, manufacturing, and physical distribution.

Coupled with materials flow is corresponding information flow. Materials-flow information is a most important factor in coordinating the diversified activities of the three manufacturing plants and attached warehouses with corporate headquarters. It must be comprehensive, thereby integrating decision making throughout the entire materials-flow process—from purchased materials to shipment of finished goods. With this integrated flow of essential information, management and operating personnel can make adjustments swiftly and effectively in response to the ever-changing business environment. The materials-flow information concept, then, is an essential part of an effective management information system.

The information flow is not restricted only to the materials area. In fact, there may well be even more information generated for activities not related directly to the materials-flow process. For example, many subparts of the corporation's corporate planning, marketing, finance, and accounting subsystems are not related directly to the manufacture of the final product. Regardless of the source or need for information, the overall distributed MIS must be

OVERVIEW OF AN
EFFECTIVE
MANAGEMENT
INFORMATION
SYSTEM—XYZ
CORPORATION

"open ended." This approach provides flexibility so that activities can be linked at minimum cost and effort. But more importantly, the open-ended approach allows for changing the direction and speed of information flow in response to management and operating personnel needs. More will be said about the information flow for selected subsystems in the following sections.

INFORMATION FLOW ILLUSTRATED. To illustrate the concept of information flow, the quarterly sales forecast and special customer orders affect the quantity of finished goods to be produced (marketing subsystem), which, in turn, affects the materials to be purchased from outside suppliers and to be manufactured within the corporation in future planning periods (manufacturing subsystem). Goods purchased or manufactured are procured on an optimum basis by using the economic order quantity (EOQ) formula. They are eventually handled by the inventory section (manufacturing subsystem). Both are requisitioned to meet the manufacturing plan in accord with the schedule of master operations (manufacturing subsystem). The operational or shop status of the final product, material, labor, and similar items is used for operations evaluation control at the manufacturing level. In some cases, operating information is significant enough for review by middle and top management. If this happens, feedback at this level of importance may make it necessary to review future plans (corporate planning subsystem). Also, it may be necessary to revise future sales forecasts. Finally, finished goods are shipped directly to customers or through plant-attached warehouses. This information flow from one subsystem to another, in particular from external and internal environment factors through shipped goods to customers or plant-attached warehouses, is depicted in figure 10.6.

Corporate Planning

Before day-to-day operational activities can function effectively, the corporate planning subsystem for the XYZ Corporation must give direction to the entire organization—that is, to the corporation's subsystems. This integrated approach requires the following modules (i.e., subparts) in order to reach the organization's objectives: (1) long-range corporate planning, (2) medium-range corporate planning, and (3) short-range corporate planning—flexible budgets. The essentials for this central subsystem are set forth in chapter 11.

The questions that can be asked of an effective MIS corporate planning subsystem that focuses on a DSS for various planning levels are innumerable. For example:

- □ What effect will a newly designed product have on sales five years hence (long-range)?
- □ What would happen to profits if certain products are redesigned and advertised quite extensively (medium-range)?
- □ What effect will the level of sales and production have on the current year's profit (short-range)?

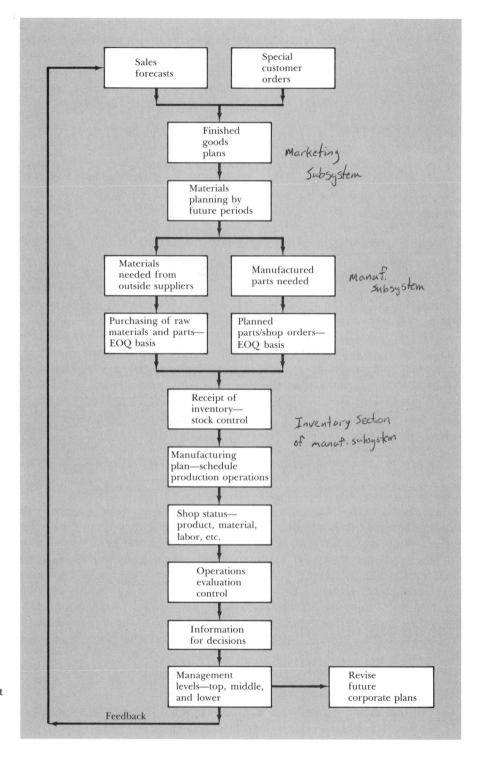

FIGURE 10.6
Flow of integrated information for the XYZ Corporation from the external and internal environmental phase to actual day-to-day operations—output from one subsystem becomes input to another subsystem.

Generally, these typical questions cannot be answered with absolute certainty. However, when the time factor is shortened, it is easier to predict the future, especially when it falls within the vista of short-range corporate planning.

Long-range plans, being the starting points for the corporate planning subsystem as shown in figure 10.7, reflect organization objectives. Likewise, they take into account the many external and internal environmental factors surrounding the corporation before being translated into more current plans; namely, short- and medium-range. By and large, the focal points of short-range

OVERVIEW OF AN
EFFECTIVE
MANAGEMENT
INFORMATION
SYSTEM—XYZ
CORPORATION

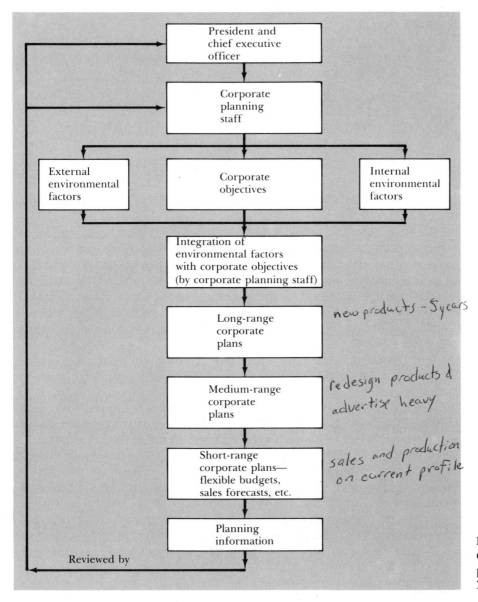

FIGURE 10.7
Overview of corporate planning subsystem—XYZ Corporation.

plans are flexible budgets designed to relate a certain level of sales to a corresponding level of production. Flexible budgets provide necessary planning information to vice presidents and their staffs. In turn, this information is forwarded to personnel who will be controlled by the budgeting process. Also, sales forecasts are used by corporate planning to fashion short-range corporate plans.

Marketing

The corporation's marketing subsystem has several modules. The more important ones are (1) sales forecasting, (2) market research, (3) advertising, (4) sales order processing, and (5) physical distribution. These essential components of the marketing subsystem are detailed in chapter 12.

Common sales order processing problems are dealt with by any effective MIS. Such a system is designed to answer these questions:

- Can this order be accepted?
- Does the corporation want to accept the order?
- When is the order actually a sale?
- Where is the order entered?
- When do the finished goods belong to be customer?
- How much is to be charged for finished goods and when?

Other questions of this type can be asked regarding sales order-processing design.

In the overview of sales order processing (figure 10.8), orders are received from customers. Appropriate order forms are prepared and edited before the customer's credit is checked. If the order is not accepted because of poor credit, it is returned to the customer and the reason is noted. Generally, the order is approved for order entry, and appropriate files (customer, pricing, and finished goods) are referenced for preparing shipping papers. Shipping papers are forwarded to the appropriate warehouses for regular shipment or to a particular plant for direct shipment.

At this point, other major subsystems interact with sales order processing (marketing subsystem). Shipping papers provide the basis for preparing customer invoices, which are eventually utilized for aging accounts receivable and processing checks received from customers (accounting and finance subsystem). In addition, they are used for assembling goods at the warehouse and plant levels. If items are available for shipment as noted by the perpetual finished goods file during the sales order processing phase, the file is changed from "finished goods on order" to "finished goods shipped" (marketing subsystem). Engineering also comes into contact with sales order processing through the receipt of special customer orders (manufacturing subsystem).

Although the foregoing procedures have concentrated primarily on sales order processing, numerous other marketing activities both precede and succeed it. More specifically, sales forecasting is employed to determine the proper levels of finished goods to have on hand in order to minimize the number of back orders experienced in order processing. In addition, advertising is

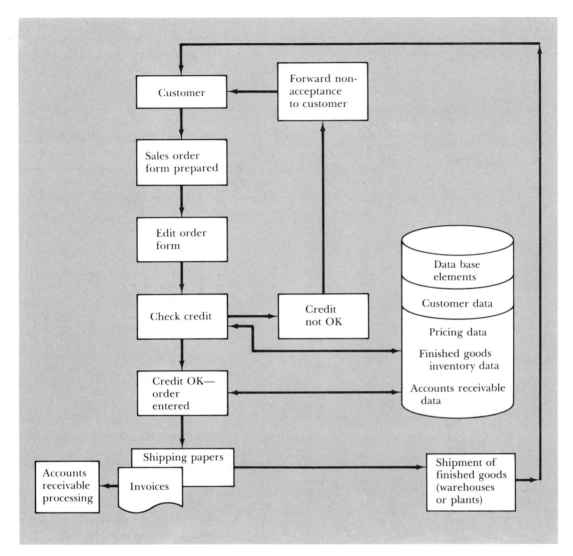

FIGURE 10.8   Overview of sales order processing within the marketing subsystem—XYZ Corporation.

determined in advance to promote the corporation's products that are on hand or will be manufactured to meet future demand. Preceding advertising activities are those pertaining to market research; that is, the determination of the appropriate products to offer XYZ's customers today as well as tomorrow.

In contrast, the last of the marketing activities—physical distribution—follows sales order processing. Shipment of finished goods, whether direct or nondirect, must be reflected in the corporation's data files. Likewise, certain data on routing finished goods are utilized in effecting the lowest total costs.

In addition, these files, as shown in figure 10.9, are referenced when finished goods are shipped to customers via order processing. As shown previously in figure 10.8, shipping papers start the customer billing and collection process (accounting subsystem).

Manufacturing

The subsystem for getting regular or special production orders produced is manufacturing. Its essential modules for the corporation in our illustration are (1) engineering, (2) purchasing, (3) production planning and control, (4) raw materials and work-in-process inventories, (5) manufacturing operations, and (6) quality control. These manufacturing activities are covered in chapter 13.

A specific order request, initiated by the customer or the corporation, must be adequately researched before the prototype model can be developed by the engineering department (figure 10.10). An important part of product

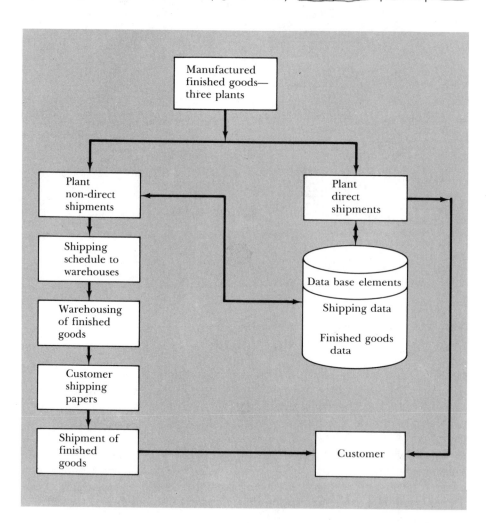

FIGURE 10.9
Overview of shipment of finished goods from plants to warehouses and customers within the marketing subsystem—XYZ Corporation.

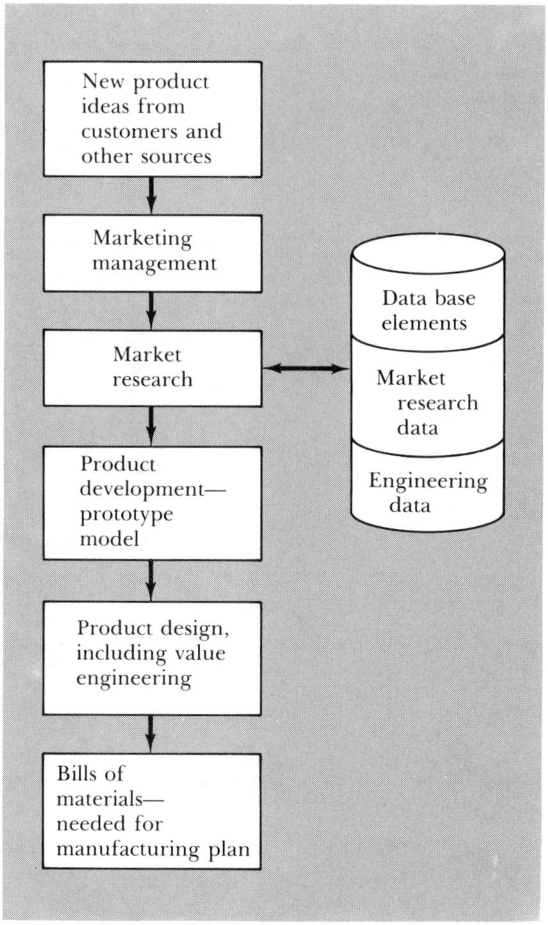

OVERVIEW OF AN
EFFECTIVE
MANAGEMENT
INFORMATION
SYSTEM—XYZ
CORPORATION

FIGURE 10.10
Overview of product
development within the
manufacturing sub-
system—XYZ
Corporation.

design is value engineering, which considers whether the parts contained in the finished product perform the required function as efficiently and inexpensively as possible. An effective MIS should answer these typical value engineering questions:

- Will the product give the customer an acceptable level of service?
- Will the service level cover the expected life of the product?
- Will internal manufacturing costs be low enough?
- Can the corporation expect to meet its expected return on investment?

Once the prototype has been developed, engineering draws the final prints that incorporate the essentials of value engineering (figure 10.10). Bills of materials are also developed for the routing of parts and subassemblies through the manufacturing centers. These detailed drawings and bills of materials are forwarded to the production planning and control department for incorporation into future manufacturing plans.

The function of purchasing, shown in figure 10.11, is to procure planned raw materials on a quarterly basis as well as to purchase items as needs arise. Quarterly purchases represent the largest dollar amount of buying activities for the next manufacturing cycle of the XYZ Corporation. Day-to-day purchases are applicable not only to manufacturing, but also to most other subsystems because various types of forms, supplies, and so forth are continually

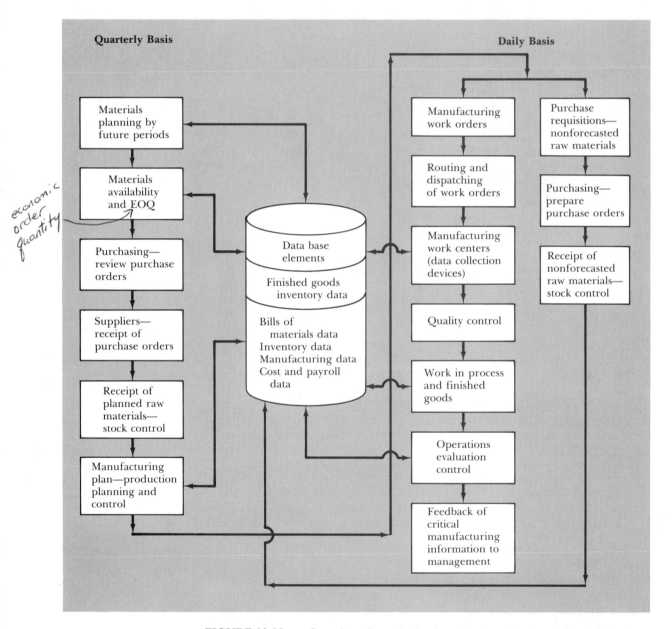

FIGURE 10.11   Overview of purchasing, production planning and control, manufacturing operations, quality control, and inventories within the manufacturing subsystem—XYZ Corporation.

OVERVIEW OF AN
EFFECTIVE
MANAGEMENT
INFORMATION
SYSTEM—XYZ
CORPORATION

needed for operations. In addition to buying activities, vendor invoices must be approved by the buyer before being forwarded to the accounts-payable section (accounting and finance subsystem).

Within the manufacturing process, the inventory module in figure 10.11 is concerned basically with planned raw materials and nonforecasted raw materials acquisition and control. Nonforecasted materials refer to items that are not forecasted on a quarterly basis, such as special production orders, experimental projects, and plant maintenance supplies. Depending on the type of inventory, data files are updated before, during, and after their movement. With this approach, data elements of inventory reflect current operations for the evaluation of actual versus standard costs. Likewise, raw materials and work-in-process data are available to other subsystems for ordering materials or requisitioning materials for production.

Fundamentally, the manufacturing phase is a continuation of forecasted finished goods (marketing subsystem). As shown in figure 10.11, raw materials are ordered on a quarterly basis (purchasing module) and, upon receipt, are placed under the supervision of stock control (inventory module). They provide input for the manufacturing plan of the production planning and control section, whose job is to schedule, route, and dispatch orders through the various manufacturing work centers. The quality control section is responsible for making appropriate tests of manufactured and finished products before forwarding them to the warehouse or customer. As illustrated, there is an interplay between physical activities and data files for operations evaluation, allowing feedback of critical information where deemed necessary.

Accounting and Finance

The sales and cost factors generated by the previous subsystems are accounted for and reported by the accounting and finance subsystem. They serve as the required inputs for the accounting and finance modules, which are (1) receivables and payables, (2) payroll, (3) cost accounting, (4) financial statements, and (5) source and application of funds. In chapter 14, these modules are thoroughly discussed.

The accounting and finance subsystem, which is responsible for keeping records, billing customers, arranging payments, and costing products, among other activities, processes a myriad of details. For accounting and finance information to assist other subsystems, it must answer these timely questions:

- ☑ Can actual cost data be compared to standard data of the various manufacturing work centers?
- ☑ Can information on the current status of customer accounts be obtained immediately if needed?
- ☑ Are all accounting and finance data in a machine-processible form for compiling current financial statements?
- ☑ Are the required funds available where and when needed?

An approach is found within an effective MIS for answering these typical accounting and finance questions.

Generally, accounting activities, as set forth in figure 10.12, center on

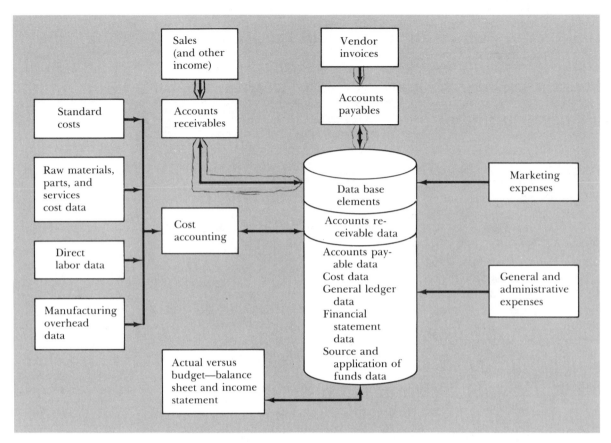

FIGURE 10.12   Overview of sales and cost data within an accounting and finance subsystem—XYZ Corporation.

recording and reporting sales and costs (expenses). Sales revenue and manufacturing costs data—on raw materials, labor, and overhead—as well as marketing and general and administrative expenses provide the necessary inputs to the general ledger for producing periodic income statements (overall and detailed). Cash, receivables, payables, and other accounts are recorded in the general ledger for producing the balance sheet. These financial statements provide inputs for intermediate and long-range analysis (corporate planning subsystem). In a similar manner, detailed income and cost analyses are helpful in determining future cash flow and capital budgets.

Sales-receivables and disbursements-payables information as displayed in figure 10.13 are projected, thereby providing cash flow information for the next month and future periods. In order to undertake large capital projects, additional sources of capital may be necessary. They may be obtained from outside sources—banks, financial institutions, bonds, debentures, and capital stock. Internal and external sources of funds should be committed only to capital projects that meet an established return on investment (ROI). However, in some cases, tangible and intangible factors must be considered for a final

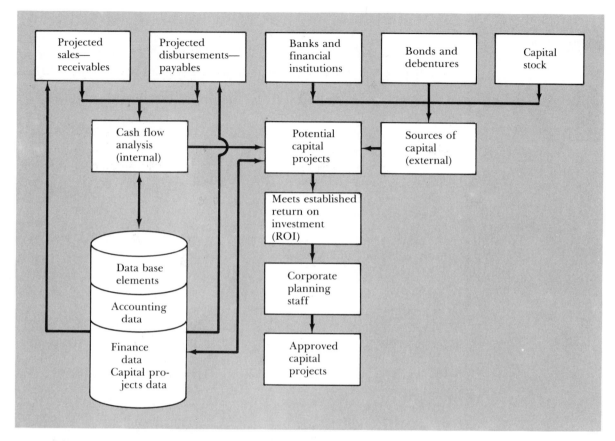

FIGURE 10.13 Overview of financial sources for capital projects within an accounting and finance subsystem—XYZ Corporation.

decision. As noted in the illustration, the capital projects and their sources of funds are integrated into the central subsystem (corporate planning subsystem) around which all others focus.

Personnel

Personnel, whose basic objective is to find "the right person for the right job," comes into contact with most other subsystems in fulfilling this stated purpose. To assist the personnel subsystem in this endeavor, certain modules are necessary: (1) skills inventory, (2) personnel selection and placement, and (3) wage and salary administration. Each area is detailed in chapter 15.

The recruitment of personnel for desired positions can be extremely difficult for any personnel department. Typical questions about recruitment are:

□ Can the position be better filled by someone within the organization?
□ Can the position be filled now as opposed to later by someone internally?

393

□ Has the best person been found for the job by exhausting internal and external recruiting procedures?

Many of these questions can be answered within an effective MIS environment, especially those dealing with internal recruitment of present employees for new job openings.

The personnel subsystem, depicted in figure 10.14, is designed to locate employees who have certain skills within the organization's operations by interrogating the skills-inventory data file. A list of potential employees for job openings is scrutinized by the personnel department for immediate action. In addition, employee files can be utilized for paying employees (accounting and finance subsystem) as well as providing a starting basis when negotiating with the labor union. The personnel subsystem, then, is an integral part of the corporation's other subsystems.

Summary—Major Subsystems of the XYZ Corporation

Corporate Planning takes into account all external and internal environmental factors surrounding the corporation in developing long-range to short-range plans that are based upon organization objectives.

Marketing initiates the product information flow. Its prime job is to contract potential customers and sell finished products through salespeople, advertising, and special promotions. Marketing is responsible for authorizing finished products to be shipped to customers from corporate-owned warehouses or via direct shipments.

Manufacturing develops new products vital to the corporation's growth and designs them from scratch. It schedules and manufactures finished products whether in anticipation of demand, upon receipt of customer orders, or some combination of these two. In addition, it procures the raw materials, supplies, equipment, and other purchase requirements necessary to meet the

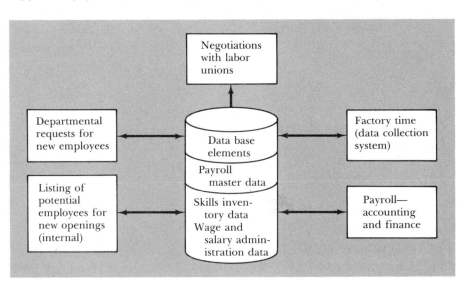

FIGURE 10.14
Overview of essential personnel functions found in other subsystems—XYZ Corporation.

corporation's operating needs. It receives, stores, and protects all materials and supplies not required for current use, and issues items for production to the authorized manufacturing departments.

Accounting and Finance collects information from other subsystems that forms the basis for the corporation's financial statements. Also, this subsystem directs its activities toward obtaining funds for operational needs and capital projects.

Personnel determines and recruits the people needed to meet present and future corporation objectives.

NEW MIS—ELIMINATING PREVIOUS SYSTEM SHORTCOMINGS

The previous information system was capable of answering many important questions confronting the organization. The system was forward-looking, with operational control in an interactive processing mode, especially at the lower- to middle-management levels (see figure 10.15). For the most part, the reasons the corporation implemented the previous information system were:

- □ better customer service and improved selling efficiency
- □ more timely and improved management information analysis and reporting
- □ improved coordination and control of the overall organization and its parts

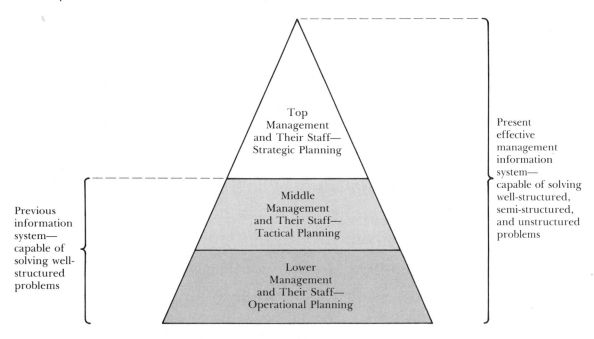

Previous information system—capable of solving well-structured problems

Top Management and Their Staff—Strategic Planning

Middle Management and Their Staff—Tactical Planning

Lower Management and Their Staff—Operational Planning

Present effective management information system—capable of solving well-structured, semi-structured, and unstructured problems

FIGURE 10.15   Comparison of previous information system with present effective management information system.

☐ better opportunity to match demand with production

☐ on-line information available for management analysis of the organization

Although the foregoing benefits were realized, management felt there were still major MIS shortcomings. For one, output from the system was received periodically, since the system was programmed to provide such reports. However, due to the fast changing times in which the XYZ Corporation was operating (and still is), this approach was much too static for management. Instead of receiving periodic reports in a static environment, there was serious need for an interface—all the way from problem formulation to solution—between the managers and staffs and their computer for the problem being solved. The capability of combining an individual's knowledge about a problem (subjectivity) with the computer's output (objectivity) throughout the problem-solving process provides the ability to look inside the problem and see what makes it "tick" as times change. From this perspective, the MIS needs to have DSS capabilities for *problem solving*.

Going one step further, the top management of the XYZ Corporation must have the capability of engaging in *problem finding* within a DSS operating mode. This is particularly necessary at the corporate planning level. In certain cases, top management of XYZ Corporation has problems that are long-term as well as continuous, where there is no final answer. Fortunately, an important characteristic of problem finding is its capability of coping with such situations—whether continuous or noncontinuous—to assist managers and their staffs at all levels in solving important corporate problems (refer to figure 10.15).

Another major shortcoming of the previous information system was its ability to provide answers only for well-structured problems, that is, for problems whose parameters are easily obtainable. When it came to answering problems that contain some semi-structured and unstructured parameters, the system proved to be inadequate. These types of problems especially arise at higher levels of management, where the planning time span involves more than one year. Most of these problem types can be thought of as executive-oriented "What if?" questions. For example, "What happens to total profits if prices are raised or lowered in the short run versus the intermediate and long run, when considering competitive reactions?" Or "What impact will the installation of mechanical robots have on production workers' morale, as well as on profits?" These typical questions contain unstructured elements that need to be evaluated over time for the XYZ Corporation. Fundamentally, the previous system was at a loss to provide adequate answers to these types of "What if?" questions. Because an effective management information system using DSS elements does utilize the decision maker's insight, intuition, judgment, and past experience at the various stages of the problem-finding and problem-solving processes, the interaction between the individual and the computer is far superior to the previous system in supporting decision making for semi-structured and unstructured problems. Problems of this type, as noted previously, tend to be continuous, their solutions tending to change over time.

OVERVIEW OF AN
EFFECTIVE
MANAGEMENT
INFORMATION
SYSTEM—XYZ
CORPORATION

Overall, the implementation of a new, effective management information system by the XYZ Corporation has helped managers and their staffs increase the successful achievement of their tasks. It allows their decisions to be improved by the support of a computerized management information system. As depicted in figure 10.15, the previous information system focused on solving well-structured problems at the lower- and middle-management levels. In contrast, the present effective management information system can assist management at all levels in a well-structured, semi-structured or unstructured problem environment. It is from this perspective that the major subsystems of the XYZ Corporation are set forth in part five of this text.

EFFECTIVE MIS PRACTICE—ESTABLISHING AN INFORMATION CENTER AT CORPORATE HEADQUARTERS

The XYZ Corporation initiated the establishment of an information center at central headquarters in Cincinnati about eighteen months ago. This center not only serves the needs of the home office, but also serves to address the DP needs at the plant level. Since plant managers and their assistants spend a fair amount of time at the home office, they have ample opportunity to get the needed information about microcomputers for use in their own operations. The interface of corporate headquarters and plant users with the information center is expected to increase in the foreseeable future.

In retrospect, a number of reasons have prompted the establishment of this information center. *First,* the use of decision support system (DSS) tools has grown tremendously as microcomputing has been introduced into the XYZ Corporation. *Second,* DSS tools are more sophisticated and easier to use, and many managers now take advantage of them to perform complex analyses of portions of their business. *Third,* DSS tools are useful in supporting managers and some operating personnel in making better decisions, and are not just systems that merely automate the decision-making function. *Fourth* and last, a wide range of tools are available to focus on specialized managerial and operational problems facing the XYZ Corporation today that were not so pronounced in the past.

A number of basic functions are offered by the information center. They are: training users, supporting users, data base maintenance, analysis of offerings, and hardware and software selection. In these areas the information center director can play a key role in encouraging effective use of micro-based DSS in the XYZ Corporation. In essence, education in modeling concepts—how to use a spreadsheet and what assumptions to make and not to make in building financial models—can be provided through this centralized information center.

Employing Current Information System Tools

At this time, a number of software packages are supported by the information center. Inasmuch as the most-used modeling tool of all organizations is the spreadsheet, its impact has also been very high at the XYZ Corporation. The utilization of Lotus 1-2-3 will be demonstrated below and throughout the remainder of the text for in-chapter materials and end-of-chapter exercises along with programs. Also, a diskette is available for use by the reader. With Lotus 1-2-3, balance sheets, income statements, and cash flows can be modeled in hours rather than days or weeks. This spreadsheet is well understood by the corporation's accountants and financial managers, many of whom found a secret wish fulfilled when they acquired the ability to build a spreadsheet that instantly showed the results of any change. As indicated above, the "What if?" facility of a spreadsheet or any DSS tool helps support the decision-making process.

Before we leave this discussion, a word of caution. An emerging problem with the use of spreadsheet models, like Lotus 1-2-3, is the lack of validation of such models before they are passed on to others. Often, assumptions are not documented in the model, and users who have not built a model may not understand the limits intended by the originator. For example, a model many not include tax tables that vary tax with amount of income; it may merely have used the marginal tax rate appropriate for the specific amounts in the first user's cases. The old GIGO (Garbarge In, Garbarge Out) rule applies as well to micros as it does to mainframes.

As well as Lotus 1-2-3, the information center supports the more popular microcomputer packages, such as WordStar and dBASE III. Additionally, it supports the micro IFPS, a fourth-generation programming language mentioned previously in the chapter, which is also available on the corporate headquarters mainframe. This language is widely used by corporate planners (refer to chapter 11) to analyze data over a long period of time, say five years. Just recently, other managers of the XYZ Corporation, especially those in manufacturing, have expressed interest in IFPS. The reason is that decision support system tools have often grown out of the operations research methodology (i.e., management science methodology) typically found in manufacturing. Linear and integer programming, queuing models, and multiple linear regression are now available on microcomputers using IFPS. Although it takes a knowledgeable user or consultant to understand how to define and structure these models, they can yield impressive results for the XYZ Corporation.

Additionally, as will be demonstrated below and in the remaining chapters, one way of making the user interface more appealing is through graphics. Graphics can be integrated for presentation, as in Lotus 1-2-3 or IFPS, or used to speed the linkage between graphic tools and other packages.

Overall, the role of the information center is to make sure that microcomputers and their software are used to maximum advantage to benefit the XYZ Corporation. When relating DSS usage to the information center, it should be noted that although DSS use will spread with or without the assistance of information center personnel, it will be most effective with their guidance, data base resources, training, and support. Getting started in micro decision support is prerequisite to the corporation's effective competition in the future.

Break-even Analysis Using Lotus 1-2-3

As the final item in this overview chapter on the XYZ Corporation, we describe the use of the electronic spreadsheet Lotus 1-2-3 for break-even analysis. Figure 10.16a shows a table that takes only about five minutes to create and can save hours of discussion and analysis. Shown is a range of possible sales volumes and variable cost percentages, along with approximate profit, break-even, or loss resulting from each combination. As the table depicts for monthly fixed costs of $40,000, the company would be at the break-even point with sales at $100,000 per month and variable costs of 60 percent for product 200. By interpolating the values in the figure, profit would be $20,000 if sales were $150,000 and variable costs remained at 60 percent, and so forth. Needless to say, this table can be tremendously revealing to managers who have never considered the implications of fixed and variable costs. It provides an easy opportunity to play "What if?" with sales and variable cost percentages.

Many variations of figure 10.16a are possible. For example, the user could divide the profits by sales to display profit margins as a percentage of sales rather than as dollar amounts. Also, yearly versions, monthly versions with yearly sales, and the like can be produced. The variation produced depends on what management wants to see. Another tool for break-even analysis is graphing the data in the table, which helps one see how well the company controls costs. A break-even graph developed using Lotus 1-2-3 is shown in figure 10.16b.

CHAPTER SUMMARY

An overview of an effective management information system for the XYZ Corporation has been this chapter's central focus. Basically, the accent at XYZ has been on integrating the information flow within the many subsystems operating in a distributed data processing mode, including DSS where appropriate. From this view, managers and their staffs are able to plan and control at the appropriate level, both local and centralized. Additionally, a conversational mode between the manager (or staff personnel) and the computer is helpful throughout the problem-finding and problem-solving processes. In fact, as the problem changes over time, this interacting process allows the problem to be redefined and solved within the revised framework. Hence, an effective management information system—as found in the XYZ Corporation—is generally never complete, but is open-ended to accommodate changing conditions.

As will be seen in this master case study, an effective MIS can support the decision maker not only in resolving well-structured problems, but also in solving semi-structured and unstructured problems as they arise in the normal course of business activities. In some cases, these problems are fundamentally *planning oriented,* but in other cases, they tend to the *control oriented.* This will be evident in the various modules of the subsystems examined in future chapters.

Breakeven Analysis

Monthly Profits When Fixed Costs Are:	$40,000
Sales Increment:	$20,000
Variable Cost Starting Percentage:	58%
Variable Cost Increment:	2%

Variable Costs

Sales	58%	60%	62%	64%	66%	68%	70%
$0	($40,000)	($40,000)	($40,000)	($40,000)	($40,000)	($40,000)	($40,000)
20,000	(31,600)	(32,000)	(32,400)	(32,800)	(33,200)	(33,600)	(34,000)
40,000	(23,200)	(24,000)	(24,800)	(25,600)	(26,400)	(27,200)	(28,000)
60,000	(14,800)	(16,000)	(17,200)	(18,400)	(19,600)	(20,800)	(22,000)
80,000	(6,400)	(8,000)	(9,600)	(11,200)	(12,800)	(14,400)	(16,000)
100,000	2,000	0	(2,000)	(4,000)	(6,000)	(8,000)	(10,000)
120,000	10,400	8,000	5,600	3,200	800	(1,600)	(4,000)
140,000	18,800	16,000	13,200	10,400	7,600	4,800	2,000
160,000	27,200	24,000	20,800	17,600	14,400	11,200	8,000
180,000	35,600	32,000	28,400	24,800	21,200	17,600	14,000
200,000	44,000	40,000	36,000	32,000	28,000	24,000	20,000
220,000	52,400	48,000	43,600	39,200	34,800	30,400	26,000
240,000	60,800	56,000	51,200	46,400	41,600	36,800	32,000
260,000	69,200	64,000	58,800	53,600	48,400	43,200	38,000

(a)

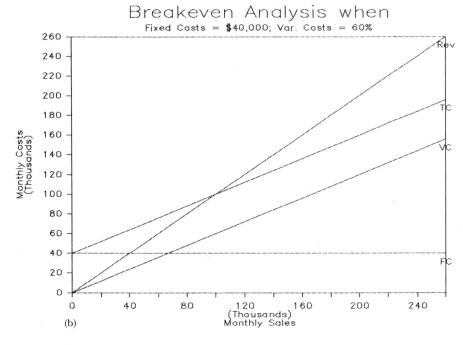

Breakeven Analysis when
Fixed Costs = $40,000; Var. Costs = 60%

(b)

FIGURE 10.16
Break-even analysis for product 200 using the Lotus 1-2-3 spreadsheet: (a) relating sales to variable cost percentages for profit, break-even, or loss, and (b) graphing to depict the break-even point for data in (a).

1. If the XYZ Corporation was a much larger company, would the MIS organization structure be different from that set forth in figure 10.2?

2. Suggest an alternative way of setting up the distributed data processing environment for the XYZ Corporation.

3. Would the various subsystems and the component parts presented in this chapter differ in an effective MIS environment (for the XYZ Corporation) versus an ineffective MIS environment?

4. How will the CRT terminals and microcomputers found at corporate headquarters and the plants be used; that is, will the focus be on transactional processing, management reporting, or both? Explain.

5. Suggest additional component parts for each of the subsystems presented in this chapter for the XYZ Corporation.

6. **a.** How important is the planning function in an effective MIS environment for the XYZ Corporation?

   b. How important is the control function in an effective MIS environment for the XYZ Corporation?

7. **a.** What shortcomings are typically found in an information system?

   b. How can they be overcome?

8. Does it appear that the information center as currently operated will be able to meet the present and future requirements of corporate headquarters users? Plant users?

9. After reexamining figure 10.2—MIS organization chart for the XYZ Corporation—develop an alternative MIS organization chart that centers on the systems analysts reporting to a systems analysts manager and programmers reporting to a programming manager. In addition, consideration should be given to the use of systems analysts and programmers as consultants to the three manufacturing plants, since the corporation is operating in a distributed data processing mode. Comparable changes should be considered for the operations side of the MIS organization chart.

10. After referring to figure 10.3, develop an alternative approach to the data communications network using a hierarchical (i.e., tree) approach for the XYZ Corporation. Consideration should be given to the fact that although one plant CPU (minicomputer) is down, the corporate CPU at the central site can be used to continue processing. Similarly, the use of an alternative plant CPU to assist the disabled CPU for a time should be considered. In your approach, utilize a distributed data processing mode for the data communications network.

11. In figure 10.4, the use of microcomputers was illustrated from two different standpoints; i.e., data base downloading and sharing peripherals for managers and their staff. Also, in figure 10.5, the use of microcomputers as front-end processors was illustrated for operating personnel. Give at least one example each to illustrate all three uses of microcomputers for the XYZ Corporation.

12. In reference to figure 10.12, an overview of sales and cost data as used by the accounting and finance subsystem of the XYZ Corporation is given. In the figure,

actual versus budget for the balance sheet and the income statement is illustrated. What data from the data base would be needed to produce budgeted amounts for the coming year? Similarly, what data would be needed to produce monthly statements that compare actual amounts with budgeted figures? How can the concept of "flexible budgets" be incorporated into the entire budgeting process? Also, of what use is cost accounting to the budgeting process?

PROJECTS

13. Using the overview of finished goods from plants to warehouses and customers within the marketing subsystem for the XYZ Corporation (as found in figure 10.9), redo the system flowchart as a data flow diagram or a Warnier/Orr diagram. Keep in mind that plant direct shipments are shipped directly to customers while plant nondirect shipments are sent to the warehouse attached to the plant. Upon receipt of customer orders, these goods are then shipped to the customer from a company-owned warehouse.

14. After considering the flow of integrated information for the XYZ Corporation from the corporate planning phase to actual day-to-day operations, develop an overall system flowchart or data flow diagram that depicts this movement of information. An underlying framework for this integrated information flow is the materials flow found in the manufacturing subsystem. To assist in the preparation of the system flowchart or data flow diagram, reference can be made to figures 10,6, 10.7, and 10.11.

15. Based upon the information set forth in this chapter, develop an overall system flowchart or a data flow diagram for the entire XYZ Corporation. The following functional areas are to be included: (1) corporate planning, (2) marketing, (3) manufacturing, (4) accounting and finance, and (5) personnel. Where deemed appropriate, the subparts of each functional area should be included for an understanding of the management information system operating in a distributed data processing mode. Additionally, consideration should be given to the appropriate data base elements that are an integral part of each functional area.

LOTUS 1-2-3 EXERCISES AND PROGRAM

16. As illustrated in figure 10.16, break-even analysis was used to determine the profitability, break-even, and lack of profitability for one of the XYZ Corporation's products. Using this as a model, develop a comparable analysis (break-even analysis and graph) for proposed product 230 using the program provided on the Lotus 1-2-3 diskette or as given in the program found for this section. The data for this product are as follows:

Selling price per unit	$10.75
Variable costs per unit	$6.25
Total fixed costs	$30,000
Practical capacity	40,000 units

Compare the profitability of this product to the one given in the chapter. Which is more profitable? In addition, should the exploration of profitability and break-even analysis be applied to the XYZ Corporation's 30 products? Why or why not?

(handwritten annotations):

Change FC to 30,000
Sales Increment: 40,000
Sales Increment %: 58%
VC Starting %: 2%
VC Increment: 2%

CM = 10.75 - 6.25 = 4.50
BE = 30,000 = 6667×10.75
BE = 30,000 / 4.50 = 71,666

Sales	58%
20,000	(30,000) (21,600)
40,000	(13,000)
60,000	(4,800) Break even
80,000	3,600 is between
100,000 402 12,000	60 + 80 thousand
260,000	79,200

This product 230 is more profitable, Yes, they may find that they aren't making profit on other products. So they may be able to do away with a product.

OVERVIEW OF AN
EFFECTIVE
MANAGEMENT
INFORMATION
SYSTEM—XYZ
CORPORATION

Sales $130
$140
Switch over between Inside + outside sales $150

	inside	outside
	15,000 x	14800
	19,000	19400 ^
	23,000	24,000 x

17. The XYZ Corporation is considering the marketing of a new product next month. The marketing vice president is considering three prices: $6.95, $7.95, and $8.95. Variable costs have been determined to be $3.25 per unit while fixed costs allocated to this product have been calculated to be $7,500. Marketing forecasts are 3,000 units at $8.95, 4,000 units at $7.95, and 4,750 units at $6.95. What price should be charged for the product to maximize its profits? Use the program provided on the Lotus 1-2-3 diskette or as given in the program found for this section. The break-even analysis of figure 10.16 can be used as a model.

18. The president of the XYZ Corporation is thinking about replacing its present marketing staff with outside sales agents. He feels that the corporation will be able to cover the same sales territory with outside sales agents. The XYZ Corporation overall financial condition can be viewed as follows:

Current Year, Just Ended

Sales	$130,000,000
Variable Costs	78,000,000
Contribution to Fixed Costs and Profit	52,000,000
Fixed Costs	37,000,000
Net Profit Before Federal Income Taxes	$15,000,000

It is assumed that sales will be the same for its present marketing staff or outside sales agents. The present cost of the marketing staff is 6 percent of sales (a variable cost), while outside sales agents would cost the corporation $8,000,000 for commissions and related expenses (a fixed cost). What should the president of the XYZ Corporation do? At what point is the corporation indifferent as to whether to add more outside sales agents or use the present marketing staff? Use the program provided on the Lotus 1-2-3 diskette or as given in the program found in this section. The break-even analysis of figure 10.16 can be used as a model.

Monthly Profits when Fixed Cost are: 37,000
Sales Incre: 10,000
VC % : 58%
VC incre: 2%

Sales	60%
20,000	(29,000)
30,000	(25,000)
40,000	(21,000)
50,000	(17,000)
60,000	(13,000)
70,000	(9,000)
80,000	(5,000)
90,000	(1,000)
100,000	3,000
150,000	23,000

LOTUS 1-2-3 PROGRAM—BREAK-EVEN ANALYSIS (DATA AND GRAPH) (PROGRAM 3)

3 zeros have been dropped

```
D1:  'Breakeven                               E11: \-
E1:  ' Analysis                               F11: \-
D2:  \-                                        G11: \-
E2:  ' --------                               H11: \-
B4:  '   Monthly Profits When Fixed Costs Are: A12: '   Sales
G4:  (C0) U 40000                              B12: (P0) U +$G$6
B5:  '   Sales Increment:                      C12: (P0) U +B12+$G$7
G5:  (C0) 20000                                D12: (P0) U +C12+$G$7
B6:  '   Variable Cost Starting Percentage:    E12: (P0) U +D12+$G$7
G6:  (P0) 0.58                                 F12: (P0) U +E12+$G$7
B7:  '   Variable Cost Increment:              G12: (P0) U +F12+$G$7
G7:  (P0) 0.02                                 H12: (P0) U +G12+$G$7
A9:  \-                                        A13: '   -----
B9:  \-                                        B13: '   ------
C9:  \-                                        C13: '   ------
D9:  \-                                        D13: '   ------
E9:  \-                                        E13: '   ------
F9:  \-                                        F13: '   ------
G9:  \-                                        G13: '   ------
H9:  \-                                        H13: '   ------
D10: '   Variable Costs                        A15: (C0) U 0
A11: \-                                        B15: (C0) (1-B$12)*$A15-$G$4
B11: \-                                        C15: (C0) (1-C$12)*$A15-$G$4
C11: \-                                        D15: (C0) (1-D$12)*$A15-$G$4
D11: \-                                        E15: (C0) (1-E$12)*$A15-$G$4
```

monthly: 45000
Sales Inc: 10,000
VC% : 52%
VC incre: 2%

Sales	54%
20,000	(35,800)
	(31,200)
	(26,600)
	(22,000)
	(17,400)
	(12,800)
	(8,200)
	(3,600)
	1,000
	5,600
	10,200
15,000	14,900

19400 29,000

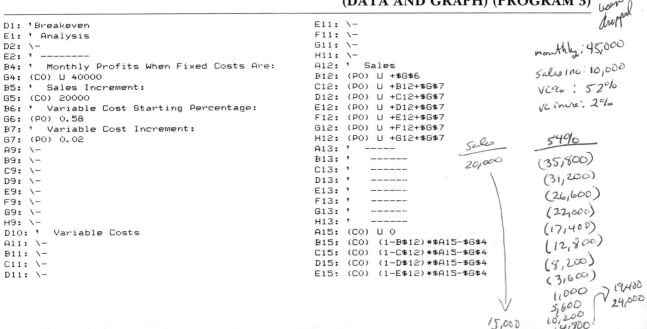

(PROGRAM 3—CONTINUED)

```
F15:  (C0)   (1-F$12)**$A15-$G$4         D22:  (,0)   (1-D$12)**$A22-$G$4
G15:  (C0)   (1-G$12)**$A15-$G$4         E22:  (,0)   (1-E$12)**$A22-$G$4
H15:  (C0)   (1-H$12)**$A15-$G$4         F22:  (,0)   (1-F$12)**$A22-$G$4
A16:  (,0)   U +A15+$G$5                 G22:  (,0)   (1-G$12)**$A22-$G$4
B16:  (,0)   (1-B$12)**$A16-$G$4         H22:  (,0)   (1-H$12)**$A22-$G$4
C16:  (,0)   (1-C$12)**$A16-$G$4         A23:  (,0)   U +A22+$G$5
D16:  (,0)   (1-D$12)**$A16-$G$4         B23:  (,0)   (1-B$12)**$A23-$G$4
E16:  (,0)   (1-E$12)**$A16-$G$4         C23:  (,0)   (1-C$12)**$A23-$G$4
F16:  (,0)   (1-F$12)**$A16-$G$4         D23:  (,0)   (1-D$12)**$A23-$G$4
G16:  (,0)   (1-G$12)**$A16-$G$4         E23:  (,0)   (1-E$12)**$A23-$G$4
H16:  (,0)   (1-H$12)**$A16-$G$4         F23:  (,0)   (1-F$12)**$A23-$G$4
A17:  (,0)   U +A16+$G$5                 G23:  (,0)   (1-G$12)**$A23-$G$4
B17:  (,0)   (1-B$12)**$A17-$G$4         H23:  (,0)   (1-H$12)**$A23-$G$4
C17:  (,0)   (1-C$12)**$A17-$G$4         A24:  (,0)   U +A23+$G$5
D17:  (,0)   (1-D$12)**$A17-$G$4         B24:  (,0)   (1-B$12)**$A24-$G$4
E17:  (,0)   (1-E$12)**$A17-$G$4         C24:  (,0)   (1-C$12)**$A24-$G$4
F17:  (,0)   (1-F$12)**$A17-$G$4         D24:  (,0)   (1-D$12)**$A24-$G$4
G17:  (,0)   (1-G$12)**$A17-$G$4         E24:  (,0)   (1-E$12)**$A24-$G$4
H17:  (,0)   (1-H$12)**$A17-$G$4         F24:  (,0)   (1-F$12)**$A24-$G$4
A18:  (,0)   U +A17+$G$5                 G24:  (,0)   (1-G$12)**$A24-$G$4
B18:  (,0)   (1-B$12)**$A18-$G$4         H24:  (,0)   (1-H$12)**$A24-$G$4
C18:  (,0)   (1-C$12)**$A18-$G$4         A25:  (,0)   U +A24+$G$5
D18:  (,0)   (1-D$12)**$A18-$G$4         B25:  (,0)   (1-B$12)**$A25-$G$4
E18:  (,0)   (1-E$12)**$A18-$G$4         C25:  (,0)   (1-C$12)**$A25-$G$4
F18:  (,0)   (1-F$12)**$A18-$G$4         D25:  (,0)   (1-D$12)**$A25-$G$4
G18:  (,0)   (1-G$12)**$A18-$G$4         E25:  (,0)   (1-E$12)**$A25-$G$4
H18:  (,0)   (1-H$12)**$A18-$G$4         F25:  (,0)   (1-F$12)**$A25-$G$4
A19:  (,0)   U +A18+$G$5                 G25:  (,0)   (1-G$12)**$A25-$G$4
B19:  (,0)   (1-B$12)**$A19-$G$4         H25:  (,0)   (1-H$12)**$A25-$G$4
C19:  (,0)   (1-C$12)**$A19-$G$4         A26:  (,0)   U +A25+$G$5
D19:  (,0)   (1-D$12)**$A19-$G$4         B26:  (,0)   (1-B$12)**$A26-$G$4
E19:  (,0)   (1-E$12)**$A19-$G$4         C26:  (,0)   (1-C$12)**$A26-$G$4
F19:  (,0)   (1-F$12)**$A19-$G$4         D26:  (,0)   (1-D$12)**$A26-$G$4
G19:  (,0)   (1-G$12)**$A19-$G$4         E26:  (,0)   (1-E$12)**$A26-$G$4
H19:  (,0)   (1-H$12)**$A19-$G$4         F26:  (,0)   (1-F$12)**$A26-$G$4
A20:  (,0)   U +A19+$G$5                 G26:  (,0)   (1-G$12)**$A26-$G$4
B20:  (,0)   (1-B$12)**$A20-$G$4         H26:  (,0)   (1-H$12)**$A26-$G$4
C20:  (,0)   (1-C$12)**$A20-$G$4         A27:  (,0)   U +A26+$G$5
D20:  (,0)   (1-D$12)**$A20-$G$4         B27:  (,0)   (1-B$12)**$A27-$G$4
E20:  (,0)   (1-E$12)**$A20-$G$4         C27:  (,0)   (1-C$12)**$A27-$G$4
F20:  (,0)   (1-F$12)**$A20-$G$4         D27:  (,0)   (1-D$12)**$A27-$G$4
G20:  (,0)   (1-G$12)**$A20-$G$4         E27:  (,0)   (1-E$12)**$A27-$G$4
H20:  (,0)   (1-H$12)**$A20-$G$4         F27:  (,0)   (1-F$12)**$A27-$G$4
A21:  (,0)   U +A20+$G$5                 G27:  (,0)   (1-G$12)**$A27-$G$4
B21:  (,0)   (1-B$12)**$A21-$G$4         H27:  (,0)   (1-H$12)**$A27-$G$4
C21:  (,0)   (1-C$12)**$A21-$G$4         A28:  (,0)   U +A27+$G$5
D21:  (,0)   (1-D$12)**$A21-$G$4         B28:  (,0)   (1-B$12)**$A28-$G$4
E21:  (,0)   (1-E$12)**$A21-$G$4         C28:  (,0)   (1-C$12)**$A28-$G$4
F21:  (,0)   (1-F$12)**$A21-$G$4         D28:  (,0)   (1-D$12)**$A28-$G$4
G21:  (,0)   (1-G$12)**$A21-$G$4         E28:  (,0)   (1-E$12)**$A28-$G$4
H21:  (,0)   (1-H$12)**$A21-$G$4         F28:  (,0)   (1-F$12)**$A28-$G$4
A22:  (,0)   U +A21+$G$5                 G28:  (,0)   (1-G$12)**$A28-$G$4
B22:  (,0)   (1-B$12)**$A22-$G$4         H28:  (,0)   (1-H$12)**$A28-$G$4
C22:  (,0)   (1-C$12)**$A22-$G$4
```

BIBLIOGRAPHY

Appleton, D. S "Very Large Projects." *Datamation,* January 15, 1986.

Cerullo, M. J. "Developing Sophisticated Computer Applications." *Journal of Systems Management,* January 1980.

Ely, E. S. "Don't Be Afraid of Computer Phobia." *Computer Decisions,* December 10, 1985.

Goldberg, E. "Applications Integration." *Computerworld,* December 30, 1985; January 6, 1986.

Gunawardane, G. "Implementing a Management Information System in an Extremely Dynamic (and Somewhat Hostile) Environment—A Case Study." *Interfaces,* November-December 1985.

Kerner, D. V. "Business Information Characterization Study." *Data Base,* Spring 1979.

Kopcych, T. "Evolution of the MIS Function." *Infosystems,* April 1986.

Leary, E. J. "Decision Support Systems Aid in Management of Operations, Resources, and Finances." *Industrial Engineering,* September 1985.

Mitchell, J. "Expanding the Small Business System." *Datamation,* November 1979. ✳

Murdick, R. G., and Fuller, T. C. "Subsystem Cycles for MIS." *Journal of Systems Management,* June 1979.

Nolan, R. L. "Managing the Crisis in Data Processing." *Harvard Business Review,* March-April 1979. ✳

Robey, D. "Computer Information Systems and Organization Structure." *Communications of the ACM,* October 1981.

Simpson, D. "Small-Business Systems Solve Big Problems." *Mini-Micro Systems,* June 1982.

Thierauf, R. J. *Distributed Processing Systems,* Englewood Cliffs, NJ: Prentice-Hall, 1978.

_____. *Decision Support Systems for Effective Planning and Control—A Case Study Approach.* Englewood Cliffs, NJ: Prentice-Hall, 1982.

Venkatakrishnan, V. "The Information Cycle." *Datamation,* September 1983. ✳

Vickers, W. H. "Source Data Processing." *Datamation,* October 1980. ✳

Sales − Variable Cost = Contribution Margin

$$\frac{\text{Fixed Cost}}{\text{Contribution Margin}} = \text{Break Even}$$

⑤

CHAPTER 11

Corporate Planning Subsystem—XYZ Corporation

ISSUES

What is the relationship between the corporate planning subsystem and the other major subsystems for the XYZ Corporation?

How important are critical success factors and problem finding to the overall corporate planning process?

What are the important functions of a corporate planning staff no matter the type of system installed?

What is the relationship of external factors to internal factors within the corporate planning function?

How important are electronic spreadsheets and financial planning packages in the corporate planning process of an effective management information system?

What is the relationship of corporate planning to control of operations within an effective MIS environment?

INTRODUCTION TO CORPORATE PLANNING

Corporate planning, the first of the major subsystems to be examined in detail for the XYZ Corporation, is the focal point of an effective MIS. Its purpose is to decide *what* to do in terms of short-, medium-, and long-range plans; *how* to implement these plans in terms of corporate resources; and *when* to execute them in order to accomplish organization goals and objectives. Important relationships and feedback interact among these three planning stages, often complicated ones. This complexity, along with revenue and cost factors, make it extremely important that management establish a systematic and analytic approach to corporate planning. The best approach for deciding what to do, how to do it, and when to do it is through systematic procedures in the corporate planning subsystem.

As in all succeeding chapters, the key elements needed for effectiveness in the major subsystem under scrutiny are set forth initially. In this chapter, these important elements—namely, critical success factors, a problem-finding approach to corporate planning, the use of corporate planning to start the continuous decision process, and mathematical and statistical packages—are explored before we present an overview of corporate planning for the XYZ Corporation. Next, the major systems for (1) long-range corporate planning, (2) medium-range corporate planning, and (3) short-range corporate planning are illustrated within an effective MIS environment. For these planning systems, the use of Lotus 1-2-3 and IFPS are illustrated. These three important functions, when performed effectively, allow information to flow upward and downward for effective corporate *planning* of the organizations's many activities. Similarly, they provide a basis for *controlling* corporation activities, as shown in subsequent chapters on the other major subsystems of the XYZ Corporation.

TYPES OF CORPORATE PLANNING

Like most organizations, corporate management at the highest level of the XYZ Corporation is charged with setting objectives; developing long-range plans; and setting marketing, manufacturing, financial, and personnel strategies, programs, and policies. It is also charged with interplant resource allocations and analysis of these plans for consistency and credibility. The plant general management of the XYZ Corporation also is involved in setting corporate objectives and, in turn, translates them into more specific objectives by functional areas. To accomplish these objectives, the management of plants and warehouses is concerned with interpreting the near-term portion of the long-range plan and translating it into short-term (annual) operating plans, as well as with allocating resources needed to achieve the objectives.

Strategy considerations relative to future market opportunities and products to fill them are basic to *long-range planning*. A distinctive characteristic of long-range planning is discovering opportunities, and then developing effective strategies and programs to capitalize on these opportunities. The long-range plans which embrace all the plants and warehouses of the XYZ Corporation and its environment provide a basis for more detailed medium-range planning.

Medium-range planning is concerned primarily with financial planning to place the organization in the best financial posture for the next several years. This fiscal planning involves developing the operating programs and associated budgets for the next several years. On the other hand, *short-range planning*, or detailed fiscal operating planning, is carried out in each plant and warehouse. In fact, within an organization that has practiced formal planning on a regular basis, it is normal for every plant and warehouse to prepare annual plans for the coming year. These plans are brought together at corporate headquarters for a detailed examination of the key measures of the business—turnover, product line, profitability, number of employees, and strength of management structure, among other factors—at a future time.

CORPORATE PLANNING CONSIDERATIONS FOR EFFECTIVE MIS

As a starting point for effective corporate planning from long- to short-range, it is helpful to examine the factors that can make or break any organization. These factors are called *critical success factors* (CSF). In turn, this discussion is related to the problem-finding approach to corporate planning. An understanding of the relationship between these important areas goes a long way toward giving direction to the XYZ Corporation, in particular, its top management and planning staff.

In addition to critical success factors and a problem-finding approach applicable to the XYZ Corporation, the importance of corporate planning starting the continuous decision process is examined. To assist management and their staff in effective long- to short-range planning, mathematical and statistical packages currently available are briefly presented as they relate to the XYZ Corporation. This orderly presentation of key considerations provides an underlying framework for the remaining sections of the chapter, namely, an overview as well as some detailed operational aspects of this particular MIS corporate planning subsystem.

Critical Success Factors

For any business, critical success factors (CSFs) are the limited number of areas in which results, if satisfactory, ensure successful competitive performance. They are the few key areas where things *must* go right for the organization

408

to flourish. A research team at the Center for Information Systems Research at MIT identified the four primary sources of CSFs as (1) industry-based factors; (2) competitive strategy, industry position, and geographic location; (3) environmental factors; and (4) temporal factors.[1] If results in these areas are not adequate, the organization's efforts for the period will be less than desired. As a result, the critical success factors are areas of activity that should receive constant and careful attention from top management and its corporate planning staff. The current status of performance in each area should be continually measured, and that information should be made available to higher levels of management.

Critical success factors support the attainment of organizational goals and objectives. Goals represent the end points that an organization hopes to reach, while critical success factors are the areas in which good performance is strictly necessary to ensure attainment of these goals. Representative goals and CSFs for the XYZ Corporation are presented in figure 11.1. In addition to determining what the critical success factors are and how to include them in the planning process, the corporate planning staff must also understand their associated activity and resource requirements. Each activity and resource, in turn, has two sets of factors that need to be identified. One set measures the level of activity or resource consumption (e.g., *activities* pending versus completed, and *resources* available versus consumed). The other set evaluates how well the results achieved (e.g., sales, plant utilization, human resources productivity, and regulatory compliance) satisfy organization goals and objectives. Overall, critical success factors provide an important input to the corporate planning process of the XYZ Corporation. They are the areas in which results, if satisfactory, will ensure success for the entire corporation.

Problem-Finding Approach to Corporate Planning

For corporate planning to be truly responsive to the information needs of top management, a problem-finding approach must be built upon the overall direction that the XYZ Corporation is taking today and tomorrow. In other words, an effective management information system should provide the kind of infor-

Desired Corporate Goals	Critical Success Factors
New product success	Timing of market entry
Increased market share	Quality dealer system
High return on investment	Fast inventory turnover
Increased earnings per share	Effective cost control

FIGURE 11.1   How the attainment of desired corporate goals is supported by critical success factors—XYZ Corporation.

[1]John F. Rockart, "Chief Executives Define Their Own Data Needs," *Harvard Business Review*, March-April 1979, pp. 81–93.

409

mation that top management and their corporate planning staff need to perform their tasks when making important corporate planning decisions. The first consideration is for critical success factors that are tied in with corporate goals. This all-encompassing system approach is possible by employing DSS elements at the corporate planning level. Such an approach is taken in this chapter. In order to understand the relationship of problem finding to corporate planning as well as to critical success factors, the following points must be considered.

In past approaches to corporate planning problems, the accent was on analytical thinking in problem solving, in which problems were identified over time. In turn, they were solved within the corporate planning time framework—the long range to the short range. However, many really important corporate planning problems were never discussed, such as "How did top management came to recognize this as an important problem?" or "Should this corporate planning problem be solved in light of critical success factors that are related to overall corporate objectives?" Hence, a new direction is necessary; that is, problem finding. In a problem-finding approach to corporate planning, the accent is on logical-analytical thinking that transcends current problem-solving efforts by identifying future problems and their impact on the XYZ Corporation today and tomorrow. Similarly, logical-analytical thinking perceives future problems as opportunities in disguise. Thus, if top management and corporate planners have comprehensively explored future problems, generally one or more opportunities can be identified without too much difficulty. In light of these facts, a problem-finding approach will be presented for long-range corporate planning in a later section of the chapter. It then is contrasted to a problem-solving approach to illustrate for the reader the distinction between the two problem approaches.

LINKAGE OF CRITICAL SUCCESS FACTORS TO PROBLEM FINDING. As indicated above, a problem-finding approach includes starting with the corporation's critical success factors that are linked to corporate objectives. CSFs help top management and corporate planners determine those areas that need attention. Also, they help to ensure that these significant factors will receive careful, continuous scrutiny. The identification of CSFs allows a clear definition of the amount of information that must be collected and be useful within the framework of problem finding. This identification moves the corporation away from the trap of building its reporting and MIS primarily around the data that are relatively easy to collect. Rather, it focuses attention on those data that might otherwise not be collected, but are significant for successful problem finding. Additionally, CSFs can be temporary; that is, they must be relevant to the present and to the future and vice versa. The DSS environment should be able to produce managerial reports to accommodate the corporation's critical success factors, which in turn are related to finding new problems for study as well as uncovering new opportunities. All in all, problem finding must be related directly to CSFs. Otherwise, the time and effort spent on problem finding that is related to non-CSFs will have very little impact on improving the corporation's operations and its related productivity as well as ensuring the corporation's profitability.

Corporate Planning Starts the Continuous Decision Process

The approach used by the XYZ Corporation for managerial decision-making can be viewed as a *continuous decision process*. It begins with setting goals and objectives, specifying the critical success factors and determining the means to achieve them, using problem-finding and problem-solving approaches, assessing the resources required, implementing a planned course of action, and controlling the plan to detect deviations. The implemented plan is then monitored to keep it on course and to correct any errors in the original assumptions that provided the basis for the plan. Revisions are usually necessary. In fact, change is integral to the nature of a corporate planning decision process. When management decides to hire 20 employees at a certain plant with certain skills—and two months later decides to increase the number to 50 because it "appears" that an increased workload is likely to be constant for a period—it is revising the plan as it relates to personnel.

Since there is a need to evaluate planning alternatives continuously for achieving stated objectives, the capability to study various aspects of a plan in its various stages becomes critical. In practical terms, this means producing many runs or variations of the same plan, using different sets of assumptions and perhaps different logic. In evaluating resources, for example, varying combinations of resources can be applied, and numerous questions concerning their nature and size can be posed: Do we have the necessary resources to achieve our objectives, or must they be acquired? If resources are to be acquired, at what cost and in what time span? Will they be operational in time to achieve the objectives within a given schedule? What are the optimum mixes of resources to satisfy different objectives under different sets of conditions? What are the likely effects of miscalculating availability and cost of equipment, personnel, or funds to acquire the needed resources? What can happen for every one percent of error in the forecast, and, therefore, how critical is it that we hold strictly to the plan?"

The anticipation of consequences of given assumptions and the evaluation of alternatives is a major activity of the corporate planning staff. The planning tools and/or models used in the process are vital, for they are the means whereby the strategic plan mirrors the real world as closely as possible. Their purpose is to help planners evaluate alternatives and (usually) choose the best one. Such evaluation has come to be known as the "what" is likely to happen "if" we take or do not take a certain course of action.

Mathematical and Statistical Packages

To assist the corporate planning staff, numerous software packages are available that often require only minimal modification to run effectively in the user's environment. Additionally, corporate planning financial packages that

411

evaluate an entire organization or some part of it can be modified to interface with other models. For example, production models can be merged with marketing and financial models to assist in total corporate planning. Software products can be used to test alternatives for capital investments and to help determine whether to lease or purchase in specific situations. Because the user, the XYZ Corporation, develops the model, it is tailored to its specific needs. And because programs are written in languages that can be readily understood, a high degree of programming expertise is not required. The net result is to add a new dimension in effectiveness to the corporate planning function, which cuts across all of the corporation's activities. Thus, the use of electronic spreadsheets and corporate planning financial packages allows the planning staff of the XYZ Corporation to support their decisions by providing better, higher-order planning information when and where needed.

Today, corporate planning financial models comprise a wide range of offerings. As noted in chapter 5, electronic spreadsheets, like Lotus 1-2-3, and financial planning packages, such as IFPS, are English-language computer systems designed to provide planning and decision support to managers. Similarly, a number of statistical packages, such as SAS, are quite useful in a corporate planning environment. In many organizations, commercially available statistical packages are employed by corporate planners to analyze external and internal data in terms of graphs, charts, and the like. In turn, these outputs serve as inputs for modeling with corporate planning financial packages. Thus, commercial corporate planning/statistical packages are available to the corporate planning staff of the XYZ Corporation, who often lack the available time to develop their own.

CORPORATE PLANNING OVERVIEW—XYZ CORPORATION

As an overview, the major functions in the corporate planning environment of the XYZ Corporation are illustrated in figure 11.2. As indicated previously, they include long-range, medium-range, and short-range planning. To facilitate planning through varying time periods, a large amount of corporate planning data is stored in the corporate data base and is retrievable upon request by the planning staff. Specifically, flexible budget data as well as current and past results of operations are capable of being extracted as input for forecasting future sales, cost values, and similar information. Also, data on product lines, distribution, technical matters, facilities, financial, and manpower planning are retrievable from the data base for corporate planning analysis using Lotus 1-2-3 and IFPS.

The corporate planning subsystem operates in a different manner from all other subsystems. Important internal environmental factors are received from the various subsystems for short-, medium-, and long-range planning purposes; certain information, in turn, is fed back to the appropriate subsystems any time major deviations from plans occur. In like manner, feedback is utilized within the corporate planning subsystem itself to alter plans at the var-

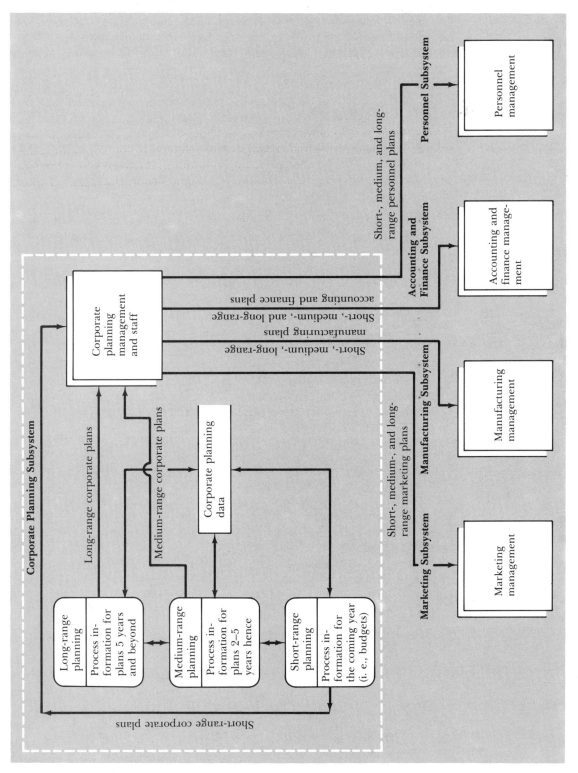

FIGURE 11.2 Corporate planning data flow diagram—XYZ Corporation.

ious levels. This overall internal data flow, along with data on the external environmental factors, provides the input for corporate planning. At the heart of the corporation's many subsystems, then, is this corporate planning function.

✳ Corporate Planning Staff

In order to optimally utilize planning information, the XYZ Corporation created a corporate planning staff (consisting of three high-level employees), which is responsible for all corporate planning activities. This group is free from day-to-day operations and is charged with the responsibility of assisting the president. Among their most important functions are:

- to establish new and challenging standards of performance that are in conformity with the corporation's goals, objectives, strategies, policies, programs, and procedures
- to assure that one- to five-year growth plans are prepared
- to assist the various subsystems in preparing one- to five-year projections
- to identify areas of product opportunity for corporate investment
- to coordinate and monitor the preparation of a plan for longer than five years
- to analyze the economic future of existing operations and to recommend programs of growth
- to analyze business, economic, and social conditions bearing on existing or prospective areas of operations

After top management has reviewed the work of this high-level staff, evaluated the one- to five-year forecast, and are convinced that the financial figures are reasonable and feasible, the composite documents thereby gathered constitute the corporate plan for the stated period of years ahead. Sometimes these "working papers" are regarded as company goals, objectives, and plans. In other cases, their significant elements are formalized into corporate goals and the various segments of the corporate plans for achievement are clearly spelled out in great detail. However, when top management concludes that the anticipated results are not adequate, it becomes imperative that the corporate planning staff create and construct a new or modified set of goals and a new plan to fulfill desired corporation objectives.

Employment of Problem Finding by Corporate Planning Staff

In view of the foregoing functions, the corporate planning staff of the XYZ Corporation must combine knowledge of today's external and internal environmental factors with a vision of the future. From this broad perspective, the problem-finding process must be employed. This approach can be best exemplified starting with the corporation's markets. The president of the XYZ Corporation recognizes that the future market for its electrical appliances may well change drastically over time. In fact, he is convinced that half of the 30 products being sold and manufactured today will not be sold five years hence. In view of this potential major upheaval in the marketplace, he has asked the corporate planning staff to get started immediately on this major area of concern.

As a starting point, the corporate planners formed a problem-finding group, consisting of the executive vice president, the vice president of marketing, four regional sales managers, and themselves. The group met for three days at corporate headquarters and initially studied problem generation (the first step of the problem-centered approach set forth in chapter 3) regarding future and present products, using a brainstorming approach. The major problem was not so much that the products were marketed under good, average, and poor economic conditions, but the changing nature of customer buying habits. Due to the continuing trend toward smaller living quarters and smaller families caused by inflation and other factors, the XYZ Corporation is faced with developing new products to reflect changes in the home market. Additionally, the group identified the trend toward more people living alone.

Based upon information generated by the group, evaluation (the second step) consisted of reviewing future marketing and its related problems. As it turned out, all of the foregoing areas were determined to be valid for managerial concern, that is, the validation stage (the third step). In sum, the continuing trend toward smaller living quarters is a major problem. Its present products are oriented toward medium- to large-size homes with ample space to accommodate them. In view of this major problem and related ones, the group spent some time establishing boundaries (the fourth step). Although the home market in foreign countries was considered viable, it was decided to "put first things first." This means channeling the corporation's resources in the development of new products for the domestic home market.

Although a number of problems need to be solved, the major one (per the above) was addressed first. Its solution lay in developing a wide range of new products over the next five years that are more compact and at the same time capable of performing a wide range of services to meet home owner needs. With this new direction, the problem-finding group worked extensively with the market research group as well as with middle marketing management, who will be in charge of selling the new home products. Overall, the problem-centered approach has resulted in identifying future product problems. In turn, these problems were brought back to the present time for solution. As a result, "management by perception" has been placed into practice by top management and corporate planners for determining future strategic marketing plans.

MIS CORPORATE PLANNING SUBSYSTEM

As noted previously, corporate planning MIS is linked directly with other subsystems. These appear as internal environmental factors in the structure shown in figure 11.3. In a similar manner, planning activities are related to external environmental factors through the organization's goals and objec-

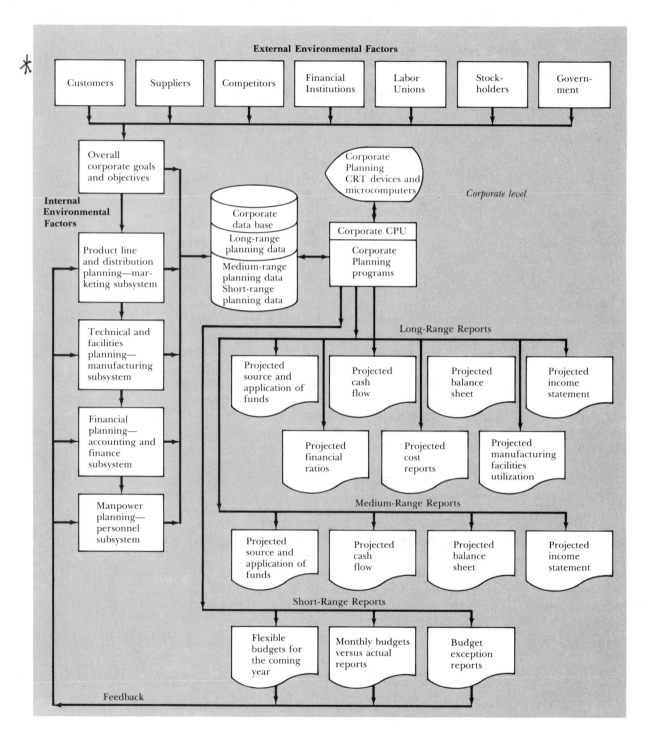

FIGURE 11.3 Corporate planning subsystem for an effective management information system—XYZ Corporation.

tives. Both internal and external factors form the basis for short- to long-range data base elements. These data elements, when used in conjunction with the appropriate program, provide the necessary corporate planning output for the various time levels. The ability to extract on-line data "now" makes this subsystem forward-looking. Information can be obtained to answering recurring and ad hoc "What if?" questions about the future. To this end, the corporate planning subsystem utilizes Lotus 1-2-3 and IFPS to answer tomorrow's questions in view of today's projections.

Use of Microcomputers to Answer "What if?" Questions

In order to answer "What if?" questions on corporate planning, the XYZ Corporation utilizes a microcomputer and mainframe approach to IFPS (refer to the prior chapter). In the micro approach, the IFPS Personal package takes advantage of the mainframe's corporate data base, thereby enhancing the analyst's job of creating "What-if" scenarios. Data from the corporate data base can be used in one of two ways. The user can either download into an IFPS model or answer a series of on-line prompts to discover the most relevant data for his or her model. As such, the wide range of data found in the corporate data base can be used in answering specific "What if?" corporate planning questions.

When answers are developed on micros (or for that matter, on mainframes), top management wants assurance that the answers are correct. This brings up the issue of quality. Automated decision support tools give top management of the XYZ Corporation all kinds of information, but the first thing the executives are going to do is question the data. They want to know if the assumptions are right and if the data are any good. The job of corporate planners is to ferret out every assumption in the data, scrutinize it, and validate it, because top management looks at information and asks "what": "What about sales?" "What about inventory?" Top management does not care *how* the information was obtained since that is the job of the corporate planners. Top management's thinking is directed toward a vision of the future and an appropriate strategy to implement that vision. In a few words, that is the "what" that top management is talking about. In turn, corporate planners are responsible for getting that strategy implemented. That represents the "how" of corporate planning, that is, the use of microcomputers to answer important recurring and ad hoc "What if?" questions.

LONG-RANGE CORPORATE PLANNING

Long-range planning starts with a realistic understanding of existing markets, products, plants, warehouses, margins, profits, return on investment, cash flow, availability of capital, engineering capabilities, and skills and capacities of personnel, to name some of the more important areas. Analysis of present operations can be performed effectively by reviewing the past few years' performance as part of the evaluation of the current year's operating and capital budget forecasts. Significant aspects of current operations, evaluated in an orderly manner, are the basis for considering how well the goals and objectives related to critical success factors are currently being met by the corporation. In like manner, explicit plans for the next five years, based on current operations and existing plans for improving operations, are an essential part of a sound corporate planning program.

Five-year Strategic Plan

For the XYZ Corporation, an outline of a five-year strategic plan includes external and internal factors enumerated in figure 11-3. The latter aspects, which are controllable by the corporation, are summarized as follows:

1. *Product line and distribution planning.* Product line planning is aimed at expanding the present product lines and entering new product markets as well as expanding the present customer base into new market segments. In contrast, distribution planning centers on the increased use of selling outlets and/or other distribution techniques to sell the corporation's products, changes in pricing policy and pricing practices to effect higher sales, and consideration of new advertising media for more effective penetration of the corporation's markets (refer to chapter 12).

2. *Technical and facilities planning.* Technical planning is geared toward creating new or improved products both for established markets and for markets in which the corporation does not participate or has such a small share as to be negligible. On the other hand, facilities planning is directed toward major facilities contemplated and improvements in processing efficiency at existing facilities. It also includes determining the percent of capacity that is now and will be employed with present facilities and machinery as well as the steps that are being undertaken to utilize excess capacity where available (refer to chapter 13).

3. *Financial planning.* Financial planning is directed toward projecting sales by product lines, gross profit (sales less manufacturing costs) by product lines, sales and general and administrative expenses, net profit by product lines, fixed and working capital needs, return on investment by product lines, and comparable financial analyses and ratios (refer to chapter 14).

4. *Manpower planning.* Manpower planning centers on the projected requirements for key management personnel and production labor when considering turnover and future growth (refer to chapter 15).

In the process of developing the above five-year strategic plan, the corporate planning staff has encountered difficulties with the corporation's managers. They found that managers first had to be educated to the need for sound long-range plans. Then they had to be taught to integrate all the events of long-range planning with their programs. In this regard, a checklist of key elements was found to be extremely helpful in ensuring that programs have been thoroughly analyzed. Generally, it includes:

- *analyses*—logical process of projecting the future
- *potentials*—skills as well as resources that are available and needed
- *problems*—apparent deficiencies
- *establishment of best alternatives*—suggested economic goals
- *coordination, implementation, and timing*—expected results in both financial and nonfinancial terms

Such a list enables managers to assess the reasonableness of their goals and objectives in order to come up with long-term policies that can realistically integrate with other corporate goals and objectives. In essence, the corporate planning staff had to impress upon managers an awareness of the importance of long-range planning as a vital part of their jobs. With this change implemented, the corporate planning staff has been able to operate effectively in their role as catalyst for the five-year strategic plan.

USE OF IFPS "WHAT IF" AND GOAL-SEEKING COMMANDS. To assist the corporate planning staff in developing a five-year strategic plan, IFPS is used on the corporate mainframe. In IFPS, the simple command WHAT IF initiates an easy-to-use process to investigate change. This command permits the corporate planning staff to make temporary changes for any data or assumption in the model and resolve a problem. As an illustration, refer to figure 11.4. A

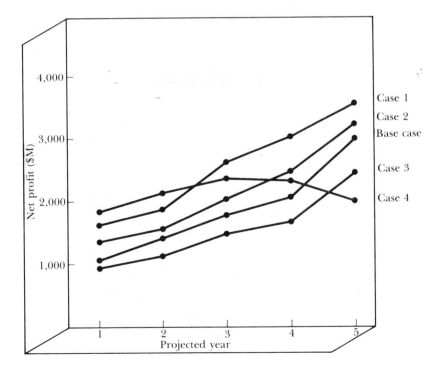

FIGURE 11.4
An example of output using the IFPS WHAT IF command. (Used with permission— EXECUCOM Systems Corporation.)

base case is used to compare possible future alternatives (cases) for the XYZ Corporation. In the cases under study, prices (case 1), volume (case 2), unit cost (case 3), and interest rates (case 4) are observed over a five-year period and compared to the base case. Hence, the corporate planning staff has the answer to its "What if?" question projected over five years. But more importantly, IFPS provides the capability to make one or more changes in the variables (prices, volume, unit cost, and interest rates) in the problem to answer new "What if?" questions.

Due to the emphasis on profitability, GOAL SEEKING has proven to be a popular command for the corporation's management and its planning staff. In essence, these leaders are concerned with what they have to do to achieve desired profit objectives. To state it another way, having set stated profit objectives, what are alternative ways for achieving them. An example of the output from using this command is shown in figure 11.5. The question "How many units need to be sold in order to increase the operating margin by ½ percent per year over the next five years?" is shown in this bar chart. This solution plus many others allow the corporation's top management, along with the corporate planning staff, to develop answers in a simple-to-use, direct, and timely manner.

Overall, the utilization of the IFPS package by management and its corporate planning staff has answered many planning questions that previously had gone unanswered. The XYZ Corporation has reaped many benefits from its use beyond those realized from the development of a five-year plan. Among these are answers to current "What if?" questions, the capability to evaluate

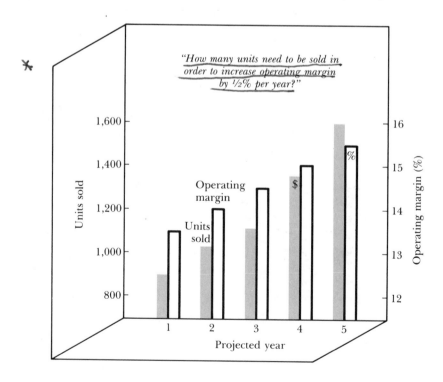

FIGURE 11.5

An example of output using the IFPS GOAL SEEKING command. (Used with permission—EXECUCOM Systems Corporation.)

many planning alternatives quickly and inexpensively, the ability to focus on crucial planning time periods, an insight into cause/effect relationships and sensitivities, the stimulation of creative and analytical thinking, and the capability for permitting more timely decision making. These important benefits to the corporation are found not only in the area of long-range planning, but are evident in medium- and short-range planning as well.

MEDIUM-RANGE CORPORATE PLANNING

Medium-range corporate planning is a subset of long-range planning, as shown in figure 11.3. The five-year strategic plan for product line and distribution, technical and facilities, financial, and manpower planning is stated in more detail. Although medium-range planning centers on the planning period of two to four years, accent in this discussion is on the second-year planning period.

Concentrate on the second year planning

The budget process for medium- (and short-) range corporate planning has several important aspects when done with the help of a computer system. First, certain assumptions about what will happen can be tested by "passing" the transactions representing these assumptions through the budget system. Second, the corporation can perceive what the financial effects of actions will be, that is, whether they are favorable or unfavorable. Third, the budget system can determine whether or not some condition or constraint has been violated—for example, if working capital availability in the future has been exceeded. An effective MIS approach to budgeting permits the corporation to respond to the dynamics of the situation. It allows changes to medium- (and short-) range budgets whenever something significant happens to alter conditions. From this view, a budget simulation model is presented.

Budget Simulation Model

In this first approach to the budgetary process by the corporate planning staff, a medium-range budget simulation model is used. Long-range corporate planning data base elements are brought into play with medium-range income and expense data elements, as illustrated in figure 11.6. Output from the budget program is selected financial information: in particular, income statement, balance sheet, cash flow, and source and application of funds. A CRT terminal can be utilized to display data to answer "What if?" questions, store new information on the data base, or change existing data elements (figure 11.7).

In developing a corporate budget model, several important factors are considered. *First, the existing budgeting system must be an excellent analogue or a measurable simulation of the corporation.* Its output mirrors the organization's physical activities. Of course, it should be recognized that some differences are inevitable between the actual accounting/budgeting system and any model of it. One of these is the way in which the values of system variables (accounts) are derived. The actual system interacts with external parties and then processes these transactions by changing the balances in the

421

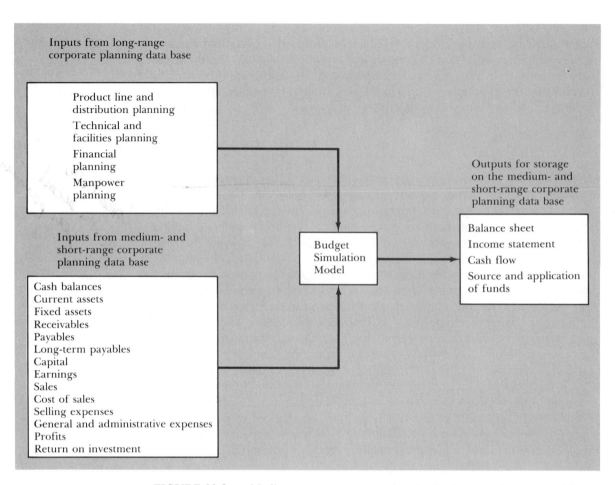

Inputs from long-range
corporate planning data base

Product line and
distribution planning

Technical and
facilities planning

Financial
planning

Manpower
planning

Inputs from medium- and
short-range corporate
planning data base

Cash balances
Current assets
Fixed assets
Receivables
Payables
Long-term payables
Capital
Earnings
Sales
Cost of sales
Selling expenses
General and administrative expenses
Profits
Return on investment

Budget
Simulation
Model

Outputs for storage
on the medium- and
short-range corporate
planning data base

Balance sheet
Income statement
Cash flow
Source and application
of funds

FIGURE 11.6   Medium-range corporate planning budget simulation model for
an effective management information system—XYZ Corporation.

appropriate accounts. In contrast, a simulation model does not have real transactions to make changes in the balances of various accounts. The user of such
a model must create artificial transactions which have a high degree of similarity to the expected real-life version. The manner of processing these transactions, then, is by formulating equations that define the values of the various
accounts.

The *second* factor in constructing a budget model is to decide the kind
of output sought. Output options are illustrated by the following questions:
(1) "Do you want the model to tell you the level of sales that must be reached
in order to achieve a predetermined profit or cash flow?" (goal seeking), or
(2) "Do you want to supply sales estimates and let the model work out the
effects on the projected levels appearing on the financial statement?" (analyzing). The second alternative is preferred because it utilizes the long- and
medium-range corporate planning data elements. Regardless of the approach,

though, the conclusion is that the desired output dictates the kind of input data that are required.

The *third* factor concerns the specifications of the model. These are the actual equations or formulas that define how the simulated account balances are derived. They are made up of variables and corresponding coefficients that represent a mathematical analogue of the account balances of budget variables that are being defined. These equations constitute the blueprint of the corporate budget model, and thereby, the essential part of the model.

The *fourth* and final factor in constructing the model is to make sure that it is valid. It must be a good approximation of reality. Here experience and intuition are indispensable. Seasoned judgment is the only way to decide finally whether or not the output of the model is reliable. Subtle relationships are discovered and new insights about the operation of the corporation are learned.

USE OF IFPS FOR A WIDE RANGE OF MEDIUM-RANGE CORPORATE PLANNING ACTIVITIES. Although the budget simulation model is widely used by the corporate planning staff, higher level managers prefer to work with the simple-to-use IFPS package. For applications such as projected financial statements several years in the future, medium-range corporate cash flow, and deciding whether to float a bond issue or sell additional stock, management has used this planning package with good results. Similarly, they have used IFPS for leasing plans versus purchasing over the next several years, as well as for merger/acquisition analysis. All in all, the Interactive Financial Planning System has been used successfully not only due to its simplicity and timeliness, but also because it allows the decision maker interfacing with it to have full control.

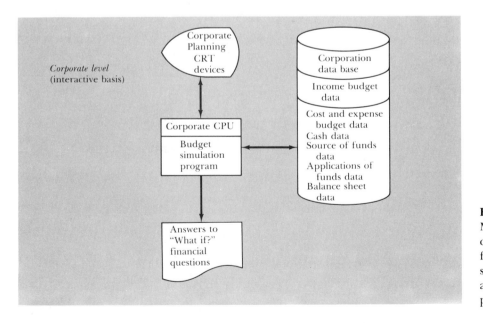

FIGURE 11.7
Medium-range corporate planning data flow for a budget simulation program in an MIS corporate planning subsystem.

Product Groups By No.	Product Group Sales as a % Total Sales	Variable Mfg Costs as a % of Total Sales	Variable Mkt Costs as a % of Total Sales
1	21.09%	62.00%	9.00%
2	17.53%	68.00%	10.00%
3	23.95%	59.00%	8.00%
4	20.48%	62.00%	9.00%
5	16.95%	68.00%	5.00%

* *

Basic Product Groups
(dollars stated in thousands)

Sales at Full Capacity $150,000
Percent of Total Capacity   70%

	Product Group by Number					Totals
	1	2	3	4	5	
Sales	$22,145	$18,407	$25,148	$21,504	$17,798	$105,000
VARIABLE COSTS:						
Manufacturing	$13,730	$12,516	$14,837	$13,332	$12,102	$66,518
Marketing	1,993	1,841	2,012	1,935	890	8,671
Contribution to Fixed Costs and Profits	$6,422	$4,049	$8,299	$6,236	$4,805	$29,811
FIXED COSTS:						
Manufacturing	$2,640	$2,420	$2,900	$2,600	$2,180	$12,740
Marketing	2,700	2,440	2,980	2,650	2,190	12,960
General & Admin	590	280	670	430	110	2,080
Net Profit Before Federal Income Taxes	$492	($1,091)	$1,749	$556	$325	$2,031
Fed. Income Taxes at 46%	226	(502)	804	256	150	934
Net Profit After Federal Income Taxes	$266	($589)	$944	$300	$176	$1,097

(a)

FIGURE 11.8 Budgeted income statements are computed at (a) 70 percent, (b) 80 percent, (c) 90 percent, and (d) 100 percent from an overall standpoint for next year—XYZ Corporation.

424

Product Groups By No.	Product Group Sales as a % Total Sales	Variable Mfg Costs as a % of Total Sales	Variable Mkt Costs as a % of Total Sales
1	21.09%	62.00%	9.00%
2	17.53%	68.00%	10.00%
3	23.95%	59.00%	8.00%
4	20.48%	62.00%	9.00%
5	16.95%	68.00%	5.00%

* *

Basic Product Groups
(dollars stated in thousands)

Sales at Full Capacity $150,000
Percent of Total Capacity   80%

	Product Group by Number					Totals
	1	2	3	4	5	
Sales	$25,308	$21,036	$28,740	$24,576	$20,340	$120,000
VARIABLE COSTS:						
Manufacturing	$15,691	$14,304	$16,957	$15,237	$13,831	$76,020
Marketing	2,278	2,104	2,299	2,212	1,017	9,909
Contribution to Fixed Costs and Profits	$7,339	$4,628	$9,484	$7,127	$5,492	$34,070
FIXED COSTS:						
Manufacturing	$2,640	$2,420	$2,900	$2,600	$2,180	$12,740
Marketing	2,700	2,440	2,980	2,650	2,190	12,960
General & Admin	590	280	670	430	110	2,080
Net Profit Before Federal Income Taxes	$1,409	($512)	$2,934	$1,447	$1,012	$6,290
Fed. Income Taxes at 46%	648	(236)	1,350	666	465	2,894
Net Profit After Federal Income Taxes	$761	($277)	$1,584	$781	$546	$3,397

(b)

FIGURE 11.8   (*Continued*)

425

Product Groups By No.	Product Group Sales as a % Total Sales	Variable Mfg Costs as a % of Total Sales	Variable Mkt Costs as a % of Total Sales
1	21.09%	62.00%	9.00%
2	17.53%	68.00%	10.00%
3	23.95%	59.00%	8.00%
4	20.48%	62.00%	9.00%
5	16.95%	68.00%	5.00%

* *

Basic Product Groups
(dollars stated in thousands)

Sales at Full Capacity $150,000
Percent of Total Capacity   90%

	Product Group by Number					Totals
	1	2	3	4	5	
Sales	$28,472	$23,666	$32,333	$27,648	$22,883	$135,000
VARIABLE COSTS:						
Manufacturing	$17,652	$16,093	$19,076	$17,142	$15,560	$85,523
Marketing	2,562	2,367	2,587	2,488	1,144	11,148
Contribution to Fixed Costs and Profits	$8,257	$5,206	$10,670	$8,018	$6,178	$38,329
FIXED COSTS:						
Manufacturing	$2,640	$2,420	$2,900	$2,600	$2,180	$12,740
Marketing	2,700	2,440	2,980	2,650	2,190	12,960
General & Admin	590	280	670	430	110	2,080
Net Profit Before Federal Income Taxes	$2,327	$66	$4,120	$2,338	$1,698	$10,549
Fed. Income Taxes at 46%	1,070	31	1,895	1,075	781	4,853
Net Profit After Federal Income Taxes	$1,256	$36	$2,225	$1,262	$917	$5,696

(c)

FIGURE 11.8   (*Continued*)

Product Groups By No.	Product Group Sales as a % Total Sales	Variable Mfg Costs as a % of Total Sales	Variable Mkt Costs as a % of Total Sales
1	21.09%	62.00%	9.00%
2	17.53%	68.00%	10.00%
3	23.95%	59.00%	8.00%
4	20.48%	62.00%	9.00%
5	16.95%	68.00%	5.00%

* *

Basic Product Groups
(dollars stated in thousands)

Sales at Full Capacity	$150,000	
Percent of Total Capacity	100%	

	Product Group by Number					Totals
	1	2	3	4	5	
Sales	$31,635	$26,295	$35,925	$30,720	$25,425	$150,000
VARIABLE COSTS:						
Manufacturing	$19,614	$17,881	$21,196	$19,046	$17,289	$95,025
Marketing	2,847	2,630	2,874	2,765	1,271	12,387
Contribution to Fixed Costs and Profits	$9,174	$5,785	$11,855	$8,909	$6,865	$42,588
FIXED COSTS:						
Manufacturing	$2,640	$2,420	$2,900	$2,600	$2,180	$12,740
Marketing	2,700	2,440	2,980	2,650	2,190	12,960
General & Admin	590	280	670	430	110	2,080
Net Profit Before Federal Income Taxes	$3,244	$645	$5,305	$3,229	$2,385	$14,808
Fed. Income Taxes at 46%	1,492	297	2,440	1,485	1,097	6,812
Net Profit After Federal Income Taxes	$1,752	$348	$2,865	$1,744	$1,288	$7,996

(d)

FIGURE 11.8 (*Continued*)

Short-range planning, the focus of which is one year, is an extension of medium-range planning. It includes the use of quarterly sales forecasts from marketing. The end result of short-range planning activities is flexible (variable) budgets developed for stated levels of possible production.

Development of Flexible Budgets

Using a microcomputer and Lotus 1-2-3, a number of levels of production capacity can be developed. In figure 11.8 (a), the overall budget for the XYZ Corporation (computed at 70 percent of capacity) is illustrated in terms of the corporation's basic product groups. Additionally, in figure 11.8 (b) through (d), the budgets are prepared for each basic product group at 80, 90, and 100 percent production. Other exhibits can be prepared, in particular, breakdowns by major subsystem or manufacturing work center. Because all of these budgets provide a basis for comparing projected to actual results, they are stored on the corporate data base as a starting point for more detailed analysis.

To provide *detailed* balance sheet and income statement data for the coming year, other financial data are fed into the corporate computer via a CRT terminal. Using a flexible budgeting program that can account for various levels of expected plant capacity, detailed financial statements are developed and printed for various capacity levels. Flexible budgeting data are also written onto the corporate data base for comparison with actual figures as they occur month by month (refer to the accounting and finance subsystem). This flexible budget data flow is depicted in figure 11.9.

Because budgeted and actual data are stored on line in the corporate data base, detailed budget versus actual reports are produced at the end of each month. During this budgeting interaction phase—shown in figure 11.9—budget exception reports are also prepared. These are the result of comparing budgeted values of the current year with current data. Where values are deemed out of line by the computer program, exceptions are highlighted on the budget exception report so that they can be evaluated for corrective action. In this manner, important exceptions are brought to the attention of management, thereby allowing the "management by exception" principle to be practiced.

USE OF LOTUS 1-2-3 FOR SENSITIVITY ANALYSIS. Going beyond its use for developing overall flexible budgets, Lotus 1-2-3 can be used for sensitivity analysis. Sensitivity analysis allows top management of the XYZ Corporation to examine the impact of a change in one or more variables. From this perspective, the spreadsheet's "What if?" capabilities can be employed. In figure 11.10, a two-variable sensitivity analysis of unit sales and selling price as they affect net income for product 309 is illustrated. Initially given in the figure are data concerning the projected income statement. As a starting point, the *first*

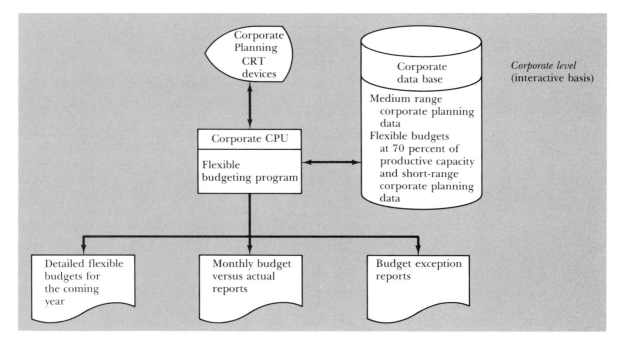

FIGURE 11.9 Short-range planning data—detailed flexible budgets for comparison with actual figures to highlight exceptions within an MIS corporate planning subsystem.

variable allowed to shift is the unit growth rate (first column); the *second* is the selling price increase (remaining columns). The first column contains a range of growth rates from the low assumption of 10 percent to the high assumption of 18 percent. The remaining columns specify a sales price increase of 4 percent to 9 percent. The value of $69,525 corresponds to the net income for the year with a unit growth of 14 percent and a 6.5 percent selling price increase for product 309. All in all, figure 11.10 is a short-run forecast for individual products of the XYZ Corporation that can be built with a micro electronic spreadsheet approach.

IFPS'S SENSITIVITY AND IMPACT COMMANDS. Just as in long-range and medium-range planning, management uses the IFPS package to answer important ad hoc "What if?" questions as they arise. A typical example from a short-range viewpoint using the IFPS approach is found in figure 11.11 where the SENSITIVITY and IMPACT commands are brought together. In this example, the first command allows the user to investigate the interplay of a change in the cost of sales percentage to operating margin (percentage) and profit before taxes in the coming year. In contrast, the second command allows the user to specify a desired percent increase in the cost of sales as the IMPACT variable and then see the effect on the selected variable, for example, profitability. According to figure 11.11, the impact of 1 percent increase in the cost of sales results in a 2½ percent decrease in profitability.

429

```
Base Year Unit Sales & Price  : Next Year's Unit Sales & Price
------------------------------:-----------------------------------
Unit Sales           200,000  : Unit Sales      10.00%    220,000
Unit Price             $2.50  : Unit Price       4.00%      $2.60
==================================================================
```

```
                      Projected Income Statement


Sales Rev.                                          $572,000

Cost of Goods Sold              65.00%               371,800
                                                    --------
Gross Profit                                        $200,200

Commissions
  Fixed                        $25,000
  Variable                       5.00%     28,600    53,600

Administrative Exp.
  Fixed                        $10,000
  Variable                       3.00%     17,160    27,160
                                                    --------
Income Before Federal
  Income Tax                                        $119,440

Federal Income Tax              46.00%                54,942
                                                    --------
Net Income                                          $64,498
```

****

```
           Sensitivity Analysis of Net Income for Next Year

             Net Income Over Selling Price Growth-Rate
           ------------------------------------------------
      Unit
      Growth
      ------
+E31          4.00%     5.25%     6.50%     7.75%     9.00%
    10.00%  $64,498   $65,460   $66,422   $67,384   $68,667
    11.00%   65,256    66,227    67,198    68,169    69,463
    12.00%   66,014    66,993    67,974    68,953    70,259
    13.00%   66,772    67,761    68,749    69,738    71,056
    14.00%   67,530    68,528    69,525    70,522    71,852
    15.00%   68,288    69,294    70,300    71,306    72,648
    16.00%   69,047    70,061    71,076    72,091    73,444
    17.00%   69,805    70,828    71,852    72,875    74,240
    18.00%   70,563    71,595    72,627    73,660    75,036
```

DATA TABLE

FIGURE 11.10　　A two-variable sensitivity analysis of unit sales growth and selling price increase as they affect net income for product 309.

Summary—MIS Corporate Planning Subsystem

Long-range corporate planning focuses on extrapolating data gathered from external and internal sources for projecting information on marketing and distribution, technical and facilities, financing, manpower, and so forth for five or more years.

　　Medium-range corporate planning addresses the same areas as long-

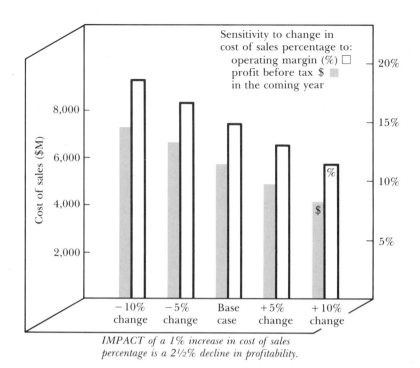

IMPACT of a 1% increase in cost of sales
percentage is a 2½% decline in profitability.

FIGURE 11.11
An example of output
using the IFPS
SENSITIVITY and
IMPACT commands.
(Used with permis-
sion—EXECUCOM
Systems Corporation.)

range planning but within a time frame of two to four years. However, the
pro forma financial statements in this time span are more detailed than those
for long-range planning.

Short-range corporate planning is an extension of medium-range planning with great emphasis on flexible budgets—forecasts related to specific
production levels for the coming year.

EFFECTIVE MIS PRACTICE—INTEGRATION OF
CORPORATE PLANNING WITH CONTROL

The net result of short-range planning activities is that the current year's fiscal
plan for the XYZ Corporation is established. When the plans for the fiscal year
are embarked upon, control is emphasized so as to realize the plan as closely
as possible. The main function of control deals with measuring performance
against plan, subsequent adjustment of plans in the light of new conditions,
and the feedback of actual experience for corporate planning in subsequent
years. It is from this view that an effective management information system
integrates corporate plans with the control function.

Overall, a continuing, cyclical planning and control process demands a
formalized corporate planning system as a logical starting point. Effective MIS
should support these planning and control activities on a continuous basis.
For the XYZ Corporation (and any other organization), the objectives of MIS
for corporate planning and control are (1) to provide top management with
support information necessary to create planning strategy that agrees with its

desired corporate objectives and critical success factors, (2) to provide analytical tools in the form of newer micro and mainframe software for evaluating alternative planning strategies in order to generate decision-aiding information, (3) to provide an effective means of sensing the impact of the external environment and thus forewarning top management of outside changes that affect the organization using a problem-finding approach, and (4) to measure the actual performance against the plans to effect better control over organizational activities by employing "management by exception." These objectives take into account past and expected conditions with major emphasis on future projections. With this framework, the corporate planning process of successive refinement results in a fiscal plan that is both forward-looking and operationally effective for control during the coming year.

CHAPTER SUMMARY

The corporate planning subsystem of the XYZ Corporation is the focal point for an effective MIS. Long-range planning data are developed internally from the various subsystems, representing the product line, distribution, technical, facilities, financial, and personnel factors. In like manner, external data are evaluated in developing plans that conform with corporation goals and objectives. Basically, the corporation's long-range strategic plans are refined in developing more specific financial plans for medium-range corporate planning. The output of this planning level serves as input for short-range corporate planning, resulting in flexible budgets for all levels of operations. Successive levels of planning provide for objectively analyzing feedback. This feedback process determines whether the management information system is doing the job it was designed for and, more importantly, provides a basis for modifying plans at the various levels if warranted.

A most important advantage of an effective MIS corporate planning subsystem is the ability to employ electronic spreadsheets, financial planning/statistical packages, and mathematical models. Corporate planning staff and corporation managers of the XYZ Corporation, for example, were shown to interact with the microcomputer and the corporate mainframe in situations where they retain full control over the human–machine interface. Likewise, they can ask and answer numerous "What if?" questions, thereby determining the effect of constant change in short-, medium-, and long-range corporate planning.

QUESTIONS

1. Distinguish among short-range corporate planning, medium-range corporate planning, and long-range corporate planning.
2. What is the importance of the following to a typical corporate planning staff?
   a. corporate goals
   b. critical success factors
   c. problem finding

3. What are the essential elements of the continuous decision process found in an effective MIS approach to corporate planning?

4. Suggest other mathematical and statistical models not set forth in the chapter that can be employed to aid the corporate planning process.

5. Referring to the section on the XYZ Corporation's long-range planning, suggest changes or improvements that would reflect an ideal MIS environment.

6. What is the relationship of long-range corporate planning to medium-range corporate planning in an effective management information system?

7. What is the relationship of short-range plans (flexible budgets) to the accounting and finance subsystem in an effective management information system?

8. Could an electronic worksheet be used just as effectively as a financial planning language for long-range corporate planning? For medium-range planning? For short-range planning? Why or why not?

PROBLEMS

9. Suppose the XYZ Corporation was service-oriented rather than manufacturing-oriented. Suggest four appropriate critical success factors related to four desired corporate goals (similar to those set forth in figure 11.1). Also, give the rationale for selecting these particular critical success factors.

10. Building upon the problem-centered approach to problem finding as presented in the chapter, develop a comparable solution using an opportunity-centered approach based upon the following facts. The approach recommended by the corporate planners of the XYZ Corporation basically centered on bringing the corporation's product line up to date in the next five years. What the report did not contain were future opportunities to make the corporation into a growth company. Based upon this mandate, explore new marketing opportunities that were not present in the first report on problem finding. Use the steps for the opportunity-centered approach in chapter 3.

11. The corporate planning subsystem of the XYZ Corporation (operating in an MIS mode) is organized into long-range, medium-range, and short-range planning modules. What other organization could have been illustrated for corporate planning? What modules from other functional areas could have been included in the corporate planning subsystem? In both situations, explore the changes necessary to ensure that the subsystems function together as an integrated whole for the entire corporation.

12. As is true of the other subsystems of the XYZ Corporation (to be presented in subsequent chapters of the text), the corporate planning subsystem is operating in a management information system environment. If the corporation desires to change to a total, thoroughgoing decision support system environment, what changes are necessary from the short-range to the long-range to effect this new operating mode? In addition, what advantages would accrue to the corporation for having made this change?

PROJECTS

13. Suppose the XYZ Corporation has just merged with a smaller company in the same industry (the surviving organization being the XYZ Corporation). As a result of the merger, we find an almost complete duplication of the information systems func-

tion (systems and operations). The individuals in each pair of like jobs are all about equally competent, but with different strengths and weaknesses. Inasmuch as the purpose of the merger is to consolidate operations and reduce personnel in the MIS area as well as other functional areas, what alternatives are available to the president and chief executive officer? In view of the alternatives, develop an appropriate block diagram or a decision tree to plot the merger alternatives of the MIS departments. Which alternative appears to be the most viable one when the human element is given the highest priority?

14. The system presented in the chapter for long-range corporate planning of the XYZ Corporation is basically a *strategic planning system* for top management because its starting point is a five-year strategic plan. A complementary *tactical planning system* for middle management could have been presented. Develop the essential requirements for such a system, that is, the inputs along with the data files and procedures to produce meaningful managerial outputs. Explore the use of color graphics to support critical tactical planning decisions where the decision maker retains control over the ongoing process. Additionally, include the use of electronic spreadsheets, financial and/or statistical packages, and/or mathematical models as tools of analysis where deemed appropriate. Use either a system flowchart or a data flow diagram to show the information flow for the tactical planning system.

15. Going beyond the tactical planning system (as set forth in the above project), develop an effective *operational planning system* for the XYZ Corporation that complements strategic and tactical planning in terms of the short run: i.e., for this week, next week, and subsequent periods. The system should provide operating management with the necessary information to support planning decisions as well as control ongoing operations. For example, programs could be developed that provide a cost analysis of each major department in the plants and office. Consideration should be given to changes occurring in product lines and distribution, in technical areas and facilities for production, in finances, and in personnel that have an impact on the current year. Current economic conditions should also be included. Include electronic spreadsheets, financial planning languages and statistical packages as well as mathematical models if they assist in making the management information system more effective for operating management and their support personnel. To show the data flow, use one or more system flowcharts or data flow diagrams for the operational planning system.

LOTUS 1-2-3 EXCERCISES AND PROGRAMS

16. In the chapter, figure 11.8 provided a means for developing the budgets of the coming year for the five basic product groups of the XYZ Corporation. The corporate planning staff has used the program provided on the Lotus 1-2-3 diskette or as given in this section. Because the values developed in the figure range from 70 to 100 percent of plant capacity, the corporate planning staff feels that there is also need for budgets that include the 5 percent intervals between 70 and 100 percent. Based upon their needs, develop this coming year's budgets that are based on 75 percent, 85 percent, and 95 percent of plant capacity. After these figures have been projected, examine the net profit after federal income taxes. Could we have saved the time of making these calculations by interpolating a value between the even levels of capacity (i.e., 70 percent to 100 percent). Why or why not for the odd levels of capacity (i.e., 75 percent, 85 percent, and 95 percent)?

17. As found in figure 11.8 of the chapter, the corporate planning staff of the XYZ Corporation has developed a budget of the corporation's five basic product groups for next year. The budgets as developed represent expected results from average economic conditions; that is, economic growth of 1 to 3 percent for next year. The president of the XYZ Corporation has just attended an important economic conference for presidents of various sized organizations. The end result was that economic forecasters are predicting good economic times, i.e., over 3 percent and possibly up to 5 percent growth for next year. The president feels that the present budgets, starting with sales, are much too conservative. He has instructed the corporate planning staff to redo all of the figures for next year based upon an expanding economy. The new facts that should be considered are given as follows:

    Sales: Total Amount $160,000,000
    Variable Costs: Manufacturing—no change in %
               Marketing—no change in %
    Federal Income Tax Rate: 46%
    Fixed Costs:

	Manufacturing	Marketing	Gen & Admin.
Basic Product Group 1	$2,680,000	$2,740,000	$610,000
Basic Product Group 2	$2,460,000	$2,480,000	$300,000
Basic Product Group 3	$2,940,000	$3,020,000	$690,000
Basic Product Group 4	$2,640,000	$2,690,000	$450,000
Basic Product Group 5	$2,220,000	$2,230,000	$130,000
Total	$12,940,000	$13,160,000	$2,180,000

To develop the new forecasts at 70 percent, 80 percent, 90 percent, and 100 percent of capacity, use the program on the Lotus 1-2-3 diskette or as given in the program found for this section.

18. In conjunction with problem 17, there is also need for budgets under good economic conditions that include the 5 percent intervals between 70 percent and 100 percent of plant capacity. Based upon the data developed in the preceding problem, develop the coming year's budgets that are based on 75 percent, 85 percent, and 95 percent of plant capacity. Use the program provided in the Lotus 1-2-3 diskette or as given in this section. Compare these values to those developed in the prior problem. Could we have saved the time of making these calculations by interpolating a value between the even levels of capacity (i.e., 70 percent to 100 percent)? Why or why not for the odd levels of capacity (i.e., 75 percent, 85 percent, and 95 percent)?

19. In the chapter, figure 11.10 provided a means for undertaking sensitivity analysis, i.e., a two-variable sensitivity analysis of units sales and selling price as they affect net income for the corporate planning staff. Using this as a model, develop a comparable analysis in terms of net income for unit growth from 5 percent to 10 percent where the increment is 1.25 percent and selling price growth rate of .25 percent to 4.25 percent where the increment is .5 percent. The corporate planning staff will use the program on the Lotus 1-2-3 diskette or the one given in this section. How do the results differ from that set forth in Figure 11.10, that is, how sensitive is the unit growth and selling price growth on the downside to changes in net income? (Note: It is necessary to use the *data table command* to solve the problem.)

20. In the chapter, figure 11.10 provided a way for undertaking a two-way sensitivity analysis of unit sales and selling price as they affect net income. Assuming that you are a member of the corporate planning staff, prepare a new sensitivity analysis such that the unit growth increment is from 10.0 percent to 14.0 percent where the increment is .5 percent and the selling growth rate is from 4.0 percent to 6.0 percent where the increment is .5 percent. What are the net income figures? Use the program provided on the Lotus 1-2-3 diskette or the one given in this section. (Note: It is necessary to use the *data table command* to solve the problem.) From another perspective, what other sensitivity analyses could have been developed as related to net income and unit growth? State one or more analyses that could have been performed in the chapter although not shown.

LOTUS 1-2-3 PROGRAMS—CURRENT YEAR BUDGETS AT 70% TO 100% OF CAPACITY (PROGRAM 4)

```
A1: 'Product
C1: 'Product Group
E1: 'Variable Mfg
G1: 'Variable Mkt
A2: 'Groups
C2: 'Sales as a %
E2: 'Costs as a % of
G2: 'Costs as a % of
A3: 'By No.
C3: 'Total Sales
E3: 'Total Sales
G3: 'Total Sales
A5: ^1
C5: (P2) U 0.2109
E5: (P2) U 0.62
G5: (P2) U 0.09
A7: ^2
C7: (P2) U 0.1753
E7: (P2) U 0.68
G7: (P2) U 0.1
A9: ^3
C9: (P2) U 0.2395
E9: (P2) U 0.59
G9: (P2) U 0.08
A11: ^4
C11: (P2) U 0.2048
E11: (P2) U 0.62
G11: (P2) U 0.09
A13: ^5
C13: (P2) U 0.1695
E13: (P2) U 0.68
G13: (P2) U 0.05
A20: '* * * * * * * * * * * * * * * * * * * * * * * * * * * * * * * * * * * *
D22: '       Basic Product Groups
D23: ' (dollars stated in thousands)
C25: '       Sales at Full Capacity
G25: (C0) U 150000
C26: (P0) '       Percent of Total Capacity
G26: (P0) U 1
D29: '  Product Group by Number
H29: ^Totals
C30: '  ------------------------------------------------
H30: '---------
C31: ^1
D31: ^2
E31: ^3
F31: ^4
G31: ^5
A33: 'Sales
C33: (C0) (C5)*(H33)
D33: (C0) (C7)*(H33)
E33: (C0) (C9)*(H33)
F33: (C0) (C11)*(H33)
G33: (C0) (C13)*(H33)
```

```
H33: (CO) +G25*G26
C34: (CO) ' --------
D34: (CO) ' -------
E34: (CO) ' -------
F34: (CO) ' -------
G34: (CO) ' -------
H34: (CO) ' -------
A35: 'VARIABLE COSTS:
A36: '   Manufacturing
C36: (CO) (E5)*(C33)
D36: (CO) (E7)*(D33)
E36: (CO) (E9)*(E33)
F36: (CO) (E11)*(F33)
G36: (CO) (E13)*(G33)
H36: (CO) @SUM(C36..G36)
A37: '   Marketing
C37: (,0) (G5)*(C33)
D37: (,0) (G7)*(D33)
E37: (,0) (G9)*(E33)
F37: (,0) (G11)*(F33)
G37: (,0) (G13)*(G33)
H37: (,0) @SUM(C37..G37)
C38: (CO) ' --------
D38: (CO) ' --------
E38: (CO) ' --------
F38: (CO) ' --------
G38: (CO) ' --------
H38: (CO) ' --------
A39: 'Contribution to
A40: '   Fixed Costs and
A41: '   Profits
C41: (CO) (C33)-(C36+C37)
D41: (CO) (D33)-(D36+D37)
E41: (CO) (E33)-(E36+E37)
F41: (CO) (F33)-(F36+F37)
G41: (CO) (G33)-(G36+G37)
H41: (CO) @SUM(C41..G41)
C42: (CO) ' --------
D42: (CO) ' --------
E42: (CO) ' --------
F42: (CO) ' --------
G42: (CO) ' --------
H42: (CO) ' --------
A43: 'FIXED COSTS:
A44: '   Manufacturing
C44: (CO) U 2640
D44: (CO) U 2420
E44: (CO) U 2900
F44: (CO) U 2600
G44: (CO) U 2180
H44: (CO) U @SUM(C44..G44)
A45: '   Marketing
C45: (,0) U 2700
D45: (,0) U 2440
E45: (,0) U 2980
F45: (,0) U 2650
G45: (,0) U 2190
H45: (,0) U @SUM(C45..G45)
A46: '   General & Admin.
C46: (,0) U 590
D46: (,0) U 280
E46: (,0) U 670
F46: (,0) U 430
G46: (,0) U 110
H46: (,0) U @SUM(C46..G46)
C47: (CO) ' --------
D47: (CO) ' --------
E47: (CO) ' --------
F47: (CO) ' --------
G47: (CO) ' --------
H47: (CO) ' --------
A48: 'Net Profit Before
A49: '   Federal Income
A50: '   Taxes
C50: (CO) (C41)-@SUM(C44..C46)
D50: (CO) (D41)-@SUM(D44..D46)
```

```
E50: (CO) (E41)-@SUM(E44..E46)
F50: (CO) (F41)-@SUM(F44..F46)
G50: (CO) (G41)-@SUM(G44..G46)
H50: (CO) @SUM(C50..G50)
A52: 'Fed. Income Taxes
A53: '  at
B53: (PO) U 0.46
C53: (,0) (C50)*($B$53)
D53: (,0) (D50)*($B$53)
E53: (,0) (E50)*($B$53)
F53: (,0) (F50)*($B$53)
G53: (,0) (G50)*($B$53)
H53: (,0) @SUM(C53..G53)
C54: (CO) ' --------
D54: (CO) ' --------
E54: (CO) ' --------
F54: (CO) ' --------
G54: (CO) ' --------
H54: (CO) ' --------
A55: 'Net Profit After
A56: '  Federal Income
A57: '   Taxes
C57: (CO) (C50)-(C53)
D57: (CO) (D50)-(D53)
E57: (CO) (E50)-(E53)
F57: (CO) (F50)-(F53)
G57: (CO) (G50)-(G53)
H57: (CO) @SUM(C57..G57)
C58: (CO) ' ========
D58: (CO) ' ========
E58: (CO) ' ========
F58: (CO) ' ========
G58: (CO) ' ========
H58: (CO) ' ========
```

NET INCOME AS RELATED TO UNIT GROWTH AND SELLING PRICE GROWTH (PROGRAM 5)

```
A1: '  Base Year Unit Sales & Price
D1: '| Next Year's Unit Sales & Price
A2: '---------------------------------
D2: '|---------------------------------
A3: 'Unit Sales
C3: (,0) U 200000
D3: '| Unit Sales
E3: (P2) U 0.1
F3: (,0) (C3)*(1+E3)
A4: 'Unit Price
C4: (C2) U 2.5
D4: '| Unit Price
E4: (P2) U 0.04
F4: (C2) @ROUND(C4*(1+E4),2)
A5: '==================================================================
C7: 'Projected Income Statement
A12: 'Sales Rev.
E12: (CO) @ROUND(F3*F4,0)
A14: 'Cost of Goods Sold
C14: (P2) U 0.65
E14: (,0) @ROUND(E12*C14,0)
E15: "--------
A16: 'Gross Profit
E16: (CO) (E12)-(E14)
A18: 'Commissions
A19: '  Fixed
C19: (CO) U 25000
A20: '  Variable
C20: (P2) U 0.05
D20: (,0) @ROUND(E12*C20,0)
E20: (,0) @ROUND(C19+D20,0)
A22: 'Administrative Exp.
A23: '  Fixed
C23: (CO) U 10000
A24: '  Variable
C24: (P2) U 0.03
D24: (,0) @ROUND(E12*C24,0)
E24: (,0) @ROUND(C23+D24,0)
E25: "--------
A26: 'Income Before Federal
A27: '  Income Tax
E27: (CO) (E16)-(E20+E24)
A29: 'Federal Income Tax
```

```
C29: (P2) U 0.46
E29: (,0) @ROUND(E27*C29,0)
E30: "--------
A31: 'Net Income
E31: (C0) (E27)-(E29)
A40: \*
B40: \*
C40: \*
D40: \*
E40: \*
F40: \*
B42: '      Sensitivity Analysis of Net Income for Next Year
B44: '        Net Income Over Selling Price Growth-Rate
B45: '      -------------------------------------------
A46: '       Unit
A47: '      Growth
A48: '      ------
A49: (T) +E31
B49: (P2) U 0.04
C49: (P2) U 0.0525
D49: (P2) U 0.065
E49: (P2) U 0.0775
F49: (P2) U 0.09
A50: (P2) U 0.1
B50: (C0) 64498
C50: (C0) 65460
D50: (C0) 66422
E50: (C0) 67384
F50: (C0) 68667
A51: (P2) U 0.11
B51: (,0) 65256
C51: (,0) 66227
D51: (,0) 67198
E51: (,0) 68169
F51: (,0) 69463
A52: (P2) U 0.12
B52: (,0) 66014
C52: (,0) 66993
D52: (,0) 67974
E52: (,0) 68953
F52: (,0) 70259
A53: (P2) U 0.13
B53: (,0) 66772
C53: (,0) 67761
D53: (,0) 68749
E53: (,0) 69738
F53: (,0) 71056
A54: (P2) U 0.14
B54: (,0) 67530
C54: (,0) 68528
D54: (,0) 69525
E54: (,0) 70522
F54: (,0) 71852
A55: (P2) U 0.15
B55: (,0) 68288
C55: (,0) 69294
D55: (,0) 70300
E55: (,0) 71306
F55: (,0) 72648
A56: (P2) U 0.16
B56: (,0) 69047
C56: (,0) 70061
D56: (,0) 71076
E56: (,0) 72091
F56: (,0) 73444
A57: (P2) U 0.17
B57: (,0) 69805
C57: (,0) 70828
D57: (,0) 71852
E57: (,0) 72875
F57: (,0) 74240
A58: (P2) U 0.18
B58: (,0) 70563
C58: (,0) 71595
D58: (,0) 72627
E58: (,0) 73660
F58: (,0) 75036
```

BIBLIOGRAPHY

Ashkenas, R. N., and Schaffer, R. H. "Managers Can Avoid Wasting Time." *Harvard Business Review,* May-June, 1982.

Bartlett, C. A., and DeLong, D. W. "Operating Cases to Help Solve Corporate Problems." *Harvard Business Review,* March-April 1982.

Bearer, J. "Technological Catch Up." *Computer Decisions,* January 1984.

Bender, P. G.; Northrup, N. D.; and Shapiro, J. F. "Practical Modeling for Resource Management." *Harvard Business Review,* March-April 1981.

Bhide, A. "Hustle as Strategy." *Harvard Business Review,* September-October 1986.

Block, Z., and MacMillan, I. C. "Milestones for Successful Venture Planning." *Harvard Business Review,* September-October 1985.

Bogue, M. C., III, and Buffa, E. *Corporate Strategic Analysis.* New York: The Free Press, 1986.

Bologna, J. "Why Managers Resist Planning." *Managerial Planning,* January-February 1980.

Booker, E. "Computers Help You Win the Game." *Computer Decisions,* September 15, 1984.

Bourgeois, L. J., III. "Strategic Goals, Perceived Uncertainty, and Economic Performance in Volatile Environments." *Academy of Management Journal,* September 1985.

Bowman, E. H. "Content Analysis of Annual Reports for Corporate Strategy and Risk." *Interfaces,* January-February 1984.

Buday, R. "MIS Works to Bridge the Gap with Corporate Management." *Information Week,* January 6, 1986.

Campbell, M. "How to Design Better Spreadsheet Forecasts." *Lotus,* May 1985.

Cassese, V.; Gruber, W.; and Hughes, M. "Planning Amid Change." *Computerworld,* December 9, 1985.

Chakravarthy, B. J., and Lorange, P. "Managing Strategic Adaptation Options in Administrative Systems Design." *Interfaces,* January-February 1984.

Chastain, C. E. "Strategic Planning and the Recession." *Business Horizons,* November-December 1982.

Coopers & Lybrand. *Business Planning in the Eighties: The New Marketing Shape of American Corporations.* New York: Coopers & Lybrand, 1985.

Crescenzi, A. D., and Reck, P. H. "Critical Success Factors: Helping IS Managers Pin-point Information Needs." *Infosystems,* July 1985.

Davis, M. "Anatomy of Decision Support." *Datamation,* June 15, 1984.

Denise, R. M. "Technology for the Executive Thinker." *Datamation,* August 1983.

Doll, D. R. "Strategic Planning." *Computerworld,* April 11, 1984.

Drucker, P. F. *Managing in Turbulent Times.* New York: Harper & Row, 1980.

Ellsworth, R. R. "Subordinate Financial Policy to Corporate Strategy." *Harvard Business Review,* November-December 1983.

Feretic, E., and Moron, T. "Forum of Executive Support: A Delicate Balance." *Today's Office,* June 1984.

Ferguson, C. R., and Dickinson, A. "Critical Success Factors for Directors in the Eighties." *Business Horizons,* May/June 1982.

Fraker, S. "High-Speed Management for the High-Tech Age." *Fortune,* March 5, 1984.

Ghemarvat, P. "Building Strategy on the Experience Curve." *Harvard Business Review,* March-April 1985.

Gold, B. "Foundations of Strategic Planning for Productivity Improvement." *Interfaces,* May-June 1985.

Goldberg, E. "Applications Integration, Have Users Caught the Fever?" *Computerworld,* December 30, 1985-January 6, 1986.

Goul, M., Shane B., and Tange, F. M. "Using a Knowledge-Based Decision Support System in Strategic Planning Decisions: An Empirical Study." *Journal of Management Information Systems,* Spring 1986.

Gray, D. H. "Uses and Misuses of Strategic Planning." *Harvard Business Review,* January-February 1986.

Gruber, W. H., and Sonnemann, G. "Information Resource Management for Corporate Decision Support." *AFIPS Conference Proceedings* (National Computer Conference) 1983.

Gunawardane, G. "Implementing a Management Information System in an Extremely Dynamic (and Somewhat Hostile) Environment—A Case Study." *Interfaces,* November-December 1985.

Hall, R. I. "The Natural Logic of Management Policy Making: Its Implications for the Survival of an Organization." *Management Science,* August 1984.

Hambrick, D. C. "An Empirical Typology of Mature Industrial Product Environments." *Academy of Management Journal,* June 1983.

Hambrick, D. C.; MacMillan, I. C.; and Day, D. L. "Strategic Attributes and Performance in the BCG Matrix—A PIMS-Based Analysis of

Industrial-Product Businesses." *Academy of Management Journal,* September 1982.

Hambrick, D. C., and Schecter, E. M. "Turnaround Strategies for Mature Industrial-Product Business Units." *Academy of Management Journal,* June 1983.

Hamermesh, R. S. *Making Strategy Work.* New York: John Wiley & Sons, 1986.

————. "Making Planning Strategies." *Harvard Business Review,* July-August 1986.

Harper, R. "Decision Support System Profits Contractors." *Computerworld,* September 1, 1980.

Harrington, D. R. "Stock Prices, Beta, And Strategic Planning." *Harvard Business Review,* May-June 1983.

Harvey, S. B. "Bridging the Planning Gap." *Infosystems,* October 1979.

Hax, A. C., and Majluf, N. S. "The Use of the Growth-Share Matrix in Strategic Planning." *Interfaces,* February 1983.

————. "The Use of the Industry Attractiveness–Business Strength Matrix in Strategic Planning." *Interfaces,* April 1983.

————. "The Corporate Strategic Planning Process." *Interfaces,* January-February 1984.

Head, R. V. *Strategic Planning for Information Systems.* Q.E.D. Information Sciences, 1979.

Hogarth, R. M., and Mahridakis, S. "Forecasting and Planning: An Evolution." *Management Science,* February 1981.

Johnson, J. R. "Enterprise Analysis." *Datamation,* December 15, 1984.

Karr, M. "Strategic Models: Where Information Means Profit." *Infosystems,* February 1985.

Kasper, G. M. "The Effect of User-Developed DSS Applications on Forecasting Decision-Making Performance in an Experimental Setting." *Journal of Management Information Systems,* Fall 1985.

King, W. R., and Rodriguez, J. I. "Participative Design of Strategic Decision Support Systems: An Empirical Assessment." *Management Science,* June 1981.

Klingman, D.; Phillips, N.; Steiger, D.; Wirth, R.; and Young, W. "The Challenges and Success Factors in Implementing Products Planning System for Citgo." *Interfaces,* May-June 1986.

de Kluyver, C. A., and McNally, G. M. "Corporate Planning Using Simulation." *Interfaces,* June 1980.

Kull, D. J. "Group Decision: Can Computers Help?" *Computer Decisions,* May 1982.

Lambrix, R., and Singhvi, S. "How to Set Volume-Sensitive ROI Targets." *Harvard Business Review,* March-April, 1981.

Larreche, J. C., and Srinivasan, V. "STRATPORT, A Decision Support System for Strategic Planning." *Journal of Marketing,* Fall 1981.

Lasden, M. L. "Long-Range Planning: Curse or Blessing?" *Computer Decisions,* February 1981.

Lewis, W. C. "Corporate Development with DSS." *Micro Manager,* November 1984.

Lewis, W. W. "The CEO and Corporate Strategy in the Eighties: Back to Basics." *Interfaces,* January-February 1984.

Liang, T. P. "Critical Success Factors of Decision Support Systems: An Experimental Study." *Data Base,* Winter 1986.

Little, J. D. C., and Findley, J. J. "Marketing Management in the 80s, Blueprint for a Revolution." *Marketing Communications,* March 1984.

MacMillan, I. C.; Hambrick, D. C.; and Day, D. L. "The Profit Portfolio and Profitability—A PIMS-Based Analysis of Industrial-Product Businesses." *Academy of Management Journal,* December 1982.

Magnet, M. "How Top Management Makes a Company's Toughest Decision." *Fortune,* March 18, 1986.

Martin, J. *Strategic Data Planning Methodologies.* Englewood Cliffs, NJ: Prentice-Hall, 1982.

Maskowitz, R. "Strategic System Planning Shifts to Data-Oriented Approach." *Computerworld,* May 12, 1986.

McIntyre, S. C.; Konsynski, B. R.; and Nunamaker, J. F., Jr. "Automating Planning Environments: Knowledge Integration and Model Scripting." *Journal of Management Information Systems,* Spring 1986.

Miesing, P., and Wolfe, J. "The Art and Science of Planning at the Business Unit Level." *Management Science,* June 1985.

Millar, V. E. "Decision-Oriented Information." *Datamation,* January 1984.

Munro, M. C., and Wheeler, B. R. "Planning, Critical Success Factors, and Management's Information Requirements." *MIS Quarterly,* December 1980.

Myers, D. "DP Managers Say DSS Needed to Tie Together Corporate Micros." *Computerworld,* October 17, 1983.

Naylor, T. H., and Neva, K. *Corporate Planning Models,* Reading, MA: Addison-Wesley Publishing Company, 1979.

———. "Design of a Strategic Planning Process." *Managerial Planning,* January-February 1980.

Nee, E. "Reaching Decisions with Micro-to-Mainframe DSS." *Micro Manager,* November 1984.

Neumann, S., and Hadass, M. "DSS and Strategic Decisions." *California Management Review,* Spring 1980.

Ohmae, K. "The Secret of Strategic Vision." *Management Review,* April 1982.

———. "See the Options Before Planning Strategy." *Management Review,* May 1982.

Oxenfeldt, A. R. "A Bridge Player's Guide to Sharpening an Executive Ability to Think and Act Strategically." *Management Review,* October 1982.

Palmer, S. "Planning with (and without) Computer Models." *ICP Software Business Review,* Spring 1982.

Pekar, P. P., Jr. "Planning in the '80s." *Managerial Planning,* March/April 1981.

Polilli, S. "Micro-Based DSS Brings Decision-Making to the Desktop." *Micro Manager,* November 1984.

Quinn, J. B. "Managing Innovation: Controlled Chaos." *Harvard Business Review,* May-June 1985.

Ramanujam, V., and Venkatraman, N. "An Inventory and Critique of Strategy Research Using PIMS Database." *Academy of Management Review,* vol. 9, no. 1, 1984.

Ramaprasad, A., and Mitroff, I. I. "On Formulating Strategic Problems." *Academy of Management Review,* vol. 9, no. 4, 1984.

Rector, R. L. "Decision Support Systems—Strategic Planning Tool." *Managerial Planning,* May/June 1982.

Rockart, J. F. "Chief Executives Define Their Own Data Needs." *Harvard Business Review,* March-April 1979.

Rockart, J. F., and Scott Morton, M. S. "Implications of Changes in Information Technology for Corporate Strategy." *Interfaces,* January-February 1984.

Rockart, J. F., and Treacy, M. E. "The CEO Goes On-Line." *Harvard Business Review,* January-February 1982.

Roman, D. R. "Executives Who Love Their Personal Computers." *Computer Decisions,* January 1983.

———. "MIS on the Attack." *Computer Decisions,* February 26, 1985.

Rout, L. "At Some Companies, Key Employees Ponder for Much of the Day." *Wall Street Journal,* December 4, 1980.

Schendel, D. E., and Hofer, C. W. *Strategic Management: A New View of Business Policy and Planning.* Boston: Little, Brown, and Company, 1979.

Seitz, N. *Business Forecasting: Concepts and Microcomputer Applications.* Reston, VA: Reston Publishing Company, 1984.

Seymour, J. "Building a Desktop Modeling/Forecasting System." *Today's Office,* November 1984.

Skinner, W. "Operations Technology: Blind Spot in Strategic Management." *Interfaces,* January-February 1984.

Steiner, G. A. *Strategic Planning, What Every Manager Must Know,* New York: The Free Press, 1981.

Susman, G. I. "Planned Change: Prospects for the 1980s." *Management Science,* February 1981.

Tharrington, J. M. "The Science of MIS Planning." *Infosystems,* June 1985.

Thiel, C. T. "What MIS Needs to Know About Strategic Planning." *Infosystems,* August 1984.

Thierauf, R. J. *Decision Support Systems for Effective Planning and Control—A Case Study Approach.* Englewood Cliffs, NJ: Prentice-Hall, 1982.

Thistlethwaite, G. E., Jr. "Strategic Planning Requires Dynamic, Ongoing Process." *Data Management,* August 1985.

Tomme, C. "What MIS Needs to Know About Strategic Planning." *Infosystems,* August 1984.

Venkatraman, N. "Research on MIS Planning: Some Guidelines from Strategic Planning Research." *Journal of Management Information Systems,* Winter 1985–86.

Wack, P. "Scenarios: Uncharted Waters Ahead." *Harvard Business Review,* September-October 1985.

Wagner, G. R. "Optimizing Decision Support Systems." *Datamation,* May 1980. ✳

Watkins, P. R. "Perceived Information Structure: Implications for Decision Support System Design." *Decision Science,* vol. 13, 1982.

Wheelwright, S. C. "Strategy, Management and Strategic Planning Approaches." *Interfaces,* January-February 1984.

Wind, Y., and Mahajan, V. "Designing Product and Business Portfolios." *Harvard Business Review,* January-February 1981. ✳

Winski, D. T. "In Search of Excellence." *Infosystems,* January 1984.

Woodwell, D. R. "Corporate Portfolios on Personal Computers." *Computer Decisions,* February 1984.

Young, L. F. "A Corporate Strategy for Decision Support Systems." *The Journal of Information Systems Management,* Winter 1984.

Young, T. R. "Who Works at Workstations." *Datamation,* April 1983. ✳

CHAPTER 12

Marketing Subsystem—XYZ Corporation

ISSUES

How can top management of the XYZ Corporation utilize information from a PIMS data base?

What is the relationship of marketing decision processes within an MIS framework to other functional areas and their decision processes?

What impact has market research software made on the area of marketing?

How can the manager-machine interface be applied to the MIS marketing subsystem for effective decision making?

How important is finished goods inventory control to the success of the XYZ Corporation?

What is the relationship of sales order processing to physical distribution in an MIS environment?

444

INTRODUCTION TO MARKETING

Marketing tends to be a controversial subject when any type of management information system is discussed. From one viewpoint, marketing is so dependent on human judgment, so involved with complex relationships, and so beset with imperfect knowledge that decisions are all too often made by sheer intuition rather than by computer analysis. In actuality, behavioral phenomena are difficult to quantify and, hence, difficult to computerize as a valid part of a marketing subsystem. However, from another viewpoint, we can admit that experience and intuition (or the behavioral aspects) are vital ingredients in marketing, but judge that their value can be greatly enhanced by quantitative computer measurement. It is from this latter point of view that the major subparts of the marketing subsystem are developed for an effective MIS.

Fundamentally, the format of this chapter follows that of the previous one. Marketing considerations underlying effective MIS are initially set forth. Specifically, they center on profit impact on marketing strategy, identifying fast-moving products, examining marketing service objectives, a problem-finding approach to marketing, mathematical models, and market research software. Next, an overview of the marketing subsystem for the XYZ Corporation is illustrated in terms of its integration with other subsystems. This background provides the underlying framework for presenting the major components of the MIS marketing subsystem, which are (1) sales forecasting, (2) marketing research, (3) advertising, (4) sales order processing, and (5) physical distribution. In the final part, the effective practice of MIS in the area of finished goods inventory control is discussed. This orderly presentation of the marketing area sets the stage for considering the other major subsystems— manufacturing, accounting and finance, and personnel—in the remaining chapters.

MARKETING CONSIDERATIONS FOR EFFECTIVE MIS

Considerations for the marketing subsystem differ from those of other subsystems because marketing captures information about the external environment in terms of market forecasts and customer orders. It is the "prime mover" from which all other subsystems either directly or indirectly receive instructions on what is to be accomplished. An important part of a marketing subsystem focuses on the data base elements themselves, specifically, what

445

they are, what the validity is for storing them on-line, how they can be stored for easy retrieval, how they can be combined with data from other subsystems, and what type of output they can produce for an interactive operating mode.

To proceed with the development of an MIS marketing subsystem (as well as any other subsystem), an order of priorities must be established in terms of what information and calculations are most valuable to marketing management. Ranking informational priorities, in particular, requires creative thinking and intuitive judgment of the highest order. For effective results, *there is a definite need for systems personnel to interact with marketing personnel,* especially marketing management and their staff, if the company seeks concrete results. From these joint efforts, the most valuable informational opportunities can be pursued and developed for mutual benefit. A helpful approach to identifying opportunities is making use of past research from the PIMS (Profit Impact of Marketing Strategies) data base.

Consideration for an effective MIS marketing subsystem must also include examining the level of customer service needed for products and identifying fast-moving products. Similarly, there is need for enlarging the perspective of the management decision process by employing problem finding in order to produce more effective decision making for the entire corporation. From this perspective, mathematical models may be helpful in improving overall corporate performance. Due to the importance of the foregoing areas, they are discussed in some detail below.

Profit Impact of Marketing Strategies

Profit Impact of Marketing Strategies (PIMS) is a computerized approach for planning market strategy that is run by the Strategic Planning Institute. It is a data pool of information on the marketing experiences of its members and encompasses more than 650 product lines.[1] Each member provides PIMS with the most intimate details on matters such as its market share, investment intensity, product quality, and total marketing and research and development expenditures. Through computer simulation, the company can then test its own market strategies against the real experiences of hundreds of comparable companies, including competitors. What it receives are answers to questions such as: "What is the normal profit rate for a business or a product line given its combination of circumstances, and why?" "If the business continues on its current track, what will its future operating results be?" "What will happen to short- and long-term performance if certain strategic moves are made?" "What changes will create the best profit or cash returns?"

Basically, what a member company wants from PIMS is to find out what it will cost to make a particular strategic move and how much better off the business will be afterward. For example, consider return on investment (ROI), which PIMS considers one of the best measures of how a business is doing.

[1]Paula Smith, "Unique Tool for Marketers: PIMS," *Management Review,* January 1977, pp. 32–34.

The PIMS models can forecast how much ROI for a business line will change because of a strategic move involving more marketing, research and development, capital equipment buildup, or whatever: both what the ROI will be immediately following the move and what it will be several years in the future.

PIMS PRINCIPLES.   Some new as well as traditional principles have emerged from PIM's computer models of the real-life experiences of its corporate members. Among them are:

- There is a set of operating rules that govern all businesses. Thirty-seven factors—including market share, capital intensity, vertical integration, and the like—jointly explain 80 percent of the success or failure of any business; only 20 percent of a business's return on investment can be attributed to factors that are unique or special, such as the quality of working relations.
- Anything more than a minimal research and development program does not make sense for a company with a weak market position. Copying competitors' products rather than investing them is probably its best bet. This can be a very profitable strategy.
- High marketing expenditures for low-quality products can have a devastating effect on profits.
- High product quality can offset a weak market position.
- Weak companies should not become vertically integrated, whereas strong ones should.
- High costs in more than one area, such as capital investment, research and development, or marketing, can ruin any business.

Extrapolating from the PIM's data base, companies should not automatically compare themselves with competitors in the same industry or business category to find out how well they are doing. According to PIMS, industry breakdowns are not all-important. A better yardstick may be the performance of companies in other industries whose total situation is comparable. A tire company, for example, may have even more in common and more to learn from the market strategies of a small appliance manufacturer than from those of another tire company.

TAILOR-MADE REPORTS.   PIMS members get three tailor-made reports for every business or product line analyzed. First, there is "The Par Report," which specifies the return on investment that is normal or "par" for the business line given the characteristics of its market, competition, position, technology, and cost structure. It reports whether the business is the kind that normally earns, say 3 percent or 30 percent, judging by the experiences of businesses with similar characteristics. It also identifies the major strengths and weaknesses of the business that account for the high or low par.

Second, "The Strategy Sensitivity Report" tests several possible strategic moves the business can make. It indicates the normal short- and long-term consequences of each move and specifies what the profit or loss is likely to be. Third, and most important, is what PIMS calls "The Optimum Strategy

Report." This report picks the combination of changes that promises to give the business the best results in terms of return on investment for the next five years, discounted cash flow over 10 years, short-term earnings, and other measures—judging by the experiences of businesses in similar circumstances. Overall, the reports are helpful to top management and its staff for giving direction to the corporate planning process.

Identifying Fast-Moving Products

For most corporations like the XYZ Corporation, a relationship exists between the number of different products offered for sale and the volume of sales. A relatively few items account for the majority of sales; a majority of items account for relatively few sales. This point (refer to figure 12.1) can be represented as follows:

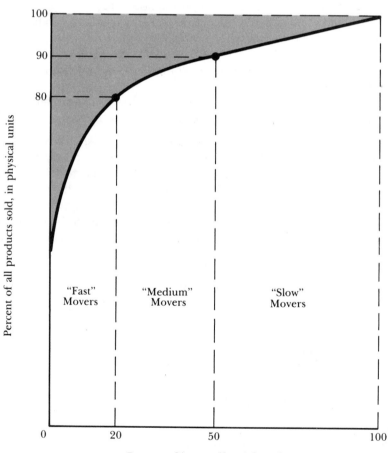

FIGURE 12.1
Application of the "20–80" rule—fast movers versus medium and slow movers of all products sold.

- About 20 percent of the items inventoried account for about 80 percent of the total sales. These are the "fast"-moving items. (This is often referred to as the "20–80" rule.)
- About 30 percent of the items inventoried account for about 10 percent of the total sales. These are the "medium" movers.
- About 50 percent of the items inventoried account for only about 10 percent of the total sales. These are the "slow" movers.

Since these relationships are recognized by marketing management of the XYZ Corporation, it provides them with an important starting point for the planning and control of operations. Specifically, sales forecasting, production, and procurement planning can be tailored to control those items that will account for most of the demand. This will allow the corporation to serve customers at a reduced cost. Of equal importance is the segregation of products, which is necessary for effective inventory control. Overall, the segregation of products into three categories is one way of "getting a handle on" what products are the corporation's sales leaders as well as where the corporation should invest in inventories to best support "fast, medium, and slow" movers.

Examining Marketing Service Objectives

Going beyond the segregation of products offered for sale, marketing management of the XYZ Corporation is concerned with two different service objectives. The *first,* in-stock service levels, focuses on having the right products in stock to supply customer needs; the *second,* speed of delivery, employs a physical distribution system that allows for timely delivery.

Regarding *in-stock service levels,* the proper in-stock conditions depend on customer needs, which must be forecasted and production planned, along with maintaining inventories at a level that will satisfy customer demand. Marketing makes use of the 20–80 rule (figure 12.1), where the relatively few items accounting for 80 percent of demand should never be allowed to be out of stock. These are the corporation's "bread-and-butter" items; customers will not stand for out-of-stock conditions. Since demand for these "fast" movers can generally be forecast more accurately—and production is (or should be) geared to manufacturing these items—the products should flow regularly through the physical distribution system, with appropriate levels of inventory.

For "medium" movers, adequate stocks should be inventoried, principally on the basis of economic production or procurement lot sizes, to guard against stockouts. A relatively low inventory should be maintained for "slow" movers. However, the cost of maintaining these inventories should be watched carefully and should not be allowed to exceed the benefit derived by the corporation. This consideration is especially true when a very large percentage of offered items represents only a small percentage of total sales.

Essentially, then, marketing management of the XYZ Corporation recognizes that there must be adequate production capabilities and inventories of fast-moving items or their customers become dissatisfied. Since the finished goods inventory is tailored to the production and distribution of these items, its in-stock position is better than if all items were treated equally.

Satisfying the service function of *speed of delivery* requires rapid delivery. Customer delivery needs should be quantified by reviewing customer ordering patterns in terms of delivery requirements and size of orders. Such an analysis enables marketing management to determine where company-owned warehouses should be located and how inventories should be allocated to best serve customers at a minimum cost. The speed of delivery and the in-stock service levels—and certain other marketing considerations—are integral parts of the problem-finding process, the subject matter of the next section.

Problem-Finding Approach to Marketing

For effective decision making that focuses on problem finding, there is need to go outside the corporation for relevant external data that can be used in planning marketing activities. Similarly, there is need to go outside the marketing subsystem within the corporation to ensure that marketing operations are coordinated with corporate planning, manufacturing, accounting finance, and personnel. From this enlarged perspective, marketing must further expand its horizons within and outside the organization. An integral part of expanding internal capabilities includes the coordination of marketing and production plans in order to reduce costs and increase profits. To effect such coordination, individual departments' actions must be compatible with corporate goals and objectives for the corporation *to have* a corporate planning process, and for marketing and manufacturing managers to recognize their dependence on the actions of others.

As an offshoot of problem finding, effective coordination can be obtained only through a conscious effort on the part of management. To illustrate this point, the XYZ Corporation's marketing manager is charged with making every effort to service customer needs so that sales will be maximized. To accomplish this, there must be sufficient inventory for seasonal sales. The production manager is charged with cost reduction and would like to smooth production and keep inventory costs down. Clearly, the objectives of these managers conflict. The problem can be expanded to include other areas, such as inventory and finance. Conflicting objectives between these sections are obvious.

Top management of the XYZ Corporation, then, is faced with resolving conflicting objectives. Marketing management seeks satisfactory solutions to their marketing problems. In a similar manner, production and financial management seek good answers to their problems. Unfortunately, each has a different and possibly narrow perspective. To manage the marketing area (as well as other areas) effectively, the corporation needs to make excellent use of problem finding as well as problem solving so that the marketing–manufacturing interface clearly produces a net overall savings. Seasonal sales can be forecast and slack periods can receive the benefit of promotional efforts in order to smooth sales and reduce variations in production and inventory levels. In addition, production savings should be compared with promotional costs, and a coordinated budget should be developed to reduce overall costs. Thus, problems of conflicting objectives, underutilization of resources, overreaction to changing economic indicators, and rigid budgetary constraints at managerial junctures that prohibit the corporation from optimizing its overall objectives can be overcome. The solution is implementing coordinated planning of the marketing function with the corporation's other functional areas, in particular, corporate planning.

Mathematical Models

Marketing managers of most organizations—including the XYZ Corporation—have developed a natural suspicion about mathematical models. There is no question that many facets of the marketing process will not submit to mathematical analysis, particularly ones that rely heavily on creativity and customer relations. However, there are other areas of marketing that respond well to systematic observation, analysis, and implementation of mathematical models. These areas offer an excellent opportunity for marketing executives willing to adopt an innovative attitude toward newer knowledge and technology.

Although mathematical models are relative latecomers in marketing, they have already paid off in areas such as sales forecasting (e.g., exponential smoothing) and new product development (e.g., venture analysis). These topics are explored below. Other marketing mathematical models include the pricing model (employing higher mathematics for optimizing profits given a certain selling price), the linear programming advertising media model (useful in determining where to spend advertising dollars), Markov chains (a brand-switching process to predict future probable market shares), PERT (a method for controlling the progress of major product projects), and Monte Carlo simulation (a queuing method to determine the optimum number of clerks to assign to a selling department).

EXPONENTIAL SMOOTHING. Exponential smoothing is a forecasting technique that is extremely accurate in predicting future market demand. The term *exponential* has a purely mathematical origin. It means that the repeated use of a smoothing constant tends to operate in a manner equivalent to an exponential multiplier. A computer program can be used so that period-to-period forecasts on many different products may be determined in a matter of minutes.

The exponential smoothing method develops a forecast of sales for the next period, for example, a quarter, by taking a weighted average of sales in the current period and a sales forecast made in the current period. The weighted values must total one. If the weight for actual current sales is set at .1, then the weight factor of the forecast made in the current period would have to be .9. The selection of the weighting factor is of utmost importance.

If it is very large (close to 1), then any fluctuation of current sales will be strongly reflected in the forecast for the next period. On the other hand, if it is set close to zero, current sales will have relatively little impact on the next period's forecast. Experience has shown that setting the weighting factor somewhere between .1 and .2 leads to reasonably favorable results. This setting smooths the extremes of current sales while allowing for definite fluctuations in sales trends. Obviously, management should experiment with various values for best results.

VENTURE ANALYSIS.   One of the most extensive and sophisticated marketing mathematical models is venture analysis, an investment planning system for analyzing new opportunities. It encompasses such techniques as probability, decision theory, and the time value of money as well as mathematical modeling. Because it is a massive system for gathering, relating, appraising, and projecting all data pertinent to a complete business venture over its life cycle, this mathematical technique stores many kinds of information. All costs involved in the product project are developed. Manufacturing costs include raw material, direct labor, depreciation, and overhead. These data are modeled for each step of the production process. For the pricing and promotion component, product prices are estimated at various sales levels in order to determine an optimum price. All promotional costs involved in marketing the product are broken down by media selected and projected. Research and development costs plus general and administrative costs are scheduled to complete the data.

Because venture analysis is very comprehensive, other links in the marketing chain—suppliers and retailers—are included. In a similar manner, key decisions that affect sales of the product, such as the introduction of similar products by competitors, are defined, related, and programmed. Also, the consumer's awareness and reaction are taken into account to make the model complete. All of the marketing factors, then, are modeled according to cause and effect. For any action on the part of a company competing in the field, the corporation estimates the reaction and effects on the other competitors. The total of all marketing interaction described above results in a sales forecast and a profitability picture. A computer simulation provides for analyzing and summarizing in a logical manner all the available information about markets, investments, costs, customers, and competitors in venture analysis.

In summary, venture analysis that relies heavily on simulation directs management in judging a new product at the market research stage by presenting analyzed information in a logically structured framework. It considers both risk and gaming factors as well as indicating the expected economic impact of various possible decision routes. Using this approach, management can reach a better decision under conditions of risk and uncertainty. In addition, the tendency of executives to delay decisions and commitments to new products will be lessened, because valuable information from a venture simulation method replaces intuition. Thus, venture analysis provides management with the means for better planning, forecasting, and decision making than would otherwise be possible.

Market Research Software

Although electronic spreadsheets and financial planning/statistical packages are available to undertake market research studies, some market research analysts prefer more specialized software. A new genre of easy-to-use menu-driven software gives them full control over the entire research project, from crunching numbers to formatting reports. Microcomputer statistics programs provide, at a fraction of the cost, the tabulation and analysis capabilities previously found only on mainframe software. A sampling of micro market research software is in figure 12.2. As a result of this software, corporations that a short time ago could not afford complex research—even some with established marketing departments—can avail themselves of sophisticated statistical data. Just as important, some companies have reduced budgets for outside research services by as much as 25 percent, and others have eliminated their dependence on such services.

Survey tabulation and data analysis software lets users design questionnaires for mail surveys or telephone and personal interviews. Data from completed questionnaires can be entered manually or read by an optical reader. The market research analyst, prompted by menus, selects parameters for cross-tabulating populations: geographic area, dollars, management responsibility, and so forth. Most packages perform typical statistical functions, such as standard deviation and error, regression, and frequency distributions. Finally, the analyst has a wide choice of table presentation and report generation features, including the type of display and headings, graphic or tabular formats, and how the information is ranked. After the analyst defines these parameters, the program processes, sorts, and produces the requested market research reports.

For the most part, using the new software does not require knowledge of a microcomputer. For example, with TeloFacts2 (figure 12.2), the research analyst can perform simple surveys in-house and send out only complex ones. In summary, market research software is extremely user friendly for the typical market research analyst and provides a quick and inexpensive way to get frequency distributions and statistical analysis.

MARKETING OVERVIEW—XYZ CORPORATION

The marketing subsystem, which is the prime source of determining what must be accomplished soon, is coordinated with the corporate planning subsystem. Its major functional subparts, shown in figure 12.3, are sales forecasting, market research, advertising, sales order processing, and physical distribution. Their design includes an interactive processing capability. Marketing data will be stored on the appropriate data base, retrievable as is or manipu-

Software Package	Vendor	Description
AIMS	Sophisticated Data Research	Automated survey interviewing system utilizing multiple CRTs
Dataprep	Personal Computers Ltd.	Survey and data analysis
MathStat	Mathematica Policy Research	Statistical analysis with graphics option
Micro-DSS/ Analysis	Addison-Wesley Publishing Co.	Data management, statistics, graphics, and report writing
MicroSURVEY	PRC Voorhees	Survey analysis
MICROTAB	M.R.A. Software Inc.	Cross-tabulation, report generator system
Profile IV	Bardsley & Haslacher Inc.	Survey analysis
Public Opinion Survey	Stolzberg Research Associates	Market research
Questab	Software Consulting Services	Data entry and report generation
Question-Writer and Answer-Tabs	Orchard Associates, Inc.	Interviewing system and survey tabulation analysis
SCAT	Cincinnati Research Systems	Survey interviewing and tabulation
SCAT	Thomas Software Corp.	Survey design and tabulation
SENTRY and TELEVIEW	Science Applications, Inc.	Data entry, telephone interviewing system
SRS	Congressional Systems, Inc.	Survey tabulation system
Super-Ranker	Media Service Concepts, Inc.	Audience ranking for sales and media
Survent and Mentor	Computers for Marketing Corp.	Survey interviewing and cross-tabulation system
Surveys Unlimited	Brown Brothers Enterprises	Survey analysis
Surveytab	Survey Tab	Cross-tabulation, data analysis
The Survey System	Creative Research Systems	Cross-tabulation, data analysis, and report generator
TABULYZER	Business Research & Surveys	Cross-tabulation and survey analysis
TELEPHONE SURVEY	Persimmon Software	Telephone interviewing and data analysis
TeloFacts2	diluthium Press	Survey and data analysis

FIGURE 12.2 Typical market research software available from vendors.

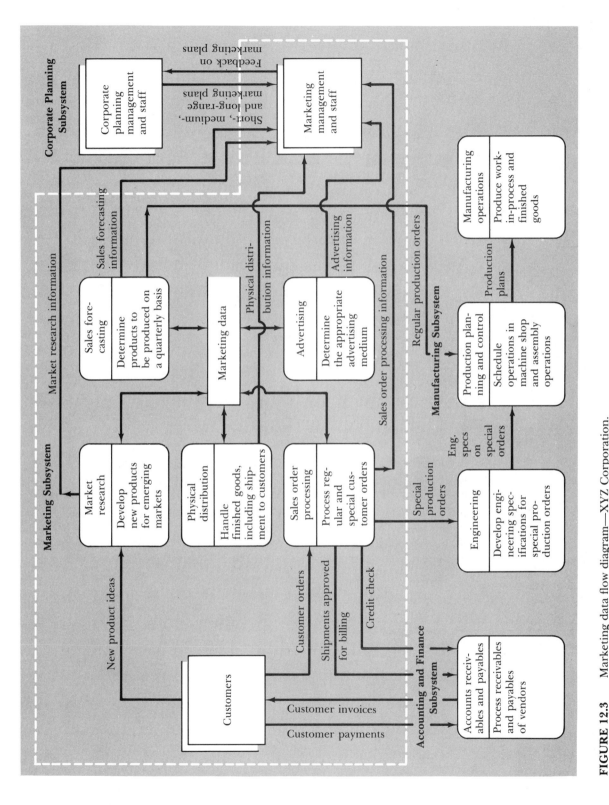

FIGURE 12.3 Marketing data flow diagram—XYZ Corporation.

lated depending on the user's needs. This capability to obtain current and exception marketing information via a CRT terminal or microcomputer makes information available when needed. With this user–machine operating mode, necessary corrective measures can be effected faster because of immediate feedback.

Marketing Intelligence—A Starting Point

Input for the MIS marketing subsystem of the XYZ Corporation comes from its customers. Not only are orders received from customers, but marketing efforts are also focused on them. The corporation's marketing executives derive their information about customers and the marketplace through marketing intelligence, formal market research, and company accounting information. *Marketing intelligence* activity is the term for the continuous effort to keep informed about current developments among customers, competing products, and the marketing environment. Similarly, *market research* centers on a more formal approach to current developments, in particular, project-oriented research. The accounting and finance subsystem generates sales and cost information in order to complement marketing intelligence and research.

Because marketing intelligence is designed to assess the marketplace in terms of its ultimate impact on the corporation, a DSS approach is needed. That is, marketing management must have the final say in key marketing decisions, as opposed to the computer providing "the answers." This is related to the fast-changing times in which the XYZ Corporation finds itself. Hence, marketing management must be able to respond to changes with the marketing intelligence evaluation process. Marketing intelligence is linked to the critical success factors discussed in the prior chapter on corporate planning. From this broad perspective, marketing intelligence picks up where corporate planning leaves off, especially in the area of the five-year strategic plan (i.e., product line and distribution planning, on down through medium-range corporate planning to short-range corporate planning). The use of a DSS approach to undertake marketing intelligence will be evident in the first of the marketing modules—sales forecasting. These introductory remarks on marketing intelligence set the stage for presenting an effective MIS marketing subsystem.

MIS MARKETING SUBSYSTEM

From an overview standpoint (shown in figure 12.4), an effective management information system produces sales forecasting, market research, and advertising information at the corporate level only. However, sales order processing and physical distribution are off-loaded from the corporate level to the plant (warehouse) level. In this manner, a desired level of customer service can be achieved through fast shipment and more accurate handling of customer

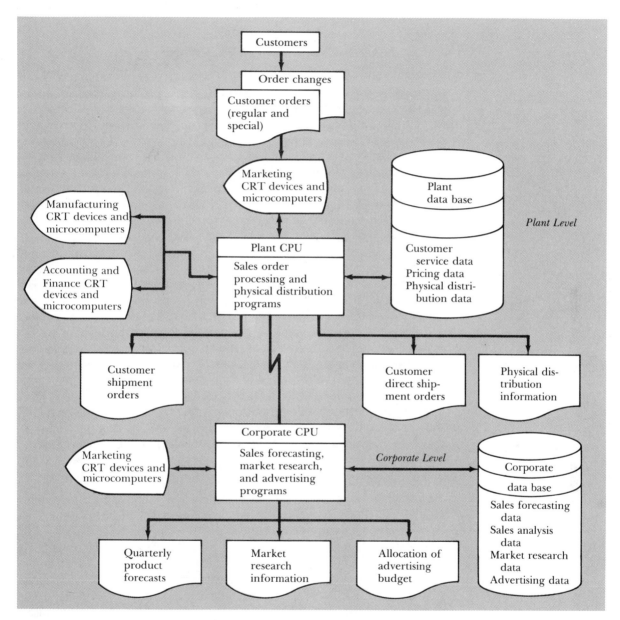

FIGURE 12.4 MIS marketing subsystem in an effective management information system—XYZ Corporation.

orders. Although these marketing modules are at different locations, they are fully integrated. The net result of this integration is that this important part of MIS will greatly enhance the support for planning and control of marketing decisions for changing times.

Use of Modeling Tools to Answer "What if?" Questions

As marketing considerations, a number of mathematical models and software packages were discussed as a way of solving marketing problems of different types. These tools, like other modeling tools, allow marketing analysts to do most of their computing off the mainframe, on their own microcomputers. This arrangement keeps marketing out of an MIS department and guarantees that system response time will remain consistently acceptable. Just as many marketing analysts are better off swapping their terminals for autonomous PCs, other microcomputer users will also profit from having mainframe modeling power on their desks. These users include departmental marketing management who periodically generate sales forecasts or budget plans, allocate promotion and advertising budgets, and justify expenditures to superiors.

Unlike marketing analysts, however, marketing managers of the XYZ Corporation need to be taught the benefits of the newer marketing tools. Having grown comfortable using Lotus 1-2-3 for their forecasting and budgeting needs to answer "What if?" questions, they may resist learning the newer modeling tools, such as IFPS (or SAS). Managers need to be shown that spreadsheets offer no analysis tools to generate sophisticated equations; users typically are forced to write their own, trying out different numbers until they find the right combination. From this perspective, marketing managers are capable of answering more "What if?" questions as they arise if they learn IFPS (or SAS).

While spreadsheets offer built-in marketing modeling capabilities, they are not as broad-based as those found in IFPS (or SAS). Such a modeling language offers many other useful techniques for marketing, a sample of which is as follows:

- *Sensitivity analysis* measures the effect of one or more variables on another. For instance, the XYZ Corporation might want to determine how fluctuations in the GNP, employment levels, inflation factors, etc. will influence future inventory levels.
- *Multiple regression analysis* uses time-series data (a series of numbers that represent values for a variable at different points in time) to produce a formula that predicts the value of a "dependent" variable on the basis of one or more "independent" variables. For example, a marketing analyst may want to determine how levels of advertising affect sales in order to time a new advertising campaign for the XYZ Corporation.
- *Goal seeking* can be described as the other side of "What if?" analysis. For example, if the XYZ Corporation spends *n* dollars in advertising and hires six new salespeople, what should the coming year's sales be to justify these new expenses?

As shown in these typical examples, IFPS (or SAS) can extend the level of problem solving for marketing management of the XYZ Corporation.

For effective sales forecasting at the XYZ Corporation, the capability to accommodate external conditions should exist. It must be able to reflect existing environments, anticipate possible environmental changes, and foresee potential policy changes. A capability to detect forecast turning points due to changes in strategy is also a requirement. The forecasting technique should provide consistent numbers for related events, such as multiple forecasts of sales, costs, and revenues. Additionally, it should be able to express the dynamic nature of the model variables, since time-dependent and interacting influences may be at work among them. Overall, the sale forecasting technique should be able to make accurate quarterly projections of demand for the corporation's products that reflect marketing intelligence.

Exponential Smoothing Method

Using these criteria for what is needed, the exponential smoothing method set forth previously will be used. The basic concept of *exponential smoothing* is that next quarter's forecast should be adjusted by employing weighting factors for current sales and the current forecast. In a sense, the weighting factors update the upcoming forecast in light of what has happened most recently to actual demand. From this viewpoint, they are smoothing constants that are derived from examining past sales experience patterns. In addition, they allow seasonal and trend adjustments to be built into the forecasting formulas to reflect marketing intelligence.

The microcomputer, illustrated in figure 12.5, is used to trigger on-line processing of exponential smoothing formulas on a quarterly basis, in conjunction with the marketing data base. For interactive processing to begin, current sales, sales forecasts in the current period, and weighting factors for each product are read in from the data base and manipulated by the exponential smoothing equations. The resulting output from the quarterly product forecast–exponential smoothing program is printed as quarterly product forecasts, as shown in figure 12.6 for a typical quarter. But equally important in terms of output is the storing of these forecasts on the common data base. Storage of quarterly sales forecasts on the corporate data base allows the possibility of their usage by the corporate planning staff plus marketing management and its staff.

To help ensure that these forecasts are representative of the future, it is useful to compare the results with prior quarters, especially of the prior year. Using micro Lotus 1-2-3, such a presentation is found in figure 12.7(a). This information is graphed in figure 12.7(b). Evaluation of the graphed information indicates that all products (100, 105, and 107) are following a seasonal pattern with a slight upward trend.

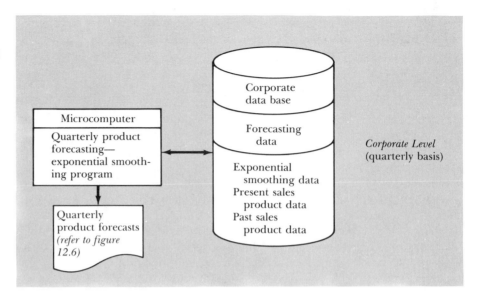

FIGURE 12.5
Quarterly product
forecasting for an MIS
marketing subsystem.

SALES FORECASTING TO ECONOMIC ORDERING.   Although it may appear that analysis ends with a forecasted product printout and on-line storage of data, actually the forecasting program is just the first of a series of on-line processing operations. Output of quarterly product forecasting–exponential smoothing program is input for the finished goods–production schedule program, which determines the number of finished products to manufacture after accounting for goods on hand and on order. This output becomes input for the linear programming program used to determine what quantities of each product should be made at which plants. It should be noted that each plant can make all products. Based on this allocation of finished products by plants, the next program—materials planning by periods—"explodes" bills of materials for the finished product's component parts and determines to what planning periods the component parts apply in order to have them available at the proper times for manufacturing operations. The program on the next level—materials availability and EOQ (economic order quantity)—evaluates the component parts in terms of requirements by planning periods after considering what is on hand and on order. Generally, it will be necessary to buy large quantities of raw materials and parts from the outside as well as to place production orders for parts to be manufactured. To keep inventory costs at a minimum, orders from within and outside the corporation are made as cost-effective as possible by using EOQ formulas. Manufacturing orders are scheduled daily by plants using a production scheduling–linear programming program. Thus, the micro sales forecasting program triggers a whole series of programs that form the basis for daily manufacturing operations and buying from outside vendors. This interaction of programs will be continued in the chapter on the manufacturing subsystem (chapter 13).

Basic Product Group	Product Number	Quarterly Forecast (Units)	Units by Basic Product Group
1	100	20,100	
	105	30,100	
	107	32,500	
	109	129,600	
	111	135,000	
	112	144,000	
			491,300
2	200	20,600	
	210	30,800	
	215	27,500	
	217	130,700	
	218	135,200	
	219	141,100	
			485,900
3	300	25,300	
	304	27,800	
	309	31,100	
	310	132,600	
	312	137,900	
	313	147,200	
			501,900
4	400	26,600	
	406	27,900	
	407	32,000	
	410	129,600	
	412	137,400	
	414	146,200	
			499,700
5	500	31,700	
	505	26,400	
	510	31,800	
	511	126,400	
	512	136,700	
	513	149,100	
			502,100
	Total quarterly forecast (units)		2,480,900

FIGURE 12.6
Output from the quarterly product forecasting—exponential smoothing program.

461

Product Forecast Information

Product Number 100		Product Number 105		Product Number 107	
Past Year's Sales & 1st Qtr.'s Forecast		Past Year's Sales & 1st Qtr.'s Forecast		Past Year's Sales & 1st Qtr.'s Forecast	
1st Qtr.	19,850	1st Qtr.	24,900	1st Qtr.	33,000
2nd Qtr.	27,500	2nd Qtr.	35,200	2nd Qtr.	36,000
3rd Qtr.	22,000	3rd Qtr.	22,500	3rd Qtr.	29,500
4th Qtr.	29,400	4th Qtr.	33,000	4th Qtr.	41,000
1st Qtr.	20,100	1st Qtr.	30,100	1st Qtr.	32,500

(a)

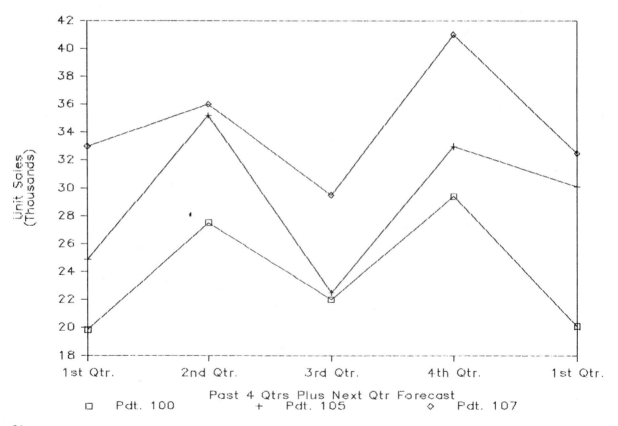

(b)

FIGURE 12.7   Sales forecasting using Lotus 1-2-3 for five quarters: (a) product forecast information for products 100, 105, and 107 (refer to figure 12.6), and (b) graph of this information.

Throughout the development, introduction, and life of a product, a corporation's marketing managers face many decisions that require accurate market assessments. Frequently, substantial resources are committed for research and development, test marketing, and other related costs prior to the critical "go or no-go" decision. If the conclusion is to market the product, the marketing executive must decide on the amount of promotional expenditures, where to allocate these expenditures among different media, when to allocate over a period of time, the amount of sales effort to be invested, and the duration of any special support for the product.

A chain reaction of other important decisions is initiated in other areas of the corporation, such as production and purchasing, because operations are geared to adjust to the new requirements. There may also be a substantial impact on research and development activities, because the potential success or failure of a new product could greatly affect the development of similar or complementary products. In this regard, the success, or even survival, of the corporation depends on the ability of the corporation's executives to anticipate the future (or at least to anticipate it better than the corporation's competitors do).

Venture Analysis

Because of the complexity of the phenomena to be predicted, the need for greater accuracy, and the dependency of outcomes on so many different variables, marketing management of the XYZ Corporation has directed that its market research activities at the corporate level utilize venture analysis on the corporate mainframe for new product development only. This approach directs the systems analysts to structure a marketing data base which will be conducive to employing this mathematical technique.

Paramount for venture analysis is the definition and evaluation of the specific variables, assumptions, constraints, and like items to be considered for inclusion in the model. For example, in terms of variables, an itemization of all candidate variables based on the subjective judgments of marketing research and other marketing personnel is necessary. Knowledge of the marketing environment and the relative importance of various factors is imperative. Then a cursory review is made of the sources of needed historical information. It is necessary to build a data base of historical data covering both the XYZ Corporation's new products and all new products introduced in the industry over the past few years for which adequate source data are available. From these data the mathematical relationships subsequently expressed in the model are derived. Thus, considerable pertinent data are needed before a new product can be effectively evaluated.

Essentially, venture analysis measures the relationships among many factors expressed in mathematical terms for the purpose of predicting the future. The underlying rationale is, that if (1) for all new products introduced over a substantial period of time, there is a strong relationship between demand levels and the specific variables considered during the early period of a product's life, and if (2) this relationship persists, the probable market activity for future new products can be estimated from corresponding early-period variables. From these interacting relationships, reliable output can be generated, which includes aggregate demand, levels of demand at various points in time, prices throughout the product's life cycle, upper and lower limits of profits that can be expected over its life, and comparable analysis as programmed into the model.

The new product should be reevaluated periodically in light of new information and current market conditions. The needs of the marketing executive for decision-making purposes—during the critical first year after the product is introduced—include systematic reevaluation and possible revision of initial demand forecasts to reflect current knowledge. These analyses need to be generated at specific intervals after introduction.

Once the foregoing venture analysis program is operational, a market researcher uses a CRT device to call in the program (figure 12.8). The researcher will then supply various estimates as they are called for by the computer, including the estimated size of the target group, recent product trial rates, repeat purchases, the promotional budget, size of the investment, target rate of return, product price, and gross profit margin. The computer will process this information and print out a forecast for the next few years of the total number of customers, corporation market share, price(s), period profits, and discounted cumulative profits. The market researcher can alter various input estimates and readily ascertain the effect of the altered data on sales, costs, and profits, such as those found in figure 12.9 for a proposed new product. Also, the individual can perform the analyses deemed appropriate for the new product under study.

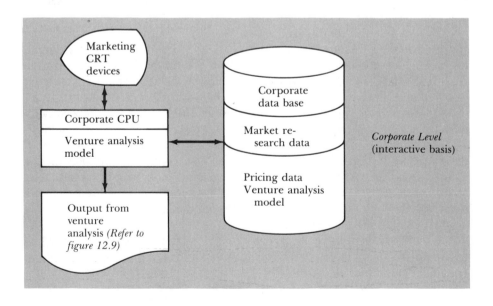

FIGURE 12.8
Market research model—venture analysis—for an MIS marketing subsystem.

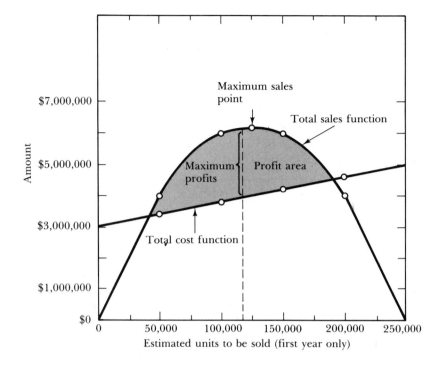

FIGURE 12.9
Estimated sales, costs,
and profits as well as
estimated units to be
sold for a proposed new
product—first year
only.

Product Strategy Analysis

Although a computer mainframe is necessary for venture analysis because of
its complexity, microcomputers are quite useful in other marketing areas. For
product strategy analysis, marketing management of the XYZ Corporation can
create a marketing strategy for next year. As a starting point, there are considerable data to work with: surveys, market tests, and market audits performed by the market research department. But none of them answer the
important questions. What would happen to contribution to fixed costs and
profit if the number of users increased next year for product 407, that is, the
"proportion usage" increased over the current year? Similarly, what would
happen to contribution to fixed costs and profit if the "rate of usage per year
" for the present number of users increased next year over the present year?

To answer these two questions, there is need to analyze the past and
future possible demand for the product and to develop a strategy based on
this analysis. Several reasons and methods exist for analyzing demand. If one
wants to look at cash flow or set inventory levels, one might analyze and forecast various elements of demand—predictable cycles, seasonal fluctuations,
and so forth—and thus come up with a sales forecast. Because a new marketing strategy must be devised, however, one wants to analyze demand in
order to understand *why* a given level of sales took place.

Once the *why* of the demand is understood, strategies are developed to
change certain events and thus increase sales. Most important is the market

465

Part — A

Demand Analysis

Historical Data
---------- ----

Year	Past 4 Years				Current Year
No. of Persons	52,250	53,100	53,246	54,125	55,157
Proportion Buying	63.0%	63.0%	64.0%	64.0%	65.0%
No. of Buyers	32,918	33,453	34,077	34,640	35,852
Rate of Buying/Yr	2.10	1.96	1.95	1.94	1.94
Total Market	69,127	65,568	66,451	67,202	69,553
Unit Price	$10.00	$10.50	$11.00	$11.00	$11.50
Revenue					$799,859
60% Variable Costs					$479,916
Contribution to Fixed Costs and Profit					$319,944

Part — B

Next Year's Strategies

	Increase in Buyers			Increase in Buying		
	#1	#2	#3	#4	#5	#6
No. of Persons	56,510	56,510	56,510	56,510	56,510	56,510
Proportion Buying	67.0%	70.0%	73.0%	65.0%	65.0%	65.0%
No. of Buyers	37,862	39,557	41,252	36,732	36,732	36,732
Rate of Buying/Yr	1.94	1.94	1.94	2.15	2.25	2.35
Total Market	73,452	76,741	80,029	78,973	82,646	86,319
Unit Price	$11.50	$11.50	$11.50	$11.50	$11.50	$11.50
Revenue	$844,695	$882,517	$920,339	$908,186	$950,428	$992,669
60% Variable Costs	$506,817	$529,510	$552,203	$544,912	$570,257	$595,601
Contrib. to Fixed Costs & Profit	$337,878	$353,007	$368,136	$363,275	$380,171	$397,068
Increase in Contrib. from current year	$17,934	$33,063	$48,192	$43,331	$60,227	$77,124
% Increase in Contrib. from current year	5.61%	10.33%	15.06%	13.54%	18.82%	24.11%

FIGURE 12.10 Product strategy analysis for product 407 using Lotus 1-2-3 to determine (a) an increase in buyers and (b) an increase in buyer usage next year under pessimistic, average, and optimistic conditions.

segment of newly formed families who are concerned about using newer electrical appliances. There are two possible strategies for increasing demand: (1) increase the proportion of buyers in this market segment, or (2) increase the usage rate of those who presently buy such a product. In addition, these strategies can be developed under optimistic, average, and pessimistic conditions.

In figure 12.10, Lotus 1-2-3 has been used to analyze the components of the problem in order to answer the preceding "What if?" questions. Historical data on the number of persons, proportion buying, and rate of buying per year are given, along with the unit price and variable costs percentage (60%). Also, the number of buyers is expected to be 56,510. To increase the proportion-using category, say from .65 to .67 under pessimistic conditions (#1 in the illustration), .70 under average conditions (#2 in the illustration), and .73 under optimistic conditions (#3 in the illustration), appropriate calculations are shown in figure 12.10 (a) for contribution to fixed costs and profit, increase in contribution from current year, and percent increase in contribution from current year. An alternative is to accept the .65 proportion and find a way to increase the usage rate, say from 1.94 to 2.15 under pessimistic conditions (#4 in the illustration), 2.25 under average conditions (#5 in the illustration), and 2.35 under optimistic conditions (#6 in the illustration) next year. The results are shown in figure 12.10 (b).

The number of possible strategies is limited only by a manager's creativity. A Lotus 1-2-3 spreadsheet approach stimulates creativity by allowing a manager to spell out alternative strategies and assumptions in a precise form. Each strategy can be translated into an estimated contribution to fixed costs and profit. Based upon the data, the best strategy is an increase in buyer usage under the various market conditions. Alternative #6 gives the greatest return—a 24.11% increase in contribution to fixed costs and profit over the current year for product 407.

ADVERTISING

The selling function by and large focuses on advertising. Selecting the best set of national magazines plus audio and visual media to communicate the corporation's advertising message to present and potential customers is a many-faceted problem. Important variables influencing the media selection process are (1) the availability of time or space in each medium, (2) the advertising budget, (3) exactly what target group the corporation wishes to reach with a given message, (4) the value of each repeat exposure, (5) the quality of the advertising medium, and (6) the discounted cost of running a selected medium. Consequently, it is no simple task to formulate an effective advertising program by identifying the key variables and quantifying the relationship among them.

To solve the advertising media problem, the XYZ Corporation turned to linear programming. The linear programming advertising media model chooses the advertising mix that will maximize the number of effective exposures subject to the following constraints: total advertising budget, specified

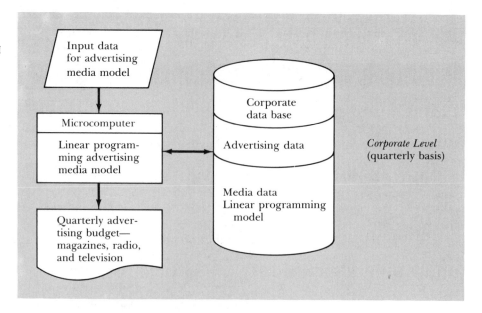

FIGURE 12.11
Advertising media
model—linear
programming—on a
quarterly basis for an
MIS marketing
subsystem.

minimum and maximum usage rates of various media, and specified exposure rates to the different market segments. The flowchart of this advertising approach on a quarterly basis is shown in figure 12.11.

Sales Campaign Modeling

The previous marketing tool examples have focused on Lotus 1-2-3; this time a sales campaign model is set up using IFPS. This model will assist the advertising manager of the XYZ Corporation in determining how levels of advertising affect sales, so that she can time new advertising campaigns to achieve maximum impact. Due to space limitations, only the model is set forth in figure 12.12. In sum, the model selects the variables to be studied, calculates the relationships between the variables, adjusts and refines the formula, selects dimensions for the model and enters assumptions, and enters values for (independent) variables. Finally, at least four sets of campaigns are developed. The sales campaign that gives the XYZ Corporation the best strategy is selected for implementation.

PERSONAL SELLING. In addition to advertising, personal selling is another method of selling the corporation's products. This is particularly true for large direct shipments to customers. The salespersons and their supervisors interact with customers, who respond to the selling effort in a complex and variable manner. This makes it extremely difficult for the company to computerize for effective control, or to run controlled experiments, or to shift salespersons,

Step 1. Select the variables to be studied. The advertising manager initially is interested in two variables: sales and advertising. She wants to be able to predict the future values of sales, the "dependent" variable, by filling in known or projected values for advertising, the "independent" variable.

Step 2. Calculate relationships between the variables. Initially create a "scatter diagram," which plots values for sales against advertising expenditures at random points in time. The program then produces a linear equation that produces a straight line whose coordinates have the least average deviation from the points in the scatter diagram. In addition, the formula is to be checked for accuracy. The scatter diagram reveals too wide a discrepancy between the ideal formula, represented by the line, and the actual numbers, represented by the scatter diagram. This means that other independent variables affecting sales must be taken into account.

Step 3. Adjust and refine the formula. The advertising manager enters housing starts as a third variable in the equation. She performs a multiple regression to determine how the two independent variables, housing starts and advertising, affect the dependent variable, sales. Essentially, the program does a series of "loops" in which it tries different numbers until it comes up with a workable three-variable equation.

Step 4. Select dimensions for the model. A dimension is any characteristic that can be used to limit or define the values for variables in a model. She decides to do a sales forecast for the next twelve months (time dimension) for a specific product (product dimension) for the western sales region (geographic dimension) for new houses costing $85,000 to $150,000 (customer income level dimension). In addition, assumptions are entered. Assumptions are facts that bear directly on the model. Some assumptions—for example, the retail price of a specific product—need periodic updates.

Step 5. Enter values for independent variables. The analyst uses a standard formula for forecasting housing start fluctuations for the next twelve months. She runs at least four iterations of the model, each a different way to distribute the advertising budget over the next four quarters. The results are then presented. The program lines up all four sets of results so that she can compare them and decide which strategy will be most effective.

FIGURE 12.12
Five steps for developing a sales campaign model.

except on a slow, evolutionary basis. As a result, using a computer-based mathematical approach to simulate changes that may or may not result in a more effective sales strategy can be both risky and expensive. For best results, selling-strategy decisions should be made within the constraints of the present organization and with changes in organizational resources taking place over time.

SALES ORDER PROCESSING

Customer sales orders presently arrive via mail, telephone, and Teletype or are hand-carried by salespersons to the three manufacturing plants. These preliminary activities are illustrated in figure 12.13. Before order processing can

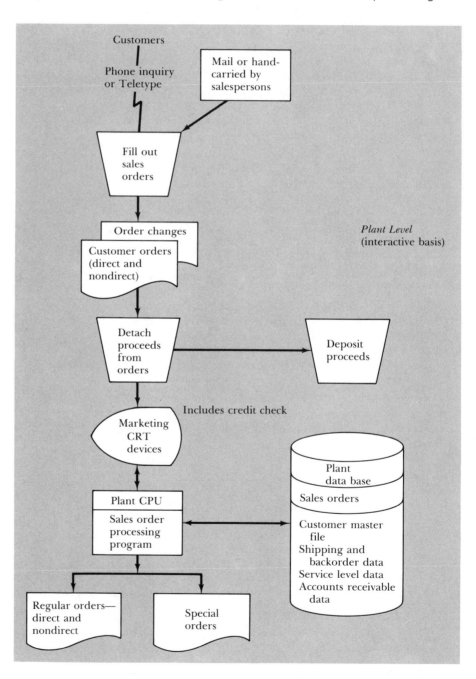

FIGURE 12.13
Sales order processing for an MIS marketing subsystem.

begin, a credit check of the customer's order must be undertaken by the credit section of the accounting department.

CRT Display of Data Entry

Once the customer's credit is approved, the order processing clerk uses a CRT terminal to enter the customer's number unless it is a new customer. In this case, the customer's name, address, and other information are entered. If the customer number is unknown for an established customer, the name is entered and the system displays a list of "sound-alike" customers from which a selection is made. The system them displays successive requests for the entry of the data pertaining to the order, as illustrated in figure 12.14. Flashed on the CRT screen are a series of questions pertaining to the following: (1) customer order number (the customer's purchase order), (2) "ship to" number and address, (3) date of order, (4) mail, phone or Teletype, (5) tax code (the customer's tax type), (6) salesperson number, (7) catalog number and number of items ordered of each product, and (8) job control number. Each keyed-in answer appears on the screen next to the question. The questions continue until the operator enters a Y for "end of order." At that point, the computer summarizes each series of answers and "plays back" the information for visual review. There is only one edit check for each item on order, and the operator verifies that an entry is correct by keying in OK (okay) or NG (no good). After an NG, the operator redisplays the particular item in question and enters changes. An editing program checks the answers against pre-established facts, and question marks flash on the screen when the program finds an answer unacceptable. For instance, if the operator fails to include the number of items ordered, the problem will flash a question mark. Or if the number of items ordered is present but the catalog number is not, another question mark will remind the operator that this information is missing.

When all questions on an order have been answered, the interactive sales order processing program accumulates finished goods requirements of the order for sales analysis and finished goods inventory. Finished goods items are not deducted from their on-line balances at this time, but are deducted by a finished goods updating program later. Awaiting shipment, finished goods amounts along with their order numbers are stored on-line. The rationale for this approach is twofold. First, because there are discrepancies between what is physically on hand and the perpetual inventory on the plant data base, the corporation has found that it is better not to deduct amounts that could result in misleading balances on-line. Second, at the end of the day a computer program can be run to trigger all unposted finished goods of the prior day, indicating errors in orders not processed and billed. Thus, the sales order processing program makes a memorandum on the plant data base concerning finished goods, which are checked against the actual items shipped before being deducted from the finished goods quantity.

Although not shown in figure 12.13, at the plant level a customer billing program is run at the end of each day whereby customer invoices are printed and mailed (refer to accounting and finance subsystem in chapter 14). Simi-

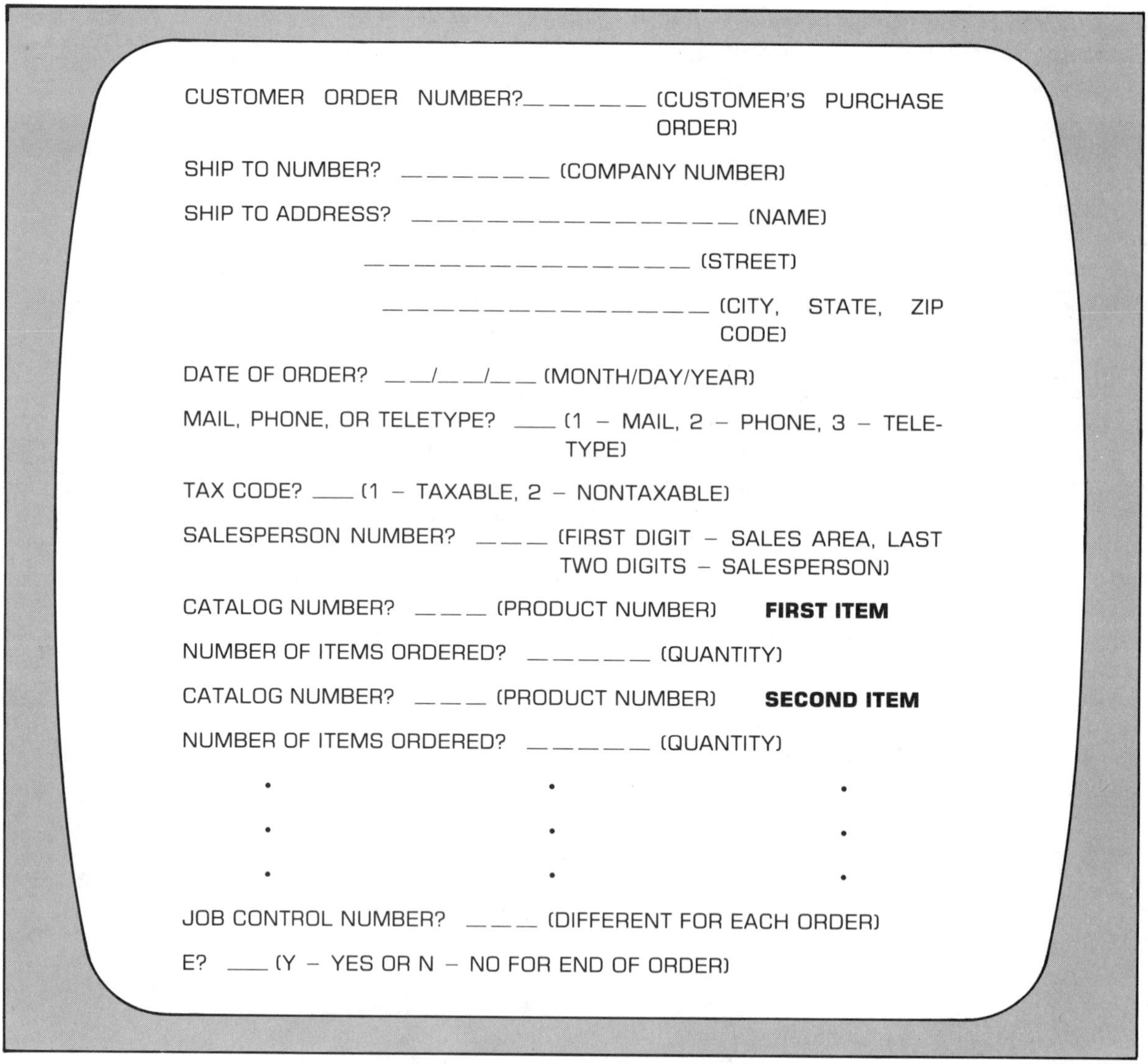

```
CUSTOMER  ORDER  NUMBER?_ _ _ _ _ (CUSTOMER'S  PURCHASE
                                   ORDER)

SHIP TO NUMBER?  _ _ _ _ _ _ (COMPANY NUMBER)

SHIP TO ADDRESS?  _ _ _ _ _ _ _ _ _ _ _ _ _ (NAME)

                  _ _ _ _ _ _ _ _ _ _ _ _ (STREET)

                  _ _ _ _ _ _ _ _ _ _ _ (CITY,  STATE,  ZIP
                                         CODE)

DATE OF ORDER?  _ _/_ _/_ _ (MONTH/DAY/YEAR)

MAIL, PHONE, OR TELETYPE?  _ _ (1 – MAIL, 2 – PHONE, 3 – TELE-
                               TYPE)

TAX CODE? _ _ (1 – TAXABLE, 2 – NONTAXABLE)

SALESPERSON NUMBER?  _ _ _ (FIRST DIGIT – SALES AREA, LAST
                           TWO DIGITS – SALESPERSON)

CATALOG NUMBER?  _ _ _ (PRODUCT NUMBER)   **FIRST ITEM**

NUMBER OF ITEMS ORDERED?  _ _ _ _ _ (QUANTITY)

CATALOG NUMBER?  _ _ _ (PRODUCT NUMBER)   **SECOND ITEM**

NUMBER OF ITEMS ORDERED?  _ _ _ _ _ (QUANTITY)

        •                 •                 •

        •                 •                 •

        •                 •                 •

JOB CONTROL NUMBER?  _ _ _ (DIFFERENT FOR EACH ORDER)

E? _ _ (Y – YES OR N – NO FOR END OF ORDER)
```

FIGURE 12.14   CRT display of data entry for sales order processing of customer orders.

larly, a sales register is printed at the end of the customer billing run as a record of daily sales. These summary sales data are forwarded to Cincinnati.

The order operations described above take about 5 to 20 minutes, depending on the complexity of the order, from the time the operator enters the customer order number. By and large, the time in which orders can be pulled after entering them interactively ranges from one to several hours. When these two times are added together, the customer service level is very high, indicating that orders in many cases can be shipped the day they are received. However, owing to unforeseen conditions, it is possible for order service time to be longer.

PHYSICAL DISTRIBUTION

Customer shipments are initiated by physical distribution (PD) at the warehouse and plant levels. Customer shipment orders, including direct shipments, are forwarded from sales order processing to physical distribution. Goods are then packed at the warehouse and plant levels for shipment to customers or warehouses. All shipment orders provide sufficient information for billing the customer and making the proper adjustments to inventory. This information is utilized for calculating finished goods inventory.

Direct shipments to customers present no real problem to physical distribution management just because the warehousing function is circumvented (figure 12.15). Basically, the PD clerk interrogates the computer for instant shipping information. Rate, route, and carrier information is available via a CRT terminal. The outgoing traffic clerk selects the appropriate means of

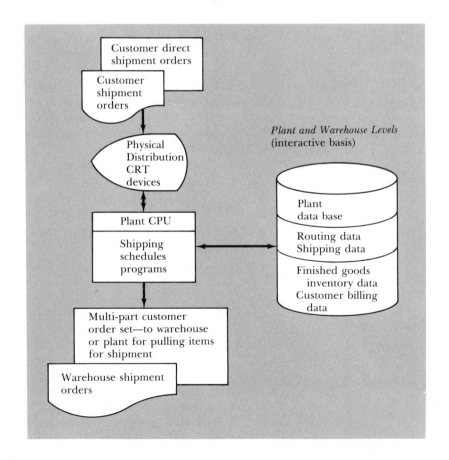

FIGURE 12.15
Shipments at the warehouses and plants for an MIS marketing subsystem.

transportation, which is stored on line for billing the customer later. The customer shipment order is completed with this information, and goods are shipped.

The procedures for customer shipment orders are similar to those for direct shipment orders, except that goods are shipped from an attached warehouse rather than directly from one of the three plants (figure 12.15). All outgoing traffic information is stored on-line for instant retrieval by the PD department via a CRT terminal. The best routing method is selected to keep costs at a minimum. These data are stored on the plant data base—specifically, in the customer billing data file—for subsequent billing.

Finished Goods Inventory Control

The objective of finished goods inventory is to have the right amount of inventory available when required by the customer. Too little finished goods inventory results in poor customer service; too much inventory ties up excess funds, resulting in a lower return on the corporation's total assets. The approach taken below considers these important factors. Customer service and finished goods cost are placed in proper balance for optimizing overall PD objectives.

The finished goods inventory system, depicted in figure 12.16, is interactive for all finished goods inventory transactions. Generally, additions to inventory result from completing production orders at the plant level, having been forwarded from the quality control and inspection department for updating the plant data base. Deductions from the finished goods data base are received via CRT terminals from the plants and warehouses, representing shipments to customers. These data plus the customer master file are utilized by the accounting subsystem for customer billing. In addition to introducing plus and minus values at the plant and warehouse levels, adjustments can be made to correct shipments, inventory, and other errors that have come to the attention of operating management. Thus, an interactive approach to finished goods keeps the plant data base up to date at all times.

Two important finished goods reports are prepared for controlling this large financial investment at the plant level. First, finished goods that are out of stock are reported immediately to physical distribution, inventory, and manufacturing management. Management may find it necessary to issue a production order if goods of this type are not on order. Second, items that must be backordered are reviewed by physical distribution management, who determine whether to fill the orders soon or cancel the orders. Hence, items that cannot be shipped are reviewed for their proper disposition.

In addition to the foregoing output, each of the three warehouses forwards summary finished goods inventory information to corporate headquarters in Cincinnati. Using a microcomputer, these data are used to prepare weekly finished goods reports which represent goods available for sale—illustrated in figure 12.17. These data are summarized monthly and provide the accounting subsystem with information for preparing monthly financial statements (figure 12.16). Also, these reports serve as an audit trail for internal and external auditors.

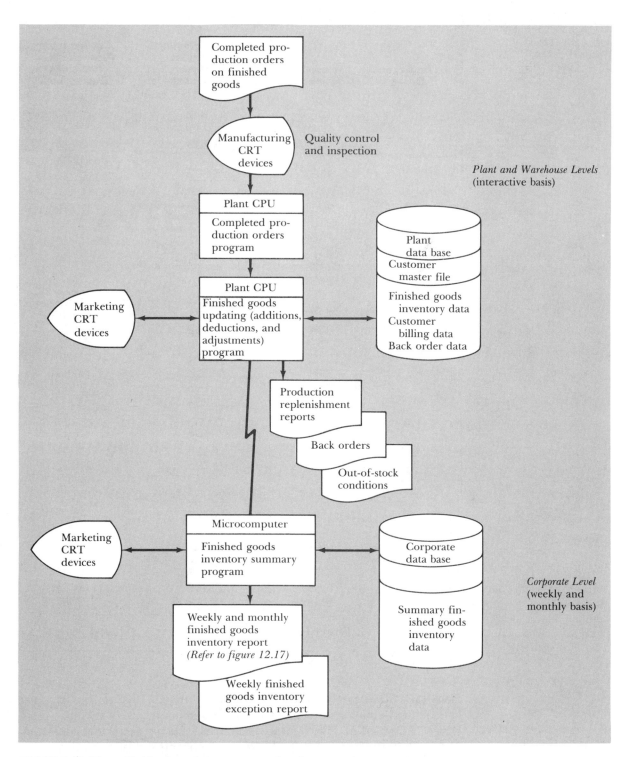

FIGURE 12.16 Finished goods inventory at the plant, warehouse, and corporate levels for an MIS marketing subsystem.

475

Basic Product Group	Product Number	Current Weekly Inventory at the Three Warehouses	Change from Prior Week— Additions (Deductions)
1	100	5,202	407
	105	6,107	(512)
	107	4,251	359
	109	6,206	372
	111	7,851	(428)
	112	8,202	601
		37,819	799
2	200	5,192	(172)
	210	4,617	312
	215	5,261	(162)
	217	6,514	412
	218	6,717	(125)
	219	8,215	1,725
		36,516	1,990
3	300	4,371	(279)
	304	5,092	(315)
	309	5,415	(210)
	310	5,371	(275)
	312	7,292	675
	313	8,165	2,212
		35,706	1,808
4	400	3,690	(192)
	406	3,785	175
	407	4,125	300
	410	3,785	(143)
	412	7,592	(412)
	414	8,057	(505)
		31,034	(777)
5	500	4,655	(212)
	505	3,575	(219)
	510	4,712	(451)
	511	3,697	(100)
	512	6,845	742
	513	9,212	1,202
		32,696	962
	Grand Totals	173,771	4,782

FIGURE 12.17
Weekly finished goods inventory report prepared for evaluation by sales management at the corporate level.

FINISHED GOODS INVENTORY EXCEPTION REPORTING. To assist marketing in determining how effective its finished goods inventory policies are, a weekly finished goods inventory exception report is micro prepared at the corporate level (figure 12.16). This report highlights out-of-stock conditions; on the other hand, overstocked goods are also starred for action by management. With such an exception report, marketing management can start corrective action, such as special sales promotions. Likewise, this weekly report can be reviewed to ensure that neither too little nor too much capital is tied up in finished goods inventory. This review is intended to ensure that customer service and the finished goods inventory are properly balanced. These reports and others, then, are designed to maximize the corporation's investment in finished goods in order to meet overall marketing goals and objectives.

Summary—MIS Marketing Subsystem

Sales forecasting is concerned with predicting what products are expected to be purchased by the corporation's customers. In turn, these forecasts provide a basis for what finished goods should be produced for the coming quarter.

Market research centers on what new products should be brought to the marketplace by the corporation. The success of the corporation depends on the ability of marketing management to anticipate the future or at least to anticipate it with new products better than the competition does.

Advertising is the major activity of the corporation's selling function. It involves selecting the best set of national magazines plus audio and visual media to communicate its advertising message to present and potential customers.

Sales order processing centers on activities necessary to get the corporation's products to its customers. Accent is on a very high level of customer service, that is, orders shipped the day that they are received.

Physical distribution focuses on the gathering and packaging of merchandise within a plant for direct shipment or within the warehouse for nondirect shipments, and concludes with the shipment of goods to the customer. Throughout the movement process, finished goods inventory is accounted for and reported on periodically.

EFFECTIVE MIS PRACTICE—UNDERLYING FRAMEWORK FOR FINISHED GOODS INVENTORY

Finished goods inventory for the XYZ Corporation acts as a buffer between customer demand and production of procurement cycles, allows for longer production runs and minimum setup expense, and provides for steady production and a stable work force. Marketing management cooperates with manufacturing management in establishing inventory levels and is responsible for managing finished goods inventory.

Without the proper management of inventory, physical distribution is merely the operation of the warehousing and transportation elements of the business. Management of these elements alone cannot provide good customer service at a minimum cost to the corporation. Finished goods inventory must be managed in full consideration of the other elements of physical distribution, namely:

477

□ *priorities—the "20–80" rule*—the value of the item to be maintained in inventory has to be considered. High-value items must be controlled more rigorously than low-value items.

□ *in-stock service levels*—the ability to supply items needed by customers is determined by these levels. They are measured by the percent of items, or units, available to fill outstanding orders at any moment of time.

□ *speed of delivery*—this factor measures the ability to get the product to the customer when the customer needs it. Some customers require very rapid service; others allow a longer lead time.

□ *penalty of being out of stock*—if items are not available when a customer orders them, the corporation pays a real or potential penalty through customer dissatisfaction or through reduced profits from either lost sales or the loss of a customer.

□ *replenishment lead time*—this is the time required to replenish an inventory. It varies by product line, time of year, availability of raw materials, and plant capacity.

□ *production or procurement lot size*—economic lot sizes must be considered in determining proper inventory levels. Unit costs generally decrease as the amount produced or procured increases. However, these advantages must be balanced against the corresponding increases in inventory costs resulting from higher inventory levels.

□ *seasonality*—seasonal variations in demand must be taken into account and anticipated if customers are to be properly supplied.

Although not set forth per se in the prior section on physical distribution, these elements are the underlying framework for finished goods inventory. From an overall viewpoint, effective control over finished goods inventory requires that marketing management along with manufacturing management incorporate the impact of these elements in their decision making. Because the elements are interacting with changing external and internal environmental factors, management must constantly evaluate them as they affect the flow of finished goods. In this way, management will be able to provide effective control over finished goods inventory.

CHAPTER SUMMARY

The marketing subsystem of the XYZ Corporation is the originator of sales order activities because it is the liaison between the corporation and its customers' needs. In the MIS subsystem at the corporate level, sales forecasting uses exponential smoothing formulas that combine past and current information in an objective manner, thereby providing a quantitative means to assist in making judgments about future sales levels to meet customer needs. Quarterly forecasts "make things happen" within the corporation by triggering inputs to many of the other subsystems. In a similar manner, at the plant level, the customer order initiates action within and outside the marketing subsystem. Whether goods are produced based on a quarterly forecast or on special order, a prime concern of the marketing subsystem is fast and reliable customer service.

An effective MIS marketing subsystem goes beyond providing interactive responses to sales forecasting, market research, advertising, sales order processing, and physical distribution. Marketing managers at the corporate level can retrieve current data in the data base and combine them with appropriate mathematical techniques for evaluating new products over their life cycles, determining appropriate prices, selecting the best advertising medium in terms of exposures and constraints, and utilizing comparable information. In essence, important marketing information is retrievable as needed. This forward-looking approach enables marketing management and their staff to make timely decisions for answering routine as well as ad hoc "What if?" questions.

QUESTIONS

1. Of the marketing considerations set forth in the chapter, which are most important from:
   a. a customer's point of view?
   b. a manager's point of view?
2. How can top management of the XYZ Corporation utilize the PIMS data base to improve its marketing operations? Discuss.
3. In terms of the functional areas presented in the chapter for marketing, where can problem finding be most effectively applied to improve the XYZ Corporation's profitability?
4. Suggest additional mathematical models not set forth in the chapter that can be used in an effective MIS marketing subsystem.
5. Can the market research group of the XYZ Corporation utilize present market research software packages? If so, how?
6. If all order processing were handled at the corporate level rather than at the plant level, would the marketing subsystem be more effective or less effective than that demonstrated in the chapter? Give reasons to support your answer.
7. Define in some detail the major parts of the MIS sales order processing computer program at the plant level.
8. Suggest an alternative method for forecasting the corporation's sales each quarter.
9. What is the rationale for placing finished goods inventory with the marketing subsystem rather than with the manufacturing subsystem?
10. Suggest an alternative method for effective allocation of the advertising budget.
11. What is the key to making a management information system responsive in supporting marketing decisions in the areas of planning and control?

PROBLEMS

12. Regarding *in-stock service levels,* the statement was made that the proper in-stock conditions depend on customer needs. Their needs must be forecasted and production must be planned to maintain the proper levels of inventories for satisfying

479

customer demand. Of great importance is the use of the 20–80 rule where relatively few items (20 percent) represent the bulk of total sales (80 percent). Suppose the XYZ Corporation did not fit these conditions and all inventory sold equally well in terms of total dollar amounts. How then should management control inventories? State what approach could be used within an effective MIS environment.

13. In the chapter, the marketing subsystem sections of sales forecasting, market research, advertising, sales order processing, and physical distribution for the XYZ Corporation were presented in an MIS operating mode. What other sections could have been illustrated for marketing? Likewise, what modules from the other functional areas could have been included in the marketing subsystem? In both cases, state what modifications would be needed to assure that these functional parts work together as an integrated whole for the corporation.

14. The MIS marketing subsystem, like the other subsystems for the XYZ Corporation, is operating in a distributed data processing system environment. If the corporation desires to change either the forecasting module or market research module to a decision support system operating mode, what changes should be made to the present MIS approach? In addition, what benefits could accrue to the corporation if either module is changed to a DSS operating environment?

PROJECTS

15. The market research department of the XYZ Corporation utilizes venture analysis to predict the success of products before they are developed. The present value of the profit over the life cycle of a certain product is estimated to be $4 million. There is, of course, a risk that profits in the later years of the life cycle will not materialize. The indicator of success in reaching desired profit levels over the life cycle of the product is believed to be only about 60 percent reliable (based upon past experience). What is the usefulness of this probabilistic information? What can be done to the given information to make it useful to marketing management in determining whether or not the product should be placed into production? Include in your answer the use of the time value of money.

16. In the section on advertising, change the system for the XYZ Corporation such that the advertising message can be more responsive to current times. Consider the merger of the internal environmental factors with the external ones so that marketing management can practice "management by perception" versus just "management by exception." Also, consider the use of mathematical models. Think in terms of how well the advertising messages communicate to the intended audience so that they can be measured and controlled effectively by marketing management. Lastly, consider the need to coordinate the selling prices with advertising strategies to achieve desired profit levels. Use either a system flowchart or a data flow diagram to show the appropriate changes.

17. Although a section on warehousing was not included in the chapter, develop a warehousing system for the XYZ Corporation that could be made to qualify this area as part of an effective management information system. When developing recommendations, there should be consideration for the fact that the warehousing system may not be the ultimate one, but rather one that will be changing over time. It is suggested that an automatic warehousing system be employed to provide fast customer service. If applicable, the utilization of mathematical models should be included. The final warehousing system should be integrated with other

parts of the marketing subsystem, in particular, transportation and finished goods inventory. Use one or more system flowcharts or data flow diagrams as a way of showing the data flow of the warehousing system.

LOTUS 1-2-3 EXERCISES AND PROGRAMS

18. As illustrated in the chapter, the output from the quarterly product forecasting–exponential smoothing program of figure 12.5 for the XYZ Corporation was used as input for the product forecast information of figure 12.6. That is, the current forecasts for products 100, 105, and 107 were related to the prior four quarter forecasts and plotted. Using this as a model, develop a comparable analysis for products 109, 111, and 112 by producing a product forecast information listing and graph. Past and current forecasted data to produce this output are as follows:

Product No. 109	Product No. 111	Product No. 112
First Qtr.—127,200	134,100	142,400
Second Qtr.—132,000	136,000	155,000
Third Qtr.—124,600	132,800	140,700
Fourth Qtr.—138,000	142,000	161,000
First Qtr.—129,600	135,000	144,000

The program to produce the desired output is provided on the Lotus 1-2-3 diskette and is shown later in this section.

19. In the chapter, the output from the quarterly product forecasting–exponential smoothing program is found in figure 12.5 for all five basic product groups of the XYZ Corporation. Taking the information for the first three products—500, 505, and 510—of the basic product group 5, develop a product forecast information listing and graph that is comparable to that found in figure 12.6. Past and current forecasted data to produce this output are as follows:

Product No. 500	Product No. 505	Product No. 510
First Qtr.—31,200	24,900	29,900
Second Qtr.—22,000	27,500	31,400
Third Qtr.—36,000	28,600	34,200
Fourth Qtr.—33,400	27,100	33,400
First Qtr.—31,700	26,400	31,800

The program to produce the desired output is provided on the Lotus 1-2-3 diskette and is given in this section.

In addition to the above requirement, compare the performance of products 100, 105, and 107 to products 500, 505, and 510. Are the forecasts more erratic or stable when comparing one group against another? What may have caused their performance to be different or similar?

20. In the chapter, the output from the quarterly product forecasting–exponential smoothing program is found in figure 12.5 for all five basic product groups of the XYZ Corporation. Taking the information for the first three basic product groups, develop a product forecasting listing and graph comparable to that found in figure 12.6. Past and current forecasted data to produce this output are as follows:

First Basic Product Group	Second Basic Product Group	Third Basic Product Group
First Qtr.—485,600	481,300	491,900
Second Qtr.—465,400	475,100	485,800
Third Qtr.—508,600	503,900	515,600
Fourth Qtr.—498,100	500,200	510,400
First Qtr.—491,300	485,900	501,900

The program to produce the desired output is provided on the Lotus 1-2–3 diskette and is given later in this section. Which of the three basic product groups is more erratic in its movement, or are they all about the same?

21. In the chapter, a method was demonstrated in figure 12.10 for determining which strategy was better for promoting a product—increasing the number of users for the product or increasing the usage rate for the product. An examination of the final values for increase in users (#1 through #3) and increase in usage (#4 through #6) indicates that strategy #6 (under good economic conditions) is the best solution. Suppose the proportion usage rate of .65 was changed to .63 for #4 through #6, would the best solution still be #6 if all other factors remained the same? In a similar manner, suppose the rate of usage per year for alternatives #1 through #3 changed from 1.94 to 2.00 and all other factors remained the same, would the best solution still be #6? Since these questions represent sensitivity analysis, suggest other forms of sensitivity analysis in this problem. Optional: undertake these sensitivity analyses. To perform sensitivity analysis, use the program provided on the Lotus 1-2-3 diskette or as shown later in this section.

22. As shown in the chapter, the XYZ Corporation has two possible strategies for its 30 product line. It can increase the number of users for each of its products or it can increase the usage rate for its products. Using product 300 as an example that will be promoted quite extensively in the coming year, develop a comparable analysis to figure 12.10 whose forecast for the coming quarter is 25,300 units (refer to figure 12.6). The yearly forecast is approximately 100,000 units. Historical data for product 300 are as follows:

Past Year	Number of Persons Always Buying Product	Proportion Buying	Rate of Buying Per Year	Unit Price
First (oldest)	62,000	.631	2.00	$8.75
Second	62,500	.640	1.96	8.85
Third	63,400	.638	2.01	9.10
Fourth	67,000	.641	1.99	9.25
Fifth (current)	69,200	.642	2.03	9.50

Also, the number of buyers is expected to be 72,000.

When reference is made to an increase in the number of users, three proportion usage rates are estimated to be .650 (under poor economic conditions), .680 (under average economic conditions), and .710 (under good economic conditions). The rate of usage per year will be the same as the latest year, i.e., 2.03. In contrast, when reference is made to an increase in usage, three rates of usage per year are estimated to be 2.05 (under poor economic conditions), 2.07 (under average economic conditions), and 2.10 (under good economic conditions). The proportion usage will remain the same as the latest year, i. e., .642. Using the program provided on the Lotus 1-2-3 diskette or as given in the program for this section, determine which approach the marketing department should follow, that is, which of the two basic approaches results in the largest dollar and percent increase in contribution.

LOTUS 1-2-3 PROGRAMS—PRODUCT FORECAST INFORMATION (DATA AND GRAPH) (PROGRAM 6)

```
C1:  '  Product Forecast Information      D10:  '2nd Qtr.
C2:  ' ---------------------------------  E10:  (,0) U 35200
A4:  '   Product Number                   G10:  '2nd Qtr.
D4:  '   Product Number                   H10:  (,0) U 36000
G4:  '   Product Number                   A11:  '3rd Qtr.
A5:  U "100                               B11:  (,0) U 22000
D5:  U "105                               D11:  '3rd Qtr.
G5:  U "107                               E11:  (,0) U 22500
A6:  'Past Year's Sales &                 G11:  '3rd Qtr.
D6:  'Past Year's Sales &                 H11:  (,0) U 29500
G6:  'Past Year's Sales &                 A12:  '4th Qtr.
A7:  '1st Qtr.'s Forecast                 B12:  (,0) U 29400
D7:  '1st Qtr.'s Forecast                 D12:  '4th Qtr.
G7:  '1st Qtr.'s Forecast                 E12:  (,0) U 33000
A9:  '1st Qtr.                            G12:  '4th Qtr.
B9:  (,0) U 19850                         H12:  (,0) U 41000
D9:  '1st Qtr.                            A13:  '1st Qtr.
E9:  (,0) U 24900                         B13:  (,0) U 20100
G9:  '1st Qtr.                            D13:  '1st Qtr.
H9:  (,0) U 33000                         E13:  (,0) U 30100
A10:  '2nd Qtr.                           G13:  '1st Qtr.
B10:  (,0) U 27500                        H13:  (,0) U 32500
```

DEMAND ANALYSIS—(HISTORICAL DATA AND CURRENT STRATEGIES) (PROGRAM 7)

```
A1:  'Part - A                            I12:  (P1) U 0.65
F2:  '      Demand Analysis               A13:  ' No. of Buyers
F3:  '      ---------------               E13:  (,0) (E10)*(E12)
F5:  '      Historical Data               F13:  (,0) (F10)*(F12)
F6:  '      ---------- ----               G13:  (,0) (G10)*(G12)
I7:  "Current                             H13:  (,0) (H10)*(H12)
A8:  'Year                                I13:  (,0) (I10)*(I12)
F8:  '       Past 4 Years                 A15:  'Rate of Buying/Yr
I8:  ^Year                                E15:  (F2) U 2.1
E9:  ' ------------------------------     F15:  (F2) U 1.96
A10:  'No. of Persons                     G15:  (F2) U 1.95
E10:  (,0) U 52250                        H15:  (F2) U 1.94
F10:  (,0) U 53100                        I15:  (F2) U 1.94
G10:  (,0) U 53246                        A16:  ' Total Market
H10:  (,0) U 54125                        E16:  (,0) (E13)*(E15)
I10:  (,0) U 55157                        F16:  (,0) (F13)*(F15)
A12:  'Proportion Buying                  G16:  (,0) (G13)*(G15)
E12:  (P1) U 0.63                         H16:  (,0) (H13)*(H15)
F12:  (P1) U 0.63                         I16:  (,0) (I13)*(I15)
G12:  (P1) U 0.64                         A18:  'Unit Price
H12:  (P1) U 0.64                         E18:  (C2) U 10
```

483

```
F18: (C2) U 10.5                      H55: (F2) U 2.25
G18: (C2) U 11                        I55: (F2) U 2.35
H18: (C2) U 11                        A56: ' Total Market
I18: (C2) U 11.5                      D56: (,0) (D53)*(D55)
A20: 'Revenue                         E56: (,0) (E53)*(E55)
I20: (C0) (I16)*(I18)                 F56: (,0) (F53)*(F55)
A22: (P0) U 0.6                       G56: (,0) (G53)*(G55)
B22: ' Variable Costs                 H56: (,0) (H53)*(H55)
I22: (C0) (I20)*($A$22)               I56: (,0) (I53)*(I55)
A24: 'Contribution to Fixed Costs and Profit   A58: 'Unit Price
I24: (C0) (I20)-(I22)                 D58: (C2) U 11.5
A40: '****************************************   E58: (C2) U 11.5
A42: 'Part - B                        F58: (C2) U 11.5
E43: '        Next Year's Strategies  G58: (C2) U 11.5
E44: '        ---------------------   H58: (C2) U 11.5
D46: '        Increase in Buyers      I58: (C2) U 11.5
G46: '        Increase in Buying      A61: 'Revenue
D47: '        ------------------------   D61: (C0) (D56)*(D58)
G47: '        ------------------------   E61: (C0) (E56)*(E58)
D48: '          #1                    F61: (C0) (F56)*(F58)
E48: '          #2                    G61: (C0) (G56)*(G58)
F48: '          #3                    H61: (C0) (H56)*(H58)
G48: '          #4                    I61: (C0) (I56)*(I58)
H48: '          #5                    A63: (P0) U +A22
I48: '          #6                    B63: ' Variable
D49: '        -----                   B64: ' Costs
E49: '        -----                   D64: (C0) (D61)*($A22)
F49: '        -----                   E64: (C0) (E61)*($A22)
G49: '        -----                   F64: (C0) (F61)*($A22)
H49: '        -----                   G64: (C0) (G61)*($A22)
I49: '        -----                   H64: (C0) (H61)*($A22)
A50: 'No. of Persons                  I64: (C0) (I61)*($A22)
D50: (,0) U 56510                     A66: 'Contrib. to Fixed
E50: (,0) U 56510                     A67: ' Costs & Profit
F50: (,0) U 56510                     D67: (C0) +D61-D64
G50: (,0) U 56510                     E67: (C0) +E61-E64
H50: (,0) U 56510                     F67: (C0) +F61-F64
I50: (,0) U 56510                     G67: (C0) +G61-G64
A52: 'Proportion Buying               H67: (C0) +H61-H64
D52: (P1) U 0.67                      I67: (C0) +I61-I64
E52: (P1) U 0.7                       A69: 'Increase in Contrib.
F52: (P1) U 0.73                      A70: ' from current year
G52: (P1) U 0.65                      D70: (C0) +D67-$I$24
H52: (P1) U 0.65                      E70: (C0) +E67-$I$24
I52: (P1) U 0.65                      F70: (C0) +F67-$I$24
A53: ' No. of Buyers                  G70: (C0) +G67-$I$24
D53: (,0) (D50)*(D52)                 H70: (C0) +H67-$I$24
E53: (,0) (E50)*(E52)                 I70: (C0) +I67-$I$24
F53: (,0) (F50)*(F52)                 A72: '% Increase in Contrib.
G53: (,0) (G50)*(G52)                 A73: ' from current year
H53: (,0) (H50)*(H52)                 D73: (P2) (D70)/($I$24)
I53: (,0) (I50)*(I52)                 E73: (P2) (E70)/($I$24)
A55: 'Rate of Buying/Yr               F73: (P2) (F70)/($I$24)
D55: (F2) U 1.94                      G73: (P2) (G70)/($I$24)
E55: (F2) U 1.94                      H73: (P2) (H70)/($I$24)
F55: (F2) U 1.94                      I73: (P2) (I70)/($I$24)
G55: (F2) U 2.15
```

BIBLIOGRAPHY

Aaker, D. A. "Developing Effective Corporate Consumer Information Programs." *Business Horizons,* January-February 1982.

Abrams, B. "Electronic Shopping Is Called Imminent, But Doubts Persist." *The Wall Street Journal,* June 23, 1983.

Armstrong, J. S. *Long-Range Forecasting, From Crystal Ball to Computer,* sec. ed., New York: John Wiley & Sons, 1985.

Bender, P. S.; Northup, W. D.; and Shapiro, J. F. "Practical Modeling for Resource Management." *Harvard Business Review,* March-April 1981.

Bonoma, T. V. "Making Your Marketing Strategy Work." *Harvard Business Review,* March-April 1984.

———. *The Marketing Edge, Making Strategies Work.* New York: The Free Press, 1986.

Buzzell, R. D. "Is Vertical Integration Profitable?" *Harvard Business Review,* January-February 1983.

Cerullo, M "Computer Control Systems in Organizations." *Data Base,* Summer 1983.

Davis, K. R. "The Process of Problem Finding: A Production-Marketing Example." *Interfaces,* November 1977.

Doyle, S. X., and Shapiro, B. P. "What Counts Most in Motivating Your Sales Force?" *Harvard Business Review,* May-June 1980.

Dubinsky, A. J., and Hansen, R. W. "Managing Sales Force Composition." *MSU Business Topics,* Spring 1981.

Dudek, V. "The Plugged In Marketers at General Foods." *Marketing Communications,* March 1984.

Farris, P. W., and Reibstein, D. J. "How Prices, Ad Expenditures, and Profits Are Linked." *Harvard Business Review,* November-December, 1979.

Fraker, S. "High-Speed Management for the High-Tech Age." *Fortune,* March 5, 1984.

Frisbie, G., and Mabert, V. A. "Crystal Ball Vs. System: The Forecasting Dilemma." *Business Horizons,* September-October 1981.

Gardner, E. S., and Dannenbring, D. G. "Forecasting with Exponential Smoothing: Some Guidelines for Model Selection." *Decision Sciences,* vol. 11, 1980.

Garvin, D. S. "Quality on the Line." *Harvard Business Review,* September-October 1983.

Georgoff, D. M., and Murdick, R. G. "Manager's Guide to Forecasting." *Harvard Business Review,* January-February 1986.

Ghemanat, O. "Sustainable Advantage." *Harvard Business Review,* September-October 1986.

Ginter, J. L.; Cooper, M. C.; Obermiller, C; and Page, T. C., Jr. "The Design of Advertising Expenditures Using Statistical Decision Theory: An Extension." *Journal of Marketing Research,* February 1981.

Gladstone, S. "Vital Statistics." *Business Computer Systems,* May, 1984.

Goslar, M. D. "Capability Criteria for Marketing Decision Support Systems." *Journal of Management Information Systems,* Summer 1986.

Hambrick, D. C.; MacMillan, I. C.; and Day, D. L. "Strategic Attributes and Performance in the BCG Matrix—A PIMS-Based Analysis of Industrial-Product Businesses." *Academy of Management Journal,* September 1982.

Hambrick, D. C., and Schechter, S. M. "Turnaround Strategies for Mature Industrial-Product Business Units." *Academy of Management Journal,* June 1983.

Hayhow, P. P. "Tools for Sales Management." *Business Computer Systems,* April 1983.

Herrmann, J. "Saving Takes the Guesswork Out of Decision Making." *Management Technology,* January 1984.

Hughes, G. D. "Computerized Sales Management." *Harvard Business Review,* March-April 1983.

———. "Electronic Hedge for Marketing Products." *Business Computer Systems,* November 1983.

———. "How to Analyze Sales Performance." *Business Computer Systems,* January 1984.

———. "When Inventory Means Sales." *Business Computer Systems,* July 1984.

Inglesby, T. "Electronic Marketing." *Micro Communications,* September 1984.

Ingram, T. N., and Bellenger, D. N. "Personal and Organizational Variables: Their Relative Effect on Reward Valences of Industrial Salespeople." *Journal of Marketing Research,* May 1983.

Janulaitis, B. V. "Gaining Competitive Advantage." *Infosystems,* October 1984.

King, W. R. *Marketing Management Information Systems.* New York: Van Nostrand Reinhold Company, 1979.

Kingston, P. L. "Generic Decision Support Systems." *Managerial Planning,* March/April 1981.

Kotler, P. "Megamarketing." *Harvard Business Review,* March-April 1986.

Kuczmarski, T. D., and Silver, S. J. "Strategy: The Key to Successful New Product Development." *Management Review,* July 1982.

Lasden, M. "Computer-Aided Decision Making." *Computer Decisions,* November 1982.

Leonard, F. S., and Sassen, W. E. "The Incline of Quality." *Harvard Business Review,* September-October 1982.

Levitt, T. "Marketing Myopia." *Harvard Business Review,* September-October 1975.

Little, J. D. C. "Decision Support Systems for Marketing Managers." *Journal of Marketing,* Summer 1979.

————. "After the Sale is Over. . . ." *Harvard Business Review,* September-October 1983.

Little, J. D. C., and Findley, J. J. "Blueprint for a Revolution." *Marketing Communications,* March 1984.

Little, J. D. C.; Mohan, L; and Hatoun, A. "Yanking Knowledge from the Numbers." *Industrial Marketing,* March 1982.

MacMillan, I. C.; Hambrick, D. C.; and Day, D. L. "The Product Portfolio and Profitability—A PIMS-Based Analysis of Industrial-Product Businesses." *Academy of Management Journal,* December 1982.

Main, J. "Help and Hype in the New-Products Game." *Fortune,* February 7, 1982.

Mayer, M. "Here Comes the Smart Card." *Fortune,* August 8, 1983.

————. "Coming Fast: Services Through the TV Set." *Fortune,* November 18, 1983.

McFarlan, E. W. "Information Technology Changes the Way You Compete." *Harvard Business Review,* May-June 1984.

McLeod, R., Jr., and Rodgers, J. C. "Marketing Information Systems in the Fortune 500." *California Management Review,* vol. 25, no. 1, 1980.

————. "Marketing Information Systems: Their Current Status in Fortune 1000 Companies." *Journal of Management Information Systems,* Spring 1985.

Monk, J. T., and Landis, K. M. "Making a Computer Part of the Sales Staff." *Business Computer Systems,* January 1984.

Munro, M. C., and Wheeler, B. R. "Planning Critical Success Factors and Management's Information Requirements." *MIS Quarterly,* December 1980.

Nulty, P. "The Computer Comes to Main Street." *Fortune,* September 6, 1982.

O'Dell, W. F.; Ruppel, A. C.; Trent, R. H.; and Kehoe, W. J. *Marketing Decision Making.* Cincinnati: South-Western Publishing Company, 1982.

Ogilvy, D., and Raphaelson, J. "Research on Advertising Techniques That Work—And Don't Work." *Harvard Business Review,* July-August 1982.

Petre, P. "How to Keep Customers Happy Captives." *Fortune,* September 2, 1985.

Porter, M. E. *Competitive Strategy, Techniques for Analyzing Industries and Competitors.* New York: The Free Press, 1985.

Ramanujan, V., and Venkatraman, N. "An Inventory and Critique of Strategy Research Using the PIMS Database." *Academy of Management Review,* vol. 9, no. 1, 1984.

Ross, E. B. "Making Money with Proactive Pricing." *Harvard Business Review,* November-December 1984.

Seymour, J. "Building a Desktop Modelling/Forecasting System." *Today's Office,* November 1984.

Shanklin, W. L., and Ryans, J. K. "Organizing for High-Tech Marketing." *Harvard Business Review,* November-December 1984.

Shapiro, B. P., and Jackson, B. B. "Rejuvenating the Marketing Mix." *Harvard Business Review,* September-October 1985.

Takeuchi, H., and Nonaka, I. "The New New Product Development Game." *Harvard Business Review,* January-February 1986.

Thierauf, R. J. *Decision Support Systems for Effective Planning and Control—A Case Study Approach.* Englewood Cliffs, NJ: Prentice-Hall, 1982.

Thietart, R. A., and Vivas, R. "An Empirical Investigation of Success Strategies for Businesses Along the Product Life Cycle." *Management Science,* December 1984.

Trigoboff, D. "Banking on Micros for That Competitive Edge." *Micro Manager,* June 1984.

Wheelright, S. C., and Makridakis, S. *Forecasting Methods for Management,* fourth ed. New York: John Wiley & Sons, 1985.

Wood, L. "Directing the Flow of Goods." *Datamation,* September 15, 1984.

CHAPTER 13

Manufacturing Subsystem— XYZ Corporation

ISSUES

How can computer integrated manufacturing (CIM) be applied to the XYZ Corporation?

What are the important considerations when developing an effective MIS manufacturing subsystem?

What are the basic components of an MIS manufacturing subsystem for the XYZ Corporation?

What is the relationship of production planning and control to manufacturing operations for the XYZ Corporation?

What is the relationship of quality control to manufacturing operations?

How important is the human-machine interface in the manufacturing work centers?

INTRODUCTION TO MANUFACTURING

The manufacture of finished goods involves many operations. Initially, the product must be designed by the engineering department. Materials and parts used in its manufacture must be acquired from outside the organization. Not only must plant, equipment, and tools be provided, but also appropriate personnel must be hired and trained to utilize manufacturing facilities. Raw materials and goods in process must be available when needed. Production must be planned, scheduled, and controlled for output that meets quality standards as well as deadlines. An effective manufacturing MIS subsystem, then, must be fully integrated in its own operations and with other functional areas to meet predetermined organization goals and objectives.

Initially, the considerations underpinning an effective MIS manufacturing subsystem are presented in the chapter. Great emphasis is placed on computer integrated manufacturing and value analysis of a product before production. Additionally, a problem-finding approach to manufacturing is highlighted along with a brief discussion of typical mathematical and statistical models and materials requirement planning software. After an overview of the tie-in of marketing with manufacturing, the major components of the MIS manufacturing subsystem are described: (1) engineering, (2) purchasing, (3) production planning and control, (4) raw materials and work-in-process inventories, (5) manufacturing operations, and (6) quality control. Last is a discussion on redesign of manufacturing operations—design to improve productivity and increase worker motivation.

MANUFACTURING CONSIDERATIONS FOR EFFECTIVE MIS

An MIS manufacturing subsystem is generally complex, requiring the use of an integrated approach using computers, that is, computer integrated manufacturing (CIM). Fundamentally, CIM means integrated manufacturing, with the computer performing the integration and with all of the information linkages being effected by computer. Within this broad framework, manufacturing activities must be coordinated with many other areas. This is particularly necessary before actual manufacturing operations can begin. More specifically, engineering must get involved in value analysis, to determine if value is being received for cost incurred. Once the product design has been finalized, purchasing must buy on an optimum basis for keeping the acquisition of materials and services at a minimum cost. In turn, these materials become an integral part of a computerized approach to the manufacturing process. Because of the importance of these topics, they are discussed below.

Building upon these considerations, management needs to look critically within the manufacturing area itself. To produce meaningful managerial and operational information for the proper planning and control of manufacturing operations, a broadened perspective is necessary; that is, the use of problem finding where deemed appropriate. In addition, appropriate mathematical and statistical models—which allow manufacturing management and line personnel to control their activities on a "now" basis—are introduced, along with current materials requirements planning (MRP-II) software. These essential areas are also explored below.

Computer Integrated Manufacturing (CIM)

As a starting point, it is helpful to look at the total framework that underlies all considerations for an effective manufacturing subsystem. This centers on *computer integrated manufacturing,* which is actually a management philosophy as opposed to a turnkey computer product. Currently, that philosophy is crucial to the survival of manufacturers, including the XYZ Corporation, because it provides the levels of planning and control for manufacturing along with the flexibility to change with the times.

The basic objective of CIM is to change management's thinking by establishing a framework within which manufacturing operations are defined, funded, managed, and coordinated. This framework requires specific mechanisms for production planning, cost control, projection selection and justification, project management, and project performance monitoring. The role of the enterprise view of CIM is to ensure the appropriate levels and types of integration. A most important concept in integration is the use of standards: both technical and data. Technical standards are set by and for the whole enterprise. They define what is sometimes called the computer systems architecture. Unlike technical standards, data standards cannot be obtained from a standards committee. They must be defined and maintained by the corporation itself to control software procurement and in-house data base development.

Computer integrated manufacturing is a technique that enables manufacturers to be more competitive. It helps improve productivity without reliance on direct labor of the past. It brings a discipline to manufacturing operations. And it provides management with real-time information that lets one be responsive to current situations. The basic components of CIM are: computer assisted design, product planning, computer assisted manufacturing, manufacturing resource planning, quality control, materials inventory control, cost control, and materials handling, which includes automatic storage and retrieval. Computer integrated manufacturing combines them all so that different solutions can be used for different needs. In addition, CIM currently includes going upstream, not only to product design, but also to process planning—computer aided process planning. It certainly includes computer aided management and management systems themselves, as well as distribution, which is the logistics aspect of getting products to customers. It includes all of the feedback of information, the linkages to the financial system through accounting for accounts receivable and payable. All of these areas fall within computer integrated manufacturing from a very broad perspective. Overall, computer integrated manufacturing is a very broad concept for more effectively managing a manufacturing enterprise. It is a way of operating a manufacturing corporation using a computer integrated business approach. In today's markets, computer integrated manufacturing is generally necessary for a manufacturing business's survival. This includes the XYZ Corporation.

Value Analysis (Value Engineering)

To assist in final product design by engineering, a manufacturer must apply *value engineering,* that is, *value analysis.* This concept requires the engineer to adopt a broader point of view and consider whether the parts contained in the finished product perform their required functions both as efficiently and as inexpensively as possible. The appraisal focuses on the function that the part—or the larger assembly containing the part—performs. To illustrate, the product is dismantled and each part is mounted adjacent to its mating part on a table. The point is to demonstrate visually the functional relationships of the various parts. Each component is studied as it relates to the performance of the complete unit, rather than as an isolated element. A value analysis checklist contains literally hundreds of questions and key ideas for reducing overall costs as well as maintaining the same level of product performance. Typical general questions in a checklist are listed in figure 13.1.

When using value engineering to appraise overall costs, possibilities for making component part design simplifications are frequently more apparent than is possible under the conventional design conditions. This in no way reflects unfavorably on the work done by the design engineer; the discovery of such potential improvements is the result of an analysis with a substantially

FIGURE 13.1
Typical value analysis (value engineering) questions (prepared by the National Association of Purchasing Management).

□ Can the part be eliminated?

□ If the part is not standard, can a standard part be used?

□ If it is a standard part, does it complement the finished product or is it a misfit?

□ Can the weight be reduced with lower priced materials?

□ Are closer tolerances specified than are necessary?

□ Is unnecessary machining performed on the item?

□ Are unnecessary finishes required?

□ Can one produce the part less expensively in the plant or should one buy from the outside?

□ Is the product properly classified for shipping purposes to obtain lowest transportation costs?

□ Can cost of packaging be reduced?

broader orientation than that possessed by the original designer. A value analysis study undertaken by the XYZ Corporation utilizes the background and skills of several people, because it is impossible to find the multiplicity of skills and experiences of that group in the person of a single designer. Resulting design changes often permit the substitution of standardized production operations for more expensive operations requiring special setup work. In other cases, an entirely different material or production process turns out to be more efficient than the one originally specified. In the final analysis, value engineering contributes to the profitability of new products.

Problem-Finding Approach to Manufacturing

The emphasis of a problem-finding approach is to provide manufacturing management with a broad view of production planning and a wide span of control over manufacturing activities. In an environment of rapid change, this is accomplished by forward information integration. External environmental information must be integrated with forecasting information. This, in turn, feeds the material requirements plan, the output of which goes into the purchasing and production planning systems. New data are captured at all points, thereby providing information for inventory and accounts payable. Although much of the thrust for information integration comes from the increased integration required of manufacturing, a larger portion is generated by the need for effective management of the production processes. Better production planning and more effective material acquisition policies demand more accurate and timely information to support their operations. Overall, the integration of information from other related subsystems with the manufacturing subsystem is a must for effective decision making.

For the XYZ Corporation, the preceding integration process starts with the five-year strategic plan. More specifically, in terms of the manufacturing area, it is related to product line planning, facilities planning, and personnel planning as developed by the corporate planning staff for top management. In turn, these manufacturing-oriented long-range plans are translated into medium-range plans and finally into short-range plans as the current-year plans. In effect, the long-term strategic plan that locates future marketing problems and solves them in terms of future opportunities is eventually refined into integrated plans for this year's manufacturing operations. From that view, it is easy to understand why timely planning and control of manufacturing resources through problem finding and the resulting information integration can be a vital factor in the long-term success of the XYZ Corporation.

To assist in the information integration process for effective decision making, the manufacturing subsystem utilizes appropriate mathematical and statistical models (some of which are explored in the next section) that assist in planning and control of its resources. It is a logical approach for overcoming common management control problems encountered in manufacturing operations, such as the misuse of available productive capacity. *Productivity* sometimes is far less than it should be or could be. Techniques to plan and control manufacturing resources are readily available, but only a few organizations have learned to use this combination of mathematical models, computerized systems, and company personnel effectively. Industrial-oriented organizations, such as the XYZ Corporation, have recently implemented these proven techniques. Now they effectively utilize their productive capacity, even in a world of persistent uncertainty and growing complexity.

Mathematical and Statistical Models

Mathematical and statistical models, when used with the corporation's data base or plant's data base, provide an excellent way to plan and control current and future manufacturing activities. For example, an important responsibility of corporate manufacturing management is to determine production loads for each manufacturing plant. From future sales forecasts, management can determine efficient manufacturing schedules. Drawing from the corporate data base via a CRT device, quarterly plant capacities can be incorporated. In a similar manner, variable costs per product group and per individual product can be calculated from the accounting subsystem data base. By utilizing the simplex method of linear programming, optimal manufacturing quotas for the three manufacturing plants can be determined based upon the forecasted period sales.

LINEAR PROGRAMMING (SIMPLEX METHOD). The approach illustrated for determining period production quotas of the XYZ Corporation is the simplex method of linear programming. Variable costs and quarterly plant capacities necessary for this mathematical technique are stored on the data base and are as follows:

Basic Product Groups	1	2	3	4	5	Quarterly Plant Capacity
Plant (Chicago)	$7	$5	$4	$8	$6	900,000 units
Plant (Los Angeles)	5	4	5	4	3	500,000 units
Plant (St. Louis)	5	3	6	5	9	1,200,000 units
						2,600,000 units

The linear programming presentation categorizes products into five basic product groups. However, the better approach is to include all of the cost factors and capacities for each of the corporation's products. In like manner, consideration should be given to the minimum number of products that must be manufactured by each plant in order that finished goods are available when needed at the attached warehouse. This approach would keep overall shipping costs between manufacturing plants and warehouses at a minimum. Although these two factors should be an essential part of the linear programming model, space limitations do not permit their presentation here.

Variations in the above quarterly plant capacities and product costs are due to differences in the number and the speed of machinery, regional wage contracts, and other manufacturing factors. Plant capacities are calculated

Basic Product Groups	1	2	3	4	5	Slack Variables	Plant Capacities
			Quantity Variables				
Plant—Chicago	X_1	X_2	X_3	X_4	X_5	X_{16}	900,000 units
Plant—Los Angeles	X_6	X_7	X_8	X_9	X_{10}	X_{17}	500,000 units
Plant—St. Louis	X_{11}	X_{12}	X_{13}	X_{14}	X_{15}	X_{18}	1,200,000 units
Artificial variables	X_{19}	X_{20}	X_{21}	X_{22}	X_{23}	X_{24}	
Basic product group requirements	400,000	550,000	600,000	400,000	550,000	100,000	2,600,000 units

FIGURE 13.2 Table for developing quantity, slack, and artificial variables in the initial linear programming tableau.

from past data and represent average outputs per machine. The marketing department has forecasted next period's (three months) product group requirements to be:

	Basic product group		
	1	400,000	units
	2	550,000	units
	3	600,000	units
	4	400,000	units
	5	550,000	units
		2,500,000	units

It should be noted that the entire capacity of the three plants (2,600,000 units) is not needed to meet next period's forecasted quotas (2,500,000 units). Thus, there is slack plant capacity of 100,000 units.

In order to express the problem mathematically, we will use a series of Xs to represent the quantities of the basic product groups to be manufactured by each plant. These are set forth as X_1 through X_{15} in figure 13.2. Plant capacities and next period's requirements are shown, as well as the slack column, which represents the 100,000 units of unused capacity. In the final analysis, the optimum solution must satisfy the column requirements and the row requirements per figure 13.2. In addition, slack variables (X_{16} through X_{18}) and artificial variables (X_{19} through X_{23}) are set forth in figure 13.2.

The optimum solution for the values set forth in figure 13.2 are obtained by applying the iterative process of the simplex method. Basically, matrix inversion is employed in determining the quantity variables. Based upon the final simplex tableau, the lowest cost production quotas by manufacturing plants for the next three months can be solved.[1]

Once the master production quotas are established, available personnel estimated, raw materials calculated, and variable costs of manufacturing determined, the job of the manufacturing manager reduces to that of a daily

---

[1]For more information on solving a linear programming problem, refer to: Robert J. Thierauf, Robert C. Klekamp, and Marcia L. Ruwe, *Management Science—A Model Formulation Approach with Computer Applications,* Columbus, OH: Charles E. Merrill Publishing Company, 1985, chapters 2 and 3.

computational procedure utilizing simulation in conjunction with linear programming. Plant manufacturing management accesses this mathematical model via a CRT terminal for printed output. The program is run at the end of the daily shift, because consideration must be given to current production bottlenecks and trouble spots as well as to where plant operations now stand—ahead of or behind schedule. Plant management can obtain the optimum production schedule and routing from the Daily Production Scheduling–Linear Programming program, thereby coordinating this information with their understudies via the plant data base (figure 13.3). Once the plant's production schedule has been set for the next day, the manufacturing work centers can function under the supervision of the production scheduling and control group.

QUALITY CONTROL ($\overline{X}$ CHART). Quality control is used to recognize and remove identifiable causes of defects and variations from set standards. Various techniques can be employed for the systematic observation of quality and the interpretation of the causes of variability. These techniques range from simple visual observations to highly statistical analyses. Inspection can consist of the application of test and measuring devices to compare manufactured parts, work in process, and finished goods with specific standards. Inspection determines whether a given item falls within specified limits of variability and is therefore acceptable. Inspection per se cannot guarantee a high quality product, but it can aid in identifying the causes of defective work.

Generally, quality standards and specifications are determined by engineers in cooperation with the marketing, manufacturing, production control, quality control, and purchasing departments. Although standards define the measurable characteristics of manufactured items, normally they allow permissible variations. These variations are called tolerances. A good set of standards, then, should include accompanying tolerances that are specific, reasonable, understandable, and achievable.

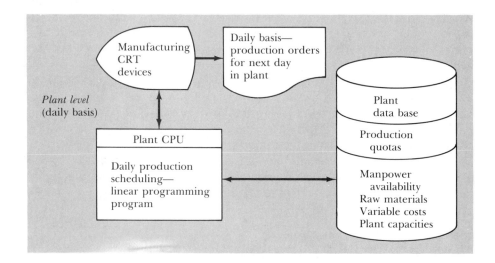

FIGURE 13.3
Daily scheduling of operational flow for each plant in an MIS manufacturing subsystem.

To illustrate the application of quality control that is statistically ori-ented, an $\overline{X}$ chart designed to facilitate the comparison of the average product manufactured to an established quality standard on an hourly basis is set forth in figure 13.4. The product in question is a manufactured part that has a desired diameter of 4.910 inches. On the $\overline{X}$ chart, the permissible tolerance is ± 0.005 (4.905 to 4.910 and 4.910 to 4.915), which represents the statistical control limits. As indicated in the illustration, a sample of the parts is taken every hour. The average of the sample is computed and plotted on the chart. Although the samples taken for the day are within established limits, at times the control limits are exceeded. This can be caused by a worn cutting tool, die, or fixture; by the loosening of a fixture; or by other factors. If some form of corrective action is not undertaken, the diameter of the part will remain out of control and will not meet the predetermined standard.

OTHER MATHEMATICAL AND STATISTICAL MODELS. Various other mathematical techniques are available for planning and controlling manufac-turing operations. Linear programming, queuing theory, and PERT/time are logical candidates. The application of linear programming, as demonstrated earlier, can be used to simplify manufacturing scheduling. The use of *queuing* and *PERT/time* will be illustrated later in the chapter under manufacturing operations.

As with mathematical models, other statistical approaches can be used in manufacturing. Probability theory, in terms of quality control, utilizes past history to determine the acceptance or nonacceptance of completed manu-factured parts and finished products. Also, custom-made statistical models can be developed to assist in sampling products as they come out of the machine shop or the minor or major assembly departments.

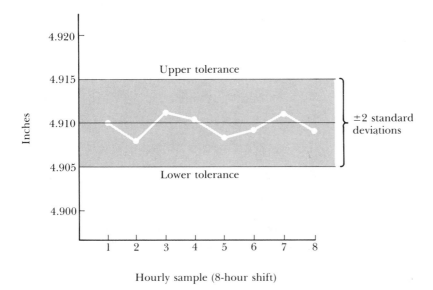

FIGURE 13.4
$\overline{X}$ chart—a statistical approach to quality control.

MRP-II Software

Materials Requirements Planning (MRP) was developed in 1978 by Oliver Wight and Darryl Landvater of Manufacturing Software Systems, Inc. It started with the development of a standard set of tools for manufacturing. It was also a better inventory control system. It became a better scheduling system when the emphasis went from merely ordering to keeping "need" dates valid and material already on order. This, in turn, became the core of what is now called the closed loop MRP system. It consists of these basic functions:

- *Production plans*—establishing the production rate in units, for each family of products.
- *Master production schedules*—breaking these plans into detailed subassemblies, components, and groups of components.
- *Material requirements plans*—using the bills of materials to define the specific components and raw materials that are needed.
- *Capacity requirements planning*—translating material planning into hours by factory work center to determine needed capacity.
- *Input/output reports*—measuring what goes into the shop and what comes out against the capacity plans to see that capacity requirements are being met.
- *Daily shop schedules*—indicating specific items that will be needed to meet the latest schedules.
- *Vendor schedules*—telling the vendors what needs to be delivered and when.

Using this material requirements planning structure as a basis, MRP-II (manufacturing resource planning) builds upon it by taking this expanded manufacturing operating system, which includes all aspects of manufacturing, and expressing it in dollars so that accounting and finance will not have a separate system that never agrees with what is really happening. Accounting and finance can monitor costs of company operations dynamically. As a result, marketing receives valid manufacturing information and is more aware of its impact in developing a valid forecast. In previous scenarios, what was really happening had nothing to do with formal schedules. The accent was on "hot" orders and information systems for getting the job done. In MRP-II, with one set of numbers, there is a combined plan and control system for manufacturing operations.

Currently, a number of software packages are available to implement MRP-II. Due to the shift today to microcomputers, software for these systems along with an illustrated example is set forth below. First, some introductory remarks about minicomputer and mainframe approaches are provided.

MRP-II PACKAGES. Typically, sophisticated manufacturing resource planning (MRP-II) tools require minicomputer or mainframe systems priced from one hundred thousand dollars into the millions. Meanwhile, costs of ongoing maintenance contracts, custom programming, peripherals, and data entry personnel further increase the cost. The cost of vendor support alone for mini-computer MRP-II packages is around forty percent of the software price for the first year or two, and ten percent per year thereafter. The result heretofore has been for most small- and some medium-sized firms to settle for the status quo: manual inventory control, with its reams of slow-moving paperwork, and a certain amount of guesswork in tracking production cycles and gauging final costs. Without the computerized controls required to better manage inventory, work-in-process, and so forth, some small firms cannot grow as fast as they would like; without generating more revenue, however, they cannot readily invest in the very tools that might make the difference.

Fortunately, solutions to this dilemma are increasingly available. Over the past five years, a handful of independent software developers have produced creditable MRP software packages for micros. Samples are listed in figure 13.5. These micro MRP-II software packages and the micro hardware they run on cost approximately 25 to 75 percent less than products at the mini end of the market.

MRP-II APPLICATION.   To illustrate the application of MRP-II, we will look at a small manufacturer who had experienced a number of unpredictable bottlenecks and considerable paperwork. There were no detailed routing slips to describe operational details. Each morning, up to two hours were spent calculating how the machines were tooled and how much each job was costing. Now, although the number of employees has nearly doubled recently, it takes 12 minutes to obtain three times as many financial comparisons on hourly production, downtime, and so forth, using an MRP-II package.

Moreover, large clients expect to know at a glance where their jobs are at any given moment. Before automating, the firm had to tell them to call back later for the information. Now, while the client is on the telephone, the job can be called up by customer name and its status checked by scanning the screen for how many set-up hours the job has so far required, pieces produced per hour, run-time dollars, pieces completed, and remaining production steps. Entering a three-digit customer code is all it takes to call up a record detailing customer name, contact, and other pertinent information. Also, every workstation has a notebook of printout containing current details on materials, fixtures, tooling, and routing slips. In effect, the operators know what to do and where to send parts next, and are taking on a greater share of responsibility.

Vital manufacturing information is obtained primarily from three reports: the daily work center dispatch; another work center report detailing what tasks machine operators performed by the week, day, or month; and a foreman's report describing the jobs coming up on machines within the week. These reports help the company to determine whether the shop is running above or below estimates and also which machines and operators run on time or behind. The MRP-II software package took three weeks to get up and running and fell into place very fast. Payback on the total investment is estimated at 12 to 15 months, and already the bottom line shows improvement.

		Bills of materials	Inventory control	Master schedule	Material requirement plan	Purchasing control	Shop floor control	Financial/accounting	Job costing	Capacity planning	Work-in-process	Order entry	Other
Company	**Product**												
DBSI Information Systems	DBSI Manufacturing Information System	x	x	x	x	x	x	x					x
Driver/Harris Systems	Matrics	x	x	x	x	x	x	x	x	x	x	x	x
Digital Microsystems	Hi-Net/MRP	x	x	x	x	x	x		x				
Bernard Giffler Associates	MR² PS: Material/ Resource Requirement Planning Systems	x	x	x	x	x	x			x			x
Helmsman Systems Inc.	HMRP	x	x	x	x	x	x	x					x
ICS Computers	Control MSG	x	x	x	x	x	x	x	x		x		
Intelligent Controls Inc.	Inman	x	x		x								x
Key Systems Inc.	Profitkey Manufacturing Control Systems	x	x	x	x	x	x	x		x			x
Martek Inc.	AIMS	x	x	x	x	x	x	x	x				x
MCBA	Base MRP			x	x		x						x
McCullough & Associates	MPAC	x	x	x	x	x	x	x	x	x	x		x
Micro Computer Consultants	INMASS	x	x	x	x	x				x		x	x
Micro Manufacturing Systems	MCS3	x	x	x	x	x	x	x	x				x
Micro-MRP Inc.	MAX	x	x	x	x	x	x						x
Pine Instrument Company	PICAM	x	x	x	x	x	x			x	x	x	x
Professional Integration Corp.	MAST	x	x			x	x	x	x				x
Resources for Software Development	PRO:MAN	x	x	x	x	x	x	x	x	x	x	x	x
Safe Computing Limited	Micro-SaFes	x	x	x	x	x	x			x			x
TCS Software	PCS Materials	x	x					x					
Tracline	M/Trac	x	x		x	x		x				x	x

FIGURE 13.5
Typical micro materials resource planning (MRP) software currently available.

The environment in which the manufacturing subsystem operates for the XYZ Corporation is illustrated in figure 13.6. The information flow throughout the system is noted in the illustration. Within this subsystem, management has the ultimate responsibility for coordinating manufacturing activities. However, the production planning and control section is the important coordinator of ongoing manufacturing operations. This group feeds back critical information, based on a programmed response, to plant foremen or to higher levels of manufacturing management as deemed necessary.

Planning of Manufacturing Activities—Quarterly Basis

The corporation's products can be produced in anticipation of demand, upon receipt of customer's orders, or in some combination of the two. If goods are being produced to order, a sales order copy—in many cases—may be the production order (regular or special). The usual arrangement is to have the production planning and control department initiate action on the order, which is then distributed to stock control, shipping, and accounting departments. However, because the bulk of the corporation's products are produced in anticipation of demand, the focus is on planning manufacturing activities on a quarterly basis.

Using MRP-II, the microcomputer procedure for determining next period's sales forecasts (three months hence)—Program A in figure 13.7—after adjusting for finished goods on order and on hand was set forth in the marketing chapter (chapter 12). Although these specific procedures will not be repeated, recall that finished goods production requirements for the next three months provide the necessary input for the manufacturing function—Program B in figure 13.7. A mathematical technique, linear programming, is utilized for determining what quantity of each product will be produced in each of the three manufacturing plants—Program C in figure 13.7.

After period requirement levels of on-line finished goods for each plant have been computed at the corporate level, the next phase is "exploding" bills of materials. The materials planning-by-periods program multiplies the quantity needed of each component times the number of final products that must be manufactured—Program D in figure 13.7. Also, it places the component requirements in the appropriate planning period, because some parts will be needed before others. In this manner, parts and materials are received just in time, that is, just-in-time inventory for production needs.

Continuing in an interactive processing mode, the output for the materials requirements by future planning periods can take two paths. One is the purchasing of raw materials and parts from outside vendors, and the other is the manufacturing of parts within the plant. The outside raw materials provide the basic inputs for manufacturing specific parts used in the assembly of the finished product. Likewise, outside purchased parts are used in the assembly of the final product. Before materials are to be manufactured or purchased, it is necessary to determine if present inventory and materials on order are capa-

499

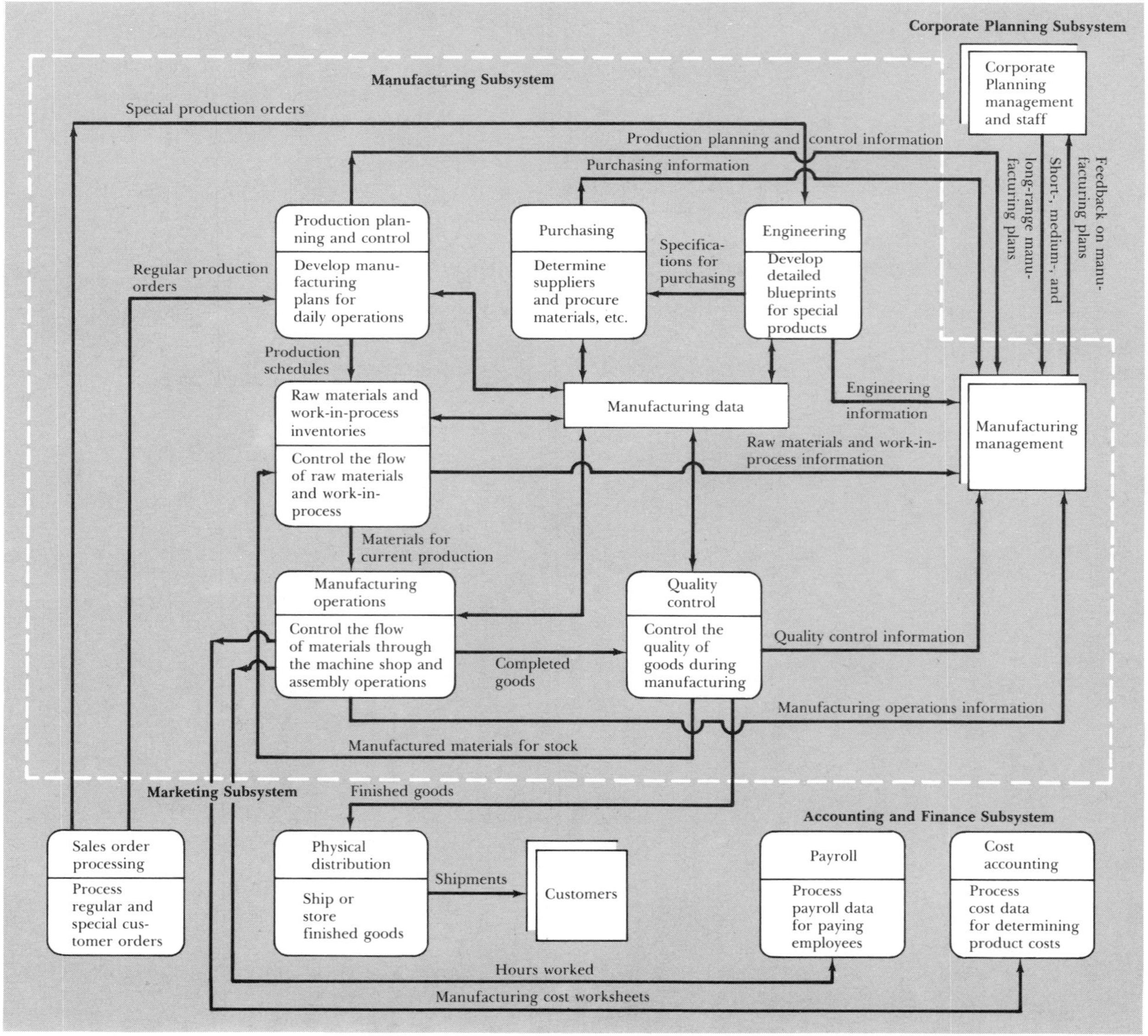

Corporate Planning Subsystem

Corporate Planning management and staff

Feedback on manu-facturing plans

Short-, medium-, and long-range manu-facturing plans

Manufacturing management

Manufacturing Subsystem

Production planning and control information

Purchasing information

Engineering — Develop detailed blueprints for special products

Engineering information

Raw materials and work-in-process information

Purchasing — Determine suppliers and procure materials, etc.

Specifica-tions for purchasing

Manufacturing data

Production plan-ning and control — Develop manu-facturing plans for daily operations

Production schedules

Raw materials and work-in-process inventories — Control the flow of raw materials and work-in-process

Materials for current production

Manufacturing operations — Control the flow of materials through the machine shop and assembly operations

Quality control — Control the quality of goods during manufacturing

Quality control information

Manufacturing operations information

Completed goods

Manufactured materials for stock

Special production orders

Regular production orders

Marketing Subsystem

Physical distribution — Ship or store finished goods

Finished goods

Shipments

Customers

Sales order processing — Process regular and special cus-tomer orders

Accounting and Finance Subsystem

Cost accounting — Process cost data for determining product costs

Payroll — Process payroll data for paying employees

Hours worked

Manufacturing cost worksheets

FIGURE 13.6   Manufacturing data flow diagram—XYZ Corporation

500

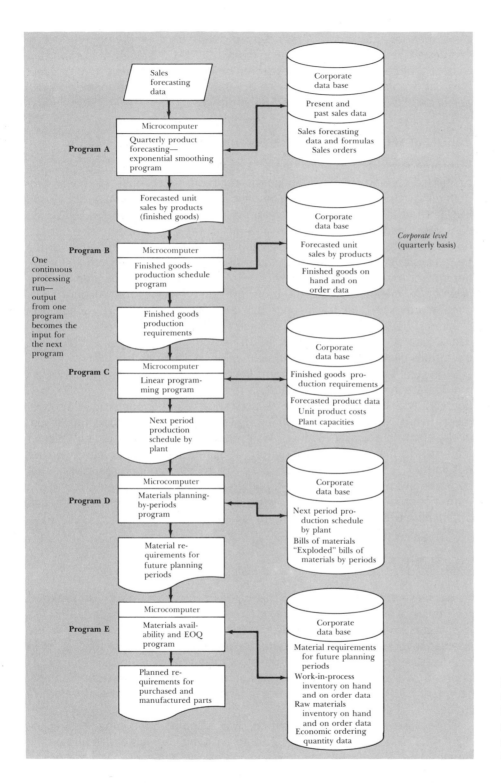

FIGURE 13.7
Quarterly planning as found in an MIS manufacturing subsystem—XYZ Corporation.

ble of meeting the corporation's needs for future planning periods. These procedures are reflected in Program E in figure 13.7. At this point, it is important to note that perpetual inventories stored on line have been adjusted to reflect physical counts in order to produce accurate output for the materials availability and EOQ (economic ordering quantity) program.

Control of Manufacturing Activities—Daily Basis

The foregoing programs—namely, (A) quarterly product forecasting—exponential smoothing, (B) finished goods–production schedule, (C) linear programming, (D) materials planning-by-periods, and (E) materials availability and EOQ (includes price breaks and vendor evaluation)—have been handled by the corporate headquarters computer in a micro interactive operating mode. By no means does the integrated operating mode stop here using MRP-II for the period under study. As shown in figure 13.8, the planned daily requirements, determined by the (F) daily production scheduling–linear programming program for all manufactured plant items, provide the means for scheduling production orders through the manufacturing work centers. Other (G) operational programs that are available to record and control daily activities include attendance, payroll, and work in process. The output of these programs provides operations evaluation reports on manufacturing activities.

In summary, quarterly programs (A) through (E) shown in figure 13.7 do not operate individually, but are integrated with daily operations, as shown in figure 13.8. Sales forecasts serve as input for finished goods product requirements, which, in turn, constitute input for the next period's production schedule by plant. In a similar manner, this output is input for "exploding" bills of materials, forming the basis for material requirements by future planning periods. In turn, this information is employed for manufacturing orders within the corporation's plants and for placing orders with outside suppliers. This input/output approach using MRP-II provides a basis for day-to-day scheduling and dispatching of various manufacturing facilities.

MIS MANUFACTURING SUBSYSTEM

As will be seen in the materials to follow, the manufacturing subsystem allows for the processing of detailed manufacturing data at the plant level because it operates in a distributed data processing mode. At the plant level, where deemed necessary, important data on manufacturing operations are forwarded directly to shop foremen. In this manner, front-line management is apprised of summary results and exception items. Fundamentally, manufacturing information at the plant level is timely due to the system's interactive mode.

Because the central point of the MIS manufacturing subsystem is the plant data base, entries are made at different time intervals depending on the type of data. The manufacturing plants in Chicago, St. Louis, and Los Angeles

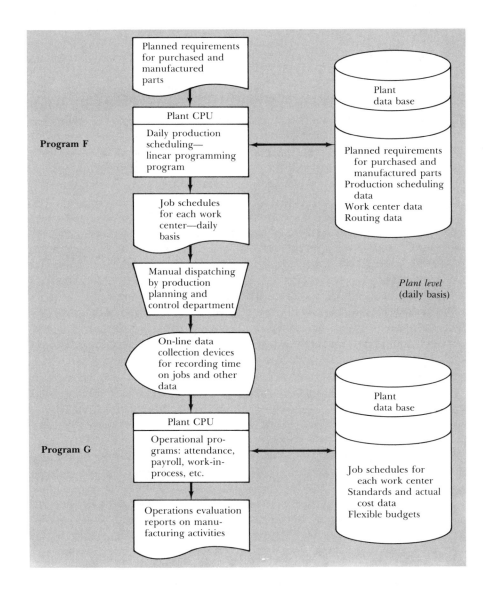

FIGURE 13.8
Daily control of
production activities as
found in an MIS
manufacturing
subsystem—XYZ
Corporation.

send data periodically (perhaps weekly or monthly) to the corporate office, where sort/merge program routines are employed to combine the latest data with past records. At that time cumulative and exception manufacturing reports are produced for corporate management. Periodic summaries and exception reports are reviewed by the plant managers and corporate management to get a firm grasp on past activities. In essence, historical reports are produced in order to review the status of budgets, orders, production, and comparable manufacturing information. Underlying this information flow is the CIM concept and MRP-II.

503

Use of MRP-II to Answer "What if?" Questions

In the previous discussion on planning manufacturing activities on a quarterly basis and control on a daily basis, the accent is on MRP-II. MRP-II makes available purchased and company-manufactured components and subassemblies just before they are needed by the next stage of production or for dispatch. This system enables managers to track orders through the entire manufacturing process and helps purchasing and production control departments to move the right amount of materials at the right time to production–distribution stages. MRP-II requires that a precise demand forecast for each product is available and that every product or subassembly's bill of materials is accurate.

Managers of the XYZ Corporation can calculate the requirements of each part or subassembly week by week and identify in advance possible delays or shortages. People in inventory control can then reschedule the affected release dates for orders to try to meet the promised deliveries. MRP-II requires that every employee—whether operator, analyst, quality inspector, salesperson, purchasing agent, or corporate planning—be thoroughly and strictly disciplined about feeding updates into the system. Without such adherence, the MRP system memory starts accumulating errors with regard to stock on hand, quantities needed, and when items are needed for specific parts or subassemblies. Everyone interacting with the MRP-II system must make all their decisions using system data at every step.

With this foregoing as a background, the MRP-II system is helpful to managers in answering "What if?" questions about customer orders, inventory levels, production orders, and so on. For example, "What is the effect on a customer shipping date if the receipt of certain raw materials and their production is delayed by three days?" or "What happens to the production schedule if work-in-process materials have to be scrapped at a certain stage in the production process?" In other words, the MRP-II is capable of answering specific "What if?" questions. In some cases, this means using sensitivity analysis to see what impact a change of one or more variables has on the final answer. In other cases, the answer may take the shape of either a line-by-line display on a video display terminal or a formal report with graphics incorporated. Thus, the MRP-II system for the XYZ Corporation is quite capable of answering recurring or ad hoc "What if?" questions.

ENGINEERING

Product design centers around the activities of mechanical and electrical engineering. The number of possible combinations for the design of complex parts is quite large. To reduce the complexity, the interaction of the engineer with the computer system is crucial, thereby resulting in a better designed product. Today, this takes the form of a CAD/CAM (Computer Aided Design/Computer Aided Manufacturing), especially for the engineering department of the XYZ Corporation. Fundamentally, CAD centers on computer powered drafting and design; CAM includes automated machine tools and systems that coordinate them. They both speed the development of new products and revision to present products as well as streamline their manufacturing operations.

CAD/CAM Systems

Although CAD and CAM systems both exist independently of each other, they are an integral part of CIM. CAD is to design what word processing is to typing. CAD workstations are linked to the corporate mainframe and automate design work, reduce design time, perform drafting and drafting revisions, and store bills of materials. They employ high-resolution screens that can display intricate graphics in color. These CAD stations feature other special devices, including plotters, light pens, and "mouse" pointing devices, that allow an engineer to "talk" to the computer. CAM, on the other hand, takes numerical data produced by CAD and puts it in a form that can be used by manufacturing. CAM is the electronic embodiment of a production technician and more, in that it includes a wide range of specialized systems, from automated machine tools to shop floor control systems.

When CAD and CAM are integrated within a CIM operating mode, they can share a data base of files containing engineering specifications, part and subassembly numbers, and instructions that enable specifications to be turned into directions for specialized tools. Hence, the CAD/CAM data base is the key element in an integrated manufacturing subsystem. The most important aspect of CAD/CAM is that the corporation's engineers can design and manufacture a product months before competition brings a product to the market. Additionally, CAD saves time by eliminating the need to redraw a product design. When an engineer wants to modify an earlier design, instead of redrawing the original, the individual retrieves it from the CAD system's data base and makes the appropriate changes.

PRODUCT (GRAPHIC) DESIGN USING CAD. Building upon the preceding, a CAD workstation is used by the engineer who displays on the screen curves interrelating the variables (figure 13.9). The variables can be cross-plotted rapidly on the display screen. The use of computer aided design techniques is an essential element of the detail drafting. For example, when the designer wishes to draw a two-dimensional mechanical assembly, the computer will be asked for a specific station cut or cross-section through the finished product. This view will be displayed on the graphics console. Using stored subroutines, the designer will draw the details of the assembly, consisting of straight lines, circular arcs, and various higher order curves. In this manner, the computer will generate various geometric features such as a draftsman would make with a standard drawing instrument. When the designer wants to utilize a standard part, it will be called up by having its part number keyed in. He or she builds an assembly using a combination of standard parts and new construction. As the interaction with the graphics display unit takes place, the computer is programmed to accumulate an up-to-date parts list on-line as part of the engineering data base which automatically indicates the part number and the num-

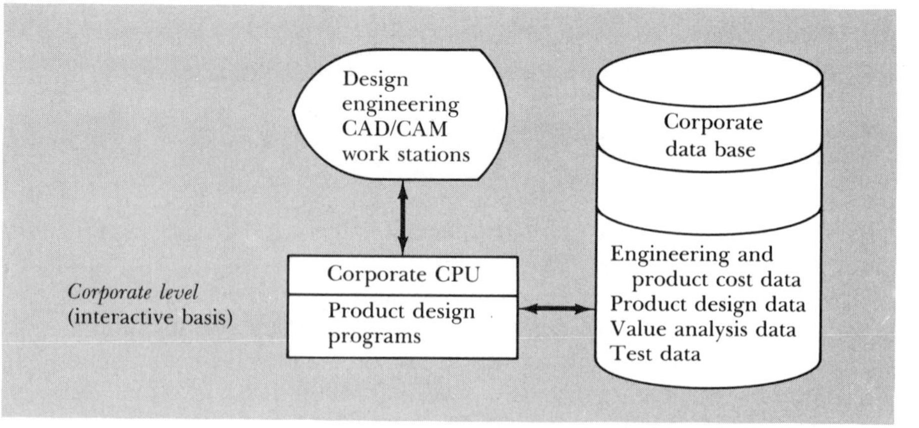

FIGURE 13.9
Product design for an
MIS manufacturing
subsystem.

ber of parts used. When the design is complete after employing value analysis, a printout can be requested of the bills of materials and master routing sheet.

Going beyond a two-dimensional viewpoint, the CAD system allows the engineer to produce three-dimensional models. Using simple commands, the engineer can create solid, three-dimensional models of products or parts. Once the engineer has created a model, the individual can view the object from different angles, "explode" it, or create a cross-section. With CAD, line drawings can be automatically generated. And as the engineer calculates measurements, the computer can be instructed to place the results of the calculations right in the drawing.

VALUE ENGINEERING. Before the product design can be finalized, engineering needs to evaluate whether the parts contained in the finished product perform the required function both as efficiently and as inexpensively as possible. This can be accomplished by using a checklist (as set forth in figure 13.1). The value analysis group evaluates the component parts under investigation with respect to each item on the checklist. Any question not answered to the satisfaction of the group becomes the starting point for a more detailed investigation. Thus the checklist assists in focusing on those factors which past experience has proved to be potentially fruitful cost reduction areas.

BILLS OF MATERIALS. Appropriate changes are made to the product's component parts—based on value analysis—before final bills of materials (refer to figure 13.10) are prepared along with the final master routing of parts through the plant's manufacturing centers. They are input to the computer system, as illustrated in 13.11. It should be remembered that data on new products have been stored on the corporate data base during the design phase. Input changes are used to update not only the corporate data base, but also the plant data base. Output at the plant level is directed toward storing bills of materials and master routing about the product on the data base as well as producing printouts of both, thereby providing each plant with essential information for manufacturing the finished product.

Component Parts for Minor Assembly

Part No.	Name	Quantity
01125	Frame	1
01150	Major bracket	1
01160	Minor brackets	4
01170	Support panels	4
01190	Heating elements	2
01222	Electric switch	1
01228	Regulator	1
01243	Catch pan	1
01250	Wiring harness	1
01260	Major bolts	4

Component Parts for Major Assembly

Part No.	Name	Quantity
02120	Main cover	1
02130	Subcovers	2
02165	Timer	1
02180	Handle	1
02190	Electric socket	1
02210	Wire and plug	1
02220	Plastic cover	1

FIGURE 13.10
Bill of materials for
product 215.

MANUFACTURING METHODS USING CAM. Going beyond the capabilities of CAD, CAM is used to determine the methods of manufacturing for the corporation's three plants. Essentially, they center on computer control of production machines. They range from machine tools running on punched-tape instructions to robots that can be programmed to perform any of a variety of industrial tasks. The XYZ Corporation has found that CAM pays off aside from any connection with CAD. More to the point, it provides speed, accuracy, tirelessness, and dependability that human operators cannot match.

PURCHASING

The actual ordering phase of purchasing consists of buying or acquiring the required materials and services, maintenance of purchase orders, and follow-up of purchase orders previously issued to vendors. In the purchasing illustration (figure 13.12), all three areas of purchasing are depicted as an essential part of MRP-II. They are also discussed in the following sections.

Buying from Vendors

An efficient purchasing operation goes beyond calculating an economic order quantity for a specific raw material or purchased part. It involves an evaluation of past vendor performance as a guide to future vendor performance. After

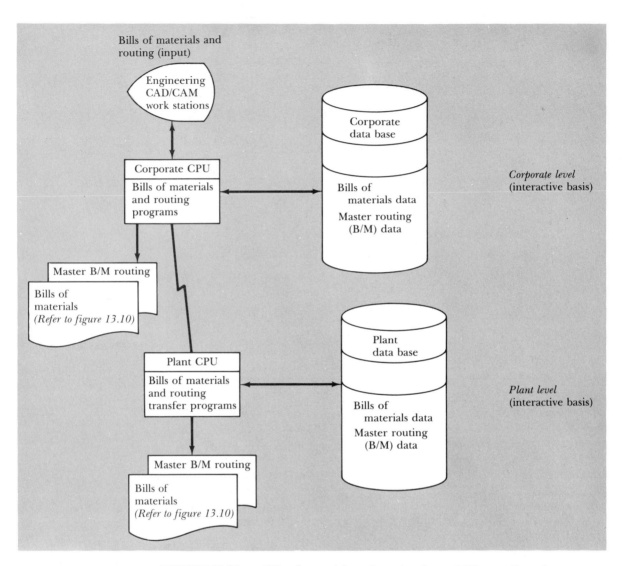

FIGURE 13.11   Bills of materials and routing for an MIS manufacturing subsystem.

the EOQ is calculated along with a computation for price breaks (if applicable), a purchase performance index (PPI) is employed to select the appropriate vendor. Basically, PPI is a weighted composite of the price (say, 50%), quality (say, 25%), and delivery (say, 25%) indexes. The vendor having the highest PPI is selected for the order under consideration, as shown in figure 13.13. All calculations are under the control of the purchase order and vendor performance evaluation program shown in figure 13.12.

The purchase order and vendor performance evaluation program employs the vendor master and inventory master data base files. The output of the ordering and evaluation program is stored on the corporate data base.

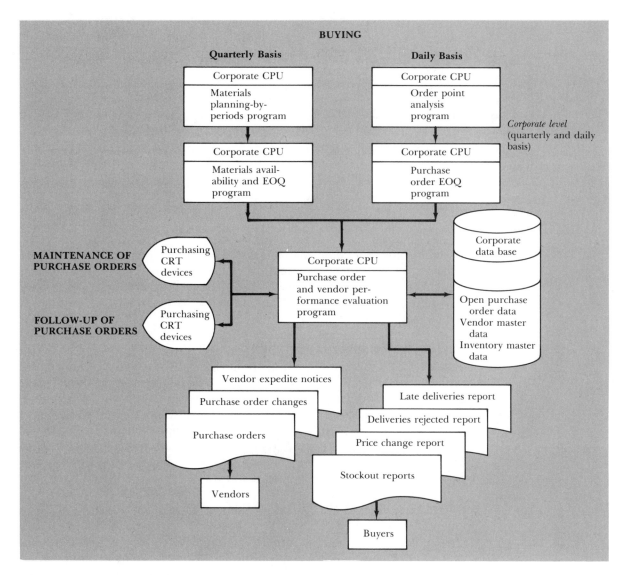

FIGURE 13.12   Purchasing—buying, maintenance of purchase orders, and follow-up of purchase orders—in an MIS manufacturing subsystem.

The purchase order data elements represent additions to the open purchase orders. Thus, the purchase order and vendor performance evaluation program uses all major purchasing data base files.

MAINTENANCE OF PURCHASE ORDERS.   Purchase maintenance involves the process of updating purchasing records, as depicted in figure 13.12. The open purchase orders, vendor master file, and inventory master file must be capable of being updated for the latest vendor additions and deletions, price and price break changes, revised vendor terms, and comparable items. In a

509

Vendor Name	Total Purchased Last Quarter	Price	Quality	Delivery	Purchase Performance Index (PPI)
Conco Supply	$46,502.75	98.25	105.00	115.15	104.2*
Mason, Inc.	26,775.21	105.78	98.25	96.54	101.6
Ideal Company	23,690.47	120.25	75.15	78.15	98.5
Teckco Corp.	55,000.50	100.50	88.75	100.20	97.5

*Vendor selected for current purchase since it has the highest past purchase performance index.

FIGURE 13.13   Vendor performance evaluation—a comparison of four vendors to determine the appropriate one.

similar manner, data base elements which are stored incorrectly on line must remain capable of being adjusted to the corrected amounts. In view of these many changes occurring outside and within the corporation, approved changes and corrections via CRT terminals at the corporate and plant levels can be made.

FOLLOW-UP OF PURCHASE ORDERS.   Purchase order follow-up, as shown in figure 13.12, keeps track of order progress. Prior-issued purchase orders are reviewed weekly by a computer program that references open purchase orders and vendor master file. Exception reports are prepared for vendors and buyers. Vendor expedite notices are prepared by corporate headquarters and reviewed by the corporation's buyers before mailing. Price changes, deliveries rejected, and late deliveries reports are issued to buyers along with copies of the vendor expedite notices. This approach gives buyers visual control over exceptions occurring in their areas.

CRITICAL PURCHASING AREAS.   Although buying, maintenance, and follow-up are concerned with merging together the external and internal purchasing factors for the XYZ Corporation, there is need to get a broader perspective of these factors using MRP-II. This can be accomplished by having purchasing management retain control over these critical areas:

- measure of idle machines and/or personnel resulting from a lack of purchased supplies
- measure of the extent of successful substitutes of materials and parts
- ratios of total purchasing salaries and expenses to total purchases and total manufacturing salaries and expenses
- value of purchase orders subjected to competitive bidding, as a percentage of total orders placed
- a number of rush orders
- quantitative measures of expediting expenses
- ratio of rejected purchases to total purchases
- savings on discounts and quantity purchases

510

□ measure of the extent of supplier technical assistance
□ measure of vendors' keeping delivery promises

Attention to the foregoing critical areas provides purchasing management with the capability of retaining control over operations as times change. Of course, it should be recognized that new critical items come into play over time and should be added to the above listing as necessary.

PRODUCTION PLANNING AND CONTROL

The production planning and control department at the plant level is responsible for all physical movements between manufacturing departments and within their respective work centers. This important department coordinates all activities concerning a production order from its initial recording, through inventory lay-up and manufacturing, to getting the finished goods ready for shipment to customers (direct shipments) or to company warehouses for shipment subsequently to customers. This module relies heavily upon the plant's data base and its communications with all manufacturing work centers. Refer to figure 13.14 for its components.

MRP-II to Simulate Production

An integral part of production planning and control using MRP-II is a simulation of the parts, minor assembly, and major assembly activities that are required, in an appropriate time sequence, to meet a production schedule. An assembly plan provides a deterministic statement of parts procurement, fabrication, and assembly activities. If production planning and control adjust capacity at the early stages to match manufacturing requirements, production activities will rarely require buffer inventories between stages. However, fluctuations in requirements from one period to the next can make production capacity management difficult. Often, the period-to-period variation is substantial. Even when the load in final assembly is reasonably level, variations in the product mix will lead to variations in load at the machine shop. The total load on the machine shop and minor assembly is the sum of the requirements by major assembly of the items produced. Despite averaging, period-to-period variations in total load on the machine shop occur. Factory foremen are quite familiar with the "feast or famine" situation. Economy of production, then, dictates smoothing of these fluctuations.

The method to smooth production is the utilization of the daily production scheduling–linear programming program (figure 13.8) mentioned in a previous section. To use this production scheduling program, all production planning and control data must be entered as they occur, thereby permitting creation of an up-to-date plant data base. Likewise, all production quotas for the present three-month period must be stored on line. It should be noted that periodically adjustments are made to period forecasts, which are reflected on the data base. Before the start of each day (the program is actually run at the

511

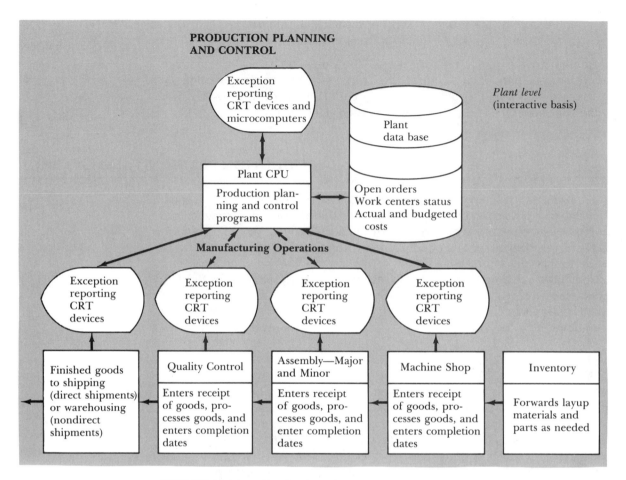

PRODUCTION PLANNING AND CONTROL

Plant level (interactive basis)

Exception reporting CRT devices and microcomputers

Plant data base

Plant CPU

Production planning and control programs

Open orders
Work centers status
Actual and budgeted costs

Manufacturing Operations

Exception reporting CRT devices

Exception reporting CRT devices

Exception reporting CRT devices

Exception reporting CRT devices

Finished goods to shipping (direct shipments) or warehousing (nondirect shipments)

Quality Control

Enters receipt of goods, processes goods, and enters completion dates

Assembly—Major and Minor

Enters receipt of goods, processes goods, and enter completion dates

Machine Shop

Enters receipt of goods, processes goods, and enters completion dates

Inventory

Forwards layup materials and parts as needed

FIGURE 13.14   Production planning and control with emphasis on exception reporting for an MIS manufacturing subsystem.

end of the prior day shift), the *computerized scheduler* initially determines what products to make for the day based on the production quotas—stated on a daily basis—by utilizing linear programming. Next, the scheduler considers where jobs are backed up or behind schedule and where production bottlenecks are currently occurring. Based on these basic inputs, the computerized on-line scheduler simulates the activities of the plan for the coming day and determines what will happen as the day begins, thereby alerting supervisors and foremen to critical areas that need attention. Because all data affecting manufacturing activities are entered as they occur, the scheduler feeds back information in sufficient time to control upcoming manufacturing operations. This daily computerized scheduler (illustrated previously in figure 13.3) also allows production control personnel to make adjustments, if deemed necessary, to accommodate last minute changes which may not have been entered as yet on the plant data base. Hence, this approach using MRP-II allows the department to retain control over the production scheduling process.

Many on-line recording techniques can aid the production planning and control department in its everyday operations. CRT devices, located in each manufacturing work center, enable the user to enter data regarding the name and location of goods in process. These keyboard entries, monitored on line by the plant computer, enable the production planning and control department to know when goods enter and leave a work center. Exception reporting alerts the department when goods are overdue from a specific work center. Delay reasons can also be entered from the individual work center CRT devices. Prolonged delays, resulting in possible shipment delay, are brought to the attention of manufacturing managers, supervisors, and foremen through exception reports. Figure 13.14 shows the data flow interaction with the production planning and control department.

The delay reports as entered onto the data base alert other manufacturing work centers about trouble areas. The work center(s) involved can enter "expected remedy" dates so that the rest of the line can make the necessary changes to the production schedule. In this manner, if noncritical parts are missing, such as power cords, the majority of the work can be performed with the part added later. Or, if critical parts are missing, such as the assembly shell, the complete order can be deleted from the daily run sheet until the part becomes available.

Once again, the adherence to set procedures using MRP-II enables the plant to operate in an efficient manner. Each work center must enter parts status when new lots are received and must clear the parts from the record of the work center when they move on to another work center. Other data, such as delay reasons, can be requested of the computer system when the expected hours within a work center exceed the normal.

RAW MATERIALS AND WORK-IN-PROCESS INVENTORIES

As stated in the last chapter, the marketing subsystem is responsible and accountable for finished goods inventory. The manufacturing subsystem, on the other hand, controls the flow of raw materials and work-in-process inventories. Due to the importance of each type of inventory, they are described separately below.

RAW MATERIALS. Using MRP-II, the raw materials inventories, maintained at the three plants, contain all the materials and subassemblies necessary for the production of the corporation's products. The data base elements consist of approximately 1,200 items. There are many small component parts, such as nuts, bolts, gaskets, and screws, which are not stored on line. These latter items do not represent a significant inventory investment and, therefore, are

513

not included in the materials planning forecast at the beginning of each three-month period. For the most part, these smaller items are controlled by the two-bin method. Under this system of inventory control, the clerk allocates one bin of materials for normal usage. When the first bin is empty and usage of the second bin begins, this individual places a new materials request. Inventory, in conjunction with purchasing, generates a purchase order for the part, stating quantity desired, price, vendor, and shipping instructions.

Inventory levels of materials are controlled from two points in the plants. The stockroom supplies data concerning the withdrawal of stocks to the systems; it also supplies the data on replenishment by the manufacturing process. All subassemblies manufactured for stock move directly into their respective storage areas along with the necessary paperwork covering the materials. The clerk checks the paperwork with the materials to ensure that everything matches. If there are differences, the exceptions are noted and the data are transmitted in corrected form to the plant CPU.

The receiving dock is another source of data for inventory control. When a vendor ships materials, they are accompanied by a packing slip which is a carbon copy of the shipping notice listing all items and quantities. Upon arrival at the dock, the receiving clerk verifies the shipment with the purchase order to insure accuracy of shipped materials. Pertinent information is keyed in via a CRT device and the system responds. If the shipment is valid, the materials are accepted and the inventory data base at the plant level is updated to include the shipment. However, if the system answers that the shipment is invalid and not due, it is refused by the receiving clerk and the carrier returns the materials to the vendor. An example of invalid vendor shipments for one day is shown in figure 13.15.

WORK IN PROCESS. Work-in-process inventory takes on an important role for the XYZ Corporation. This type of inventory is no longer controlled by an analysis of sample back orders and downtime (as in the prior information system). In the system's operations, work in process is controlled by MRP-II, that is, a simulation model of the plant work flow. The model evaluates the relationship of downtime and the total work-in-process inventory levels.

The information flow of the work-in-process inventory is recorded by on-line data collection devices in each of the manufacturing work centers as shown in figure 13.16. Personnel using these terminals are responsible for recording the time and labor involved in each manufacturing operation. The materials used for each manufacturing order are recorded via CRT terminals located in the stock control room. Between these sets of on-line terminals, a complete record of work in process is obtained on a "now" basis.

The work-in-process inventory gives management a complete, up-to-date picture of a plant's operations. The inventory system is of great value in maintaining customers' goodwill by quickly locating their orders in a plant by keying in the customer's order number from any of the on-line terminals. The user desiring the information receives back the location of the order in the plant along with an estimated shipment date.

Order Date	Purchase Order No.	Vendor Name	Date Rec'd	Quantity Ordered	Quantity Received	Part No.	Reason for Invalid Shipment
4/18/8X	21941	Perkins Corporation	5/18/8X	1,000	1,200	01170	Units not ordered were returned
5/2/8X	22027	Vin Vac Company	5/18/8X	450	450	01255	Units delivered three weeks in advance
4/17/8X	21907	Cincinnati Metals	5/18/8X	600	600	02166	Units not completed according to requirements stated on purchase order
4/2/8X	21869	Kenwall Company	5/18/8X	2,200	2,225	02211	Units were damaged in shipment—need to be reworked by vendor
4/15/8X	21891	Johnson Sheet Metals	5/18/8X	750	750	02188	Units delivered were the wrong color per the purchase order

FIGURE 13.15   Invalid vendor shipments for a typical day at one plant—output from the raw materials inventory control program.

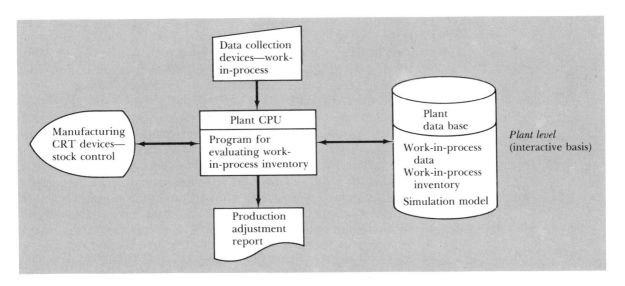

FIGURE 13.16   Work-in-process flow for an MIS manufacturing subsystem.

Work-in-Process Simulation

The value of the MRP-II work-in-process simulation model mentioned above is its ability to adjust the production cycle when fluctuations unexpectedly appear. Even though the production cycle is normally a planned period, it is not able to cope with the small variations that occur during the production cycle. For example, if four or five personnel are missing from a key department, this leaves the next department with downtime owing to the lack of incoming work. The job of the inventory simulation model is to adjust the production flow and return the system to normal. As indicated previously, the work-in-process level in figure 13.16 is created by data collection in manufacturing work centers and in the stockroom. Because the work-in-process levels are always up to date, the simulation model can be used at any time for determining the production adjustment. Generally, the simulation model is used once a day.

MANUFACTURING OPERATIONS

The manufacturing operations of the XYZ Corporation comprise its physical manufacturing process. Its major parts in an MIS environment are the machine shop and assembly (major and minor). In separate sections that follow, each will be explored in terms of its essential operations.

Machine Shop

The machine shop, being the first department to start a production order in terms of the manufacturing process (figure 13.14), requests parts from inventory-stock control. Completion dates from all other departments and work centers depend on the availability of parts from the machine shop. Using MRP-II, scheduling of its operations follows the same path as that through other manufacturing departments and work centers. The data base is updated when parts enter and leave the department, and the master schedule shows expected work loads and dates.

Many advanced manufacturing methods are used. Automated processes, including industrial robots, numerical-control machine tools, and computer-monitored processes are typical ones. With the feedback mechanism of these advanced techniques, machine utilization reports are no problem. A small minicomputer in the shop area monitors all processes and reports back to the plant computer (figure 13.17). Exception reports are made available on-line by the minicomputer in order to assure immediate corrective action. A typical daily exception report is shown in figure 13.18. Any time the storage capacities of the minicomputer are exceeded throughout the day, this condition is reported to the plant computer. Daily summary reports are produced for the supervisor of the machine shop. Weekly summary reports are sent to the superintendent of manufacturing operations and the plant manager. They are also transmitted to the corporate data base for future reference.

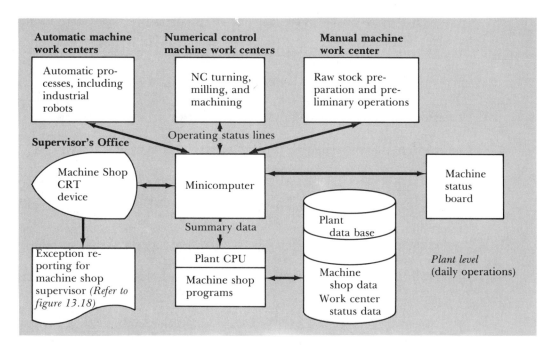

FIGURE 13.17   Minicomputer control of machine shop operations in an MIS manufacturing subsystem.

Because the machine shop is the heart of the manufacturing area, management has decided that it must know the status of all machines constantly. A "machine status board" has been installed in the supervisor's office under the control of the minicomputer. Through feedback lines attached to all plant machines, the computer knows if the machines are operating, idle, or in setup.

MACHINE SHOP EXCEPTIONS—7/22/8X

Part Number	Quantity	Exceptions Items
01172	150	Materials received from vendor do not meet specifications for milling machine
01259	350	Machine operator incorrectly milled the first 50 units of the production order
01161	400	Materials returned to stock control since they are the incorrect part number
02210	250	Production order called for only 200 units although 250 units were machined
01216	200	New machine operator spoiled 20 units of the production order

FIGURE 13.18
A typical daily exception report for a machine shop supervisor at one plant.

Green, red, or yellow lights are illuminated, respectively, on the board for the proper condition. A manual key-in station, similar to the keyboards in other departments, allows the machine operator to enter the reason for machine idle time.

The numerical control (NC) machine work centers have a great impact on the manufacturing subsystem. The advent of computer controlled machine tools brought about the added efficiency of operations. Complete and accurate status reporting can be made without manual intervention and operator knowledge. This will eliminate "beat the game" tactics by operators and labor problems relating to "watchdog" activities.

The automatic processes in the machine shop consist of robot operations and fixed-cycle machine tools, such as plastic injection molding machines. By examining capital equipment utilization reports, the XYZ Corporation has justified the use of robot operations for constant, large-lot-size, monotonous jobs. Past history showed that manual operations are boring, thereby adding to scrap problems and health hazards. The robots do these jobs with ease. The minicomputer monitors the robots and produces exception reports to the machine shop's supervisor and the foremen when operations go out of control.

Fixed-cycle machines are becoming more commonplace for this corporation. They can do repeated operations without manual supervision. Parameters are input by dials on the machine, and the process begins. The minicomputer again monitors the actions of these machines and produces exception reports when tolerance limits are exceeded. The supervisor of the machine shop receives these exception reports by use of the status board and CRT device (figure 13.17). This enables the supervisor to take corrective action before a complete parts lot has to be scrapped. Also, the minicomputer contacts other responsible people for corrective action at the appropriate times. With CRT devices in the tool crib and in the plant and machine-maintenance department, exception reporting schemes allow for corrective action.

Assembly—Minor and Major

Even though the minor and major assembly departments constitute separate areas using MRP-II, they will be treated together because their data flow needs and applicable mathematical models are the same. Their data flow was shown previously in figure 13.14. As in the machine shop, a minicomputer is used to monitor the automatic minor assembly and conveyor lines. Their status is reported on a "machine status board" in the supervisor's office. Exception reporting takes place via CRT terminals, as was illustrated for the machine shop.

Mathematical models to assist management decisions concerning machine loading, systems operations, and comparable activities include PERT/time, queuing, and linear programming (described previously under production planning and control). The locations of individual assembly areas can be implemented with the aid of PERT/time charts. The sequence of operations can also be determined by utilizing this technique. For example, it is inefficient to place a 30-minute operation in the middle of assembling the product, resulting in holdups down the line, when the same operation can be performed toward the end of the sequence. PERT/time, then, is employed to highlight bottlenecks and dependent functions, thereby leading to improved manufacturing operations in the assembly areas.

MINIMIZING COSTS OF DELAYS. The bottleneck problem can also be solved by using queuing or waiting-line theory, which permits the user to minimize costs of delays. Total assembly department operations can be improved by careful analysis of existing procedures. For example, an operator has the job of keeping ten automatic assembly machines in operation. The machines periodically require attention, such as refilling an empty hopper, relieving a choke, or making adjustments. Because chokes and out-of-adjustment conditions occur at random, the servicing requirements cannot be scheduled. It has been determined, however, that each machine requires an average of six minutes attention per hour by the operator, and that during this time, it is nonproductive. It is then assumed that

$$\text{Downtime} = 100\% \times (6 \text{ minutes}/60 \text{ minutes}) = 10\%$$
$$\text{Efficiency} = 100\% - 10\% = 90\%$$

However, this assumption is not always correct, because one or more of the machines may be idle while another is being serviced. By using a table of queuing loss factors, it can be determined that if there are ten machines, the resulting queuing loss is 12.4 percent. Thus,

$$\text{Efficiency} = 90\% - 12.4\% = 77.6\% \text{ per machine}$$

By hiring another operator to help service the machines, the number of machines per operator becomes five. The comparable queuing loss factor from the table becomes 2.8 percent per machine.

Before manufacturing management can decide whether or not the hiring of another operator is justified, it must determine the new operator's cost. If it is assumed that the operator's wages plus fringe benefits are $200 per week, and that the contribution to fixed costs and profits from the output of ten machines is $60 per hour, then the cost of an extra operator must be related to the reduction in queuing loss for hiring this operator. Thus

$$12.4\% - 2.8\% = 9.6\% \text{ (approximately 10\%)}$$

Based on a forty-hour week and 10 percent gain in output as a result of the reduced queuing loss, there is an approximate gain of four hours per week. The increase in contribution is

$$4 \text{ hours/week} \times \$60/\text{hour contribution} = \$240$$

The cost savings possible by using two operators, then, is

$$\$240.00 - \$200.00 = \$40.00 \text{ per week}$$

519

This example once again points out the necessity of an accurate data base in terms of efficiency rates, dollar costs, and times of manufacturing operations.

Feasibility of New Equipment

In order to improve the productivity of its three manufacturing plants, the vice president of manufacturing must continually appraise the onslaught of new machinery and equipment. This involves comparing several new pieces of equipment against the present equipment. Similarly, it involves a very complex feasibility study justifying automated equipment. Both of these approaches will be demonstrated below using Lotus 1-2-3.

INDIFFERENCE ANALYSIS. This first method used to determine the feasibility of new equipment is called *indifference analysis* because there is a point at which the individual is indifferent between the purchase of one or more pieces of machinery. In other words, the indifferent points represent the rates of substitution for one alternative versus another. For example, the XYZ Corporation is currently operating an older drill press at its St. Louis plant. Its costs (alternative A) along with the costs for the two alternatives (B and C) are as follows:

Alternative Type Machine	A Hand Operated	B Semi- Automated	C Completely Automated
Variable costs per unit	$2.00	$1.00	$0.50
Fixed costs	$0	$3,000	$9,000

These data are set forth in figure 13.19(a) along with the *x* and *y* coordinates for plotting the data in figure 13.19(b). As shown, the analysis indicates that alternatives A and B are indifferent at 3,000 units, alternatives A and C are indifferent at 6,000 units, and B and C are indifferent at 12,000 units. In addition, the data can be interpreted as follows: in the first year, use alternative A for production up to 3,000 units, use alternative B for production between 3,000 units and 12,000 units, and use alternative C for production over 12,000 units. The factor determining the machine to purchase is the expected sales of units to be produced. If the expected sale is 9,000 units, the best alternative is B. However, if the expected sale is 15,000 units, the best is C.

FEASIBILITY STUDY JUSTIFYING AUTOMATED EQUIPMENT. The second alternative (in determining which type of automated equipment to buy) centers on assembling detailed facts concerning the equipment today and tomorrow. More specifically, it involves analyzing the life-cycle of new machinery for manufacturing present and/or approved new products. For example, the vice president of manufacturing wants to know whether the corporation should invest in new machinery to produce two new products—A (314) and B (315)—at its Los Angeles plant. The data needed include income, product costs, common costs, and other important factors. They are as follows:

Income	Product A (314)	Product B (315)
Anticipated annual revenue	$250,000	$400,000
Product Costs		
Initial outlay for equipment	$500,000	$1,000,000
Annual equipment maintenance	$75,000	$30,000
Annual labor hours	4,100 hours	2,000 hours
Floor space (per square feet)	200	220
Power consumed (kwh)	4.5	6.2
Common Costs	**Dollars**	**Yearly Inflation**
Labor per hour	$24.50	6%
Floor space (per square foot)	$16.00	6%
Power (kwh)	$0.09	8%
Maintenance inflation		7%

Other Important Factors (for Both Products)

Cost of money	16%
Incremental tax rate (federal, state, and local)	43%
Service life	5 years
Salvage value (% of initial cost)	8%

Using the Lotus 1-2-3 approach as found in figure 13.20 (page 524), neither investment—considering the time value of money—should be made because the return is too low: neither meets the corporation's established rate of return, 20 percent.

QUALITY CONTROL

The quality control department is the most critical control point in an MIS manufacturing subsystem. The internal workings of this department are illustrated in figure 13.21 for completed manufactured parts and finished products. Because the deadline of customer shipments and available labor make 100 percent sampling of the corporation's output impossible, statistical tools, utilizing such techniques as those set forth earlier in the chapter, come into play.

To employ a statistical technique, a CRT device in the quality control department is connected to the plant computer (figure 13.21). By keying in the proper codes and part numbers, the statistical analysis model (originally developed on a micro) comes on line to direct the quality control section on the number of parts to check, depending on the last part checked. The computer can relay the necessary information to the quality control department in order to make the decision on acceptance or rejection. Typical reasons for rejection of manufactured parts and finished products are in figure 13.22. If there are conditions that have not been taken into account by the statistical technique, the human–machine interface allows the quality control person to override the answer to accept or reject the manufactured goods. Hence, the MIS approach to quality control allows for changing conditions as they arise.

```
                    Indifference Analysis
                    ---------------------

Alternative A                             Equation for Alt. A
-------------                             -------------------
Keep the current equipment.               TC(A) =      $0 + $2.00 N
Fully depreciated, hand operated machines.
Fixed costs are equal to      $0.00 per year.
Variable  costs  equal        $2.00 per unit.


Alternative B                             Equation_for Alt. B
-------------                             -------------------
Purchase semiautomatic machines.          TC(B) = $3,000 + $1.00 N
Fixed costs increase to  $3,000.00 per year.
Variable costs reduce to      $1.00 per unit.


Alternative C                             Equation for Alt. C
-------------                             -------------------
Purchase completely automatic machines.   TC(C) = $9,000 + $0.50 N
Fixed costs increase to  $9,000.00 per year.
Variable costs reduce to      $0.50 per unit.



Substitution
------------
Equation A
When X is..       Y equals..
        0               0
    3,000           6,000
    6,000          12,000
    9,000          18,000 Alt A

Equation B
When X is..       Y equals..
        0           3,000
    3,000           6,000
    6,000           9,000
    9,000          12,000
   12,000          15,000
   15,000          18,000 Alt B

Equation C
When X is..       Y equals..
        0           9,000
    3,000          10,500
    6,000          12,000
    9,000          13,500
   12,000          15,000
(a) 15,000          16,500 Alt C
```

FIGURE 13.19   (a) Indifference analysis for equipment alternatives A, B, and C and (b) a graph of the results—St. Louis plant of the XYZ Corporation.

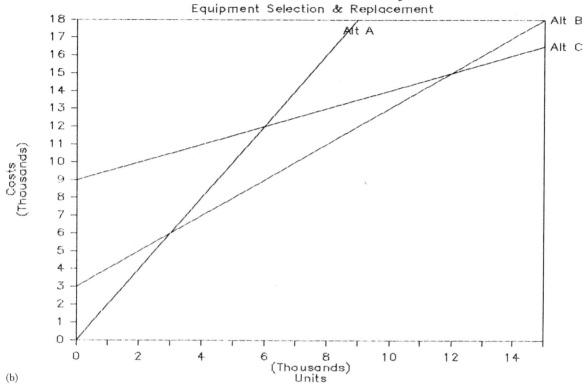

(b)

FIGURE 13.19   Continued

Summary—MIS Manufacturing Subsystem

Engineering centers on the design of new products using mechanical and electrical engineering. Included is value engineering, which is useful in evaluating whether the parts contained in the finished product perform the required function both as efficiently and inexpensively as possible.

    Purchasing consists of buying required materials and services, maintenance of purchase orders issued in the buying process, and follow-up with the appropriate vendors.

    Production planning and control is responsible for all physical movements between manufacturing departments and within their respective work centers. It uses MRP-II to coordinate all activities concerning a production order from its initial recording, through inventory lay-up and manufacturing, to getting the products ready for shipment.

    Raw materials and work-in-process inventories center on the proper recording and control of inventories from the stock room, to the manufacturing work centers, and through quality control. The conversion of raw materials

523

```
                  Return on Investment - Net Present Value Method

                            Individual Machine Costs
                            ----------------------------
                              A                    B
Initial Cost                $500,000             $1,000,000
Salvage Value                 40,000                 80,000
Net Cost                    $460,000               $920,000
Maintenance Cost              75,000                 30,000
Labor in Hours                 4,100                  2,000
Floor Space (sq ft)              200                    220
Power Usage (kwh)                4.5                    6.2


                            Costs Common To Both Machines
                            -------------------------------
Common Costs                Inflation      Cost of Money      16.0%
Labor (per hour)   $24.50     6.0%         Incr Tax Rate      43.0%
Floor Space        $16.00     6.0%         Service Life           5
Power               $0.09     8.0%         Salvage Value       8.0%
Maintenance Inflation         7.0%
-----------------------------------------------------------------------------


                 Year 1      Year 2     Year 3      Year 4      Year 5
Machine A        ------      ------     ------      ------      ------

Maintenance     ($42,750)   ($45,743)  ($48,944)   ($52,371)   ($56,037)
Operator Labor   (57,257)    (60,692)   (64,333)    (68,193)    (72,285)
Floor Space       (1,824)     (1,933)    (2,049)     (2,172)     (2,303)
Power             (2,022)     (2,184)    (2,359)     (2,547)     (2,751)
Depreciation
  Tax Effect      43,000      43,000     43,000      43,000      43,000
Revenue         $250,000    $250,000   $250,000    $250,000    $250,000
Salvage                                                          40,000
Total cash flow
  from operations $189,147   $182,448   $175,314    $167,716    $199,624
Present Value of
  cash flows from operations . . . . . . . . . . . .           $598,635
Net Present Value of cash flows
  from operations less initial net cost . . . . . . . . . .    $138,635
Return on investment - percentage per year . . . . . . . . .     6.03%
-----------------------------------------------------------------------------


                 Year 1      Year 2     Year 3      Year 4      Year 5
Machine B        ------      ------     ------      ------      ------

Maintenance     ($17,100)   ($18,297)  ($19,578)   ($20,948)   ($22,415)
Operator Labor   (27,930)    (29,606)   (31,382)    (33,265)    (35,261)
Floor Space       (2,006)     (2,127)    (2,254)     (2,390)     (2,533)
Power             (2,786)     (3,009)    (3,250)     (3,510)     (3,791)
Depreciation
  Tax Effect      86,000      86,000     86,000      86,000      86,000
Revenue         $400,000    $400,000   $400,000    $400,000    $400,000
Salvage                                                          80,000
Total cash flow
  from operations $436,177   $432,961   $429,536    $425,887    $502,001
Present Value of
  cash flows from operations . . . . . . . . . . . . . . . . .$1,447,184
Net Present Value of cash flows
  from operations less initial net cost . . . . . . . . . .    $527,184
Return on investment - percentage per year . . . . . . . . .    11.46%

-----------------------------------------------------------------------------
Return on investment A vs B . . . . . . . . . . . . . . . . .     5.43%
```

FIGURE 13.20   A feasibility study using Lotus 1-2-3 to justify or reject the new equipment for the Los Angeles plant.

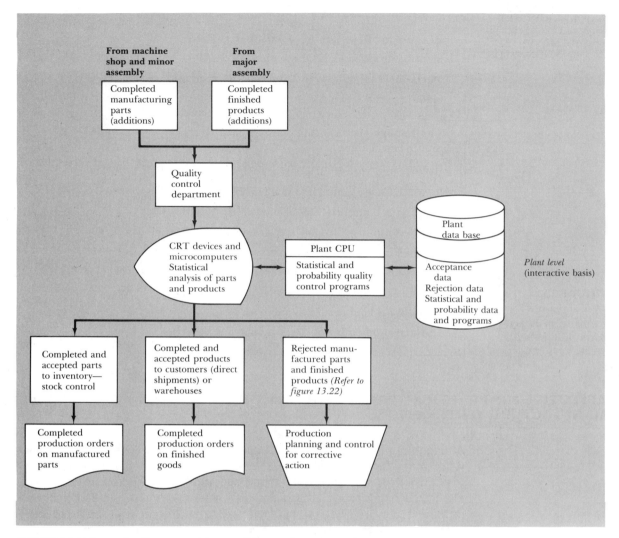

FIGURE 13.21   Quality control in an MIS manufacturing subsystem.

inventory to work-in-process inventory finally results in the output of finished goods.

   Manufacturing operations comprise the essential part of the MIS manufacturing subsystem. Its major parts are the work centers in the machine shop, minor assembly, and major assembly. The machine shop uses raw materials for machining parts which, in turn, along with other purchased materials and parts are used as input for minor assembly. These assemblies, using still other materials, are finally put together as the finished product in major assembly.

   Quality control comprises the critical control points in the manufacturing process—within the machine shop, minor assembly, and major assembly—where the quality of the goods is checked for conformance to predetermined standards.

525

Reasons for Rejection of Manufactured Parts

Manufactured batch does not meet acceptable quality standards.

Machining of castings indicates holes on their surfaces.

Manufactured batch lacks the appropriate part or parts per the bill of materials.

The number in the manufactured batch is less than that called for by production planning.

Incorrect parts have been machined for a specific part number.

Reasons for Rejection of Finished Products

Finished products have been incorrectly assembled.

Finished products do not operate—manual and/or electrical failings.

Finished product lacks one or more parts per the bill of materials.

Covers on the finished product do not fit properly.

There is a mismatch of colors on the finished product.

Improper wiring for foreign export.

Finished product is not clean enough for shipment.

FIGURE 13.22
Typical reasons for rejecting manufactured parts and finished goods.

EFFECTIVE MIS PRACTICE—WORK REDESIGN OF MANUFACTURING OPERATIONS

Although production planning and control are essential within an MIS framework, many times its effectiveness can be improved by delegating some of the detailed aspects of manufacturing operations to line personnel, for example, to machine shop operators and assemblers. Although not demonstrated in the chapter, it is helpful, for instance, to allow machine operators more autonomy over the start-up and stopping of their machines. This procedural change increases operating effectiveness since operators previously had to get a foreman's approval before beginning a production run or stopping a machine for maintenance. The operators are also permitted to perform minor maintenance on their machines without supervisory approval. These work redesign changes are extended to provide the machine operators with more complete jobs and more responsibility for their work.

Permitting machine operators to shut off their machines and perform minor maintenance work, such as making machine adjustments and replacing parts, can result in less overtime and fewer cost overruns on jobs. The machine shop is averaging approximately 11 minutes to accomplish adjustments which averaged 3½ minutes of actual maintenance work. The additional 7½ minutes are consumed by delays while the operator gets the attention of a supervisor and the supervisor gets hold of a maintenance technician. At times, the delay is substantially longer. Given that each operator will routinely experience two or three delays a day, the cumulative impact of such delays represents a significant loss of production over an eight-hour period. Under work redesign, operators will be permitted to shut down machines and perform many of these tasks themselves, resulting in substantial cost savings. These cost reductions will be the result of less overtime work, fewer cost overruns, and an improved maintenance program. A last benefit will be that maintenance workers have more time to overhaul machinery on a preventive maintenance schedule.

A key element in the machine shop redesign efforts is providing the workers with more feedback about their work. Often, new performance or quality measurements are initiated. The end result is a body of information relevant to performance that previously was not available. This information at times reveals problems not otherwise apparent to either management or the workers involved. For example, in the production operation described above, machine shop operators might begin recording machine stops to monitor performance of their machines on a weekly basis. Along with a maintenance person, each operator might identify any machine requiring an unusual number of stops. As a result, several problems may be identified. Correction of these maintenance problems will likely result in increased production.

Just as work redesign increases productivity for machine shop operators, the same can be said for assembly departments. In work redesign for minor and major assembly, setting up work on a user basis is a central part of the work restructuring process. This restructuring results in direct communication between the persons completing the work and the persons who receive the work. Complaints, questions, and adjustments can often be accomplished without the intervention of a third party (i.e., a supervisor). This reduces the communication problems that emerge when a person attempting to resolve the problem is not the person most familiar with the intimate details of the work.

The most important aspect of work redesign efforts for the minor and major assembly departments, however, is the incorporation of checking, inspection, and expediting tasks into the jobs of the workers doing the actual work. The employee responsible for assembling a part is also made responsible for inspecting it. In contrast, arrangements where the work is regularly checked by employees other than the ones doing the actual work can result in higher costs. Hence, work redesign results in a reduction of inspectors or expeditors required in quality control. In addition, it allows the assembler more ''self control'' over his or her working environment, thereby allowing one more use of individual talents on the job. Many times, this approach is instrumental in increasing the worker's motivation to do a better job.

CHAPTER SUMMARY

The manufacturing subsystem has witnessed many exciting recent developments. The automated factory, industrial robots, microcomputers, minicomputers, and other new processes are important advances in the manufacturing process. In addition to the employment of advanced manufacturing methods and machines, MRP-II, CAD/CAM, and mathematical models have helped to bring an entirely new approach to the MIS manufacturing subsystem. New mathematical and statistical techniques—several of which were outlined in the chapter—are capable of producing fast and accurate results for management.

For the foregoing hardware and technical advances to be effective in an MIS manufacturing subsystem, a computer integrated manufacturing approach must be used. As discussed in the chapter, the products must be engineered properly by utilizing value engineering. Similarly, purchasing must buy on an optimum basis and, at the same time, ensure that the quality requirements of incoming materials are proper for manufacturing operations. In the functioning of these vital premanufacturing activities, there is need for timely responses, whether they be for line personnel, operating management, or higher management. Only in this manner can the MIS manufacturing subsystem operate in a way that allows effective decision making over manufacturing activities.

QUESTIONS

1. What important items must be considered in the development of an effective MIS manufacturing subsystem?

2. Why is computer integrated manufacturing (CIM) regarded as a management tool rather than a type of manufacturing software? Explain.

3. What are the essential elements of value engineering?

4. How important is problem finding in manufacturing versus corporate planning in terms of the total corporation?

5. What is the relationship of manufacturing-oriented mathematical and statistical models to CIM?

6. **a.** What are the essential elements of MRP-II?
    b. How can MRP-II be used to answer recurring and ad hoc "What if?" questions for manufacturing of the XYZ Corporation?

7. **a.** Define the role of engineering management in an effective MIS environment.
    b. How useful is CAD/CAM to the engineering department of the XYZ Corporation?

8. **a.** Define the role of purchasing management in an effective MIS environment.
    b. What is the function of the purchase performance index (PPI)?

9. What information is helpful to production planning and control to oversee current manufacturing operations?

10. How important is planning and control over work-in-process inventories?

11. What managerial reports are helpful in controlling raw materials and work-in-process inventories within an MIS manufacturing subsystem?

12. What is the tie-in between manufacturing operations and quality control in an MIS manufacturing subsystem?

13. State the various types of manufacturing information that can be and possibly should be batch processed in an effective management information system.

14. To assist the engineering group of the XYZ Corporation, value engineering, or value analysis, is used to determine whether the parts contained in the finished product perform their required functions as efficiently and inexpensively as possible. To instill this important concept in the engineering department, describe how it should be incorporated in individual engineering project groups. Include in your answer the timing factor in terms of its usefulness to the product's final design.

15. The modules of the manufacturing subsystem of the XYZ Corporation were set forth in the chapter: engineering, purchasing, production planning and control, raw materials and work-in-process inventories, manufacturing operations, and quality control. What other sections could have been developed for the MIS manufacturing subsystem? Also, what modules from the other subsystems—corporate planning, marketing, and accounting and finance—could be included in the manufacturing subsystem? For both situations, explore what modifications would be necessary to make these functional parts work as an integrated system for the entire corporation.

16. As illustrated in the chapter, the MIS manufacturing subsystem of the XYZ Corporation is operating in a DDP mode. What changes are necessary to change either the engineering or quality control module to a total decision support system operating mode? In addition, what advantages would accrue to the corporation for a DSS operating mode versus an MIS operating mode?

17. To improve the manufacturing operations of the XYZ Corporation, develop alternative approaches that might be used to improve assembly operations—minor or major. Include in your answer what effect the changes would have on the quality of the final product as well as what changes might be required in the quality control department. The suggested alternatives should recognize the importance of keeping overall production costs as low as possible and increasing final product quality. Additionally, consideration should be given to increasing both productivity and employee morale. In a similar manner, the worker should be allowed more participation in decisions that affect him or her directly.

18. Since only a brief reference was made in the chapter to receiving, set forth a receiving system within an effective MIS environment for the XYZ Corporation. This can take the form of a system flowchart or a data flow diagram. Include the need for a human–machine interface as normally found in an effective MIS operating mode. Consideration should be given to the fact that the receiving area is an integral part of the numerous manufacturing activities. Additionally, consideration should be given to the utilization of exception reporting on incoming items.

19. A data collection system, normally an integral part of the manufacturing process, was not illustrated in the chapter of the XYZ Corporation. Fundamentally, a data collection system permits data to be fed directly into the computer system via data collection devices which are conveniently located for all job production personnel. When a factory employee starts a job, the individual inserts a plastic identification badge into a reader, which designates the work center and departmental number. The person then places a punched card (a traveler card accompanies every production order as it progresses through the plant) into the same reader, which identifies the job being worked on. The data are transmitted to the computer. Upon completion of the job, the above process is repeated, along with the keying in of the number of units produced. The data are automatically transmitted to the computer, where they are stored by job number for cost analysis, paying the employees, making the necessary adjustments to production schedules, and inventory balances.

Based upon this information, develop a detailed system for this area. Include in your answer one or more systems flowcharts or data flow diagrams to diagram the informational flow. Consideration should be given to outputs that are helpful to management not only in controlling current operations effectively, but also for assisting management in "getting a handle on" improving productivity in the plant.

LOTUS 1-2-3 EXERCISES AND PROGRAMS

20. As demonstrated in the chapter, indifference analysis is useful to determine which type of machine should be purchased. This approach was shown in figure 13.19. Using this as a model, develop a comparable analysis (substitution analysis and graph) for data which are given as follows:

Alternatives for Machine Shop
1. Existing process—foot-operated press
   Original cost $3,000 (fully depreciated)
   Variable cost per piece $0.25
2. Proposed process—solenoid-operated press
   Original cost $3,500
   Variable cost per piece $0.15
3. Proposed process—dial-type motor press
   Original cost $10,000
   Variable cost per piece $0.10

The graph should not only show the range of volumes for which each process would be used, but also reflect the fact that the equipment is highly specialized and has no salvage value. Based upon the output from the Lotus 1-2-3 program, what should the plant superintendent do, purchase one of the new presses or keep the old one? The program for this problem is provided on the Lotus 1-2-3 diskette or as given in the program found in this section. Additionally, does this equipment analysis lend itself to another graphic approach? If so, what might it be? Optionally, develop a Lotus 1-2-3 program to prepare the graph.

21. In the chapter, indifference analysis was presented in figure 13.19 as a useful way of determining which type of machine should be purchased. Using this approach as a model, develop a comparable analysis (substitution analysis and graph) for the data given as follows. The XYZ Corporation is currently operating an older machine (machine 1) in its Machine Department of the Los Angeles plant for stamping parts with a variable cost of $10.00 per unit and a zero book value (completely depreciated). In addition, the cost of removing the older press equals its salvage value. Being considered in its place are two different presses manufactured by E. W. Bliss Company. The faster press (machine 2), an industrial robot, will increase hourly production, but it will increase fixed costs by $10,000 per year and reduce variable costs by $4.00 per unit. An even faster press (machine 3), another industrial robot, will increase fixed costs by $12,500 per year, but reduce variable costs by $5.00 per unit. Long-run forecast for sales indicates that sales will not fall below 5,100 units per year for the next five years. At what point is the XYZ Corporation indifferent as to which press to purchase? Should the old press be kept or should one of the two proposed presses be purchased? The program for this problem is provided on the Lotus 1-2-3 diskette or can be found in this section. In addition, does this equipment analysis lend itself to another graphic approach? If so, what might it be? Optionally, develop a Lotus 1-2-3 program to prepare the graph.

22. The vice president of manufacturing for the XYZ Corporation has just received a feasibility study justifying automated equipment at the Los Angeles plant. He must now analyze the life-cycle costs of new machinery that meet his manufacturing needs for new products 415 and 416. Using figure 13.20 as a model, develop a comparable analysis for both products to determine whether they are worth the large initial investment, that is, should the corporation undertake the investment even though the equipment has been justified? The program is provided on the Lotus 1-2-3 diskette or can be found in this section. The data compiled for this analysis are as follows:

Product Costs	Product 415	Product 416
Initial outlay for equipment	$250,000	$500,000
Annual equipment maintenance	$ 37,500	$ 15,000
Annual labor hours	2,050 hours	1,000 hours
Floor space (per square feet)	100	110
Power consumed (kwh)	2.25	3.10
Anticipated annual revenue	$125,000	$200,000

Common Costs	Dollars	Yearly Inflation
Labor per hour	$12.25	6%
Floor space (per square foot)	$ 8.00	6%
Power (per kwh)	$ 0.05	8%
Maintenance inflation		7%

Other Important Factors (for Both Products)

Cost of money	16%
Incremental rax rate (federal, state, and local)	43%
Service life	5 years
Salvage value (% of initial cost)	8%

23. Referring to the preceding problem, suppose the initial outlay for equipment was less than that shown, that is, the equipment cost for product 415 was $200,000 and the equipment cost for product 416 was $400,000. What should the vice president of manufacturing for the XYZ Corporation do? Using figure 13.20 as a model, develop new values to determine whether the large initial investment is justified. The program is provided on the Lotus 1-2-3 diskette or can be found in this section.

Suppose the large investment outlays still are not feasible, what approach should the vice president of manufacturing use to determine the feasibility of undertaking the production of products 415 and 416? In other words, how should *sensitivity analysis* be undertaken to resolve the vice president's dilemma?

LOTUS 1-2-3 PROGRAM—INDIFFERENCE ANALYSIS (DATA AND GRAPH) (PROGRAM 8)

```
C1:  'Indifference Analysis              A20: 'Variable costs reduce to
C2:  '--------------------               C20: (C2) U 0.5
A3:  'Alternative A                      D20: 'per unit.
E3:  'Equation for Alt. A                A23: 'Substitution
A4:  '-------------                      A24: '------------
E4:  '-------------------                A25: 'Equation A
A5:  'Keep the current equipment.        A26: 'When X is..
E5:  'TC(A) = 0                          B26: '     Y equals..
G5:  (C0) (C7)                           A27: (,0) U 0
H5:  '+                                  B27: (,0) ($C$7)+($C$8*A27)
I5:  (C2) (C8)                           A28: (,0) U 3000
J5:  'N                                  B28: (,0) ($C$7)+($C$8*A28)
A6:  'Fully depreciated, hand operated machines.   A29: (,0) U 6000
A7:  'Fixed costs are equal to           B29: (,0) ($C$7)+($C$8*A29)
C7:  (C2) U 0                            A30: (,0) U 9000
D7:  'per year.                          B30: (,0) ($C$7)+($C$8*A30)
A8:  'Variable  costs  equal             C30: 'Alt A
C8:  (C2) U 2                            A32: 'Equation B
D8:  'per unit.                          A33: 'When X is..
A10: 'Alternative B                      B33: '     Y equals..
E10: 'Equation for Alt. B                A34: (,0) U 0
A11: '-------------                      B34: (,0) ($C$13)+($C$14*A34)
E11: '-------------------                A35: (,0) U 3000
A12: 'Purchase semiautomatic machines.   B35: (,0) ($C$13)+($C$14*A35)
E12: 'TC(B)                              A36: (,0) U 6000
F12: '=                                  B36: (,0) ($C$13)+($C$14*A36)
G12: (C0) (C13)                          A37: (,0) U 9000
H12: '+                                  B37: (,0) ($C$13)+($C$14*A37)
I12: (C2) (C14)                          A38: (,0) U 12000
J12: 'N                                  B38: (,0) ($C$13)+($C$14*A38)
A13: 'Fixed costs increase to            A39: (,0) U 15000
C13: (C2) U 3000                         B39: (,0) ($C$13)+($C$14*A39)
D13: 'per year.                          C39: 'Alt B
A14: 'Variable costs reduce to           A41: 'Equation C
C14: (C2) U 1                            A42: 'When X is..
D14: 'per unit.                          B42: '     Y equals..
A16: 'Alternative C                      A43: (,0) U 0
E16: 'Equation for Alt. C                B43: (,0) ($C$19)+($C$20*A43)
A17: '-------------                      A44: (,0) U 3000
E17: '-------------------                B44: (,0) ($C$19)+($C$20*A44)
A18: 'Purchase completely automatic machines.   A45: (,0) U 6000
E18: 'TC(C)                              B45: (,0) ($C$19)+($C$20*A45)
F18: '=                                  A46: (,0) U 9000
G18: (C0) (C19)                          B46: (,0) ($C$19)+($C$20*A46)
H18: '+                                  A47: (,0) U 12000
I18: (C2) (C20)                          B47: (,0) ($C$19)+($C$20*A47)
J18: 'N                                  A48: (,0) U 15000
A19: 'Fixed costs increase to            B48: (,0) ($C$19)+($C$20*A48)
C19: (C2) U 9000                         C48: 'Alt C
D19: 'per year.
```

LOTUS 1-2-3 PROGRAM—LIFE-CYCLE ANALYSIS (PROGRAM 9)

```
A1:  '          Return on Investment - Net Present Value Method
C3:  '     Individual Machine Costs     C9:  (,0) U 75000
C4:  '     ----------------------       E9:  (,0) U 30000
C5:  U ^A                               A10: 'Labor in Hours
E5:  U ^B                               C10: (,0) U 4100
A6:  'Initial Cost                      E10: (,0) U 2000
C6:  (C0) U 500000                      A11: 'Floor Space (sq ft)
E6:  (C0) U 1000000                     C11: (,0) U 200
A7:  'Salvage Value                     E11: (,0) U 220
C7:  (,0) U +C6*($F$19)                 A12: 'Power Usage (kwh)
E7:  (,0) U +E6*($F$19)                 C12: U 4.5
A8:  'Net Cost                          E12: U 6.2
C8:  (C0) U +C6-C7                      C14: '    Costs Common To Both Machines
E8:  (C0) U +E6-E7                      C15: '    ----------------------------
A9:  'Maintenance Cost                  A16: 'Common Costs
                                        C16: ^Inflation
```

```
D16: '     Cost of Money
F16: (P1) U 0.16
A17: 'Labor (per hour)
B17: (C2) U 24.5
C17: (P1) U 0.06
D17: '     Incr Tax Rate
F17: (P1) U 0.43
A18: 'Floor Space
B18: (C2) U 16
C18: (P1) U 0.06
D18: '     Service Life
F18: U 5
A19: 'Power
B19: (C2) U 0.09
C19: (P1) U 0.08
D19: '     Salvage Value
F19: (P1) U 0.08
A20: 'Maintenance Inflation
C20: (P1) U 0.07
A21: \-
B21: \-
C21: \-
D21: \-
E21: \-
F21: \-
B23: ^Year 1
C23: ^Year 2
D23: ^Year 3
E23: ^Year 4
F23: ^Year 5
A24: 'Machine A
B24: ^------
C24: ^------
D24: ^------
E24: ^------
F24: ^------
A26: 'Maintenance
B26: (C0) -C9*(1-F17)
C26: (C0) +B26*(1+$C$20)
D26: (C0) +C26*(1+$C$20)
E26: (C0) +D26*(1+$C$20)
F26: (C0) +E26*(1+$C$20)
A27: 'Operator Labor
B27: (,0) -C10*B17*(1-F17)
C27: (,0) +B27*(1+$C$17)
D27: (,0) +C27*(1+$C$17)
E27: (,0) +D27*(1+$C$17)
F27: (,0) +E27*(1+$C$17)
A28: 'Floor Space
B28: (,0) -C11*B18*(1-F17)
C28: (,0) +B28*(1+$C$18)
D28: (,0) +C28*(1+$C$18)
E28: (,0) +D28*(1+$C$18)
F28: (,0) +E28*(1+$C$18)
A29: 'Power
B29: (,0) -24*365*B19*C12*(1-F17)
C29: (,0) +B29*(1+$C$19)
D29: (,0) +C29*(1+$C$19)
E29: (,0) +D29*(1+$C$19)
F29: (,0) +E29*(1+$C$19)
A30: 'Depreciation
A31: '     Tax Effect
B31: (,0) (+$C$6/$F$18)*$F$17
C31: (,0) (+$C$6/$F$18)*$F$17
D31: (,0) (+$C$6/$F$18)*$F$17
E31: (,0) (+$C$6/$F$18)*$F$17
F31: (,0) (+$C$6/$F$18)*$F$17
A32: 'Revenue
B32: (C0) U 250000
C32: (C0) U 250000
D32: (C0) U 250000
E32: (C0) U 250000
F32: (C0) U 250000
A33: 'Salvage
F33: (,0) +F19*C6
A34: 'Total cash flow
A35: '     from operations
B35: (C0) @SUM(B26..B33)
C35: (C0) @SUM(C26..C33)
D35: (C0) @SUM(D26..D33)
E35: (C0) @SUM(E26..E33)
F35: (C0) @SUM(F26..F33)
A36: 'Present Value of
A37: '  cash flows from operations . . . . . . . . . . .
F37: (C0) @NPV(F16,B35..F35)
A38: 'Net Present Value of cash flows
A39: '  from operations less initial net cost . . . . . . .
F39: (C0) +F37-C8
A40: 'Return on investment - percentage per year . . . . .
F40: (P2) ((F39)/(C8))/5
```

```
A41: \-
B41: \-
C41: \-
D41: \-
E41: \-
F41: \-
B43: ^Year 1
C43: ^Year 2
D43: ^Year 3
E43: ^Year 4
F43: ^Year 5
A44: 'Machine B
B44: ^------
C44: ^------
D44: ^------
E44: ^------
F44: ^------
A46: 'Maintenance
B46: (C0) -E9*(1-F17)
C46: (C0) +B46*(1+$C$20)
D46: (C0) +C46*(1+$C$20)
E46: (C0) +D46*(1+$C$20)
F46: (C0) +E46*(1+$C$20)
A47: 'Operator Labor
B47: (,0) -E10*B17*(1-F17)
C47: (,0) +B47*(1+$C$17)
D47: (,0) +C47*(1+$C$17)
E47: (,0) +D47*(1+$C$17)
F47: (,0) +E47*(1+$C$17)
A48: 'Floor Space
B48: (,0) -E11*B18*(1-F17)
C48: (,0) +B48*(1+$C$18)
D48: (,0) +C48*(1+$C$18)
E48: (,0) +D48*(1+$C$18)
F48: (,0) +E48*(1+$C$18)
A49: 'Power
B49: (,0) -24*365*B19*E12*(1-F17)
C49: (,0) +B49*(1+$C$19)
D49: (,0) +C49*(1+$C$19)
E49: (,0) +D49*(1+$C$19)
F49: (,0) +E49*(1+$C$19)
A50: 'Depreciation
A51: '     Tax Effect
B51: (,0) (+$E$6/$F$18)*$F$17
C51: (,0) (+$E$6/$F$18)*$F$17
D51: (,0) (+$E$6/$F$18)*$F$17
E51: (,0) (+$E$6/$F$18)*$F$17
F51: (,0) (+$E$6/$F$18)*$F$17
A52: 'Revenue
B52: (C0) U 400000
C52: (C0) U 400000
D52: (C0) U 400000
E52: (C0) U 400000
F52: (C0) U 400000
A53: 'Salvage
F53: (,0) +F19*E6
A54: 'Total cash flow
A55: '   from operations
B55: (C0) @SUM(B46..B53)
C55: (C0) @SUM(C46..C53)
D55: (C0) @SUM(D46..D53)
E55: (C0) @SUM(E46..E53)
F55: (C0) @SUM(F46..F53)
A56: 'Present Value of
A57: '  cash flows from operations . . . . . . . . . . .
F57: (C0) @NPV(F16,B55..F55)
A58: 'Net Present Value of cash flows
A59: '  from operations less initial net cost . . . . . . .
F59: (C0) +F57-E8
A60: 'Return on investment - percentage per year . . . . .
F60: (P2) ((F59)/(E8))/5
A61: \-
B61: \-
C61: \-
D61: \-
E61: \-
F61: \-
A62: 'Return on investment A vs B . . . . . . . . . . . .
F62: (P2) (F60)-(F40)
```

BIBLIOGRAPHY

Aggarwal, S. C. "MRP, JIT, OPT, FMS?" *Harvard Business Review,* September-October 1985.

Agin, G. J. "Computer Vision Systems for Industrial Inspection and Assembly." *Computer,* May 1980.

Aleksander, I. *Designing Intelligent Systems.* New York: Unipub, 1984.

Appleton, D. S. "The State of CIM." *Datamation,* December 15, 1984.

Armstrong, D. J. "Sharpening Inventory Management." *Harvard Business Review,* November-December 1985.

Baker, E. F. "The Changing Scene on the Production Floor." *Management Review,* January 1983.

Batt, R. "DP Seen Critical to Manufacturing Productivity." *Computerworld,* May 18, 1981.

————. "Machine Intelligence Eyeing Automation Mart." *Computerworld,* August 17, 1981.

Baumann, E. W. "Test Robot Work Cells With Graphic Systems." *Computerworld,* March 26, 1984.

Becker, R. H. "All Factories Are Not the Same." *Interfaces,* May-June 1985.

Begg, V. *Developing Expert CAD Systems.* New York: Unipub, 1984.

Bernhard, R. "Robotics—Too Many Vendors, Too Few Applications." *Systems & Software,* August 1984.

Bernstein, A. "A Case for Quality." *Business Computer Systems,* March 1984.

————. "Micro MRP Gets It Together." *Business Computer Systems,* October 1984.

————. "Innovating with Shop-Floor LANs." *Business Computer Systems,* April 1985.

————. "Computer-Based Manufacturing." *Business Computer Systems,* July 1985.

Braue, J. "GM MAPS The Future." *Computer Decisions,* December 17, 1985.

Bruno, C. "Labor Relations in the Age of Robotics." *Datamation,* March 1984.

Buffa, E. S., and Miller, J. G. *Production—Inventory Systems: Planning and Control.* Homewood, IL: Richard D. Irwin, 1979.

Burt, D. N., and Soukup, W. R. "Purchasing's Role in New Product Development." *Harvard Business Review,* September/October 1985.

Bylinsky, G. "America's Best-Managed Factories." *Fortune,* May 28, 1984.

————. "GM's Road Map to Automated Plants." *Fortune,* October 28, 1985.

Cashin, J. "Benefits of Micro CAD/CAM, CAE: Lower Cost, Better Design." *Software News,* July 1986.

Catalano, F. "Emerging Low-End CAD Market Attracts Attention." *Mini-Micro Systems,* October 1983.

Cornelison, J., and Chandra, D. "Top Management Policies Can Destroy MRP." *Production & Inventory Management and APICS News,* March 1981.

Cox, J. F., and Clark, S. J. "Problems in Implementing and Operating a Manufacturing Resource Planning Information System." *Journal of Management Information Systems,* Summer 1984.

Davis, D. "New Projects: Beware of False Economies." *Harvard Business Review,* March–April 1985.

De, S.; Nof, S. Y.; and Whinston, A. B. "Decision Support in Computer-Integrated Manufacturing." *Decision Support Systems,* January 1985.

Desmond, J. "Shaking Smokestacks: Software in Manufacturing." *Software News,* June 1986.

Dicasali, R. L. "Integration Coming to Shop Floor Automation." *Computerworld,* March 26, 1984.

————. "Functional Integration Is Key to Factory of Future." *Industrial Engineering,* September 1984.

————. "MIS Gets into Manufacturing." *Computerworld Focus,* March 19, 1986.

Dizard, J. W. "Machines That See Look for a Market." *Fortune,* September 17, 1984.

Dolan, S. S., and Williamson, R. F., Jr. "Factories Adopting Distributed Intelligence." *Computerworld,* March 26, 1984.

Dooley, B. "Study: U.S. Slips on High-Tech Implementation." *Management Information Systems Week,* March 20, 1985.

Donovan, R. M., and Appleby, H. H. *Planning and Controlling Manufacturing Resources.* New York: AMACOM, 1979.

Fersko-Weiss, H. "Expert Systems, Decision-Making Power." *Personal Computing,* November 1985.

Fine, C. H., and Hax, A. C. "Manufacturing Strategy: A Methodology and an Illustration." *Interfaces,* November-December 1985.

Foulkes, F. K., and Hirsch, J. L. "People Make Robots Work." *Harvard Business Review,* January-February 1984.

Foundyller, C. M. "Technology Continues to Define Leaders of CAD/CAM and CAE Market." *Mini-Micro Systems,* August 1984.

Gand, A., and Cook, M. E. "Choosing an MRP System." *Datamation,* January 1983.

Gardan, Y., and Lucas, M. *Interactive Graphics in CAD.* New York: Unipub, 1984.

Gerwin, D. "Do's and Don'ts of Computerized Manufacturing." *Harvard Business Review,* March-April 1982.

Gervarter, W. R. *Intelligent Machines, An Introductory Perspective of Artificial Intelligence and Robotics.* Englewood Cliffs, NJ: Prentice-Hall, 1985.

Gessner, R. *Manufacturing Information Systems.* New York: John Wiley & Sons, 1984.

Ghemawat, P. "Building Strategy on the Experience Curve." *Harvard Business Review,* March-April 1985.

Gold, B. "CAM Sets New Rules for Production." *Harvard Business Review,* November-December 1982.

————. "Foundations of Strategic Planning for Productivity Improvement." *Interfaces,* May-June 1985.

Goldhar, J. D. "Computer Integrated Flexible Manufacturing: Organizational, Economic, and Strategic Implications." *Interfaces,* May-June 1985.

Gould, L. "Planning Ahead." *Digital Review,* December 1984.

————. "Still Planning Ahead." *Digital Review,* January 1985.

Gray, C. "MRPII Software." *Computerworld,* January 27, 1986.

Gunn, T. "The CIM Connection." *Datamation,* February 1, 1986.

Hapgood, F. "Inside a Robotics Lab: Avoiding Obstacles." *Technology Illustrated,* May 1983.

Harty, P. "Manufacturers Migrate to MRP, JIT." *Software News,* June 1985.

Hawkins, D. F. "Toward the New Balance Sheet." *Harvard Business Review,* November-December 1984.

Hayes, R. H., and Wheelwright, S. C. *Restoring Our Competitive Edge: Competing Through Manufacturing.* New York: John Wiley & Sons, Inc., 1984.

Hehnen, M. T., et al. "An Integrated Decision Support and Manufacturing Control System." *Interfaces,* September-October 1984.

Heinritz, S. F., and Farrell, P. V. *Purchasing Analysis and Application.* Englewood Cliffs, NJ: Prentice-Hall, 1981.

Hertz, D. B. "Artificial Intelligence and the Business Manager." *Computerworld,* October 24, 1983.

Hinze, W. "CIM: The Future of Factory Management Automation." *Computerworld,* September 9, 1985.

Hodder, J. E., and Riggs, H. E. "Pitfalls in Evaluating Risky Projects." *Harvard Business Review,* January-February 1985.

Howie, R. L. "Criteria for Purchasing Automation to Its Fullest." *Computerworld,* March 26, 1984.

Hunsche, M. A. "The Three Challenges of Factory Systems Integration." *Infosystems,* April 1986.

Jaffe, M. "Decision Support Systems for Manufacturing." *Infosystems,* July 1983.

Jordon, H. H. "Improving Corporate Profits with Inventory Management." *Purchasing World,* March 1981.

Kantrow, A. M. "Industrial R&D: Looking Back to Look Ahead." *Harvard Business Review,* July-August 1986.

Kaplan, R. S. "Must CIM Be Justified by Faith Alone?" *Harvard Business Review,* March-April 1986.

Keller, E. L. "Industrial Automation: Awaiting the Final Link—Standards." Special *Systems & Software,* June 1984.

Kerr, J. "Made in the U.S.A." *Business Computer Systems,* December 1985.

Kleutghen, P. P., and McGee, J. C. "Development and Implementation of an Integrated Inventory Management Program at Pfizer Pharmaceuticals." *Interfaces,* January-February 1985.

Knickerbocker, C. "Integrating AI and Unix Applications." *Systems & Software,* November 1984.

Kolodziej, S. "Micro-Based CAM Systems—From Plan Vanilla to Thirty Flavors." *Computerworld Focus*, June 19, 1980.42

———. "Computer-Integrated Manufacturing: The Key Word Is Integrated." *Computerworld Focus*, June 19, 1985.

———. "Users Move Toward MRP." *Computerworld Focus*, March 19, 1986.

LaCoe, D. "Expert Systems: An Answer to Factor Management." *Robotics World*, October 1984.

Lampert, A. "Expert Systems Get Down to Business." *Computer Decisions*, January 1982.

Landvater, D. "The Rise and Fall of Just-in-Time." *Infosystems*, November 1984.

Lee, T. H.; Fisher, J. C.; and Yau, T. S. "Is Your R&D on Track?" *Harvard Business Review*, January-February 1986.

Leonard, F. S., and Sasser, W. E. "The Incline of Quality." *Harvard Business Review*, September-October 1982.

Li, L. "Computer-Aided Design—The Offer Architects Can't Refuse." *Business Computer Systems*, March 1984.

Liberatore, M. J., and Miller, T. "A Hierarchical Production Planning System." *Interfaces*, July-August 1985.

Lusa, J. M. "Manufacturing Systems, Aiming for More Productivity." *Infosystems*, February 1981.

Macfarlane, M. L. "The Automated Factory, An Analysis." *Micro Manager*, April 1984.

Main, J. "The Battle for Quality Begins." *Fortune*, December 29, 1980.

———. "Under the Spell of the Quality Gurus." *Fortune*, August 18, 1986.

Major, M. J. "New Technologies Are Finding Their Way to the Factory Floor." *Software News*, June 1985.

———. "Wading Through the Transition in CAD/CAM, CAE." *Software News*, September 1985.

Marks, P. A. "Putting CAD/CAM Into Place." *Computerworld Focus*, March 19, 1986.

McKibbin, W. "Will AI Clash with MIS in the Factory?" *Infosystems*, August 1983.

Meal, H. C. "Putting Production Decisions Where They Belong." *Harvard Business Review*, March-April 1984.

Michaelsen, R., and Michie, D. "Expert Systems in Business." *Datamation*, November 1983.

Michie, D. *Machine Intelligence and Related Topics*. New York: Gordon and Breach Science Publishers, 1982.

Miller, J. G., and Vollmann, T. E. "The Hidden Factory." *Harvard Business Review*, September-October 1985.

Mizlo, J. "LAN Tightens Factory Floor Control." *Mini-Micro Systems*, December 1985.

Monk, J. T., and Landis, K. M. "Getting Inventory Up and Running." *Business Computer Systems*, August 1984.

O'Dell, P. "MRP: Look Before You Implement." *Computer Decisions*, August 27, 1985.

Orr, J. "Picking the Best Cadd System for You." *Computerworld*, June 10, 1985.

Peterson, R., and Silver, E. A. *Decision Systems for Inventory Management and Production Planning*. New York: John Wiley & Sons, 1979.

Phillips, T. E., and White, K. R. "Minimizing Inventory Cost." *Interfaces*, August 1981.

Pont, J. W. "Collecting and Using Shop-Floor Data." *Infosystems*, August 1985.

Putnam, A. O. "A Redesign for Engineering." *Harvard Business Review*, May-June 1985.

Rauch-Hindin, W. "Expert System to Plan PC Board Assembly in the Factory." *Systems & Software*, August 1984.

Reeve, R. C. "Where Are the Robots?" *Computerworld*, June 10, 1985.

Richardson, P. R.; Taylor, A. J.; and Gordon, J. R. M. "A Strategic Approach to Evaluating Manufacturing Performance." *Interfaces*, November-December 1985.

Rifkin, G. "A Look at Robotics in the U.S." *Computerworld*, October 7, 1985.

Riggs, J. L. *Production Systems: Planning, Analysis, and Control*. New York: John Wiley & Sons, 1981.

Ritzman, L. P.; King, B. E.; and Krajewski, L. J. "Manufacturing Performance Pulling the Right Levers." *Harvard Business Review*, March-April 1984.

Roberts, S. K. "Computers Simulate Human Experts." *Mini-Micro Systems*, September 1983.

Rowe, J. C. "Programmable Controllers Altering Shop Floor." *Computerworld*, March 26, 1984.

Schmitt, R. W. "Successful Corporate R & D." *Harvard Business Review,* May-June 1985. ✗

Skinner, W. "Operations Technology: Blind Spot in Strategic Management." *Interfaces,* January-February 1984.

——. *Manufacturing: The Formidable Competitive Weapon.* New York: John Wiley & Sons, 1985.

Stamps, D. "The Micros Move Into Manufacturing." *Micro Manager,* April 1984.

Steele, L. "Managers' Misconceptions About Technology." *Harvard Business Review,* November-December 1983. ✗

Stix, G. "Computers Accelerate Manufacturing." *Computer Decisions,* September 15, 1984.

——. "Manufacturing Resource Planning Keeps You on Time, On Target." *Computer Decisions,* October 1984.

——. "Has GM Found the Missing Link?" *Computer Decisions,* December 1984.

Taylor, W. "Why Automatic Factories Are Not." *Computerworld,* April 8, 1985.

Teicholz, E. "Computer Integrated Manufacturing." *Datamation,* March 1984. ✗

Teicholz, E., and Kilburn, P. "Low-Cost CADD at Work." *Datamation,* January 1983. ✗

Thierauf, R. J. *Distributed Processing Systems.* Englewood Cliffs, NJ: Prentice-Hall, 1978.

——. *Decision Support Systems for Effective Planning and Control—A Case Study Approach,* Englewood Cliffs, NJ: Prentice-Hall, 1982.

Trigoboff, D. "Micros Proliferating in Manufacturing Marketplace." *Management Information Systems Week,* March 20, 1985.

Tucker, M. "Software Development Fires Up Workstations." *Mini-Micro Systems,* July 1986.

Wakefield, B. D. "MRP Works: Here's Proof You Can Use in Planning." *Production,* February 1981.

Walleigh, R. C. "What's Your Excuse for Not Using JIT?" *Harvard Business Review,* March-April 1986. ✗

Wheelwright, S. C., and Hayes, R. H. "Competing Through Manufacturing." *Harvard Business Review,* January-February 1985. ✗

White, L. "On the Shop Floor With Micro MRP." *Computerworld Focus,* March 19, 1986.

Wight, O. W. "MRP II: Manufacturing Resource Planning." *Computerworld,* September 28, 1981.

Williamson, R. "Black-Box Technique Automates Quality Control." *Computerworld,* December 16, 1985.

Winston, P. H., and Predergast, K. A. *The AI Business, The Commercial Uses of Artificial Intelligence.* Cambridge, MA: The M.I.T. Press, 1984.

CHAPTER 14

Accounting and Finance Subsystem—XYZ Corporation

INTRODUCTION TO ACCOUNTING AND FINANCE

The functions of accounting and finance in an effective management information system for the XYZ Corporation center around recording, classifying,
and summarizing transactions and events that are—in part at least—of a
financial nature and interpreting the results. Standard double entry is utilized
to reflect the in- and out-flow of cash and noncash transactions. Accounting
and finance data are stored on some machine-processible medium at the
appropriate level, that is, plant (warehouse) or corporate headquarters. In
turn, these data provide the necessary input for producing the type of management information desired at the plant and corporate levels. With this context, the essential components of an effective MIS accounting and finance
subsystem are developed in this chapter.

    The first part of the chapter discusses important considerations on mak-
ing the accounting and finance subsystem effective. These include return on
investment, financial ratios and statistics, a problem-finding approach to
accounting and finance, and mathematical models, along with micro software. After presenting an overview of accounting and finance for the XYZ
Corporation, the second part of the chapter centers on the essential elements
of this subsystem: (1) receivables and payables, (2) payroll, (3) cost accounting, (4) financial statements, and (5) source and application of funds. Finally,
the integration of corporate planning with accounting and finance for the XYZ
Corporation is examined from the viewpoint of effective MIS practice.

ACCOUNTING AND FINANCE CONSIDERATIONS FOR EFFECTIVE MIS

MIS considerations for the accounting and finance subsystem go beyond its
own boundaries. Customer billing is initiated by marketing; vendor invoices
are received from purchasing. Payroll, whether factory or office, also originates outside the accounting subsystem. Similarly, feedback of product cost
data is forwarded from the manufacturing work centers and inventory. The
only real accounting and finance functions that are generated within their
own operation are financial statements and sources of funds. Financial state-

ments are forwarded to all subsystems for managements' review and appropriate corrective action. They form the basis for financing capital projects and current operations. Thus, most other subsystems must be considered in developing an effective management information system.

Not only must the accounting and finance subsystem enlarge the scope of its activities by going outside its traditional boundaries, it also must achieve new management goals. Among these are improved access to accounting and finance data for answering new "What if?" questions, more analytical managerial information to evaluate the changing environment, improved flexibility for meeting changing demands placed upon the accounting and finance areas, and improved capability for providing a faster closing cycle of all financial transactions. The incorporation of these goals into the MIS accounting and finance subsystem results in a new way of viewing ongoing operations.

Based upon the foregoing considerations for effective MIS, the emphasis below is on return on investment, financial ratios and statistics, and micro investment software. This is followed by a discussion of a problem-finding approach, mathematical models, and integrated micro accounting systems. This background provides an underlying framework for developing a management information system for planning and control over accounting and finance activities.

Return on Investment

Because ROI is a sound measure of good, average, or poor performance, management of the XYZ Corporation should consider ways of improving its return. Acquisition of investments that have a high return, pruning of low-return product lines, cost reduction and profit improvement, improving asset utilization, and changing the financial structure are constructive measures to increase the corporation's return on its investments. An optimum allocation of financial resources that considers these alternatives for increasing ROI is a must for reaping a higher return. However, there is a word of caution. If such an allocation means raising ROI, it also means balancing long-term commitments and noneconomic constraints like social responsibility. Hence, reduction of commitments seems preferable to taking on a whole series of marginal projects that will, in the long run, reduce the corporation's return on investment.

Regarding the last point, research findings indicate an overall relationship between ROI and investment intensity: the higher the ratio of investments to sales, the lower the return on investment tends to be.[1] This conclusion was drawn from a survey of 57 corporations controlling 620 diverse businesses. The survey indicated that businesses with high investment intensities cannot achieve profit margins sufficient to effect the greater amounts of investments they require to sustain a given volume. Another important finding from this same study is that market share is a major influence on profita-

---

[1]Sidney Schoeffler, Robert D. Buzzell, and Donald F. Heany. "Impact of Strategic Planning on Profit Performance." *Harvard Business Review*, March-April 1974, p. 143.

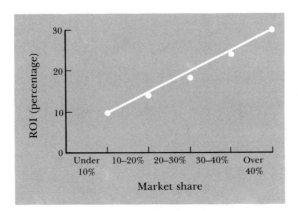

FIGURE 14.1
Relationship between market share and pretax return on investment.
SOURCE: Robert D. Buzzell, Bradley T. Gale, and Ralph G. M. Sutten, "Market Share—A Key to Profitability." *Harvard Business Review*, January-February 1975, p. 98.

bility.[2] ROI goes up steadily as market share increases. On the average, business with market shares above 36 percent earned more than three times as much, relative to their investment, as businesses with less than 7 percent of their respective markets. Subsequent research strongly supports the proposition that market share is positively related to the rate of return.[3] This fact is illustrated in figure 14.1. Three possible explanations given are economics of scale, market power, and the quality of management. Also, research data indicate that the advantages of a large market share are greatest for businesses selling products that are purchased infrequently by a fragmented customer group.

Financial Ratios and Statistics

The MIS accounting and finance subsystem of the XYZ Corporation is quite capable of producing important financial ratios and statistics. Overall, operational ratios available immediately from a microcomputer are presented in figure 14.2. These ratios are of great value for financial analysts as well as for the corporate planning staff. Specifically, they can be calculated as needed and serve as the basis for financial management by exception when appropriate ranges are assigned to each ratio. For example, the ratio of current assets to current liabilities should be about 2:1.

As shown in figure 14.2, the corporate data base contains the information needed to prepare the profit and loss statement and the balance sheet as well as appropriate formulas for calculating financial statistics and ratios. When the user requests a specific statistic or ratio, the calculations are automatically performed to obtain the required results. These statistics and ratios provide an insight for measuring actual results against the short-range plans.

---

[2]Ibid.,p. 141.

[3]Robert D. Buzzell, Bradley T. Gale, and Ralph G. M. Sutten. "Market Share—A Key to Profitability." *Harvard Business Review*, January-February 1975, pp. 97–106.

Microcomputer

Financial ratios and statistics programs

Corporate data base
Balance sheet data
Income statement data
Statistics and financial data

Utilization parameter	Data requirements and calculations	Data requirements and calculations	Utilization parameter
Management efficiency Capital turnover	Sales ÷ assets employed	Net income ÷ sales	*Operation efficiency* Return on sales
Liquidity status Current ratio	Current assets ÷ current liabilities	Annualized sales ÷ average inventory	*Inventory utilization* Inventory turnover
Measure of solvency Investment status	Investment ÷ total assets	Backlog ÷ sales/day	*Days of sales in backlog* Undelivered commitments
Investment utilization Return on investment	Annualized net income ÷ average investment	Shareholders equity ÷ total debt	*Credit strength* Net worth debt ratio
Asset profitability Return on assets used	Sales return percent × asset return percent	Cash + securities + net receivables ÷ current liabilities	*Immediate liquidation* Acid test ratio
Receivable investment Average collection period	Accounts receivable ÷ net credit sales × 365	Pretax income + interest expense ÷ total assets	*Percent earnings available* Stockholders' earnings status

Management effectiveness can be measured by the capital turnover ratio, asset profitability, and return on investment. Also, the corporation's performance can be gauged through the return on sales, days of sales in backlog, inventory utilization, and receivable collections.

Micro Investment Software

Going beyond the evaluation of internal operations via financial ratios and statistics, finance managers of the XYZ Corporation using microcomputers are making a profitable assault on the financial market by using sophisticated programs to screen investments and keep portfolios up to date. Sophisticated investment software enables them to access electronic data banks replete with the latest financial news. Finance managers can use these programs to systematically track and screen any type of investment possibility—stocks, bonds, commodities, savings certificates, etc.

More specifically, finance managers can now:

- obtain up-to-the-minute securities price quotes, financial news, and corporate reports (including those mandated by government regulations) over telephone lines.
- translate current and historical stock statistics into charts and graphs of the investments' past performance and projected future activity.
- keep portfolios current by recording the day's closing quotes and trading transactions, and by making daily accounting entries, including portfolio cash value, short- and long-term realized and unrealized gains and losses, and maturities and expirations.
- screen potential investments, using criteria (such as "quality," risk, and yield) selected by the user.

How the finance managers get the latest data on the above depends on the particular investment-management programs being used.

For some investment-management programs, stock quotes are keyed in by hand. For others, a data base on a floppy disk is used and replaced each month with an updated version. These monthly data disks are provided by the software distributor for a yearly subscription fee. The data in these packages, already compiled and arranged, can be massaged to produce the fullest picture of a potential investment's past performance. Two such products are Microscan (from Isys Corporation) and Stockpack (from Standard & Poor's Corporation). Still other sources include on-line commercial data banks, which provide the latest quotes from different securities markets as well as financial information from various publications and company reports. To extract data from these sources requires a modem. In addition to the cost of this hardware, users are billed for use of the telephone line and the data bank's computer.

Some of the information utilities that provide such stock-market data are

---

FIGURE 14.2   Typical financial ratios and statistics as calculated within a microcomputer environment.

The Source and CompuServe, Inc. The Source (from Telecomputing Corporation of America) carries the United Press International (UPI) news wire and data from all major stock exchanges. CompuServe (a subsidiary of H & R Block) carries the Associated Press wire, news from ten U.S. daily papers, and quotes from the leading stock exchanges. The Dow Jones News/Retrieval Service, in Princeton, N.J., is another popular commercial data bank available to microcomputer users.

Currently, there are more than 100 different microcomputer programs available for investment planning, stock market research, securities selection, and portfolio management. A sample list of these micro investment software programs is found in figure 14.3 on pages 545 and 546.

Problem-Finding Approach to Accounting and Finance

As an introductory approach to problem finding in the area of accounting and finance, electronic spreadsheets such as Lotus 1-2-3 can be used. These "calc" programs do away with much of the tedious analysis associated with investment management. They also help managers plan their next steps, thus functioning as planning aids. A manager might set up the vertical column headings as years and the horizontal rows as elements of potential profit. The manager can then estimate the annual return on investment by a single element, such as long-term capital gains, dividends, interest, or some form of income. A single spreadsheet can be built for each type of security, commodity, property, option, and so forth. Of course, it is up to the finance manager to make reasonable market judgments to project future earnings for each investment in the portfolio. From this perspective, the electronic spreadsheet is useful for problem solving.

Going beyond problem solving, the Lotus 1-2-3 spreadsheet can also be helpful in problem finding. For example, the XYZ Corporation's goal is to double the value of its investments in five years. The finance manager can sum the bottom lines of individual spreadsheets for each portfolio component to get the estimated aggregates for the period. If the total return does not attain the corporation's goal, the finance manager can easily determine which of the individual profit contributors is likely to fail to produce its share of gains, and make adjustments. The net result is that the spreadsheet analysis approach is useful for identifying future potential investment problems before they happen. In turn, the portfolio model can be quickly recalculated based on these changes, and the effect on the aggregate gains is seen immediately. Overall, the finance manager uses electronic spreadsheet analysis to perceive future investment alternatives and their relevant problems and bring them back to the present time for solution.

Mathematical Models

Many mathematical models have been developed for the various areas of accounting and finance. However, the main topics addressed here are financial

Product	Distributor	Data Source	Features
Compu Trac	Compu Trac Inc.	Interactive Data Corp. for stock data; Commodity Systems, Inc. for commodity data	Integrated investment package that provides graphics-oriented technical analysis of data
Dow Jones Market	RTR Software Inc.	Dow Jones News/ Retrieval	Technical analysis charting and graphing of present and historical data
Dow Jones Portfolio Evaluator	Apple Computer inc.	Dow Jones News/ Retrieval	Allows user to store, modify, and update portfolios
Dow Jones Portfolio Management System	Commodore Business Machines, Inc.	Dow Jones News/ Retrieval	Maintains multiple security portfolios and updates values of portfolios, graphs performance of selected stocks, and generates reports for tax purposes
Microcash	Future Technologies International, Inc.	Dow Jones News/ Retrieval, The Source	Cash management package that includes 14 modules and performs a wide range of treasury functions; interfaces with word processor
Investor's Micro Messenger	Investor's Micro Messenger	Manual entry of quotes or on-line retrieval from data bank	For a yearly fee, an IMM member gets software that analyzes stock and commodities markets, simulates trades as buys and sells, prints out profit and loss statements, graphically shows buys and sells over time, and suggests trades for the next day
Microscan	Isys Corp.	Data base on disk	Allows user to screen data base of 1,400 securities after determining investment criteria
On-Balance Volume Charting	Stock Market Software, Inc.	Warner Computer Systems, CompuServe, Dow Jones News/ Retrieval	Comprehensive menu-controlled package that provides automatic log-on storage and analysis of quotes

FIGURE 14.3   Microcomputer investment software.

Product	Distributor	Data Source	Features
PEAR	Pear Systems	Manual entry of quotes or Dow Jones News/Retrieval	Automatic updating of portfolios via master securities file
SMART	Software Resources Inc.	SRI	Technical analysis using graphics, evaluation of systematic trading approaches, historical market research, automatic data base updating
Stockfocus	Centennial Software, Inc.	Manual entry of quotes	Determines historical highs and lows of stocks, and projects future highs and lows
The Stock Manager	Omni Software Systems, Inc.	Manual entry of quotes	Manages portfolio of 500+ stocks, with 30 items in each stock listing, generates reports, including 1040
Stock Market Monitor	Logical Systems, Inc.	Manual entry of quotes	Compares keyboard high/low/close/volume data to general market activity
Stock Market System	RTR Software, Inc.	Manual entry of quotes	Allows up to 5 stocks to be plotted at once to show relative performance over user-determined time period
Stockpak	Tandy Corp's Radio Shack stores, Standard & Poor's Corp.	Data base on disk	Package includes 3 program diskettes, performs portfolio management and allows user to screen data base

FIGURE 14.3   Continued

statements and cost areas. For example, linear programming has been helpful in evaluating overall performance as a supplement to standard procedures for comparing actual to budgeted amounts. Numerous cost formulas have been developed to evaluate current manufacturing performance. Also, simulation models have been widely used in such areas as in predicting profits, analyzing future costs, examining the variances of costs, and projecting corporate taxes.

LINEAR PROGRAMMING MODEL.   An interesting application of mathematical modeling for MIS is to structure the accounting subsystem on a linear programming model. This approach goes beyond a comparison of actual with flexible budgeted amounts. Specifically, the differences between what the corporation accomplished with its available resources for the month and what it should have accomplished with these same resources is calculated in terms of overall contribution. Thus, a true overall efficiency of operational variances can be determined using the linear programming model, thereby giving the managers a new tool for overall control of operations.

This approach requires the development of the objective function and constraint equations as found in any linear programming problem. Actual time available in the various manufacturing work centers for the month under study, manufacturing times for each product, contribution for each product, quantities that can be sold, and minimum sales requirements are the necessary input. The introduction of these variables for one plant means that about one hundred equations with several hundred variables must be developed before computer processing can begin. Because most of these data are already stored on the data base, the problem is simplified. The program references these data elements plus other data that can be entered via a CRT terminal. There is no need to list all the intermediate solutions (i.e., tableaus) in the problem—a printout of the first and last tableaus is sufficient. It should be pointed out that a mathematical model of this magnitude takes considerable memory space and computation time. For this reason, it is advisable to perform such calculations during a non-operating shift when there are few or no demands on the computer.

COST ACCOUNTING MODELS. Manufacturing cost analysis, overall, is directed toward its major components—material, labor, and overhead variances. Many more variances can be developed. Some can be reported as they happen, while other variances are reported on a daily, weekly, monthly, or some other logical period-evaluation basis. In general, mathematical cost accounting models can give management and their staff more effective control over current costs.

Typical cost accounting models for a specific work center are illustrated in figure 14.4. The first cost accounting model (equation 14.1) is the materials-usage variance percent, which measures daily the deviation of materials used during the manufacturing process for a production order in a specific work center.

The summation (Σ) of all actual materials used to produce a manufacturing order within any work center is accumulated on the data base during manufacturing. It is then compared to the total standard materials cost when the manufacturing process is complete. The number of manufactured items is multiplied by the standard unit materials cost to arrive at total standard costs. The resulting value must be multiplied by 100 to convert it to a percent.

The second model (equation 14.2) focuses on labor reporting by work center. All actual direct labor costs accumulated by shift for each work center are divided by standard time calculations to evaluate labor costs. As in the previous calculation, the resulting value is multiplied by 100 to convert it to a percent.

Overhead variances, like raw materials and labor, can take many forms in reports of timely information. One such variance—the third model (equa-

1) Materials-usage variance percent $= \dfrac{\Sigma\text{AM}}{(\text{SM} \times \text{AU})} \times 100$ **(Equation 14.1)**

where ΣAM = total cost of all actual materials used for a production order within a specific work center

SM = standard unit materials cost for a production order within a specific work center

AU = actual units for a production order within a specific work center

2) Labor variance percent $= \dfrac{\Sigma\text{ADL}}{(\text{SH} \times \text{SLR})} \times 100$ **(Equation 14.2)**

where ΣADL = total actual direct labor cost (includes fringe benefits) by a specific work center for a shift

SH = standard hours by a specific work center for a shift

SLR = standard labor rate (includes fringe benefits)

3) Overhead variance percent $= \dfrac{\Sigma\text{AOC}}{(\text{AH} \times \text{SOR})} \times 100$ **(Equation 14.3)**

where ΣAOC = total actual overhead costs by a specific work center

AH = actual hours worked by a specific work center

SOR = standard overhead cost rate by a specific work center

FIGURE 14.4   Cost accounting models for a specific work center—materials usage, labor, and overhead variances (in percents).

tion 14.3)—is a weekly comparison of actual summarized overhead costs versus standard amounts. Actual overhead costs by a work center are divided by the actual hours times the standard overhead work center rate. The calculated value is multiplied by 100.

Numerous other variances can be developed for materials, labor, and overhead. Basically, these deviations highlight specific areas of manufacturing operations. Equally important are variances that analyze overall operations, such as production and work centers. Hence, a wide range of variances can be tailored to meet the managerial needs of the XYZ Corporation (or any other organization).

Integrated Micro Accounting Systems

Before concluding our discussion on considerations for effective MIS, it is helpful to look at current integrated micro accounting systems. If a corporation does more than $1 billion a year in sales, accounting on a microcomputer cannot be performed. In fact, a microcomputer may not be adequate once a corporation has more than three or four concurrent users, a heavy volume of transactions, or more than 1,000 different items in stock. But if the corporation has 50 employees or less, fewer than 4,000 transactions per month, and can take most orders over a single telephone line, an integrated micro accounting system is highly viable. As such, the XYZ Corporation does not qualify for such a system. However, this overview of micro accounting packages in figure 14.5 should be of interest since the microcomputer is widely used for accounting functions.

An integrated accounting system has two major advantages. The first is *consistency*—all reports draw on a single integrated data base. The second is the *savings* in personnel time. It takes less time to complete an order-entry form when most of the information can be filled in automatically from a customer and stock file. Posting to the ledger, a tedious task of double-entry when done directly from the general ledger module, can be largely automated when done through special-purpose modules like accounts payable or accounts receivable.

		Modules				
Product	**Vendor**	**Payroll**	**Inventory**	**Order Entry**	**Pt. of Sales**	**Time/ mat'l**
Accounting Plus	Micro Plus	x				
BPI	BPI Systems	x				
Business Library	Software Libraries	x	x			
Excalibur	Armor Systems	x	x	x	x	x
Great Plains	Great Plains Software	x	x	x		
Inmass	Microcomputer Consultants		x	x		x
Integrated Accounting$	Pearlsoft	x	x			
Realworld Business Software	Realworld Corporation	x	x	x		
Red Wing	Redwing Business Systems	x	x			
Software 16	Softran Corporation		x	x		
Solomon III	TLB, Inc.	x	x	x		x
State of the Art	State of the Art	x	x	x		x
Step 1	Commercial Micro Systems		x	x		

FIGURE 14.5   A sample of integrated accounting systems for microcomputers.

Typically, three criteria can help identify the micro accounting systems best suited for a company's needs. They are:

- The *scope* of the business: Are there several partners? enterprises? divisions?
- The *nature* of the business: Is the primary product services, or goods? Is the bulk of income derived from a large number of small purchases or a small number of large purchases? Does the company have a small or a large number of products to keep track of?
- The *volume* of business that the company does: Is it large or small?

Based upon the answers to these criteria, one of the integrated micro software systems set forth in figure 14.5 can be selected, with good results.

ACCOUNTING AND FINANCE OVERVIEW—XYZ CORPORATION

The major functions of accounting and finance in the XYZ Corporation are shown in figure 14.6. The include receivables and payables, payroll, cost accounting, financial statements, and source and application of funds. Accounting and finance data are stored on the plant and corporate data bases, retrievable as is or after manipulation, depending on the user's needs. The system can calculate this information on a current basis. Management is always able to retrieve current cost data, financial operating ratios, and cash balances.

Other subsystems can benefit from the financial statements prepared by the accounting and finance subsystem. The corporate planning staff can evaluate current trends in profitability for last-minute budget changes. Also, manufacturing management can evaluate its inventory investment in light of current operating conditions. Likewise, manufacturing management can appraise its overall ability to keep raw materials cost at a minimum. The ability to extract current accounting and finance information via a CRT terminal can indicate changes to the user as they occur. Corrective measures are effected much sooner.

Control Over the Accounting and Finance Subsystem

Management decision processes in an MIS accounting and finance framework focus on *control decisions*. Fundamentally, control decisions are concerned with implementing management's plans as well as achieving organization goals and objectives. Management cannot wait until the end of the month to find out how well it is doing in relation to the corporate short-range plans; they need the capability to obtain performance reports that let them see where they stand today. It is the responsibility of the MIS accounting and finance subsystem to provide not only timely and meaningful performance reports at regular intervals, but also to provide the facility to produce appropriate management reports upon demand where the manager or staff member

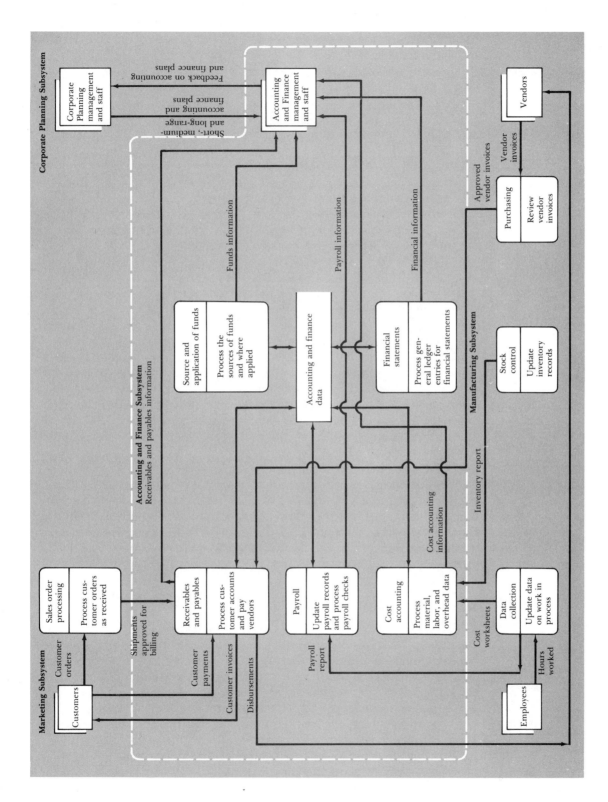

FIGURE 14.6 Accounting and finance data flow diagram—XYZ Corporation.

can interact with the system such that he or she has control over the decision-making process.

In an effective approach to the decision-making process in the area of cost accounting, the subsystem can develop analytical cost information for supporting managerial decision making. This approach utilizes cost accounting formulas to generate pertinent information that is germane to problem solving at a higher level of management. Hence, important cost information that needs to be acted upon by the appropriate level of management is generated. Also, an effective MIS approach provides the capability to make changes to the cost accounting system in order to highlight cost areas that may have been unimportant in the past. Other areas where changes can be made to support the accounting and finance decision processes include: accounts receivable, accounts payable, payroll, financial statements, and sources of funds—the subject matter of this chapter.

MIS ACCOUNTING AND FINANCE SUBSYSTEM

The previous summation of the important considerations for effective MIS serves as a background for presenting the component of accounting and finance. Data elements should be structured so that information to be displayed or printed can be easily extracted from the corporate or plant data bases. Similarly, they should be able to serve the needs of all other subsystems that need accounting and finance data. Proper employment of these data elements, then, is an essential, integral part of an effective MIS.

An overview of the accounting and finance subsystem is found in Figure 14.7. The input from other subsystems, along with the accounting-generated information, provides management and their staff with desired output. In addition, accounting and finance exception reports are produced on an interactive basis if so desired. But just as important is the feedback of instantaneous information to operational levels that utilize accounting and finance information for comparing actual operations to budgeted amounts or standards.

Relating a Responsibility-Oriented Approach to "What If?" Analysis

Because an effective MIS provides relevant financial information to management for supporting decision making, it can provide managers with information for each responsibility center of the corporation. From this view, it is a *responsibility-oriented approach,* integrating planning or budgeting with control of performance reporting. Such a system is based on knowledge of cost behavior. It recognizes the significance of standards and flexible budgeting in improving the quality of the information provided for all management levels. Generally, it is not too difficult to justify the cost of developing and operating an effective MIS accounting and finance subsystem when managers and their

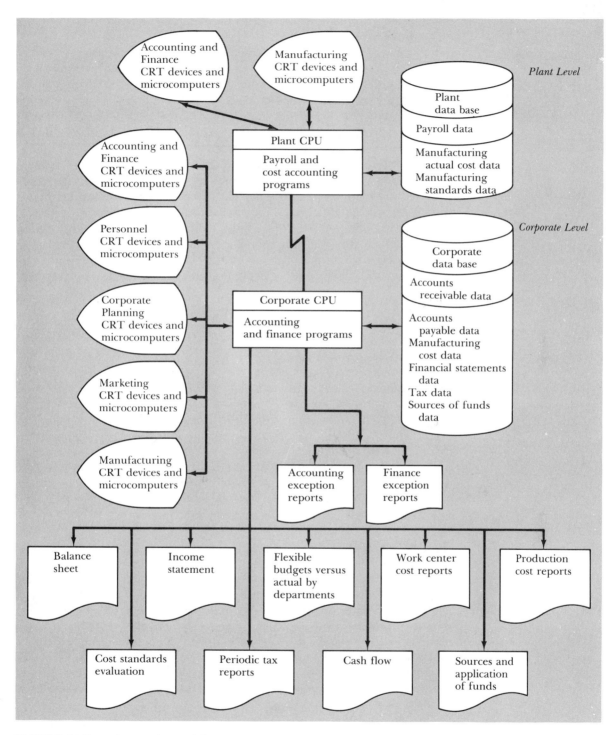

FIGURE 14.7   Accounting and finance subsystem for an effective management information system—XYZ Corporation.

staff find the information provided to be extremely useful to their planning and control decisions.

Within the framework of a responsibility-oriented approach, accounting and finance take on a new perspective. By going beyond the traditional role of reporting on what has happened, it adds a new dimension by providing a means of synthesizing a myriad of data for answering key "What if?" questions for one or more areas of responsibility. Typically, such questions include "What happens to net profits before federal income taxes if variable costs of producing certain products are decreased by a capital investment? What impact do interest rate changes have on net profits if funds must be borrowed on the outside?" or "What is the best method—borrowing from a bank, selling stock, or floating a bond issue—for financing large capital projects if future economic conditions are uncertain?" Although answering these type questions generally requires the use of mathematical models or software packages, an effective MIS accounting and finance subsystem is entirely capable of supplying answers to these difficult questions for assigned responsibility. In light of this capability, the accounting and finance subsystem is set forth below.

RECEIVABLES AND PAYABLES

The data flow for customer billing does not originate with the accounting function, but with sales order processing. By way of review, after the accounts receivable section has approved the customer's credit, the sales-order operator enters the customer order via a CRT terminal. The individual then interrogates the finished goods inventory file and/or enters the production order for any desired items not available from the warehouses. Data are accumulated on the plant data base regarding warehouse shipments and back orders. Each day, at the plant level, a customer billing program is triggered and customer invoices are printed and mailed to the customers. Likewise, a sales register is printed immediately following the customer billing run.

ACCOUNTS RECEIVABLE ACTIVITIES. As shown in figure 14.8, the foregoing procedures form the basis for charging the customer accounts at the plant level. A CRT terminal is employed to post customer payments. This time, however, they are entered by the accounts receivable section. All legitimate complaints on customer accounts are handled as they are received, and appropriate adjustments are made to the plant data base, thereby reflecting the correct (current) accounts receivable balances. Daily, a cash-receipts program is initiated after all customer payments have been posted, resulting in a cash-receipts register. In addition, daily exception reports are triggered at the end of the day, including customer overpayments and adjustments—debits and credits. Entries are automatically made to the general ledger stored on the plant data base.

Reports are prepared on a micro monthly. These include aging of

554

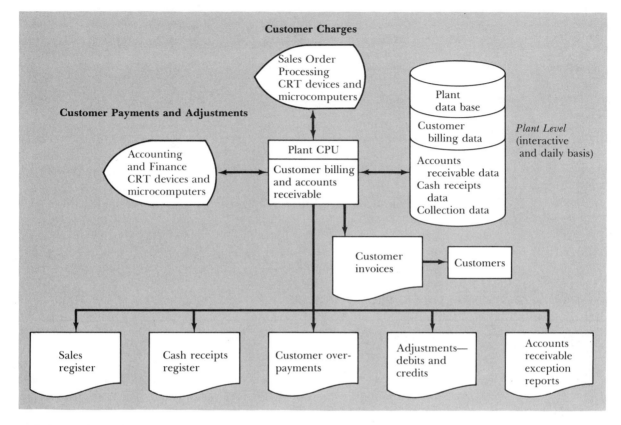

Customer Charges

Sales Order Processing CRT devices and microcomputers

Customer Payments and Adjustments

Plant data base
Customer billing data

Plant Level (interactive and daily basis)

Accounting and Finance CRT devices and microcomputers

Plant CPU
Customer billing and accounts receivable

Accounts receivable data
Cash receipts data
Collection data

Customer invoices → Customers

Sales register

Cash receipts register

Customer over-payments

Adjustments—debits and credits

Accounts receivable exception reports

FIGURE 14.8 Customer billing and accounts-receivable data flow for an MIS accounting subsystem.

accounts receivable (refer to figure 14.9 for a typical aging report) and the preparation of customer statements. Although an aging list is printed once a month, a CRT terminal can be used to retrieve information on accounts, thereby making customer account data available interactively.

ACCOUNTS PAYABLE ACTIVITIES. Although the basic accounts receivable functions are handled daily, the same time frame is not necessary for all accounts payable activities. Essentially, vendor invoices are entered by the accounts payable section of the accounting department (figure 14.10) at the plant level after review by purchasing. Daily entry is via a CRT terminal for storage on the data base. Twice a week, a voucher register is prepared for invoices received since the preparation of the previous register, as illustrated in figure 14.11 on page 558.

The XYZ Corporation pays its bills on the 10th and 25th of the month, thereby scheduling cash disbursements and voucher-check runs on these days (figure 14.10). The cash disbursements register is a listing of checks to be paid and payments that will take advantage of cash discounts offered. After a brief

Customer Name	Current Balance	30 Days and under Balance	Over 30 Days and up to 60 Days Balance	Over 60 Days and up to 90 Days Balance	Over 90 Days Balance
ABC Stores	$26,550.50	$18,905.50	$7,645.00	—	—
Adams Company	46,916.75	31,405.37	8,968.70	$6,542.68	—
Aromis, Inc.	15,267.92	9,205.72	4,200.51	1,650.77	$210.92
Baker Company	1,592.48	1,592.48	—	—	—
Consolidated Stores	92,165.22	62,982.42	29,182.80	—	—
.	.	.	.	.	.
.	.	.	.	.	.
.	.	.	.	.	.
Totals	$22,207,512.20	$12,572,178.15	$5,981,574.50	$3,106,717.65	$547,041.90

FIGURE 14.9   Aging of accounts receivable by periods report.

review by the accounts payable section, voucher checks are computer-prepared. At the end of the run is a listing of prior overpayments to specific vendors.

Monthly, a list of unpaid vouchers is prepared at the plant level. Also, a vendor overpayments/credits listing is printed for review by the accounts payable manager. It should be noted that current accounts of individual vendors, like customers, can be interrogated for current information at any time from a CRT device.

PAYROLL

Factory payroll is an essential part of the data collection system in the manufacturing subsystem. When a factory employee enters the work center in the morning, a plastic badge is inserted by the individual into a badge-reader remote terminal. Such terminals are connected to an area station, which, in turn, is connected to the plant CPU through a transmission control unit. When it is time for the employee's shift to begin, the foreman activates the area station to receive a printout of work center attendance.

The employee's current work assignment is entered via the terminal. The employee makes a setting on the terminal to indicate the type of transactions he or she is entering (work assignment). Next, the employee badge number is entered in the selector dial and a prepunched job card is inserted in the card-

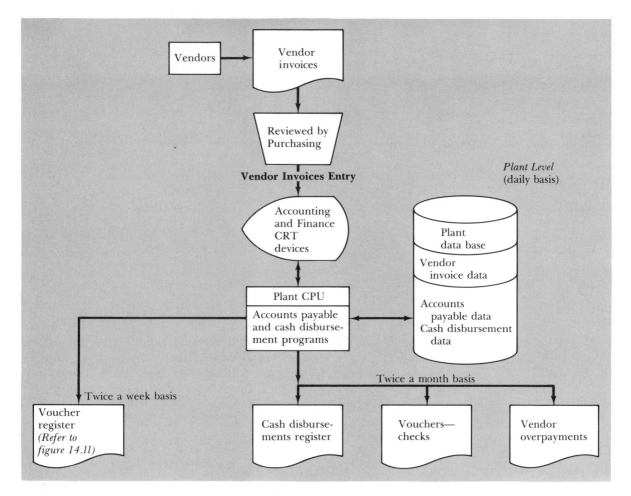

FIGURE 14.10   Accounts payable and cash disbursements data flow for an MIS accounting subsystem.

reader slot. The individual presses the entry level, and the data are recorded on the data base. As the employee changes from one job to another, entry via the remote terminal is used to indicate the end of a job. Likewise, the new production order to be worked on is also entered. In this manner, the plant data base contains data for weekly payroll processing as well as for the costing of production orders.

As shown in figure 14.12, daily production-time data base elements are accumulated on a weekly basis and are summarized to produce a weekly time, gross pay, and exception report. A typical report is shown in figure 14.13. Approved payroll changes are made via a CRT terminal in accounting before final processing occurs. The payroll register and checks, including earnings statements, are then produced and distributed to factory employees.

Payroll activities do not end with weekly processing at the plant level,

Vendor Name	Vendor Invoice Number	Date	Amount	Previous Balance	Current Balance
Argone Supply Co.	15F – 9250	4/15/8X	$6,875.50	—	$6,875.50
Aristocraft Metals	227 – 429	4/13/8X	4,298.27	$8,247.95	12,546.22
Atone Company	A 97347	4/16/8X	11,315.45	11,515.45	22,830.90
Billings, Inc.	146791	4/14/8X	2,118.90	18,272.50	20,391.40
Blenish Corp.	B 00448	4/15/8X	975.55	—	975.55
•	•	•	•	•	•
•	•	•	•	•	•
•	•	•	•	•	•
		Totals	$1,647,297.49	$6,875,423.12	$8,522,720.61

FIGURE 14.11   Voucher register of invoices received since the preparation of the previous register.

but must be carried forward for quarterly and yearly reports. Weekly figures are automatically posted to the general ledger stored on-line at the corporate level for producing monthly statements. Quarter-to-date earnings are used in preparing quarterly reports on federal income and FICA taxes withheld. Finally, year-to-date figures are the basis for preparing W2s.

COST ACCOUNTING

Cost accounting for effective MIS depends on data generated throughout the work day at the plant level. Usage of raw materials and parts is recorded by the manufacturing subsystem and can be retrieved by cost accounting. In a similar manner, work center data collection devices within the manufacturing subsystem provide the input for costing analysis at the plant level. The raw materials and labor data are compared to standards stored on the plant data base.

Direct Costing

In order for cost accounting to provide useful information for supporting managerial decision making, the management information system is based on the assignment of responsibility within the organization. The system must be tied to responsibility centers, whether they be in the office or plant. This *responsibility-oriented approach* provides the foundation for the technique called *direct costing*. Direct costing segregates *variable costs* from *fixed costs* (as opposed to *absorption costing,* which combines them). Hence, selling price

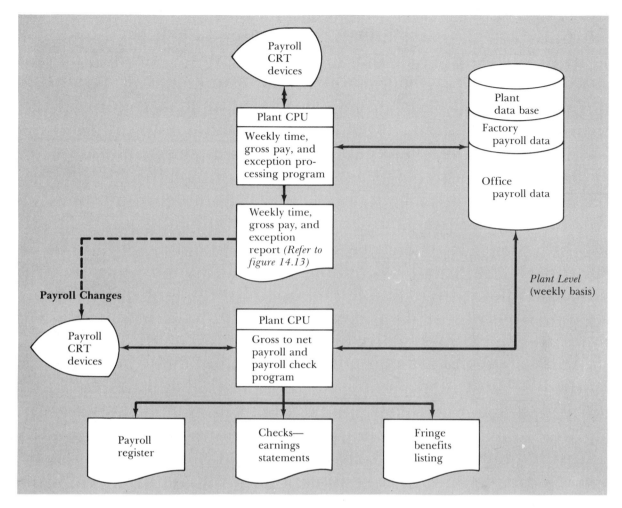

FIGURE 14.12   Overall payroll data flow for an MIS accounting subsystem.

less variable costs equals contribution to fixed costs and profits before federal income taxes. In turn, this value less fixed costs equals net profits before federal income taxes. Direct costing is concerned primarily with the elimination of arbitrary allocations of common or joint costs. It emphasizes the benefits of tracing costs to individual cost centers and then measuring them.

With an accurate segregation of variable and fixed costs to determine product contribution, the cost accountant can determine which products really contribute to overall profits and which do not. Similarly, the total contribution for each of the corporation's five product lines can be calculated. It may well be that this cost information should be forwarded to a higher level of management for review. There may be a changing pattern among the products and product lines in terms of total contribution. The capability of the cost accountant to interact with the computer to detect changing cost trends is

Employee Name	Employee Number	Hours Worked	Hourly Rate	Exception Item
John P. Ambrose	0025	42	$8.60	This department has worked 40 hours this week; investigate 2 hours of overtime.
William J. Black	0046	40	9.05	The maximum rate for the first shift is $8.95; investigate the reason for the higher rate— second shift?
Richard L. Brand	0054	40	6.75	The minimum rate for this department is $7.05; investigate the reason for the lower rate.
Joseph E. Cosgrove	0063	39	8.60	This department has worked 40 hours this week; investigate 1 hour under the regular forty hours.
. . .	. . .	. . .	. . .	. . .

FIGURE 14.13
Weekly time, gross pay, and exception report.

the purpose of cost accounting. In addition, since the XYZ Corporation does take on marginal orders, it is helpful to use the direct costing method before accepting them. If the order does not cover at least variable costs (i.e., out-of-pocket costs), it should not be accepted. On the other hand, if the order covers variable costs and does make a contribution to fixed costs, it probably should be accepted. The rationale is that the contribution would offset some of the overhead (i.e., fixed costs) and hopefully, make some contribution to profits.

COST STANDARDS. Going beyond the concept of direct costing to answer a series of "What if?" questions regarding contribution, the use of cost standards can be expanded in an MIS. Basically, *cost standards* are carefully determined estimates of what costs (and revenues) should be for a given time period. Properly determined standards can be used for several different purposes: profit planning using flexible budgets, performance evaluation and control, product costing and income measurement, pricing, and the like. From this enlarged perspective, management is not concerned with cost control in the sense of minimizing costs, but rather with cost effectiveness—that is, how effective are current operations? Management needs information on the increasing or decreasing productivity of its manufacturing operations.

As an example of utilizing cost standards, a daily work center cost report generated at the plant level is illustrated in figure 14.14. Daily variances by work center are calculated for materials usage, labor, and overhead. Other reports, such as work center time attendance and exception reports, are generated daily and on an interactive basis, respectively. A program is triggered at the end of each week to transfer summary cost information from the plant to corporate headquarters. These cost figures are used for longer-range analysis, in particular, to improve the operations of a specific plant as well as to compare one plant against another. Also, these analyses verify cost standard accuracy or the lack of it.

Weekly costs analyses are processed at the corporate level. They include production cost variance, labor standard rate variance, and overhead variance. Of special interest is the weekly production cost report (figure 14.15) that

---

Work Center No. 15

Materials-Usage Variance Percent (Equation 14.1)

$$\frac{\text{Total cost of actual materials used}}{(\text{Standard unit materials cost} \times \text{actual units})} \times 100$$

$$\frac{\$3,150}{(\$3.09 \times 1000)} \times 100 = 102\% \text{ or } \$60.00 \text{ unfavorable variance}$$

Labor Variance Percent (Equation 14.2)

$$\frac{\text{Total actual direct labor cost}}{(\text{Standard hours} \times \text{standard labor rate})} \times 100$$

$$\frac{\$1,410}{(220 \times \$6.00)} \times 100 = 107\% \text{ or } \$90.00 \text{ unfavorable variance}$$

Overhead Variance Percent (Equation 14.3)

$$\frac{\text{Total actual overhead costs}}{(\text{Actual hours} \times \text{standard overhead cost rate})} \times 100$$

$$\frac{\$2,500}{(230 \times \$10.00)} \times 100 = 108\% \text{ or } \$200.00 \text{ unfavorable variance}$$

FIGURE 14.14
Daily work center cost report—analysis for work center 15.

WEEKLY PRODUCTION COST REPORT
(PER UNIT BASIS)
ANALYSIS OF PRODUCT 210

| Work Center | Materials | | Labor | | Overhead | | Week Ending 5/18/8X Total Costs | | |
	Actual	Standard	Actual	Standard	Actual	Standard	Actual	Standard	Quantity
15 – Machine Shop	$2.60	$2.55	$2.41	$2.35	$1.64	$1.60	$6.65	$6.50	3,000
36 – Minor Assembly	2.04	2.05	1.60	1.60	1.45	1.45	5.09	5.10	3,000
53 – Major Assembly	2.26	2.25	2.26	2.25	1.76	1.75	6.28	6.25	3,000
74 – Inspection	—	—	1.17	1.15	1.12	1.10	2.29	2.25	3,000
	$6.90	$6.85	$7.44	$7.35	$5.97	$5.90	$20.31	$20.10	

FIGURE 14.15   Weekly production cost report (per unit basis)—analysis of Product 210.

brings together information generated on other reports. This report is reviewed by manufacturing and accounting management. Generally, the information contained in this report is the basis for weekly management meetings and evaluation at the corporate and plant levels.

In addition to the above cost reports, other period analyses are generated at the corporate level. A monthly listing of materials, labor, and overhead costs to be absorbed by the financial statements is prepared. Also, a listing of raw materials, work in process, and finished goods is processed. On a quarterly basis, a cost analysis, similar to figure 14.15, is run. Standard costs are evaluated in view of rising costs and are changed to reflect current operations. Where costs are continually out of line, this information is reviewed by corporate and plant manufacturing management to determine what corrective action can be taken to ensure that future costs are reliable for determining cost effectiveness.

FINANCIAL STATEMENTS

Financial statements are prepared at the corporate level based on general ledger data in the corporate data base, which have been forwarded from the three manufacturing plants. The general ledger updating program, shown in figure 14.16 at the corporate level, is used throughout the month to keep the data base updated. Data are fed from within and outside the accounting and finance subsystem. At the end of the week, a listing of general ledger entries is produced by the computer to indicate the various debits and credits to specific accounts. In a similar manner, after all transactions have been processed

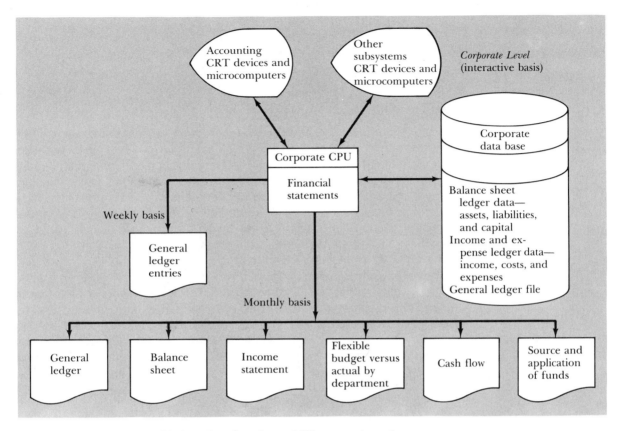

FIGURE 14.16   General ledger data flow for an MIS accounting subsystem.

for the last day of the month, general ledger balances and their detailed trans-actions are printed as well as written onto a separate section on the data base. This step is performed because this month's general ledger items must be capable of being processed against the corporate data base the next work-ing day. Thus, the previous month's general ledger can be changed later to effect corrections and entry of special items. Where applicable, changes made to the previous month can also be made to the current month's data base for uniformity of accounting data.

The monthly financial statements, namely, balance sheet, income state-ment, and flexible budgets by departments, are computer processed. Although the essential elements for balance sheet items may originate outside the accounting department, their physical flow is reflected in accounting entries that are summarized on the month-end balance sheet. Similarly, income and expenses are the result of activities in other departments, which flow into the corporate data base under program control, as general ledger entries. The resulting income and expenses form the basis for the income statement for the entire corporation. In turn, actual values are compared to flexible budgeted values for meaningful analyses. The responsibility for main-

563

taining budgeted data base elements belongs to the corporate planning subsystem. The profit after taxes, in the form of retained earnings and depreciation plus specific balance sheet items, provides the source of funds for the corporation which, in turn, are applied to financing specific projects.

Responsibility-Oriented Approach

From the foregoing presentation, you can see that financial statements are forwarded to all levels of management on a timely basis. But equally important to management is the responsibility-oriented approach (mentioned previously), that is, the provision for timely exception reports which highlight income and expenses that fall outside predetermined limits, for the purpose of holding managers responsible. Interactive processing can, for example, compare actual sales against typical patterns and control limits, leading to identification of *in-control* and *out-of-control* conditions as they occur. The same approach can be applied to costs and expenses. Comparisons, then, can be retrieved upon demand.

The approaches outlined above for financial statements are also applicable to the preparation of tax returns. By and large, data can be extracted from the data base as of a closing date and written onto magnetic tape. At a later date, tax returns can be prepared in a batch-processing mode. Thus, governmental reports and returns on the federal, state, and local levels present no major obstacle for the XYZ Corporation.

SOURCE AND APPLICATION OF FUNDS

Cash, the vital ingredient for sustaining the corporation's day-to-day operations, must be available when needed. Because cash is an expensive commodity, it is important that it not be wasted and that any excess be employed as profitably as possible. The cash manager must keep the corporation solvent while at the same time increasing profits through efficient cash management, that is, investing excess cash in short-term investments. Thus, it is important to be continually aware of changes in the corporation's cash balance.

The present system of cash flow is an integral part of the accounts payable and accounts receivable sections. Each plant forwards daily totals to corporate headquarters. Daily, two reports are generated by the computer and forwarded to the cash manager. These reports—Cash Transactions Data and Summary and Bank Balances—are used in determining appropriate actions to be taken regarding the present cash condition.

The cash manager, with the assistance of a financial analyst, examines the reports and compares them to the original projected cash flow analysis statement (to be explained below). In addition, a determination is made regarding the adequacy of working capital. If not enough cash is available for normal business operations in the period ahead, the cash manager informs the treasurer who, in turn, takes the necessary action to ensure that ample cash will be forthcoming. The treasurer might, for example, sell some treasury bills or borrow on a short-term basis from a bank. On the other hand, if it is found that too much cash is on hand, the cash manager will take action to invest it in some safe but profitable investment.

Projected Cash Flow Analysis

For a longer term view, cash flow analysis is projected for the coming quarter. The information from preceding day-to-day operations along with the data used in the preparation of financial statements provides a basis for determining cash flow for the coming quarter. An example of projected cash flow for the coming quarter is in figure 14.17. Using a micro Lotus 1-2-3 package, pro-

```
                                      X Y Z Corporation
                                  ----------------------

                                July          August        September
                              ----------    ----------    ----------

RECEIPTS:
   Accounts Receivable
      Collections From Sales in:
         May                   $325,000       ----          ----
         June                  3,791,667      325,000        ----
         July                  7,500,000      4,375,000      375,000
         August                ----           7,500,000      4,375,000
         September             ----           ----           7,500,000
                              ------------   ------------   ------------
            Total Receipts     $11,616,667   $12,200,000    $12,250,000
                              ------------   ------------   ------------

DISBURSEMENTS:
   Accounts Payable            $5,227,500     $5,490,000     $5,512,500
   Payroll                     5,576,000      5,856,000      5,880,000
   Dividends                   495,000        ----           ----
   Federal Income Tax          ----           ----           1,725,000
   Capital Improvements        ----           530,000        ----
                              ------------   ------------   ------------
      Total Disbursements      $11,298,500    $11,876,000    $13,117,500
                              ------------   ------------   ------------


SUMMARY:
   Excess Receipts Over
      Disbursements            $318,167       $324,000       ($867,500)
   Balance Beginning
      of Month                 20,000         338,167        662,167
   Balance End of             ------------   ------------   ------------
      Month                    $338,167       $662,167       ($205,333)
                              ============   ============   ============
```

FIGURE 14.17   Projected cash flow analysis—receipts and disbursements—to determine ending cash balance for the coming quarter.

jected receipts are spread over three months, based upon collections in the current months and collections from the past two months. (Collections were calculated as follows: May—$\frac{1}{12}$ of year × $130,000,000 annual sales × .03 collection percentage; June—$\frac{1}{12}$ × $130,000,000 × .35 + $\frac{1}{12}$ × $130,000,000 × .03; July—$\frac{1}{12}$ × $150,000,000 × .6 + $\frac{1}{12}$ × $150,000,000 × .35 + $\frac{1}{12}$ × $150,000,000 × .03; August—$\frac{1}{12}$ × $150,000,000 × .6 + $\frac{1}{12}$ × $150,000,000 × .35; and September—$\frac{1}{12}$ × $150,000,000 × .6.) Projected disbursements are also determined for the coming quarter. (Accounts payable were calculated at a .45 percent rate and payroll at a 48 percent rate based upon collections in the month. Disbursements were given for dividends—$495,000—and for capital improvements—$530,000. In addition, federal income taxes were derived by taking annualized sales of $150,000,000 for the current quarter times 10 percent profit times 46 percent tax rate times one fourth of the year.)

The summary shown at the bottom of the figure indicates that the XYZ Corporation will not be solvent over the quarter since the cash balance will be negative ($205,333) at September 30. This has been caused by the quarterly tax payment. Based upon the negative cash flow, the treasurer would be well advised to sell short-term securities or establish a line of credit with one or more local banks in light of the anticipated negative balance.

Capital Investment Decisions

For each project or group of projects that requires substantial sums of funds for implementation, the cash manager—under the direction of the treasurer—decides on the optimal financing method. After reviewing an analysis of the capital project (a typical request is set forth in figure 14.18), the cash manager interrogates the corporate data base for financial structure data, which is primarily of a long-term nature (figure 14.19). A financial structure report is generated for review by the cash manager. That individual is now prepared to make a financing recommendation after considering the current debt–equity ratio, current borrowing rates, interest charges for which the corporation is currently committed, and current and projected sales, as well as other factors pertinent to the decision.

Once a decision, such as bank borrowing, has been made regarding financing, the cash manager incorporates this information into the analysis of the capital project. The formal report is prepared and then forwarded to the corporate planning staff. The prescribed channels for endorsement and approval of large capital projects are the vice president of the department initiating the project, the vice president of accounting and finance, and the executive vice president. When the project is finally approved, a copy of the approval is forwarded to the cash manager, who takes the necessary steps to obtain the funds for implementation. If the project is rejected, it is forwarded with the reasons to the capital budgeting manager who, in turn, contacts the initiating department and reviews the reasons for rejection.

Capital investment "What if?" questions can benefit from a thorough

Capital Investment Proposal	
Project 122	

Department – Machine Shop

Plant – #2

Project Title – Plastic Molding Machine

Estimated Cost – $105,000

Estimated Return on Investment – 30% (after taxes)

Objective: To replace existing plastic machine #1575 with a new and more efficient one.

Economic Justification: Machine 1575 is 15 years old, fully depreciated, and operating at 60% of its rated capacity. The quantity and quality of products produced on this machine have resulted in a below-average contribution to plant profits.

The cost of the new machine is $105,000. Not only will the new machine be more efficient, but it will consistently produce a higher-quality product at a lower unit cost.

Title of Initiator: <u>Marvin D. Bullock, Production Supervisor</u>   Date 6/26/8X

Financial Analyst: <u>Russell E. Thompson</u>   Date 6/28/8X

FIGURE 14.18   A typical project request for capital equipment.

analysis of financing alternatives or other factors using Lotus 1-2-3. In figure 14.20, a simplistic model is shown that evaluates the purchase of a new piece of equipment costing $30,000. Expected savings are estimated to be $10,000 annually, and the equipment has an expected useful life of five years. Figure 14.20(a) includes these assumptions and also shows a discount rate of 12.5 percent, which the company would have to pay on money borrowed to finance the purchase. Using the present value method, this investment would bring future savings that have a present value of $35,606, or $5,606 more than the investment cost. Given this set of assumptions about savings, useful life, and discount rate, the equipment should be purchased.

On the other hand, estimates for interest rate, annual savings, and useful life might deviate from these assumptions. To illustrate, assume that the interest rate has been projected accurately but the useful life and annual savings estimates are more suspect. Lotus 1-2-3 allows the user to perform either a one- or two-way sensitivity analysis to examine potential changes. The one-way analysis allows looking at changes in only one variable, but evaluating the range of values generated for a number of equations. To perform this analysis, list the alternative values of the variable in a column. The example in figure 14.20(b) uses the first column to store a range of values for annual savings.

567

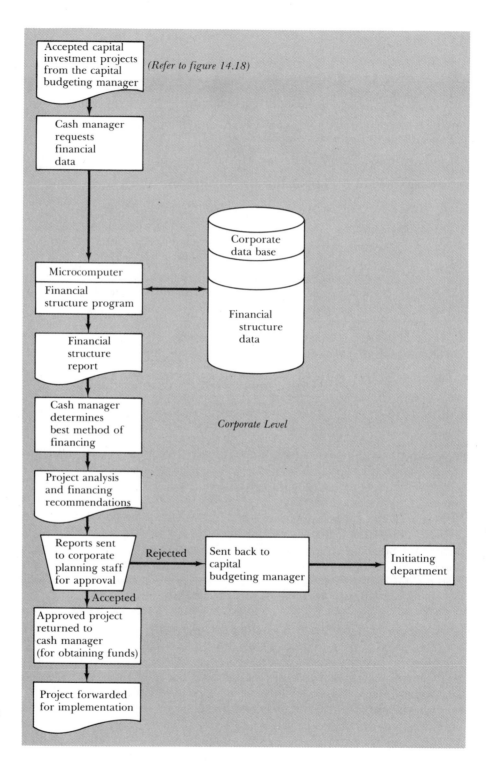

FIGURE 14.19
Current source of capital data flow for an MIS accounting and finance subsystem.

Part A

```
                Capital Investment Decision
                ------- ----------- --------
           Purchase Price              $30,000
           Useful Life                       5
           Cash Savings - Annual Basis  $10,000
           Discount Rate                 12.50%
                                        ----------

           Present Value               $35,606
```

* *
Part B

```
                     Cash      Present
                    Savings     Values
                                 +E10
                    $7,000     $24,924
                     8,000      28,485
                     9,000      32,045
                    10,000      35,606
                    11,000      39,166
                    12,000      42,727
                    13,000      46,287
```

* *
Part C

Present Values Over Useful Life (Years)

Cash Savings +E10	3	4	5	6	7	8
$7,000	$16,669	$21,039	$24,924	$28,377	$31,446	$34,174
8,000	19,051	24,045	28,485	32,431	35,938	39,056
9,000	21,432	27,051	32,045	36,485	40,431	43,938
10,000	23,813	30,056	35,606	40,538	44,923	48,820
11,000	26,195	33,062	39,166	44,592	49,415	53,702
12,000	28,576	36,068	42,727	48,646	53,908	58,585
13,000	30,957	39,073	46,287	52,700	58,400	63,467

FIGURE 14.20   Capital investment decision using Lotus 1-2-3 for equipment
that costs $30,000: (a) present value over 5 years at 12.5% discount rate with annual
savings of $10,000, (b) a one-way sensitivity analysis such that the present value
changes in response to a variation in annual savings, and (c) a two-way sensitivity
analysis such that the present value changes in response to two different variables—
cash savings and useful life (years).

The answers in the next column show the savings of less than $7,000 and
$8,000 make buying the equipment a bad idea because the present value of
savings would be less than the current cost.

In figure 14.20(c), a two-way table allows one to look at the results of
only one formula but vary two variables in one calculation. As an example,
leave the values for the first variable as is (cash savings) in the first column.

569

Next, place values for the second variable (useful life in years) in the remaining columns, and let the spreadsheet make the columnar calculations for present values. The table shows that the final results are sensitive to changes in both variables. If one prepared another two-way analysis that examined discount rate and years of useful life, the results would be much more sensitive to changes in the useful life than in the discount rate, evidenced by larger changes in results as the useful-life projections changed. Thus, "What if?" questions can be answered about present values when related to cash savings and years of useful life or discount rate and years of useful life.

Summary—MIS Accounting and Finance Subsystem

Receivables and payables—accounts receivables center on charging the customer accounts for orders shipped (as the result of sales order processing) and the resulting collection of payments. On the other hand, accounts payables process the invoices for goods and services received as well as making these payments.

Payroll is an essential part of the data collection system of the manufacturing subsystem. Time reporting in an on-line mode is used to pay factory employees weekly. Also, all other organizational personnel are paid via payroll processing procedures.

Cost accounting is concerned with costing the corporation's products as they are produced. Its underlying method is direct costing, which segregates fixed costs from variable costs.

Financial statements are the end result of bringing together monthly operations in terms of sales and costs. Balance sheet, income statement, and flexible budget versus actual by departments are the focal points of reporting financial results.

Source and application of funds focuses on obtaining the needed funds for application to capital projects and current operations. An integral part of source and applications of funds is the cash flow now and in the future.

EFFECTIVE MIS PRACTICE—INTEGRATION OF ACCOUNTING AND FINANCE WITH CORPORATE PLANNING

To improve accounting and finance decision making, financial managers and their staff must enlarge the scope of their thinking and relate it to corporate planning. At times, this means getting involved in problem finding. This will allow them to "get the big picture" so that there is optimization of resources for the entire corporation versus one or just a few parts of it. The success which the XYZ Corporation has in attaining its short- to long-range goals and objectives depends on the degree of integration of its operations. Enlargements of the scope of organization activities as well as the acceptance of responsibilities that lie outside the boundaries of traditional accounting and finance are illustrated below for capital investment planning.

Because the commitment of the corporation's money is directed to capital projects, investment planning is concerned mainly with providing the various manufacturing capacities called for in the corporation's long-range plans. It consists of the comparative evaluation of alternative projects requiring the commitment of corporation capital. While long-range plans provide the framework for capital investment planning, it is at the investment stage that managers and their staff commit portions of the corporation's pool of capital to specific projects. Hence, individuals responsible for investing corporation resources need an understanding of financial concepts and models in order to use them effectively for decision making. They must be able to select and apply those concepts and models that indicate the expected profitability of proposed investments, that is, capital projects.

Because capital projects are based on future estimates, they involve some degree of risk. Managers and their assistants are in a position to make better decisions if they know something of the risk involved in individual projects. Aided by the computer and using a capital project (simulation) model, they can prepare a probability profile of the rate of return for each investment proposal. Also, within this model, the time value of money can be employed to show the true worth of future income dollars—significantly less than dollars today. It is only in the last few years that the time value of money has been formally included to measure the investment project's profitability. Basically, the model provides a meaningful economic appraisal of proposed capital projects over the long term. In like manner, it allows management to tie in these projects with the corporation's long-range plans.

The cost of capital is a necessary cost of operations. Accounting for these costs is essential for the meaningful appraisal of capital project proposals. To make wise decisions on the selection and approval of investment proposals, managers need to know how effective individual projects promise to be in using the corporation's capital to generate a satisfactory return over the long run. Projects that do not offer a return at least equal to the corporation's cost of capital should be rejected—or at least have to be justified on other than economic grounds.

Going beyond financial considerations, accounting concepts and assumptions which were developed and accepted as appropriate for the periodic measurement of net income generally may not be relevant for appraising the profitability of investment proposals. Accrual accounting procedures introduce allocations irrelevant to profit planning. They tend to negate the reliability of project profitability measures computed on that basis. Each capital project should be considered a separate financial entity, and the relevant period is the economic life of the project. The incremental cash flow is the relevant concept for measuring the return on investment. Since planning relates to future activities, only future cash flows are relevant to the capital project analysis. Thus, corporate planning for capital projects requires modification of traditional accounting procedures to measure the ROI correctly over the long term.

CHAPTER SUMMARY

The accounting and finance subsystem of the XYZ Corporation is an integral part of the corporate planning, marketing, manufacturing, and personnel subsystems within an effective MIS environment. Corporate planning is the starting point for flexible budgets for the coming year. Marketing is linked to accounts receivable, purchasing to accounts payable, manufacturing to payroll, and inventory to cost accounting. Despite this high degree of integration, numerous other methods and procedures operate within the accounting and finance subsystem without reference to other subsystems.

As demonstrated in the chapter, an effective MIS accounting and finance subsystem centers on timely information using a responsibility-oriented approach. Management and their staff can retrieve current accounts receivable data for checking customer credit, checking on the status of overpayments to or credits due from vendors, determining the accuracy of plant personnel attendance, analyzing actual versus standard costs, retrieving current general ledger balances, determining sources of funds, and investing excess cash funds, among other things. In essence, information can be evaluated *now* about other subsystems as well as the accounting and finance function itself, enabling the XYZ Corporation to be forward-looking in problem finding and problem solving. Of equal importance to timely accounting information are the flexibility to meet changing needs, the capability to upgrade the level of managerial reporting, improved access to data, and the capability to provide more analytical information.

QUESTIONS

1. Contrast the role of the plant controller in accounting with that of the corporate treasurer in finance.
2. Of what importance is return on investment and comparable financial ratios and statistics to top management? To operating accounting and finance managers?
3. **a.** What impact has micro investment software made on operating accounting and finance managers?
   b. What impact have integrated micro accounting systems made on the XYZ Corporation?
4. List other mathematical models not discussed in the chapter that have been successfully used to plan and/or control accounting- and finance-oriented activities.
5. Why does the management decision process for accounting and finance focus on control decisions?
6. Determine the major parts of the customer billing program in an MIS environment.
7. List additional cost accounting formulas found in an effective MIS.
8. What is the relationship of flexible budgets (as set forth in chapter 11 under short-range planning) to the MIS accounting subsystem?
9. Of what significance to management is knowledge about next month's cash flow?

10. **a.** How can an electronic spreadsheet be used to evaluate capital investment decisions?

    b. What is the function of sensitivity analysis using an electronic spreadsheet to evaluate capital investment decisions?

PROBLEMS

11. The accounting and finance subsystem of the XYZ Corporation, as set forth in this chapter, emphasized *control decisions,* that is, decisions that are concerned with implementing management's plans as well as achieving organization goals and objectives. In effect, this subsystem provides managerial performance reports to let management know where they stand today. From another perspective, develop appropriate methods for the accounting and finance subsystem that can help management do a better job of planning the future. Include in your answer the development of plans from the short range to the long range.

12. In the accounting and finance subsystem set forth in the chapter for the XYZ Corporation, the following areas were included: receivables, payables, payroll, cost accounting, financial statements, and source and application of funds. What other related modules could have been included that logically fit in with the accounting and finance subsystem? Additionally, what modules from other functional areas of the corporation could be included in the accounting and finance subsystem? In both cases, discuss what modifications are necessary to make these systems function together as an integrated whole.

13. Inasmuch as the MIS accounting and finance subsystem of the XYZ Corporation is operating in a distributed data processing mode, what changes would be made in either the accounts receivable or the cost accounting systems to qualify them as operating in a decision support mode? In your answer, include not only what changes would be necessary in the two systems, but also if it would be beneficial to make the changes from an MIS operating mode to a decision support system operating environment.

PROJECTS

14. In the chapter, the use of mathematical models was illustrated for accounting and finance. Incorporate the mathematical model of linear programming for a specific area within the accounting and finance subsystem for the XYZ Corporation. Include in your answer the type of equations that would have to be developed as constraints. State the objective to be achieved, i.e., maximizing profits or minimizing costs. Also state why this technique is a better approach than the current method or technique.

15. Referring to the MIS cost accounting system for the XYZ Corporation, determine reports that support management's ability to detect changing costs over time. If appropriate, include the use of standard mathematical models as well as cost accounting formulas. A starting point might be the cost accounting formulas presented in the chapter. Show the appropriate changes in the form of a system flowchart or a data flow diagram.

16. Capital budgeting per se of the XYZ Corporation was not treated in the chapter, although reference was made to the capital budgeting manager (e.g., in figure 14.19). Using this information as background, develop an MIS capital budgeting system that gives high-level managers effective control and feedback for recommended capital budgets. Consider using a manager–machine interface for faster support of decision making on the feasibility or infeasibility of capital projects. Also, include the possibility of using standard software packages and mathematical models to develop an effective capital budgeting system. Where appropriate, use system flowcharts or data flow diagrams to show the data flow from one area to another for the capital budgeting process.

LOTUS 1-2-3 EXCERCISES AND PROGRAMS

17. In the chapter, the projected cash flow for the coming quarter (July, August, and September) was depicted in figure 14.17. Using this figure as a model, develop a comparable analysis for January, February, and March of next year. Use the program provided on the Lotus 1-2-3 diskette or the program found in this section. The data needed for this program are as follows:

Collections from Sales in:

November of prior year	$\frac{1}{12} \times \$130,000,000$ (annualized sales) $\times .03$ (collection %)
December of prior year	$\frac{1}{12} \times \$130,000,000 \times .35 + \frac{1}{12} \times \$130,000,000 \times .03$
January	$\frac{1}{12} \times \$140,000,000 \times .6 + \frac{1}{12} \times \$140,000,000 \times .35 + \frac{1}{12} \times \$140,000,000 \times .03$
February	$\frac{1}{12} \times \$140,000,000 \times .6 + \frac{1}{12} \times \$140,000,000 \times .35$
March	$\frac{1}{12} \times \$140,000,000 \times .6$

Disbursements for:

Accounts payable—January, February, and March	45% of total monthly collections on sales
Payroll—January, February, and March	48% of total monthly collections on sales
Dividends—January	$495,000
Capital improvements—February	$530,000
Federal income taxes—March	$140,000,000 (annualized sales for January, February, and March) $\times \frac{1}{4}$ (first quarter of the year) $\times$ 10% (profit on sales before federal income taxes) $\times$ 46% (federal income tax rate)

Is it possible to develop a program that compares cash flow analysis for these three months with the previous three-month period? If so, describe what the graph would look like. Optionally, develop a Lotus 1-2-3 program to prepare the graph.

18. As illustrated in the chapter, the projected cash flow for the coming quarter (July, August, and September) was depicted in figure 14.17. Using this figure as a model, develop a comparable analysis for October, November, and December. Use the program provided on the Lotus 1-2-3 diskette or the program found in this section. The data needed for this program are as follows:

Collections from Sales in:

August	$\frac{1}{12}$ × $150,000,000 (annualized sales) × .03 (collection %)
September	$\frac{1}{12}$ × $150,000,000 × .35 + $\frac{1}{12}$ × $150,000,000 × .03
October	$\frac{1}{12}$ × $130,000,000 × .6 + $\frac{1}{12}$ × $130,000,000 × .35 + $\frac{1}{12}$ × $130,000,000 × .03
November	$\frac{1}{12}$ × $130,000,000 × .6 + $\frac{1}{12}$ × $130,000,000 × .35
December	$\frac{1}{12}$ × $130,000,000 × .6

Disbursements for:

Accounts payable—October, November, and December	45% of total monthly collections on sales
Payroll—October, November, and December	48% of total monthly collections on sales
Dividends—October	$495,000
Capital improvements—November	$530,000
Federal income taxes—December	$130,000,000 (annualized sales for October, November, and December) × ¼ (fourth quarter of the year) × 10% (profit on sales before federal income taxes) × 46% (federal income tax rate)

It is possible to develop a program that compares cash flow analysis for these three months with the previous three months period? If so, describe what the graph would look like. Optionally, develop a Lotus 1-2-3 program to prepare the graph.

19. As highlighted in the chapter, the projected cash flow for the coming quarter (July, August, and September) was shown in figure 14.17. Based upon this model, develop a comparable analysis for April, May, and June of next year. Use the program provided on the Lotus 1-2-3 diskette or the program found in this section. The data needed for this program are as follows:

Collections from Sales in:

February	$\frac{1}{12}$ × $140,000,000 (annualized sales) × .03 (collection %)
March	$\frac{1}{12}$ × $140,000,000 × .35 + $\frac{1}{12}$ × $140,000,000 × .03
April	$\frac{1}{12}$ × $130,000,000 × .6 + $\frac{1}{12}$ × $130,000,000 × .35 + $\frac{1}{12}$ × $130,000,000 × .03
May	$\frac{1}{12}$ × $130,000,000 × .6 + $\frac{1}{12}$ × $130,000,000 × .35
June	$\frac{1}{12}$ × $130,000,000 × .6

575

Disbursements for:

Accounts payable—April, May, and June	45% of total monthly collections on sales
Payroll—April, May, and June	48% of total monthly collections on sales
Dividends—April	$495,000
Capital improvements—May	$530,000
Federal income taxes—June	$130,000,000 (annualized sales for April, May, and June) × ¼ (second quarter of the year) × 10% (profit on sales before federal income taxes) × 46% (federal income tax rate)

Is it possible to develop a program that compares cash flow analysis for these three months with the previous three months period? If so, describe what the graph would look like. Optionally, develop a Lotus 1-2-3 program to prepare the graph.

20. In the chapter, a capital investment decision method using Lotus 1-2-3 for the XYZ Corporation was presented in figure 14.20. Using this figure as a model, develop a comparable analysis for (a) and (b) parts only; that is, (a) determine a single present value and (b) a series of multiple present values (i.e., one-way sensitivity analysis) for the following data:

    (a) Purchase price $50,000
         Useful life   8 years
         Annual cash savings $8,500
         Current interest rate   11.0%

    (b) Cash savings on an annual basis:

$5,500	$8,500	$11,500
6,500	9,500	
7,500	10,500	

The program is provided on the Lotus 1-2-3 diskette and in this section. What is the best alternative (i.e., yields the highest present value) based upon the data given? Is it necessary to undertake other financial analysis to answer this question?

From another perspective, is it possible to develop a graph that compares the cash savings on an annual basis for part (b) of this exercise? If so, describe what the graph would look like. Optionally, develop a Lotus 1-2-3 program to prepare the graph.

21. As illustrated in the chapter, a capital investment decision method using Lotus 1-2-3 for the XYZ Corporation was presented in figure 14.20. Using this figure as a model, develop a comparable analysis for (a) and (c) parts only; that is, (a) determine a single present value and (b) a series of cash savings over the investment's useful life (i.e., two-way sensitivity analysis) for the following data:

    (a) Purchase price $110,000
         Useful life   6 years
         Cash savings on an annual basis $28,000
         Current interest rate   11.5%

    (b) Cash savings on an annual basis:

$24,000	$30,000	$36,000
26,000	32,000	
28,000	34,000	

(c) Useful life in years:

3	6
4	7
5	8

The program is provided on the Lotus 1-2-3 diskette and is given in this section. What is the best alternative (i.e., highest present value)? Is it necessary to undertake other financial analysis to answer this question? From another perspective, is it possible to develop a graph that compares the best of the present values for cash savings on an annual basis over the number of useful years (3 to 8) for part (b) of this exercise? If so, describe what the graph would look like. Optionally, develop a Lotus 1-2-3 program to prepare the graph.

LOTUS 1-2-3 PROGRAMS—CASH FLOW ANALYSIS (PROGRAM 10)

```
D1: '              X Y Z Corporation        D19: (,0) U (0.48)*(D15)
D2: '              ------------------        E19: (,0) U (0.48)*(E15)
D4: ^July                                    F19: (,0) U (0.48)*(F15)
E4: ^August                                  A20: '    Dividends
F4: ^September                               D20: (,0) U 495000
D5: ^----------                              E20: (,0) U ^---
E5: ^----------                              F20: (,0) U ^---
F5: ^----------                              A21: '    Federal Income Tax
A6: 'RECEIPTS:                               D21: (,0) U ^---
A7: '   Accounts Receivable                  E21: (,0) U ^---
A8: '      Collections From Sales in:        F21: (,0) U (150000000)*(0.1)*(0.25)*(0.46)
A9: '         May                            A22: '    Capital Improvements
D9: (CO) U (1/12)*(130000000)*(0.03)         D22: (,0) U ^---
E9: (CO) U ^---                              E22: (,0) U 530000
F9: (CO) U ^---                              F22: (,0) U ^---
A10: '        June                           D23: (CO) '-------------
D10: (,0) U (1/12)*(130000000)*(0.35)        E23: (CO) '-------------
E10: (,0) U (1/12)*(130000000)*(0.03)        F23: (CO) '-------------
F10: (,0) U ^---                             A24: '       Total Disbursements
A11: '        July                           D24: (CO) @SUM(D18..D22)
D11: (,0) U (1/12)*(150000000)*(0.6)         E24: (CO) @SUM(E18..E22)
E11: (,0) U (1/12)*(150000000)*(0.35)        F24: (CO) @SUM(F18..F22)
F11: (,0) U (1/12)*(150000000)*(0.03)        D25: (CO) '-------------
A12: '        August                         E25: (CO) '-------------
D12: (,0) U ^---                             F25: (CO) '-------------
E12: (,0) U (1/12)*(150000000)*(0.6)         A27: 'SUMMARY:
F12: (,0) U (1/12)*(150000000)*(0.35)        A28: '    Excess Receipts Over
A13: '        September                      A29: '       Disbursements
D13: (,0) U ^---                             D29: (CO) (D15)-(D24)
E13: (,0) U ^---                             E29: (CO) (E15)-(E24)
F13: (,0) U (1/12)*(150000000)*(0.6)         F29: (CO) (F15)-(F24)
D14: (CO) '-------------                      A30: '    Balance Beginning
E14: (CO) '-------------                      A31: '       of Month
F14: (CO) '-------------                      D31: (,0) 20000
A15: '          Total Receipts               E31: (,0) +D33
D15: (CO) @SUM(D9..D13)                       F31: (,0) +E33
E15: (CO) @SUM(E9..E13)                       A32: '    Balance End of
F15: (CO) @SUM(F9..F13)                       D32: (CO) '-------------
D16: (CO) '-------------                       E32: (CO) '-------------
E16: (CO) '-------------                       F32: (CO) '-------------
F16: (CO) '-------------                       A33: '       Month
A17: 'DISBURSEMENTS:                           D33: (CO) +D29+D31
A18: '   Accounts Payable                      E33: (CO) +E29+E31
D18: (CO) U (0.45)*(D15)                        F33: (CO) +F29+F31
E18: (CO) U (0.45)*(E15)                        D34: (CO) '============
F18: (CO) U (0.45)*(F15)                        E34: (CO) '============
A19: '   Payroll                              F34: (CO) '============
```

CAPITAL INVESTMENT DECISION (PROGRAM 11)

```
A1:  'Part A
B2:  '      Capital Investment Decision
B3:  '      ------- ---------- --------
B4:  'Purchase Price
E4:  (C0) U 30000
B5:  'Useful Life
E5:  (F0) U 5
B6:  'Cash Savings - Annual Basis
E6:  (C0) U 10000
B7:  'Discount Rate
E7:  (P2) U 0.125
E8:  '-----------
B10: 'Present Value
E10: (C0) @PV(E6,E7,E5)
A20: "* * * * * * * * * * * * * * * * * * * * * * * * * * * * * * * * *
A21: 'Part B
C24: ^Cash
D24: ^Present
C25: "Savings
D25: ^Values
D26: (T) +E10
C27: (C0) U 7000
D27: (C0) 24923.978391
C28: (,0) U 8000
D28: (,0) 28484.546732
C29: (,0) U 9000
D29: (,0) 32045.115074
C30: (,0) U 10000
D30: (,0) 35605.683415
C31: (,0) U 11000
D31: (,0) 39166.251757
C32: (,0) U 12000
D32: (,0) 42726.820099
C33: (,0) U 13000
D33: (,0) 46287.38844
A40: '* * * * * * * * * * * * * * * * * * * * * * * * * * * * * * * *
A41: 'Part C
C45: "Present Values Over Useful Life (Years)
A46: ^Cash
C46: '----------- --------- ------ -------- ----- --------
A47: "Savings
A48: (T) +E10
B48: U 3
C48: U 4
D48: U 5
E48: U 6
F48: U 7
G48: U 8
A49: (C0) U 7000
B49: (C0) 16669.410151
C49: (C0) 21039.47569
D49: (C0) 24923.978391
E49: (C0) 28376.869681
F49: (C0) 31446.106383
G49: (C0) 34174.316785
A50: (,0) U 8000
B50: (,0) 19050.754458
C50: (,0) 24045.115074
D50: (,0) 28484.546732
E50: (,0) 32430.708207
F50: (,0) 35938.407295
G50: (,0) 39056.36204
A51: (,0) U 9000
B51: (,0) 21432.098765
C51: (,0) 27050.754458
D51: (,0) 32045.115074
E51: (,0) 36484.546732
F51: (,0) 40430.708207
G51: (,0) 43938.407295
A52: (,0) U 10000
B52: (,0) 23813.443073
C52: (,0) 30056.393842
```

```
D52:  (,0)  35605.683415
E52:  (,0)  40538.385258
F52:  (,0)  44923.009118
G52:  (,0)  48820.45255
A53:  (,0)  U 11000
B53:  (,0)  26194.78738
C53:  (,0)  33062.033227
D53:  (,0)  39166.251757
E53:  (,0)  44592.223784
F53:  (,0)  49415.31003
G53:  (,0)  53702.497805
A54:  (,0)  U 12000
B54:  (,0)  28576.131687
C54:  (,0)  36067.672611
D54:  (,0)  42726.820099
E54:  (,0)  48646.06231
F54:  (,0)  53907.610942
G54:  (,0)  58584.54306
A55:  (,0)  U 13000
B55:  (,0)  30957.475995
C55:  (,0)  39073.311995
D55:  (,0)  46287.38844
E55:  (,0)  52699.900836
F55:  (,0)  58399.911854
G55:  (,0)  63466.588315
```

BIBLIOGRAPHY

Albert, W. W. "Value Based Strategic Investment Planning." *Interfaces,* January-February 1984.

Balachondron, B. V., and Zoltners, A. A. "An Interactive Audit–Staff Scheduling Decision Support System." *Accounting Review,* October 1981.

Beehler, P. J. *Cash Management: Principles and Practices for the '80s.* New York: AMACOM, 1980.

Benoit, E. "What's Your Financial Position?" *Business Computer Systems,* November 1982.

Bowman, M. J. "Human Diagnostic Reasoning by Computers: An Illustration from Financial Analysis." *Management Science,* June 1983.

Briggs, G. "Micros Help Manage the Money at First National Bank of Chicago." *Micro Manager,* June 1984.

Brock, T. L. "Cash Flow Statements on Lotus 1-2-3." *Journal of Accountancy,* April 1986.

Campbell, M. "Sensitivity Analysis—A Structured Approach to What-If." *Lotus,* July 1985.

Cerullo, M. "Computer Control Systems in Organization." *Data Base,* Summer 1983.

Chalos, P., and Bader, A. H. "Higher-Tech Production: The Impact on Cost Reporting Systems." *Journal of Accountancy,* March 1986.

Desmond, J. "Breaking Down the Barriers: Financial Packages Integrate." *Software News,* February 1986.

Dinman, S. B. "The Secret to Building More Effective Budgets." *Lotus,* May 1985.

Donnelly, R. M. "The Changing Role of the Controller." *Financial Executive,* April 1982.

Dooley, B. "Micros; Changing the Face of Accounting." *Micro Manager,* October 1984.

du Toit, D. F. "Confessions of a So-So Controller," *Harvard Business Review,* July-August 1985.

Earl, M. J. "Prototype System for Accounting Information and Control." *Data Base,* Winter-Spring 1982.

Eiler, R. G.; Goletz, W. K; and Keegan, D. P. "Is Your Cost Accounting Up to Date?" *Harvard Business Review,* July-August 1982.

Erengil, B. "What Every Financial Planner Needs in a DSS." *Software News,* December 1984.

Frank, J., and Schnabel, J. "Timing of Borrowing Decisions—A Decision Support System." *Journal of Systems Management,* April 1983.

Freedman, D. H. "Banking's MIS Dilemma." *Infosystems,* January 1986.

Frisco den Hertoz, J. "Information and Control Systems: Roadblock or Bridge to Renewal." *Data Base,* Winter-Spring 1982.

Gessford, J. E. *Modern Information Systems Designed for Decision Support.* Reading, MA: Addison-Wesley Publishing Company, 1980.

Good, P. "Integrated Applications: There's Something for (Nearly) Everyone." *Software News,* April 1985.

Green, J. H. "Using Life-Cycle Analysis." *Lotus,* August 1985.

Handmaker, D. "Bright Futures." *Business Computer Systems,* July 1983.

Hansen, J. V., and Messier, W. F. "A Relational Approach to Decision Support for EDP Auditing." *Communications of the ACM,* November 1984.

Harrington, D. R. "Stock Prices, Beta, and Strategic Planning." *Harvard Business Review,* May-June 1983.

Hickingbotham, D., and Field, T. "Calculating ROI on an IBM PC, 'What if'." *Business Software Review,* February 1986.

Jablonsky, S. F., and Dirsmith, M. W. "Is Financial Reporting Influencing Internal Decision Making?" *Management Accounting,* July 1979.

Janulaitis, M. J. "Gaining Competitive Advantage." *Infosystems,* October 1984.

Juris, R. "Electrifying Cash Flow." *Computer Decisions,* January 28, 1986.

———. "Well-Connected Accounting." *Computer Decisions,* June 17, 1986.

Keen, P. G. W. "DSS & OA, Insights & Challenges." *Computerworld,* December 7, 1983.

Kingston, P. L. "Generic Decision Support Systems." *Managerial Planning,* March/April 1981.

Kolojeski, G. "How to Use a Microcomputer to Do Personal Financial Planning." *Computers in Accounting,* July/August 1985.

Kucis, A. R., and Battaglia, S. T. "Matrix Accounting for the Statement of Changes in Financial Position." *Management Accounting,* April 1981.

Kyd, C. W. "Scheduling Your Cash Requirements." *Lotus,* August 1985.

Lacob, M. "Computers Put Corporate Cash to Work." *Computer Decisions,* September 15, 1984.

Lasden, M. "Computer-Aided Decision Making." *Computer Decisions,* November 1982.

Leavitt, D. "Finetuning Through Job Accounting Packages." *Software News,* March 1986.

Lockman, A., and Minsky, N. "Designing Financial Information Systems for Auditability." *Journal of Management Information Systems,* vol. 1, no. 1, Summer 1984.

Mauer, R. J. "Micros in Personal Trusts." *Micro Manager,* June 1984.

Miles, J. B. "Toward a Model Modeler." *Computer Decisions,* July 15, 1985.

Moscone, S. A., and Simkin, M. G. *Accounting Information Systems Concepts and Practices for Effective Decision Making.* New York: John Wiley & Sons, 1981.

Myers, S. C. "Finance Theory and Financial Strategy." *Interfaces,* January-February 1984.

Needle, S. "Multiuser Accounting Systems: The Pros & Cons of Sharing." *Journal of Accountancy,* February 1986.

Pearson, M. A. "A Primer on Managerial Accounting." *Infosystems,* May 1986.

Post, D. "General Ledger's Bottom Line." *Business Computer Systems,* July 1984.

———. "Striking a Balance." *Business Computer Systems,* August 1984.

Sandretto, M. J. "What Kind of Cost System Do You Need?" *Harvard Business Review,* January-February 1985.

Smith, R. E. "You Know My Name, Look Up the Number." *Datamation,* May 15, 1985.

Snyder, C. "Integrated Accounting Systems . . . Are They All They're Cracked Up to Be?" *Business Software Review,* September 1986.

Thierauf, R. J. *Decision Support Systems for Effective Planning and Control—A Case Study Approach.* Englewood Cliffs, NJ: Prentice-Hall, 1982.

Verschoor, C. C. "Personal Financial Planning and the CPA." *The Journal of Accountancy,* January 1985.

Wagner, G. R. "Optimizing Decision Support Systems." *Datamation,* May 1980.

Walker, E. S. "Accounting Packages: Selection and Management." *Datamation,* August 1981.

Wilkinson, J. W. *Accounting and Information Systems,* sec. ed. New York: John Wiley & Sons, 1986.

Woodwell, D. R. "Corporate Profits on Personal Computers." *Computer Decisions,* February 1984.

Wright, W. F. "Cognitive Information Processing Biases; Implications for Producers and Users of Financial Information." *Decision Sciences,* vol. 11, 1980.

Young, H. "The Wall Street-Desktop Connection." *Business Computer Systems,* September 1984.

Zanakis, S. H.; Marrides, L. P.; and Roussakis, E N. "Applications of Management Science in Banking." *Decision Sciences,* vol. 17, 1986.

Zuber, G. R.; Elliott, R. K.; Kinney, W. R., Jr.; and Leisenring, J. J. "Using Materiality in Audit Planning." *Journal of Accountancy,* March 1983.

Zuboff, S. "New Worlds of Computer-Mediated Work." *Harvard Business Review,* September-October 1982.

CHAPTER 15

Personnel Subsystem—XYZ Corporation

ISSUES

How important is it to take a broad perspective of the personnel function within an effective MIS framework?

What are the essentials of a human resource management system in the personnel function?

How important are staffing and mathematical models in personnel decision making?

How can an effective MIS in the area of skills inventory assist management in retaining qualified personnel?

How do the short-run and long-run approaches to personnel selection and development differ?

What are the important elements of wage and salary administration within an effective management information system?

For the personnel function to be effective, it must be capable of providing "a good fit" among the employee, the task, and the organizational unit. If there is "a poor fit," the employee will not be as productive as possible, not to mention the cost to management of motivating the individual to at least a satisfactory level of performance. Hence, the underlying thrust of the personnel function as presented in this chapter is providing a good fit for personnel throughout the organization.

Like the previous subsystems of the XYZ Corporation, the personnel function does not operate alone, but is thoroughly integrated with every other subsystem. Management wants a work force capable of handling the corporation's current and future work volumes. Implied in this statement is the requirement for flexibility: a permanent work force is maintained for normal operations, that is, supplemented by an auxiliary force for peak work loads or emergency conditions. In this manner, the XYZ Corporation can keep its personnel costs at a minimum while servicing the required business functions and their related subfunctions necessary to accomplish its goals and objectives.

The same structure used in prior chapters also serves to explore the personnel function. Specifically, important considerations underlying an effective MIS personnel subsystem are discussed. These include the human resource management system (HRMS), manpower planning, a problem-finding approach to personnel, and typical mathematical models oriented toward personnel. These items provide a framework for presenting personnel's major components, which are (1) skills inventory, (2) personnel selection and placement, and (3) wage and salary administration. Finally, the effective MIS practice of integrating the personnel function with corporate planning concludes the chapter.

PERSONNEL CONSIDERATIONS FOR EFFECTIVE MIS

Considerations relevant to the personnel function within an effective MIS environment go beyond its own basic structure. Payroll master data provide a starting point in terms of present personnel cost. Production planning and control requires the proper placement of factory personnel to effect the desired level of output. Similarly, shipment of finished goods considers the number of warehouse personnel handling current customer orders. Thus, an effective personnel subsystem must relate to other subsystems in order to provide the necessary human resources for accomplishing organization objectives.

Because the personnel function is so all-encompassing, organizations need to expand their managerial decision-making processes. Not only is it necessary to develop short- to long-range plans in this area, it is also extremely important to mesh these plans with other subsystems encompassing marketing, manufacturing, finance, and operations. Competition and technical innovations portend far more than new packaging, engineering, or merchandising programs. The "people element" is indispensable to the corporation. Personnel management and their staff must display a high level of analytical ability to provide useful solutions for a wide range of people problems confronting the corporation.

In addition to expanding the scope of managerial decision making, personnel considerations for effective MIS include staff planning in future years to meet anticipated growth. Similarly, there is need to exercise control over the personnel function. To effect improved planning and control, mathematical models are available that lend themselves to the personnel function.

Human Resource Management System (HRMS)

Since any corporation's most valuable resource is its employees—like the XYZ Corporation—every employee represents an obligation by the corporation to utilize that resource in the most beneficial way. Also, every employee represents a vast amount of record keeping, not only for the corporation's internal needs, but also for governmental (external) needs. In the past, all human resources management was done manually. Hours were spent searching files to locate the specific information needed for a list or report. Today, however, performing these tasks manually can bury the personnel department under an avalanche of details, increasing government and labor union compliance demands, and a growing assortment of employee benefits.

Computerized human resource management systems are available to fit the needs of any size corporation—including the XYZ Corporation—and operate on a wide variety of hardware. They are inexpensive, easy to install, and pay for themselves in terms of time saved and penalties avoided. These systems are staking a vital claim in the structure of corporate planning. Human resource management systems can be used in various ways to meet internal needs. They can track such information as skills, prior employment, and training courses to aid in career path planning. They can be used for recruiting, training, and educating employees. They can track and administer employee benefits and monitor absences.

Custom-designed human resource management systems can be very expensive. Thus, "Why re-invent the wheel?" A good packaged system should be flexible enough to meet a corporation's unique needs. It should be easy and economical to install as well as to learn and use. Most packaged human resource management systems offer an interface into the payroll system. This expanded data base then allows even more access into employee records. The systems are on-line so records are viewed on a computer terminal. Reports may be formatted and written through the use of a report writer. As corporations continue to grow and employee data record-keeping needs increase, they are turning to the computer and packaged human resource management systems to assist in utilizing their people resources to best advantage.

FEATURES OF HRMS. Most HRMS packages are programmed to monitor salary ranges—a universal need for all corporations. This is particularly important for union and non-union departments of a typical corporation. Most packages enable managers to measure performance with pay. It answers the question: "Are we paying the right money to the right people?" Along with salary monitoring, human resource packages can be the perfect tools for tracking performance reviews and succession planning. The XYZ Corporation with 3,000 employees, for example, finds it simple to track the top ten percent of its employees using a human resource package. The elements of succession planning—performance reviews, salaries, and employees' educations—are typical features of micro-based packages.

Security is another important consideration in human resource software. Outsiders cannot use the telephone to access information from a micro as they can from a mainframe. Access to most packages is controlled by operator passwords, and many use a horizontal-and-vertical password system. This lets a human resource director block all departments but his or her own out of certain fields, and prohibits nonmanagerial personnel workers from accessing sensitive information.

When narrowing down the list of vendors, the cost of the basic package should not be the first consideration. It is important to look for hidden costs as well. Besides installation, user training, and maintenance, there is the price of optional features. Job-applicant tracking—another desirable feature—may also cost extra. Keeping a record of applicants and their skills is important to many human resource directors, particularly those in industries with a high turnover. It is wise for personnel directors to incorporate word processing, spreadsheet, and graphics software (like Lotus 1-2-3) with human resource software. For example, if one wants to maintain detailed records of job applicants, as well as use a word-processing system to respond to them, one may or may not be able to purchase these features as separate constituents in a single integrated system. Hence, another consideration when purchasing human resource software is how easily it interfaces with other software.

A final consideration is how easily the software can be linked to a mainframe. Most human resource software offers only one-way linkage to a mainframe. Two-way linkage, ideal for a large corporation, has been slow to arrive, although some packages now offer it. Experts anticipate this will be an element of growth in human resource software development. A typical list of HRMS software is in figure 15.1.

LIMITATIONS OF HRMS. Typically, HRMS software packages will not solve all of the problems facing a personnel director. These packages were developed only recently, and they still have limitations. One major limitation is the small memory capacities of most micros. The personnel manager should determine the needs of his or her employer's human resource department before purchasing a system. The manager should beware of vendors that claim their software has capacities for up to 2,000 employees. First of all, only limited information about that many employees would fit on a micro. Second, managing such information without a multi-user system would be a time-consuming chore. In addition, sorting records on a micro is slow and difficult. On the other hand, the microcomputer's inability to handle all of a corporation's per-

Vendor	Package Name	Description	Hardware
Charles Russ Associates Inc.	CARE-FOR	Manpower planning and succession planning system with capacity for forecasting expected vacancies over a 5-year period.	IBM PC XT
Corporate Education Resources Inc.	Executive TRACK	Succession, development, and replacement planning system with capacity to match candidates with open positions and to generate 14 major reports.	IBM and Wang personal computers
Cresap, McCormack & Paget	HR FORECAST	Mainframe modeling program that simulates employee flow and calculates supply and demand for "What if?" scenarios. Accessed through on-line connection with consultant's computer for first year. At the end of first year may be installed on user's own IBM mainframe.	IBM mainframe
Criterion, Inc.	Job Trak	Succession planning system that creates organizational chart files and interfaces with existing personnel data bases.	IBM PC, XT, AT, or compatibles
GAI Systems	CHRIS	Human resource planning and information system available in six versions ranging from a simple package supporting a maximum of 250 employees to full-featured packages for administration supporting up to 5,000 employees and expandable through optional modules for analysis, planning, forecasting, and modeling.	IBM PC to IBM System/38
Hoffman Research Associates	Human Resource Analysis Package	Mainframe package consisting of several analytical packages dealing with compensation, employee movement, EEO problems, task inventories, labor force projections, and succession planning issues.	IBM PC or XT

FIGURE 15.1   Typical human resource management systems available from vendors.

Vendor	Package Name	Description	Hardware
Human Resource Management Associates	HR-FLOW	Planning system which performs a Markov analysis of manpower supply and allows the user to input assumptions regarding manpower demand. Written in BASIC.	Wide range of personal computers
Human Resource Technology	MSP/OSA	Planning system utilizing coded color graphics for analysis of key position candidates and vacancies, proficiency indicators, and performance standards according to either tiered or pool designations.	IBM PC or compatible
Microanalytic Management Systems	PADDSS	Personnel accounting and development decision support system individually tailored to handle functions, such as job analysis and design, candidate search, organizational and personnel needs analysis, training and needs development analysis, job and personnel financial evaluations.	IBM PCs and mainframes and others
Pacesetter Software	Organization Map	Integrated product consisting of two systems—a human resources decision support system and an organization analysis and productivity improvement support system. Assists with control of compensation costs, manpower and succession planning, organizational restructuring, affirmative action planning, and organizational charting.	IBM PC or XT
Personnel Technology	JOURNEY	General purpose English-like modeling language that can be used to build an HRP flow model to forecast supplies of and demands for personnel. Standard report tables include procurement and outplacement costs, current	IBM PC

FIGURE 15.1   Continued

Vendor	Package Name	Description	Hardware
		organizational staffing structures, vacancies, workloads, and likely career pathing.	
Randell-Heiken Inc.	OPTEM	Integrated, modular data base management system for human resource planning and tracking. Utilizes dBase III. Supported functions include manpower planning and forecasting, succession planning, organizational design, performance management, executive development, and affirmative action.	IBM PC, XT, At or compatibles
SwiftSure Data Systems Inc.	MICROPROSPECT	Manpower planning system designed by the British Institute of Manpower Studies. Allows modeling of stocks and flows of various personnel groups for analysis of staffing needs, recruitment efficacy, promotion policies, etc.	IBM PC and compatibles

FIGURE 15.1   Continued

sonnel data does not erode the benefits of micro based software. These systems are valuable when used in conjunction with a mainframe.

Microcomputers, then, can become valuable human resource systems when linked with a mainframe. They handle subsets of information quite well. Down-loading information from a mainframe and using a micro to do calculations is a common use for human resource software. In other words, the micro can be used as an intelligent terminal. For high volume, a mainframe makes sense. For problem solving and manipulating data, a micro makes sense for HRMS.

Manpower Planning

A most important element related to HRMS is personnel planning—commonly referred to as "manpower planning"—which involves predicting future personnel requirements. Manpower planning is greatly needed because of the decreasing supply of high-talent personnel. In the past, as well as currently, the Research Institute of America has stated that management not only is the most urgent need of the future, but will be the most critically short resource.

As a result, planning must be aimed toward management development. Not only will management be in short supply, but so also will be personnel with high levels of technical knowledge. This latter shortage is due to rapid technological change. It is difficult for even a qualified professional to keep abreast of any field, a fact which may cause obsolescence of technical manpower. The increasing shortage of management and technical personnel, together with their high cost, has forced the XYZ Corporation to recognize that manpower itself must be considered a resource as important as other corporate resources. Therefore, planning is required to ensure that full value for each personnel dollar will be realized, especially in managerial and technical positions.

Manpower planning refers to the complex task of forecasting and planning for the right *numbers* and the right *kinds* of personnel at the right *places* and the right *times* to perform activities that will benefit the organization in accomplishing its goals and objectives, besides helping its members satisfy their own needs. Manpower planning is successful to the extent that it properly coordinates these elements.

An essential component of the manpower planning system is a personnel forecasting technique capable of anticipating the future size and nature of the work force. Two aspects of the forecasting task require attention: (1) anticipating organizational demand for human talent of various types, and (2) anticipating available personnel supply within the organization. Personnel models simplify the forecasting components of manpower planning by manipulating available data using mathematical techniques. They provide a simplified and logical view of the levels and flows of personnel throughout an organizational system. They focus on variables considered by managers to be significant and consider assumptions or parameters underlying system behavior. Mathematical techniques make it possible to evaluate the relative importance of the many factors that influence an organization's personnel needs and availability. Due to their importance, these factors are covered later in the chapter.

Problem-Finding Approach to Personnel

The personnel function of the XYZ Corporation is called upon to assist top management in new ways that result in more effective use of both human resources and the capabilities of the personnel subsystem. This enlarged perspective necessitates that the personnel decision process change from just problem solving to problem finding.

Because problem solving has been the present emphasis by personnel management of the XYZ Corporation, there is need to expand on this approach to provide for the impact of human factors on organizational success and productivity. This realization leads to drafting human resource specialists into corporate planning. Once admitted, these specialists begin to shift administration's orientation from *reactive* administration to *proactive* management and planning. The corporation and its personnel department begin to think in terms of projected labor needs, five-year hiring plans, anticipatory

589

talent development, employee recycling, productive task distribution, and cost accountability.

Since these issues had for the most part not been seriously contemplated before, the XYZ Corporation (like many corporations) found that it had neither the collected data nor the analytical capability to tackle them, and so turned for assistance to outside consultants. The consultants, in turn, developed tools to help create the forecasts and models that clients were requesting. Only recently have some of these tools begun to appear as HRMS packaged commodities (refer to figure 15.1).

The message should be clear. The real value of a human resource planning system is not after-the fact analysis, but its anticipatory capability. The critical need is to solve problems before they arise. The personnel subsystem of the XYZ Corporation, then, must be increasingly aware of the significance of the corporation's human resources today and tomorrow. It must review the efficient use of existing personnel at its present and future level of development, assess the level of present and anticipated performance of corporation employees, and concern itself with the enhancement of the individual's skills and talents currently and in the future in order to improve productivity and overall contribution of the work force.

With this general orientation for problem finding, the personnel function has an excellent opportunity to contribute to the growth and success of the corporation in still other ways. Personnel is able to help identify and ease potential pressure points and adverse trends related to the organization's human resources. For example, a human resource specialist can provide management with counsel and assistance that can help it meet the intense pressure generated by equal employment legislation and affirmative action programs. No longer can equal employment be indiscriminately lumped in with the sundry group of activities included under corporate social responsibility. With corporations' expanded responsibility in this area, it is imperative that personnel managers be qualified to provide the advice desperately needed by the corporation.

The personnel function is able to spot adverse trends in turnover and absenteeism. This responsibility does not end with problem identification. The goal is to determine the causes of these problems and what is actually needed to help the organization solve them. The personnel department has to be more creative (i.e., proactive) in those areas of its responsibilities, and its staff needs to become involved in providing managers with advice that is workable and useful.

In addition, the personnel department has become increasingly oriented toward growth and efficiency of the corporation instead of merely administering traditional personnel activities. This means greater emphasis upon planning the structure of the future organization and its personnel requirements, identifying and selecting the right people to meet these expected needs, developing and utilizing the organization's present-day human resources, and assessing and rewarding performance. The purpose of these activities is to ensure growth of both the corporation and the individual employee.

Mathematical Models

Numerous mathematical models have been successfully applied to the personnel function. Techniques such as simulation and Markov analysis permit manipulation of important historical data for critical variables. Specifically, modeling enables managers to explore aspects of systems that cannot be observed directly—for example, the movement patterns of employees between different jobs in an organization over time, or the reactions of personnel to changes in management policies and individual employment decisions. In this section, the above techniques (simulation and Markov analysis) are discussed, with an eye toward analyzing future personnel requirements by job classifications.

WORK FORCE SIMULATOR. The Work Force Simulator, developed by IBM, is an example of a mathematical model used to evaluate personnel plans. The effects of new hiring, transferring, and retraining programs are tested against the data stored on line in a skills inventory system. Basically, the skills inventory contains the following data:

- *employee profile*—contains data about the employee, such as home address, marital status, and number of dependents
- *employment history*—shows the positions the employee has held within the company, salary over the years, and appraisals
- *resumé and significant achievements,* including previous employment
- *education data* with major and minor fields of concentration
- *skills data,* including on-the-job training and experience

These blocks of skills inventory data provide reports on a regular basis to management in the areas of salary benefits analysis, education and training planning, placement resumés, and appraisal scheduling. Once a year, the basic data are printed for each employee in order to update them. After review and appropriate corrections, the Work Force Simulator is employed to determine upcoming personnel requirements by major subclassifications. In this manner, personnel with desired technical skills can be hired in conformance with the corporation's plans.

MARKOV ANALYSIS. Markov analysis is a way of analyzing the current movement of certain variables in order to forecast their future movement. When applied to projecting future personnel needs, this means analyzing current personnel skills—highly technical, technical, semi-technical, and non-technical—with the goal of predicting future personnel requirements. The firm needs to know the causes of gains and losses, as well as their percents or probabilities, before future needs can be projected.

To illustrate this mathematical technique, certain concepts must be explained. The "hard-core component" describes employees who do not move from one job level to another. Personnel who switch from one level to another represent "gains" from the previous level. In a similar fashion, those who move to a lower level job for one reason or another are represented as "losses." Retentions (hard-core component), gains, and losses are calculated in figure 15.2 for the corporation's manufacturing plant in St. Louis. Note that zeros on the diagonals mean one group can incur neither gains nor losses from itself. Also, the losses columns represent transpositions of the gains in the rows.

The next step is to convert the data developed in figure 15.2 (retentions, gains, and losses) to matrix form. The problem is represented in this form in figure 15.3 for ease of mathematical calculations. The rows in the matrix show the retention rates and the gains of company (A, B, C, and D) personnel, while the columns depict the retention rate and the loss of personnel to a different positional level. In this figure, the first matrix is stated in terms of the actual number of personnel. The second matrix is shown in terms of transition probabilities. In reading the rows, row 2 indicates that technical personnel are retained at a .767 rate, while gaining .091 from highly technical personnel (caused by declining skills of older personnel), .109 from semi-technical personnel, and .060 from non-technical personnel. Note that non-technical personnel enter at their respective levels, but then acquire more formal education and on-the-job training, enabling them to rise to a higher level. Reading down the second column, the retention rate of technical personnel is again .767, while .133, .017, and .083 of its employees are lost to highly technical, semi-technical, and non-technical positions, respectively. In effect, all the basic gain and loss relationships can be observed.

The foregoing matrix calculations have focused on the changes from one period to the next period, that is, from one month to the next. What is needed from the above analysis is an equilibrium state that can be reached in the future. Specifically, what are the final or equilibrium personnel percents

Type of Personnel	Period One, Number of Personnel	Gains From				Losses To				Period Two, Number of Personnel
		A	B	C	D	A	B	C	D	
A—Highly technical	220	0	40	0	10	0	20	10	15	225
B—Technical	300	20	0	25	15	40	0	5	25	290
C—Semi-technical	230	10	5	0	10	0	25	0	0	230
D—Non-technical	250	15	25	0	0	10	15	10	0	255
	1,000									1,000

FIGURE 15.2 Retentions, gains, and losses of personnel in Markov analysis for the manufacturing plant in St. Louis.

	Type of Personnel				Period Two			Type of Personnel			
	A	B	C	D	Number	Percent		A	B	C	D
A	175	40	0	10	225	22.5%	A	.796	.133	.000	.040
B	20	230	25	15	290	29.0%	B	.091	.767	.109	.060
C	10	5	205	10	230	23.0%	C	.046	.017	.891	.040
D	15	25	0	215	255	25.5%	D	.067	.083	.000	.860
								1.000	1.000	1.000	1.000
Period One:											
Number	220	300	230	250	1,000						
Percent	22%	30%	23%	25%		100.0%					

FIGURE 15.3   A calculated matrix of personnel transition probabilities.

approximately one year hence? By utilizing the above matrix, the following equations are developed:

$$A = .796A + .133B + .000C + .040D$$
$$0 = -.204A + .133B + .040D \qquad \textbf{Equation 15.1}$$
$$B = 0.91A + .767B + .109C + .060D$$
$$0 = .091A - .233B + .109C + .060D \qquad \textbf{Equation 15.2}$$
$$C = .046A + .017B + .891C + .040D$$
$$0 = .046A + .017B - .109C + .040D \qquad \textbf{Equation 15.3}$$
$$D = .067A + .083B + .000C + .860D$$
$$0 = .067A + .083B - .140D \qquad \textbf{Equation 15.4}$$
$$1.0 = A + B + C + D \qquad \textbf{Equation 15.5}$$

The final equation is employed to show that the four personnel categories equal 1.0.

Solving for equilibrium (approximately one year hence) by simultaneous equations yields the following values:

Type of Personnel	Equilibrium	Period One	Differences Plus (Minus)
A—Highly technical	22.8%	22%	.8%
B—Technical	26.8%	30%	(3.2%)
C—Semi-technical	23.7%	23%	.7%
D—Non-technical	26.7%	25%	1.7%
	100.0%	100%	0.0%

The results indicate that there is need to hire highly technical, semi-technical, and non-technical personnel at the St. Louis plant. Thus, Markov analysis is a method of analyzing movements of personnel from one group to another in order to determine where future recruiting efforts should be directed. This technique allows management to allocate and develop available talent within the corporation by evening out future indicated surpluses and shortages of personnel.

One final comment is in order regarding Markov analysis. It should be used with discretion because probabilities employed are principally extensions of past experience, and past experience may not be representative of future trends.[1]

PERSONNEL OVERVIEW—XYZ CORPORATION

The personnel subsystem of the XYZ Corporation is seen in figure 15.4 interacting with other subsystems. These relationships can be viewed in three distinct overlapping phases. *Phase one* covers the skills inventory of present employees. *Phase two* centers around the recruitment, screening, and selection of employees before and throughout their employment. *Phase three* covers the obligation to the corporation in the form of wage and salary administration, and to the individual for accurate verification of employment when necessary.

Within the framework of these basic phases, authorized staff have the ability to extract current personnel information via a CRT device or a microcomputer. With this capability, corrections and appropriate actions are effected much sooner. In this type of operating mode (i.e., an on-line and up-to-date data base), future personnel projections can be made relatively easily with mathematical models as described above.

Control Over the Personnel Function

To assist in control over the personnel function, an organization needs to have an up-to-date personnel data base. Personnel data are stored in the corporate and plant data bases according to type. Of prime importance is quick accessibility for instantaneous display of pertinent personnel data via a CRT terminal. In this manner, the personnel subsystem can meet the demands placed upon it with immediate responses.

On the plant data base, *skills inventory* information consists of employee name, number, educational background, on-the-job training, specific skills, and time spent developing and using these skills. In turn, the payroll master file supplements these data base elements—specifically, adding the employee's address, earnings-to-date, and various taxes withheld. Personnel history and training data elements consist of additional detailed information necessary to highlight the specific skills of a plant employee. This information is helpful in *personnel selection and placement,* that is, in placing present employees in new jobs. From this view, internal recruitment precedes external recruitment, thereby showing the concern of management for promoting

[1]For more information on Markov Analysis, refer to Robert J. Thierauf, Robert C. Klekamp, and Marcia L. Ruwe, *Management Science—A Model Formulation Approach with Computer Applications.* Columbus, OH: Charles E. Merrill Publishing Company, 1985, chapter 8, Markov Analysis.

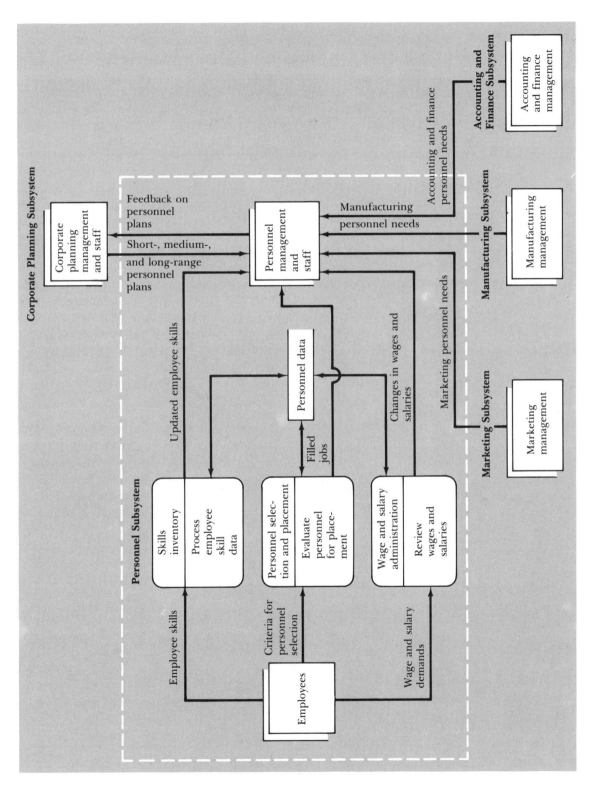

FIGURE 15.4 Personnel data flow diagram—XYZ Corporation.

from within as well as providing an atmosphere for assisting organization personnel to achieve their personal career goals.

Moving up the corporate data base, data elements for personnel comprise *wage and salary administration,* that is, data on negotiations, cost studies, and the like. Wage and salary data are used to determine the labor costs for flexible budgets within the corporate planning subsystem. These data can be employed when management is negotiating with the union. The offers made by management include wage improvements, changes in fringe benefits, work rules, and comparable items. Applications can be developed for company negotiators to test alternative proposals based upon the corporate data base elements.

As shown in figure 15.5, CRT terminals and microcomputers at the corporate level and the plant level make it possible to retrieve vital personnel data on an interactive basis. For example, skills inventory information regarding a specific employee can be retrieved instantaneously via a CRT terminal device. In like manner, personnel history listings for selection and placement of present employees in new positions can be produced via a microcomputer. In addition, wage and salary information by departments and in total are retrievable immediately, making the personnel data base usable for a wide range of purposes. Last, but not least, microcomputers can be linked to the corporation's data base in order to answer recurring and ad hoc "What if?" questions.

MIS PERSONNEL SUBSYSTEM

Input for the MIS personnel subsystem of the XYZ Corporation originates partly in other subsystems—particularly in the accounting and manufacturing subsystems. However, skills inventory, personnel selection and placement, and wage and salary administration originate within the personnel function. Regardless of the originating data, these input sources are combined with the existing data base—skills inventory, payroll master, personnel history, and training data—to produce desired personnel reports. In addition, various personnel forms are maintained, such as personnel history and promotion records and personnel requisition forms.

Use of HRMS to Answer "What if?" Questions

The personnel subsystem of the XYZ Corporation must be able to answer "What if?" questions as they arise. By using a human resource management system, such questions can be answered; for instance, "What is the cost of laying off a shift in a particular plant?" The HRM system is able to provide an answer on the basis of labor contract. The other part of the HRMS centers on answers to questions that relate to the rules, that is, the policies, contracts, and federal regulations that govern the way people within the corporation can do things. When these rules are incorporated into the system, appropriate "What if?" questions can be answered and decisions administered properly. If the corporation has a policy of hiring only people with a particular back-

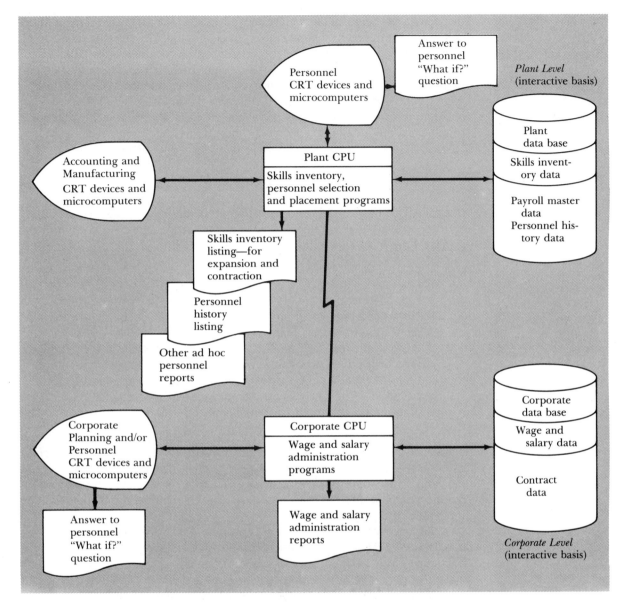

FIGURE 15.5   Personnel subsystem for an effective management information system—XYZ Corporation.

ground at a certain level, for example, management needs to have its MIS enforce this. From this perspective, the HRMS serves top management as well as the personnel department.

In addition, the HRMS should allow corporation executives to produce ad hoc or special reports. The HRMS should be able to provide top management with an answer to such a question as: "If a five percent increase were given to all salaried personnel employed by the corporation for over three years, an eight percent increase given to all employed over eight years, and a four percent increase to nonsalaried personnel, what do salaries look like for the next year?" The real value of the system, then, is how its output can be related back to management. This is where the emphasis has changed in recent years. With such a system, the XYZ Corporation's vice president of accounting and finance or personnel can fill in a few parameters and get a report promptly to answer "What if?" questions.

SKILLS INVENTORY

Capable of serving as a basis for an automated skills inventory system, a library or thesaurus of "skill catalogs" of employees, stored on the plant data base (figure 15.6), includes the following items:

- □ employee number (for basic reference)
- □ employee name
- □ formal education
- □ current occupation of employee
- □ on-the-job training
- □ fields of professional specialty and specific concentrations within it
- □ type of products or services involved in the employee's current job
- □ types of equipment on which the employee has experience
- □ past and current projects the employee has undertaken
- □ what work the employee would like to perform

Updating of the skills inventory system is relatively straightforward. New employees complete a checklist containing the foregoing items, which is often entered on the data base, as part of their orientation procedures. As individuals terminate employment, all skills data relating to their permanent numbers are dropped from disk storage. These simplified procedures assume timeliness of reports.

Requests of the on-line skills inventory system, as seen in figure 15.6, are handled by a CRT device or a microcomputer at the plant level. Micro output from the system can take several forms. For example, reports issued quarterly include a skills inventory listing by employee names, an alphabetic listing of all plant employees, a departmental listing of employees by years of service (refer to figure 15.7), and biographical sketches of employees. These are reviewed by plant supervisors to ensure that the plant data base is accurate— that is, to see that all changes in job levels have in fact been recorded. This checking also ensures that the employee is paid properly and, ultimately, makes possible an accurate costing of products manufactured.

The system described here is designed to generate specific reports to meet the employer's needs; a cross-referenced printout in booklet form is produced quarterly. This is prepared from data stored on the plant data base. Individual employee dossiers, which are useful as auxiliary documents for other personnel-related functions, can also be readily prepared from the plant data base.

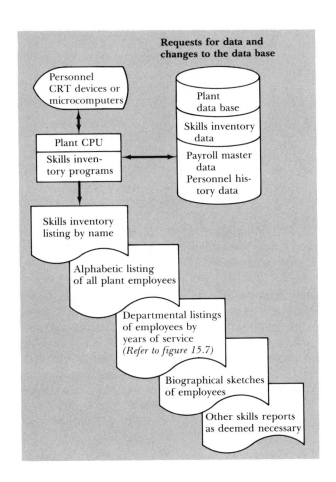

FIGURE 15.6
Skills inventory data flow for an MIS personnel subsystem.

| | Employee | | Years of |
Department	Name	Number	Service
08 – Lathe Work Center			
	Michael J. Cuttingham	0075	18
	Larry E. Gordon	0101	15
	Michael E. Pleva	0110	14
	Frank F. McVay	0135	12
	•	•	•
	•	•	•
	•	•	•

FIGURE 15.7
Employee department listing by years of service.

Trimming the Work Force

Although the skills inventory system is designed to assist in personnel selection and placement (refer to the next section) as the XYZ Corporation grows, there is no guarantee that the corporation will continue in a positive direction. Generally, the XYZ Corporation has found that over the last two decades a weakening job market keeps a downward pressure on wages, thereby producing a softening in consumer spending. But it also helps pave the way for a smooth, orderly transition from an economic boom to a period of moderate long-term growth. In view of these factors, the XYZ Corporation must be prepared at any time to trim its work force at its three manufacturing plants and warehouses.

A starting point for reducing the size of its blue-collar labor force is to relate the leading economic indicators to the corporation's sales forecasts. When leading indicators are tending to move downward, the forecasts of the corporation's 30 products take this into account. In turn, the number of products to be produced each quarter is lowered. This information is then downloaded from the corporate data base along with the skills inventory data to a micro by a personnel analyst. A thorough analysis is undertaken using a model called "readjusting personnel requirements." Actually, the personnel analyst is trimming the size of the workforce at the plants and warehouses. Thus, the personnel department of the XYZ Corporation is responsible for being proactive concerning the hiring of new workers so that plants' and warehouses' personnel reduction is kept to a minimum when it occurs. From this enlightened perspective, the personnel department can employ its skills inventory data to their best advantage when "the chips are down."

PERSONNEL SELECTION AND PLACEMENT

Personnel selection and placement for the XYZ Corporation is concerned with three important phases. *First,* the MIS needs to forecast personnel needs. This can be accomplished by using one of the mathematical models set forth previously in the chapter. *Second,* this department recruits personnel to meet organizational needs. Properly managed, the MIS furnishes information on skills required for all current and upcoming corporation programs. An essential part of personnel selection is information about inventory of skills available in the corporation. *Third,* although not described below, the personnel subsystem matches available personnel with current labor assignments in order to use employees most effectively.

Forecasting Work Force Requirements

Personnel management must continually review and evaluate alternative personnel plans brought about by changing work loads and/or technological advances. Decisions in this area should be quantitatively analyzed so that the people hired today can begin the kind of training necessary to fill new positions or vacancies as they occur. A Work Force Simulator (similar to that set forth previously) can be employed for determining personnel information under varying future conditions.

The Work Force Simulator, being a broad-based planning model, involves two basic concepts—namely, a phase approach and a matrix structure. In the phase approach, the interaction of different work-force factors is considered. A decision concerning a mandatory retirement age is stated. Also, an estimate of attrition due to reasons other than retirement is set forth. Factors for recruiting new personnel are added and provisions are made for internal transfers of employees because of promotion or retraining.

In the matrix structure of the Work Force Simulator (figure 15.8), consideration of job levels over a period of time is included. Each column of the matrix represents a different time period, such as a year or a five-year span. Each row of the matrix represents a different job level. At each intersection of rows and columns, one job level at a certain time period is represented.

The simulator is started by entering policy factors and data about the current plant-level work force—age, experience, education level, and comparable data. By utilizing data about current employees from the plant data base (figure 15.9), the start of the simulation depicts the situation as it actually is. In the first phase of the model, the loss of personnel by retirement

Job Level	Time Period—Years				
	One	Two	Three	Four	Five
Highly Technical:					
Job 1	①	②	③	④	⑤
Job 2	⑥	⑦	⑧	⑨	⑩
· · ·	etc.				
Job n					
Technical					
Jobs 1 through n					
Semi-Technical					
Jobs 1 through n					
Non-Technical					
Jobs 1 through n					

FIGURE 15.8 Matrix structure of the Work Force Simulator—columns represent different time periods and rows represent different job levels. Circles represent the number (n) of employees in each category.

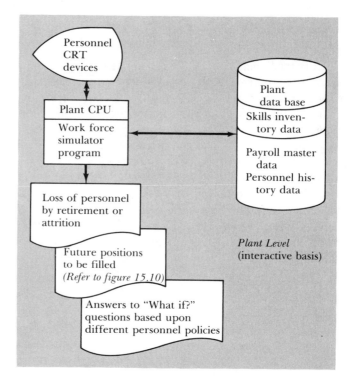

FIGURE 15.9

Personnel selection and placement data flow for an MIS personnel subsystem.

and attrition can be observed. In the next phase, future positions to be filled are determined under certain stated policies (refer to figure 15.10). Additionally, answers to ad hoc "What if?" questions based upon different personnel policies can be answered (figure 15.9). The net effect of this Work Force Simulator is that it allows a hypothetical test of different personnel policies. This example of an imaginative use of the personnel subsystem in an effective MIS environment provides corporate planners with long-range information.

An alternative approach to forecasting the work force by Markov analysis was illustrated in an earlier section. As noted there, it can predict future personnel needs by type—highly technical, technical, semi-technical, and non-technical. The data in the illustration represented the St. Louis plant (the largest one) consisting of 1,000 employees. For next year, the results indicated that highly technical (0.8%), semi-technical (0.7%), and non-technical (1.7%) needed to be hired to replace existing personnel. Hence, the hiring process should start with internal recruitment before going to the outside.

Internal Promotion—Matching Employees to Jobs

Going beyond a forecasting approach to manpower planning, an effective MIS is designed to assist manufacturing plant supervisors and foremen in matching present employees to job openings. The starting point is utilizing the skills inventory data stored on the plant data bases. Having on-line personnel records available (at each of the three plants), the system is designed to go

Job Classification (Level)	Location			
	Chicago	St. Louis	Los Angeles	Total
HIGHLY TECHNICAL				
Senior Engineers	2	4	3	9
Junior Engineers	2	4	3	9
Production Control Personnel	1	1	1	3
Totals	5	9	7	21
TECHNICAL				
Factory Foremen	1	—	1	2
Engineering Assistants	2	—	2	4
Tool and Die Makers	1	—	1	2
Totals	4	—	4	8
SEMI-TECHNICAL				
Machinists	3	3	4	10
Assembly Personnel— Minor	2	4	3	9
Totals	5	7	7	19
NON-TECHNICAL				
Assembly Personnel— Major	10	15	12	37
Receiving and Stock Control Clerks	1	2	1	4
Totals	11	17	13	41
Grand Totals	25	33	31	89

FIGURE 15.10
Future personnel positions (engineering and manufacturing) to be filled for next year—output of the Work Force Simulator program.

beyond keeping these records up to date. Besides serving many other uses, such as EEO (Equal Employment Opportunity) reporting on employees and printing weekly in-house payroll reports, the system is used for employee–job matching. Job postings for factory positions, printed weekly, are posted on factory bulletin boards in each of the three plants. For the people who apply, a job applicant review profile is generated by the system. Also included are copies of the performance evaluation that the potential supervisor and/or foreman reviews. This current information gives factory management (supervisor or foreman) a complete picture about the employee. It should be noted that the job-applicant review profile can be used as a turnaround document when a person actually gets selected for the job. It also enables factory management to avoid using personnel folders that might contain personal and confidential information.

The preceding approach to matching employees to jobs is but one part of the "placement and selection" process. If one or more job openings go unfilled for two weeks, the factory manager interrogates the plant data base to screen possible applicants who might be candidates. If none are available within the requesting plant, the data bases at the other two plants are interrogated. The output—the job-applicant review profile—becomes the basis for a possible transfer of one or more employees. On the other hand, if no one is available internally or if the available personnel are not interested, it is generally necessary to go outside for recruiting the appropriate factory personnel. For high-skill jobs, this access capability is extremely helpful to factory management.

Overall, the foregoing procedures for matching employees (current and prospective) to job openings is very responsive to the task of meeting the newer skills required in a changing manufacturing environment of the XYZ Corporation. Throughout the process, the factory supervisor or foreman brings certain personal parameters (intuition, past experiences, judgment) to the employee–job matching process. The factory manager has total freedom and flexibility to accept or reject the employee under consideration. With this view, the individual's subjective feelings are integrated with the objective findings via the job search program.

Use of Micro Package for Assessing Personnel Costs

A variation of problem finding centers on the XYZ Corporation acquiring a microcomputer package to assist in determining pertinent information on the possibility of locating a new warehouse in the southeast part of the United States. It has engaged the services of Cresap, McCormick and Paget, a major consulting firm, which currently offers a number of stand-alone microcomputer products for human resource planning in conjunction with its consulting services (refer to figure 15.1). It was decided that a program called Relevant Labor Pool (RLP) is to be utilized. It is configured for independent operation on a microcomputer with dBASE III.

RLP was useful in assessing (i.e., comparing) projected business sites in terms of availability and cost of labor for the new warehouse because of its projected space utilization and relative efficiency to yield significant operational savings. What the analysis of projected need against available labor supply revealed, however, was that any hoped-for savings would be more than offset by higher-than-expected pay rates and the necessity of offering such incentives as transportation and child care to attract workers in a high-employment area. Based on these RLP findings, top management of the XYZ Corporation decided to search for another location with a cheaper and more plentiful labor supply. Although alternative sites are still being considered, it is expected that one will be selected within the next three weeks using RLP.

WAGE AND SALARY ADMINISTRATION

The last of the major personnel functions, wage and salary administration, involves working with selected data and ratios at corporate headquarters. A wage and salary analyst, for example, determines salary and wage curves by job classifications and supplies this wage and salary information to higher levels of management. The analyst's participation in salary surveys is relatively brief because wage and salary data are maintained on the corporate data base. In essence, the MIS approach is basically extracting wage and salary data as is or manipulating the data for desired results.

The wage and salary data on the corporate data base and comparable wage and salary data from other industries plus other selected data are also needed to produce the reports illustrated in figure 15.11. Typical management reports produced are salary surveys (refer to figure 15.12), salary curves by job classifications, comparable wage and salary data from other industries, and other selected wage and salary data.

Annual Salary Analysis

To gain a better understanding of the XYZ Corporation's annual salary survey, it is helpful to use the data to make meaningful comparisons, that is, to com-

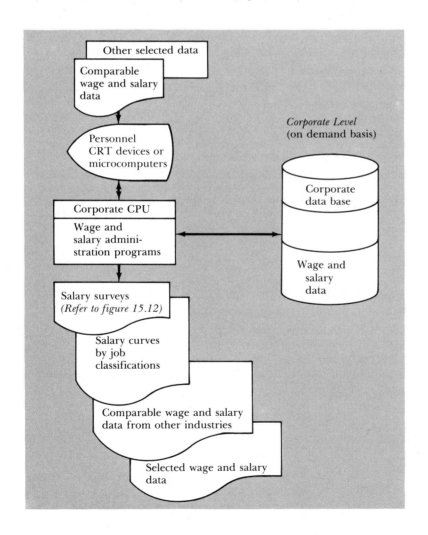

FIGURE 15.11
Wage and salary administration data flow for an MIS personnel subsystem.

Job Classification (Level)	Industry Average	Manufacturing Plants		
		Chicago	St. Louis	Los Angeles
HIGHLY TECHNICAL				
Senior Engineers	$39,500	$38,100	$36,400	$40,400
Junior Engineers	28,500	27,500	26,400	30,500
**Production Control Personnel	31,500	28,000	26,500	30,500
TECHNICAL				
**Factory Foremen	30,800	29,400	29,100	30,400
Engineering Assistants	22,400	20,300	19,500	22,800
*Tool and Die Makers	25,500	26,700	25,800	27,500
SEMI-TECHNICAL				
Machinists	24,500	23,900	23,000	24,800
*Assembly Personnel— Minor	20,100	20,600	20,200	21,000
NON-TECHNICAL				
Assembly Personnel— Major	19,500	19,600	18,900	20,000
**Receiving and Stock Control Clerks	17,000	16,100	15,000	16,700

*All manufacturing plants above the industry average
**All manufacturing plants below the industry average

FIGURE 15.12   Industry salary survey (engineering and manufacturing) by job classifications as compared to the XYZ Corporation—three manufacturing plants. *Note:* all figures have been rounded to the nearest hundred.

pare the industry average with salaries paid in the three manufacturing plants (Chicago, St. Louis, and Los Angeles). This is accomplished in figure 15.13(a) and graphed in (b), using Lotus 1-2-3 on a microcomputer, for highly technical personnel in engineering and manufacturing. Comparable comparisons could have been performed for technical, semi-technical, and non-technical personnel. These data indicate that the XYZ Corporation is overpaying its engineering and manufacturing personnel.

In addition, the wage and salary analyst can evaluate how wages and salaries in each plant and warehouse compare to budget, how the cost of wages and salaries compares to sales, and how one plant or warehouse ranks against other plants or warehouses and against the corporation average.

Depending on the needs of management, the analyst can also delve into other personnel issues by evaluating reports on

Job Classification (Level)		Manufacturing Plants		
Highly Technical	Industry Average	Los Angeles	Chicago	St. Louis
Sr. Eng	$39,500	$40,400	$38,100	$36,400
Jr. Eng	28,500	30,500	27,500	26,400
Production Control	31,500	30,500	28,000	26,500

(a)

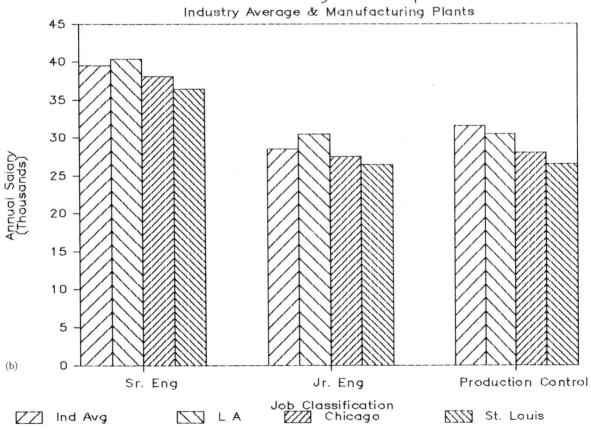

(b)

FIGURE 15.13 (a) Annual salary survey for highly technical personnel—industry average versus the three manufacturing plants of the XYZ Corporation, and (b) a graph of the same data using Lotus 1-2-3.

607

□ the promotability of employees
□ the corporation's progress toward affirmative action
□ department goals and progress toward realizing them
□ plant and warehouse goals and progress toward realizing them
□ budget management
□ backup of key positions

Overall, personnel data base elements can be extracted, manipulated, and printed to answer specific managerial "What if?" questions directed toward wage and salary administration.

Summary—MIS Personnel Subsystem

Skills inventory focuses on keeping track of employee skills for the purpose of retrieving specific information on a specific employee, promoting from within, preparing periodic reports to meet the corporation's needs, and so forth.

Personnel selection and placement is concerned with forecasting future personnel needs, recruiting personnel to meet organizational needs, and matching available personnel with current labor assignments in order to make effective use of available personnel.

Wage and salary administration involves working with selected data and ratios to determine appropriate wage and salary curves by job classifications, and supplying this information to higher management.

EFFECTIVE MIS PRACTICE—INTEGRATION OF PERSONNEL WITH CORPORATE PLANNING

The personnel function centers around skills inventory, personnel selection and placement, and wage and salary administration. From an effective MIS perspective, these personnel activities must be integrated into the organization's overall corporate planning process. Instead of a melange of diverse activities, the personnel department must be an integrated management activity responsible for the effective utilization of the organization's human resources. It must be sensitive to the requirements of the organization and committed to making the organization more effective. Specifically, the skills inventory system speeds up considerably the location of qualified employees for full-time and part-time special assignments. If in-house personnel cannot be located, the personnel selection and placement function takes over hiring from the outside. Included in this function is personnel planning for the short, intermediate, and long run. Additionally, wage and salary administration must be concerned about equitable pay for its employees. Wages and salaries must fairly reflect employee positions and skills required. The personnel function can best be performed, then, in the context of an effective MIS environment by relating its activities from the outset to the corporate planning process.

The MIS personnel subsystem of the XYZ Corporation is related directly to other subsystems because all functional areas depend on the human factor to accomplish the corporation's objectives. In terms of data used, personnel relies heavily on the payroll function of the accounting subsystem. Similarly, information available from the manufacturing subsystem, such as technical skills required for a specific job and the apprenticeship requirements for a certain job level, are of great help to the personnel function. However, despite this important level of integration, many methods and procedures evolve from the personnel function itself. Overall, the development of a personnel subsystem is a difficult undertaking because such a variety of approaches can be used to provide timely management information for changing conditions. The attendant circumstances must be surveyed for applying the most appropriate approaches to an MIS personnel subsystem.

QUESTIONS

1. **a.** What are the essential elements of a human resource management systems? Explain fully.
   b. How does an HRMS differ from a manpower planning system? Explain fully.
2. It has been said that the use of a human resource management system is to control turnover. Explain what is meant by this statement.
3. Of what help is manpower planning to operating managers at the plant level? How does it help the personnel department at the plant level?
4. How can a problem-finding approach be applied to the personnel subsystem of the XYZ Corporation?
5. What are the essential control elements of an effective personnel subsystem?
6. Suggest other mathematical models that can be employed by an MIS personnel subsystem to make it more effective.
7. Explain the relationship of skills inventory to personnel selection and placement in an effective MIS environment.
8. Referring to the section on personnel selection and placement, suggest an alternative approach to determining the number of personnel needed for future positions.
9. What are the essential elements comprising an effective wage and salary administration system within an MIS personnel subsystem?
10. What is meant by the statement that "an effective MIS personnel subsystem is directly responsible for coordinating the planning, employment, training, and compensation functions so as to maintain an equilibrium between external and internal environmental personnel factors." Explain thoroughly.

PROBLEMS

11. In the first part of the chapter, attention was focused on a human resource management system for all corporations, followed by the use of HRMS to answer spe-

cific "What if?" questions for the XYZ Corporation. Suggest at least three other "What if?" questions that are answerable by employing an HRMS for the corporation. Are these questions more easily answered by approaches other than a human resource management system?

12. The use of manpower planning was stressed in this chapter for the XYZ Corporation. Fundamentally, manpower planning refers to predicting future personnel requirements. This is particularly important because of the tightening supply of highly educated personnel in specialty areas. If the corporation cannot attract professional people from the outside through regular channels, what approaches can be used to ensure that an adequate supply of qualified personnel are available? Include in your answers ways to meet the needs of the functional areas of the organization, including the personnel department itself.

13. In the chapter, the skills inventory, personnel selection and placement, and wage and salary administration modules were developed for the MIS personnel subsystem of the XYZ Corporation. Although these sections are typically found for personnel, what others could have been developed for personnel that logically fit in this area? In addition, what MIS subsystems normally interface with the MIS personnel subsystem? Is it possible that their component parts could be an integral part of the personnel subsystem? If so, discuss how the MIS personnel subsystem can be modified to integrate these modules.

14. Presently, the MIS personnel subsystem operates in a distributed data processing mode. Going beyond this type of information processing mode, what changes could be made in either the personnel selection and placement system or the wage and salary administration system to make it qualify as a total decision support system? Include in your answer both the appropriate DSS changes that you would recommend for one of the two modules and whether the XYZ Corporation would be better off operating in an MIS or a DSS operating mode.

PROJECTS

15. To assist management in predicting future personnel needs of the XYZ Corporation, Markov analysis can be used to project future personnel needs for next year, the following year, and so forth. The assumption in this mathematical model is that the future will be comparable to the past in terms of gains and losses of personnel at the various levels, whether they be highly technical, technical, semi-technical, or non-technical workers. Suppose the future is expected to be quite different from the past. What changes could be made to the mathematical model to ensure that the answer is reasonably accurate? Consider alternative approaches to accurately predicting future personnel needs. Additionally, list the benefits and shortcomings of each approach, and select the one that appears most promising for predicting future manpower requirements.

16. Augment the personnel selection and placement system of the XYZ Corporation in such a way that it matches the available personnel with current labor assignments to make effective use of available personnel on a daily basis. Consideration should be given to employing mathematical models. Also, consider merging data generated by other subsystems with internally generated personnel data. As a way of bringing all these changes together, use either a system flowchart or a data flow diagram.

17. Training and education were not addressed in this chapter. Develop the essential elements that would qualify as part of the MIS personnel subsystem for the XYZ Corporation. For possible inclusion in your answer is the role of computer assisted instruction (CAI), which allows managers control over the quality of instructional information, thereby giving them increased confidence in the proficiency level of their employees. From another perspective, consideration might be given to using a software package (refer to chapter 5) as a basis for evaluating employees for their current as well as future responsibilities. Use one or more system flowcharts or data flow diagrams as a means for depicting the data flow for the training and education system.

LOTUS 1-2-3 EXERCISES AND PROGRAMS

18. In the chapter, industry salary survey (engineering and manufacturing) by job classification as compared to the three manufacturing plants of the XYZ Corporation was illustrated in figure 15.12. In turn, the analysis for highly technical personnel (senior engineers, junior engineers, and production control personnel) was shown in figure 15.13(a) along with a graph of this analysis in figure 15.13(b). Using this as a model, develop a comparable analysis for technical personnel (factory foremen, engineering assistants, and tool and die makers) based upon the program provided on the Lotus 1-2-3 diskette or as given in the program found in this section. How do the results of this exercise compare to those given in figure 15.13? Is it possible to show the graph of this problem differently using Lotus 1-2-3? If so, state what the graph might be. Also, use Lotus 1-2-3 to prepare an alternative graph.

19. As illustrated in the chapter, industry salary survey (engineering and manufacturing) by job classifications as compared to the three manufacturing plants of the XYZ Corporation was given in figure 15.12. In turn, the analysis of highly technical personnel (senior engineers, junior engineers, and production control personnel) was shown in figure 15.13(a) along with the graph of this analysis in figure 15.13(b). Using this as a model, develop a comparable analysis for non-technical personnel (assembly personnel—major and receiving and stock control clerks) based upon the program provided on the Lotus 1-2-3 diskette or as given in the program in this section. How do the results of this exercise compare to that given in figure 15.13? Is it possible to show the graph of this problem differently using Lotus 1-2-3? If so, state what the graph might be. Also, use Lotus 1-2-3 to prepare an alternative approach.

20. The vice president of personnel for the XYZ Corporation is wondering how the company compares to its competition in what it pays for all of its technical personnel. In figure 15.12, "Industry Salary Survey by Job Classifications," the categories of interest are the highly technical, technical, and semi-technical categories. Using the data in figure 15.12, sum the data for each of three technical categories for each plant and develop a comparable analysis for all categories of technical personnel (i.e., highly technical, technical, and semi-technical) based upon the program provided on the Lotus 1-2-3 diskette or as given in the program found for this section. What should she do regarding the Lotus 1-2-3 output? That is, should she initiate a study to analyze the wage and salary structure further, do nothing, or pursue some other avenue of analysis? State an appropriate path for her to follow.

LOTUS 1-2-3 PROGRAM—ANNUAL SALARY SURVEY (DATA AND GRAPH) (PROGRAM 12)

```
D1: '        Annual Salary Survey
D2: '        --------------------
A5: 'Job Classification
B6: "(Level)
F6: '        Manufacturing Plants
A7: '--------------------
F7: '------------------------------------
D8: "Industry
A9: 'Highly Technical
D9: "Average
F9: "Los Angeles
H9: "Chicago
J9: "St. Louis
A11: '   Sr. Eng
D11: (C0) U 39500
F11: (C0) U 40400
H11: (C0) U 38100
J11: (C0) U 36400
A12: '   Jr. Eng
D12: (,0) U 28500
F12: (,0) U 30500
H12: (,0) U 27500
J12: (,0) U 26400
A13: '   Production Control
D13: (,0) U 31500
F13: (,0) U 30500
H13: (,0) U 28000
J13: (,0) U 26500
```

BIBLIOGRAPHY

Bender, P. S.; Northup, W.; and Shapiro, J. "Practical Modeling for Resource Management." *Harvard Business Review,* March-April 1981. ✳

Betts, M. "Flexibility Key to Bendix HRMS." *Computerworld,* July 22, 1985.

Campbell, C. R. "HRMS Features, Functions Fairly Easy to Identify." *Software News,* March 1983.

Edelman, F. "Managers, Computers & Productivity." *MIS Quarterly,* September 1981.

Fombrun, C.; Tichy, N. M.; and Devanna, M. A. *Strategic Resource Management.* New York: John Wiley & Sons, 1984.

Fraser, N. M., and Hipel, K. W. "Computer Assistance in Labor-Management Negotiations." *Interfaces,* April 1981.

Gallant, J. "HRMS Meet Personnel Data Needs." *Computerworld,* May 13, 1985.

George, R. "Avoiding Confusion in HRMS Selection." *Software News,* March 1984.

Gessford, J. E. *Modern Information Systems Designed for Decision Support.* Reading, MA: Addison-Wesley Publishing Company, 1980.

Glatzer, H. "Once Mainframe HRMS Begins Its Migration." *Software News,* February 1985.

Goldmacher, E. S., and Mitchell, J. A. "Personnel Record Systems Present Own Pitfalls." *Computerworld,* August 25, 1980.

Harty, P. "Users Cite Productivity Access as HRMS Assets." *Software News,* February, 1985.

Holloran, T. J., and Byrn, J. E. "United Airlines Station Manpower Planning System." *Interfaces,* January-February 1986.

Juris, R. "Managing Human Resources Online." *Computer Decisions,* May 1984.

Kelleher, J. "Human Factors." *Business Computer Systems,* August 1985.

Keough, L. "Managing Personnel the Micro Way." *Computer Decisions,* March 12, 1985.

Kull, D. "People Programs." *Computer Decisions,* January 29, 1985.

LaBelle, C. D.; Shaw, K.; and Hellensack, L. J. "Solving the Turnover Problem." *Datamation,* April 1980. ✗

Leavitt, D. "Multiple Influences Interact in Selection of HRMS: Survey." *Software News,* March 1983.

Mackey, C. B. "Human Resource Planning: A Four-Phase Approach." *Management Review,* May 1981.

Major, M. J. "HRMS: Last of the 'General' Computing Frontier." *Software News,* January 1986.

Mercer, Z. C. "Personal Planning: An Overlooked Application of the Corporate Planning Process." *Managerial Planning,* January-February 1980.

Miller, E. M. "Personnel Selection in the Presence of Uncertainty." *Personnel,* September-October 1980.

Mills, D. O. "Planning with People in Mind." *Harvard Business Review.* July-August 1985. ✗

Morecroft, J. D., W. "Rationality in the Analysis of Behavioral Simulation Models." *Management Science,* July 1985.

Muczyk, J. "Comprehensive Manpower Planning." *Managerial Planning,* November/December 1981.

Nadler, L., ed. *The Handbook of Human Resource Development.* New York: John Wiley & Sons, 1984.

Post, D. W. "Computers as Counselors." *Business Computer Systems,* January 1985.

Robinson, T. "Human Resource Management Systems, Traditional Data Leading to More Real Information." *Software News,* March 1983.

Santarelli, M-B, ed. "Executive Views on Human Resource Systems." *Software News,* March 1984.

Skinner, W. "Big Hat, No Cattle: Managing Human Resource." *Harvard Business Review,* September-October 1981. ✗

Snyders, J. "Human Resource Management: A Dynamic Field for Software." *Infosystems,* August 1985.

Sterpos, P. "Productivity, Work Force Availability, and Rational Production Scheduling." *Interfaces,* August 1980.

Sullivan, F. L. *How to Calculate the Manufacturer's Costs in Collective Bargaining.* New York: AMACOM, 1980.

Thierauf, R. J. *Decision Support Systems for Effective Planning and Control—A Case Study Approach.* Englewood Cliffs, NJ: Prentice-Hall, 1982.

Vaughan, L. L. "How Do You Choose a Personnel System?" *Computerworld,* January 30, 1984.

Walton, R. E. "From Control to Commitment in the Workplace." *Harvard Business Review,* March-April 1985. ✗

Walton, R. E., and Lawrence, P. R. *HRM, Trends and Challenges.* Hagerstown, MD: Harvard Business School Press, 1984.

Winter, F. W. "An Application of Computerized Decision Tree Models in Management-Union Bargaining." *Interfaces,* March-April 1985.

INDEX

WE VALUE YOUR OPINION—PLEASE SHARE IT WITH US

Merrill Publishing and our authors are most interested in your reactions to this textbook. Did it serve you well in the course? If it did, what aspects of the text were most helpful? If not, what didn't you like about it? Your comments will help us to write and develop better textbooks. We value your opinions and thank you for your help.

Text Title _____ Edition _____

Author(s) _____

Your Name (optional) _____

Address _____

City _____ State _____ Zip _____

School _____

Course Title _____

Instructor's Name _____

Your Major _____

Your Class Rank _____ Freshman _____ Sophomore _____ Junior _____ Senior

_____ Graduate Student

Were you required to take this course? _____ Required _____ Elective

Length of Course? _____ Quarter _____ Semester

1. Overall, how does this text compare to other texts you've used?

_____ Superior _____ Better Than Most _____ Average _____ Poor

2. Please rate the text in the following areas:

	Superior	Better Than Most	Average	Poor
Author's Writing Style	_____	_____	_____	_____
Readability	_____	_____	_____	_____
Organization	_____	_____	_____	_____
Accuracy	_____	_____	_____	_____
Layout and Design	_____	_____	_____	_____
Illustrations/Photos/Tables	_____	_____	_____	_____
Examples	_____	_____	_____	_____
Problems/Exercises	_____	_____	_____	_____
Topic Selection	_____	_____	_____	_____
Currentness of Coverage	_____	_____	_____	_____
Explanation of Difficult Concepts	_____	_____	_____	_____
Match-up with Course Coverage	_____	_____	_____	_____
Applications to Real Life	_____	_____	_____	_____

3. Circle those chapters you especially liked:
   1   2   3   4   5   6   7   8   9   10   11   12   13   14   15   16   17   18   19   20
   What was your favorite chapter? _____
   Comments:

4. Circle those chapters you liked least:
   1   2   3   4   5   6   7   8   9   10   11   12   13   14   15   16   17   18   19   20
   What was your least favorite chapter? _____
   Comments:

5. List any chapters your instructor did not assign. _____

6. What topics did your instructor discuss that were not covered in the text?_____

   _____

7. Were you required to buy this book? _____ Yes _____ No

   Did you buy this book new or used? _____ New _____ Used

   If used, how much did you pay? _____

   Do you plan to keep or sell this book? _____ Keep _____ Sell

   If you plan to sell the book, how much do you expect to receive? _____

   Should the instructor continue to assign this book? _____ Yes _____ No

8. Please list any other learning materials you purchased to help you in this course (e.g., study guide, lab manual).

   _____

9. What did you like most about this text? _____

   _____

10. What did you like least about this text? _____

    _____

11. General comments:

    May we quote you in our advertising? _____ Yes _____ No

    Please mail to: Boyd Lane
                      College Division, Research Department
                      Box 508
                      1300 Alum Creek Drive
                      Columbus, Ohio 43216

    Thank you!